EVALUATION STUDIES REVIEW ANNUAL
Volume 2

Evaluation Studies

EDITORIAL ADVISORY BOARD

Review Annual

Malcolm W. Klein, *Department of Sociology and Anthropology, University of Southern California, Los Angeles*
Kenneth J. Lenihan, *New York City*
Henry M. Levin, *School of Education, Stanford University*
Sar A. Levitan, *Center for Manpower Policy Studies, George Washington University*
Joseph H. Lewis, *Police Foundation, Washington, D.C.*
Richard J. Light, *Public Policy Program, Kennedy School of Government, Harvard University*
Trudy Lucas, *RANN Program, National Science Foundation, Washington, D.C.*
Laurence E. Lynn, Jr., *Public Policy Program, Kennedy School of Government, Harvard University*
Kathleen V. McNally, *Joint Council on Economic Education, New York*
John D. Montgomery, *Kennedy School of Government, Harvard University*
David Mundell, *Education and Manpower Planning Board, Congressional Budget Office, Washington, D.C.*
Irving Piliavin, *Institute for Research on Poverty, University of Wisconsin-Madison*
Henry W. Riecken, *School of Medicine, University of Pennsylvania*
H. Laurence Ross, *Program Director, Law and Social Sciences, National Science Foundation, Washington, D.C.*
Peter H. Rossi, *Department of Sociology, University of Massachusetts, Amherst*
Susan E. Salasin, *Chief, Research Diffusion and Utilization Section, National Institute of Mental Health, Rockville, Maryland*
John W. Scanlon, *The Urban Institute, Washington, D.C.*
Robert Schrank, *Division of National Affairs, The Ford Foundation, New York*
Herbert C. Schulberg, *Office of Education and Regional Planning, Western Psychiatric Institute and Clinic, University of Pittsburgh*
Frank P. Scioli, Jr., *Division of Advanced Productivity Research and Technology, National Science Foundation, Washington, D.C.*
Michael Scriven, *Department of Philosophy, University of California, Berkeley*
Lee Sechrest, *Department of Psychology, Florida State University*
Robert E. Stake, *School of Education, University of Illinois at Urbana-Champaign*
Elmer L. Struening, *School of Public Health, Faculty of Medicine, Columbia University*
Ernest W. Stromsdorfer, *Deputy Assistant Secretary for Research and Evaluation, U.S. Department of Labor, Washington, D.C.*
Michael Timpane, *Director, Center for Educational Finance and Governance, The Rand Corporation, Washington, D.C.*
Carol H. Weiss, *Bureau of Applied Social Research, Columbia University*
Jack Wiener, *Division of Extramural Research Programs, National Institute of Mental Health, Rockville, Maryland*
Marvin E. Wolfgang, *Center for Studies in Criminology and Criminal Law, University of Pennsylvania*

Evaluation Studies

Review Annual

Volume 2   1977

Edited by Marcia Guttentag

With

Shalom Saar

SAGE PUBLICATIONS / BEVERLY HILLS / LONDON

For information address:

SAGE Publications, Inc.
275 South Beverly Drive
Beverly Hills, California 90212

SAGE Publications Ltd
28 Banner Street
London EC1Y 8QE

Printed in the United States of America

International Standard Book Number 0-8039-0724-9

Library of Congress Catalog Card No. 77-81156

SECOND PRINTING

CONTENTS

ABOUT THE EDITORS

MARCIA GUTTENTAG is President of the newly founded Evaluation Research Society. In 1976, she was President of the Division of Personality and Social Psychology of the American Psychological Association, and is a Past President of the Society for the Psychological Study of Social Issues. A developmental social psychologist, she is the coeditor of the *Handbook of Evaluation Research,* and the author of many articles on evaluation theory and methods. Most recently she has coauthored *The Evaluation of Training in Mental Health, Undoing Sex Stereotypes,* and *Women and Sanity: Fact and Fiction.*

SHALOM SAAR is a doctoral candidate at the Harvard University Graduate School of Education. He is involved in research in policy planning and program evaluation. He received his A.B. from Swarthmore College and an M.P.A. from the John F. Kennedy School of Public Administration at Harvard University. Mr. Saar is currently active in conducting program evaluations for the Department of Health, Education and Welfare and is writing a book on the evaluation of manpower programs.

INTRODUCTION

By

MARCIA GUTTENTAG and SHALOM SAAR

Evaluation research is quickly achieving greater maturity as a discipline. Although it is still the newest social science field, developments within it have been quite rapid. It is, for example, no longer preoccupied with self-definition. There is little discussion about what evaluation is and is not, and how it should be differentiated from other forms of research. Considerable consensual validation now exists about the domain of evaluation, and its distinctive features, even if minor differences remain about the exact definition of evaluation research. Evaluation research is a discipline which now has immense spread throughout every sector of society. Evaluators are being used to assess the impact of public programs on many of the social, economic, psychological, and political aspects of our lives. The new federal emphases on zero-based budgeting and on accountability have accelerated policymakers' reliance on evaluation.

Within evaluation research, these trends have led to a new and more sophisticated emphasis on issues of data aggregation and data integration, i.e., the inferences that can be made from evaluative information, inferences relevant to policy decisions. This second volume in the *Evaluation Studies Review Annual* series reflects this shift in emphasis within evaluation. The papers in this volume reveal this current stress on information integration and the relevance of evaluation to policy.

HOW VOLUME 2 WAS PLANNED

In keeping with the pattern established for Volume 1 of this series, an Editorial Advisory Board was used for Volume 2 of the *Evaluation Studies Review Annual, 1977.* Individuals on the board represented all of the social science disciplines and a variety of different substantive fields. Each Editorial Advisory Board member was asked to survey both published and unpublished material in his or her field and to submit nominations of the best work in evaluation done during the year 1976. In some instances, Editorial Advisory Board members also nominated works which had been recently published (though not in 1976), works which they believed were significant enough to be reprinted.

In keeping with the tremendous growth of the evaluation field, a great many more recommendations of excellent papers were made than could be included in the current volume. In fact, nearly three times the number of papers which do appear in this volume were judged to be of sufficiently high quality to have been included had space been available.

Choices of individual papers were also made on the basis of the major emphases of this volume. Those works which illuminated methods of data aggregation and data integration were given priority. Those studies which advanced conceptual or methodological links between evaluation and policy were also favored. Even within these categories, a number of excellent papers could not be included because of their length, of their technical content. Readers interested in problems in the use of analysis of covariance, for example, might contact the Stanford Evaluation Consortium *Occasional Papers* for a copy of L.J. Cronbach et al., *Analysis of Covariance: Angel of Salvation or Temptress and Deluder?* From the same source, an excellent analysis of data aggregation problems can be found in Cronbach et al., *Research on Classrooms and Schools: Formulation of Questions, Design, and Analysis.* The Police Foundation has a fine series of evaluations which were also too lengthy to include. Particularly noteworthy in 1976 were: *Police Response Time: Its Determinants and Effects* by Tony Pate, Amy Ferrara, Robert A. Bowers, and Jon Lorance, and *Three Approaches to Criminal Apprehension in Kansas City: An Evaluation Report* by Tony Pate, Robert A. Bowers, and Ron Parks. A forthcoming volume of the National Academy of Sciences on Social Research and Development, edited by Laurence Lynn, includes a number of insightful papers on the relationships between social R&D and policy. These are just a few illustrations of the valuable and abundant new literature in the evaluation field.

EVALUATION RESEARCH NOW

Uninformed decision making can be costly to society. Currently the major thrust of evaluation research is the conceptual and methodological attempt to integrate and aggregate data so that realistic and timely inferences can be made from evaluative information. There is little disagreement among policymakers about the urgent need for information. The challenge and responsibility for evaluation research is how to provide policymakers and the general public with the most accurate and relevant information. Information must be timely if it is to be used in the planning and decision-making process. Methodological discussions about evaluation research problems have not, in the past, been dissimilar from those in other types of research, i.e., focused on the most reliable and valid ways with which to generate data. The emphasis has been on data production. Now, both the large amount of information naturally available from many programs and concerns about costs of information generation have required evaluators to exercise caution about the use of resources for massive data generation operations. What do the data mean? Who will use the information? When? Why? These, increasingly, are the questions which evaluators must confront when making design choices.

At the same time, the facile data aggregations which routinely were done with large-scale evaluations have increasingly been questioned by statisticians and methodologists. Data aggregation issues are particularly acute now. Block grants and the decentralization of large programs have made patently absurd the fiction that a national program is analogous to an independent variable. If data cannot be aggregated across diverse sites and diverse programs, how then can national decisions be made about the value of national programs? There are growing methodological and statistical attempts to answer this key question. This volume includes a number of the most recent, thoughtful approaches to this issue.

In contrast to the evaluation research literature of even a few years ago, evaluators no longer decry the political context within which evaluation takes place. Instead, they now work with an acute awareness of the need for the policy utilization of their findings. The political context of evaluation is no longer seen as a foreign element. It is, instead, treated as another dimension of the evaluative context which must, like others, be considered at every point in the evaluation research process. Evaluators have not only paid heed to the political context of evaluation, they have also developed methodologies which permit the political realities and the multiple conflicting goals of various groups to be integrated within the evaluation research progress. The debate between policymakers and evaluators is ever livelier and more open. Another indication of the field's growing maturity is that the discussion is focused more on *how* to integrate evaluation and policy than on *whether* these two should be integrated. To reflect this emphasis, Part 1 and Part 3 of this volume are directly concerned with the relationships between evaluation and policy. In each of the substantive areas which have been chosen for this volume, the stress is also on methodologies which bridge the gap between evaluation and policy. A clear illustration of the interplay between evaluation and policy can be found in Part 4—*Evaluation in Education*—where the Coleman-Pettigrew and Green debate begun in Volume 1 is continued in Volume 2.

As one reviews the evaluation literature in a number of substantive areas, it no longer is so easily possible to know in which discipline the evaluation researcher received his training. Evaluation research now is a discipline which in informed by methods from all of the social sciences. Because of this interdisciplinary breadth, the methods of each discipline, and the assumptions which underlie them, have been subjected to critical scrutiny, and have benefited from the revisionism of these new perspectives. Such modifications of standard methodologies are also reflected in the articles in this volume.

Education is one of the most highly researched evaluation fields. It was difficult to select only a few articles for this section, since the quantity and quality of nominated studies were exceptionally high. Educational programs are massive, use many resources, feed ideological biases, and effect almost everyone in modern society. Public reaction to educational evaluations is often immediate and frequently intense.

The Coleman-Pettigrew-Green debate on "white flight" opens this section. The debate highlights both methodological issues and the interpretation of evaluation data. The policy issues are critical, and are deeply related to how the data are evaluated. Evaluators are placed in highly responsible public roles.

The educational evaluation studies which have been included analyze the impact of teaching, the effect of schooling and of the treatment of behaviorally disturbed pupils. These studies illustrate methodological innovations and data utilization ideas.

How can the effects of a major program like Title III, which varies greatly in each site, be assessed? The Weathersby et al. study provides a comprehensive model, which, in this case, assesses the impact of Title III on students' decisions to attend an institution of higher learning, but has greater generalizability to the evaluation of many federal programs of this type.

The recognition that the forces of supply and demand are not flexible enough to achieve full employment compelled policymakers to design programs aimed at helping the unemployed and the poor. Since their establishment, manpower programs have changed in content, goals, and government expenditures. The change in emphasis was a function of economic conditions, political considerations, and the social environment. Evaluations of manpower training programs suffered a great deal of criticism regarding their validity and reliability. Most evaluation studies have suffered from serious methodological handicaps such as lack of control groups, randomization procedures, and data interpretations. As a result, it was difficult to determine if the recorded changes were actually the direct results of the programs.

The alarming rate of unemployment during the early 1970s and the need for assimilating diversified manpower programs led to the Comprehensive Employment and Training Act legislation of 1973, whose aim was the decentralization of manpower programs. It provided local authorities with the power to decide on the content of the programs to relate them to local needs.

Some argue that the lack of conclusive answers to the impact of manpower programs has been the consequence of methodological problems rather than the actual performance of the programs.

Evaluation of manpower programs has basically looked into a narrow definition of outcomes, primarily wage gain, while neglecting other potential outcomes as a result of participation in the program. The delegation of the responsibility of manpower programs to local authorities holds the potential of programs evaluated against better defined goals. It should also minimize the macrolevel aggregations which in the past had limited relevance to local policies.

In criminal justice evaluation there is often almost too much data and the question is how to make sense out of it. Time series have been effectively used in criminal justice evaluations. In this section some of the wisest and most complex new thinking about the organization and analysis of naturally generated data in the criminal justice field is presented. In mental and physical health evaluations, although there have been no major new breakthroughs of evaluation methodologies, a more sophisticated and appropriately honed use of known evaluation methods is apparent. The match between method and content has never been better, as witnessed by the selections in this volume, each of which convincingly captures relationships which are difficult to establish.

This volume, we hope, reflects some of these newest and most important trends in evaluation research.

PART 1
THINKING ABOUT EVALUATION

1

THE PRESENT STATUS OF EVALUATION RESEARCH

By

HOWARD E. FREEMAN

This paper is a review of the field of evaluation research. The major focus of the paper is on the various methodological procedures currently used in the evaluation of social and cultural action programs. Both strengths and weaknesses of various approaches to evaluating the program implementation and outcome are examined. Further, suggestions are offered for improving the state of the art in evaluation research. Since evaluation research impacts on policy development and planning, the technical discussion is imbedded in a social policy perspective.

From Howard E. Freeman, "The Present Status of Evaluation Research." Prepared for the 1976 UNESCO Evaluation Research Conference, Washington, D.C.

PROLOGUE

In 1935, an obscure sociologist, teaching at a then small state university in the southern United States, published a paper pleading for the experimental evaluation of Franklin D. Roosevelt's New Deal social programs.[1] This little known article is quite remarkable. Deletion of the term "New Deal" and substitution of the slogan "Great Society" would have made it timely in the U.S. in the 1960s. While the United States has not had a catchy phrase to describe its human-resource and social-welfare programs since then, the message of the article still holds. Indeed, this 1935 plea for evaluation research is relevant to social and cultural program activities in all countries, regardless of differences in ideological outlook and the deficits in the human condition that are given priority by different nations. The message is clear: unless policymakers, social planners, and the public know the consequences of efforts at planned social change and social innovation, broad-scale programs of social action cannot be judged rationally.[2]

Certainly, a search of the world's literature would turn up numerous similar statements, some probably predating the article cited. The point, however, is that evaluation research, in the very contemporary use of the term, has a history going back at least to the days of the Great Depression. Its emergence is related to the development and refinement of modern social research methodologies; and also, of course, to revised outlooks on social responsibility and the expanded role of governmental and international groups in the amelioration of medical and social problems and the improvement of human living conditions (Bremner, 1956; see also Frankel, 1976).

At the same time, evaluation research is a very new social invention. Evaluation research has been "discovered," as Merton (1965) has informed us about all inventions, because of the social-structural circumstances of our times. There is no need to belabor the defects in the human condition and the social milieux of the world, of our most industrialized countries and of our lesser-developed nations. The challenge to innovate, experiment, and *evaluate* is rooted in the realization that most human resource, health improvement, and social development programs —regardless of geographical location and sponsorship—have been misguided, misconceived, badly implemented, and ineffective. Both the historical trajectory of evaluation research and its current fashionableness require some elaboration in order to appraise the current state of the field.

A BRIEF HISTORICAL OVERVIEW

Even in the 1930s there were precedents for advocating the application of rigorous social research methods to the assessment of programs (see Bernstein and Freeman, 1975:ix-xiii, for relevant references). Dodd's water boiling experiment in the Middle East was part of the sociological literature; Lewin's field studies and Lippett and White's work on democratic and authoritarian leadership were well known to psychologists; and the famous Westinghouse Electric study that contributed the term "Hawthorne Effect" to the social science literature was undertaken during this decade.

A historical trajectory can be constructed. Lewin's contributions continued during the 1940s. There was the monumental "American Soldier" applied research program of Stouffer and his associates during World War II that included a number of evaluation research studies, and there were similar efforts in Great Britain and elsewhere. The immediate post-World War II period saw massive inputs of resources to remedy unattended problems and unmet needs for urban development and housing, technological and cultural education, occupational training, and preventive health activities. Then too, this was the initial period of major commitments to international programs of family planning, health and nutrition, and rural community development. Resource expenditures were huge, and these commitments were accompanied by continual cries for "knowledge of results."

By the 1950s, certainly, large-scale evaluation programs were commonplace. Evaluations of delinquency prevention programs, penal-rehabilitation projects, psychotherapeutic and psychopharmacological treatments, public housing programs, and community organization activities were being undertaken in Europe as well as in the United States. Many of the programs of family planning in Asia, of nutrition and health care in Latin America, and of agricultural and community development increasingly had their evaluation components.[3] Knowledge of the methods of social research, including the art of the social survey and the technology of computer-assisted statistical analysis, became widespread. "Outside" evaluation studies, during the 1950s and 1960s, began to be supplemented and supplanted by investigations undertaken by nationals from many nations.

During the 1960s, papers and books on the practice of evaluation research also grew dramatically. Suchman's (1967) review of methods of evaluation research, Hayes's (1959) monograph on evaluation research in lesser-developed countries and Campbell's (1969:409-429) call for social experimentation are but illustrations. By the late 1960s—in the U.S. and internationally—evaluation research, in the words of Wall Street, had become a "growth industry!"

It is impossible to estimate the current volume of evaluation research activities. In the United States, by the beginning of the 1970s, there were about 300 new studies begun each year with direct federal support and with average budgets of about $100,000 each. By now, the number of evaluations started each year has probably doubled, and dollar costs have risen markedly. While not usual, studies may have budgets as great as 10 to 20 million dollars, as in the case of on-going evaluations of compensatory education in the U.S. Evaluations in other countries also have increased dramatically in number and cost. The aggregated assessments of family planning programs in Asian countries, supported by both national governments and international groups, represent one of the most expensive and extensive set of evaluation efforts ever undertaken. An on-going review by the World Bank has identified 19 experiments between 1950 and 1974 in India alone.[4] Evaluation research in Latin America on the relations between nutrition and cognitive development also is in the multimillion dollar category (Klein et al., 1972:219-225). In brief, at local, national, and international levels, with major support from governments and foundations, evaluation research has become a robust and continuing endeavor.

The extensive interest in evaluation research is manifest in several ways. Some of the research conducted over the past five to ten years has provided a stream of additional studies, secondary reanalyses and critiques. Take one example: since its creation in 1968, the educational TV program *Sesame Street* has been adopted and adapted for use in countries around the world. The original program, during its first two years on TV in the United States, was subjected to two independent evaluations by the Educational Testing Service. Their optimistic appraisals of its impact have since been countered by a secondary analysis of the ETS data by Cook and associates (1975) at Northwestern University, other studies in the United States, and those conducted elsewhere.[5] Recently Diaz-Guerrero and his associates (1976:145-154) in Mexico have completed two major true experiments which provide important insights into the differences in impact findings from study to study.

In the first of the Mexican studies, a quasi-laboratory evaluation, small groups of urban, preschool children, with adult monitors present, watched the educational program. Others saw cartoons instead. Extensive differences between pretest and posttest scores on a variety of cognitive and knowledge tests were found between the randomly selected experimental and control children.

In the second study—a field experiment—randomly selected experimental and control children watched either the program or cartoons in day-care settings in urban areas and public buildings in rural ones. This time there were no major systematic differences between the experimental and control children. Why? An important difference between the two evaluations is that, in the second experiment, groups of children assigned to each TV set were much larger than in the first, and there was much less "adult monitoring." Thus, the strong hint that children's educational TV programs, unless accompanied by efforts to sustain attention (or in more general terms, to maintain motivation), are of minimal utility.

In general, the sets of evaluations on *Sesame Street* were well done and conducted by skilled investigators. This certainly is so for the ETS, Northwestern, and Mexican investigations. From the standpoint of a program of evaluations, the cumulative effort is an illustration of the usefulness of evaluation research. While the Children's Television Workshop, creators of the program, may not entirely appreciate the findings that followed the original evaluations, taken together these studies have (1) stimulated interest in the use of TV for early child education, (2) identified the limits of such educational programs, (3) suggested the need for additional program elements to maximize impact, and (4) contributed to general knowledge on the factors related to the development of educational and intellectual achievement.

I cite the set of evaluation studies on *Sesame Street* because it is an example of work of interest to a broad international community. It is valuable because of both positive and negative findings; it is important because results have cross-national generalization utility; and it indicates that controversy and disagreement, when conducted in an open forum by persons of integrity and competence, can contribute to social and cultural program development.

Not all intervention programs have the glamor of *Sesame Street* and not all evaluation efforts are undertaken as competently as the research done on this TV educational effort. But in such areas as primary health care, professional education, work training, income security, and public safety, to name a few, there has been a rapid accumulation of studies which have been broadly disseminated and which are of widespread usefulness.[6]

Also, the past five or so years have seen the publication of texts (Weiss, 1972), books of readings (see, for example, Caro, 1971; see also Rossi and Williams, 1972), critiques of the methodological quality of work (Bernstein and Freeman, 1975), and discussions of the organizational and structural constraints that limit the successful conduct of evaluation research (Riecken and Boruch, 1974; see also Wholey et al., 1970). Last year, a major handbook—of some 1,500 pages—was published.[7] In the United States, the magazine *Evaluation* has an estimated readership of 20,000, and there are both competing journals and specialized ones, some with international editorial boards and readerships.[8] The spurt of publications, national and international conferences, the formation of professional evaluation-research associations, and special sessions at the meetings of academic and practitioner groups are testimony to the growth and development of the field.

Finally, there are expanded organizational arrangements for the conduct of evaluation research, with the economic and structural outlines of different countries shaping the settings in which evaluation researchers work. In the U.S., for example, a large number of profit-making groups compete with university and nonprofit organizations for contracts and grants. In other nations, such as Great Britain, the traditional links between government and university professors found in other research areas have been extended to the evaluation research field. In still others, organizations have emerged with varying linkages to one or more governments.[9] The growth and institutionalization of organizational settings is another indication of the sustained interest of a broad community in evaluation research.

This brief historical sketch hopefully illuminates the continuity of development of the field, at least since 40 years ago or so, when an Arkansas sociology professor pleaded for program evaluation. But history can obscure as well as illuminate. For, while there is continuity in the development of the evaluation field, a qualitative change has occurred. Even as late as 1967, Suchman's (1967) definition that evaluation research is the application of social research techniques to the study of large-scale human service programs was a useful and sufficient delineation of the field. Now, however, it is clear that evaluation research is more than the application of methods. It is a political activity, an input into the complex mosaic from which emerges policy decisions and allocations for the planning, design, implementation, and continuance of programs to better the human condition.

POLICY DEVELOPMENT AND EVALUATION RESEARCH

Some years ago, Sheldon and I (1970:97-111) described the emerging field of social indicators as a "social movement." The same characterization applies to the evaluation research field; rather, perhaps, it is useful to think of both sets of research activities as part of a broad social movement to maximize rationality in social policy and human resource program development (Freeman and Bernstein, 1975). The point should be made sharply; evaluation research is not a benign social science activity, it is a political decision-making tool.

The prosperity of evaluation research does not stem primarily from dedicated social researchers undertaking technically sophisticated studies. Rather, it is because of a growing commitment to orderly policy development and implementation. Certainly social scientists and intellectuals have contributed to this outlook in their efforts to create the "policy sciences" and in their personal activities to achieve progressive social change (Berk and Rossi, 1976). But, the major impetus for rational policymaking and program development are political and pragmatic, and it is the politician, the planner, and the foundation executive who exercise the leadership in the evaluation research field. It is persons of power and influence, not academicians, who are the evaluation research lobby and who are responsible primarily for the widespread growth of the evaluation endeavor.

It is clear that nations and communities have not adopted a rational policy outlook with uniformity. Moreover, it is naive to hold that crude political expediency and the press of various interest groups are unimportant determinants of policy development and program implementation. Rather the social movement that includes an emphasis on evaluation research is an evolving one, with fleeting contextual circumstances rather than rational policy analysis often dominating policy decisions.

But the general direction of activities in most countries is clear. Whatever be the social values and the program goals and objectives of those in powerful positions, information on program efficiency, efficacy, and accountability are persuasive inputs to the elusive influence and decision-making processes that surround policy development and implementation. These are the products of evaluation research, and it is their political worth that has encouraged its remarkable growth.

Some policymakers and planners advocate evaluation research because of their strong conviction about the need for rational policymaking, and because their career and educational socializations have stressed the difficulties and limitations in the long run of relying primarily on either their emotions or crude political expediency in program planning, design, and implementation. Others adopt an evaluation research posture because of the presence of individuals and groups whose support is essential to their daily activities, and of advocacy organizations who insist upon disclosure of the way programs are conducted and their impact, and who may sometimes undertake evaluations themselves. For example, in a number of major program areas, the U.S. Congress has directed the secretaries of such departments as Health, Education, and Welfare to provide evaluation research findings in order to receive consideration of subsequent budgets. In the international field, there is considerable questioning currently of both governmental and foundation programs, and one way of defending activities is to provide evidence of their utility.

Whether or not persons in key roles voluntarily opt to support evaluation studies is unimportant. The consequences are the same: there is growing recognition at a policy and planning level that affective appeals and arguments of persuasion simply are insufficient. Evaluation researchers work in a political context, and it is persons with aspirations to direct the course of social life and the rhythm of social change who stimulate the demand for evaluation research. Thus, evaluation researchers necessarily are either proponents or protagonists of particular value positions and social action philosophies.

Evaluation researchers, in undertaking their studies, as Berk and Rossi (1976:349) have noted, "are *always* choosing sides before empirical findings are produced." But they are doing more than that; they are accepting a different or at least a second set of criteria on which to judge the evaluation research undertaken. Evaluation researchers are not conventional investigators whose sole concern typically is the peer assessment of others in their field regarding whether or not they did the work properly.

Any critique of the present state of evaluation research then must not only examine issues of method but of policy relevance as well. Take two examples: the matters of time required for completion of studies and the selection of variables for outcome measures. As Coleman (1972) has indicated, research for policy purposes remains an idle aspiration if the findings are not available when needed for political decision-making. Well-designed and carefully executed studies are worthless if they do not contribute to the decision-making process. Thus, designs need to be judged not only in terms of a puristic set of standards but in terms of the pragmatic concern with timely utilization.

To turn to the second example: dominant ideologies and political realities affect the definitions of evaluation criteria. To use Berk and Rossi's (1976:339-340) illustration, the guaranteed annual income experiments have emphasized how much of a work disincentive is induced by substituting income security for public welfare, not whether income security impacts on the health, morale, or family stability of the poor. Evaluation research is judged useful if it contributes to moving social policies in the direction advocated by planners and politicians and to tailoring their future positions on these social programs. Most consumers of evaluation research are unconcerned about whether or not it contributes to either theoretical understanding or some integrated intellectual view of the workings of a society or a particular subsystem in it.

Methodological excellence and policy relevance, then, are both frames of reference which have to be taken into account in judging the present state of the field, and appraisals based on one framework may conflict with those based on the other. This is not the only arena in which the application of a scientific outlook to the management and amelioration of pressing problems raises the issue of conflicting norms in assessing worth. Many life-saving, therapeutic interventions in medicine, for example, are the result of research regarded as less than rigorous by biomedical scientists. But in the realm of social research, the dual pressures of methodological rigor and policy utility have never before been as strongly experienced as in the evaluation research field.

BOUNDARIES OF THE EVALUATION RESEARCH FIELD

There are considerable differences of opinion as to what constitutes evaluation research. From one standpoint, any body of information that allows one to reach decisions on programs, treatments, and interventions can be considered to be evaluation research. This is such a broad definition, however, that it is not useful. Under it, first, one could include the application of "conventional wisdom" or "common sense." For example, if it is repeatedly observed that large numbers of children in a school do not bring their lunch, and a school lunch program is initiated and the children eat at school, the latter fact becomes a "commonsense evaluation." The problem is, however, that many such efforts lead to faulty conclusions. Take the commonsense evaluation just noted: if the parents of the children are indeed desperate for funds, and consequently their families have inadequate diets, knowledge that their children are receiving a meal in school can result in a redistribution of the food provided family members at home. The result is that the school lunch program becomes a substitute for what the children would have received at home, rather than a supplement to their normal diet.

A second type of activity often referred to as evaluation research under a broad definition are judgments on whether or not certain activities, treatments, and interventions occur in conformity with generally accepted professional standards. So-called evaluations of many medical care, educational, social welfare, and similar programs are so conducted. For example, an evaluation of a school health program might be based on whether or not a child receives an annual physical examination. Of course, many professional programs operate on the basis of evidence that clearly points to the desirability of certain practices. Many practices, however, go on because of tradition and professional values, and without knowledge of their utility. This is the case for the example cited above about annual physical examinations for school children. The evidence, at best, is ambiguous whether or not a child between the age of 6 and 12 benefits in terms of current and future health from annual physicals. Yet, this is generally a criterion today for assessing school health programs, and heavy commitments are made to encourage health examinations.

A third type of activity often regarded as evaluation consists essentially of clinical and impressionistic judgments of programs. For example, an experienced educator may review the usefulness of a new set of textbooks by sitting in a classroom and judging whether what takes place is better, the same, or worse than what he or she regards as "usual" on the basis of experience. Clinical assessments are often seriously defective because of the great variations that occur in the assessments of different judges, and because there rarely is a systematic sample of programs and their participants in these clinical-type efforts.

Increasingly, persons in the evaluation research field do not include any of the activities discussed above as evaluation research. It should be emphasized that it is not necessarily desirable to evaluate, in the narrow sense of the term, all human resource programs. Indeed, many human resource programs, because of political, structural, practical, and cost considerations, cannot be evaluated well, if at all. Under these circumstances, policymakers, planners, and program people must, of course, rely on paraevaluation activities.

At the same time, however, it is important to maintain reasonable boundaries in the evaluation research field. In my view, evaluation research is best defined as activities which follow the general mandates of social research, compromising these as minimally as possible because of the realities of the political and pragmatic environment in which investigators work. In other words, evaluation research is the application of social science methodologies to the assessment of human resource programs, so that it is possible to determine, empirically and with the confidence that results from employing scientific procedures, whether or not they are useful. Three terms are generally used in the field to describe evaluation activities: process evaluation, impact evaluation, and comprehensive evaluation.

Process Evaluation

Fundamentally, there are two questions that one is concerned with in doing evaluations. The first is whether or not a particular program, intervention, or treatment was implemented according to its stated guidelines; the second is whether or not a program made a difference. The former type of evaluation is referred to as "process evaluation." A process evaluation generally is centered on two questions (Bernstein and Freeman, 1975:18-19, 65-81):

(1) Has the program been directed at the appropriate and specified target population or target area?

(2) Were the various practices and intervention efforts undertaken as specified in the program design or derived from the principles explicated in that design?

The reasons for evaluating process are obvious. First, from the standpoint of the administration of human resource programs, it is critical to know that what presumably was paid for or deemed desirable is actually undertaken. Second, there is no point in being concerned with the impact or outcome of a particular program unless one knows that it did indeed take place, and on the appropriate target group.

Many programs are not implemented and executed in the way originally designed. Sometimes personnel and equipment simply are not available; sometimes persons engaged in the program are prevented by political or other reasons from undertaking what they intended. Individuals who are part of the program staff may not have the motivation or know-how to carry out their tasks as outlined. There are also instances in which the intended program targets do not exist in the numbers required, cannot be identified precisely, or will not be cooperative. For example, in certain suburban communities, funds have been provided for various types of programs in which the target population is identified as children with past histories of juvenile delinquency. In some instances, after such studies have been started, it is found that there are simply very few delinquents, or that the police and courts are not willing to provide identifying data and cooperation in locating them, or that the juveniles concerned simply refuse to take part in the program. Process evaluation provides a systematic assessment of whether or not a program operates in conformity to its design, and whether or not it reached the specific target population.

Impact Evaluation

Impact evaluation is concerned with gauging the extent to which a program effects a change in the desired direction. It implies that there is a set of prespecified, operationally defined goals and criteria of success; measured impact refers to movement or change toward the desired objectives. These objectives may be social-behavioral ones, such as reduction of parole violation or decline in the rate of admissions to hospitals; they may be community-related measures, such as the frequency of crime reported to the police or reported in sample surveys by community members; or they may be physical changes such as the amount of carbon monoxide in the air or the number of buses that conform to a planned time schedule.

In terms of impact evaluation, a design is required that allows the investigator, in a persuasive way, to demonstrate that the changes which occur are a function of the particular program, intervention, or treatment and cannot be accounted for in other ways. Sometimes, a variant of the classic experimental design, in which there are control and experimental groups that receive different treatments, is used. Often it is necessary, however, to employ statistical approaches rather than experiments for practical reasons, such as either the use of longitudinal designs with comparisons over time or the employment of adjusted quasi-control groups (Gilbert et al., 1975). In general, most evaluation researchers take the position that experimental designs are the most appropriate way of measuring impact, since they provide known means of controlling external biases.

Comprehensive Evaluation

The term "comprehensive evaluation" refers to studies that include both a process and an impact evaluation. Ideally all evaluations should contain both process and impact components. That is, for the purposes of policy determination, as well as for contributions to basic social science knowledge, the most appropriate evaluation is one that includes the study of both process and impact. A comprehensive evaluation, then, is defined as one in which appropriate techniques and ideas have been utilized so that it is possible (1) to determine whether or not a program, intervention, or treatment is carried out as planned, and (2) to assess whether or not the program resulted in changes or modifications consistent with the intended outcomes.

The position I advocate—that it is important usually to undertake evaluations that include measurement of both process and impact—is a controversial one. Clearly, there are cases where it is foolish to invest in studying impact when there is much reason to believe programs are not being undertaken as planned or where groups of programs are known to be pluralistically implemented. In such cases, it may be strategic to devote resources to studying process first. Then, too, there are cases where programs are either cut and dried or there is a body of evidence on their implementation available so that most resources can be devoted to impact evaluation. But impact evaluation without knowledge of what took place can fault a vital program and result in poor policy decisions; just as huge expenditures of public funds may continue because the program is implemented as planned, and responsible officials regard this as sufficient evidence of worth even though there is no evidence of impact.

A general criticism of the present state of evaluation research is the failure, much too often, to undertake process evaluations. In the study Bernstein and I (1975:65-82) conducted of U.S. Department of Health, Education, and Welfare evaluations, we found that approximately one-quarter of these studies did not include the measurement of process. The percentage is much higher in studies emanating at local levels in both the United States and elsewhere.

Failure to study process is serious. There may be many programs that offer significant solutions to defects in the human conditions that have been passed over because the evaluation failed to show an impact. Yet, in fact, the real reason for lack of impact was that the program was never implemented fully well, or at all. There is an important analysis of educational performance contracting by Gramlich and Koshel (1975) that is informative in this respect. The bold idea of providing payment to organizations implementing programs on the basis of the extent to which they actually improved students' educational skills was abandoned because the impact evaluation failed to show systematic benefits. In fact, while there were faults with the impact evaluation undertaken, it is unlikely that any impact evaluation would have shown benefits since a variety of conditions prevented a regular and full implementation of the program.

If I had to single out one major reason that so few evaluations demonstrate positive impact findings, I believe it is the failure of proper program implementation and consequently the incorrect assumption that different groups received different treatments. As will be discussed, process evaluations are difficult to undertake well, and it is this area of evaluation activity that needs the most refinement. Nevertheless, avoiding process evaluations is not the solution.

Lack of Impact Findings

In general, systematic evaluation studies fail to identify policy-significant program impacts. As I have observed, less than adequate program implementation, often unstudied, sometimes accounts for lack of program impact. It should be recognized, however, that many social programs, even those with long established traditions, are actually of limited or no efficacy. In the mental health field, for example, there have been strenuous efforts to change attitudes toward mental illness, via group discussions, films, and the like. Such programs continue even today. In many countries there is a body of findings however, going back at least a decade, that strongly indicate that while such programs do increase knowledge of mental illness and its treatment, they only minimally change attitudes toward the mentally ill (Scott and Freeman, 1963).

Let me cite another example. There is major emphasis, certainly in the U.S. and in other industrialized countries as well, on occupational training in order to reduce the number of community members with inadequate skills for employment. Numerous evaluations of such programs strongly suggest that they are, at best, minimally effective (National Academy of Sciences, 1974). The same observation can be substantiated in terms of other program areas of interest to UNESCO and participants in this meeting.

The explanation for the limited efficacy commonly found can be stated quite simply, but the solution is hardly easy. Most programs, by their design and because of the interests of policymakers, planners, and program implementors, are directed at a narrow band of community members' life space. Since programs generally are lodged in a usually unchanged overall social structure, their specific benefits tend to be vitiated by other forces. The point is obvious: no program directed at reducing youth crime that is narrow in focus will markedly affect illegal behavior when poverty, defects in the cultural and environmental conditions, and corrupt values dominate life in urban centers. It is an awareness of this point that has led to broad-scale, "integrated" programs which include a variety of program elements. This structural change outlook was reflected strongly in the early Great Society programs in the U.S. It likewise underlies efforts in Great Britain and other parts of Europe to develop "new towns," and is the rationale for broad community action projects in lesser developed parts of Latin America, Asia, and Africa.

The often meritorious efforts of persons with special program interests, who undertake social action efforts of a narrow sort, without recognizing the impingement of general social structure, need to be put in a proper perspective. It is clearly a matter of balance. In many parts of the world, there are strong feelings that nothing short of a major remodeling of the general social structure of communities can achieve very much. Everyone has their personal ideological feelings on this matter, and the participation of evaluation researchers in programs that fail to take into account the general societal defects is an impossible matter on which to set specific guidelines (Berk and Rossi, 1976). There is an outside limit, however, when the possibility of an effective program is so unlikely because of an overwhelmingly defective social environment that the evaluation researcher must reject the opportunity to undertake a study. It can be argued that a proper role for evaluation researchers is to force early abandonment of impotent programs, for many evaluation investigators have a considerably broader understanding of social structural constraints than the professionals who design programs. Evaluation researchers, at least sometimes, may be less blind to the realities of the general social structure than individuals fully embedded in the establishments that dominate policy and program development.

Further, it should be observed that many programs are developed by individuals with strong professional biases. Professionals in such fields as recreation, psychotherapy, community organization, and so on have been indoctrinated during their academic socializations and careers to accept on faith the utility of their work. The end result is over-enthusiams and under-questioning of the efficacy of the programs they advocate. Sometimes "professional territoriality" results in keeping out program inputs that are inconsistent and antagonistic to their doctrines. It may lead to persons with different professional outlooks competing so vigorously to dominate large, comprehensive action efforts that the in-fighting takes precedence over responsible program planning and development. There is little likelihood in such situations of a successful evaluation in the sense of policy-significant positive results. As evaluation research increases as a factor in the determination of policy and program decisions, and as the policy sciences in general increasingly affect the planning and program development processes, evaluation researchers risk being judged as conservatives, for they often are involved in narrowly developed and professionally doctrinaire program activities that fail to address the overall social-structural change issue (Berk and Rossi, 1976).

Role of the Evaluation Researcher

Indeed, ideas about the role of the evaluation researcher, and organizational relations between evaluation researchers, policymakers, and program implementors, are changing. Formerly, it was generally felt that the ideal organizational arrangement was to have the evaluation researcher separated from the action group, and it was held that organizational independence of evaluation researchers led to objectivity (Bernstein and Freeman, 1975:99-134). Increasingly, questions are being raised about this viewpoint. First, such separation diminishes the likelihood that evaluation researchers will contribute to the development of detailed defined objectives and program designs, requisites for conducting sound studies. Second, the evaluation researcher may extend the "neutral role" to the point where the investigator is studying so weak an action effort that impact is impossible to achieve, but has no way of strengthening the intervention.

There are strong advocates now of "participatory evaluation research," and the fuller involvement of the evaluator in the program development and implementation process. Further, there are increased calls for program feedback. There is no agreement on the extent to which evaluation researchers should feed back process and impact findings during the life of evaluations. Clearly, on the one hand, if feedback leads to such extreme program modifications that the evaluation design is fully negated, then feedback participation has been too great. On the other hand, feedback that is constructive and allows for program modification within the framework of an evaluation design may increase the likelihood of positive findings.

Indeed, in view of the experience of the failure of most evaluations to come up with positive impact findings, evaluation researchers probably would do well to encourage the "biasing" of evaluations in the direction of obtaining positive results. I am not, of course, advocating either the fabrication of results or violation of the ordinary social research rules as they apply to evaluation studies. Rather, it has to do with such elements as concentrating evaluations on targets most amenable to change when treated and to stressing unusually strong program interventions rather than minimal ones. Zeal to apply a program to everyone and every location and enthusiasm for a particular intervention by policymakers, planners, and program personnel may be counterproductive to obtaining positive results. The designing of an intervention so that it has the greatest potential of demonstrating impact thus may fall upon evaluation researchers, and isolation and independence from programming does not facilitate such efforts.

These comments lead to a last set of observations about program involvement of evaluation researchers. Despite the growth of evaluation research as a specialty and an increased emphasis in academic training on relevant techniques, there is an extremely short supply of sophisticated researchers. In many cases, evaluation research experts find themselves in the role of expert consultant and part-time advisor to studies that are then carried by persons with various levels of training and research proficiency. The model of the outside, part-time expert does not work as well when one conceives of the evaluation researcher being fully involved in policy development, planning, and program implementation as it does when he or she is working with the evaluation team independently. In nations which have a short supply of evaluators, the issue is an exceedingly important one. Appropriate educational and career-training programs for increasing the number of "indigenous" evaluation researchers have not been well thought through, although there is increased discussion of this matter. Maintaining "old-fashioned" ideas on the role of the evaluation researcher and on organizational arrangements, however, is no solution. There is a priority need for much more conceptual thinking and experienced understanding of the utility of different roles and organizational relations for evaluation researchers.

THE PRESENT STATE OF PROCESS EVALUATION

Evaluation research, as noted, needs to consider two important process questions: (1) whether or not programs are delivered in ways consistent with the intended intervention or action effort and (2) whether or not these programs are delivered to appropriate targets. As discussed earlier, inadequate knowledge of these matters prevents an understanding of lack of program impact, since it is not possible to ascribe negative results to either program efficacy or to implementation. Also, of course, in the case of programs that are innovative, and which are being tested in order to decide upon their widespread applicability and utility, failure to know about the implementation process limits reproducibility and broad implementation.

Assessing Program Implementation

There is an ideal way of conceptualizing social programs in order to study the process of their implementation; it is to operationally define each specific program development. If this is accomplished, it solves many of the problems surrounding the assessment implementation. For example, if a program is designed to increase community members' awareness of contemporary social and political issues, and it consists of special daily TV programs with contents well described, weekly discussion groups with interpersonal process clearly outlined, and biweekly individual conferences with purposes sharply explicated, it is then possible to use a variety of research approaches to examine program implementation. If, however, program specifications are not operationalized, then it is necessary to undertake a much more ambitious and risky set of research tasks in order to do a process assessment.

There are two reasons that probably explain the difficulties of program element specifications. First, oftentimes planners and program implementors do not conceive their efforts in segmented parts, and are reluctant to specify elements. In the minds of some, doing so may have undesirable consequences, for program elements when viewed independently are more open to criticism than if a total, defuse package is described.

Second, many of the inputs of the programs are so-called professional know-how, and the style of work in many professions runs counter to explicating what exactly takes place. Many professionals claim they operate on "initiative branching," depending upon the contingencies turned up in dealing with each particular target of an intervention. For example, stating that individualized education development plans will be formulated for each person in the program is a way of avoiding the specification of work in terms of actions and steps. Particularly professionals, with status and prestige, are offended and affronted by the idea that they must expose what they do. Medicine is, of course, a clear case. As Freidson (1972) had noted, most physicians practice in privacy, and there is great pressure not to have anyone invade the examining room. Medicine may be the extreme case, but the ideology of autonomy and individual judgment is found among educators, social workers, and other specialists. There is inevitable conflict between the need to specify program elements and the way many who are engaged at the firing line in various kinds of social change efforts carry out their mission.

Most of the experience suggests that opportunities for rigorous process evaluations are strengthened when there are explicit agreements, literally of a contractual nature, between the evaluation research team and program persons. The very process of developing such contractual arrangements often is a valuable way of clarifying and explicating programs and of describing them in terms of elements. Also, of course, the consequences of such contracts is a commitment to process assessment that is much more difficult to gainsay later. If this matter of commitment to process evaluation is not dealt with forthrightly and openly, a process evaluation may not be completed satisfactorily because of differing assumptions between the evaluation research group and program staff on what was expected.

There are three usual means of collecting process data. One is some form of observation of the actual program in which either recordings of various sorts or field notes are taken. A second set of data sources is either interviews or other secondhand accounts of what takes place from either the targets of action programs or the persons delivering and rendering services. The third approach is the use of records, which may vary from the scribbles of practitioners to computerized record-keeping systems on attendance and activities. Not enough attention has been paid to the costs and benefits of different ways to obtain process information. Thus, there are no guidelines of a general enough nature to set forth. It depends not only upon resources available for process assessment, but on the particular content of the programs. But it is important to note that a small quantity of reliable and valid information is much better than large amounts of data without these qualities. Further, it is almost always better to have smaller samples of information from multiple sources than larger samples from a single source.

Consistent with the view expressed about the full involvement of the evaluation researcher in policy and program implementation, it is evident that process evaluations stand the most chance of receiving cooperation if staff involved in the program understand the importance of the assessment. Process evaluations must be constructed in ways that minimize extra work on the part of program persons and, ideally, which reduce their total work loads. For example, it is possible in many cases for the data required by process evaluators to serve the functions of client records and program reporting at the same time. Oftentimes, process evaluations have included the duplicate collection and reporting of the data that program people are collecting anyway for their own purposes. Implementing a process evaluation in ways that maximize cooperation requires, of course, not only understanding the goals and purposes of the evaluation by the parties involved in it, but an understanding of the dynamics of the program by the evaluation researchers. Otherwise, how can they seriously expect the cooperation of program implementors?

There is an interesting difference in evaluations in which economists have a strong influence compared with those done by persons with other disciplinary orientations. Economists stress appropriate resource expenditures required for programs. Programs of all sizes compete with each other for scarce resources. As will be discussed subsequently, it is frequently important in impact evaluations not only to examine the efficacy of programs but their efficiency or costs to benefits as well. Process evaluations, therefore, often must include data on the costs of providing different program elements.

In most human resource fields, there is unsatisfactory development of the notion of "units of service" and this limits analyses of costs to benefits. Some attention is being paid to this problem, but it is essential to devote more effort to a development of units of service in various fields, particularly for action programs that consist of more than one program element. Evaluation research may not in the near future reach the levels of sophistication of large hotel corporations which have detailed cost data for each service and item they provide their guests. But certainly many programs are amenable to more sophisticated practices in this respect than ones now utilized.

There is another reason, in addition to knowing about the costs of programs for cost-benefit analyses purposes, to be concerned with resource expenditures. There is, increasingly, insistence on fiscal accountability in intervention programs. Massive programs frequently are undertaken without their sponsors and the groups providing the resources being able to trace the actual delivery of program elements to particular targets. There is widespread dissatisfaction with providing resources solely on the basis of a postprogram audit that consists of listing salaries paid and overhead costs. Rather, there is increasing pressure to be able to relate costs to services delivered.

Traditionally, many implementors of human resource programs have rejected accountability notions that require the same types of information that are common in production-type industries. But, increasingly, there is clamor for such information. Protagonists of both established and innovative programs, particularly in the face of tight resource situations and increasing program costs, are insisting upon data on accountability. Process evaluations, in a sense, can be thought of as a "management tool" and the accountability function of process evaluations is on the increase.

It is important to recognize that the conduct of process evaluations raises a number of problems on the protection of human subjects. Process evaluations often invade the privacy of program staff and participants. Also, process evaluation activities may involve access to names and identifiable characteristics of persons. Recently, the National Academy of Sciences and other governmental groups have been seeking guidelines for the protection of subjects in evaluation research (see, for example, Bennett and Lumsdaine, 1975; see also Sjoberg, 1975). There is great variation, of course, in the outlooks of different countries and program specialty groups regarding protection of human subjects in social research in general, and in evaluation research in particular. As evaluation research increases in prominence, this is another area of realistic and emotional concern.

Target Identification

The identification and selection of targets is equally as important to assess as program implementation. In most programs, targets are groups of individuals that share a common status, i.e., grammar school children, retired workers, and so on. In some instances, they are aggregates of individuals such as the persons who make up families, work groups, and recreational clubs. In still others, they are organizations of various sizes and complexities, such as hospitals, prisons, neighborhoods, and regional associations.

It is not unusual, when evaluation research programs are undertaken, to find that to meet sample size requirements, extensive and expensive case finding is required, or target definitions need to be liberalized. For example, including teenage bed-wetters and poor school performers in the target population of a program to prevent criminal acts among adolescents with a high risk of committing them is, in the minds of many, questionable (although an example of an actual study recently undertaken that I do not care to reveal by name). The theme emerges again: unless evaluation researchers enter the development and planning of action programs early enough and with sufficient influence, inadequacies in target population definition may render useless other aspects of the endeavor.

In most cases, it should be recognized, social action programs are dealing with rare events and rare conditions. There are exceptions, of course, such as programs in areas where economic, educational, and cultural difficulties dominate. But, in general, small proportions of drawing groups are usually "at risk." Failure to have adequate screening devices for target population selection results in having only a small proportion of a group potentially able to benefit from a particular program, or markedly increasing program and research costs to the point that they become impractical ventures. It is obvious that to have a special learning disability program for *all* children in a school makes no sense when only 5%, say, of the children have learning disabilities. Program costs aside, unless the school is of huge size, differences in learning from pretest to posttest are unlikely to be revealed.

The issue raised has some deep philosophical and political aspects. Let me name a few. First, efficient identification of target populations that have a condition with stigmatizing aspects raises serious ethical considerations. For example, effective screening to locate mildly retarded children for a special program may result in so invidious a labeling of them by their peers and teachers that any gains from the program are far overshadowed by the negative effects of the labeling process.

Second, when programs include opportunities, goods, and services valued by all community members, and only those with particular characteristics or who live in particular circumstances are admitted, then both policymakers and community members may have to bear considerable antagonism and loss of community support. These may include anything from selective admission practices to recreational and cultural events to unique access to intensive educational and medical services. Many times there is intense pressure brought upon policymakers to increase flexibility and modify target population requirements, and these are sometimes yielded to on pragmatic grounds. There is no guideline again, but evaluation researchers must recognize the conflict that exists between defining a target population on evaluation design grounds and on political grounds.

Consistent with the point made earlier, target population selection is a critical place where it is possible to bias programs toward success or failure. For example, programs of sex education and family planning that are predicated on, say, having the equivalent of sixth-grade educational skills would do well to exclude those without this skill level from the target population, although naturally any inferences would have to be restricted to persons of this level of educational background. The press to constantly open up programs to those for whom they were not designed, or who have extremely low potential for movement in the program-desired direction, is one feature of evaluation efforts that leads to so many findings of no impact.

Identification of the target population is not enough. Except for some institutional populations, most program participation is either voluntary or at least partly so. Most social programs require a high degree of cooperation from targets. Persons who plan and implement programs may continue to be surprised about the matter, but it is evident that many individuals and groups simply do not wish to participate in various human resource activities. There are limits, of course, to the techniques and procedures that can be used to obtain target population cooperation. Protection of human subjects, and political and humanitarian concerns do set boundaries. But these boundaries vary greatly from action field to action field and from one geographical area to the next.

In any event, it is important as part of the process evaluation not only to estimate probabilities of cooperation, but to be able to identify the characteristics of nonparticipants and those who drop out of programs at various points in time. Reasons for dropouts, which have considerable bearing on the definitiveness of impact evaluations, vary, depending both upon the duration of the program and the particular characteristics of the locality in which the program is conducted. For example, in the evaluation of the Mexican version of *Sesame Street* discussed earlier, about one-third of the study group children were lost to both the program and the evaluation during the six-month period in which the program was on the air. High rates of residential mobility and fluctuations in economic conditions are major determinants of program participation in virtually every large center in the world. In rural areas, where labor intensive work varies with agricultural growing seasons, many action programs suffer large losses in their target populations around harvest times. It is clear that unless one makes estimates of program participation and dropout rates that are fairly accurate, it is not possible to undertake effective evaluation research. Further, for both innovative and established programs, knowledge of differences in the characteristics of regular participants, sporadic participants, and nonparticipants is essential in making inferences and generalizations about efficacy and efficiency. Information on subgroup characteristics of a target population, as with the measures obtained for target selection, need to be valid, reliable, and reasonably modest in cost and effort to collect.

The research operation required for adequate target identification and tracking includes both use survey research procedures and oftentimes special diagnostic and screening procedures. Such operations, done well, may appear to be expensive and time consuming and may require considerable technical sophistication. Consequently, target population identification is frequently undertaken inadequately in evaluation research studies. But the use of ill-designed and unsystematically located target groups renders questionable either statements regarding program implementation or impact. Numerous examples can be cited of costly programs in which failure to undertake necessary target population research vitiated important evaluation research efforts.

Perhaps the major concern with knowledge of targets and their behavior during the delivery of a program is the consequences of the assignment of targets to different action program modalities. Forced assignment occurs in many on-going and innovative programs simply because of the resources available to the action effort. For example, there may be a very simple program that has the goal of teaching adolescents to play musical instruments. But only so many children can have access to the trumpets and saxaphones available; some must settle for the flute. The major issue, however, is when persons and groups are assigned to different program modalities for experimental purposes, or in the extreme, when part of the target population is treated as a control group and receives no intervention or a placebo.

Subsequently, the advantages and problems of implementing experimental designs will be discussed as part of the review of the state of impact evaluation. Here, however, it is important to point out that target cooperation clearly may differ depending upon the particular treatment modality to which targets are assigned. Resistance and strain to the random assignment of targets for experimental purposes is found among practitioners and planners, among target populations, and among evaluation investigators themselves. All three groups, generally, have a commitment to the protection of human subjects and argue strongly against target assignments that may have deleterious effects.

It is certainly true that investigators in evaluation research studies, sometimes with the connivance of action persons, have undertaken evaluations in which either control or comparison groups have been negatively impacted upon. These rare cases, generally in medical evaluations, have tended to sensitize in the extreme large numbers of persons connected with the evaluation research endeavor about the negative consequences of target assignments for experimental purposes. While the risks to human subjects in most social evaluations are minimal, concern with negative impacts and side effects should and must continue to be a major issue in the promotion of experimental designs. Not only is there the humanitarian issue with reference to the participants in any particular experiment, but there is also the need not to deflate confidence in evaluation research by the discovery of studies in which inadequate attention has been paid to the human subjects' problem.

But, by far, resistance to experimental assignment of the targets is related to the views and outlooks of practitioners and policymakers. They are concerned with the political and public relations consequences of differential assignment and there is some grounds to the position, particularly when randomization is the technique employed. Neither policymakers nor the general public are always convinced of the fairness of random assignment. For example, Wolfle (1970) reports the experience at the University of Illinois at which some 3,350 new students were selected randomly from the available pool of 4,200 well-qualified applicants. Public reaction to this procedure was so negative that the university ultimately was forced to admit all 4,200 students.

Actually, little is known about the conditions under which either policymakers, the general public, or potential targets accept or reject assignment to different experimental treatments or to experimental and control groups. There are two common assumptions which must at best be regarded as hypotheses. The first is that such assignments are most acceptable when the intervention is looked upon as what might be referred to as a "positive add-on," i.e., an intervention that enhances the capacities of an individual or the quality of social life. For example, an innovation in which students from a school with an outstanding reputation are accepted on a random basis for a special school program designed to even further their educational growth. Under such circumstances, it is generally assumed that neither teachers, students, nor parents will become exceedingly vocal about the evaluation plan. Contrast this to an experiment in a low-income barrio of Bogotá in which there is a known high prevalence of acute intestinal illnesses and malnutrition among children because of inadequate sanitary conditions. Under these circumstances, random selection of families for a program is asserted most often to raise serious resistances to the assignment procedure. There is no evidence to support this position. Certainly, it depends upon the awareness of various groups to what is going on and their expectations regarding entitlements and equitable distribution of additional resources.

A second assumption is that there will be less resistance to assignment for evaluation purposes if there is a scarcity of the resources required for fuller program implementation. It is argued that, under these circumstances, persons are more sympathetic to random assignment of targets. At least one study, conducted admittedly on a limited population of U.S. college students, suggests that this is not the case (Hillis and Wortman, 1976). Subjects in this study tended to react more negatively when scarcity of resources was a reason mentioned for differential assignment, than when it was not. The authors of this study suggest that the explanation of scarcity of resources results in antagonism toward program personnel who were then blamed for not being able to garner sufficient resources to include all potential targets in the program.

There are some who are optimistic that, with increased understanding of the process of program evaluation research and a general "scientific orientation," the resistance to assignments for research purposes will diminish. Certainly, it is unlikely to decline in the short-term future and remains a pervasive concern, whether real or not, in negotiations between evaluation researchers, policymakers, and program implementors concerning the design of studies.

Then, too, there may be differential participation and dropouts from programs because of assignment considerations. Participation in various types of action programs are not always pleasurable and, in addition, are often demanding in terms of time for program involvement and research data collection, as well as requiring modification in the customs and routines of targets. It may not be, of course, the "experimental treatment" that is necessarily the unattractive condition, but one or more of the comparative interventions that is viewed with disdain. Also, in experiments using true control groups, failure to sustain contact or have knowledge of the whereabouts of targets so assigned may result in differential maintenance of the integrity of these groups.

HOWARD E. FREEMAN [39]

In any event, there are few large-scale evaluations that end up entirely pure, from an experimental design standpoint, even when they start out with the randomized assignment of targets to particular treatment modalities. Many evaluation efforts need to make exceptions for political and public relations purposes, if not to protect human subjects at the outset. These impurities are almost always followed by contaminating differences in dropout rates from program initiation to program completion. As a consequence, it bears repeating, knowledge of relevant characteristics of targets is essential.

What may represent a desirable body of knowledge either about targets or the program process from the standpoint of research methodology may not be acceptable in terms of the interest, resources, and time demands of persons in the arenas of policy development, planning, and implementation. It is critical that persons involved in the policy process understand as fully as possible, as Hilton and Lumsdaine (1975) note in discussing population programs, that a thorough process evaluation is an important factor in assuring that program impacts will not be compromised or attenuated (see also Cowling and Steeley, 1973).

At the same time, the evaluation researcher has a responsibility to be as economical as possible in the development of a plan for assessing process and studying the characteristics of the target population. There are no rules, of course, and the statement that process evaluation needs to be well conceptualized and carefully designed is pretty much an ad hominem. Nevertheless, the state of the art with respect to process evaluation in many areas of program interest to this conference is exceedingly underdeveloped. I do not think it is too bold a position to argue that, if one has to choose between directing efforts now at the improvement process or impact evaluation procedures, the former has the higher priority.

PRESENT STATUS OF IMPACT EVALUATION

The measurement of impact requires procedures that allow the evaluator (1) to document the extent to which the social-action program has or has not achieved its stated goals; (2) to attribute any effects or changes that are discovered to the implementation of the action program, ruling out rival hypotheses which might alternatively explain identified changes; (3) to delineate, if possible, the conditions or combination of conditions under which the program is most efficient (i.e., those that yield maximum benefits and minimum costs); and (4) to delineate, if possible, any unanticipated consequences or side effects of the implementation of the program.

One example is an evaluation of a pretrial court diversion project, aimed at routing first offenders out of the criminal justice system early in the legal processing of offenders. An evaluator assessing the effectiveness of such a program should be able to provide information on the following: (1) whether or not the program was effective in attaining its specified objectives, such as fewer subsequent appearances in court, fewer subsequent official legal contacts, and fewer and shorter prison sentences; (2) whether or not findings obtained are a demonstrable result of the pretrial diversion program; (3) what were the costs per case of this intervention compared with alternative ways of handling first offenders; and (4) any negative consequence such as reducing the threat of a prison term precipitating a rise in the number of new first offenders. While this is an oversimplified account, it pinpoints the kind of information that ideally the evaluator should provide. Naturally, this information should be provided with the greatest degree of certainty that the use of the existing research craft can provide. Accordingly, it is expected that the evaluator will select, from among methodological and design procedures available, those which give him or her the greatest confidence about the reliability and validity of results, within the confines of having to operate in a real-life social and political setting.

Most impact evaluations are rooted in the idea of an experiment, and the basic outlook is no different in evaluation research than when the procedures are undertaken in any of the sciences. The experimental approach, however, serves often only as a point of departure in evaluation studies, since in most evaluations there is limited control over the research process compared with such fields as agriculture. Rather, there are many more partially contaminated experiments and quasi-experiments undertaken than studies that are pure in their experimental design and execution.

Quasi-experiments are essential because either randomization is not possible or practical, or the time demands of policymakers require ex post facto evaluations rather than prospective ones. Because of the difficulties of achieving true experiments in evaluation research, a vast body of methodological literature is developing that extricates sophisticated procedures for approximating as closely as possible the rigor of true experiments. Every suggestion brings critics to the fore, who argue against the utility of each newly invented statistical procedure to approximate the true experiment.

It should be noted that, while most evaluations are either experimental or quasi-experimental in their frameworks, there are other approaches that have their advocates. One is a decision-making view based upon the application of Bayesian statistics. Essentially, such efforts attempt to approximate by successive determinations a set of decision-alternatives, making use of available data that oftentimes include judgments and crude estimates (Edwards et al., 1975).

There are also advocates of a simulation approach in which various values are assumed and the different outcomes that occur, depending upon the assumed values, are examined. The idea of simulating social and behavioral systems in whole or part has been around for a considerable time. Wilkins, for example, in discussing evaluations in the area of penology has noted (1969:135): "It is often possible to obtain estimates of likely payoff from the selection of alternatives where the situation does not exist in fact but is simulated in some way. From simulation it may be possible to select one or two strategies for change that are both acceptable and seem (from the results of simulation studies) to have a high probability of success."

It is not necessary, of course, to use a decision-making or simulation approach independent of an experimental model, although this is usually the case. In general, while there are advocates of alternative approaches to the experimental one, most evaluation researchers argue strongly that, consistent with the overarching validity of the experimental method in scientific work, the evaluation research field requires experimentation whenever possible. There are, however, a wide variety of viewpoints on the worth of pure designs—that is, true experiments that are without contamination—in comparison with compromise designs which may either forgo complete randomization or rely heavily on statistical manipulations. Discussion on this matter needs to be placed in the contexts of two views about significance of results.

Policy and Statistical Significance

Scientific researchers in every field rely on measures of statistical significance and confidence intervals in making inferences. Statistical significance cannot be ignored, of course, in evaluation research, since clearly probability estimates are extremely critical if evaluation findings are to be utilized in deciding about implementing or continuing major programs of action and social change.

At the same time, however, statistical significance is not at the heart of the inference process in evaluation research. The notion of policy significance, while a less precise term, must guide the thinking of evaluation researchers. One question to be asked is whether or not the differences are important, i.e., large enough to be considered useful compared with other interventions and programs in a particular field.

Programs may have efficacy, but it may be so limited that it is unimportant. The difficulty in providing guidelines about the magnitude of impact that renders an intervention policy significant rests on the availability of other action strategies in a field, and the values that surround requirements for human service resource allocations. It is obvious, for example, that a program which reduces the rate of serious crimes against persons by even 1% or 2%, when placed in terms of number of lives saved or number of hospital days reduced for victims, may well be regarded as a large program discovery. But, a 1% to 2% reduction in the educational deficits of preschool children, when placed in terms of number of letters of the alphabet recognized, say from M to N, may be regarded to be of little or no significance.

Judgments of the policy significance of the magnitude of an impact is an activity policymakers and planners as well as evaluation researchers must engage. There is considerable difficulty in the sharing of results between the parties, and in achieving a consensual judgment of utility from a policy standpoint. In part, it is a matter of the partisanship of many program supporters in comparison with the somewhat more neutral outlooks that evaluation researchers frequently assume. It also is difficult to communicate statistical findings in ways that allow substantive interpretations. Take, for example, the large nutritional interventions program being conducted in rural Guatemalan villages by the Institute for Nutrition in Central America and Panama. Preliminary findings suggest that, when social and economic factors are taken into account, a twice daily high-calorie supplementation program explains about 1% to 2% of the variance in the cognitive development of preschool children (Klein et al., 1972). Is this a policy significant finding or not? Clearly it has to be first translated into what this means substantively, and judged in relative terms by persons who know about competing means for increasing cognitive skills in young children.

Further, size of effect and policy significance of results in each field must be judged in resource expenditure terms. In general, with the exception of economists, evaluation researchers have focused their attention on the efficiency of interventions. Certainly, cost-benefit analyses have their limitations, both psychologically because there is a tendency to put everything in money terms and technically because of the limitations of data and of analytical procedures used. But for policy purposes, certainly, costs per unit of improvement is a major consideration. As Levin (1975) notes:

> The focus of cost-effectiveness analysis in evaluation research is to determine that strategy or combination of strategies that maximizes the desired result for any particular resource or budget constraint. In order to understand this concern more fully, it is necessary to consider the fact that government agencies and other institutions are faced with finite budgets and other resources for achieving their objectives. Although each agency may have a relatively narrow set of goals, such as reducing crime, improving educational results, curbing pollution, improving nutrition, reducing infant mortality, and so on, there are presumably alternative methods for accomplishing these tasks. Traditionally, evaluation research has occupied itself only with comparing these alternatives with respect to their results. The costs of alternatives have not been considered. Yet it is obvious that the less the cost of obtaining any particular set of results, the greater will be the contribution of the program toward achieving agency goals because the limited resources will provide a greater impact. . . . Perhaps the willingness to nominate for policy consideration any program that shows statistically significant results in outcomes over alternatives derives from the fact that only too rarely can such differences be found. Under these circumstances, any differences are thought to be important and worthy of being used for policy recommendations by researchers. But such zeal may provide a very misleading answer once costs are taken into account. That is, the alternative that appears to yield better results in terms of comparative effectiveness may have costs that far outweigh its superiority in results.

Moreover, the policy significance of effects needs to be judged in terms of political considerations. Here one must rely mainly on the intuition and experiential knowledge of persons who know the arena and location of the social-action programs. Sometimes, however, it is possible as part of formative evaluations to undertake surveys much like the "product acceptability" studies done in market research; other times there is ethnographic information available. Every nation and community, and subgroup within them, has its own normative rigidities which include everything from restrictions on examining parts of the body to times of the day and week when persons are willing to cooperate in different programs. It is obvious that programs that do show substantial efforts and are cost-beneficial in one community may not be exportable to others. This is one of the arguments for the use of persons who know the culture in which an action program is taking place. At the same time, there are risks that those indigenous to particular communities may seem to know what is going on, while actually, their understanding of social and cultural dynamics is less than that of an outsider who has made an effort to understand the locale and its people. Also, indigenous evaluation researchers may overestimate cultural rigidities in an effort to maintain their humanistic posture regarding "their people." In any event, policy significance does have to take into account the implementation realities for action programs.

Finally, there is the question of undesirable side effects. There is a growing concern, for example, in the health field about intervention programs which increase the dependency of persons on the medical organization and diminish their independence of judgment and coping behavior. Certainly, it is possible in virtually every area of action concern to consider whether or not highly professionalized programs and delivery systems will have long-range undesirable consequences in terms of increasing dependency.

But that is only one of the issues of unintended side effects. Programs in the United States directed at reducing school segregation, for example, are held by many to have increased "white flight" from major cities. Similarly, the housing program efforts in many places of the world, whether useful or not from the standpoint of an improved housing environment, have severely tampered social networks of family members (Wilner et al., 1962).

These remarks about the need for concern with policy significance are relevant to judging evaluations of programs from the standpoint of decisions on implementation but need to be considered in the process of critically reviewing pieces of evaluation research. Certainly, it is important for the development of the art and science of evaluation research to be as rigorous as possible, in study design and conduct, and it is essential that there be full review of studies so that the field advances from a technical standpoint.

Unfortunately, however, many of the critical methodological debates that have occurred over individual studies ignore the issue of policy significance. The debate about the Head Start evaluation is a good case in point. Since the original study inferred program failure, there have been a number of additional analyses suggesting that the original evaluation report may have underestimated the impact of Head Start (Williams and Evans, 1972). Certainly, there is a validity to many of the criticisms made about sample selection and statistical analyses. But the point is, if one is interested in Head Start as a broad-scale program to improve children's potential for gaining education skills, then the original report's conclusions are sensible. At best, there is only limited impact and the program's effects vary by group characteristics and locality. From the standpoint of policy significance, whether or not there were more statistically significant differences between Head

Start and non-Head Start children than first reported is only of minor importance. The position that methodological critiques need to be undertaken with policy-significance in mind can be generalized, providing it is not overextended. The point is that while ideally one wants to make certain studies as rigorous as possible, since programs in most fields involve very large resource expenditure systems, small disparities between an original analysis and replications and reanalyses usually have no meaning to policymakers. I want to emphasize that I am not arguing for sloppy research. But, somehow, there needs to be a balance between the nit-picking that often occurs in the face of finding insignificant effects from a statistical point of view and the need to direct energies to creative reprogramming in order to be able to develop efficacious and efficient programs from a policy perspective.

Criteria Variables

The discussion of policy significance is relevant to a consideration of criteria or outcome variables of impact evaluations. It is, of course, essential that outcome variables for impact investigations be developed so they are reliable and valid. But there are two particular issues that relate to a policy prospective on evaluation research. One is that they reflect the political concerns of policymakers. It was indicated earlier, for example, that the major outcome variable of the well-known New Jersey reverse income tax study is the extent a guaranteed wage creates a disincentive to work. Academically oriented social scientists may argue that from a social system perspective this measure is of minimal interest. It is a political fact, however, that the issue of income security leading to lower work-force participation is of critical concern. There are, unfortunately, a number of evaluation studies in which investigators have imposed their own criteria variables, only to find that the results, positive or negative, are of limited interests in the policy area. Blame must be shared on both sides. The choice of outcome measures by politically insensitive evaluation researchers is part of the explanation. The failure of policymakers and planners to explicate goals clearly and the ways they allow operationalizing them is the other part.

There are certain guidelines here. In the first place, policymakers are most likely to be concerned with social behaviors not psychological ones, and with measures of performance not of capacity. A work-training program may increase skills but in the face of extant social structural constraints have little or no impact on employment. Evaluation research in which attitude changes are the outcome measure is rarely likely to excite the policymaker as much as modifications in community and interpersonal behavior. Second, policymakers are interested in enduring changes rather than transitory ones. For example, action programs that lead to, say, a year's gain in educational skills at age five, if everyone plateaus anyway at age ten, probably will be regarded as unimportant from a policy perspective. Third, policymakers are concerned with measures they can understand in terms of their concreteness. Many of the measures employed in evaluation studies are expressed in either relative terms or adjusted scores and they have little meaning except to sophisticated experts in a particular field.

The second major issue in the development of dependent variables is the need for uniform outcome variables. In most fields, including crime, health, labor-force participation, and the like, different measures of outcome are often used. Even slightly different criteria variables impede comparisons between studies. It presents full comparison of a spectrum of completed studies to determine program priorities. A noteworthy effort to address this problem is the International Association for the Evaluation of Educational Achievement (IEA) study which provides educational performance data on a range of countries that vary in their development. Strenuous effort went into developing culture-free measures. While the effort may not be completely successful, it does allow for comparisons with considerable confidence between children exposed to different programs who live in various cultures (Kiros et al., 1975).

The matter is of a deeper social and intellectual concern. It raises the question of whether or not, despite cultural variability, there are social processes that have broad if not universal saliency. Certainly if one is concerned with the utility of social programs across groups and countries, and believes that the body of knowledge from evaluations should contribute to social progress in many nations, then attention has to be paid to the conceptual and functional equivalence of outcome measures (Freeman, 1972; see also Berry and Dasen, 1974). A glaring case where this is essential is in the study of early child development, where there are literally hundreds of intervention efforts concerned with the outcome of action programs on the cognitive performance of children. Yet, both the use of a hodgepodge of outcome measures and outcries of cultural chauvinism have reduced the generalization potential of work in the area. It is clear that much discussion and measurement effort is required in order to maximize opportunities for comparative analyses.

Research Design

As noted, the model of the true experiment is rarely realized in evaluation research. Most persons in the evaluation research field agree that the ideal of random assignment of subjects and appropriate pre- and posttest measures should be strived for. I quote from Campbell and Boruch (1975:208):

> If an experiment is not randomized, assumptions must be made that are often untenable and are even more frequently unverifiable. In addition, a mélange of parameters must be identified and estimated based on insufficient theory and data. These two problems in themselves are sufficiently formidable (and at times untractable) to justify eliminating them at the outset, by assuring through randomization that groups are identical to one another with respect to unknown parameters. The problems of making inferences based on nonrandomized data are not new, of course, nor are they confined to the evaluation of social programs. Their formal origins are evident in Galton's attempt to identify the size and stability of the effects of various plant fertilization methods based on some of Charles Darwin's observational data. Galton overestimated the conclusiveness of his own results, in part because he assumed that clever statistical manipulation would make possible essentially the same inferences one might obtain on the basis of randomization data.

In the article from which the above quotation was taken, Campbell and Boruch identify a number of pitfalls of quasi-studies. The risks are impressive when statistical manipulations are required in order to compensate for not having a true experimental design. Let me cite the six major categories of problems noted by Campbell and Boruch (1975:209-275) and extensively discussed in their paper:

1. *Systematic Underadjustments of Preexisting Differences.* Artifacts that occur when one seeks to correct for pretreatment differences between experimental and comparison groups. These occur whether either matching covariance or multi-regression analysis is undertaken to equate.

2. *Differential Growth Rates.* For a wide variety of measures used in evaluations, such as compensatory educational programs, it is reasonable to presume that groups higher on a pretest are higher because of their more rapid growth rate in previous years, and that these more rapid growth rates will continue during the period of the experiment. If quasi-experimental studies are undertaken, there needs to be at least some logical data on which to estimate growth curves of unevenly rated groups, otherwise making inferences from these evaluations is hazardous.

3. *Differences in the Reliability of the Scores of Different Age Groups.* Based upon the experience in education where age of subjects is related to reliability, if there are differences such as age between experiment and comparison groups, these may affect inferences on impact.

4. *Lower Reliability in the More Disadvantaged Group.* Not only may age affect reliability and differential inferences, but other characteristics that differ between experimental and comparison groups such as socioeconomic status, may result in the same occurrences.

5. *Grouping Feedback Effects.* Nonrandomized experimental and comparison groups are often a result of assigning aggregate populations to different treatments, such as workers in two factories. Under such circumstances, the relations between the persons in one group may be advantageous to doing well on evaluation measures in comparison with the other, and this raises major problems of inferences. Campbell and Boruch (1975:274-275) cite the illustrations that if children from school A have much higher vocabularies than children from school B at the outset of the experiment—the same school-age children may learn vocabulary from each other—inter-child learning could account for the differences found in an experiment.

6. *Test-Floor and Test-Ceiling Effects.* In a number of areas, the outcome variables may be either too easy or too difficult at pretest administration. Again, use the example of Campbell and Boruch. If the degree of deficit is underestimated for a school group and the test used is too difficult, this produces a test-floor effect resulting in underestimation of the deficit on the pretest, particularly for the more disadvantaged group. If the same children were tested on the same measure at another point in time, the expected difference in abilities would have reduced the floor-effect, making the differences between two comparison groups appear different in magnitude on the second testing.

There are compelling reasons then to undertake true experiments when possible. Gilbert, Light, and Mosteller (1975:64-134), three expert methodologists, have reviewed a large number of studies and rated their design and execution. Studies on income security, court treatment of accused persons, emergency medical assistance, and recovery from tonsillectomy, to name a few, were among the true experiments that they gave high marks. When they rated quasi-experiments, the proportion that received high ratings is much lower. As we have noted, in some fields such as employee training quasi-experiments have been pretty much a waste of time.

But confining evaluation research as true experiments cuts down on opportunities to undertake important policy-relevant investigations. Let me cite two illustrations. The first is the Coleman report (Coleman et al., 1966) on school desegregation, which has had important impacts on educational policy in the United States. The second is the study of public housing on social, psychological, and health conditions which has been important in dampening enthusiasm for public housing as a panacea for all social and medical ills. Neither of these studies could have been done as a true experiment. The former did not lend itself to prospective analysis, given the changing conditions with respect to desegregation and the time demands of policymakers. The latter could not be undertaken as a true experiment because of the impossibility of convincing housing authorities to randomly assign families to experimental and control groups.

Undoubtedly, nonexperimental efforts, particularly when they fail to demonstrate impact effects that either highly organized professional groups or conventional wisdom suggests is apparent, will continue to draw fire from methodologists and program groups. In an important paper, Cain (1975) points out, however, that economists have been doing nonexperimental studies, using structural equations and multiple-regression analyses for a considerable period of time.[10] It is difficult to argue about the utility of economic analyses, since many of our broad-scale programs hinge upon findings of these studies. He argues persuasively that nonexperimental designs are useful when *the investigator has knowledge of and can model the selection process by which subjects for analyses are assigned to various groups.* In other words, Cain's view is that analyses of nonexperimental data rooted in theoretically justified models can provide useful and meaningful evaluation results.

A major problem with quasi-experiments, particularly those in the social rather than economic sector, is that there is often unknown confounding of selection and treatment. I quote the example of Campbell and Boruch (1975:203-204):

> If a quasi-experimental study shows that people who have had psychotherapy have a higher suicide rate than matched cases who have not had psychotherapy, one is correctly reluctant to conclude that psychotherapy causes suicide. It is clear that no amount of matching can completely correct for the fact that those seeking psychotherapy are more suicide prone. As another example, consider an experiment done with failing students, some of whom are randomly assigned to a group that receives twenty hours of high-quality tutoring. The results would show that this tutored group does better than

those randomly assigned to the control group. However, if a correlation study were performed, it would show that the students who had more hours of tutoring got poorer grades on the subsequent final examination. This is because of the strong tendency for those students who do poorly to seek out the most tutoring. While this tutoring no doubt helps, it is not sufficient to correct the selection bias. Although the study needs to be done, we doubt if any amount of matching, covariance or regression adjustment on previous grades and other covariates would change the negative correlation into the correct positive one.

In these two examples, common-sense background knowledge would prevent the conclusion that psychotherapy and tutoring were harmful. But in many other settings, evaluation researchers are packaging similar under-adjusted selection differences as though they were treatment differences.

What is clear is that quasi-experiments which use regression analyses of one sort or another to equate groups not only need to be undertaken with sophistication, but that major responsibility of the investigators involved is to alert consumers of their research about the potential limitations of the work. There is simply no way to insist that all studies be true experiments. As discussed much earlier, many studies that have a basic experimental approach end up as a quasi-design because of study groups losses during the research process, and many others simply cannot have random designs given time demands and pragmatic considerations. Undoubtedly, developmental work will continue, creating more powerful structural equation procedures, one which will increase the utility of quasi-experimental studies.

EPILOGUE

In this paper, I have tried to weave together my enthusiasm about the contributions of evaluation research with realism about the current technical state of the field. The criticisms offered do, of course, constitute a plea for increased technical sophistication and rigor in execution of studies. But that is only part of the needed development of the field. There are examples of good work. Enough "for instances" exist that the observation I made several years back no longer holds fully that it is the promise of evaluation research, not studies themselves, that have excited so many about the field (Bernstein and Freeman, 1975:xii).

But, in a large number of cases, evaluation studies still are not utilized or are underutilized in policy development and program implementation. The major reason is that we have not fundamentally solved the organizational and orchestrational problems that currently limit the potential of evaluation research. The extensive time requirements to do sound studies, resource constraints, political blockages to conducting work, and administrative barriers are much more serious defects than the extant limitations in methods. These matters are receiving some but not enough attention, as I noted in an earlier part of this paper.

The plea some 45 years ago was to initiate evaluations of social action programs, the plea now is for addressing the political and contextual problems that inhibit successful completion and utilization of them. This is the contemporary challenge to evaluation researchers, as well as, of course, to our colleagues in policy, planning, and program implementation. To rephrase a line from a general discussion of the responsibilities of science, we must get up and face the wind, confront the future (Bevan, 1976).

NOTES

1. Stephan, 1935:515-521. Ross and Cronbach claim that the idea of program evaluations actually goes back to the turn of the century. Ross and Cronbach, 1976:81-107.
2. Throughout this paper, I draw upon the book I published last year with Professor Bernstein. See Bernstein and Freeman, 1975. I have also drawn upon Freeman and Sherwood, 1970.
3. See Hayes (1959:112-116) for a representative set of references to these studies.
4. This study is located in the Population and Human Resources Division, Development Economics Department, the World Bank. A report will be forthcoming in 1977.
5. For a report on the original ETS study, see Lesser, 1974.
6. Not all sets of evaluations are so "successful," of course. For example, a blue-ribbon review of manpower training programs in the U.S. notes that, although over 180 million dollars has been spent in evaluating these programs, little is known of their effects on job-ceiling and job-holding. See National Academy of Sciences, January 1974.
7. Struening and Guttentag, 1975, Volumes 1 and 2. For a more specialized reference book, see Anderson, Ball, and Murphy, 1975.
8. See, for examples, *Evaluation*, published by the Minneapolis Medical Research Foundation, Inc., in collaboration with the National Institute of Mental Health, and *Studies in Educational Evaluation*, published by the School of Education, Tel-Aviv University, Israel, Center for Study of Evaluation, University of California at Los Angeles, and the Institute for Science Education of the University of Kiel, West Germany.
9. For example, the Instituto Nacional de Ciencias del Comportamiento y de la Actitude Publica, A.C., which did the Mexican Sesame Street study, is a completely independent organization. The Institute of Nutrition of Central America and Panama, a PAHO affiliate, is partly supported and policy-directed by Central American governments.
10. In addition to the approach of economists, a wide variety of other designs that are nonexperimental have been used. See the excellent discussion by Cook and Campbell, 1976.

REFERENCES

ANDERSON, S.B., BALL, S., and MURPHY, R.T. (1975). Encyclopedia of educational evaluation. San Francisco: Jossey-Bass.
BENNETT, C.A., and LUMSDAINE, A.A. (1975). "Social program evaluation: Definitions and issues." Pp. 29-33 in C.A. Bennett and A.A. Lumsdaine (eds.), Evaluation and experiment. New York: Academic Press.
BERK, R.A., and ROSSI, P.H. (1976). "Doing good or worse: Evaluation research politically re-examined." Social Problems, February, 23(3):337-349.
BERNSTEIN, I.N., and FREEMAN, H.E. (1975). Academic and entrepreneurial research. New York: Russell Sage Foundation.
BERRY, J.W., and DASEN, P.R. (1974). "Introduction: History and method in the cross-cultural study of cognition." Pp. 1-20 in J.W. Berry and P.R. Dasen (eds.), Culture and cognition: Readings in cross-cultural psychology. London: Methuen.
BEVAN, W. (1976). "The sound of the wind that's blowing." American Psychologist, 31(7):491.

BREMNER, R. (1956). From the depths: The discovery of poverty in America. New York: New York University Press.

CAIN, G.G. (1975). "Regression and selection models to improve nonexperimental comparisons." Pp. 297-317 in C.A. Bennett and A.A. Lumsdaine (eds.), Evaluation and experiment. New York: Academic Press.

CAMPBELL, D.T. (1969). "Reforms as experiments." American Psychologist, 24(April): 409-429.

CAMPBELL, D.T., and BORUCH, R.F. (1975). "Making the case for randomized assignment to treatments by considering the alternatives: Six ways in which quasi-experimental evaluations in compensatory education tend to underestimate effects." In C.A. Bennett and A.A. Lumsdaine (eds.), Evaluation and experiment. New York: Academic Press.

CARO, F.G. (ed., 1971). Readings in evaluation research. New York: Russell Sage Foundation.

COLEMAN, J.S. (1972). Speech delivered in December to the American Association for the Advancement of Science, Washington, D.C. Reported in Footnotes, 1(March):1.

COLEMAN, J.S., CAMPBELL, E.Q., HOBSON, C.J., McPARTLAND, J., MOOD, A.M., WEINFELD, F.D., and YORK, R.L. (1966). Equality of educational opportunity. Washington, D.C.: U.S. Government Printing Office.

COOK, T.D., APPLETON, H., CONNER, R.F., SHAFFER, A., TAMKIN, G., and WEBER, S.J. (1975). "Sesame Street" revisited. New York: Russell Sage Foundation.

COOK, T.D., and CAMPBELL, D.T. (1976). "The design and conduct of quasi-experiments and true experiments in field settings." Pp. 223-325 in M.D. Munnette (ed.), Handbook of industrial and organizational research. New York: Rand McNally.

COWLING, T.M., and STEELEY, G.C. (1973). Sub-regional planning studies: An evaluation. Oxford: Pergamon Press.

DIAZ-GUERRERO, R., REYES-LAGUNES, I., WITZKE, D.B., and HOLTZMAN, W.H. (1976). "Sesame Street around the world/Plaza Sesamo in Mexico: An evaluation." Journal of Communication, 26(2):145-154.

EDWARDS, W., GUTTENTAG, M., and SNAPPER, K. (1975). "A decision-theoretic approach to evaluation research." Pp. 139-181 in E.L. Struening and M. Guttentag (eds.), Handbook of evaluation research, vol. 1. Beverly Hills, Calif.: Sage.

FRANKEL, C. (1976). "Introduction." Pp. 3-30 in C. Frankel (ed.), Controversies and decisions. New York: Russell Sage Foundation.

FREEMAN, H.E. (1972). "Outcome measures and social action experiments: An immodest proposal for redirecting research efforts." American Sociologist, 7(November):26-30.

FREEMAN, H.E., and BERNSTEIN, I.N. (1975). "Evaluation research and public policies." Pp. 9-25 in S.S. Nagel (ed.), Policy studies and the social sciences. Lexington, Mass.: D.C. Heath.

FREEMAN, H.E., and SHERWOOD, C.C. (1970). Social research and social policy. Englewood Cliffs, N.J.: Prentice-Hall.

FREIDSON, E. (1972). "The organization of medical practice." Pp. 343-358 in H.E. Freeman, L.G. Reeder, and S. Levine (eds.), Handbook of medical sociology. Englewood Cliffs, N.J.: Prentice-Hall.

GILBERT, J.P., LIGHT, R.J., and MOSTELLER, F. (1975). "Assessing social innovations: An empirical base for policy." In C.A. Bennett and A.A. Lumsdaine (eds.), Evaluation and experiment. New York: Academic Press.

GRAMLICH, E.M., and KOSHEL, P.P. (1975). Educational performance contracting. Washington, D.C.: The Brookings Institution.

GUTTENTAG, M., and STRUENING, E.L. (eds., 1975). Handbook of evaluation research, vol. 2. Beverly Hills, Calif.: Sage.

HAYES, S.P., Jr. (1959). Evaluating development projects. Paris: UNESCO.

HILLIS, J.W., and WORTMAN, C.B. (1976). "Some determinants of public acceptance of randomized control group experimental designs." Sociometry, 39(2):91-96.

HILTON, E.T., and LUMSDAINE, A.A. (1975). "Field trial designs in gauging the impact of fertility planning programs." Pp. 322-323 in C.A. Bennett and A.A. Lumsdaine (eds.), Evaluation and experiment. New York: Academic Press.

KIROS, F.G., MUSHKIN, S.J., and BILLINGS, B.B. (1975). Educational outcome measurement in developing countries. Washington, D.C.: Public Services Laboratory.

KLEIN, R.E., FREEMAN, H.E., KAGAN, J., YARBROUGH, C., and HABICHT, J-P. (1972). "Is big smart? The relation of growth to cognition." Journal of Health and Social Behavior, 13(September):219-225.

LESSER, G.S. (1974). Children and television. New York: Random House.

LEVIN, H.M. (1975). "Cost-effectiveness analysis in evaluation research." Pp. 89-90 in M. Guttentag and E.L. Struening (eds.), Handbook of evaluation research, vol. 2. Beverly Hills, Calif.: Sage.

MERTON, R. (1965). On the shoulders of giants. New York: Harcourt, Brace and World.

National Academy of Sciences (1974). Final report of the Panel on Manpower Training Evaluation. The use of Social Security earnings data for assessing the impact of manpower training programs. Washington, D.C.: Author.

RIECKEN, H.W., and BORUCH, R.F. (eds., 1974). Social experimentation. New York: Academic Press.

ROSS, L., and CRONBACH, L.J. (1976). "A review by a Task Force of the Stanford Evaluation Consortium of the Handbook of Evaluation Research." The National Academy of Education, 3:81-107.

ROSSI, P.H., and WILLIAMS, W. (eds., 1972). Evaluating social programs. New York: Seminar Press.

SCOTT, J.F., and FREEMAN, H.E. (1963). "The one night stand in mental health education." Social Problems, 10(3):277-284.

SHELDON, E.B., and FREEMAN, H.E. (1970). "Notes on social indicators." Policy Sciences, 1:97-111.

SJOBERG, G. (1975). "Ethics and evaluation research." Pp. 29-51 in M. Guttentag and E.L. Struening (eds.), Handbook of evaluation research, vol. 2. Beverly Hills, Calif.: Sage.

STEPHAN, A.S. (1935). "Prospects and possibilities: The New Deal and the new social research." Social Forces, 13:515-521.

STRUENING, E.L., and GUTTENTAG, M. (eds., 1975). Handbook of evaluation research, vol. 1. Beverly Hills, Calif.: Sage.

SUCHMAN, E. (1967). Evaluative research. New York: Russell Sage Foundation.

VAN DUSEN, R.A., and ZILL, N. (eds., 1973). Basic background items for U.S. household surveys. Washington, D.C.: Social Science Research Council.

WEISS, C.H. (1972). Evaluation research. Englewood Cliffs, N.J.: Prentice-Hall.

WHOLEY, J.S., SCANLON, J.W., DUFFY, H., FUKUMOTO, J.S., and VOGT, L.M. (1970). Federal evaluation policy. Washington, D.C.: Urban Institute.

WILKINS, L.T. (1969). Evaluation of penal measures. New York: Random House.

WILLIAMS, W., and EVANS, J.W. (1972). "The politics of evaluation: The case of Head Start." Pp. 249-264 in P.H. Rossi and W. Williams (eds.), Evaluating social programs. New York: Seminar Press.

WILNER, D.M., WALKLEY, R.P., PINKERTON, T.C., and TAYBACK, M. (1962). The housing environment and family life. Baltimore: Johns Hopkins University Press.

WOLFLE, D. (1970). "Chance, or human judgment?" Science, 167:1201.

2

EVALUATION AND SOCIETY

By

MARCIA GUTTENTAG

Evaluation research flourishes in a postindustrial society where the dominant emphasis is on human services. This discussion focuses on the multiple perspectives which must be represented in evaluations which are conducted in a context of decentralized programs.

From Marcia Guttentag, "Evaluation and Society." *Personality and Social Psychology Bulletin,* 1977, *3*(1):31-40.

There are no agreed upon definitions of units when one moves away from individuals as targets, despite the considerable body of knowledge in the sociology of organizations. Regardless of the level of organization of the targets, it is essential that there be sufficient identifying data about them that allow their delineation from the nontargets in a community or locale.

In the case of individuals, targets usually are identified in terms of social and demographic characteristics or in terms of the problems, difficulties, and conditions they share—or both. When aggregates other than individuals are the targets, they are variously defined in terms of the characteristics of the individuals that comprise the groups or the organizations, their formal and informal collective properties, or their shared problems and deficiencies. Thus, for example, the targets of a program in which individuals are pivotal might be defined as follows: male adolescents between ages 15 and 18 who reside in "X" district and who are between one and three years behind their normal grade in school. An example of a definition of an organizational target might be as follows: formally incorporated clubs of at least 10, and no more than 30, members, which restrict membership to persons over 60, and which, in Y city, live in areas where there is neither television reception nor a movie theater within a one-mile walk for at least 75% of its members.

These are illustrations of targets fairly well defined in operational terms. In most cases, however, definitions of targets often include more diffuse and ambiguous characteristics, or characteristics difficult and expensive to measure. For example, add to the individual definition noted above the additional requirement that targets live in households in which there is a high degree of marital conflict; or, in the case of the second definition, groups contain a large proportion of alienated and socially isolated individuals.

In many evaluation research studies, characteristics difficult to measure validly and reliably, as in the examples above, predominate in descriptions of target populations. In these cases programs may lose duplicability and expandability.

It is important to remember that only last year common agreement was reached among survey researchers on standard items to measure such social characteristics as education and occupation (Van Dusen and Zill, 1973). Given this state of affairs, there is no wonder that in the evaluation research field there are major problems of operational definition and few standardized measures. It is necessary, for continuity of work in evaluation research, that attention be paid to this matter.

A major reason it is necessary to have a rigorous definition of the target population is to estimate the "take" for a particular program. Practitioners and planners in most human resource fields, naturally enough, tend to overestimate the incidence and prevalence of target groups for which they have program investments. Those with loyalties to, say, physically handicapped persons, and who are interested in providing culturally stimulating programs for them, have unrealistic notions of how large the population is in a community who are both physically handicapped and culturally deprived. The same is true when one is dealing with either medically diagnosed or socially labeled groups, or a particular demographic slice of community members.

Abstract. Evaluation research requires a different paradigm than classical experimental research. It requires a paradigm in which it is possible to use the multiple objectives of different groups as the framework within which decisions about data gathering are made. It requires decision-oriented rather than conclusion-oriented research, although experiments and other forms of data generation can be used. This article discusses the unique characteristics of evaluation research and the decision theoretic (Maut-Bayesian) paradigm which fulfills these special requirements.

Evaluation research is in the midst of a major paradigm shift. This shift is related to a much larger social change--the movement from an industrial to a post-industrial society. Daniel Bell has pointed out that the epistemological status of science is changing in correspondence with this societal movement, and with it as well, the role and requirements of scientists.

Let us first briefly categorize the characteristics of industrial and post-industrial societies, the roles men and women play in such societies, and then comment on the distinctive problems and contexts of science, especially social science, in these societies.

The nature of the research paradigm developed within the context of an industrial society will be commented upon, and then the characteristics of an evaluative research paradigm which are required in a post-industrial society. Evaluation research is the social science which is in the vanguard position in these societal changes because it is intimately linked with the thrust of a society as expressed in its social and human services. To illustrate the paradigmatic change, a number of what appear to be methodological problems, which are currently being debated actively in the evaluation research literature, will be presented. These problems are closely linked to, and revelatory of, the paradigm shift. Then the decision theoretic approach to evaluation will be briefly discussed. It will be argued that its peculiar features are, perhaps, uniquely suited to the conditions and epistemological requirements of evaluation in a post-industrial society.

Three Types of Societies

These societies as ideal types might be characterized in the following ways:

Pre-industrial. "Life in pre-industrial societies--still the condition of most of the world today--is primarily a game against nature. The labor force is overwhelmingly in the extractive industries: agriculture, mining, fishing, forestry. One works with raw muscle power, in inherited ways, and one's sense of the world is conditioned by the vicissitudes of the elements--the seasons, the storms, the fertility of the soil, the amount of water, the depth of the mine seams, the droughts and the floods. The rhythms of life are shaped by these contingencies."

Industrial societies. "Industrial societies, producing goods, play
a game against fabricated nature. The world has become technical and
rationalized. The machine predominates and the rhythms of life are
mechanically paced; time is chronological, mechanical, evenly spaced
by the divisions of the clock. Energy has replaced raw muscle and
provides the basis for the large leaps in productivity, the mass output
of standardized goods which characterizes an industrial society. Energy
and machines transform the nature of work. Skills are broken down into
simple components, and the artisan of the past is replaced by two new
figures: the engineer who is responsible for the layout and flow of
work, and the semi-skilled worker who is the cog between the machines
until the technical ingenuity of the engineer creates a new machine
which replaces him as well. [Ideally,] it is a world of scheduling
and programming in which the components are brought together at exact
moments for assembly. It is a world of coordination in which men,
materials, and markets are dovetailed for the production and distribution of goods. [Ideally,] it is a world of organization--of hierarchy
and bureaucracy--in which men are treated as things because one can
more easily coordinate things than men."

Post-industrial society. "A post-industrial society, because it
centers on services--human services, professional and technical
services--is a game between persons. The organization of a research
team, the relation between doctor and patient, teacher and pupil,
government official and petitioner--a world, in short, where the
modalities are scientific knowledge, higher education, community organization, and the like--involves cooperation and reciprocity rather than
the coordination and hierarchy. [Ideally,] the post-industrial society
is also a communal society in which the social unit is the community
organization rather than the individual and decisions have to be reached
through some polity--in collective negotiations between private organizations, as well as government--rather than the market. But cooperation
among men is more difficult than the mangement of things. Participation
is a condition of community; and when many different groups want too
many different things and are not prepared to bargain, then increased
conflict or deadlock results. There is either a politics of consensus
or a politics of stymie" (Bell, 1976, pp. 147-148). This is, of course,
Daniel Bell's thesis.

Of course, these societies necessarily coexist, even within the
same country in the modern world. What is described is the major thrust
of change. In the United States we are still producing steel and industrial products--but the emphasis, the direction of society, is post-
industrial. One look at the Occupational Outlook Handbook for 1976-77
confirms the rapidity of our movement into a post-industrial society.
A growth of nearly 30% of white-collar employment is projected for 1985--
that includes professionals, managers and technical workers. Blue-collar
work will expand only 13% (Levine, 1976).

What is it that man seeks to understand and to master in these
different kinds of societies? In pre-industrial society, "the first
confrontation was with nature, and for most of the thousands of years
of human existence, life has been a game against nature, to find a
strategy which keeps nature at bay: to find shelter from the elements,
to ride the waters and the wind, to wrest food and sustenance from the
soil, the waters, and other creatures. The coding of much of man's
behavior has been shaped by the need to adapt to these vicissitudes"
(Bell, 1976, p. 148).

In industrial society, "man . . . sought to make things, and in making things he dreamt of reworking nature. To be dependent on nature was to bend to its caprices. To remake nature, through fabrication and replication, was to enhance man's powers. The industrial revolution was . . . an effort to substitute a technical order for the natural order, an engineering conception of function and rationality. . . ."

"The post-industrial order turns its back on both. In the salient experience of work, men live more and more outside nature, and less and less with machinery and things; they live with, and encounter only, one another. The problems of group life, of course, are among the oldest difficulties of human civilization. . . . But now the context has changed. The oldest forms of group life were within the context of nature, and the overcoming of nature gave an external, common purpose to the lives of men. The group life that was hitched to things gave men a huge sense of power as they created mechanical artifacts' to transform the world. But in the post-industrial world, for the majority of persons, the older contexts have disappeared from view. In the daily round of work, men no longer confront nature, either as alien or beneficent, and few handle artifacts and things.

"For most of human history, reality was nature, and . . . men sought to relate themselves to the natural world. In the last 150 years reality has been technics, tools, and things made by men. . . . Now reality is becoming only the social world, excluding nature and things" (Bell, 1976, pp. 148-149). This is the thesis that Bell eloquently presents.

What of the role of science in these societies? The development of the physical sciences and engineering preceded and made the Industrial Revolution possible. The physical sciences and industrial society interacted synergistically. The problems of the industrial society--the mastery over and creation of things--from plastics to space probes, provided the problems and contexts for scientific solutions.

The origins, nature, methods and focus--i.e. the epistemology of science--are deeply embedded in the societal context, and concerns, out of which they develop. Let us therefore examine more closely the epistemology of the scientific paradigm which led to and prospered in the context of an industrial society.

Science in an Industrial Society

"The technical world is defined by rationality and progress" (Bell, 1976, p. 151). As Bacon put it, "The end of our foundation is the knowledge of causes, and secret motion of things; and the enlarging of the bounds of human empire, to the effecting of all things possible" (Bacon, 1628).

There is a non-accidental unanimity of purpose in the model of the physical sciences and the aims of an industrial society. The search is for the invariant laws which govern the interaction of "things"--the physical, material things and processes. It is mind over matter. The surfaces of matter are penetrated to find the true relationships between things. The aim is explanation. And when scientific advances are made, these are often quickly translated into technological applications. The invariances that are sought--the laws--are key. The same chemical reactions must reliably recur if industries are to be based upon them. A variable, when it is unchanged, must be the same over time and place, though of course it may interact with various environmental conditions, etc. Most, if not all, of the variables chosen for study in this model of science have such properties.

The scientists' role is very much in keeping with the remaking of nature required by the technical order of the industrial world. It is entrepreneur-like in its emphasis on mastery over nature. The powerful community of scientists is trained to accept the same norms for the definition of variables, for measurement, for hypothesis testing, and the criteria for the acceptance of a scientific explanation. With these common, explicit definitions, a scientist in any laboratory, in principle, should be able to completely replicate the procedures of a colleague anywhere else in the world. Informed by the collective work of other scientists, one individual can, hopefully, in his own laboratory, achieve a scientific breakthrough--in the explanation and/or creation of new physical interactions--such as, for example, the recent announcement of Khorana's synthesis of a gene.

Even the language in which scientific discoveries are couched reveals the underlying role of the scientist as the entrepreneur who masters the invariant secrets of nature (physical reality) and bends them to his will--e.g. "cracking the genetic code." Only one way of coding genetic information--now discovered! This is the stuff of Nobel Laureates, and is, of course, the paradigm of science with which we are all familiar, the one that so intrigued the logical positivists. It still, of course, remains, and its epistemology is still appropriate to the industrial society's aim of explaining, controlling, and eventually synthesizing and creating new variants of matter and nature.

But, as has been pointed out, we are now moving toward a post-industrial society where the emphases and contexts have shifted from the mastery over things toward the problems inherent in the "creation of settings" (Sarason, 1976) and of human services--professional, technical, informational, social.

Quine (1950) has remarked, "Truths are as plentiful as falsehoods . . . but scientific activity is not the indiscriminate amassing of truths; science is selective and seeks the truth that counts for most, either in point of intrinsic interest or as instruments for coping with the world."

If the key issue of the post-industrial society is mastering and understanding the "game between persons" (Bell, 1976), organizations and the variety of decision-making social units, then it is not surprising that there would be a paradigm shift from the older scientific model toward one which is oriented more toward this new set of problems and contexts.

Some Symptoms of the Paradigmatic Malaise

It is not surprising that much recent work in the philosophy of science is critical of some of the root assumptions of the older scientific paradigm. The orientation of these criticisms is of interest. Keep in mind that in the post-industrial society the diversity of social groups is an important problem. This diversity and heterogeneity of decision-making groups must be acknowledged in the creation and organization of services--whether those of a research team or of a national health program. As Festinger (1954) saw years ago, social reality (really realities) are based on social comparison processes, without the possibility of reference to single, outside empirical standards.

Much of the recent criticism and revisionism in the philosophy of science concerns itself with this intrinsic diversity of views, and the difficulty or impossibility of unambiguous interpretations. Feyerabend (1975) and many others maintain that hypothesis testing itself is an

open-ended process, that observations themselves do not imply or allow
for any single unambiguous interpretation.

Toulmin (1971) and others have described the shift in the philosophy of science away from emphases on the "logical, formal relationships within particular intellectual cross-sections of science; toward
an emphasis on the ways in which scientists, as people, "give up one set
of concepts in favor of another." This historicism is reflected in
Kuhn's view of science as a social enterprise in which consensus
changes over time. The focus on historicism in the philosophy of
science is only one aspect of the paradigm shift toward an emphasis on
multiple perspectives--in this case, different perspectives over time.
Another aspect of this shift in the philosophy of science is the retreat
from prediction and control towards a greater concern with "understanding."

Still another way in which the post-industrial social focus is
reflected in shifts within the scientific paradigm, particularly in the
social sciences, surfaces in the new emphasis on dialectic, which can
be seen in the Marxist critiques of "value free" sociology, and the
multiple perspectives methodologies explored in the recent work of
Levine & Rosenberg (Note 1) and Mitroff (in press). These critiques,
and the dialectical methods, topple the scientist from his previously
secure role as the knowledge entrepreneur, and legitimate a diversity
of perspectives, each with its distinctive interpretation of social
realities.

Yet another reflection of the paradigmatic shift in the concerns
of science in a post-industrial society is the focus on the structure
and contents of the minds of men (rather than the nature of physical
reality)--with the emphasis on structuralism as a scientific concern--
from Piaget's genetic epistemology to the structuralism of the anthropo-
logists, linguists and psychoanalysts (at least the French ones). The
major orientation in the social sciences now is: "How do people define
their (subjective) world?" Subjectivity has been reintroduced, as it
must be, to handle the diversity of perspectives. Even social psychology has been influenced by these paradigm changes--from a new self-
consciousness about its own historicity (Gergen, 1973) to a redefinition
of how the person is considered (influenced by the human action philosophers)--which has led to changes even in the laboratory methods used
in social psychology (Harre and Secord, 1975).

In summary, then, there are many indications of a paradigm change,
particularly in the social sciences, a shift which seems integrally tied
to the major concerns and problems of a post-industrial society--"the
game between persons"--centered on services. Earlier, I said that
evaluation research, of all the social science fields, is, fortunately
or unfortunately, in the vanguard position in a post-industrial society.
That is because the very content of the discipline is the social programs
and services and the decisions which have to be reached about them, by
the various, diverse, participating groups of the society.

Requirements of an Evaluative Paradigm
in a Post-industrial Society

What would such an evaluative paradigm be like? First, it would
have to respect within its formal structure the perspectives of these
diverse, decision-making groups. The objectives of these groups would
determine the kinds of information produced. No longer would the
scientist's view of what was important be dominant. His would be only
one voice of the various constituencies. Since in a post-industrial

society power rests more significantly on information, decision over
what information to produce must be egalitarian, rather than entrepreneurial. The information itself must be related to the inferences about
the extent to which programs fulfill the various objectives of the
different groups. Methodologies and statistical systems must be used
which do not make false assumptions about the character of social
realities, and which permit the inferential combination of the variegated, diverse, sloppy, qualitative data that human beings leave in
their trails. Most important, the paradigm should fit the requirements
of the evaluative problem, such as the need for information for decisions which may be intermittent, and non-regular.

There is a sharp test for such proposed evaluative paradigms. If
they produce information that is not used in program decisions--then
they are not adequate paradigms. Later an approach to evaluation will
be described which does fulfill these requirements, namely the decision-
theoretic approach.

As you can tell, we do not agree with some of our colleagues that
evaluation research is a pallid, warmed-over version of applied social
research. On the contrary, its scientific, intellectual problems are
distinctively new, because of the new contexts, orientations and issues
confronted in post-industrial societies. Note that in the discussion
which follows, we are always referring to primary evaluations, not to
secondary evaluations. Primary evaluation means going out and doing
the evaluation yourself. In secondary evaluation, the evaluator critically reanalyzes a primary evaluation which has been conducted by
someone else. There now are industries which do either one or both.
It will soon be clear why the questions that have been addressed in
secondary evaluations keep them--at what appear to be a safe distance
away--from the paradigmatic concerns which are inescapable in primary
evaluations.

In order to illustrate the differences between an evaluation
paradigm for a post-industrial society, and the research paradigm
developed within the industrial society's context and problems, we will
turn to six methodological issues that continue to receive extensive
discussion in the evaluation literature. These recurrent issues are
troubling because of the failure to recognize the paradigm shift. The
six points are:

1. Is a social program an independent variable?
2. How can the objectives of multiple decision-making groups be
   dealt with?
3. Who shall control--decide--what information is produced?
4. Can data be aggregated nationally?
5. Must evaluation use experimental or quasi-experimental designs?
6. How can diverse types of data be integrated?

Independent variables are the mainstay of the older scientific
paradigm, developed for the mastery and control of physical realities.
Part of the definition of an independent variable is that it is the same
over time and place. Hydrogen is hydrogen. Independent variables are
the sine qua non of experimentation, which is, of course, one of the
key methods of that model of science.

Is a social program an independent variable? Maybe. Sometimes.
Gilbert, Light, & Mosteller (1975) have argued that the analogy between
independent variables and medical, socio-medical, and social programs
is strong, and the latter can be treated as though they were independent

variables. We disagree. Certainly, the Salk vaccine was an independent variable—as is any medical program which consists of carefully measured equal doses of a chemical. But when one turns to most of the human service programs of a post-industrial society, the independent variable analogy is impossible. A program like CETA (Comprehensive Employment and Training Act), or Model Cities, is different in every city; indeed, the requirement that it be different is written into the enabling legislation. Even within the same city, social programs differ greatly over time, and it is often unlikely that any two individuals will receive the same treatment.

(Some psychologists have made the inverse of the argument presented here. Since social programs may not be independent variables, they suggest that perhaps all social variables, even those manipulated in controlled laboratory experiments, suffer from the lack of representativeness, the lack of "sameness" (Bonoma, Note 2). But these arguments are outside the focus of the present discussion.)

One way in which this issue has been handled by researchers trained in the older model, is not to have anything to do with a program unless program administrators promise to make it an independent variable. That is where the famous fights arise. And the researcher's illusions. Nevertheless, the fuzzy, variegated, and changeable nature of many social programs create social realities radically different from physical ones. When it is demanded that problems be forced to fit methods, rather than vice versa, then the need for a paradigm shift is patently clear.

Without independent variables, what then is the problem in evaluation? The answer is a bewildering further question. It is not what is the problem, but whose problem is it? In the older scientific paradigm the scientist as a representative of the scientific community defined the problem and hypotheses to be investigated, in keeping with the aim of focused mastery over physical reality.

In the post-industial society, social realities are as variable as the groups that define them. The "insider-outsider's" perspectives which are of concern to modern philosophers of science are directly confronted in the evaluation of human service programs. Multiple perspectives of diverse decision-making groups are the everyday reality in evaluation. The scientist is no more than a representative of one group of knowledge producers; his perspective receives no special priority. For the evaluation of human services in the post-industrial society, a scientific paradigm is required which permits each of the decision-making groups to propose its distinctive perspective on how the problem itself is to be defined.

Until now, we have left the term "evaluation" undefined, although this is a discussion of evaluation research. Evaluation is an aspect of decision making. The evaluative scientific problem in a post-industrial society is how to provide the information relevant to the continuous decisions which must be made by these heterogeneous groups—about which human services to adopt, which to discontinue, and which to change.

Despite the concerns of the philosophers, the older scientific paradigm has no legitimated means for including the diverse perspectives of different groups in the very definition of the problem. When the older paradigm shapes the discussion in the evaluation literature, then, these multiple groups are relegated to the annoying, interfering category of "the politics of evaluation"—which researchers believe often interupts what they think to be the proper conduct of evaluative research.

From another point of view, these groups often evoke the ire of these evaluators, because often they do not use the data that evaluators have so laboriously obtained, in making their decisions. Altogether, evaluators trained in the older paradigm find these diverse groups to be disagreeable and difficult.

Our view on this is harsh. If evaluative data is not used by the decision-making groups, then the evaluator has failed--has failed to gather the information relevant to the criteria which will be used in making the decisions. The most important criterion of how good an evaluation is, is the extent to which the information it produces is actually used in making decisions.

It should be clear, then, that the question which never arises in the older paradigm, because its answer is so obvious--who decides what information shall be produced?--is of the utmost import in evaluation. And the answer is that if the decision-making groups' objectives do not shape the decisions about what information will be produced, then the evaluation will not be used by them for program decisions, and by our criteria which we have just given, the evaluation will be a failure.

Thus far we have been concerned with problem definition and multiple perspectives. The last three "methodological issues" seem to be closer to true methodological and statistical problems. And they are.

First, the data aggregation problem. If, as we have just described, a great many national social programs are not at all analogous to independent variables, but are quite different over sites and within sites over time, then how can data about the program be aggregated? The answers proposed by the older paradigm are to treat the legislation for the program as though it had created an independent variable, and to ignore these differences, or to take a complete "black box" approach, as for example, economists do in Manpower evaluations, where they say in effect, "I don't care what was done to them, I'm only going to look at outcomes."

Once again, we disagree. Even if a paper fiction is accepted or program differences are completely ignored, it is still a violation of the core assumptions of classical statistics (Newmann-Pearson, Fisherian) to add apples and oranges. Is there any alternative, other than complete disaggregation? We think there is. It is to aggregate inferences rather than data. Lest this sound mysterious, methods for this have been developed.

A similar issue arises about data integration. There simply is no way, using classical statistics, to integrate data which varies widely in source, type and quality. If, however, such diverse data is used to progressively modify inferences, then all such variegated data can be both used and integrated. Of course, we are following Bayesian statistics, in which data of any type can be used to revise prior probabilities (the certainty with which decision makers hold their hypotheses) into posterior probabilities.

Must evaluation use experimental or quasi-experimental designs? This seems a straightforward design question. Or is it? We want to be sure that it is understood that in these remarks we have been concerned with alternative paradigms, a level of abstraction above that of choices between alternative designs. Choices about the methods that will be used to generate the relevant data follow and do not precede decisions about what information is relevant. Put another way, the choice of paradigm is the primary and initial choice. Then there are a wide variety of methods from which to choose so that the researcher can generate the desired information. We have not been arguing against the experimental method, or quasi-experimental designs. Using a decision theoretic evaluation paradigm, a researcher might want to use these experimental methods in the data gathering process. What has been argued is whether the older scientific paradigm in which experimental methods were the sine qua non, was an appropriate paradigm for evaluation in a post-industrial society. Obviously, we do not think it is. But frequently the methods generated within a scientific paradigm can be the technologies which can be chosen within another paradigm. So, experimental or quasi-experimental designs are two of the methodological choices which are available to the researcher--after decisions about what kind of information is needed have been made. Unfortunately, in much evaluation research literature, there is a confusion between paradigmatic and methodological issues, and paradigm differences are obscured by the concentrated focus on design choices.

Decision Theoretic Evaluation Paradigm

Initially we said that we would explain the decision theoretic approach to evaluation and argue that its peculiar features are, perhaps, uniquely suited to the conditions and epistemological requirements of evaluation in a post-industrial society.

Detailed discussions of the steps in decision theoretic evaluations, especially multi-attribute utilities and Bayesian combinations, will be presented later. What we will do here is briefly discuss the general characteristics of the decision theoretical approach which make it perfectly appropriate to the paradigm required for evaluation in a post-industrial society.

Decision theoretic approaches permit the formal explication and prioritization of the objectives of diverse groups. There is no need to pool or in any other way blend this diversity. Each group defines and prioritizes its own objectives for any program. Thus the "multiple perspectives requirement" is formally and structurally the starting point of the evaluation. Choices about what information is to be generated are determined by the most important objectives of each group. Information is provided by researchers for at least the most important objectives of each decision-making group. That takes care of who decides which information shall be generated.

Bayesian, rather than classical, statistics are used to link the prioritized objectives to inferences about the actual states of the world, i.e. programs. Data is used to change the prior probabilities--the certainty with which hypotheses are held--into posterior probabilities given data. Inferences are aggregated rather than data. The Bayesian system is data inclusive, so that it can use all of the data generated through experimental methods, as well as qualitative, archival, anecdotal, and other variegated forms of information--it is just that the diagnosticity of the data will vary. A further characteristic of the Bayesian system is that data gathering can be continuous, intermittent, irregular. At any point in time, prior probabilities can be revised into posteriors, given whatever data exists. Thus a feedback information system is possible so that evaluation information (whatever there is) can be given to decision makers whenever they need it for decisions.

Perhaps it is a lucky accident that there is an approach with the characteristics which so aptly fit the needed paradigm. Perhaps it is not an accident, since most modern work on the development of these approaches has taken place within the past few years.

To be working in a discipline at the forefront of the major paradigmatic scientific change in the post-industrial society is exciting. It _is_ as a new ball game. Do join it!

Reference Notes

1. Levine, M., & Rosenberg, N. S. An adversary model of fact finding and decision making for program evaluation: theoretical considerations. Unpublished paper, 1976.
2. Bonoma, T. Social psychology and social evaluation. Unpublished paper, February 1975.

References

Bacon, F. The new atlantis, 1628.

Bell, D. The cultural contradictions of capitalism. New York: Basic Books, 1976. Esp. chap. 4, "Toward the great instauration: religion and culture in a post-industrial age," pp. 146-171.

Festinger, L. A theory of social comparison processes. Human Relations, 1954, 7, 117-140.

Feyerabend, P. Against method: Outline of an anarchistic theory of knowledge. Atlantic Highlands, N. J.: Humanities Press, 1975.

Gergen, K. Social psychology as history. Journal of Personality and Social Psychology, 1973, 26, 309-320.

Gilbert, J., Light, R., & Mosteller, F. Assessing social innovations: An empirical base for policy. In C. A. Bennett & A. A. Lumsdaine (Eds.), Evaluation and experiment. New York: Academic Press, 1975.

Harre, H., & Secord, P. F. The explanation of social behavior. Totowa, N. J.: Littlefield, Adams & Co., 1973.

Levine, C. C. Occupational outlook handbook in brief, 1976-77 edition. U.S. Dept. of Labor, reprinted from the Occupational Outlook Quarterly, Vol. 20, No. 1, Spring 1976.

Mitroff, I. I. On evaluating scientific research: The contribution of the psychology of science. Journal of Technological Forecasting and Social Change (in press).

Quine, W. V. O. Methods of logic. New York: Holt, Rinehart & Winston, 1950.

Sarason, S. The creation of settings and the future societies. San Francisco: Jossey-Bass, 1972.

Footnotes

1. Reprint requests should be addressed to Dr. Marcia Guttentag, Read House, Graduate School of Education, Harvard University, Cambridge, Mass. 02138. Delivered as the Presidential Address to the Division of Personality and Social Psychology, American Psychological Association, Washington, D. C., September 5, 1976.

3

POLICY RELEVANT SOCIAL RESEARCH:
WHAT DOES IT LOOK LIKE?

By

LAURENCE E. LYNN, Jr.

In a penetrating and original analysis Laurence Lynn tackles the most difficult problem of all—that of choosing the criteria of policy relevance. By what criteria should social R & D be judged? This analysis of the types of knowledge which different projects provide, clarifies how the choice of criteria depends on values and perceptions of the appropriate federal role.

From Laurence E. Lynn, Jr., "Policy Relevant Social Research: What Does It Look Like?" *Policy Analysis on Major Issues,* prepared for the Commission on the Operation of the Senate, 1977.

In 1976 the Federal Government invested more than $1.8 billion in knowledge production and utilization relating to the identification and solution of social problems. Included in this figure are research, statistics, evaluations, demonstrations and experiments. Though the need for large-scale Federal support of social R. & D. is widely accepted. questions concerning the relevance of social R. & D. to the making of social policy have become more insistent in recent years. What are we learning? Who is making effective use of what we learn?

The beginning of systematic Federal support for social R. & D. can perhaps be traced to the creation of the Federal Bureau of Ethnology in 1881.[1a] During the following four decades, motivated by the Progressive Era's concern for social problems and the need for scientific advice generated by World War I, Federal support for social R. & D. emerged in recognizable form. The Depression Era's social problems and World War II further stimulated Federal spending for social research, which reached a level of $53 million in 1937 and exceeded $60 million by 1953.[1b] Growth was slow during the 1950's, when social R. & D. concentrated on problems of national security and health. Stimulated by another burst of governmental energy to solve social problems, it accelerated sharply during the 1960's, with present levels of spending being reached only in the last few years.

EMERGENCE OF THE RELEVANCE PROBLEM

As federal support for social R. & D. reached significant levels, controversies began. To oversimplify a complex history, there had been two principal sources of concern: legislators distrustful of "social engineers" who promote radical ideas and pursue irrelevant academic interests, and social scientists worried that dependence on government might compromise their independence.[2]

---

*This article is adapted from "Introduction" and "Interpreting Policy Relevance" by Laurence E. Lynn, Jr., in Knowledge and Policy: The Question of Relevance. Laurence Lynn, Jr., editor. National Academy of Sciences, Washington, D.C., 1977.
[1a] Perhaps the classic beginning of policy relevant, federally supported social R. & D. is the Lewis & Clark Expedition. See Appendix, "The Lewis & Clark Expedition: A Social R. & D. Paradigm," below.
[1b] Kathleen Archibald, "Federal Interest and Investment in Social Science," in U.S. House of Representatives, "The Use of Social Research in Federal Domestic Programs," part I, Committee on Government Operations, 90th Cong., 1st sess., April 1967, p. 328.
[2] An early manifestation of this concern was contained in the 1938 report of the National Research Committee, "Research—A National Resource." This report recommended that "research within the Government and by non-governmental agencies which cooperate with the Government be so organized and conducted as to avoid the possibilities of bias through subordination in any way to policy-making and policy-enforcing." A series of quasi-official reports. beginning with the 1938 report of the National Resource Committee, have discussed national policies for the support of research to solve complex social problems. These reports have urged the federal government to play a major role in supporting social R. & D. and have discussed a variety of the problems that arise when the government undertakes such support. See, for example, President's Science Advisory Committee, "Strengthening the Behavioral Sciences" (Washington, D.C.: 1962); U.S. House of Representatives, Committee on Government Operations, "The Use of Social Research in Federal Domestic Programs," 90th Cong., 1st sess. 1967 (Washington, D.C.: U.S. Government Printing Office, 1967); National Academy of Sciences, "The Behavioral
(Continued)

In the early 1970's, however, concerns were increasingly heard from a relatively new source: Federal policymaking officials whose agencies supported social R. & D. Many of these officials believed that a raison d'etre for the growing amounts being spent was the production of knowledge that would be useful in their policymaking roles. Based on their experience in looking for and using knowledge from research, they expressed doubts that federally supported social R. & D. produced much useful knowledge or that usable knowledge was actually used often enough to justify the cost of obtaining it.

Disappointment in social R. & D., for example, was expressed by then Secretary of Health, Education and Welfare Elliot Richardson, whose department accounted for nearly half of federally supported social R. & D. In reviewing the sums spent by HEW, he observed that:

> Too much of this money has gone into poorly conceived projects, too few of the results have been rigorously assessed, and our means of disseminating the worthwhile results have been too feeble. This means that we know less than we should, that we're less sure of what we know, and that too few people share the knowledge we do possess.[3]

The following criticism of social R. & D. sponsored by the Defense Department appears in a 1971 report by the National Research Council.

> High-level officials, both in the Department of Defense and in the former Bureau of the Budget, believe that research should be more useful to them than it is. Non-mission-oriented basic research is considered to have lacked policy pay-offs and to have constituted both a subsidy to producers and a source of difficulty and irritation with the Congress. Research producers are sometimes viewed as being more interested in furthering their academic disciplines than providing operational help to the Department of Defense.[4]

After surveying a large number of government officials and social scientists, Fortune magazine reported in 1972 that "no one in government is much tempted by the fruits on social science's tree of knowledge."[5]

The Nixon Administration's statement of support for Federal research and development programs for fiscal year 1974 stressed the importance of recognizing that "how we spend our resources for research and development is just as important as how much we spend." It placed emphasis on "encouraging the focusing of research and development on specific problems within areas of special national need" and on insuring that "the American people get a proper return on the dollars they invest in Federal research and development."[6]

Such concerns have given rise to specific questions:

(Continued from p. 59.)
Sciences and the Federal Government" (Washington, D.C.: The National Science Foundation, 1968); National Academy of Sciences, "The Behavioral and Social Sciences, Outlook and Needs" (Washington, D.C.: National Academy of Sciences, 1969); National Science Foundation, "Knowledge Into Action: Improving the Nation's Use of the Social Sciences" Washington, D.C.: National Science Foundation, 1969).

[3] U.S. Department of Health, Education and Welfare, "Responsibility and Responsiveness." Washington, D.C., 1972, p. 11. One of Richardson's early acts at HEW was to have his planning and evaluation staff review HEW supported social R. & D. and identify tested ideas that were awaiting adoption and promotion. Though a few ideas were identified, his staff concluded, contrary to Richardson's expectations, that "(1) There probably are no hidden jewels coming out of our R. & D. that are awaiting to be discovered if we just look enough, and (2) if such jewels do exist, our [R. & D.] bureaus are not apt to find them given the present reporting procedures."
For a further discussion of HEW's efforts to improve the relevance of its social R. & D., see Laurence E. Lynn, Jr., "Improving the Usefulness of Social R. & D.: Easier Said Than Done."

[4] National Academy of Sciences, "Behavioral and Social Science Research in the Department of Defense."

[5] Tom Alexander, "The Social Engineers Retreat Under Fire," Fortune, October 1972, p. 132.

[6] Special Analyses, Budget of the United States Government, fiscal year, 1974 (Washington, D.C.: U.S. Government Printing Office, 1973), pp. 251-257.

Should the allocation of social R. & D. resources among social problem areas be changed, e.g., more on evaluation and experimentation and less on social science research; more on randomized, controlled field trials and less on uncontrolled demonstrations; more on research done by universities and research institutions and less on analysis done by profit-making firms; more on long-term grants and less on short-term contracts?

Should the support of social R. & D. by the Federal Government be organized and administered differently? For example, should research administration be more centralized; should there be a greater use of formal planning processes; should there be more intramural research: should the potential users of research be more involved in research planning; should there be more interagency coordination?

The emergence of executive concern about the usefulness of social R. & D. is neither surprising nor disturbing. Any Federal activity competing for scarce budgetary resources will be subjected to critical evaluation by budget examiners. program evaluators, congressional committees, and policymakers. This has been especially true during the chronic budgetary squeezes of the early 1970's. Moreover, disillusionment with social R. & D. has in many respects been a reflection of post-Great Society disillusionment with social programs.

Paradoxically, however, recent insistence by Federal officials on relevance and accountability from the social R. & D. community is a partial reflection of the success the community has had in penetrating government. Following years of urging by social scientists, the policy world now takes it for granted that the social sciences have a contribution to make in government. Policymakers have come to depend on "social engineers" or "research brokers" to communicate expert knowledge. As assistant secretaries, deputy assistant secretaries and deputy undersecretaries for research and program development, research brokers are now fixtures in virtually every Federal agency. Professors and researchers from the social science community are regularly appointed to Cabinet posts. The staffs of numerous government bureaus and congressional offices have been "upgraded" by the addition of younger members with graduate education and the ability to read, criticize, and evaluate research reports. Through the Congressional Budget Office, the General Accounting Office. the Congressional Research Service and the Office of Technology Assessment. Congress is developing its own institutionalized cadre of trained policy analysts and social scientists.

These research brokers often exert pressure on the social R. & D. community to produce results relevant to policymaking.[7] Moreover, now that analysts and social scientists are part of the permanent government, it is unlikely that their insistence on relevance will ever abate. In fact, it is likely to increase at all the "right" times. i.e.. when knowledge is most needed to clarify complex policy choices. Thus, it would be a mistake to regard "the relevance problem" as aberrant or transitory.

[7] A similar point was made in a recent study of social science utilization by the University of Michigan's Institute for Social Research. "The notion that more and better contact [between social scientists and policy makers] may result in improved understanding and greater utilization may be true. but there are also conditions where familiarity may breed contempt rather than admiration." See Center for Research on Utilization of Scientific Knowledge. "The Use of Social Science Knowledge in Policy Decisions at the National Level. A Report to Respondents" (Ann Arbor: Institute for Social Research of the University of Michigan, 1975), p. 50.

Managing for Results

The pressure for relevance is more than just talk. It has taken a variety of concrete forms:

Increasing reliance in many agencies on competitively awarded contracts (and on "sole source" contracts with favored performers) instead of grants, and on grant arrangements that involve collaboration between grantor and grantee;

Pressures from policy, management, and budget personnel to improve contract and grant administration and research monitoring, dissemination, and utilization;

Increasing opposition to the use of peer review panels and community-oriented research advisory councils; and

A growing popularity for the forms of social R. & D. that seem most immediately useful to policy makers—program evaluation, policy analysis, expert consultation, and social experimentation—with a correspondingly lower priority accorded to traditional social science research performed at universities.

In addition, some agencies are experimenting with systematic methods for planning and setting priorities for their social R. & D. activities. Occasionally, other management devices have been tried. They include "policy implications papers" prepared in conjunction with completed research projects [8] and the appointment of research consumers to research advisory committees.

Unfortunately, we lack systematic evidence as to whether these steps are having the results their sponsors hope for. There are indications, however, that dissatisfaction with the usefulness of social R. & D. is not abating. For example, a recent report by the Federal Council for Science and Technology Task Group on Social R. & D. states the following:

There are indications that too little social R. & D. is relevant to policymaking and that too much research, even if relevant, is not available to and utilized by the appropriate decision makers." [9] A 1976 National Research Council review of the National Science Foundation's applied social science research concluded that "the quality of the work is highly variable, and that on average it is relatively undistinguished with only modest potential in useful application." [10]

In general, social R. & D. continues to receive criticism from Congressmen, executive branch officials, and social scientists because it is neither good nor well-managed research, and because it has little potential for use.

Although this continued criticism reflects the persistence of the problems that led to criticism in the first place, many in the social R. & D. community believe that recent pressures for policy relevance have actually been counterproductive. In their view, the attempt to manufacture socially useful knowledge to order—to treat the acquisition of knowledge like any other government procurement—has flooded the market with shoddy products. The resulting poor quality research, nonreplicable demonstrations, ambiguous experiments, useless data, and biased evaluations have neither policy value nor scien-

[8] For an interesting example, see Marcia Guttentag and Kurt Snapper, "Plans, Evaluations, and Decisions," Evaluation, Vol. 2, No. 1 (1974), p. 58ff.
[9] Report of Federal Council for Science and Technology Task Group on Social R. & D., Mar. 5, 1976, p. 3.
[10] "Social and Behavioral Science Programs in the National Science Foundation" (Washington, D.C.: National Academy of Sciences, 1976), p. 77.

tific merit. In the view of others, nothing has changed but the name of the game.

For example, one psychologist strongly committed to socially useful research notes that:

> Paradoxically, when funding agencies under the edicts of conservative Federal administrations have pressured for relevance, the effect has often been just the opposite from that which was intended—an increase occurred only in pseudo-relevancy and much rewriting of project proposal to use the [relevant] terminology took place.[11]

This unsatisfactory state of affairs has stimulated still more ideas for reforming social R. & D. management. One idea is to tighten the management of social R. & D. still further by centralizing social R. & D. administration, restricting Federal funding mainly to high priority subjects and projects, subjecting individual project proposals to greater scrutiny, and weakening or eliminating peer review [12] and what is asserted to be its parochial emphasis on methodology and performer reputation. At the other extreme, some would abandon direct approaches to achieving policy relevance altogether and return the making of social R. & D. policy to the scientific community. Those holding this view would strengthen, not weaken, peer review and leave the choice of subjects for research, the selection of research methods and performers, and decisions to disseminate research findings to those with scientific qualifications. By thus promoting quality and scientific merit, they believe, the government would be enhancing the social utility of social R. & D. in the most fundamental sense.

What do we know?

In the face of such divergent views, it seems wise to pause and take stock. What knowledge do we possess that is relevant to the formulation of social R. & D. policy? To what extent and in what manner is knowledge used in resolving social policy problems? By what strategies can the most useful forms of knowledge be obtained?

Regrettably (and ironically), we possess little knowledge obtained through research that will help answer these questions. As Albert Biderman has noted, ". . . social scientists . . . are only slightly more predisposed to rate social scientific knowledge about their business as one of their most critical needs than are people in those social endeavors that social scientists seek a mandate to inform." [13] Most studies addressing Federal social R. & D. policy have been promotional; that is, preoccupied with the extent of Federal financial support of social sciences at academic institutions and with the number of social scientists influential in government. Though there is a growing body of social science research on organizational behavior and change, the diffusion of innovations, and the nature of bureaucratic decisionmaking, this research has seldom influenced main arguments or recommendations.

There is recent evidence that this situation may be changing. The study by Nathan Caplan and Associates helps fill in the large gaps in our understanding of how the use of social science information influences Federal Government policy. The National Institute of

[11] Martin Deutsch, "On Making Social Psychology More Useful," Social Science Research Council, Items, Vol. 30, No. 1 (March 1976), p. 2.
[12] See Thane Gustofson, "The Controversy Over Peer Review," Science, Vol. 190 (12 Dec. 1975), pp. 1060–1066.
[13] Albert D. Biderman, "Self-Portrayal," Science, Vol. 169 (11 Sept. 1970), p. 1067.

Mental Health has initiated several studies aimed at understanding policymaking processes and the role of social R. & D. institutions in shaping them. The National Academy of Sciences published "Knowledge and Policy in Manpower," a landmark study of the manpower research and development program in the Department of Labor.[14] In a study sponsored by the Commission on the Organization of the Government for the Conduct of Foreign Policy, Professor Alexander L. George analyzed the entire body of social science knowledge on decisionmaking and developed ideas on how foreign policy formulation could make better use of information.[15]

Despite these efforts, few of the proposed solutions to the relevance problem have been based on a clear conception of what the terms "relevant to policy" or "socially useful" mean.

WHAT IS POLICY RELEVANCE?

Many who believe that social R. & D. ought to be more useful to policymakers base their views on an idealized policy process something like the following:

Policymakers realize that they have some responsibility for existing social problems. How can we reduce youth crime or curb drug addiction? How can we raise the educational attainment of poor children? How can we enhance productivity and the availability of jobs for the able-bodied unemployed? How can we provide a decent home and a suitable living environment for all Americans? How can we insure access to health care for the poor, and spare all Americans the strains imposed by rapidly rising health care costs? Recognizing such problems, policymakers begin seeking advice and assistance on what to do about them.

Among the sources of advice to policymakers is the social R. & D. community, which consists of the producers of social knowledge. In the best of all worlds, this community is continuously and systematically engaged in the study of individual, group, institutional, and social behavior. Its members develop models of behavior and empirically test hypotheses derived from these models. Based on their theoretical and empirical studies, they can explain, for example, why people commit crimes or become addicted to drugs, why prices rise while there is substantial unemployment, or what the effects of unequal educational opportunity are.

Even more to the point, the social R. & D. community is capable of predicting consequences of altering the factors affecting behavior. They can, for example, predict the consequences of various policy measures which change the incentives influencing relevant groups and institutions. They can predict what will happen if the price of natural gas is deregulated, if mandatory sentences are adopted for habitual

---

[14] Though not addressed to the problems of managing social R. & D., a recent study of Federal biomedical research is of considerable methodological interest. "Our project has only one goal." stated the authors: "to demonstrate that objectives, scientific techniques— instead of the present anecdotal approach—can be used to design and justify a national biomedical research policy." Through a rather rigorous empirical process, their study identified what they believed to be the types of research that underlay the top ten clinical advances in cardiovascular and pulmonary medicine and surgery in the last thirty years. See Julius H. Comroe, Jr. and Robert D. Dripps, "Scientific Basis for the Support of Biomedical Science," Science, Vol. 192, No. 4235 (Apr. 9, 1976), pp. 105–111.

[15] U.S. Commission on the Organization of the Government for the Conduct of Foreign Policy, "Appendix D: The Use of Information" (Washington, D.C., U.S. Government Printing Office, 1975).

offenders, if property tax relief is granted to elderly homeowners, if mandatory busing is used to achieve school desegregation, and the like. Once they come to understand the policy problem, they can assist in designing policies which will bring about socially desirable behavioral outcomes, and in estimating the costs of achieving those outcomes. They can compare different policies in various terms meaningful to policymakers (e.g., the effects of different policies on the cost of living, on family stability, on industry profitability, or on patterns of racial segregation).

Moreover, the social R. & D. community may discover social pathology. Social researchers may identify the extent and causes of poverty, the potential for violence among urban minorities, or the extent of occupationally-related mental illness. Thus, the social R. & D. community will be in a position to provide policymakers with early warnings of potential policy issues and with the questions they should be asking.

Even in this ideal world of knowledge-seeking policymakers and knowledgeable social researchers, problems of social R. & D. management would exist. Through what channels should communications between policymakers and researchers take place? How should the research community be organized and supported while doing its work? When social knowledge is lacking on an existing problem, when researchers disagree, or when their results are ambiguous, what should policymakers do while additional knowledge or clarification is being acquired? When resources to support social R. & D. are scarce, how should priorities among research objectives be established?

Moreover, even in ideal circumstances it is not clear what the indicators of policy-relevant research should be. Research useful to policymakers will probably be the cumulative result of many theoretical, methodological, and empirical investigations. It makes little sense to say that only empirical or applied research is relevant to policy if they depend for their validity on theoretical and methodological developments. Nor does it seem sensible to pass judgment on the policy relevance of every individual study. Policy relevance is an attribute of a broad research program in which the accumulated efforts of researchers are leading toward useful answers for policymakers. But who is to decide whether a research program is likely to yield useful answers? Who are to be the arbiters of policy relevance, and how will they function?

Thus, under the best of circumstances, managing social R. & D. for policy relevance would be a difficult task. It becomes more difficult when the complexities of actual policymaking are considered.

The elusive policymaker

Who makes income maintenance policy, or crime control policy, or mental health policy? The answer, of course, is that in our system of government there is no single, authoritative policymaker. In the case of most social problems, the power to influence or shape policies and programs is fragmented among the executive branch, the legislative, the judiciary, and organized private interest groups. Fragmentation is exacerbated by the specialization of organization and function characteristic of the executive and legislative branches of government. Thus, eleven committees of the House of Representatives, ten of the Senate and nine executive departments or agencies have some jurisdiction over income maintenance programs.

Participants in policymaking have different roles, constituencies, values, interests, perspectives, and abilities. Their attitudes toward research also differ; some value it and some do not. Moreover, among those that value it, some are genuinely open-minded in seeking and using research findings, others attempt to mobilize these findings for partisan or legitimizing purposes, and still others view research in a tactical, rather than substantive context—a research program may be a device for keeping an issue alive or for delaying action.

Policymaking that takes place within the framework of an adversary process can hardly be scientific or rational. Policy decisions are made through bargaining and compromise by participants with widely divergent perspectives. If policy relevance has any general meaning, it means relevance to the participants in a complex political process. From the point of view of participants, policy-relevant research is research which helps them fulfill their chosen roles and achieve goals they consider important.

This situation poses dilemmas for the producers of social knowledge. For a researcher to be relevant in the sense of consciously contributing to a partisan political process may seem incompatible with objective scientific inquiry. Moreover, with so many different participants and perspectives, someone is bound to be dissatisfied and critical concerning the nature and results of virtually any social R. & D. activity, no matter how useful it may be to a particular participant or how scientifically valid it may be in the eyes of the researcher's professional peers.

On the other hand, there is abundant evidence, as we noted above, that the research community cannot remain aloof or isolated from policymakers and continue to receive Federal financial support. Sooner or later someone—a Congressman, a budget examiner, or a newly appointed executive—will find it advantageous to ask why continued support of irrelevant research is in the agency's, the Government's, or the public interest. Unless the scientific community has the political muscle to suppress such questions (but are lobbying and special pleading in such a cause compatible with objective science?), some concept of accountability must be developed. The thorny questions of relating knowledge production to a pluralistic political process remain.

Policy: A moving target

Policymaking is not an event. It is a process that moves through time-consuming stages, beginning with public recognition that a problem exists, to the establishment and operation of a program or a combination of programs aimed at dealing with aspects of a problem— which may take a long time and may never happen—to evaluation, review, and modification (but seldom death).

In moving through various stages, policymaking does not usually wait for relevant knowledge to become available. Under the pressure of events and constituencies, legislation is passed, programs are started, regulations and guidelines are written, and funds are authorized, appropriated, and spent whether or not relevant analysis and research findings are available. Indeed, the process often works the other way around: the systematic accumulation of knowledge on an appropriate scale may not begin until policies and programs are implemented. Once established and in operation, operating programs legitimize the large-scale expenditure of public funds for research. This process has been true, for example, with issues such as income maintenance, environmental protection, and energy development.

Social problems are seldom solved by a single decisive act or policy declaration; rather, policies to deal with them are fashioned incrementally over time in a series of measures which are partial and not necessarily irreversible. In fact, perceptions as to the basic nature of the problem may change as time passes, causing the evolution of policy to change trajectory. For example, the proper Federal role in the financing of health care has been debated for four decades. Important steps, including the Kerr-Mills Act and Medicaid, have been taken. Yet debate continues and further major developments are almost a certainty.

The time-consuming, action-forcing, incremental, and adaptive nature of the policymaking process has several important but conflicting implications for social R. & D.

First, despite the immediate pressure of events, there is usually time for significant social R & D. The immediate questions may change over time, but the need for research on fundamental issues will be a continuing one. Though individual policymakers usually have short time horizons, the policy process has much longer ones, a circumstance hospitable to the time-consuming nature of knowledge production.

Second, however, the farther in the future the research is focused, the less related it is to immediate issues; and the more remote its usefulness, the smaller the current constituency for the work. Policymaking is concerned with current issues and problems. Policymakers with short time horizons would rather commit resources to obtain immediate help than invest in an uncertain future when they may not be around. They will be more impatient with future-oriented research, more likely to cut it back in favor of research with immediate impact.

Third, each incremental step that adds to the complexity of our public laws and programs makes future significant action, especially if it involves institutional change, that much more difficult. As time passes and programs evolve, policymaking becomes more and more preoccupied with existing programs and institutions and with the vested interests surrounding them. Thus, except in a newly emerging policy area, short-run use of policy ideas derived from research may be low because policymakers must ultimately contend with the political realities of programs, laws, and the organized interests that support them, with the need to strike bargains when they might prefer to be introducing innovations.

The dilemma for the social R. & D. manager or the researcher interested in policy relevance is clear. He can invest in the future by supporting basic research, which usually has little current interest but the possibility of significant long-run payoffs, or he can meet his client's near-term needs with research which has greater support but perhaps a questionable prospect of weighing heavily in the balance. Should he concentrate on discovering and researching questions and problems where there may be little current interest and thus possibly limited and unstable funding, or should he deal with the familiar agenda of social problems, where approval and funds for additional social R. & D. are easier to obtain? It is a precarious existence.

The criterion problem

In this complex world of policymaking, what would a policy relevant research program look like? By what criteria of policy relevance could social R. & D. be judged?

As an example of how this problem might be approached, let us pose several questions with respect to a particular social R. & D. project:

(1) Have the findings of this study been incorporated into policy?

(2) Have the findings of this study been analyzed and discussed by someone influential in the policy process?

(3) Are the findings of this study potentially relevant to a current policy debate?

(4) Are the findings of this study potentially relevant to future policy debates?

(5) Has this study shed light on the nature of a social problem or condition or on how society or its members function?

(6) Has this study contributed to the formulation, design and conduct of other research projects, the findings of which will be helpful in the making of current or future policy?

(7) Does this study advance an intellectual discipline in a way that will enhance the social usefulness of research conducted within that discipline's framework?

(8) Does this study have scientific merit in the opinion of qualified social scientists?

The choice of criteria will depend on one's values and perceptions concerning the appropriate Federal role in supporting social R. & D. These perceptions will in turn be influenced by where one sits: one's specific obligations and responsibilities. For example, if an agency R. & D. manager can answer yes to questions (5) through (8), he may argue, "All our social R. & D. projects are policy relevant." The parent department's management personnel are likely to have more "results-oriented" criteria; research is policy relevant only if they can answer yes to questions (1) and (2). The staff of a Congressional committee or members of a department's policy analysis staff, who are likely to have a broader substantive orientation than management personnel but be less "academic" than research managers, may regard research as policy relevant if they can answer yes to questions (3) and (4). In contrast to the above official views, an academic social scientist might judge all projects for which the answer to (8) is yes to be "socially useful," and therefore worthy of Federal support.

These clusters of views represent distinct evaluation philosophies. Each has merit, particularly in the context of allocating scarce resources. Which should actually be used?

The problem of choosing criteria of policy relevance is even more complicated. As noted above, the initiation of research may be intended as a holding or delaying action in the political process. It may be a symbolic act, signalling concern or adumbrating future actions. Initiating research may be a way for an executive or a legislator to placate or support a colleague who needs to show that "something is being done" about a problem. In these circumstances, it may matter less that research is producing useful results than that research is being done at all.

Is research launched for these reasons to be judged irrelevant? Some believe that it is irrelevant. John H. Noble, Jr., for example, advocating a new, more rigorous system of peer review, argues that

Most important would be the effect that a new system might have by unmask-ing and curtailing the use of scarce R. & D. funds for service subsidy and the seeking of influence. . . . Projects serving mixed purposes create ambiguity and, because of the servicing requirements they impose, distract and dissipate the energies of technically qualified R. & D. administrators. . . .[16]

Whatever the merits of this view, it ignores the realities governing Federal support for social R. & D. Research activities of various kinds will continue to be initiated for reasons that are branded as "political" by scientists. Superintending such activities with appropriate diligence may be the price research executives must pay for the discretion to conduct research more in line with their interests. The suggestion here, however, is that the social R. & D. community as well as Federal re-search executives might go beyond merely putting up with "political research" and recognize its legitimacy in the policymaking process, not to mention making the most of the opportunity to learn something useful.

Unfortunately we are not yet through with complications. The act of choosing and applying criteria of policy relevance is itself subject to political and bureaucratic pressures. An example from my own ex-perience illustrates the problem.

In 1972, officials from the Department of Health, Education and Welfare's Planning and Evaluation Office, the Social Security Admin-istration, the Department of Labor, and the Office of Economic Oppor-tunity began meeting to agree on a design for evaluating the Family Assistance Program, the enactment of which was thought to be a good possibility. All agreed that the evaluation research should produce knowledge useful for income maintenance policymakers. But what knowledge? At the time, the official Administration goal for welfare reform was the reduction of welfare rolls. There was also hostility in the Office of Management and Budget, the White House, and elsewhere to intrusive and expensive data collection for research purposes. This climate created problems for researchers who believed that policy-rele-vant knowledge included evidence about work effort, family stability, consumption, and self-esteem collected from an appropriate sample on a longitudinal basis. Moreover, issues such as these mattered a great deal to some agencies and not at all to others. Though the group was composed mainly of competent researchers, scientific issues had to com-pete for attention with bureaucratic and political ones.

Similarly, a recent attempt by OMB to improve the relevance of evaluation research findings to program decisionmaking by including an evaluation plan and the specification of objectives in all legislation brought worried reactions from many agency officials. They rightly perceived that deciding what knowledge is relevant to policymaking is a political as well as a scientific judgment. To act as if policymaking is scientifically rational when it is not is to risk saddling research ad-ministrators with wholly inappropriate objectives and constraints.[17]

The many faces of policy relevance

With so many dimensions to policy relevance, it might seem that anything goes: a plausible justification can be advanced for virtually any current research project, demonstration, or experiment if 'political

[16] John H. Noble, Jr., "Peer Review: Quality Control of Applied Social Science," Science, Vol. 185 (13 September 1974), p. 920.
[17] See Susan Salasin and Laurence Kivens, "Fostering Federal Program Evaluation: A Current OMB Initiative," Evaluation (Vol. 2, Number 2, 1975), pp. 37–41.

projects' or the pursuit of false leads are permitted. What, then, is the problem?

The problem, as it emerges from studies of Federal social R. & D. management, is twofold: First, few if any relevance criteria are applied during the planning of social R. & D. Too little thought is given to the types of knowledge that will be most useful to the agency, to Congress, to third parties, or to supporting disciplines prior to the commissioning of research projects. Little attention is given to developing the priorities for guiding project selection. Second, research management typically focuses on individual projects—in fact on each year's "new starts"—rather than on multi-year, multi-project research programs. Only infrequently are research projects "part of an overall effort to . . ." achieve a significant increase in knowledge valued for explicitly stated reasons. This type of management virtually precludes the use of criteria that stress the cumulative and reinforcing effects of research.

Thus, federally supported social R. & D. seldom seems to add up to anything. Ad hoc, ex post facto justifications are rarely adequate to vindicate, in the eyes of skeptical policymaking and management officials, research activities that lack a strong and well-thought-out rationale.

Ironically, the unsatisfactory outcomes of this type of research management often lead to administrative actions that make matters worse. Attemps are made to tighten up individual project management, and to apply specific, utilitarian criteria and strict deadlines to each one. Because valuable new knowledge is usually obtained through a cumulative, iterative, time-consuming, and often inefficient process of investigation, the results of applying procurement methods to knowledge production may deepen the disillusionments with social R. & D.

If this analysis is correct, the solution to the relevance problem will have two aspects. First, officials involved in social R. & D. activities must recognize the complexities of the knowledge-into-policy process and the central insight that follows from it—that many criteria are appropriate to assessing the relevance of social R. & D. to policy-making. Second, criteria of relevance must be consciously applied in the formulation of social R. & D. agendas, before projects are selected and funded, if social R. & D. activities are to have coherence and purpose.

Successful implementation of such a solution will require relatively sophisticated oversight and management of social R. & D. It is admittedly a tall order, especially because it almost certainly cannot be imposed by fiat on a set of activities that are decentralized, diverse, and uncoordinated. If social R. & D. is to surmount the criticism it continues to receive, and if investments in the production and utilization of useful social knowledge are to yield the desired results, it is a solution that those concerned with the health of the social R. & D. enterprise are well advised to pursue.

APPENDIX

The Lewis & Clark Expedition: A Social R. & D. Paradigm

Historians of science have noted the Enlightenment-influenced, empirically-minded spirit in which the Nation was founded. Of Washington, Jefferson and Franklin, Don K. Price writes, "The first effect of their leadership was to destroy the traditional theory of hereditary sovereignty, and to substitute the idea that the people had the right, by rational and experimental processes, to build their governmental institutions to suit themselves." [18] Gene M. Lyons adds that the scientific spirit of the Founding Fathers "was also shaped by a pragmatism and utilitarianism that grew out of the practical demands of settling a new land and that have characterized American society science from the beginning." [19]

As President, Thoms Jefferson was responsible for perhaps the first major federally supported social research. ". . . [Perhaps] the most important fact about the Lewis and Clark expedition . . . is the degree to which it was 'programmed,' or planned in advance, down to the smallest detail by Jefferson and his scientific associates in Philadelphia . . ." [20] In the view of historian William H. Goetzman, the Lewis and Clark expedition can reasonably be regarded, at least in part, as basic, as opposed to applied, social R&D. ". . . Lewis and Clark might almost be considered a logical extension of the American Philosophical Society, which existed to promote the general advancement of science and 'the useful arts'." [21] The results were unquestionably in the 'applied' category, however. The expedition "replaced a mass of confusing rumors and conjectures with a body of compact, reliable and believable information on the western half of the continent which caught the imagination of the country." [22]

The systematic exploration and survey of the American West in many ways represents a paradigm for the relationship of public policymaking and scientific research. In the case of the Lewis and Clark expedition, for example, Jefferson sought relevant, documented knowledge in the face of pressures to act in furtherance of American ambitions in the West, but prior to major policy developments. He was systematic in organizing and training an interdisciplinary team to assemble new knowledge on behalf of a broad social goal. "Jefferson's instructions, in their detail, their insistence on astronomical observation, attention to nature history and the Indians, and above all its reiterated admonition to keep every possible record, set a scientific tone for this expedition and for the many that would later copy the pattern he set." [23]

[18] Don K. Price, "Government and Science, The Dynamic Relation in American Democracy" (New York: New York University Press, 1954). p. 4.
[19] Gene M. Lyons, "The Uneasy Partnership, Social Science and the Federal Government in the Twentieth Century" (New York: Russell Sage Foundation. 1969), pp. 2–3.
[20] William E. Goetzman, "Exploration and Empire, The Explorer and the Scientist in the Winning of the American West" (New York: Vintage Books, 1966), p. 5.
[21] Ibid., p. 5.
[22] A Hunter Dupree, "Science in the Federal Government, A History of Policies and Activities to 1940" (Cambridge, Massachusetts: Harvard University Press-Belknap Press, 1957), p. 27.
[23] Ibid., p. 26.

4

DOING GOOD OR WORSE:
EVALUATION RESEARCH POLITICALLY REEXAMINED

By

RICHARD A. BERK and PETER H. ROSSI

In a fresh view which takes seriously the extent to which evaluation research rests on moral and political value judgments, Richard Berk and Peter Rossi, in a novel use of decision theory, show how these judgments can be made explicit and used in the choice of research design alternatives.

From Richard A. Berk and Peter H. Rossi, "Doing Good or Worse: Evaluation Research Politically Reexamined." *Social Problems,* February 1976, *23*(3), 337-349.

This paper argues that all evaluation research must necessarily rest on significant moral and political value judgments. These and other methodological factors in turn affect social problem definitional processes surrounding ongoing social programs. Moreover, evaluation research implicitly endorses particular ideological perspectives and therefore has broader implications for social change. The paper argues, however, that despite these serious weaknesses, evaluation research may play a progressive role if one is prepared to employ research designs that capitalize on inevitable value judgments, rather than ignore them.

The late sixties found American social science under severe attack from within its own ranks. On the one hand, social science was indicted for irrelevance: at worst, for a trained incapacity to make contributions towards the betterment of humanity, and at best, for being too mired in its own brand of scholasticism to care. On the other hand, social scientists were accused of selling out: perhaps as courtesans exchanging useful expertise for status and contact with the powerful, or more likely, as ordinary whores peddling cheap favors to anyone with ready cash. Whether handsomely paid and respected or poorly paid and held in contempt, the charge was the same: collaboration with the "Establishment."

The apparent contradiction between these two critiques did not escape notice. If social scientists were pillars of the status quo, they could hardly be irrelevant. If they merely debated arcane trivialities, they could scarcely be shoring up the foundations of society. Yet, there was a synthesis which contended that evil and irrelevance could enjoy a compatible marriage. One might work only on issues defined by the powerful and be irrelevant to critical problems ignored by those interests. One might work on the "real" problems, and perhaps even "radical" solutions, but be so far removed from the political arena that one's only audience was other equally isolated academics. Perhaps most important, researchers who did not actively oppose the status quo were criticized as its tacit supporters. Consequently, it was not necessary to be a courtesan to sell out, one might merely be a court jester, magician, or priest, kept for amusement, astonishment, or ritual purification. Nor was it necessary to be paid through invoices. The sinecures of tenure could be regarded as long term, generous subsidies for supportive irrelevance.

The flowering of evaluation research in the late 1960's and the consequent

---

* This paper has benefited from numerous discussions with many colleagues over the years. In particular, we wish to thank Sarah F. Berk, Howard S. Becker, Allan Schnaiberg, Richard Hay, Alice S. Rossi, Peter E. Rossi, and John Walton for comments on earlier drafts. We also want to acknowledge the generosity of the Russell Sage Foundation for its support of both authors in work on Evaluation Research.

enlargement of applied research opportunities promised at least a partial response to these challenges. First, evaluation research openly took the status quo as problematical. Programs, practices, and institutions were to be judged according to their effectiveness in meeting their goals. Hence, researchers might be free from the charge of pandering or soliciting. Second, evaluation research was to be more closely linked to a variety of people who might actually use its findings to make decisions. To the degree that such people were interested in honest assessment of "relevant" aspects of our society, evaluation research might be more relevant as well. Finally, evaluation research is technically challenging, presenting as many if not more difficulties to be surmounted than the usual academic research. Hence evaluation research might do good and do it elegantly.

Sufficient time has now elapsed since the first burgeoning of evaluation research to enable one to stand back a bit and partially assess some aspects of the experience. This paper is such an effort based on our two decades of involvement (shared somewhat unequally among the two authors) in applied research. The main issue of the paper is whether it is possible to do good and do it well.

We will address both technical issues and political issues. These two realms are in fact inseparable, although most discussions of evaluation research have typically tackled one or the other. When research methods and politics are jointly considered, the emphasis has usually been on the ways political questions influence technical questions (e.g. Moynihan, 1973; Johnson, 1974; Riecken et al., 1975). We shall mention such effects, but we shall be as concerned with forces operating in the opposite direction: the political implications of evaluation research. Finally, we are also concerned (perhaps obstinately) with the possibility of improvement. What can be done to make applied research reach the limits of its better capabilities both as a technical apparatus and as a device for social improvement?

EVALUATION RESEARCH METHODOLOGY: TOOL OR SHAFT?

The term "social program" can be plausibly applied to almost any organized state activity ranging from those formally defined as meliorative—the welfare system, social security, compensatory education—to those more restricted to maintenance of the national organism—military defense, the federal reserve system, and income taxation. In practice, however, the term "social program" is usually reserved for activities aimed at helping the disadvantaged segments of our society.

Although evaluations can be made, in principle, of any concerted governmental effort, in practice, evaluation research is employed most frequently in the assessment of social programs (in the narrow sense) and of new programs rather than those that have been operational for some years.[1] In addition, the role assigned to evaluation research necessarily implies skepticism about our attempts at remediation, and to the extent that this perspective is reinforced by findings showing "null" or trivial effects, evaluation research contributes to a growing sense of social problem intractability. In other words, evaluation research becomes part of the social problem definitional process (Kitsuse and Spector, 1973).

---

[1] Almost all are "monitored" in the sense that operational reports are required, which casts some light on the operations of the system involved. Perhaps the major "social program" that comes closest to being unevaluated and unmonitored is the Central Intelligence Agency.

Given this almost inevitable political role for evaluation research, it is important to recognize that most common designs possess an inherent conservative bias. When they are imposed on existing programs with treatment content fully determined, the resulting findings are obviously constrained by an empirical reality already in place. Alternative social interventions that have been rejected for implementation cannot be evaluated, and effects of treatment characteristics beyond the range of existing variation cannot be directly assessed. Hence, the common finding that class size has marginal effects on learning obtains *only* within the range of class sizes customarily found within American schools. The finding that manpower training is a relatively impotent treatment holds only for conventional manpower retraining programs. Moreover, since the types of programs enacted and funded are clearly limited by political feasibility, evaluation research may find itself rejecting potential solutions when the real blame may lie with timid or conservative policy makers responsible for the program's boundaries.

It might appear that when evaluation researchers can participate in decisions about treatment content, the inherent conservatism of evaluation designs may be moderated. However here too, political feasibility intervenes. Thus, the field experiments on the negative income tax considered a rather restricted range of income guarantees and tax rates, the boundaries being fixed in part by what *experimenters* thought were politically viable.

In short, social programs rarely exceed the limits of dominant political ideologies. Indeed, when public officials puff up their programs bv dubbing them "innovative" and "pioneering," they are usually referring to programs that go little beyond conventional wisdom.[2] Therefore, the intractability of social problems in the face of what appears to be all-out efforts at reform may merely reflect the timidity of policy makers. The almost consistent finding of evaluation researchers that programs work weakly, if at all, may bolster a view that social problems are considerably more intractable to ameliorative efforts than in fact may be the case were bolder programs enacted.[3]

Dominant ideologies also affect the definitions of evaluation criteria. Thus, the main efforts of the negative income tax experiments were expended on how much work disincentive income guarantees would induce, an issue thought paramount in the minds of conservatives in Congress who would have to enact a negative income tax proposal. Other objectives such as improved health, or enrichment of leisure time, were either neglected entirely or downplayed in published assessments. In other words, evaluation research may validate a particular view of social problems by emphasizing certain outcomes as opposed to others. The implied political message of the negative income tax experiments is that the main problem with the poor is their potential laziness.

There are other perhaps more subtle ways that evaluation research methodo-

---

[2] In a condescending way, Moynihan tells about a Boston black woman who asked him why it was that "they only fund the programs that don't succeed?" Moynihan introduces the anecdote to show how naive the person in the street may be, not to question the conservative cast of social programs in the Great Society series (Moynihan, 1968:3).

[3] Of course, if one accepts the view that reforms are linearly related to amelioration effects, then all that is necessary is to try a weak treatment since the effects of a strong treatment would be simply linear extrapolations. The criticism expressed in the text implies a non-linear world, in which there are thresholds, kinks, knots and more complicated nonlinear relationships between reforms and ameliorative effects.

logy contributes to the definition of social problems; virtually all technical issues have an ideological side. For example, assessment requires measurement and hence those goals that are more easily measured tend to be those that get assessed. Outcomes that can be counted easily tend to be listed as the outcomes desired: How long was the parolee out of prison before being re-arrested? How many hours a week was the income maintenance recipient working? What was the reading level of children in schools? More subtle and possibly as important outcomes tend to be underplayed because they are difficult to measure: the quality of jobs, the parolee's job and wage prospects in comparison to his expected take from illegal activities, what children read as well as how well they read.[4]

Equally significant is the fact that applied social researchers are more technically proficient in the study of individuals than in the study of organizations, and therefore, social research tends to be more social psychological than social structural. Thus, there is a conventional scale for measuring the alienation of individuals, but not for the alienating tendencies of work organizations. Whether our preference for technical devices centering on individuals is a function of problem definitions or whether our technical deficiencies determine our research interests is diffficult to discern. Obviously this is another way the political and technical merge.

Finally our standard evaluation tools tend to neglect historical and social processes. Elaborate factorial experimental designs can only handle a relatively small number of causal factors and, perhaps more important, independent variables are purged (through randomization) of correlations with other phenomena in the world to which they are inevitably linked. A desire to maximize what Campbell and Stanley (1963) have called "internal validity" (or minimize what sociologists call "spuriousness") has spawned research methodologies which in effect make social programs orthogonal to other social forces that might cause differential outcomes between experimental and control groups. Time series designs and processual approaches add an important longitudinal dimension to evaluation research, but one would be hard pressed to call such work historical. The time period is simply too short and the variables are usually more social psychological than structural.[5] Similarly, while in theory, systems approaches using structural equations have the potential to reduce some of these difficulties (e.g. see Goldberger and Duncan, 1973), there are still enormous technical difficulties to be overcome before they live up to advance billing. A major hurdle is that the critical assumptions necessary to make the statistical

---

[4] This is not an argument for qualitative research methods, since the latter are not without their own technical biases. Even the most astute observer can only see what is visible or what people are willing to reveal. Thus, one can easily record the dialogue occurring during group therapy sessions in a prison, since all the action is taking place at one location, in plain view and through verbal interaction. Related processes occurring in separate cells after lock up, events occurring simultaneously during the therapy session, and non-verbal therapeutic interaction may well be missed. Outcomes that are hard to record, thus tend to be ignored in qualitative assessments of program effects.

[5] It is very instructive to examine the recent *Design and Analysis of Time-Series Experiments* by psychologists Gene V. Glass, Victor L. Wilson, and John M. Gottman. The technique of "differencing" is suggested as a means to remove non-stationary processes before examining treatment effects. This procedure in essence purges the time-series of its systematic historical characteristics and is thus analagous to randomization.

solutions tractable are often at variance with empirical reality (e.g. assumptions about the nature of measurement error).

While it is hard to judge how much evaluation research methods are determined by a pre-existing astructural world view, it is clear that they reinforce such perspectives. The New Jersey-Pennsylvania Income Maintenance Experiment, for example, was superimposed upon an existing welfare structure and food stamp program, plus a wide range of ethnic, geographical, and class variations. Yet, such factors were ignored in a research design which focused almost exclusively on work effort of households. The implicit model of society was clear: social structure is composed of modules relatively independent of one another and therefore subject to alteration without producing any important ripples throughout the system.[6] In principle, most social scientists subscribe to a very different notion of society, but this classroom posture has simply not been translated into evaluation research practice.[7]

If the astructural, ahistorical bias in social research methodology were only a reflection on the scientific community, it might be dismissed as a manifestation of uneven development. But when this bias appears in evaluation methodology that is by design meant to affect political decisions, the bias has a broad political message: The basic structural features of our society are by and large functioning smoothly. Social programs are mainly fine tune-ups on a sound engine. Thus, manpower retraining programs are predicated on the diagnosis of unemployment in which there is a mismatching of labor supply and demand, a sort of friction in the working of the labor market that can be reduced by altering the mix of skills. Or the WIN program assumes in training welfare women for jobs, that the jobs then available would be more attractive than welfare, a notion that clearly contradicts the facts, especially with respect to income.

In summary, evaluation methodology in usual practice implicitly endorses an incremental notion of social change. Change occurs only in small amounts and then only with respect to one area at a time. The "clumping" of social change (i.e., the fact that some changes can have catalytic or synergistic effects on other areas) is ignored. Regardless of the accuracy of incremental perspectives, their ideological values are clear. First, attention may be diverted away from fundamental issues of power and privilege to detailed debates over the relative merits of minor variations in negative income tax plans. Income Maintenance in turn becomes solely a question of appropriate minimum and maximum levels of support for the needy, rather than consideration of income redistribution across all levels of American society. Second, if change is incremental, it is far more difficult to accuse society of being unresponsive to the needs of all its citizens. One can argue that "meaningful" change occurs every day. Finally, and perhaps most important, the astructural, ahistorical biases of evaluation methodology reinforce the idea that the rationale for social change can rest on impartial and

---

[6] When ripples are sent throughout the system, then political flak is sent up. Thus, Moynihan (1969) criticizes the Community Action Program because its authors did not appreciate that community organizations were not going to stop with pressuring social agencies but would quickly move to put thorns in the sides of mayors and city councils. Implicitly Moynihan would prefer programs that worked on independent modules rather than ones that had the potential of upsetting larger systems.

[7] A promising exception is Jerald Hage *Communication and Organizational Control*, N.Y. John Wiley & Sons, 1974. Hage's monograph is still more program than fulfillment.

objective assessments of societal performance. Evaluation findings are put forward as judgments above politics, based on scientific data, not organized interests. The implicit message is that if the "truth" can be revealed, decision makers will respond to it. Again, whether this is accurate or not, it is clearly a political statement in which social change becomes increasingly a technological question to be decided by the outcome of scientific investigation, conducted by dedicated scientists who are above "mere politics."

CAN ONE DO GOOD WELL?

We have been arguing that social programs introduced over the past decade have typically had only incremental and segmental change as their objective, tinkering with the system rather than addressing fundamental redesign. In addition, the process of evaluation at least implicitly endorses certain ideological positions of debatable merit. Is there any point then to undertake serious evaluations of social programs? We will argue that in many cases the answer is yes, but that one should move to more self-conscious applications of certain methodological perspectives on research designs.

Evaluation research has some of the same liberating potential as other social science activities. Good social science is at least a demystifying activity. The very questioning of common assumptions about the nature of society means that one is less likely uncritically to accept any dogmatic world view. If common assumptions are tested with data, skepticism is reinforced by increased understanding. (We are well aware of phenomenological arguments which ultimately make social science itself problematic. But we will assume, perhaps naively, that something useful can be learned from social science, at least until a better set of procedures come along.) To the degree that skepticism and understanding can be widely communicated, social science may even be subtly subversive.

As an application of social science, evaluation research has substantial potential for demystification. Rigorous assessments of social programs can provide important data with which to question conventional wisdom. For example, the Income Maintenance Experiment, illustrates this promise: Puerto Ricans in the experimental group showed the effect of lessened work effort as classical economic theory predicted, while whites showed virtually no effects and blacks *increased* their work effort (obviously showing themselves to be the most imbued with the work ethic!). Similar demystification tasks were accomplished by the Coleman Report when it showed that schools made smaller contributions to the learning of children than family background.

The demystifying function of evaluation research may be materially aided by the fact that so few programs show important effects. Of course, such null outcomes are exactly what we would expect, given our critique of current social programs as piecemeal and lightweight. The failure of program after program if *effectively* documented, can contribute to an empirically grounded critique of American society.

Ironically, it is the scientific "authority" of evaluation research that produces its greatest impact. Regardless of the ultimate validity of the social science enterprise, the rules of evidence stressed by at least its more quantitative practitioners are the very rules many public officials have come to voice (perhaps, ambivalently) as criteria for deciding on the life expectancy of social programs. For example, federal legislation of late has increasingly required some specified percentage of program funds (typically 1%) to be allocated to "rigorous" evaluation of those programs. While practice has not always followed preaching (the program implications of evaluation findings may often be over-ridden by political exigencies), the scientific character of evaluation research makes results a bit harder to dismiss. In other words, competent evaluation research practitioners can play the game under rules which all sides will likely take as fair (at least in theory) and often correctly show that most programs make little difference.[8]

Along with the political advantage of its scientific trappings, evaluation research often has the additional asset of being politically mandated research. To the degree that program assessments are required under law or requested by public officials, they acquire a cloak of legitimacy which other kinds of social science may lack. Ivory tower academics may be dismissed as dreamers and Ralph Nader types may be labeled publicity seekers or trouble makers. In contrast, when evaluation researchers are invited to assess a social program, a modicum of credibility is built into their findings from the start. Policy makers are in effect saying in advance that the resulting data will be useful and hence might play an important role in decision-making. To charge later that the findings are irrelevant or based on shoddy procedures raises the embarassing question of why the evaluation was supported at all.

The effectiveness of evaluation data is often further enhanced when program partisans can be encouraged to participate in the research design and when relevant measures are in metrics which policy makers take as valid. For example, in a classic parole study by Kassebaum, Ward, and Wilner (1971), the evaluation design was so tight that it was almost impossible to escape its inevitable conclusions. The treatment was several different kinds of group therapy thought to maximize what its advocates called a "Therapeutic Community." A randomized experiment was used, testing therapeutic programs which met as closely as possible the optimum specifications desired by program supporters.[9] In other words, the researchers in effect asked what program advocates would want in the best of all possible worlds, provided for those needs, and then assessed this "ideal" program. In addition, the outcome measures included results (e.g. re-arrest) which the State Adult Corrections Authority took as valid. Therefore, when the findings showed "no effect" it was much harder to dismiss them. Although the state prison system was not immediately changed, this and other research findings began a process which led to major alterations in state prison policy (Berk et. al., forthcoming).

Of course, demystification merely strips away the crust of conventional wisdom. The same set of startling findings can be interpreted in either a conservative or more radical direction. Thus, Colemen's findings can be interpreted to mean that we should put less money into education, since more expensive education is no more effective than less expensive systems. Or, it could be interpreted to mean that the educational experience to which American

---

[8] Note that this is inherent in the close fit between much evaluation methodology and the public positions of many policy makers. Hence, it operates even if the evaluation researcher is an outsider who has not been encouraged (let alone invited) to assess a program. This means that evaluations by academics or citizens groups using evaluation technology may have more legitimacy and therefore, impact, than social science using other approaches (other things equal).

[9] Additional funds were obtained to support treatments that were thought to be the best possible implementation of the group therapy idea.

children are typically exposed is insufficiently intense to make much of an impact. While evaluation research is political, it is no substitute for politics. Social science can demystify, but it remains the task of politics to interpret the meaning of demystification for direction of political policy.

The moment one begins to take demystification seriously, a number of methodological issues appear. For example, it is clear from the assessment of Sesame Street that the program does aid pre-school children, and it certainly provides much amusement to numbers of children and adults. Yet if we examine closely the *size* of the effects achieved by a year of viewing, we note that children exposed to the program are on the average able to recognize about two more letters of the alphabet and to count further a correspondingly small distance in the number scale. Sesame Street does produce *statistically significant* effects, but they are of little *substantive significance.*

It is in the difference between substantive and statistical significance that a role begins to emerge for the methodologically sophisticated researcher bent on demystification. To begin, it is critical to communicate this distinction since even some well-trained quantitative researchers often confuse the two, and most policy makers will automatically interpret "significant" as substantively significant.[10]

But more important, by using principles from Decision Theory[11] and Bayesian thinking one can work *within the boundaries of conventional scientific norms* to design evaluation research so that such confusions are minimized. And once one starts to build on these widely endorsed though typically ignored practices (see for example Wonnacott and Wonnacott, 1970: chapter 10), a number of other possibilities emerge. We turn to these issues now.

Figure 1 shows a matrix familiar to any student in an introductory statistics course. The categories along the left margin indicate whether program effects really exist (or more generally, whether the null hypothesis is really true or false). The categories along the top of the table indicate whether one's research implies that the program effects really exist (or more generally, whether the null hypothesis appears true or false). The cells represent all possible crossings of

---

[10] Indeed a good case can be made for the substitution of the less misleading term "statistically reliable" for the often misinterpreted "statistically significant."

[11] In essence, Decision Theory builds on (1) one's expectations of the likelihood that certain events will occur, (2) a set of actions one can choose among and (3) one's preference or utilities for various joint outcomes of one's actions and the events. The purpose of Decision Theory is to develop a strategy to maximize one's utilities by choosing the action or actions (if all are not mutually exclusive) for which the sum of the products of event probabilities and appropriate utilities are the highest. In other words, one generates an expected value (or expected payoff) for each action and then chooses the one with the best expected value. (Chernoff and Moses, 1959:10-11). For example, suppose one wanted to decide whether or not to carry an umbrella to work. The expected return for carrying the umbrella would be the utility of carrying it if it rained times the probability it might rain plus the utility of carrying it if it did not rain times the probability it might not rain. The expected return for not carrying the umbrella would be the utility of not carrying the umbrella if it rained times the probability it might rain plus the utility of not carrying the umbrella if it did not rain times the probability it might not rain. One would then decide whether to carry the umbrella based on the highest expected payoff.

Decision Theory is increasingly used in a variety of contexts. In this paper we will be talking about using Decision Theory to assist in making a number of *technical* decisions about evaluation research *designs.* This should not be confused with Marcia Guttentag's important work (1975) which employs Decision Theory much more broadly from the determination of program goals to the generation of policy recommendations.

FIGURE 1

Matrix of Evaluation Research Outcomes

Judgment of the existence
of program effects

		Yes	No
Program Effects	Yes	A Correct Judgment (True positive)	B TYPE II ERROR (False negative)
	No	C TYPE I ERROR (False positive)	D Correct Judgment (True negative)

judgments with the actual situation. Type I and Type II errors fall along the minor diagonal while correct assessments fall along the major diagonal.

Given a fixed sample size and the choice of statistic, Blalock (1972) for example, tells the student that "it is impossible to minimize the risks of both types of errors simultaneously." Therefore, "The decision as to the significance level selected depends on the relative costs of making the one or the other type of error and should be evaluated accordingly. Sometimes a practical decision must be made according to the outcome of the experiment" (Blalock, 1972:160). In an example discussed in Blommers and Lindquist's *Elementary Statistical Methods* (1960:282-283), the costs of incorrectly endorsing a school program which in fact does not facilitate learning (a Type I error) are listed as:

Purposeless expenditure of a large sum of tax money when other important needs for this money exist and, when the error becomes known, the attendant:

1. public criticism;
2. loss of school board member's confidence;
3. loss of staff members' confidence;
4. possible creation of staff dissension resulting from singling out one building for special aid;
5. general overall damage of professional reputation;
6. possible loss of superintendency.

Other costs are then discussed for failing to demonstrate real program effects when they actually exist: failure to provide needed services, public criticism, and so on. In other words, it is common to recommend building one's expectations about various research outcomes along with their utilities into decisions about the size and location of the region of rejection for significance tests.

The basic notion of designing research to correspond in part to various *a priori* subjective assessments is recommended in other situations besides choosing the criticial level for significance tests. Sampling texts (e.g. Kish, 1967) counsel the investigator to choose both the sample size and mode of selection based on *a priori* judgments of the magnitude of effect sought, the cost of alternative designs, anticipated variance in the population, and a host of other consequences (i.e. the probability of various events and their utilities). Specialists in research design broaden still further the range of acceptable discretion urging researchers to build their empirical work on the "best" mix of decisions which maximize some combination of scientific and practical considerations (Campbell and Stanley, 1963; Cook and Campbell, 1974; Riecken et. al., 1975). Thus, if "informed consent" cannot be obtained from subjects without telling them a great deal about the research (and risking considerable reactivity), one might choose to provide extensive information at the cost of weakening both internal and external validity. Similarly, if the ramifications of one's measures seem especially critical (e.g. in intelligence testing), one might choose to allocate one's limited resources far more heavily toward shoring up construct validity even at the cost of weakening other forms of validity. The basic point is that design tradeoffs always exist, subjective judgments must necessarily intrude, and therefore one should consciously consider these complexities in planning research.

Another way of partially approaching these considerations is to refer again to Figure 1 and in particular the cells representing true positives and true negatives (cells A and D). In the same way that false negatives (Type II errors) and false positives (Type I errors) produce outcomes with expected payoffs, true positives and true negatives *also* generate mixes of costs and benefits with various probabilities. For example, while it may always be desirable in theory to find real program effects when they exist, one might be faced with rather high and unacceptable costs if the design revealing those effects risked serious injury to subjects. Thus one might try a new drug only on volunteers even though external validity might be greatly reduced. Or, one might abandon randomization if some people in immediate need of treatment effects (however dubious) would be bypassed. In other words, one might choose seriously to jeapordize some aspects of scientific validity if a "greater good" is served. Note however, that both the probability and worth of that greater good are clearly subjective assessments laden with moral and political judgments.

Thus a combination of inevitable budget constraints, the resulting necessity of making choices about allocating scarce resources, and the consequent requirement of using non-scientific criteria in such decisions (as all applied methodologists recommend), invite the use of broadly *political* desiderata in the design of evaluation research. Indeed, we have been arguing that evaluation research is highly political in any case and moreover, the lines between moral, practical and political research constraints would be impossible to draw. Therefore, one might justifiably choose to design research to maximize demystification (or any of a number of other political objectives). This implies that *all four cells* in the table are worthy of attention in a Decision Theory perspective, not just the cells representing Type I and Type II errors. More broadly, any "scientific" design goals one might favor in theory (internal or external validity) can be made the subject of a searching cost-benefit analysis.

How might one apply a Decision Theory perspective to research designs where demystification was a major objective and where one would in addition try to minimize many of the negative implications of evaluation research discussed earlier? Take the example of behavioral modification applied to convicted felons, an approach that certainly attracts controversy. Suppose that one is convinced on moral grounds that behavior modification poses a serious threat to individual freedom because it encourages "Big Brother" solutions to deviant behavior, supports yet another cadre of "helping" professionals, has great potential for misuse, and fosters the belief that the felon, not the criminal justice system is the problem. At the same time, one might at least entertain the possibility that behavioral modification with extensive safeguards could be appropriate for a few highly dangerous felons. Now, if one expected some positive effects from a behavioral modification program (e.g. lower re-arrest rates), one would want to be very sure that these outcomes were large relative to the program's potential costs (on the grounds that only dramatic effects could justify the use of a method that is morally controversial). How might this be accomplished?

To begin, one would be careful to distinguish between *substantively* and *statistically* significant effects as mentioned earlier. But perhaps one might believe that in the current climate of fear about crime such subtleties would be ignored and prison administrators and public officials would seize on any program promising even a hint of crime reduction. Thus, one's assessment of the consequences of a true positive for trivial treatment effects projects very high costs relative to potential benefits. Under these circumstances one might decide to apply what Decision Theory counsels and make one's research design responsive to subjective probabilities of various research consequences and their utilities (just as one might if the preferred design risked injury to subjects).

One strategy would be to reduce the power of any significance tests seeking to distinguish real effects from sampling error. This might be accomplished by using smaller samples, higher alpha levels, two tail rather than one tail tests, less efficient estimators[12] and perhaps even instruments with greater amounts of random measurement error. To the degree that any of these tactics reduced the dollar costs of doing the research, one might decide to invest the savings to improve the quality of the sample of subjects, enhancing external validity. Thus, should treatment effects appear, one might have a better notion of the kinds of felons for whom the treatment might be appropriate. In other words, one consciously "weakens" the design on some dimensions while strengthening it on others to maximize the "usefulness" of research results.

A second strategy involves less tampering with the research design but also makes the findings easily re-analyzed and hence, vulnerable to the ambitions of overzealous policy makers. One might replace the conventional null hypothesis of no difference between treatment and control groups with a null hypothesis based on some minimum level of *substantive* significance. After working out anticipated costs and benefits for various amounts of reduction in recidivism, one might decide that a 10% difference was the minimum non-trivial effect.

Finally, perhaps the greatest danger to a "proper" assessment of the program's outcomes involves the application of research designs in which it is impossible to unscramble program effects from other sources of change. Social programs are particularly susceptible to self-selection and administrator selection biases. In our example, one could imagine prison officials and behavioral modification professionals placing their "best risks" into the treatment group. This would argue for the use of true experiments where assignment to treatment and control groups was done randomly. In summary, were one to evaluate programs like

---

[12] There is clearly a great deal that could be said about strategies for reducing the efficiency of estimators. Any good statistics book will have lots of advice on making estimators more efficient and all one has to do is reverse the suggestions. To take an extreme example, one might choose to assume nothing about the sampling distribution of an estimator (often a reasonable position for small samples) and use Tchebycheff's Inequality instead of the more common normal curve.

behavioral modification for felons, one might design research to have *high* internal validity and *low* conclusion validity.

What would happen if rather than anticipating a reduction in recidivism, one anticipated an increase in recidivism? Assuming the same political assessment described above, one would then want to consider a different kind of research design. For example, since any demonstration of greater recidivism from the treatment would effectively kill the program, one would prefer a research design where even very small differences between treatment and control groups would be revealed. Therefore, one would want to maximize the power of any significance tests by using large samples, lower alpha levels, one tail tests, more efficient estimators and the best measurement instruments possible. One would also want to employ a true experiment so that false negatives through selection biases would be unlikely to appear. Further, one might decide to weaken external validity (invest heavily in the randomization process rather than getting a more representative sample) if internal and conclusion validity could be substantially improved.

CONCLUSIONS

Without going through any additional examples, it should be clear the kinds of design strategies we are suggesting. The application of social science methodology to evaluate social programs or investigate any empirical phenomena must inevitably address the real world of practical, moral and political imperatives. Applied methodologists from the days of R.A. Fisher have argued that research designs must be responsive to these pressures. We have simply been applying logical extensions of their views.

Some researchers will undoubtedly argue that while subjective biases are inevitable in social science research, one should attempt to incorporate the biases of the policy makers (or any other employer) for whom the research is being done, or avoid evaluations where one's value premises are not shared. These are more difficult questions to handle, especially given the space available here (See Berk, forthcoming). Nevertheless, some tentative rejoinders can be briefly suggested.

First, to avoid evaluations unless one can work comfortably with the people for whom the research is being undertaken is clearly a political and moral decision with political and moral consequences. By failing to participate one has loaded the dice so that results will likely reflect the preferences of the active parties. Clearly, withdrawal may be equivalent to implicit support.

Second, to see oneself simply as a hired hand and incorporate the values of employers into research designs is to abdicate one's moral and political responsibilities to others. All professionals place limits on the uses to which their skills may be put: many physicians will refuse to "pull the plug" on terminal patients, many defense lawyers will not argue a case in ways inconsistent with their understanding of the facts. We are simply arguing that social scientists engaged in applied research exercise similar judgments.

In summary, it should be clear that political and methodological considerations are inextricably linked. Although the logic and mathematics of research designs may well be neutral, the moment they are applied to social programs, claims of scientific objectivity become totally unjustified. It is simply impossible to be a neutral technician; applying the technology necessarily implies ideological positions with political consequences. Evaluation researchers are *always* choosing sides even before empirical findings are produced.[13]

REFERENCES

1. Berk, Richard A., Selma Lesser, Harold Brackman, *Compromised Justice: An Empirical Study of the Changing Criminal Law.* Academic Press, 1976.
2. Berk, Richard A., "Doing Good Well: A Perspective on Applied Research," Forthcoming.
3. Becker, Howard S., Irving Louis Horowitz, "Radical Politics and Sociological Research: Observations on Methodology and Ideology" AJS, Vol. 78, No. 1, (July, 1972), pp. 48-67.
4. Blalock, Hubert, *Social Statistics,* New York: McGraw-Hill, 1972.
5. Blommers, Paul, E. F. Linquist, *Elementary Statistical Methods,* Boston: Houghton, Mifflin, 1960.
6. Campbell, D. T., Julian Stanley, *Experimental and Quasi-Experimental Designs for Research,* Chicago: Rand McNally, 1963.
7. Chernoff, Herman and Lincoln E. Moses, *Elementary Decision Theory,* New York: John Wiley, 1959.
8. Cook, T. P., D. T. Campbell, "The Design and Conduct of Quasi-Experiments and True Experiments in Field Settings," in *Handbook of Industrial and Organizational Research,* M. O. Dunnette (ed.), Chicago: Rand McNally, 1974.
9. Edwards, Ward, Marcia Guttentag and Kurt Snapper, "A Decision Theory Approach to Evaluation Research" in Elmer L. Struening and Marcia Guttentag (eds.), *Handbook of Evaluation Research,* Sage Publications, Beverly Hills, 1975.
10. Glass, Gene V., Victor L. Wilson, John M. Gottman, *Design and Analysis of Time Series Experiments,* Colorado University Press, Boulder, 1975.
11. Goldberger, Arthur S., Otis Dudley Duncan, *Structural Equation in the Social Sciences,* New York: Seminar Press, 1973.
12. Hays, William L. *Statistics,* Holt, Rinehart and Winston: New York, 1973.
13. Johnson, Earl Jr., *Justice and Reform: The Formative Years of the OEO Legal Services Program,* New York: Russell Sage Foundation (1974).
14. Johnston, J., *Econometric Methods,* McGraw-Hill: New York, 1972.
15. Kassebaum, Gene, David Ward, and Daniel Wilber, *Prison Treatment and Parole Survival: An Empirical Assessment,* New York: John Wiley and Sons (1971).
16. Kish, Leslie, *Survey Sampling,* New York: John Wiley, 1967.
17. Kitsuse, John, I., and Malcolm Spector, "Towards a Sociology of Social Problems: Social Conditions, Value Judgements and Social Problems", *Social Problems* (Spring): 407-419.
18. Moynihan, Daniel P., *The Politics of a Guaranteed Income,* Random House: New York, 1973.
19. Moynihan, Daniel P., "The Professors and the Poor," in Daniel P. Moynihan (ed.) *On Understanding Poverty,* Basic Books: New York, 1968.
20. Moynihan, Daniel P., *Maximum Feasible Misunderstanding,* Free Press, New York, 1969.
21. Riecken, H. W., Boruch, R. F., Campbell, D. T., Caplan, N., Glenwan, T. K., Pratt, J., Rees, A., and Williams, W., *Social Experiments for Planning and Evaluation,* Academic Press: New York, 1974.

---

[13] There are many other benefits that might emerge from evaluation research such as gaining understanding for its own sake. We have not addressed these other outcomes since they are not special to evaluation research but common to all good social science. For a provocative discussion of these issues see Becker and Horowitz, 1972.

PART 2

EVALUATION METHODOLOGY
AND DATA INTEGRATION

5

REGRESSION AND SELECTION MODELS TO IMPROVE NONEXPERIMENTAL COMPARISONS

By

GLEN G. CAIN

Statistical analyses of uncontrolled experiments can be biased and therefore lead to faulty inferences. Glen G. Cain proposes regression and selection models which minimize them, and convincingly shows how, if the investigator has knowledge of and can model the selection process, such bias may be minimized whether or not the assignments have been random. In many evaluations it is nonexperimental data which must, of necessity, be analyzed. The author's wise expansion of a theoretically justified model for such analyses is germane and timely.

From Glen G. Cain, "Regression and Selection Models to Improve Nonexperimental Comparisons." Pp. 297-317 in *Evaluation and Experiment, Some Critical Issues in Assessing Social Problems*, New York: Academic Press, 1975.

I. INTRODUCTION

This chapter is organized around two points.[1] The first is a restatement of the main thesis of the preceding chapter by Campbell and Boruch in the framework of a regression model. The second concerns strategies for obtaining unbiased estimates of parameters of interest from nonexperimental data. Before developing these points, let me raise briefly a larger and perhaps philosophical issue of whether there are lessons offered by economic research for the problems with which we are dealing. At the conference on which this volume is based, I was struck by the emphasis on the necessity for "true" experiments as a way of getting unbiased measures of the effects of various programs or

_____

[1]Roughly the first half of this chapter adheres fairly closely to my oral presentation at the 1973 Battelle conference. The last half attempts to summarize points which emerged during the discussion with the conference participants. One section, noted in the text, has been added to help clarify a point. I am grateful to my colleague, Arthur S. Goldberger, for a number of clarifying comments on a first draft.

program inputs. If this impression is correct, then I see an implicit but definite challenge to economic research, or at least to empirical economics.

In my view economics is an empirical science. There is very little predictive power that can be derived directly from economic theory--solely, that is, from axiomatic economic theory. Even the simple proposition that demand curves slope downward is an empirical proposition, not a theoretical one. The predictive power, therefore, depends on the measurement and estimation of relationships among variables. This essential task of measurement is all done with nonexperimental data. The negative income tax experiment, with which I have been associated, is quite exceptional.[1]

Like evaluation research, economic research seeks to measure the effects of policy variables--taxes, subsidies, training programs, etc.--which are part of programs of intervention in the social processes. If we conclude that controlled experimentation is the only trustworthy way to measure the effects of these social-action programs, a shadow of doubt is cast on empirical research in economics. On the other hand, we could reach a contrasting and optimistic conclusion if evaluation research were approached from the perspective of a "believing" economist. That is, if the

---

[1] A report of the negative income tax experiment, formally entitled "The Graduated Work Incentive Experiment," is provided in the Spring 1974 issue of The Journal of Human Resources. The issue includes six articles which describe the experiment and some of its principal research results.

research findings of economics are valid and reliable, then this may indicate that the necessity for experimentation is overdrawn. This is not an issue that can be resolved in this volume, but it may serve as an interesting and perhaps provocative perspective.

II. AN ALTERNATE APPROACH TO BIAS IN TREATMENT EFFECTS

I will now turn to the substance of the previous chapter. The main thesis may be summarized and, I think, clarified, in the framework of a regression model. We can look upon the outcome of a program as the dependent variable, y, and the program itself (or, perhaps, some specified set of program inputs) as the independent variable, T. Let us adopt the simplest specification of T: T = 1 if the person is in the treatment group, and T = 0 if the person is in the control group. There is, of course, an error term, e, which will include all the omitted variables, X_1, X_2, ... X_k, which affect y and "pure" measurement error in y. Thus:

$$y_i = f(T_i) + e_i$$

(i = 1,2 ... N subjects in the sample).

This function may be represented by a linear model, $y_i = a + bT_i + e_i$, without sacrificing the generality of the argument. If we randomly assign groups to treatment and control status, we are assured that the measured relationship, $\partial y / \partial T (= b)$, is an unbiased measure of the effect of T on y.[1] Formally, we are assured of the unbiasedness of b because randomization assures us that T is uncorrelated with the error term in the sample, and, therefore, the estimated b is what we can expect to observe if T were changed in replications of the program. Changes in T correspond, of course, to administering the program to previously untreated members of the population.

Let me digress briefly to discuss the strategy of trying to include some of the omitted "X" variables as explicit independent variables in models which assume random assignments. Clearly, we never design an experiment without any theory; we have some a priori knowledge of variables (besides the treatment) that affect the outcome. Generally, there are compelling reasons for including some of these other variables in a multiple regression model used to estimate the relationship.

First, including relevant X variables will reduce the amount of error variance, and in so doing increase the precision of our estimates of the effect of T on y. Clearly, we seek a significant reduction in error variance which

---

[1] I use "unbiasedness" to mean that the effect we measure is, on the average, the same as the effect that would emerge from an application or implementation of the program to the relevant population. Some degree of ambiguity in the term may arise when there is uncertainty about whether the estimated model accurately represents the process or experiment about which we wish to make inferences. The issue will be discussed further below. Hopefully, the term will be sufficiently clear in context.

reduces the standard error of estimate and thus makes up for the loss in degrees of freedom when using more independent variables.

Second, there are often scientific or policy reasons for measuring the effects of the X's upon y for their own sake. The X's may be variables measuring father's education, mother's education, family income, the subject's health status, and so on. Some of these variables are amenable to policy manipulation. Others, like age, are not, but there may be some scientific interest in measuring their relationship. Moreover, in the light of our principal interest in the treatment (or program) effect, we might be interested in interaction effects between the treatment and some of these other independent variables; these interactions could be estimated explicitly in the multiple regression model.

Finally, by including the important X variables we afford ourselves some protection from misestimating the **treatment effect, in the event a sample correlation exists** between T and one or several of the X's. Given the high costs of controlled experiments, we can seldom rely on replications to "wash out" these sample correlations and the resulting biases in measured treatment effects.

Now let me turn to the main point of Campbell's and Boruch's argument, which concerns the biases in treatment effects that can result from statistical analysis of uncontrolled experiments. The general problem is precisely that the assumption of zero correlation between the error term, e, and the treatment variable, T, is incorrect; that the nonrandom assignment to treatment and control groups has resulted in some variable or set of variables (that affect

y) being correlated with T. If these go unmeasured or (if they are included in the model) are mismeasured, then we will in general get a biased estimate of the treatment effect. If the omitted variables are essentially unmeasurable, then the problem may be intractable.

The bias can be displayed with our linear, additive regression model. Let y measure educational achievemeht, and let "true ability," A, and the treatment (the program), T, be variables determining y, along with an error term which is assumed to be uncorrelated with A and T. In the regression equations written below, I will drop the subscript i and suppress all constant terms, which are irrelevant to the analysis. Thus,

$$y = a_1 T + a_2 A + e.$$

An unbiased measure of the effect of T on y would be obtainable from this model, if we could measure A. Without this measured variable, we have instead:

$$y = bT + e',$$

where $e' = a_2 A + e$ is correlated with T if A is correlated with T.

Now, there is a well-established relationship between the correct measure of treatment effect, a_1, and the observed measure, b; namely:

$$b = a_1 + ca_2,$$

where c denotes the regression coefficient in the auxiliary regression of ability on treatment:[1]

$$A = cT + u.$$

If we know the signs of these two parameters, c and a_2, then we know the direction of the bias in b. Clearly, the sign of a_2, the effect of true ability on achievement, is positive. The sign of c, the relation between treatment and true ability, can be plus, minus, or zero. It would be zero if treatments were assigned randomly with respect to true ability, and then there would be no bias. It would be minus in the case that Campbell and Boruch have discussed, where the most disadvantaged children (i.e., those with the lowest true ability) receive the treatment. Finally, the sign of c would be positive in the case of "creaming." There are many social programs for which we have reason to suspect such positive selectivity. Clearly, the magnitude of the bias in b will depend on the magnitude of a_2 (the size of the omitted variable's effect on y) and c (the size of the relation between A and T).

It will come as no surprise to note that the problem in avoiding the bias in the measure of T in the model with nonrandom assignments is that we are never able to measure the "true ability" variable, A. Note that A is merely a one-variable representation of all the unmeasured factors

---

[1]The auxiliary regression measures a sample relationship between A and T, but it does not purport to express "causality" as between the two variables.

that vary in the process described by the program and that systematically affect the outcome (y). So defined, A would generally represent test-taking ability in educational program evaluations, earning ability in manpower training evaluation, the "ability" to avoid some specific disease in a disease prevention program, and so on.

Now that I have presented the thesis of the preceding chapter using regression notation, let me summarize this thesis in words. Campbell and Boruch are certainly correct to claim that: 1) if two populations differ in mean true ability; 2) if one is the source of a treatment group and the other of a control group; and 3) if we do not control for this difference in ability when measuring the treatment effect, then the treatment-control difference will be confounded with the ability differences. Phrased in this terse way, the point will probably strike many readers as quite obvious. Furthermore, it is also intuitively clear that 4) if partially controlling variables are used, the bias (in the measured treatment effect) will be small or large as the control variables do a good or a bad job in controlling for the ability difference.

We can distinguish two types of selection processes that are relevant to this question of a bias in the measured treatment effect; namely, those that are known and those that are unknown to the investigator. Indeed, the critical difference for avoiding bias is not whether the assignments are random or nonrandom, but whether the investigator has knowledge of and can model this selection process. Recall that the sufficient condition for achieving no bias is that T and e are uncorrelated. Random assignment is just one way of knowing the selection process and ensuring the zero correlation between T and e. There are other ways of selecting subjects for treatment and control groups, and these ways may be fully specified in a regression model, in which case we could again attain the desired goal of a zero correlation between T and e.[1]

I will discuss a polar case in which no random assignments are permitted. (Mixed models are mentioned below.) For example, let the selection procedure be one in which the order of application for admission is the sole basis for assignment to the treatment group. If the order--1st, 2nd, ... 100th, etc.--is available, then the first 50, say, could be assigned to the treatment group. Let us assume that the order of application is correlated with true ability, although we do not need to prejudge the sign of this correlation. If, for example, the most "able" parents were the early applicants, the correlation would be positive; if, say, mothers on welfare first heard about the program and applied earlier, then the correlation could be negative. In either case, the fact that only order of application determines the assignment permits an unbiased measure of the treatment in the model:

$$y = b_1 T + b_2 X + e,$$

where X is the order or position number in the queue.

---

[1] My understanding of the material in the following several paragraphs has been improved by references to two papers by Arthur S. Goldberger (1972 [a] and [b]).

For another example, assignment to the treatment group could be made strictly and solely on the basis of family income--only subjects in families with incomes below a certain level are treated. Family income could then be the X variable in the above model. It is only slightly more complicated in form, if not in substance, to think of a well-defined set of indicators which determine the subject's assignment and which could then be included in the model as a vector of control variables.

Finally, a convenient illustration of modeling the selection procedure is offered by using a pretest score as a basis for assignment to an education program. Suppose all children who score less than X_0 are assigned to the treatment group. Here, X will represent that part of ability which is related to the treatment. Note that there is an ability component, $v = X - A$ (where A, as before, is the "true-ability" score for an individual), but this component is unrelated to the treatment. If the linear and additive specification of X and treatment is reasonably correct, then the following model (Figure 1) will provide an unbiased measure of the effect of T:

$$y = c_1 T + c_2 X + e.$$

Figure 1 is obviously drawn on the basis of an optimistic assumption that the treatment has a positive effect on y. Also, the flatter-than-45° slope of $\partial y/\partial X$ $(= c_2)$ is intended to capture the realistic assumption that the pretest score, X, is a fallible measure of (test-taking) "ability." In principle, the assumptions of additivity and nonlinearity are not crucial, although if an interactive,

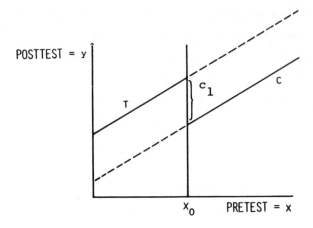

Fig. 1. Nonrandom assignment to T and C groups, based on a pretest score, X. Dashed lines represent non-observed extrapolations of y, given X and the treatment/control status.

nonlinear model applies there may be practical difficulties in getting reliable estimates of the more complicated parameter, $\partial y/\partial T$.

One shortcoming with the model graphed in Figure 1 is that the precision of the estimate of $\partial y/\partial T$ is less than in the case of random assignments (in which T is independent of ability and, of course, independent of X). Also, if "true ability" were known and included in place of X, the precision of $\partial y/\partial T$ would be further increased.[1] But these short-comings can be offset by larger sample sizes or by various

---

[1] These statements are made without proof. See Goldberger (1972 [a] and [b]) for further discussion. Intuitively, uncorrelatedness between X and T provides for a larger

ways of reducing the error variance in the model, such as stratifying the sample or improving the accuracy of measures of y.

I should make clear a point which led to some misunderstanding during the discussion at the conference. The design shown in Figure 1 provides for a nonzero (indeed, negative) correlation between T and X, a correlation which is larger in absolute value than that between T and A. However, the correlation is not perfect: if one knows the value of T (either 1 or 0), one cannot perfectly predict the pretest value (X). If, on the other hand, the selection variable was also dichotomous--i.e., boys or girls, black or white, passed-the-pretest or failed-the-pretest--then our design would break down. A perfect correlation between T and X would exist, and we could not estimate $\partial y/\partial T$, given X, nor $\partial y/\partial X$, given T.

---

residual variance in T (i.e., the variance in T, holding X constant), and the larger residual variance in T produces a more reliable estimate of the regression coefficient of T. The claim that using A instead of X improves the reliability of the estimates of T is explained, again intuitively, as follows: Because A is a true measure of ability, using it would increase the R^2 more than would X (a fallible measure of ability). This higher R^2 means that the error variance in the model is less, and a significant reduction in error variance serves to increase the reliability of estimated regression coefficients.

At this point it is instructive to consider a mixed selection model, in which some randomization is combined with nonrandom selection. Let the probability, P, of selection depend on X, such that:

$$0 < P(X) < 1.$$

Note that the previous examples of nonrandom selection required that the probability of receiving the treatment was 1 if $X < X_0$, and 0 if $X \geq X_0$. In the mixed model thé program administrators might select more disadvantaged children for the program, but not all such "low X" children would be placed in the treatment group and not all "high X" children would be placed in the control group. Given this stratification, however, some randomization would be necessary to determine which low-X (or high-X) children were assigned to the treatment and control groups. The selection process is fully represented by a random assignment that is conditional upon a known value of X. The previously defined regression model, with T and X as independent variables, allows as before an unbiased measure of the treatment effect, but with more precision than in the previous case of only an X-based assignment. The mixed model is very close to the "regression discontinuity" model Campbell has suggested as an acceptable quasi-experimental design (Campbell, 1969).

With a mixed model, even a dichotomous X variable and a dichotomous treatment/control status would not produce a perfect correlation between X and T, as discussed above. The polar case of a completely nonrandom selection process is nevertheless instructive, because we see explicitly the

nonessentiality of randomization for the purpose of estimating an unbiased treatment effect.

Given the potential control that program directors have
over the selection and allocation procedures, the model just
described may have great practical significance under conditions when randomization is not feasible; again, see
Campbell's discussion (1969). The model and example also
serve to illustrate that a post hoc observed difference
between treatment and control groups--i.e., they differ in
population mean values of y--does not necessarily produce a
situation in which the treatment effect is biased. The
contrary impression is given by Campbell's articles on the
problem. (This issue will be further discussed below.)

III. ESTIMATION OF MODELS UNDER CONDITIONS OF UNKNOWN BIAS

Now let us examine the second of the two fundamental
situations in an evaluation design, wherein the selection
process is not fully known. We cannot escape the requirement that the correlation between T and e must be zero (or,
of course, small enough to be ignored) if we are to accept
as unbiased the measured effect of T. Therefore, the burden
falls on the theoretical specification to provide the relevant set of X variables. Generally, all those X's that are
correlated with both y and T must be included, although
special contrary cases, mentioned below, may arise which
preserve a zero correlation between T and e. Whether this
task of theoretical specification is feasible obviously
depends on the given problem. Each program is intended to
be operated in a certain way and in a specified environment.

Consequently, the task of the model builder is limited, at least, to a specification that applies only to these contexts.

There is no question but that the theory must convincingly "close" the system defined by the process and environment of the program.[1] In other words, the model must be "complete" in the following sense: variables correlated with y must be 1) included in the model as "control variables; or, if excluded, they must be 2) known to have a net or partial zero correlation with T; or 3) known to be unvarying in the given environment or process; or 4) known to be themselves completely determined by included variables (in which case we could say that the former have no "net" relation to y); or 5) known to be part of a set of omitted variables which tend to "offset" each other in their effects on y--i.e., where the expected value of y, given the omitted X's, is zero.

The informational requirements for such a complete model are formidable, of course. Incidentally, I would not object if someone claimed that the requirements amount to

---

[1] The term "closed system" was used by F. Mosteller, who raised the question at the conference and in subsequent correspondence of whether the theory provided a closed system (i.e., a complete model) for the purpose at hand. Mosteller quite properly remarked that the question of "bias" in the effect of a given variable, whether T or some other variable, has no meaning in the absence of such a complete model.

knowing the "selection" process in a more fundamental sense than that which is narrowly implied by the "direct selection" procedures which are determined by the administration of the program. If economists, for example, claim to estimate the net effect of labor unions on wages, we must have a model to "capture" (specify) the selection mechanism which distinguishes union member from nonunion member (or, perhaps, a worker covered by a union contract compared with one not covered). Here, the union status variable represents the T variable in our evaluation model, and all the caveats for estimating a union effect in a context of nonrandom assignments must apply. As I mentioned at the outset of this discussion, whether economics provides examples of credible empirical models--credible in the context in which they are intended to apply--is a large question.

Campbell's and Boruch's criticism of the estimated treatment effect in models where the selection process is not directly or explicitly specified is most effective when they are able to persuade their audience of a specific selection bias. Recall (from Figure 1) that an unconditional difference in population means is not sufficient to produce a bias; the difference in means must be one that is conditional upon the variables which appear in the theoretical model but are not included in the empirical model actually employed. There are undoubtedly many cases when there is sufficient knowledge about the selection procedures that the qualitative judgment about the difference in conditional means is warranted.

However, as I view the Campbell-Erlebacher criticism of the Head Start evaluation by the Westinghouse Learning Corporation (Campbell & Erlebacher, 1970), I find that their source of information about the selectivity bias is unclear. How do they know that the Head Start and control children, who came from the same neighborhood, differ in their conditional mean ability? A negative selectivity among children from the same neighborhoods for participation in compensatory education programs is not inevitable. We can visualize circumstances in which the Head Start administrators might "cream" or, what comes to the same situation, exclude "hopeless cases" or "disruptive" children.

If Campbell's and Erlebacher's "knowledge" comes solely from some observable characteristics (or set of characteristics) then we have a right to ask: If these are the characteristics that discriminate between the two groups, then why not use these variables in the model? If they "know" because there are nonmeasurable variables which are known to discriminate between the two groups--perhaps on the basis of some subjective or testimonial expressions of opinion--why don't they make clear that this is the source of their knowledge and permit the reader to assess this ad hoc judgment? Actually, I suspect that many observers would share Campbell's judgment that in the WLC Head Start study, differences in abilities between the Head Start and control groups remained even after the WLC control variables were used. That is, a net difference remains. But this conclusion is based on our subjective empirical impressions of the Head Start selection procedures. Such a conclusion should not be a product of an analysis of a hypothetical model in which the net difference is assumed at the outset, which it was in the simulation model used by Campbell and Erlebacher in their paper.

It may be helpful to consider adopting an explicit convention which, I believe, expresses the Campbell position on the question of selectivity bias. The convention is that whenever the treatment and control groups differ in observed indicators of ability, in situations where the selection procedure is unknown, we should simply assume that this difference understates the "true" difference. Thus, the mean differences in preprogram test scores (if available) could be assumed to understate the true ability difference. If the treatment group's preprogram score were lower, we would assume that they are even worse off than indicated; if their preprogram test score were higher, they would be assumed to be "creamed" to a greater extent than was revealed by their test score advantage.

In the WLC Head Start study, there was no preprogram test score, but in a reanalysis of this data by Barnow, a measure of gross differences in ability was obtained as follows:[1] Using the <u>control</u> group, the postprogram test score, y_C, was regressed on a large number of ability indicators, such as child's age, parents' income, and parents' education, which we shall label X's. The regression equation measured the effect of these commonly used predictors of cognitive achievement on a test score that was, of course, unaffected by the Head Start program. Now, assuming the coefficients of these X's are the same for the treatment group, a predicted mean score, $\bar{\bar{y}}_T$, for the treatment group was calculated based on these coefficients and the treatment

---

[1]This procedure is specified in detail by B. S. Barnow (1973). The suggestion for this procedure came from my colleagues, Robert Avery and Harold Watts.

group's own X-values. A comparison of $\bar{y}_C (=\hat{\bar{y}}_C,$ by construction) and $\hat{\bar{y}}_T$ reveals the extent to which the control and treatment groups differed in the set of ability indicators, where the ability indicators (the X's) are "weighted" by their effects (i.e., regression coefficients) on y_C. This method of comparing the abilities of the two groups seems to us to be far superior to any simple or multiple comparison of X values, per se, since we do not know whether a difference in a given X--say, "mother working,"--has a plus, minus, or zero effect on y. The regression-prediction equation not only combines the various X's but does so in a way that takes into account their effect on y.

Recall that controlling for the X's in the test of the Head Start program provokes Campbell to claim that the treatment group (whose $\hat{y}_T$ was less than $\hat{y}_C$) is still worse off. If this view is maintained consistently, it is equivalent to saying that any mean difference in indicators understates the true difference, when, to repeat, we have no relevant information about how the selection procedures "really" discriminated on ability. Perhaps we could adopt this convention as a "conservative" procedure in evaluation studies. I am not persuaded, however, that it is justified in general, although perhaps it was appropriate for the WLC study.

I would conclude by agreeing with Campbell and Boruch on the general desirability of random assignments. I would agree also to be suspicious of evaluations in which we know little about the selection methods, although I am more hesitant to assert a direction of bias in these circumstances. On the other hand, I am undoubtedly more sympathetic to the

use of theoretically justified models for analysis of nonexperimental data. This sympathy is not totally owed to my
membership in the economics profession. I am one of the few
members who has hedged his bets with research in a controlled experiment.

REFERENCES

Barnow, B. S. The effects of Head Start and socioeconomic
status on cognitive development of disadvantaged children. Unpublished doctoral dissertation, University of
Wisconsin, Department of Economics, 1973.

Campbell, D. T. Reforms as experiments. American Psychologist, April 1969, 24(4), 409-429.

Campbell, D. T., & Erlebacher, A. How regression artifacts
in quasi-experimental evaluations can mistakenly make
compensatory education look harmful. In J. Hellmuth
(Ed.), Compensatory education: A national debate (Vol.
3, Disadvantaged child). New York: Brunner/Mazel, 1970.

Goldberger, A. S. Selection bias in evaluating treatment
effects: Some formal illustrations (Discussion paper
123-72). Madison: Institute for Research on Poverty,
1972. (a)

Goldberger, A. S. Selection bias in evaluating treatment
effects: The case of interaction (Discussion paper
129-72). Madison: Institute for Research on Poverty,
1972. (b)

6

THE PRIORITY SCORE ALLOCATION DESIGN

By

**HENRY W. RIECKEN, ROBERT F. BORUCH,
DONALD T. CAMPBELL, NATHAN CAPLAN, THOMAS K. GLENNAN, Jr.,
JOHN W. PRATT, ALBERT REES, and WALTER WILLIAMS**

Regression-discontinuity designs are in frequent use by evaluators. In the many evaluation situations where "random assignment of eligibles is not regarded as acceptable," this quasi-experimental analysis is done. Riecken and associates show how, while still adhering to administrative restrictions about eligibility, various manipulations of eligibility criteria may be done which can serve to strengthen this design, to permit stronger inferences.

From Henry W. Riecken et al., "Assignment to Treatment by Priority Scores: The Regression Discontinuity Design." Pp. 88-97 in H.W. Riecken and R.F. Boruch (eds.), *Social Experimentation: A Method for Planning and Evaluating Social Intervention.* New York: Academic Press, 1974.

The basic ideas behind the Regression–Discontinuity design can be more easily understood if we begin by considering first a strong and then a weak form of a true experiment both of which are applicable to the type of situation which is also appropriate for a Regression–Discontinuity quasi-experiment. Recall an earlier remark that one of the necessary conditions for a social experiment is that the ameliorative treatment be in short supply, thus guaranteeing that there are more experimental units (persons, schools, cities, etc.) available for the treatment than are going to be treated. This condition regularly occurs for pilot programs in which a new program is tried out on a limited population. It often occurs for specialized programs applied to eligible subgroups of the population, such as specialized opportunities based on merit, or compensatory programs based on need. If such programs are in short supply, with more eligibles than program space, it provides one of the conditions for using some of the eligible applicants as a control group.

Under these circumstances, the best strategy would be a true experiment in which random assignment of units occurred *across the full range of eligibility*. Let us consider, for example, a Neighborhood Youth Corps training program in which needy unemployed or under-employed young adults receive training for specific, well-paying jobs. Eligibility for the program might depend (as it once did) on per capita earnings of the applicant's family. If there are a larger number of eligible applicants than the program can handle, the experimentally oriented administrator could randomly select from all those eligible the number for which there was space in the program. By keeping records on the randomly equivalent remainder for use as a control group, he could, at a later time, collect data on earnings of trained and not trained individuals in order to measure the effect of training.

Now, there are many situations in which random assignment of eligibles is not regarded as acceptable. Eligibility, it is argued, occurs in degree, not as a dichotomous quantum: Those most eligible, those most needy, should get the treatment if there are not facilities to take care of all those eligible. This argument against randomization is often stated as though existing assignment procedures *did* meet the equity requirements on which random assignment fails. Careful examination of almost any agency operation will usually show that they do not. There is regularly lacking any procedure for ranking those who are potentially eligible in order of need as a basis for admissions decisions. The casual procedures of recruitment and admission allow ample room for cronyism and administrative convenience. New facilities are deliberately given minimal publicity in order to avoid a surplus of applicants. If a first-come, first-served rule is employed, the most needy will rarely be among those most alert to new facilities. Those first to apply will have learned about the opportunity by informal informational sources prior to public announcement. In contrast with existing practice, a thorough publicizing of program opportunities, resulting in a surplus of eligibles who are then assigned at random to treatment or control status, is a highly moral procedure, over and above the value of making possible experimental evaluation.

Nevertheless, if resistance to full-scale randomization cannot be overcome, it is still possible to give explicit attention to degree of eligibility in a weak form of experiment, namely a *tie-breaking randomi-*

zation experiment. Let us suppose that rather than being spread out over the entire range of eligibles, the job training program was instead concentrated on those most in need; and that the program could accommodate all of those with family incomes of $22 per person per week and below, plus half of those with incomes of $23 a week. Even under the constraint to give the treatment to the neediest, it would now be justifiable to assign randomly to treatment or nontreatment those persons who were tied at $23. Thus a small-scale true experiment could be carried out. This is a weak experiment on two counts. First, a very small number of cases may be available and thus a difference reflecting a genuine effect might not be statistically significant, or might even be reversed by sampling fluctuations. One would want to maximize the number of persons who were tied at the cut-off score and a useful way to do this would be to adopt relatively large class intervals within which scores could be regarded as equal for all practical purposes. Thus, in the present example a $2 per week interval would yield a larger number of ties than would, say, a 50¢ per week interval, as well as avoiding the excessive and meaningless precision of the latter calculation. The second weakness of this experiment is that it explores the treatment effect only for a narrow range of eligibility and thus provides a very limited base for estimating the effects over the whole range of treatment (see Figure 4.1). On the other hand, the narrow range that it does explore is presumably similar to the adjacent ranges where expansion and contraction of the program would take

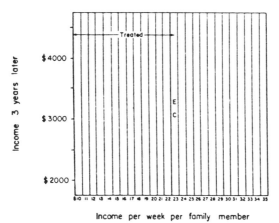

Income per week per family member

Figure 4.1 Illustrative outcome for a hypothetical tie-breaking experiment in which some applicants with a per capita weekly family income of $23 are assigned at random to the Neighborhood Youth Corps while others are randomly assigned to control group status. All those with incomes of $22 and below get the training. Means for each group on average earnings subject to witholding 3 years later are indicated by the location of the E for Experimental Group and C for Control Group.

place, and thus it is relevant to an important problem for administrative decision making.

REGRESSION-DISCONTINUITY DESIGN

In considering Figure 4.1, let us ask what might be found if one did a follow-up study of eligibility units adjacent to the experiment. Assuming the training to have been effective, one could expect the all-treated group with eligibility scores of $22 to have later incomes very similar to those of the Experimental (E) subgroup of $23, slightly lower perhaps as a concomitant of their slightly lower starting income, but still higher than the Controls (C) of $23—similarly for scores of $21, $20, or less. On the other hand, later incomes among those with eligibility scores of $24, all untreated, should be very similar to those of the controls of category $23—slightly higher, but not as high as the experimentals of category $23, etc. The hypothetical data of Figure 4.2 extend such a follow-up study across the whole range of income categories.

Comparison of Figure 4.2 with Figure 4.1 suggests that one should be able to infer what the results of a hypothetical tie-breaking experiment would have been from analysis of the effects of nonrandomly assigned treatments across the total range of eligibility. Thus, if the cutting point for eligibility had been set at $22 and below, with all of the $23 group going untreated, and if the outcome had been as in Figure 4.3, we could be quite confident that a tie-breaking experiment would have shown the results found in Figures 4.1 and 4.2. On the other hand,

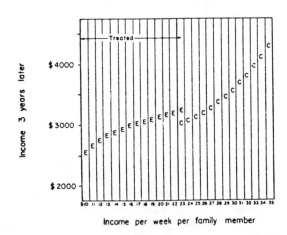

Income per week per family member

Figure 4.2 Hypothetical tie-breaking experiment of Figure 4.1 plus values for those in other family income classes, all of whom either got Neighborhood Youth Corps training if at $22 or below, or did not if at $24 and above.

were the results to be as in Figure 4.4, we could be confident that the treatment had no effect.

Figures 4.3 and 4.4 illustrate Regression–Discontinuity design (Thistlethwaite and Campbell, 1960; Campbell, 1969; and from a different methodological tradition, Goldberger, 1972, pp. 14–21). It is a quasi-experimental substitute for the tie-breaking randomization experiment shown in Figure 4.1, rather than for full-range randomization. The results of Regression–Discontinuity design do not serve as a basis for estimating effects at all levels of eligibility, but only as a basis for extrapolating to the results of a hypothetical tie-breaking experiment at the cutting point. For example, it appears in Figure 4.3 that the income effect drops off among the most eligible, a conclusion which comes from an implicit assumption that without treatment the outcomes would have shown a straight line slope over the whole range. This need not be the case, of course, and curvilinear functions may be at least as common as linear ones in such settings.

The Regression–Discontinuity design is quasi-experimental in that more unverifiable assumptions have to be made in interpreting it than would be required for the tie-breaking randomization. For example, one has to assume a homogeneity of the measurement units on both sides of and across the cutting point. One also has to make assumptions about the underlying mathematical function. A suggested mode of statistical analysis (Sween, 1971) is to fit a curve separately to the two segments of the data above and below the cutting point and to obtain

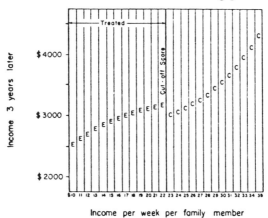

Income per week per family member

Figure 4.3 Hypothetical outcome for a Regression–Discontinuity design showing a degree of effect from Neighborhood Youth Corps similar to that illustrated in Figures 4.1 and 4.2. This figure is essentially the same as Figure 4.2, except that there is no randomized category and no tie-breaking randomization. Instead, all at income level $22 and below have been admitted to the program.

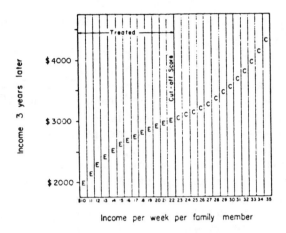

Figure 4.4 Hypothetical outcome for a Regression–Discontinuity design in the setting of Figures 4.2 and 4.3, but in which the treatment has had no effect.

from each the intercept value at the cutting point, thus literally extrapolating from each side to the cutting point. The magnitude of the difference between these two extrapolated values will obviously depend upon what form of curve is assumed for each of the two parts. If the basic underlying curve is sigmoid, as illustrated in Figures 4.3 and 4.4, then fitting a linear function to a null condition represented by Figure 4.4 will produce a pseudo-effect. One should also graph the results and distrust the statistical results if visual inspection makes plausible a continuous function with no discontinuity at the cutting point. Of course, an arbitrary coincidence of an independent jump in the underlying curve with the cutting point is always a possibility, but an unlikely one if the assumption of equality of intervals in the measurement scale is justified and the variation within intervals is homogeneous.

While the illustrations provided deal with a single dependent and a single independent variable, multivariate versions of the design would often be preferable, as long as the feature of a sharp cutting point on a quantified decision criterion is not lost. Pooling many eligibility variables into a single eligibility score is discussed in the following. Multivariate outcome variables would be usable in several forms. A single dependent variable, such as later earnings, could be statistically adjusted to eliminate differential effects of various socioeconomic background variables, except those used to quantify eligibility. Or, a composite outcome variable constructed by multiple regression techniques could be employed.

PROBLEMS IN QUANTIFYING ELIGIBILITY AND
ADMINISTRATING ADMISSION PROCEDURES

The basic situation is a common one: an ameliorative program in short supply; a basic decision that it should go to the most needy; a desire to see the program scientifically evaluated. For this situation, if random assignment among equally eligible subjects is ruled out, the Regression-Discontinuity design is probably the best one available and thus should frequently be used. To use it requires a quantified eligibility criterion and other special admission procedures and controls.

For some ameliorative programs a quantitative variable is already included among several eligibility criteria. Family income in Neighborhood Youth Corps is but one example. Test scores, as on a reading readiness test, provide another class of examples. Where these exist, a Regression-Discontinuity design can be used among that subsample of applicants who meet all other requirements and for whom this quantitative criterion is thus decisive. In such cases, the Regression-Discontinuity design could be used with present administrative machinery. What is required is (1) adherence to a sharp cutting point, allowing no exceptions for the set of applicants for which the score is to be the sole and uniform decision rule, and (2) keeping full records of eligibility scores and identification data on both those accepted and those rejected by this criterion. Some illustrations of likely biases will help make the admissions procedures clearer.

One source of bias is in the fact that, in most treatment programs, there occur cases which must be admitted to the program regardless of their eligibility as defined by the cut-off score. This may be because of the compelling nature of the person's needs as seen by the staff, because of political considerations, or for other reasons. Such cases should be identified and removed from the research sample without examining their eligibility score and without regard to whether they fall in the treated or the untreated group. Otherwise, they produce bias. The bias arises because administrators typically strive to minimize the number of exceptions to the rules and to invoke special privilege only if the special case would have been rejected for treatment by imposition of the cut-off score. If only those who would have been rejected are then removed from the study, this "purifies" the untreated group without a parallel purification of the treated group. That is, the treated group retains persons who, had their scores fallen instead in the no-treatment range, would have been admitted anyway. Such a process of selective elimination tends to make a compensatory program look good. If these cases cannot be eliminated in advance, one could leave them in the analysis but classify them as their eligibility scores *would* have assigned them, e.g., ineligibles who were assigned to treatment being labeled for analytic purposes as not having received the treatment. While this leads to an underestimate of treatment effects, it avoids letting selection biases produce pseudo-effects. (See the more extended treatment in Chapter III of modes of analysis where not all of those randomly assigned to a treatment accept it.) For the procedure of allowing exceptions by falsifying the crucial scores, there is no methodological cure. One should, however, be able to estimate the direction of bias in many situations. For example, where the program is compensatory, the process would usually exaggerate its effectiveness.

Another potential bias comes from the existence of an official, publicized cut-off score, a practice often followed if there is room for all of those eligible. In the Neighborhood Youth Corps program, the requirement that family income be below the poverty level might have been such a criterion. When this score is something that the potential applicant can ascertain about himself (as income or age), there results a self-selection among ineligible applicants that is not paralleled among the eligibles. Thus, the agency meets and gets initial records on persons in the ineligible region who have not had adequate information about the cut-off point. From this group, therefore, many of the more alert and able have removed themselves. For a compensatory program, this bias is in the direction of making the treatment look good through a sampling bias that reduces the level of competence of the untreated. In the case of a legally fixed cut-off which the applicant cannot himself determine precisely before applying, such as an achievement test score, this source of bias is not likely. Even if there is some tendency in such a case for the alert ineligible not to apply, it is unlikely to produce an abrupt discontinuity in applicant quality right at the cutting point.

The preceding considerations have been presented as though admission were being decided for sizable batches of applicants at one time. Where a new facility is going to open on a specific date or where an instructional program is organized into terms with fixed starting dates, then this is feasible. One can compare the number of spaces with the number of applicants and set the cutting point in a Regression–Discontinuity design. However, the design is also usable for "trickle processing" situations, in which new applicants appear at any time and are admitted or not depending upon their qualifications and the number of beds available—short waits and empty beds being tolerated but kept to a minimum. Under trickle processing, batchlike time periods must be established within which a cut-off criterion is adhered to. If too many empty beds are accumulated or if waiting times become too long, then for the next time period a corrective readjustment is made, for example, by lowering the admission score. Each time period contains a complete quasi-experiment. But individual periods will frequently include too few cases to be interpretable in isolation. Combining time periods or batches requires careful rules to avoid selection biases. Since different cutting points have been used, pooling requires that the data be converted into units above and below the cutting point. (At least four such steps on each side would seem a minimum; more are, of course, desirable.) All batches must contribute in equal proportion to all steps used, otherwise batch-to-batch sampling differences will create bends in the composite curve. But identity in the size of the units from batch to batch is not required.

Many ameliorative programs lack any official quantitiative criteria for admission to treatment. To apply the Regression–Discontinuity design to them, a quantitative ordering of eligibility priority is essential. Two widely useful procedures are ranking and rating. Ranking can only be used if applicants are being handled in large batches. Within each batch, all applicants can be ranked in need by each of the admissions staff and a combined ranking generated. The top n eligibles would be admitted. Alternatively, eligible individuals can be rated as to need by each staff member and the average of all ratings taken. When several criteria are available, they can be combined statistically into a single eligibility score.

In large batch processing the cutting point can be decided after all candidates have been rated, and it can be chosen so as to provide exactly the same number of candidates as there are spaces (randomizing if there are ties at the cutting point). In trickle processing, the cutting point for a given time period must be set in advance on the basis of past experience, including past rate of applicants, typical eligibility, and rater idiosyncracies.

In summary, the Regression–Discontinuity design is an important quasi-experimental analysis, available where program administrators are willing to specify precisely the order of eligibility and to adhere meticulously to it. Because of the requirement of quantifying eligibility, it represents a significant additional procedural burden over ordinary admission procedures, a burden usually as great or greater than that required for randomization from a pool of eligible applicants larger than the facilities can accommodate. Such randomization is to be preferred on grounds of both statistical efficiency and the fewer background assumptions that have to be made. But where randomization is precluded, the Regression–Discontinuity design is recommended.

References

Campbell, D. T. Reforms as experiments. American Psychologist, 1969, 24, 409-429. (No. 4, April)

Goldberger, A. S. Selection bias in evaluating treatment effects: Some formal illustrations. Discussion Papers, #123-72. Madison: Institute for Research on Poverty, University of Wisconsin, 1972.

Sacks, J., & Ylvisaker, D. Linear estimation for approximately linear models. Discussion paper Number 9, Center for Statistics and Probability, Northwestern University, October, 1976.

Spiegelman, C. H. Two methods of analyzing a non-randomized experiment "adaptive" regression and a solution to Reiersöl's problem. Unpublished Ph.D. Dissertation, Northwestern University, Mathematics Department, June, 1976.

Sween, J. A. The experimental regression design: An inquiry into the feasibility of nonrandom treatment allocation. Unpublished Doctoral Dissertation, Northwestern University, August 1971.

Thistlethwaite, D. L., & Campbell, D. T. Regression discontinuity analysis: An alternative to the ex post facto experiment. Journal of Educational Psychology, 1960, 51, 309-317.

7

FOCAL LOCAL INDICATORS
FOR SOCIAL PROGRAM EVALUATION

By

DONALD T. CAMPBELL

Donald Campbell has been a pioneer in the use of time series for evaluative purposes. In this elegant and abundantly illustrated article he shows how focal local social indicators, including administrative records, can be used in program evaluation. The argument for keeping aggregate statistics so they can be retrieved for lists of persons is a persuasive one.

From Donald T. Campbell, "Focal Local Indicators for Social Program Evaluation." *Social Indicators Research,* *3*(1976), 237-256.

ABSTRACT. An important role for social indicators is in the evaluation of the impact of specific social programs. This requires (in the absence of randomized experiments) extended time-series of social indicators. Such series will usually only be available for administrative records (both public and private). It is in the national interest that these be made flexibly research-retrievable by local region, by frequent time interval, and in fine topical breakdown. The ability to report aggregate statistics retrieved for lists of persons adds still greater precision in program evaluation, and can be done with no loss of privacy and without any release of individual data. For this purpose, the use of uniform individual identification numbers add efficiency without increased risk to privacy.

Of the many uses to which social indicators may be put, perhaps the most important in the long run will be in *evaluating the impact of specific social reforms*, ameliorative programs, changes in laws, pilot programs, demonstration programs, and the like. Such use raises many problems and requirements not met with when social indicators are employed to assess the status of a whole nation. Some of these are flagged in the wording of the title.

It seems useful to begin with a number of concrete illustrations of this use of social indicators, and Figures 1 through 15 have been provided for this purpose. It is hoped that the captions are sufficiently informative to make these disparate studies comprehensible.

1. LOCAL

Most programs that call for evaluation are applied to social units smaller than a nation as a whole. This is particularly true for demonstration programs, and for programs initiated by or in cooperation with city, county, state, or provincial governments. Even national programs are better evaluated if the introduction can be staged so that some regions get it a year before others, providing during that year an 'experimental' region and comparison regions. For program evaluation purposes, a federal system has the advantage that single states or provinces often try out new programs, with adjacent

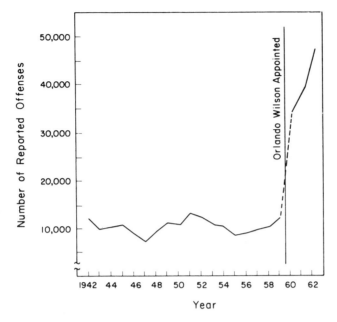

Fig. 1.   Number of reported larcenies under $50 in Chicago (data from *Uniform Crime Reports for the United States*, 1942–62). Presumably the jump in crime rate represents a change in reporting quality rather than a crime increase (Campbell, 1969).

provinces available as comparisons. In a more centralized nation, these effective quasi-experimental designs might be precluded. (See Figures 5 and 6 for actual illustrations.) Thus we need *local* statistics, available on the unit receiving the new program and on comparable units not receiving it.

The kinds of social indicators that might be useful are as varied as the social programs our local, provincial, and national governments generate. Statistics on deaths, days hospitalized, days lost from work, traffic accidents, unemployment, achievement test scores, and crime, illustrate the kinds of indicators that can be useful when made available by schools, census tracts, police districts, city, county, or province.

Potentially, the computerization of administrative records, if properly augmented by research-retrieval capabilities, should make such regional breakdowns readily available. At the present time, it is extremely costly and usually impossible to get regional data on any units other than those routinely used in administrative reports. For urban programs, it is now

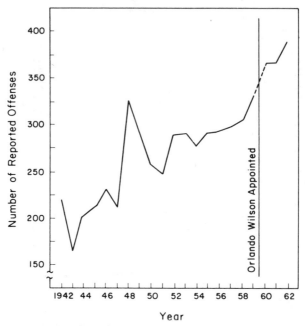

Fig. 2. Number of reported murders and nonnegligent manslaughters in Chicago, Illinois, from 1942 to 1962 (data from *Uniform Crime Reports for the United States*, 1942,62). Presumably these data are unaffected by the 1942–59 reporting bias shown in Figure 1 (Campbell, 1969).

usually impossible to break out the data by census tract, police precinct, election precinct, school system district, single school boundaries, medical service boundaries, etc. Creating such capacity is an urgent public need. It will be costly to set up initially, but low cost to keep going once established. Not only should relevant government administrative records be made research-retrievable in this way, it is also in the public interest that this capacity be created for records of insurance companies (hospitalization, medical, automobile, life), major educational testing firms, hospitals, schools, etc. Government funding of one statistician and one computer programmer for each major private record center would be a very wise investment in augmenting our ability to determine whether or not our ameliorative programs are working (as nine times out of ten, at the present time, we cannot). It must be emphasized that these uses can be achieved with no increase in jeopardy to individual privacy, as is discussed below.

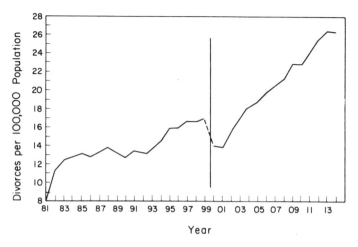

Fig. 3.   Divorce rate for German Empire, 1881–1911. Does the law of 1899 make divorce less frequent, but also a poorer indicator of marital stability? (Glass, *et al.*, 1971).

The social indicator movement is rightly spending a great deal of effort in the development of subjective social indicators in which people report on the quality of their lives as they see it, achieved through public opinion survey methods. These face special problems when used for program evaluation. Surveys designed to monitor national well being do not provide useful local data. It is a frustrating statistical reality that one needs as large a sample

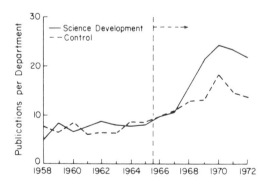

Fig. 4.   Departmental publication rates in mathematics for Science Development and control institutions. Most Science Development funding was initiated for the recipient schools on various dates during 1965–68 (Drew, 1975).

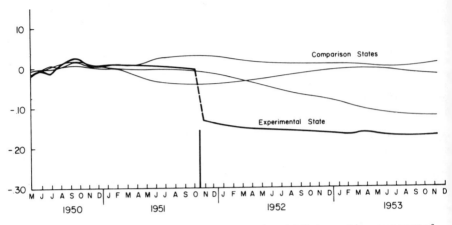

Fig, 5.   Effect of introducing a law in the Experimental State requiring repayment of welfare costs from the deceased recipient's estate on the old age assistance case loads. Monthly data have all values expressed as a percentage of the case load 18 months prior to the change of the law. (Modified from Baldus, 1973, p. 204, Figure 1.)

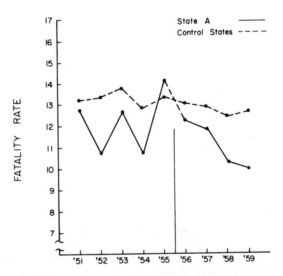

Fig. 6.   Traffic fatalities per 100,000 of population in State A prior to and after a strong crackdown on speeding initiated in 1956, compared with the average of four neighboring states (Campbell, 1969, p. 419, Figure 11). The fact that the crackdown was in response to the unprecedented rise in fatalities in 1955 complicates the interpretation. The 1957–59 trend is more clearly indicative of genuine impact.

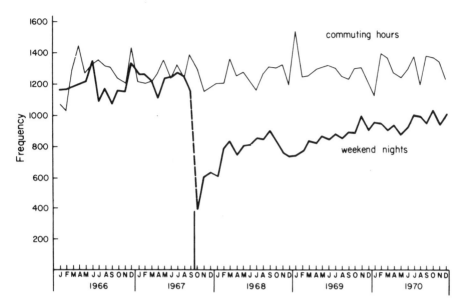

Fig. 7. British traffic casualties (fatalities plus serious injuries) before and after the British Breathalyser crackdown of October 1967, seasonally adjusted (Ross, 1973, Figures 10 and 11 combined). Bars were closed prior to and during commuting hours.

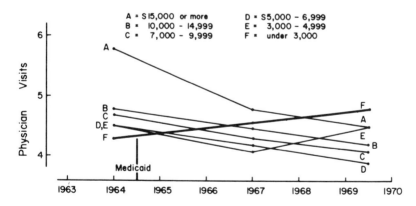

Fig. 8. Possible evidence for the effect of Medicaid on the contacts with doctors of persons in low-income families. The first data set is based on weekly surveys carried out between July 1963 and June 1964. The second set come from July 1966–June 1967. The third wave is entirely within 1969. (Wilder, 1972, p. 5, Table B.)

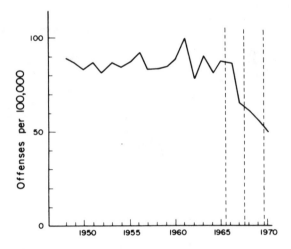

Fig. 9. Incidence of all sex offenses (except incest) known to the police in Denmark during the period 1948–1970 (Kutchinsky, 1973, p. 164). Kutchinsky gives reasons why the drop may be a co-effect rather than caused by relaxation of laws against pornography in 1965, 1967, and 1969.

(e.g., 2500) to document an improvement in morale in Silver Springs, Maryland as one does for the whole United States. However, the instruments designed for national surveys can be specially administered to local samples before and after a new program is tried out, and at the same time to some appropriate comparison region not getting the program. (This is not to say that survey data are never useful in program evaluation. Note the dramatic impact of U.S. Medicaid legislation shown in Figure 8.)

2. FOCUSED ON FREQUENT TIME PERIODS

The real world of social ameliorative efforts is an imperfect laboratory at best. If a change is noted, there are usually many alternative explanations for the effect not ruled out by the data collection effort. Planning and improved research methodology can greatly improve this situation. The randomization of assignment to treatment which provides optimal clarity of results will usually be impossible, certainly for changes in laws that affect all persons within a governmental jurisdiction. For such settings, reviews of non-randomized research designs (Campbell and Stanley, 1963–6; Campbell,

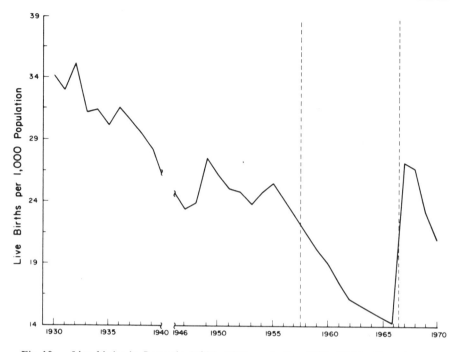

Fig. 10.   Live births in Romania (1930–1970, excluding 1941–1945). (Data from David, 1970.) The sudden prohibition of abortions in October, 1966, clearly had an immediate, if not necessarily permanent effect on birth rates. However, the legalization of abortion in 1957 may not have affected the steadily downward trend.

1969; 1975; Riecken et al., 1974) point to the interrupted time series design with comparison series as the most powerful of quasi-experimental designs. For tests of significance to be used, many time points are needed (Box and Tiao, 1965; Glass et al., 1975). For most reforms and legal changes, monthly or weekly data are needed, annual data do not provide enough degrees of freedom. Because of strong weekend effects, and because months vary from each other and from year to year in how many weekends they have, weekly data (even if combined into 4-week units) is much superior to monthly data (e.g., Ross et al., 1970; Ross, 1973). When as in Figure 7, the crackdown starts in the middle of the month, analytic 'months' differing from calendar months, are desirable. Thus to our computer retrieval capacities for administrative records, public needs for program evaluation would be best served by retrieval capacity providing fine-grained time detail and flexible alternative aggregation units.

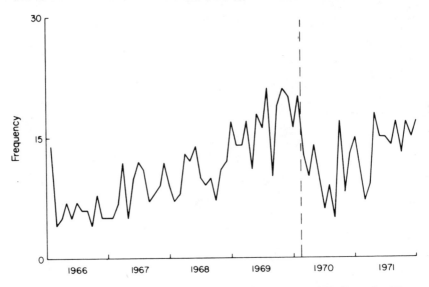

Fig. 11. Gun homicides by month, Washington, D.C., 1966–1971. 'Operation Disarm the Criminal' operated January–June, 1970 (Zimring, 1975, p. 189).

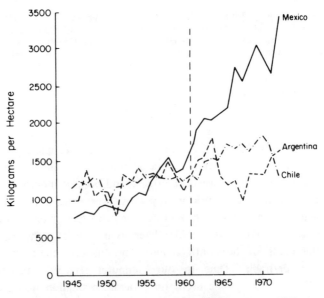

Fig. 12. Introduction of Semi Dwarf HYV Wheat in Mexico in 1961. Argentina and Chile are presented as controls (Hoole and Job, 1975, p. 21).

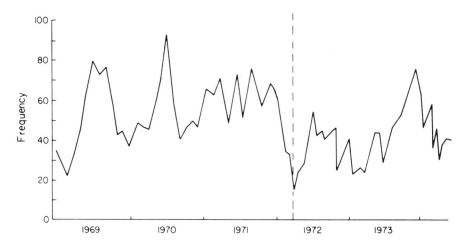

Fig. 13. The impact of 'Operation Whistlestop' on thefts from automobiles, Hyde Park area of Chicago. The 'Whistlestop' campaign, initiated in March of 1973, encouraged the carrying of whistles and blowing then on seeing anything suspicious, or when victimized oneself. (From Hook *et al.*, ms. in preparation.) While the rate of this crime seems lower during Whistlestop than before, the sharp drop just prior to the start of the campaign makes it highly equivocal evidence of program impact.

The desirability of fine-grained time series on local units accents the special usefulness for program evaluation of administrative records, which are being collected anyway, and on complete populations rather than samples. We cannot hope to achieve such local and frequent observations using subjective social indicators.

3. TOPICALLY FOCUSED

Ideally, for evaluating any new program, there would be a range of social indicators representing both the benefits expected by the advocates of the program and the harms expected by its opponents. We can move in this direction, but we must remember that all indicators are imperfect and that all are composite products of many causes, many of which are irrelevant to program impact. We can make social indicators based on administrative records more useful if we can break down global indicators into topically specific statistics more focally related to the topic at hand. Thus in evaluating the impact of the British Breathalyser Crackdown of 1967, shown in

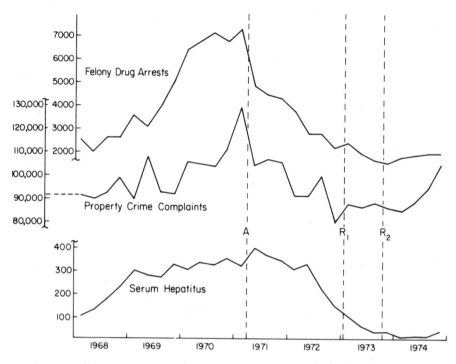

Fig. 14. New York City records of possible relevance to drug abuse (courtesy of Anthony F. Japha, Drug Law Evaluation Project, The Association of the Bar of The City of New York).

A. In March of 1971, the Police Department initiated a major change of policing effort, increasing attention to drug suppliers, decreasing attention to drug users.

R_1. January 1973, Governor Rockefeller announces proposed new stricter drug laws and criminal penalties.

R_2. September, 1973. Rockefeller drug laws take effect.

Felony Drug Arrests. (Quarterly frequency.) The sharp drop after *A* presumably shows the anticipated change in police arrest activity rather than a drop in drug use necessarily.

Property Crime Complaints. (Quarterly, seasonally adjusted.) Commonly regarded as an indicator of drug addiction. Is the drop at point A evidence of impact of the police campaign against suppliers? Comparison data from Hoboken, Boston, and Philadelphia would help.

Serum Hepatitus. (Quarterly. Excludes transfusion-based and infectious hepatitis.) This type of hepatitis is spread at least in part through hypodermic needles used in shooting drugs. Is the decline a delayed effect of policy change at A? Or is it due to a decrease in vigilance in reporting hepatitis cases (as the parallel drop for infectious hepatitis, not shown, might indicate)?

At the present time, drug abuse indicators are probably too much influenced by police effort and unknown forces, and reform programs are too delayed in their effects, or too weak, to produce clear-cut evidence of program impact. But the data are encouraging enough to justify the refinement of indicators, the search for new more direct measures less influenced by extraneous forces, and the use of comparison series from jurisdictions not impacted by the program under study.

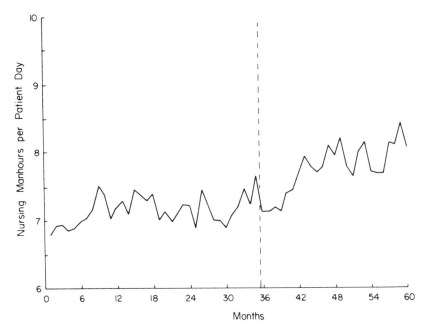

Fig. 15. Effect of hospital merger on nursing work hours per patient day, seasonally adjusted (from Whittaker, 1974). The merger on the 35th month produced a significant *increase* in hospital costs, using the Box and Tiao (1965) statistics. Similar increases were also shown on other indicators using both monetary and work time units. Note that these findings go directly against the hopes and indeed the official reports from merger programs, where analysis of this detail have not been made. Roos (1973) reports similar findings, and points out that, with comparison hospitals added, this is the best evaluation method available, randomized assignment of hospitals to mergers being out of the question.

Figure 7, it would have been useful to have separate data on driver fault, blood alcohol of driver, and fatalities separate from nonfatal serious accidents. It added tremendous power to the analysis that the data were retrievable by time of day. For crime statistics, details of type of crime should be retrievable; for hospital records, details of illness and medication, etc. Improving the topical specificity of retrievable administrative records is an urgent public need if we are to achieve the ability to learn the effects of our new governmental programs.

For topical focus, subjective social indicators, as achieved by interviews and questionnaires, will always have a great advantage in flexibility and subtlety over administrative records. We will usually want to use such methods, even if only once before and once afterwards, and in conjunction with the longer fine-grained time series coming from administrative records. We should also consider augmenting administrative records to include the judgments of the many human participant observers at all levels of the institution. Thus in factories, schools, welfare agencies, and government bureaus we should consider instituting brief multi-topic 'Annual Reports for Program Evaluation' to be filled out by every person. Thus teachers, students, and parents might rate the effectiveness of the school in teaching reading, writing, arithmetic, music appreciation, etc. These ARPE's would avoid evaluating any persons (not pupils, nor teachers, nor principals, nor parents) limiting themsleves instead to rating the program alternatives available (Campbell, 1971). Such ARPE's would be topically specific enough to evaluate changes in textbooks, as well as more fundamental modifications of the educational system. Forms have been developed for public schools (Weber *et al.*, 1971; Anderson, 1973a, b) and for social welfare settings (Gordon and Campbell, 1971). We cannot expect these to produce monthly data, but with comparison regions and cross-topic control comparisons they would provide relatively unequivocal evidence for many changes.

It seems clear from Figures 1–15 that the interrupted time-series methodology has great promise for program evaluation. More work is needed by statisticians on appropriate models for tests of significance. For example, the Box-type models (Glass, *et al.*, 1975) fail to show significance in Figure 11, perhaps because they weight the most recent observations too heavily. Handling seasonal trends and combining experimental and control series in tests of significance remain problems. Public needs for hard-headed information on program effectiveness require further methodological research in these areas.

Methodological considerations also provide recommendations to legislatures and administrators for the optimal use of this method. Here are five.

(1) Introduce a new program decisively with adequate advance publicity. If a new program is gradually introduced, the gradual effects are apt to be indistinguishable from the ordinary kinds of trend changes that would be apt to occur anyway. Delayed starting dates may facilitate this. Figure 7 provides a good example. The bill was passed in May for a September starting date which was well publicized (Ross, 1973).

(2) Keep the record-keeping systems constant, if they are any good at all.

Too often the new reform also reforms the data system, resulting in changes which are uninterpretable as program effects. Figure 1 illustrates the problem, although in a setting where it was probably unavoidable. Dual record-keeping, old style and new, would be recommended for an extended overlap period.

(3) Legislative and administrative actions attacking chronic problems are more easily evaluated than quick responses to acute problem flare ups. This is due to a complex problem in statistical inference, illustrated, if not explained, in Figure 3 (Campbell, 1969; Riecken, et al., 1974).

(4) Evaluation money should often be invested in assembling comparison statistics from other neighboring governments, as other provinces in evaluating one province's legislation, or in Canadian statistics for evaluating United States programs and vice versa.

(5) Where available administrative records are inadequate for the evaluation of major program goals, and where evaluation of the program has high priority, as in pilot programs, the enabling legislation should provide one-year delays in program start-up so that pre-program data can be obtained on newly developed social indicators specifically designed for the program.

4. FOCUSED ON PERSONS

Figures 1 through 15 and the preceding sections bear an obvious relation to 'social indicators' as commonly understood. In the present section we pick up the theme of *administrative records used for program evaluation*, and move into an application that may be outside of the social indicator movement as usually delineated, but is of such high potential that it needs mention in any program evaluation context.

The interrupted time-series method described so far is available only for program *changes*, it cannot be used to evaluate on-going programs. However, if administrative records can be made available as averaged data on lists of specified persons, then these records can be used as social indicators of program effectiveness on a wide range of *ongoing* social programs.

So great are contemporary concerns with individual privacy, with a corresponding abhorrence of combining individual data from two record systems, that it seems important to start out by making clear that this use of administrative records can be done, and done effectively, without breaching individual privacy, without releasing any individual data to anybody from any record file. The details are available in the current U.S. National Research

Council report of the Committee on Federal Agency Evaluation Research (Rivlin *et al.*, 1975. See especially Appendix A by Campbell, *et al.*, 1975). But since the recommended technique is not widely known, it seems important to present here a brief overview of 'mutually insulated' statistical linkage between data files, achieved without file merger, that is, without expanding either file's data on individuals.

Let us use as a concrete illustration a U.S. Job Corps training program, eligibility for which is determined by a variety of requirements such as age, unemployment, family income, etc. When there is a surplus of eligible applicants, priority is given to those with the lowest per-person family income. The Job Corps training center classifies applicants on this basis, among others, filling up its training class from the most needy among the eligible, using randomization to break ties, and keeping records also on those applicants above the cutting point for use as a comparison in measuring program effectiveness.

As illustrated in Figure 16, these applicants, admitted and rejected, are grouped into lists of 10 or so persons each, each list homogeneous on per-person family income. Each list is randomly given a meaningless code letter or number, e.g., A through U in Figure 16. These lists of names are then sent to the U.S. Social Security Administration research retrieval staff, which randomly deletes one name from each list, retrieves for the other names the desired information (such as earnings subject to social security deductions or withholding tax and unemployment compensation claims for various time periods), statistically combines these data into statistical composites (such as averages, standard deviations, numbers of cases for which data are availaable, etc.), and returns only these statistical products for each list code to the local Job Corps evaluation staff. The evaluators then reassemble the lists in meaningful order, pooling the statistics for lists of the same income value , producing results such as shown in Figure 17. The Job Corps Staff would have learned nothing about individual earnings, nor the SSA have learned anything about individual training status or reported family earnings.

The general feasibility of such procedures have been demonstrated by Heller (1972) and Fischer (1972), but unfortunately, not where the assignment of applicants to programs had been done in a systematic way that made program effects estimable. Under normal operating procedures, the grounds for admission are imprecise, variable, unrecorded, and with no records kept on those rejected. Formalizing eligibility requirements, with the

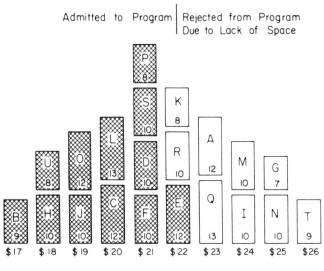

Admitted to Program | Rejected from Program Due to Lack of Space

Weekly Income per Family Member

Fig. 16.   Lists of applicants to a Job Corps program organized by family income, producing an approximate frequency distribution (imaginary data). The lists have been randomly labeled by letters A through U. The number below the letter indicates the number of persons in the list. The cross-hatched lists are to receive the program, priority being given to those of lower income. There is space for only 12 of those persons at $22.00 per week. These twelve are chosen at random from the 30 available at $22.00, making up list E, the remainder going into lists K and R. (The design is also usable in the absence of tied cases and tie-breaking randomization.)

admission decision hinging (for some subgroups at least) on a quantified eligibility score (such as family income, reading skill scores, the sum of admission interviewers' ratings on several priority dimensions, or even time of application) makes possible the 'regression discontinuity design' just illustrated (Campbell, 1969; Riecken et al., 1974). (If it is feasible, randomized admissions of eligibles for the whole pool rather than just for tie-breaking cases at the cutting point is, of course, still better from the standpoint of statistical inference, particularly for estimating program effects for the whole range of income levels.)

No manpower program has as yet been as well or as validly evaluated as by the method illustrated in Figures 16 and 17. If it went no further, settling just for administrative records unaugmented by follow-up interviews, it would be

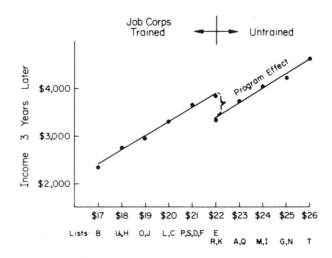

Fig. 17.   Subsequent income as a function of training and pretraining family income,
(same imaginary study as Figure 15). Training increases income by an estimated $500
per year, estimated with most confidence for those applicants near $22.00 per week in
per-person family income.

extremely inexpensive also. Heller (1972) reports retrieval costs of $1.00 per
person. But even if it were ten times that, it would still be cheap, as
interviews will run $100.00 or more per person. Rate of follow-up contact by
interviewers in manpower studies has run as low as 50%, and with more cases
lost from the control group than for the trained group. SSA retrieval would
probably be much better than this, and certainly less biased. Thus such use of
administrative records would be a valuable low-cost adjunct even for a
follow-up evaluation study employing interviews.

This type of program evaluation is potentially available wherever
ameliorative programs have more eligible applicants than they are funded for.
This is certainly the case for most federal and local programs targeted to
special needy groups. It is usually only by failing to give these opportunities
proper local publicity that program administrators avoid a surplus of
applicants. Such programs are very expensive, and can be carried out in a
wide variety of ways. It is in the highest public interest that we create the
capacity to evaluate such programs by these means. To do so we must expand
the research retrieval capacity of our major administrative files relevant to
program evaluation, including again such private files as medical insurance

and educational testing services. To do so we must also (when evaluation is wanted) formalize program admission procedures and keep records on those rejected as well as those accepted.

Does present or proposed privacy legislation in the United States and elsewhere jeopardize such program evaluation? Certainly privacy legislation should be carefully scrutinized to determine whether or not it needlessly precludes such procedures. For example, in the case of Figures 16 and 17 it would certainly decrease the cost of retrieval and reduce the frequency of errors in the United States if Social Security numbers accompanied names on the lists. The U.S. Privacy Act of 1974 would not preclude this in the Job Corps case, since salary or subsistence payments are being made to the trainee. But the language of the bill would seem to preclude the use of Social Security numbers if we were evaluating a medical rehabilitation program or a nonpaying training program, for example. In the Job Corps case it might well preclude the retention of Social Security numbers for applicants for whom there was no space and thus got no funds, thus making the analysis impossible, needlessly.

A unified national data bank would jeopardize privacy through increasing the pay off to a blackmailing employee. Like most program evaluation methodologists today, the present author opposes such a super-file. What is proposed instead is that all existing files be kept separate, or even split up further, but that each have the capacity for "mutually insulated" negotiation with other files in ways precluding the transfer of individual data from one file to another.

The use of a universal identifying number, such as the U.S. Social Security number almost is and could become, must not be confused with a unified data bank. The latter can be prohibited directly, as can all kinds of sharing of individual data between files. Social Security numbers do not as a rule facilitate the misuse of data in files, and have not been involved in the bad examples of using files to invade individual privacy. They add little to the convenience of retrieval of private information or gossip on a single person, but greatly facilitate mass statistical retrievals in which individuals are anonymous. Their social value for program evaluation greatly outweighs the very slight, if any, increase in the danger of misuse they incur.

NOTE

* Supported in part by U.S. National Science Foundation Grant GSOC-7103704. Prepared for a planned volume on social indicator research supported by the National Science Foundation, Murray Arborn, Editor.

BIBLIOGRAPHY

Anderson, J. K., 'Evaluation as a Process in Social Systems', Unpublished doctoral dissertation, Northwestern University, Department of Industrial Engineering & Management Sciences, 1973. (a)

Anderson, J. K., 'The Use of Annual Reports in Program Evaluation', Duplicated report (25 pp.), 1973. (b)

Baldus, D. C., 'Welfare as a Loan: An Empirical Study of the Recovery of Public Assistance Payments in the United States', *Stanford Law Review* 25 (1973), 123–250.

Box, G. E. P. and Tiao, G. C., 'A Change in Level of Non-Sationary Time Series', *Biometrika* 52 (1965), 181–192.

Campbell, D. T., 'Reforms as Experiments', *The American Psychologist* 24 (1969), 409–429.

Campbell, D. T., 'Methods for the Experimenting Society', Paper presented to the American Psychological Association, Washington, Washington, D.C., September 1971; to appear in *The American Psychologist* after revision.

Campbell, D. T., 'Assessing the Impact of Planned Social Change', in G. M. Lyons (ed.), *Social Research and Public Policies*, The Public Affairs Center, Dartmouth College, Hanover, NH: 1975.

Campbell, D. T., Boruch, R. F., Schwartz, R. D., and Steinberg, J., 'Confidentiality-Preserving Modes of Access to Files and to Interfile Exchange for Useful Statistical Analysis', Appendix A to A. M. Rivlin *et al.*, *Protecting Individual Privacy in Evaluation Research*. A report of the Committee on Federal Agency Evaluation Research of the National Academy of Sciences, National Research Council, Washington, DC, 1975.

Campbell, D. T. and Stanley, J. C., 'Experimental and Quasi-Experimental Designs for Research on Teaching', in N. L. Gage (ed.), *Handbook of Research on Teaching*, Rand McNally, Chicago: 1963. (Also published as *Experimental and Quasi-experimental Designs for Research*, Rand McNally, Chicago, 1966.)

David, H. P., *Family Planning and Abortion in the Socialist Countries of Central and Eastern Europe*, The Population Council, New York, 1970. Romanian data based primarily on *Anuarul Statistic al Republicii Socialiste Romania*.

Drew, D. E., *Science Development: An Evaluation Study*, Publishing & Printing Office, National Academy of Sciences, Washington, DC, 1975. (National Board on Graduate Education, Technical Report No. 4)

Glass, G. V., Tiao, G. C., and Mcguire, T. O., 'Analysis of Data on the 1900 Revision of German Divorce Laws as a Time-Series Quasi-Experiment', *Law and Society Review* 4 (1971) 539–562.

Glass, G. V., Willson, V. L., and Gottman, J. M., *Design and Analysis of Time Series Experiments*, Colorado Associated University Press, Boulder, 1975.

Gordon, A. C. and Campbell, D. T., 'Recommended Accounting Procedures for the Evaluation of Improvements in the Delivery of State Social Services', Duplicated manuscript, 1971. Center for Urban Affairs, Northwestern University.

Hook, J., 'Operation Whistlestop: An Interrupted Time-Series Analysis of a Community

Crime Prevention Program', Department of Psychology, Northwestern University, in preparation.

Hoole, F. W. and Job, B. L., 'Progress Report on MUCIA Project on the Application of the Experimental Method to the Design and Evaluation of Technical Assistance Projects', Duplicated, 52 pp. Department of Political Science, Indiana University, March 1, 1975.

Kutchinsky, B., 'The Effect of Easy Availability of Pornography on the Incidence of Sex Crimes: The Danish Experience', *Journal of Social Issues* 29 (1973), 163–181.

Riecken, H. W., Boruch, R. F., Campbell, D. T., Caplan, N., Glennan, T. K., Pratt, J., Rees, A., and Williams, W., *Social Experimentation: A Method for Planning and Evaluating Social Intervention*, Academic Press, New York, 1974. (For the Social Science Research Council.)

Rivlin, A. *et al.*, *Protecting Individual Privacy in Evaluation Research*, A report of the Committee on Federal Agency Evaluation Research of the National Academy of Sciences, National Research Council, Washington, DC, 1975.

Roos, N. P., 'Evaluating the Impact of Health Programs: Moving from Here to There'. Duplicated research report (40 pp). Department of Social and Preventive Medicine, University of Manitoba, Winnipeg, Canada, July, 1973.

Ross, H. L., 'Law, Science, and Accidents: The British Road Safety Act of 1967', *Journal of Legal Studies* 2 (1973), 1–78.

Weber, S. J., Cook, T. D., and Campbell, D. T., 'The Effects of School Integration on the Academic Self-Concept of Public School Children', Paper presented at the meeting of the Midwestern Psychological Association, Detroit, 1971.

Whittaker, G. F., 'An Economic and Statistical Evaluation of the Performance of Hospitals in a Merged System: An Application of a Quasi-Experimental Design,' Northwestern University, Ph.D. Dissertation, Department of Accounting and Information Systems, 1974.

Wilder, C. S., *Physician Visits, Volume and Interval Since Last Visit, U.S., 1969*, National Center for Health Statistics, Rockville, Maryland, Series 10, No. 75, July 1972 (DHEW Pub. No. (HSM) 72–1064).

Zimring, F. E., 'Firearms and Federal Law: The Gun Control Act of 1968', *The Journal of Legal Studies* 4 (1975), 133–198.

8

DETERMINING AN OPTIMUM LEVEL OF STATISTICAL SIGNIFICANCE

By

STUART S. NAGEL and MARIAN NEEF

Stuart Nagel and Marian Neef provide a clearly reasoned and simply worked out method for considering the optimum level of statistical significance in terms of the costs and benefits of type 1 and type 2 errors. This application of decision theory to the issue has a strong rationale and is computationally straight forward; thus eminently useable.

From Stuart S. Nagel and Marian Neef, "Determining an Optimum Level of Statistical Significance." Unpublished manuscript, 1976.

The weather is something about which many people complain, but about which few people do anything. Likewise, statistical significance levels are also something about which there are complaints of arbitrariness, inflexibility, conservatism, deceptiveness, and other complaints.[1] Like the weather, however, few of the complainers or other social scientists do anything feasible to lessen the causes of those complaints, although some statistical analysts do offer general suggestions as to what ought to be done.[2] Typical reactions to determining a desirable level of statistical significance include Hubert Blalock's statement that "The decision as to the significance level selected depends on the relative costs of making the one or the other type of error and should be evaluated accordingly."[3] Most statistical analysts, like Sidney Siegel, agree that "Although the desirability of such a technique for arriving at decisions is clear, its practicality in most research in the behavioral sciences at present is dubious, because we lack the information which would be basic to the use of loss [i.e., cost] functions."[4]

The purpose of this article is to discuss a meaningful and feasible approach to determining the optimum level of statistical significance to use in any statistical inference situation in order to choose the level that will maximize perceived benefits minus perceived costs. More specifically, the article will first deal with choosing an optimum level of significance in light of an inventory modeling perspective whereby one seeks to minimize the sum of the holding costs (or type 1 error costs) and the outage costs (or type 2 error costs). The article then deals with choosing an optimum level in light of a decision theory perspective whereby one seeks to maximize the expected value of accepting or rejecting a hypothesis or presumption. Both perspectives are meaningful, but only the decision theory perspective seems feasible with regard to the simple data it needs in order to be applied.

We will illustrate the concepts and methods involved in these two perspectives by applying them to the decisional problem of what is the optimum threshold probability of guilt to merit a conviction in criminal procedure, and to the statistical hypothesis that black defendants are treated the same as white defendants in sentencing or other aspects of criminal procedure. The first problem is referred to as the conviction criterion problem, and the second problem as the racial disparity problem. Each perspective or approach to determining an optimum significance level can be graphically applied to each of the two problems, resulting in the four graphs or figures which summarize the basic ideas of this article.

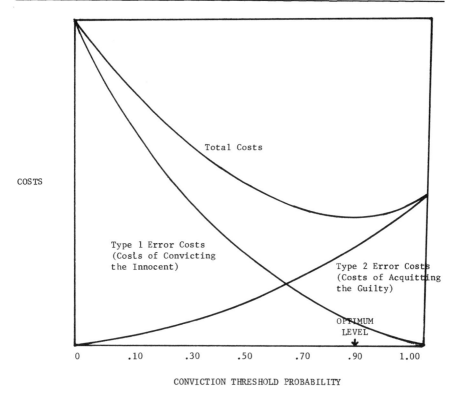

The above cost curves are consistent with the cost considerations of those who consider an optimum conviction threshold probability to be about .90.

Figure 1: AN INVENTORY MODELING APPROACH TO DETERMINING AN OPTIMUM THRESHOLD PROBABILITY: As Applied to Criminal Convictions

because it sounds most like minimizing the sum of type 1 error costs and type 2 error costs as used in conventional statistical language.

The type 1 and type 2 error cost curves reflect the relative or absolute value of a type 1 error versus a type 2 error which the influential legal commentator William Blackstone evaluated at a 10 to 1 ratio.[6] Those error cost curves also attempt to reflect the empirical reality of the relation between the required threshold level and the making of such errors. That empirical reality is virtually impossible to know. For that reason, it is virtually impossible to go from curve-drawing to determining an optimum threshold level rather than to go as we have done from an accepted optimum threshold level to drawing curves. Bear in mind that there are an infinite number of shapes for type 1 error cost curves and type 2 error cost curves that when summed will bottom out over the .90 level.

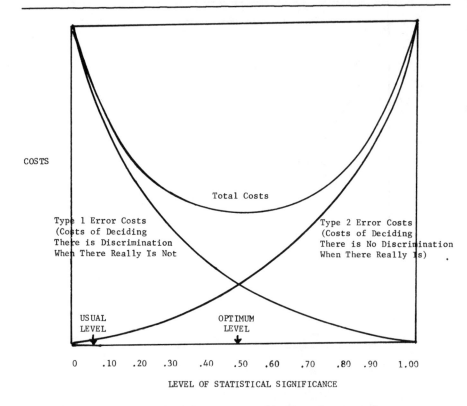

COSTS

Total Costs

Type 1 Error Costs
(Costs of Deciding
There is Discrimination
When There Really Is Not

Type 2 Error Costs
(Costs of Deciding
There is No Discrimination
When There Really Is)

USUAL
LEVEL

OPTIMUM
LEVEL

0   .10   .20   .30   .40   .50   .60   .70   .80   .90   1.00

LEVEL OF STATISTICAL SIGNIFICANCE

The above curves are consistent with the cost considerations of a person who considers it equally undesirable to make a type 1 or type 2 error in this context. Since the presumption is one of no difference, falsely rejecting that presumption is a type 1 error and falsely accepting that presumption is a type 2 error.

Figure 2: AN INVENTORY MODELING APPROACH TO DETERMINING AN OPTIMUM LEVEL OF STATISTICAL SIGNIFICANCE: Applied to the Hypothesis that Black Defendants are Treated the Same as White Defendants

B. The Racial Disparity Problem

The racial disparity problem is also like an inventory level problem because if we set the statistical significance level too high, then we are likely to make the mistake of deciding there is no discrimination when there really is. Likewise, if we set the significance level too low, then we are likely to make the mistake of deciding there is discrimination when there really is not. Those concepts are graphically illustrated by Figure 2. The two error cost curves are drawn with equal although rising slopes to reflect the values of a person who considers it equally undesirable to make a type 1 error of wrongly rejecting the hypothesis or presumption of sameness and a type 2 error of wrongly accepting the hypothesis of sameness.[7]

Given the equality of the two types of error costs, it logically follows that the optimum level of statistical significance is .50 rather than the usual level of .05. Either Figure 2 or Figure 1 is capable of nicely illustrating that working with a .05 significance level results in relatively high type 1 error costs and relatively low type 2 error costs. In other words, by working with the conventional .05 level, we are in effect requiring the equivalent of proof beyond a reasonable doubt before we will reject the hypothesis that discrimination does not exist, or accept the hypothesis that it does exist. We are also in effect requiring the equivalent of what is legally referred to as a mere scintilla of proof in order to accept the hypothesis that discrimination does not exist or reject the hypothesis that it does exist.

Although Figures 1 and 2 are useful in understanding the basic concepts involved in an optimum conviction criterion or significance level, they are virtually useless as a feasible method for arriving at an optimum level except for business inventories or industrial quality control where accurate accounting or engineering data is available for generating equations to express the curves. Merely saying that the type 1 error costs are equal to or twice as important as the type 2 error costs does not tell us the shape of the curves since those curves reflect both (1) the value of a type 1 error versus a type 2 error and (2) the unknown empirical relation between various significance levels and the occurrence of such errors. In other words, total type 1 error cost for any probability level combines both a price per unit or per error, and a quantity of errors at that level. Thus, the inventory modeling perspective, while meaningful, lacks feasibility as a simple, widely applicable method for determining optimum significance levels.[8]

II. A DECISION THEORY APPROACH TO DETERMINING AN OPTIMUM LEVEL OF STATISTICAL SIGNIFICANCE

What is needed for determining an optimum conviction criterion or significance level is a method whereby one does not have to know the empirical relation between different criteria or levels and various costs or benefits, but only the relative value of a type 1 error versus a type 2 error. In other words, what we need is a meaningful way of translating Blackstone's 10 to 1 error ratio into a threshold probability or the 1 to 1 error ratio in the racial disparity problem into a level of statistical significance without needing any intermediate curve drawing or empirical data.

Decision theory provides an approach for doing that. Decision theory can be defined as a procedure whereby one chooses among alternatives in order to maximize benefits minus costs in light of probabilistic or uncertain events. In this context, the choices are to accept or reject the hypothesis or presumption. The uncertain event is whether the hypothesis or presumption is true or false.

A. The Conviction Criterion Problem

The method can be nicely illustrated by the conviction criterion problem, as is shown in Figure 3. That figure indicates we have a choice of acquitting or convicting a defendant who may be innocent or guilty. To determine an optimum

PROBABILITY OF DEFENDANT
BEING INNOCENT

		Defendant Guilty (P)	Defendant Innocent (1-P)	EXPECTED VALUE
	Accept Hypo i.e., Acquit	-B e.g., -10 (Type 2 error)	+A e.g., +100 (Type 2 accuracy)	$EV_A = (-B)(P) + (+A)(1-P)$ $= (-10)(P) + (+100)(1-P)$
ALTERNATIVE DECISIONS AVAILABLE	Reject Hypo i.e., Convict	+B e.g., +10 (Type 1 accuracy)	-A e.g., -100 (Type 1 error)	$EV_R = (+B)(P) + (-A)(1-P)$ $= (+10)(P) + (-100)(1-P)$

General Presumption: Defendant is innocent. Type 1 error rejects presumption when true. Type 2 error accepts presumption when false.

The values in this table are those for William Blackstone, who said 10 guilty persons should go free rather than convict one innocent person.

Optimum level for Rejection: $P^* = A/(A+B) = 100/(100+10) = .91$, meaning Blackstone would require greater than .91 probability of guilt before he would convict.

Figure 3: A DECISION THEORY APPROACH TO DETERMINING AN OPTIMUM THRESHOLD PROBABILITY: As Applied to the Hypothesis or Presumption that a Defendant is Innocent

threshold probability for someone like William Blackstone, we could go through the following steps:

1. Prepare a four-cell payoff matrix with accept and reject on the vertical axis and hypothesis true or false on the horizontal axis.

2. Of the four cells or possible outcomes, have the person whose values are relevant indicate which outcomes are undesirable and which outcomes are desirable. Blackstone would say cells 1 and 4 reading across are undesirable outcomes and cells 2 and 3 are desirable ones.

3. Of the two undesirable outcomes, which one is the more undesirable? Blackstone would say cell 4 which involves convicting an innocent defendant rather than cell 1 which involves acquitting a guilty defendant.

4. If we anchor the more undesirable outcome at −100, then on a scale of 0 to −100, where would you put the less undesirable outcome? Blackstone would say at −10 since he has said it is 10 times as bad to convict an innocent defendant as it is to acquit a guilty defendant.

5. If our respondent is a logically consistent person, then whatever value he assigns to a type 1 error (wrongly rejecting the hypothesis) should also be assigned to a type 2 accuracy (rightly accepting the hypothesis), but opposite in sign. Likewise, whatever value he assigns to a type 2 error (wrongly accepting the hypothesis) should also be assigned to a type 1 accuracy (rightly accepting the hypothesis), but opposite in sign. In other words, the benefits of accepting a true

hypothesis consist of avoiding the costs of rejecting a true hypothesis, and the benefits of rejecting a false hypothesis consist of avoiding the costs of accepting a false hypothesis. Thus, the payoff matrix for William Blackstone would involve values of -10, $+100$, $+10$, and -100 reading across.

6. Determine the expected value of accepting the hypothesis by summing the expected positive benefits ($+A$ or $+100$ for Blackstone discounted by the probability that the defendant is innocent) and the expected negative costs (-10 discounted by the probability that the defendant is guilty). This is the equivalent of the expected benefits minus the expected costs. Also determine the expected value of rejecting the hypothesis by determining the expected benefits ($+10$ discounted by or multiplied by P) and the expected costs (-100 discounted by 1-P). To express these expected values does not require knowing the probability that the defendant is innocent, but only requires having an algebraic symbol like P to complete the expression.

7. Given the expected value of accepting the hypothesis and the expected value of rejecting the hypothesis in light of our respondent's indication of the relative undesirability to him of a type 1 and type 2 error, now set those two expected values equal to each other and solve for P. Doing so will tell us the value of P when those two expected values are equal. That algebraically determined value of P is the optimum threshold probability in the sense that when the perceived probability of guilt is above that figure, the respondent should reject the hypothesis of innocence and convict; and when the perceived probability is below that figure, the respondent should accept the hypothesis of innocence and acquit. If the respondent follows the decision rule, he will always be choosing the alternative between the two alternative choices that gives him the highest expected benefits minus expected costs. Solving for P in the algebraic expression $(-B)(P) + (+A)(1-P) = (+B)(P) + (-A)(1-P)$ yields the fact that the equilibrium P, optimum P, or P* equals $A/(A+B)$. Thus, Mr. Blackstone's threshold probability would be $100/(100+10)$ or .91, meaning he would require greater than a .91 probability of guilt before he would convict.[9] If Blackstone had valued a type 2 acquittal error at more than 10 (e.g., 20 to 100), then his .91 probability would have been lower, but raised if Blackstone had valued a type 2 acquittal error at less than 10 (e.g., 5 to 100, rather than 10 to 100 or 1 to 10).[10]

B. The Racial Disparity Problem

The same simple responses and reasoning can be applied to determining an optimum significance level as is illustrated in Figure 4. The only difference is that the optimum level for the conviction probability threshold is normally stated in terms of the probability level above which one *rejects* the hypothesis of innocence, whereas the optimum level for statistical significance is normally stated in terms of the probability level above which one *accepts* the hypothesis of no difference. The simplified formula for the former optimum level is $A/(A+B)$, and the simplified formula for the latter optimum level is the complement or $B/(A+B)$. Assuming a type 1 error is anchored at -100 as the more undesirable of the two errors, then all

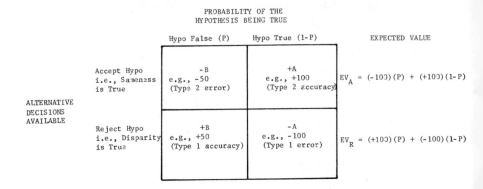

PROBABILITY OF THE
HYPOTHESIS BEING TRUE

		Hypo False (P)	Hypo True (1-P)	EXPECTED VALUE
ALTERNATIVE DECISIONS AVAILABLE	Accept Hypo i.e., Sameness is True	-B e.g., -50 (Type 2 error)	+A e.g., +100 (Type 2 accuracy)	EV_A = (-100)(P) + (+100)(1-P)
	Reject Hypo i.e., Disparity is True	+B e.g., +50 (Type 1 accuracy)	-A e.g., -100 (Type 1 error)	EV_R = (+100)(P) + (-100)(1-P)

General Presumption: There is no difference between black and white defendants.

The values in this table are those of a person who considers it twice as undesirable to make a type 1 as a type 2 error in this context.

Optimum Level for Acceptance: P* = B/(A+B) = 50/(100+50) = .33, meaning that a difference between matched black and white defendants that has a chance probability greater than .33 should be accepted as a real difference rather than a chance difference, and the converse for a difference with less than a .33 chance probability. Matching should generally be done at least on the crime and having a prior record.

Figure 4: A DECISION THEORY APPROACH TO DETERMINING AN OPTIMUM LEVEL OF STATISTICAL SIGNIFICANCE: As Applied to the Hypothesis or Presumption that Black Defendants are Treated the Same as White Defendants

one has to do is determine one number, namely on a 0 to −100 scale what is the relative undesirability of a type 2 error or the value of B. In other words, the optimum significance level can be considered as simply equal to B/(100+B). Applying that simplification to a person who considers it twice as undesirable to make a type 1 error as a type 2 error, we arrive at a P* or optimum significance level of 50/(100+50) or .33. Sometimes a type 2 error may be considered more undesirable than a type 1 error, and then we use the original formula of B/(A+B) which then becomes 100/(A+100).[11]

This decision theory approach is obviously far more simple and thus more feasible to apply than any approach that involves determining type 1 error costs and type 2 error costs for different levels of statistical significance. It is also far more simple than alternative decision theory approaches which require placing in the payoff cells absolute units like dollars, rather than purely relative units like we have used. It is also simpler than alternative decision theory approaches which require placing in the cells probabilities that the various kinds of errors or accuracies will occur.[12]

This approach also allows one to work backwards and say what a given threshold probability means in terms of the relative undesirability of a type 1 error versus a type 2 error. For example, if we start with the .05 level as a given, what does that tell us about how social science researchers have in effect or implicitly been evaluating type 1 and type 2 errors? Answering that question simply involves solving for B in the equation $.05 = B/(100+B)$. The value of B in that equation is 5.26 (or $5/.95$) meaning the traditional .05 significance level implies that a type 1 error is 100 to 5.26, or 19 to 1 times as undesirable as a type 2 error.

Another related purpose for this approach is for translating a chance probability into an undesirability ratio. For example, if we find that a difference or a relation has a .33 chance probability, we can say that such a relation ought to be accepted as a real rather than as a chance relation if we are willing to accept a type 2 error as being only half as bad as a type 1 error rather than the usual 1/19 times as bad. What we in effect did is solve for B in the equation $.33 = B/(100+B)$, which yields a B of 50 or half the A of 100.

Perhaps the best approach when discussing the statistical significance of one's findings is to do so in terms of both the conventional .05 and .01 tests and the kind of benefit-cost approach presented here, rather than use this approach to replace the conventional tests. Our approach is a benefit-cost approach in the sense that we seek to accept the hypothesis if the expected benefits [i.e., $A(1-P)$] minus the expected costs [i.e., $B(P)$] of accepting are greater than the expected benefits [i.e., $B(P)$] minus the expected costs [i.e., $A(1-P)$] of rejecting. In using the benefit-cost or decision theory approach to arriving at an optimum P^* value, one should be as explicit as possible in describing how one determined the relative values of A and B, i.e., the ratio between the type 1 and type 2 error costs. One might also indicate how one's conclusions that certain findings are statistically significant would be affected or not affected by changes in the values of A and B.

With this kind of decision theory approach for determining an optimum level of statistical significance, there should no longer be any reason for complaining about the arbitrariness, inflexibility, conservatism, deceptiveness, and other defects of the .05 or .01 levels of statistical significance. Instead, one should be able to evaluate most major research hypotheses in terms of the relative undesirability of a type 1 error versus a type 2 error, and then use the expected benefit-cost maximization formula to determine the optimum level of significance probability in light of that relative undesirability. One could further indicate the significance level that would correspond to various relative undesirability ratios, and one could also express the ratio that would have to exist in order to accept a relation or difference given its chance probability. The approach does seem to make meaningful Hubert Blalock's recommendation of determining a desirable level of statistical significance by evaluating the costs of making the one or the other type of error, contrary to other statistical analysts who say it cannot be done.[13]

APPENDIX: BASIC FORMULAS IN DETERMINING
AN OPTIMUM LEVEL OF STATISTICAL SIGNIFICANCE

This appendix pulls together on a more abstract symbolic level the basic formulas which are mainly presented verbally and illustrated with concrete examples in the article. By seeing the formulas on a more abstract level their interrelations and generalizability are further clarified. This appendix also briefly refers to some important general matters which did not seem so appropriate to discuss in the text given the emphasis on verbal presentation and concrete illustrations.

I. Basic Symbols

P = The probability that a given finding could be due to chance sampling error, or the probability that a hypothesis or presumption is true (or false).

P^* = The probability level above which a hypothesis or presumption is rejected (or accepted) and below which it is accepted (or rejected), i.e., a statistical significance level.

TC = Total costs, i.e., the sum of the type 1 error costs of rejecting a true hypothesis or presumption, plus the type 2 error costs of accepting a false hypothesis or presumption.

A = Type 1 error costs. One can try to express these costs in dollars or other absolute units, or simply in relative terms, i.e., relative to the type 2 error costs.

B = Type 2 error costs. One can try to express these costs in dollars or other absolute units, or simply in relative terms, i.e., relative to the type 1 error costs.

II. An Inventory Modeling Approach to Determining Optimum P^*

(1) Optimum $P^* = P$ where $\Delta TC/\Delta P = 0$

(2) If $TC = A + B = a_1(P)^{b_1} + a_2(P)^{b_2}$ where $b_1 < 0$ and $b_2 > 0$, then $\Delta TC/\Delta P =$

$$b_1 a_1(P)^{b_1-1} + b_2 a_2(P)^{b_2-1}.$$

(3) If point 2 above is true, then when $\Delta TC/\Delta P = 0$, optimum $P^* =$

$$[-(a_1 b_1)/(a_2 b_2)]^{1/(b_2-b_1)}.$$

III. A Decision Theory Approach to Determining Optimum P^*

(1) Optimum $P^* = A/(A+B) = X/(X+1)$ where $X = A/B$, if the significance level or probability threshold is stated in terms of the probability level above which one *rejects* the hypothesis or presumption.

(2) Optimum $P^* = B/(A+B) = 1(X+1)$ where $X = A/B$, if the significance level or probability threshold is stated in terms of the probability level above which one *accepts* the hypothesis or presumption.

NOTES

1. James Skipper, Anthony Guenther, and Gilbert Nass, "The Sacredness of .05: A Note Concerning the Uses of Statistical Levels of Significance in Social Science," 2 *The American Sociologist* 16-18 (1967); Hanan Selvin, "A Critique of Tests of Significance in Survey Research," 22 *American Sociological Review* 519-527 (1957); Denton Morrison and Ramon Henkel (eds.), *The Significance Test Controversy: A Reader* (Aldine, 1970); Stephen Spielman, "The Logic of Tests of Significance," *Philosophy of Science* 211-225 (1974).

2. General suggestions such as the need to consider the relative costs of type 1 and type 2 errors are mentioned in Sanford Labovitz, "Criteria for Selecting a Significance Level: A Note on the Sacredness of .05," 3 *The American Sociologist* 200-222 (1968); William Hays and Robert Winkler, *Statistics: Probability, Inference, and Decision* 375-443 (Holt, Rinehart and Winston, 1970).

3. Hubert Blalock, *Social Statistics,* 160 (McGraw-Hill, 1972).

4. Sidney Siegel, *Nonparametric Statistics for the Behavioral Sciences* 8 (McGraw-Hill, 1956).

5. Rita Simon and Linda Mahan, "Quantifying Burdens of Proof," 5 *Law and Society Review* 319 (1971).

6. William Blackstone, 4 *Commentaries* 358 (1761).

7. For a discussion of the problems involved in determining whether black defendants are treated the same as white defendants (other than the problem of how much of a difference constitutes a statistically significant difference), see S. Nagel and M. Neef, "Racial Disparities that Supposedly Do Not Exist: Some Pitfalls in Analysis of Court Records," 52 *Notre Dame Lawyer* 87-94 (1976).

8. In algebraic terms, the inventory model in effect says there is a type 1 error cost curve of the form $A = a_1(P)^{b_1}$ where b_1 is negative, and there is a type 2 error cost curve of the form $B = a_2(P)^{b_2}$ where b_2 is greater than one. The parameters for those power functions or log-linear functions could theoretically be determined by creating a data matrix of numerous situations in which we somehow know the type 1 error costs (A), the type 2 error costs (B), and the statistical significance level that was used (P). We would then use the log of A as a dependent variable and the log of P as the independent variable in one linear regression, and then use the log of B as a dependent variable and the log of P as the independent variable in a second linear regression. After so determining the values of a_1, b_1, a_2, and b_2, we could then determine that the value of P where the total costs bottom out is a simple function of those four parameters, as is shown in the appendix to this article. That function follows from setting the slope of the total costs relative to P equal to zero and then solving for P, as is also shown in the appendix. One could assume for the sake of simplicity that a_1 equals a_2. One cannot, however, insert 3 in place of b_1 and 1 in place of b_2 in order to show that the type 1 error costs are 3 times as undesirable as the type 2 error costs. This is so because the value of A to B is not simply a function of the value of b_1 to b_2. The A/B ratio, for example, changes if b_1/b_2 is 6 to 2 rather than 3 to 1.

9. The proof for the formula for finding the threshold P is as follows:

$(-B)(P) + (A)(1-P) = (+B)(P) + (-A)(1-P)$

$-BP + A - AP = BP - A + AP$ (Removing parentheses)

$A + A = BP + AP + BP + AP$ (Transposing)

$2A = 2BP + 2AP$ (Combining terms)

$A = BP + AP$ (Dividing by 2)

$A = P(B + A)$ (Factoring)

$P^* = A/(B + A)$ (Dividing by B + A)

10. One could further simplify the formula $P^* = A/(A+B)$ by algebraically reducing it to $P^* = X/(X+1)$ where X is the A/B ratio. Thus, if Blackstone had a 10 to 1 ratio, this simplified formula would reduce to $10/(10+1) = 10/11 = .91$. The simplified formula has the advantage that the user does not have to determine separate quantities for A and B, but only the one quantity of how many more times A is valued than B.

11. One could further simplify the formula $P^* = B/(A+B)$ by algebraically reducing it to $P^* = 1/(X+1)$ where X is the A/B ratio. Thus, if one considers it equally bad to make a type 1 or type 2 error in the racial disparity problem, this simplified formula would reduce to $1/(1+1) = 1/2 = .50$. As mentioned previously, the simplified formula has the advantage that the user does not have to determine separate quantities for A and B, but only the one quantity of how many more times A is valued than B.

12. See Hays and Winkler, *supra* Note 2, especially pages 383-399.

13. See Notes 3 and 4, *supra*.

9

DISTRIBUTING FEDERAL EDUCATION AID TO LOW ACHIEVEMENT PUPILS: THE PREDICTED ACHIEVEMENT METHOD

By

MARTIN FELDSTEIN

The current method of distributing Title I grants is based on the number of children in poverty in each district. According to Martin Feldstein, this method of funding can be improved if the distribution of the grants be based on students' predicted achievement. In his study, he uses a multiple regression prediction equation in order to change the method of distribution of funding for low achievement pupils. As an economist, Professor Feldstein is concerned with what he considers appropriate distribution of public resources. He suggests using pupils' predicted achievement scores to decide upon careful dissemination of Title I programs, as he believes this method will be more responsive to low achievement pupils.

From Martin Feldstein, "Distributing Federal Education Aid to Low Achievement Pupils: The Predicted Achievement Method." Unpublished Discussion Paper no. 528, December 1976.

Title I of the Elementary and Secondary Education Act is the primary form of Federal aid to students before the college level. In fiscal year 1977, the Title I program will provide grants of nearly two billion dollars to local education authorities for educational spending on low income pupils. The rules of the program and its legislative history indicate that its primary purpose is to increase the expenditure on these pupils and not to redistribute income, to equalize educational spending among districts, or to compensate communities for the difference between educational spending on low income pupils and the local taxes that their families pay either directly or indirectly.

Although the program is formally stated in terms of low income levels, it is more logical to regard the current method of distributing Title I funds on the basis of the number of children in poverty in each area as an indirect way of providing funds for children with low educational achievement levels.[1] In this paper I explain how the targeting

---

*Professor of Economics, Harvard University. I am grateful to Daniel Erdmann and Daniel Frisch for their assistance, to the Department of Education of the Commonwealth of Massachusetts for providing the data on test scores, and to the Compensatory Education Division of the National Institute of Education, Department of Health, Education and Welfare for financial support.

[1]The current method of distribution also adjusts for differences among states in the cost of education. I will assume that this adjustment will be maintained in the future and will not discuss it explicitly.

of Title I funds to low achievement pupils could be improved by using a multiple regression prediction equation. This method would make the distribution of Title I funds depend on several demographic and economic variables that are currently collected by the Census. The evidence for Massachusetts presented here indicates that the predicted achievement method can be substantially more effective than the current Title I method at directing funds in relation to achievement.

The first section of this paper discusses the logic of the predicted achievement method and the way that it would be implemented in practice. Section 2 describes the Massachusetts data used in the current analysis. The third and fourth sections present results for mean achievement scores and low achievement scores. There is a brief concluding section.

1. The Predicted Achievement Method

Consider the problem of distributing a fixed amount of Title I funds among the school districts within a state; the issues and methods that arise in this context can be extended to the more general problem of distributing national funds among the states. The goal accepted in this paper is to distribute these funds on the basis of "educational need" as measured by poor performance on standard tests of educational achievement or ability.

The most direct approach would obviously be to administer a standardized test to all students in the state and then distribute funds on the basis of the resulting test scores. I will refer to this as the "measured achievement method" to distinguish it from the "predicted achievement method" that is developed below. To be more specific, the measured achievement method might give more funds to school districts with low mean achievement scores or to school districts in which a higher proportion of students had scores below a given standard.

The obvious problem with this method is that it gives school districts an incentive to attain test scores that understate the true ability of their students. If the reward for poor performance is great, the resulting bias in reporting is also likely to be great. Test scores can be depressed by intentionally poor test conditions, by explaining to students that their school will be rewarded with extra resources if they do poorly, etc. Since poor performance is easily achieved, the resulting test scores are likely to be without value as a measure of students' true abilities. The measured achievement method must therefore be rejected as unworkable.

The predicted achievement method would also begin by administering a standardized test to all students in the state and calculating the mean score for each school district.[1] These mean achievement scores are then related by a multiple regression equation to some of the economic and demographic characteristics of the school district that are collected by the Census of Population. The estimated regression equation is used to "predict" the mean test score that each district would be "expected" to achieve on the basis of its population characteristics. Title I funds are distributed among the districts according to these predicted test scores.

The predicted achievement method is thus able to use information on test scores without giving school districts an incentive to report a biased measure. Each school district knows that the aid that it will receive will depend on its population characteristics as reported by the Census. The test scores of its students have only a very small and indirect effect on the amount of aid received through the influence that the district's test score would have on the estimated coefficients of the regression equation. With a large number of districts, the influence of any single district's score on the coefficients will be imperceptibly small and the incentive to distort can safely be ignored.[2]

The current method of distributing Title I funds on the basis of the number of pupils in poverty can be regarded as a simple form of

---

[1] Other summary measures, such as the proportion scoring below some arbitrary level, might also be used. I return to this below.

[2] Even this small incentive to distort can be eliminated by giving a small reward for high measured test scores while giving substantial aid on the basis of low predicted test scores.

the predicted achievement method based on a single variable. A higher proportion of pupils in poverty is generally associated with a lower mean achievement score in the district. By making the aid per pupil that is given to a district proportional to the percentage of pupils in poverty, the current Title I program generally distributes more aid per pupil in districts with lower mean achievement scores. However, the association between the percentage of pupils in poverty and the district's mean achievement score is a relatively weak one; in the evidence for Massa-chusetts presented below, the correlation between these variables is -0.40. This implies that, if aid per pupil is distributed in proportion to the percentage of pupils in poverty, the correlation between per pupil aid and mean achievement will also be -0.40. By using additional population characteristics that are associated with low achievements, the multiple regression form of the predicted achievement method obtains a much closer targeting of funds; the Massachusetts evidence implies that adding four more variables increases the correlation from 0.40 to 0.60. The details of this multiple regression form and other measures of low achievement will be discussed after the data are described.

2. The Data

The predicted achievement method is illustrated in this paper with data for 310 Massachusetts school districts. The analysis combines information on individual pupil achievement test scores and ability test scores with 1970 Census information on the population characteristics of their school districts. This section describes the data and presents a few summary statistics.

In 1971, each of the school districts in Massachusetts administered the same achievement and ability tests to all of their fourth grade pupils.[1] The tests used were the McGraw-Hill Comprehensive Test of Basic Skills and the California Mental Maturity Test. Three separate achievement test scores were calculated for each pupil: reading achievement, language achievement and mathematics achievement. Although no official single summary achievement score was defined, the mean of the three individual scores will be used in this study and will be referred to as the achievement score. In addition, three ability test scores were calculated for each pupil: a verbal ability score, a non-verbal ability score and a combined ability score. The Massachusetts Department of Education provided a computer tape with these test scores for each of the 80,814 fourth grade pupils in the state.

The analysis in this paper will focus on the two summary scores: the combined achievement score and the overall ability score. For each

---

[1] Although it would obviously have been better if test scores were available for all grades, the current data are sufficient for the present illustrative purpose.

score, two different types of measure of poor achievement are considered: the mean score in the school district and the percentage of pupils scoring below various "low score" thresholds. These measures of poor achievement were calculated for the 310 Massachusetts school districts for which Census information could also be collected; these districts include 87 percent of the Massachusetts population.

Table 1 presents state summaries of the achievement and ability measures for the 310 school districts. The achievement test is scored to produce a national average of 400. The average of the Massachusetts district scores is 423.2. District averages ranged from a low of 364.5 to a high of 464.4. It must be borne in mind that these scores are district means of individual pupil scores; there would, of course, be much more variation among individual pupil scores. The second row of the table shows that on average 24.3 percent of the pupils in a school district scored below 390. The percentage of low scoring pupils (by the 390 criterion) varied widely; the minimum and maximum values imply that in at least one district no pupil scored below 390 while in another more than 80 percent were low scorers. The next two lines of the table show corresponding summaries for two lower achievement standards.

The ability test is scored to produce a national average of 100. In Massachusetts, the mean of the district averages was 107.0. The other figures presented in lines 5 through 8 of Table 1 can be interpreted like the achievement score summaries in the top part of the table.

The basic population characteristics that are likely to affect pupil achievement and ability scores are the education and income of the parents in the school district. Other possible influences include the

I. AN INVENTORY MODELING APPROACH TO DETERMINING AN OPTIMUM LEVEL OF STATISTICAL SIGNIFICANCE

In deciding an optimum inventory level for a business firm, one must be careful not to have too much inventory because that will generate unduly high storage and spoilage costs. Likewise, one must be careful not to have too little inventory because that would generate unduly high outage costs whereby orders are lost because they cannot be met. Operations researchers have developed meaningful quantitative techniques for arriving at an inventory level for a given product of a given firm that minimizes the sum of the holding costs and and the outage costs.

A. The Conviction Criterion Problem

The conviction criterion problem is like an inventory level problem because if we set the threshold probability of guilt too high, then too many truly guilty defendants will be acquitted, analogous to having too high an inventory level. Likewise, if we set the threshold probability of guilt too low, then too many truly innocent defendants will be convicted, analogous to having too low an inventory level. The prevailing conviction criterion level in the United States is usually stated in words like "beyond a reasonable doubt." When it is expressed quantitatively, the figure of about a .90 probability of guilt is usually given by judges.[5]

Those concepts are graphically illustrated in Figure 1. The horizontal axis shows conviction criteria or threshold probabilities from zero to 1.00. The vertical axis shows the three kinds of costs. As the conviction threshold probability goes up, there is an increase in type 2 error costs or the costs of acquitting the guilty. Those costs probably rise at an increasing rate as the criterion approaches 1.00. As the threshold probability goes down, there is an increase in type 1 error costs or the costs of convicting the innocent, probably at an increasing rate. The type 1 error costs are likely to rise more steeply than the type 2 error costs because it is customary to consider a type 1 error of convicting an innocent defendant to generally be more costly than a type 2 error of acquitting a guilty defendant. The total cost curve is simply the sum of the two separate cost curves. It bottoms out over the .90 threshold probability in light of what we previously said about what is generally considered the optimum threshold probability. That may be higher than the usual threshold probability applied by actual jurors or judges.

This perspective is the equivalent of saying the optimum probability is the one that maximizes benefits minus costs. Any given threshold probability corresponds to a certain amount of conviction benefits, which consist of acquittal costs avoided by rightfully convicting. Likewise any given probability corresponds to a certain amount of acquittal benefits, which consist of conviction costs avoided by rightfully acquitting. Thus, the optimum threshold probability can be equally stated as the probability that (1) maximizes conviction benefits plus acquittal benefits, (2) maximizes conviction benefits minus conviction costs, (3) maximizes acquittal benefits minus acquittal costs, or (4) minimizes conviction costs plus acquittal costs. The fourth alternative is the one expressed in Figures 1 and 2

Table 1

School District Test Scores and Population Characteristics

	State Mean of Districts	Standard Deviation	Minimum	Maximum
Achievement Score				
1. District Average	423.2	14.5	364.5	464.4
2. Percent below 390	24.3	12.2	0.0	81.8
3. Percent below 370	13.1	8.9	0.0	48.5
4. Percent below 350	6.5	5.9	0.0	33.3
Ability Score				
5. District Average	107.0	4.0	92.8	116.2
6. Percent below 95	18.4	9.5	0.0	51.5
7. Percent below 90	9.7	6.7	0.0	45.5
8. Percent below 85	4.4	4.0	0.0	25.0
Population Characteristics				
9. School Children in Poverty (%)	7.3	6.1	0.0	59.2
10. Families with High Income (%)	5.9	6.3	0.0	46.2
11. Families with Low Income (%)	27.3	9.8	6.6	63.4
12. Adults with High School Diploma (%)	61.8	13.8	25.6	90.4
13. Adults with Any College (%)	26.3	13.1	0.0	64.9
14. Children per Family	0.95	0.19	0.46	1.58

Statistics refer to 310 Massachusetts school districts in 1971; see text for further explanation.

number of children per family, the size of the community, and the occupational mix of the population. [1] Since school districts in Massachusetts have the same boundaries as towns and cities, Census data for individual districts are available for all districts above a very small minimum size. As noted above, the 310 districts used in this study include 87 percent of the state population.

The percentage of school children from families below the poverty line corresponds approximately to the poverty criterion used by the current Title I formula. For the 310 Massachusetts towns, an average of 7.3 percent of children age 6 to 17 were in families below the poverty line. Line 9 of Table 1 provides other measures of the distribution of this variable.

Although the percentage of children from poverty families may be the best single measure of income to use in predicting low achievement and ability scores, the predictions can be improved by using additional measures of the district's income distribution. [2] The equations presented below use the percentage of "high income" families (i.e., families with incomes above $25,000 in 1969) and the percentage of "low income" families (i.e., families with incomes below $8,000 in 1969). The state averages and distributions of these variables are shown in lines 10 and

---

[1] In Massachusetts there are too few districts with substantial numbers of non-white pupils or Spanish-speaking pupils to examine the influence of these factors.

[2] Note that the Census information relates to all children while test scores are for fourth grade pupils only. For an actual application of the predicted achievement method, it would obviously be desirable to have test scores for all grades. Similarly, it would be good if possible to have Census information on families with school age children rather than all families.

11 of Table 1.

Parental education is likely to have a positive effect on pupils' achievement scores. Two measures of the education of the adult population of the community are included in the prediction equations presented below: the percentage of adults over age 25 who are high school graduates and the percentage of adults over age 25 who have had any college education. More detailed measures of education, e.g., distinguishing those with a college degree from those with any college education, did not improve the statistical prediction equation.

A large number of children per family can be expected to lower pupils' mean achievement scores. An increase in family size reduces both the financial resources and parents' time available per child. The evidence presented below supports this presumption.

The other variables that were studied, including the size of the community and the occupational structure, were not statistically significant. It may of course be possible to find yet other variables that are important, especially when test scores are available for children of all ages. But the current set of income, education and family size variables is sufficient to illustrate the potential use of the predicted achievement measure.

3. Distribution According to Mean Achievement and Ability Scores

This section considers the implication of distributing Title I funds on the basis of the districts' mean achievement or ability scores. More specifically, let A_i be the number of dollars of aid per pupil given to school district i and let S_i be the measured average score on the achievement test. The "measured ability method" of distributing Title I funds could take the form:

$$(1) \qquad A_i = a_0 - a_1 S_i .$$

The parameters of this formula (a_0 and a_1) must be chosen in a way that is consistent with the available Title I aid per pupil for the state as a whole, $\overline{A}$. Since equation 1 implies that $\overline{A} = a_0 - a_1 \overline{S}$ where $\overline{S}$ is the average score in the state,[1] equation 1 can be rewritten as

$$(2) \qquad A_i = \overline{A} - a_1(S_i - \overline{S}) .$$

A district's aid per pupil is equal to the available average aid per pupil ($\overline{A}$) plus or minus an amount that depends on the difference between the average score in the district and the state average score. The parameter a_1 could be chosen to make the distribution of aid as sensitive or insensitive to S_i as the policy officials wish. If this method were workable, it would provide perfect targeting of funds to districts with low mean achievement; i.e., the correlation of A_i and S_i would be exactly minus 1.

As I explained in section 1, this measured achievement method is not workable because of the incentive that it contains for distorted

---

[1] Note that $\overline{A}$ and $\overline{S}$ are weighted averages of A_i and S_i, weighting by the corresponding numbers of pupils.

measurement of S_i. The predicted achievement method can be operated in an exactly similar way without the incentive for distorted measurement of S_i. In place of equation 1, the aid formula is

(3) $\qquad A_i = a_0 - a_1 SP_i$

where SP_i is the score <u>predicted</u> for district i on the basis of the multiple regression equation and a_0 is chosen to satisfy the Title I budget constraint.[1] Since the actual and predicted scores are not equal, the targeting of aid according to score will be less accurate than it would be if the S_i could be used directly. More precisely, the correlation between aid and actual score if equation 3 is used as the aid formula is equal to the correlation between SP_i and S_i in the regression equation.

Table 2 presents the equations relating the mean achievement and ability scores in each district to the five income and education variables described above. For comparison with the implications of the current method, equations are also presented in which the percentage of school children below the poverty line is the only independent variable.

Equation 2.1 shows that the district mean achievement scores respond in the anticipated ways to all five independent variables. A district tends to have lower achievement scores when a higher percentage of children are in families below the poverty line, when a higher percentage of families have incomes below $8000, and when there are more children per family. Note that although the two measures of

---

[1] Equation 2 cannot be used here because the <u>weighted</u> average of the SP_i is not equal to $\overline{S}$.

Table 2

Equations Predicting Mean Achievement and Ability Scores

Equation	Dependent Variable	Independent Variables						Constant	R
		Children in Poverty	Low Income Families	High Income Families	High School Graduates	College Attendees	Children Per Family		
2.1	Mean Achievement	-0.558 (0.125)	-0.286 (0.108)	0.192 (0.188)	0.274 (0.119)	0.065 (0.149)	-11.2 (4.6)	426.0	0.595
2.2	Mean Achievement	-0.961 (0.124)						430.3	0.404
2.3	Mean Ability	-0.190 (0.028)	-0.059 (0.025)	0.038 (0.043)	0.049 (0.027)	0.098 (0.034)	-3.3 (1.1)	107.4	0.735
2.4	Mean Ability	-0.315 (0.032)						109.3	0.485

See text for definitions. Standard errors are shown in parentheses.

income are obviously correlated, there is sufficient independent variation to make both of them statistically significant and useful variables in the equation. The regression coefficients also indicate that districts tend to have higher achievement scores when a higher percentage of adults are high school graduates and have had some college education; more families with high income raise the district mean score but the effect is not statistically significant.

As I indicated above, the individual regression coefficients are less important for the current purpose than the goodness of fit of the equation as a whole. The multiple correlation coefficient of $R = 0.60$ implies that the correlation between the 310 measured mean achievement scores and the corresponding mean achievement scores predicted by equation 2.1 is 0.60. This in turn implies that if Title I funds are distributed according to the predicted achievement formula of equation 3, the correlation of aid per pupil and actual score will be -0.60. This is true no matter how intensely aid is made to respond to predicted score as long as a_i is not equal to zero.

The current method of distributing Title I aid in proportion to the number of children in poverty is exactly equivalent to using a form of equation 3 but basing the predicted score on a regression using the percentage of children in poverty as the only variable. Distributing Title I aid in proportion to the number of children in poverty implies

(4) $$A_i N_i = k \, POV_i \ ,$$

i.e., the total aid received by the district $(A_i N_i)$ is k dollars per pupil in poverty (POV_i). This is clearly equivalent to

(5)
$$A_i = k\left(\frac{POV_i}{N_i}\right) ;$$

aid per pupil is proportional to the percentage of pupils in poverty. A regression equation relating predicted score to the poverty percentage can be written

(6)
$$SP_i = \beta_0 - \beta_1\left(\frac{POV_i}{N_i}\right)$$

where β_0 and β_1 are the estimated regression coefficients. Substitute 6 into 3 to obtain a distribution formula based on predicted achievement:

(7)
$$A_i = a_0 - a_1\beta_0 + a_1\beta_1\left(\frac{POV_i}{N_i}\right) .$$

By choosing a_0 and a_1 to make $a_0 - a_1\beta_0 = 0$ and $a_1\beta_1 = k$, equation 7 is identical to the current rule as expressed by equation 5.

Equation 2.2 of Table 2 presents the regression coefficients for predicted achievement based on the percentage of children in poverty. The correlation coefficient is only $R = 0.40$. This implies that the correlation between aid per pupil and average score is only -0.40 with the current method of distributing aid in proportion to the number of children in poverty. The multiple regression method of equation 2.1, with its correlation of 0.60, is clearly more successful at targeting aid to districts with low average achievement.

It is worth noting that the distribution of funds differs substantially between the two methods. The correlation between the aid per pupil that would be distributed on the basis of equation 2.1 and the aid per pupil that is distributed in proportion to the percentage of pupils in poverty is only 0.68.

Equations 2.3 and 2.4 of Table 2 present the corresponding coefficients for the predicted ability equations. Again the multiple regression equation can provide substantially better targeting of aid than the distribution in proportion to the percentage of children in poverty.[1]

---

[1]Appendix Table A-1 presents equations corresponding to 2.1 and 2.3 for the individual components of the achievement and ability tests.

4. Distribution According to Low Score Proportions

Although the mean score of the pupils in a district is the most natural summary of the test scores of all of the pupils, it may be more appropriate to focus Title I aid on districts with larger numbers of low scoring pupils and to disregard high scorers. If so, the mean score is a less suitable criterion than the proportion of pupils with scores below certain levels. This section examines the feasibility of using multiple regression equations to predict the proportion of pupils with low scores. Table 1 above showed the average proportions falling below the thresholds that will be used for the achievement and ability tests.

The aid formula now takes the form

(8) $$A_i = b_0 + b_1 \text{ PPB390}$$

where PPB390 is the predicted percentage of pupils scoring below 390 on the achievement test. Analogous distribution equations could be written for the other thresholds and for the ability scores.

Since the interpretation and properties of this equation are essentially identical with the analysis of section 3, we can turn directly to the results presented in Table 3. Column 1 indicates the dependent variable for each equation and column 2 reports the mean of that variable for the state as a whole. The multiple correlation coefficient reported in column 10 is also equal to the correlation between aid per pupil and the percentage of pupils below the critical threshold if aid is distributed on the basis of the predicted proportion of low-scoring pupils. For comparison column 11 presents the correlation between the percentage of pupils below the critical threshold and the percentage of children in

Table 3

Equations Predicting Proportion of Pupils with Low Achievement and Ability Scores

Equation	Dependent Variable	Children in Poverty	Low Income Families	High Income Families	High School Graduates	College Attendees	Children Per Family	Constant	R	Correlation of Dependent Variable with Children = Poverty
				Independent Variables						
3.1	Achievement below 390 (%)	0.611 (0.111)	0.295 (0.096)	-0.152 (0.167)	-0.152 (0.106)	0.009 (0.132)	14.7 (4.1)	7.91	0.531	0.414
3.2	Achievement below 370 (%)	0.335 (0.086)	0.202 (0.074)	-0.093 (0.129)	-0.114 (0.082)	0.031 (0.102)	8.9 (3.2)	3.50	0.440	0.331
3.3	Achievement below 350 (%)	0.162 (0.059)	0.140 (0.051)	-0.073 (0.089)	-0.049 (0.057)	0.037 (0.071)	4.6 (2.2)	-0.32	0.350	0.259
3.4	Ability below 95 (%)	0.633 (0.079)	0.120 (0.068)	-0.061 (0.119)	-0.076 (0.076)	-0.123 (0.094)	7.0 (2.9)	12.21	0.622	0.522
3.5	Ability below 90 (%)	0.423 (0.576)	0.128 (0.050)	-0.033 (0.087)	-0.066 (0.055)	-0.051 (0.069)	6.3 (2.1)	2.75	0.595	0.498
3.6	Ability below 85 (%)	0.098 (0.039)	0.108 (0.034)	-0.038 (0.058)	-0.068 (0.037)	0.035 (0.046)	2.8 (1.4)	1.56	0.421	0.284

poverty; this correlation is also the correlation between aid per pupil and the percentage of pupils below the critical threshold when aid is distributed in proportion to the number of children in poverty.

Four conclusions emerge from Table 3. First, the multiple regression method always results in a substantially better targeting of aid to low-scoring pupils than the current method of distributing aid in proportion to the number of children in poverty. Second, the correlation values are lower than for the mean scores discussed in section 2: it is easier to target funds to districts with lower mean scores than to target funds to districts with a high percentage of low-scoring pupils. Third, the problem of targeting becomes more difficult as the critical score is lowered, i.e., as attention focuses on smaller and smaller fractions of all pupils. Fourth, the relative gain from using the multiple regression method becomes greater as the critical score is lowered.

5. Conclusion

This paper has examined the feasibility of distributing Federal aid among school districts according to the educational achievement of pupils in each district. I began with the very negative conclusion that it would be impossible to give aid to districts directly on the basis of low test scores because doing so would induce districts to distort the scores that they obtain and report. However, the indirect "predicted achievement method" is potentially free of such distortion. It would permit the distribution of aid on the basis of population characteristics in a way that, on average, directs more funds to communities with more low achievement pupils. The evidence for Massachusetts that is analyzed in this paper indicates that the multiple regression predicted achievement method would provide a significantly better targeting of funds to low achievement districts than the current method of distributing funds according to the number of children in poverty.

Table A-1

Equations Predicting Mean Achievement and Ability Scores by Type

Equation	Dependent Variable	Independent Variables						Constant	R
		Children in Poverty	Low Income Families	High Income Families	High School Graduates	College Attendees	Children Per Family		
A.1	Reading Achievement	-0.651 (0.141)	-0.234 (0.122)	0.220 (0.212)	0.345 (0.134)	0.241 (0.168)	-11.7 (5.2)	427.2	0.663
A.2	Language Achievement	-0.754 (0.151)	-0.390 (0.131)	0.074 (0.228)	0.364 (0.144)	-0.070 (0.180)	-11.9 (5.6)	440.1	0.550
A.3	Arithmetic Achievement	-0.269 (0.117)	-0.236 (0.101)	0.281 (0.177)	0.114 (0.112)	0.025 (0.140)	-10.1 (4.3)	410.6	0.437
A.4	Language Ability	-0.171 (0.028)	-0.088 (0.025)	0.077 (0.043)	0.035 (0.027)	0.092 (0.034)	-3.85 (1.05)	109.0	0.743
A.5	Non-Language Ability	-0.181 (0.030)	-0.010 (0.026)	-0.004 (0.045)	0.055 (0.029)	0.082 (0.036)	-2.07 (1.10)	104.2	0.636

10

CUI BONO?
MEASURING INCOME-REDISTRIBUTION EFFECTS
OF CAPITAL PROJECTS

By

JOHN D. MONTGOMERY and MARTIN KATZMAN

What the intended beneficiaries of a program perceive as its consequences is an important issue in evaluation. Though lip service is paid to this problem, few evaluations can be found which have addressed both the actual and the perceived consequences of a program. In an evaluation of a new water supply system in a developing country, John Montgomery and Martin Katzman have shown, with admirable clarity, how the "critical incident" technique and other methods can be used to measure discrepancies between actual and perceived effects, in this case those of income-redistribution.

From John D. Montgomery and Martin Katzman, "Cui Bono? Measuring Income-Redistribution Effects of Capital Projects." Unpublished paper, 1977.

ABSTRACT: *Evaluation of the income-redistributing performance of a capital project in the Third World produced evidence on four counts that the system was in fact operating to benefit rural and urban poor: (1) The management had attempted to reduce "hidden costs" otherwise borne by the poor by subsidizing the extension of services to outlying areas and by providing low-interest credit for household connections. (2) The poor were using the services as fully as well-to-do households were, the actual consumption being related significantly to family size and not income. (3) The progressive rate structure used in the project bore more heavily on the rich than on the poor in general, though this "transfer effect" would have been greater if rates had combined a flat fee with a small surcharge based on the appraised value of the property. (4) A "critical incident" study of experience among users showed that all groups, regardless of ethnic origin, socioeconomic status, or location, perceived the project to be beneficial to the entire society, and especially to the rural poor. Information about these effects can be used by policymakers in international agencies for devising appropriate loan terms for utility-type projects. It can also guide project managers in the design of rate structures, the setting of user charges, and the assignment of priorities for the future expansion of services.*

Many governments and international lending agencies now give very high priority, in rhetoric at least, to development projects that have a potential for redistributing income. They have not abandoned "trickle-down" projects, of course, and they still accept the probability that most of their investments will benefit the rich before they do the poor. Concern over social equity has nevertheless introduced changes in development strategies, calling for increased emphasis on projects that benefit the poor while also contributing to economic growth. But how can such projects be identified? What principles should guide managers and operators in financing such capital projects?

It is sometimes argued that political leaders themselves are the principal saboteurs of efforts to implement social equity or income-redistributing projects. For they have little hope of reaping an immediate political reward for helping the poor, who are rarely organized for effective political action. In any case, rural and urban poor are usually unaware of the relatively small benefits they would receive from development projects, and they operate on a shorter time horizon than that required to punish politicians who are accused of selling out to the rich. These facts of life are cited to explain the cynicism that seems to dominate the choices that governments make in designing and implementing national plans. But there are exceptions: several noted politicians have made or staked their careers on poverty programs in recent times. Moreover, increasing numbers of economic plans, derived from technicians but processed at cabinet levels, now discuss progress in terms of measurable indicators of social equity. Trade unions, farmers' associations, and liberal intellectual leaders in many countries are creating public pressures for redistributive policies so as to compensate for some of the organizational weaknesses and political indifference of the poor. Planners and bureaucrats are deriving considerable satisfaction from the use of their professional talent to improve social justice. Finally, international conferences and international donors are providing added impetus to the movement in favor of income-redistributing projects as important elements in economic and social development. There is a corresponding rise in professional interest in some of the analytical approaches that are now being used to evaluate the social equity consequences of capital projects.

Social equity and income redistribution are not, of course, identical concepts. Indeed, social dissatisfaction with the general state of social equity tends to rise as income distribution improves in real terms. The phenomenon of rising frustrations in the face of rising income is as well documented as the parallel fact that perceived relative privation is a more important cause of social conflict than "actual" privation.[1] Planners and evaluators should therefore be prepared to ask not only whether their projects are *actually* meeting income redistributing criteria, but whether the intended beneficiaries so *perceive* the consequences.

There are at least four major sources of discrepancy between intended and perceived equity gains. For the sake of clarity, we shall designate them as "hidden costs," "distributive disabilities," "social distortions," and "perceived privation."

(1) *The "Hidden Costs" Thesis.* Planners may ignore the special costs the poor often have to bear in gaining access to project outputs. These costs include not only direct outlays of time and money, but also the cost of complementary investments necessary to utilize the project. For example, the government of India once offered sanitary privies free to all comers, but the poorest villagers had no means of transporting them to rural areas. The time lost in voting or in visiting health service centers may be a significant burden on the intended beneficiaries. Foregoing the earnings of minor children may be a sacrifice paid for free education.

(2) *"Distributive Disabilities."* Planners may perceive these "hidden" costs, but be unaware of their incidence or magnitude. For example, new roads tend to provide special benefits to those who can afford automobiles and tolls; rural electrification benefits those wealthy enough to afford electrical appliances; free higher education facilities tend to benefit the more affluent who can afford to invest in primary and secondary education.

(3) *"Social Choice" Distortions.* Planners may work out means of distributing services equally, but find that their ethnocentric or class-based preferences have misled them and that the services themselves are unimportant to the poor. For example, state subsidies to urban amenities may not benefit ethnic groups that occupy rural areas, where living standards are generally lowest. Import subsidies for baby foods are of little benefit to the poor even though the shelves of the retailers are open to all.

(4) *"Perceived Privation."* The poor may misperceive the intentions or true

benefits of a project. For example, they may resent the fact that the facilities provided for them below cost are available on the same terms to others who can afford to pay; or they may doubt the good faith of the government; even in the absence of observed discrimination, they sometimes suspect that they are being victimized because they expect to be; or they may resent the paternalism implied by the government's benevolence even when it is well intentioned.

Such discrepancies, probably far more widespread than planners realize, have to be dealt with on both political and administrative levels, often on a continuing basis, and sometimes by use of less than "optimal" arrangements for popular participation in the assignment of project benefits and responsibilities.

All of these circumstances were examined in a recent evaluation of a state water supply system in Justicia. (The name of the country is fictitious; the facts are real.) This US$14 million project involved the construction of a barrage, storage reservoirs, and transmission mains. Half of the project was financed by the government of Justicia; half by an international development agency. What was unusual about this postevaluation was the researchers' opportunity (1) to interview planners extensively about their intentions, assumptions, and perceptions; (2) to test these assumptions by analyzing water-use behavior; and (3) to measure the experiences and perceptions of the intended beneficiaries, after the project, by the "critical incident" technique and other survey methods.

SOCIAL EQUITY GOALS IN JUSTICIA

Justicia is a multiethnic society with a slight majority of Indigenes (53%), and significant Settler (35%) and Migrans (11%) communities. While there are enormous disparities within each community, ethnicity is highly related to location, occupation, and income. Although disproportionately rural, poor, and less educated, the Indigenes acquired the perquisites and symbols of political power through a constitutional process commencing with an independence movement after World War II. The coming of independence to Justicia in the 1950s, the formation of the political union in the 1960s, and a constitutional change following some racial disturbances, were the products of a political accommodation among these ethnic groups, in which the "legitimate interests" of the Migrans and Settler communities as well as the "special position" of the Indigenes were recognized. This accommodation has permitted the economically more advantaged non-Indigene communities to accept policies that would increase access of Indigenes to commercial and professional opportunities, in exchange for self-restraint on the part of the Indigenes against pushing too far in a confiscatory direction. This form of compromise emphasizes "distributive" as opposed to "redistributive" politics: the growing economy has made it possible to work toward social equity and Indigene advancement without undermining political stability.

The Second and Third Justicia Plans carefully articulated the goals of eradicating poverty and eliminating the ethnic income inequality. On the one hand the continuation of the nation's rapid economic growth (averaging 6% per annum in the previous decade) has been pursued by macroeconomic policies favorable to export expansion and import substitution. And since the benefits of past growth had trickled down very slowly to the Indigenes (indeed, the perceived ethnic gap may have widened in favor of the Settlers), more specific distributive mechanisms were called for. Public facilities such as schools, water, and electricity were to be dispersed as evenly as possible between city and countryside, and the fiscal system as a whole was to redistribute a significant share of the national income in a pro-poor direction. Admissions quotas and the language of instruction at higher levels of education were designed to insure entry of Indigenes in proportion to their share of the population. Public business corporations were being established in trust for the Indigene population. The goals of Justicia's public policy are explicitly to increase the share of income enjoyed by the poor, disproportionately Indigene, citizens.

THE STATE WATER SUPPLY PROJECT

The State Water Supply Project under review was clearly in the income-redis-tributing tradition, though to be sure it would benefit the rich along with the poor. One of the oldest and best public systems in Asia, it served the major urban areas and some adjacent rural areas. But it was becoming obsolete. By 1965, projections of the water supply and demand and rates of population increase and industrial-ization showed clearly that future shortages were inevitable; already by 1972 water rationing had to be instituted during the dry months. If such conditions were to continue, the poor would have suffered more: the rich could have afforded to dig the wells, build the cisterns, and buy the bottled water necessary to continue a reasonably comfortable existence, and the poor would have been compelled to line up at public standpipes, use unfiltered water, and collect the rain in stagnant pools and mosquito-breeding containers. Parallel circumstances observed in other Third World cities such as Bangkok provide a vivid picture of life under these circumstances.[2] Moreover, the rural areas, where the largest proportion of Indigenes live, could not have been served by the system at all unless the supply could be increased.

The enlarged system made possible by the international and federal loans aimed primarily at protecting the existing users against future shortages while extending the services to rural areas. Like the other major expansions of public services in postindependent Justicia—access to the university, entry into the civil service, and the control of the new system of state enterprises, for example—the State Water Supply Project was conceived as a mechanism whose benefits were targeted primarily at the urban and rural poor, especially the ethnic Indigenes. Operating policies of the state-run water authority expressed the same goal. The structure of water rates was designed to impose the costs progressively. Prior to 1973, separate urban and rural rate schedules guaranteed that large-scale industrial users would pay considerably more than households using small amounts of water. The project loan necessitated a rate increase in 1973, but to attenuate the burden on the poor, urban and rural schedules were unified and a new schedule was established, distinguishing residential and business consumers, the latter paying higher rates; within the residential category, however, smaller and presumably poorer users paid less per thousand gallons than the larger and presumably richer users (Table 1).

A second feature of the water authority's policies was the decision to reinvest 5% of all revenues in water main extensions. The state is divided into five zones of roughly equal population, and investments in mains were allocated nearly equally among them. Despite the recognition that service in lower-density areas is not commercially profitable, extensions to the rural areas were justified as a "social dividend" which a public monopoly owes the people.

Third, the areas that were not yet served by distribution pipes were supplied for the most part with public standpipes, which were metered and charged to the local government council. Since these standpipes served mostly low-income (and Indigene) villages, this policy was clearly redistributive since the entire population bears the cost through a progressive tax system. Squatters who requested piped-in water could receive service also if after one year the local housing board declined to order demolition of the squatments (in the meantime, many would purchase water illegally, usually at high prices, from a neighbor). And finally, although the authority required households to pay for connections to the water mains, the water authority provided interest-free loans for this purpose, which were amortized over a period of five years.

In many developing countries, public utilities are subsidized from general tax revenues, and when international financing is sought, the lenders require an increase in utility rates to guarantee financial and managerial autonomy. The State Water Department was already run on a self-financing basis, but engineering requirements for expansion and international inflation necessitated a substantial increase in water rates from $0.60 per thousand gallons in 1968 to $0.95 per thousand after the project.

TABLE 1. RESIDENTIAL RATE STRUCTURES BEFORE AND AFTER REVISION*

Monthly Rate per Thousand Gallons	Thousands of Gallons Consumed per Month					
	Urban			Rural		
	0-5	5-10	10-30	0-5	5-10	10-30
Old rate, J$	.50	.50	.55	.60	.60	.60
New rate, J$	.60	.95	.95	.60	.95	.95
% change	20	90	73	0	58	58

*Excluding rates charged to industrial-commercial consumers and residential consumers of more than 30,000 gallons. Average charge before the rate increase was J$ 0.60 per thousand gallons; after the increase, J$ 0.95.

PLANNERS' PERCEPTIONS OF
INCOME-REDISTRIBUTION THROUGH USER CHARGES

Public utility projects are especially amenable to serving income-redistribution goals because they produce "necessities"—i.e., goods with low income-elasticity of demand—and because they permit price discrimination on the basis of where, when, and to whom benefits are delivered. To the extent that welfare economic theory condones redistribution through pricing, it favors higher surcharges for goods consumed by the wealthy. Explicit welfare-economic theorems assume that consumption varies directly with family income, but ignore the influence of other characteristics such as family size and age composition.[3] By deduction, then, larger consumers are therefore wealthier.

This is clearly the model the planners had in mind. The investment in expanded water-production facilities and distribution mains was clearly intended to benefit the poor, both directly, by providing an important necessity to the rural areas, and indirectly, through the employment-providing industrialization that would be made possible by an increased water supply. And a progressive rate structure was designed to insure that the poor would not bear a disproportion of the burden.

A progressive rate structure for water is an efficient income-redistributing device when there is a high correlation between family income and consumption. If this correlation were perfect, and if the price-elasticity of demand for water were low, then efficient redistribution could be achieved simply by manipulating the steepness of the rates. But in this state the simple correlation between water consumption and income was found to be only .16, while that between water consumption and family size is .62. Since family size proved to be essentially uncorrelated with income ($r = -.09$), there were a substantial number of poor-but-large families, paying higher water bills than wealthy-but-small families (Table 2).[4]

Despite the fact that usage charges at the very low end of the scale did not increase much, and not at all for the rural population, the significant increases at

TABLE 2. RELATIONS AMONG INCOME, WATER CONSUMPTION, AND
WATER BILLS, 1972

Monthly Income[a]	Number of Cases	Percentage Distributions						
		Monthly Consumption[b]			Monthly Water Bill[a]			
		0-5	5-10	10+	1-3	4-5	6-8	9+
0-150	249	41.8	38.9	19.3	51.4	26.4	10.1	12.1
150-500	641	20.7	47.8	31.5	27.2	32.5	24.3	16.3
500-800	189	16.9	50.8	32.3	18.1	33.0	28.2	20.9
800 plus	242	12.0	45.4	42.6	7.1	23.4	39.2	30.3

a. in J$

b. thousand gallons

Chi-square for income distribution = 99.0, $p < .001$; Cramer's V = 0.188

Chi-square income versus bill, 136.8, $p < .001$, Cramer's V = 0.221

TABLE 3. REDISTRIBUTIVE EFFECTS OF CHANGE IN WATER RATES
OCCURRING IN 1973

| | Mean Monthly Income J$ | % of Income Expended on Water* | | Net Change |
		Before	After	
Very poor	125	4.0	6.2	2.2
Poor	325	1.6	2.4	.3
Medium	650	1.0	1.6	.6
Rich	800	1.0	1.5	.5

*Calculated for urban consumers.

SOURCE: Unpublished water consumption survey, 1972.

the middle and higher end of the use schedule hit the average poor family relatively hard. This regressive effect was not a result of planner's malice, but a consequence of unawareness of the consumption patterns of the poor. In fact, despite the progressiveness of the rate structure, the rate increase resulted in a greater burden on the poor, in proportion to their income, than on the rich (Table 3). This difficulty could have been partially offset by increasing the breakpoint between low and high rates on the schedule, but because of the low correlation between consumption and income, the problem could not be eliminated entirely by manipulating the rates.

BENEFICIARIES' PERCEPTIONS

Measuring the benefits perceived by different groups of users is, of course, a more difficult process. The geographical distribution of facilities provides evidence in this state that the squatter-occupied areas of the city and that rural areas were, in fact, being well-served.

But before planners can gain much appreciation of the popular perception of the benefits, the public has to express its experience and opinions directly, either collectively or individually. In the absence of individual complaints, riots, punitive political action, indignant speeches, or conversely, of spontaneous feasts, marches, and celebrations, political leaders may know little of the public's real perceptions. But such expressions in the wake of a development project are rare indeed. Evaluations of perceived benefits must therefore depend on specific research undertakings.

During the evaluation study of this project, it was possible to reach 7,760 households (7% of the total number) by distributing a questionnaire through the public school system. The fact that nearly all children in the state up to the age of 14 were enrolled in school, and the cooperative spirit of the education authorities, provided an economical means of sampling the public experience with the system. The survey was prepared in the four languages in use in Justicia, and the questionnaires handed out and collected by teachers to pupils about 14 years old, the highest age group enrolled in compulsory schooling. The teachers had been instructed previously about the purpose and importance of the survey, and the expectation was that since the data to be gathered were easily observable by the pupils, there would be little distortion even if they themselves filled out the survey rather than, as requested, their parents.[5] The questionnaire included data about the household and its physical condition (the number of taps or water outlets being a surrogate for income), opinions about effects of the water supply system, and, most important of all, actual experience with the system (making use of a method that draws on behavior as contrasted with opinions of the respondents).[6] Responses were supplied by all identifiable elements of the population—all ethnic groups, rural and urban residents, households that had access to the system only through public standpipes, and groups that did not use the public water supply at all.

The results were both illuminating and surprising: in the public's mind, the planners' intentions of helping the poor and the rural populations were even stronger than their deeds. For in 1976, when the survey was conducted, the ethnic Indigenes were still more likely to be excluded from the system altogether, or to use only the public standpipes, than the non-Indigene population, simply because more of them were living in the rural locations that were less adequately served than the cities. But they, along with other groups, reported that the water supply system was generating more or less equal benefits to all groups. The objective incidence of the relative benefits distributed to different groups did not affect their perceptions.

Improvements in the system can be perceived in many dimensions—the reliability of flow and pressure, the quality of water, and the availability of the facilities being the most important. The survey turned up 4,723 incidents, of which 40% were concerned with rationing or adequacy of supply; about 25% with quality (including, especially, taste and pressure); and 10% with cutoffs and service. The references to rationing were overwhelmingly favorable (1,930 versus 12), while those to quality were rather unfavorable (418 versus 822), and those about cutoffs and service overwhelmingly unfavorable (58 versus 408). These responses suggest that simply having water was a salient event to consumers, certainly in the Justicia setting; it was more important than concerns over its quality and reliability. The policy implications support the decision to continue investing in mains to extend service.

Availability increased most rapidly in the rural areas and poor neighborhoods, but the other dimensions pertain to all users. Only 23% of the population reported any actual improvement in service; those using standpipes were somewhat more likely (30%) to perceive improvements than those with piped-in water (23%), and of course much more than those without access to the public system (13%).

The causes of the perceived improvements are complex. A higher proportion among those using standpipes (37%) than among those having their own piped-in water (28%) have received service for the first time only within the past five years. Thus in terms of availability, presumably rural and poor families benefited more. But others also perceived benefits: families with piped-in water experienced fewer cutoffs after the new system began operating (only 46% in 1975 as opposed to 63% in the old system).

TABLE 4. DISEASES AFFECTED BY WATER SUPPLIES (IN THE STATE)

Diseases		1966	1967	1968	1969	1970	1971	1972	1973	1974	1975[b]
Cholera:	No.	—	—	3	1	63	—	16	3	127	—
	Rate[a]					8.11		1.97	0.36	14.96	
Dysentery:	No.	117	69	54	43	30	43	71	56	45	21
	Rate		9.17			3.86	5.42	8.75	6.75	5.30	2.42
Food Poisoning: (Salmonella)	No.	NA	NA	NA	50	56	44	17	23	17	20
	Rate					7.21	5.54	2.09	2.77	2.00	2.30
Infectious Hepatitis:	No.	NA	NA	NA	367	204	202	217	243	143	108
	Rate					26.26	25.44	23.73	29.28	16.85	12.45
Typhoid and Paratyphoid	No.	NA	NA	NA	14	41	59	118	94	44	34
	Rate					5.28	7.43	14.53	11.33	5.19	3.92

a. Rate per 100,000 population.
b. 1975 data through November only.
NA = not available
SOURCE: Data supplied by Director, Health Department, State Medical and Health Services, January 1976.

The degree to which individuals perceived their own situation as improving did not vary much with location or ethnicity. These self-assessments are paralleled by perceptions of the distribution of benefits. Nearly 90% of the respondents believed that the benefits of the system were distributed equally, with little difference between Indigenes and non-Indigenes; those with piped-in water were somewhat more likely (90%) to perceive benefits as being distributed equally than those using standpipes (85%), and 90% of those with no access to the system nevertheless thought all were benefited equally.

Few respondents reported in answer to another question that they perceived unequal distribution of benefits. The vast majority could not perceive any particular group that benefited more, though rural people were perceived somewhat more frequently than urban dwellers as the primary beneficiaries.

Special surveys are also valuable in reporting direct social benefits that cannot be measured in any other way. For example, public health advantages from improved water supplies are assumed by planners and sometimes the impacts are crudely quantified in theoretical statements of social costs and benefits. But except for situations in which polluted water is replaced by purified water, or where scanty supplies are replenished to the point where personal hygiene and sanitation can be measurably improved, there are usually no clearly identifiable changes in the incidence of disease that can be traced to new dams, reservoirs, and delivery systems. Both public health officials and water supply engineers in the state were convinced that the new system contributed to public health, but were unable to prove it (except, perhaps, by extrapolating the consequences of interruptions and rationing that would have been necessary in a few years if the system had not been enlarged). But the evaluation procedure provided evidence that confirmed these assumptions. While there were no statistically significant decreases in water-borne or -related diseases (Table 4), the public *perceptions* of improved health and environmental conditions were unmistakable. In response to questions about what differences the system made in their own lives or in the neighborhood environment, 26% indicated improved health, which was in most cases attributed to the new system. It is significant that the greatest decline in illness was reported by those using public standpipes. Of the 4,723 experiences with the water supply system that were reported in the survey, only one could be interpreted (by a mild stretch of the imagination) as negative in terms of health (someone found a dead python in the reservoir). In contrast, 106 postive experiences were cited.[7]

DISCREPANCIES IN SOCIAL EQUITY EFFECTS

None of the four sources of discrepancy between intended and realized equity benefits of the water supply project posed insuperable obstacles to achieving its redistributive goals. The fact that evidence was obtained on all four counts has now made it possible for project managers to improve their performance marginally, and it has offered confirmation to planners who believe that capital projects can be both selected and managed to serve social equity purposes. There remain important areas of comparison and choice among capital projects, and some immediate policy issues about which further study is necessary. Moreover, the transferability of both these operational decisions and the evaluation procedures employed here is still open to question. But the data gathered on this relatively small capital project provide some reassurance about the direction in which current development policy is moving.

The project can hardly be accused of ignoring the hidden costs to the poor of participating in the system. Despite the costs of connection financing was arranged by the water authority, with the result that the poor increased their participation in the system. The rural poor were able to connect to new distribution mains, and the urban poor to the new lines serving the squatter settlements. And those who were not served by piped-in water had increased access to publicly financed standpipes.

Nor can the project be accused of providing a service for which the poor had low preferences; social distortions were not important. The very fact of continued connection and the high levels of use, which varied only slightly with income and ethnicity, indicate that this good enjoyed an important place on the list of priorities of the poor.

Nor did the poor feel alienated or nihilistic toward the system. The fact that cutoffs for as short as three hours elicit direct complaints from all groups suggests that the users feel the system is responsive to their wants. Indigenes reported themselves as somewhat more likely to telephone complaints (30%) than non-Indigenes (23%).

The only short fall of the system, as an income-redistribution project, was the unintended discrimination against the poor as a result of the altered incidence of costs. Although the progressive rate structure was designed with the welfare of the poor in mind, the planners were unaware of the degree to which consumption levels were dictated by family size, which tended to place poor-but-large households in the high rate categories.

The financial burden on the poor would have been reduced if the water rates had remained constant and the deficits financed by the generally progressive tax system already in effect. This method, however, conflicts with the lender's requirement that the project be self-financing on the basis of user fees, in order to protect the utility from political manipulation. One alternative would be to increase the progressivity of the rate structure by lowering the charge for the first consumption block, by raising its limits, and by increasing the charge for succeeding blocks. This change would help *small* poor families, but the low correlation between income and water consumption implies that such a rate schedule would also penalize poor-but-large families and benefit rich-but-small families. A better alternative would be to use a two-part tariff, with a flat user fee, and a basic charge proportional to the value of residential property, which is highly correlated with income ($r = 0.68$) and almost uncorrelated with water consumption ($r = 0.04$).[8]

POLICY IMPLICATIONS

General policy recommendations for achieving income redistributive goals flow from this experience, both for evaluation procedures and for project selection and design. Selecting projects whose outputs are "necessities" and establishing progressive rate structures are not sufficient guarantee of achieving efficient income redistribution. Current assumptions about levels of use, and therefore relative distribution of benefits, need to be verified in each instance, to insure that the progressive rate structure turns out in practice to distribute the burden of payments as intended. "Hidden costs" of access borne by the poor must also be adequately assessed. And public responses, both attitudinal and behavioral, need to be followed carefully if the social equity objectives of public investment are to bring political rewards. Political leaders do respond to their constituencies; most of them would like to serve the public, but find greater satisfaction in doing so if the public is aware of these services and regards them favorably.

One is left with an ironic puzzle: Would government financing that was immune from requirements of fiscal autonomy for each project have permitted the project to respond more directly to the needs of the poor by relying on tax revenues for capital charges? The answer depends on the basic tax structure of the country (which, in Justicia, is clearly progressive), and on alternative methods of financing (the private capital market would have required higher interest rates, but a grant or interest-free loan from the government of Justicia might have increased the income-redistributing effects in this case). The costs would have to be borne by the tax-paying public, presumably those more well-to-do elements, especially. But that change would raise the most durable of all issues in public policy: whose ox is to be gored? Cui malo?

NOTES

1. Ivo K. Feieraband, Rosalind L. Feieraband, and Ted Robert Gurr (eds.), *Anger, Violence and Politics: Theories and Research* (Englewood Cliffs, N.J.: Prentice-Hall, 1972); Nazli Choucri, *Population Dynamics and International Violence* (Lexington, Mass.: D.C. Heath, 1974), Part II.

2. Camp, Dresser, and McKee, *Master Plan, Metropolitan Bangkok, Thailand: Water Supply and Distribution* (Boston, 1970), Vol. 1, Summary.

3. Martin S. Feldstein, "Distributional Equity and the Optimal Structure of Public Prices," *American Economic Review*, 62(March 1972):32-36; Martin S. Feldstein, "Equity and Efficiency in Public Sector Pricing: The Optimal Two-Part Tariff," *Quarterly Journal of Economics*, 86(May 1972):175-187; Gerard R. Faulhaber, "Cross Subsidization: Pricing in Public Enterprises," *American Economic Review*, 65(December 1975):966-978; Julian LeGrand, "Public Price Discrimination and Aid to Low-Income Groups," *Economica*, 42(February 1975):32-42.

4. Based on a water consumption survey in the form of unprocessed computer cards, produced in April 1972. The multiple R^2 of water consumption against income and family size is approximately .45 (n = 1,321). These results are strikingly similar to findings in Canada both in magnitude of R^2 and relative importance of family size vis-à-vis income. Angelo P. Grima, *Residential Water Demand*, Geography Research Monograph no. 17 (Toronto: University of

Toronto Press, 1972), pp. 101-106. One possible explanation for high consumption in poor households in Justicia might have been the illegal practice of retailing water to neighbors who are unwilling or unable to obtain their own connections. But only 10% of the households in this area were without direct service. Even if all of them were connected to a "poor household," the resulting excess use in those households would not explain more than a small proportion of the difference. But it is known that most of the unconnected households had other sources of water.

5. Internal evidence suggests that a very large number of parents did at least supply the children with some of the responses.

6. The "critical incident" method, as used here, provided an important supplement to the survey questionnaire format that seek opinions or other data from carefully selected respondents representing a known "universe" of individuals or households. The critical incident data bank represents human experience relating to the subject under investigation; the collective experience itself, not the respondents, constitutes the "universe" that is sampled. To obtain a representative sample, the procedure is to ask the respondents to describe the most recent incidents (not the most important or dramatic ones) that they experienced in connection with the subject under investigation. Each experience is recorded in the respondents' own words, not through a multiple-choice form. The incidents are classified into as many unique categories as the data define. Additional incidents are collected until all categories are filled (i.e., no "new" types of incidents are supplied). The method was first used in World War II to explore the "experience" of effective aircrew performance to improve pilot selection and training. Since then it has had hundreds of applications in the United States and abroad. Unfortunately, there is no comprehensive history of its use (and abuse). For the early history of the method, see John C. Flanagan, *Measuring Human Performance* (Palo Alto: American Institutes for Research, 1962, 1974, Chapter IV and Appendix, Bibliography for Chapter IV).

7. To put the public health incidents in perspective, only 110 events out of 4,723 concerned public health benefits; in other words, the amenity value of water seemed more salient than the public health benefits.

8. This argument assumes that the full incidence of the surcharge is borne by the renter. If part of the surcharge is borne by the landlord, who is usually richer than the tenant, the results are even more progressive than we assumed.

11

ACCUMULATING EVIDENCE:
PROCEDURES FOR RESOLVING CONTRADICTIONS
AMONG DIFFERENT RESEARCH STUDIES

By

RICHARD J. LIGHT and PAUL V. SMITH

This has been one of the most frequently cited and influential studies in the evaluation literature. That popularity attests to the importance of concerns about data integration of both researchers and policymakers. As a substitute for "taking a vote," Richard Light and Paul Smith propose an integrative schema—"the cluster approach" that provides such integration in an economical and statistically compelling manner.

From Richard J. Light and Paul V. Smith, "Accumulating Evidence: Procedures for Resolving Contradictions Among Different Research Studies." *Harvard Educational Review,* November 1971, *41*(4), 429-471.

Significant knowledge in the social sciences accrues ever too slowly. A major reason is that various research studies on a particular question tend to be of dissimilar designs, making their results difficult to compare. An even more important factor is that social science studies frequently produce conflicting results, which hinder theoretical developments and confuse those responsible for the implementation of social policies. In this pioneering effort the authors suggest criteria for determining when data from dissimilar studies can be pooled. Methods for recognizing fundamental differences in research designs, and for avoiding the creation of artificial differences, are offered. A paradigm, labeled the "cluster approach," is proposed as a means of combining the data of studies from which conflicting conclusions have been drawn. Major emphasis is placed on ways that the paradigm might solve problems presently faced by educational researchers, and several studies comparing the effectiveness of pre-school programs are used to illustrate the cluster approach.

Partial support for Richard J. Light's work was provided by a grant from the Spencer Foundation.

> The thirteenth stroke of a clock is not only
> false of itself, but casts grave doubts on the
> credibility of the preceding twelve.
>
> Mark Twain, *Autobiography*

Mark Twain's statement captures a striking part of the experience of doing educational research. It seems that for every twelve studies reaching a specific conclusion, it is always possible to find a thirteenth that disagrees. Mark Twain's solution might well have been to put all thirteen behind him, and light out for the Territories. The research equivalent of Mark Twain's action would be to discard the conflicting evidence, and initiate a new study. But this action would entail three costs. First, a great deal of information, much of which might be potentially valuable, would be thrown away. Second, a decision would be postponed for at least the length of time required by the new research. Third, from the point of view of the next reviewer of the literature, this new research would simply be the fourteenth in the set of studies. No matter what its results, for the next reviewer the contradictions remain. Thus, for any researcher, it is worth making an attempt to find a way to combine and reconcile conflicting studies.

The traditional starting point for finding such a way, in both educational and scientific research, is a review of the existing literature. These reviews frequently contribute to educational policy decisions. Essentially they involve three steps. First, all the relevent empirical studies are gathered together. Second, studies with inadequate sampling procedure, measurement and instrumentation, or methods of analysis are identified and discarded. Third, the conclusions from the remaining studies are assembled and compared in an effort to find consistent results. The third step often encounters contradictions; similar studies frequently produce contrary results.

When the purpose of the literature review is primarily theoretical, inconsistencies in the results of various studies can be disconcerting. When the purpose of the review is to develop specific policies, however, such inconsistencies can paralyze attempts at public action. In a recent address to the American Educational Research Association, Senator Walter Mondale, speaking in the context of school integration, put the issue clearly:

What I have not learned is what we should do about these problems. I had hoped to find research to support or to conclusively oppose my belief that quality integrated education is the most promising approach. But I have found very little conclusive evidence. For every study, statistical or theoretical, that contains a proposed solution or recommendation, there is always another, equally well documented, challenging the assumptions or conclusions of the first. No one seems to agree with anyone else's approach. But more distressing: no one seems to know what works. As a result I must confess, I stand with my colleagues confused and often disheartened.[1]

The Senator's quandary is understandable. Further, his description of the lack of consistency in educational findings unfortunately applies not only to research on integration, but to many other issues in educational policy as well. Even apart from the formulation of educational policy, the contradictions we encounter among similar studies with different conclusions cripple a fundamental component of the scientific process: the systematic accumulation of knowledge.

Most readers who are familiar with educational research journals, as well as other social science journals, will recognize the following paradigm. An author reports the results of his research, and concludes his article with a statement that reads, "While I have found X, Y, and Z, further research on this subject is needed." What does this statement imply? It implies the author is interested in seeing further results, collected by himself or by others, which will either corroborate or contradict his own findings. Thus, the author must believe, as most researchers and policy makers do, that evidence and knowledge should be cumulative. But for evidence to be cumulative, there must be accessible procedures for accumulating it. Currently, there appear to be few systematic efforts to accumulate information gradually from a set of disparate studies.

We present here the outlines of a strategy for accumulating information. We call this strategy a "cluster" approach, because it flows from the ideas of cluster sampling originally developed in the field of sampling theory. We wish to stress that our presentation will in no way be "complete"; we are not able to offer a long list of suggestions on what to do in every conceivable situation. We are currently working on a number of specific technical suggestions, however, and hope that others who consider this problem an important one will begin similar work.[2]

In this essay, then, we focus first on some background issues which lay the foundation for the cluster approach to combining studies. We discuss methods currently used to combine studies, a number of defects of these methods, and some general costs of combining studies improperly. These costs can become

---

[1] Address given to the American Education Research Association's annual meeting, February, 1971, New York City.

[2] We believe this general problem of combining studies is as important to the non-statistician as to the statistical community. We have therefore kept the text relatively free of technical arguments, and confined such points to footnotes.

prohibitively high. Second, we give some examples taken from the literature of educational research that illustrate conflicting results. Third, we discuss the unique nature of educational settings and why classic experimental procedures should be modified for them. The fourth section begins a discussion of procedures for combining educational studies. The cluster approach enables us to represent a wide range of possible effects. Also, this section contains the main body of our argument: a list of the major ways in which clusters (for example, classrooms within schools) can differ. We argue that when major differences among samples are fully represented in an analysis, seeming contradictions among the samples can be resolved and converted into valuable findings. Finally, in the fifth section, we look at two examples of the kind of insights provided by adopting the cluster approach.

Combining Studies: What Is Done Today?

The issue of combining studies is not new. There are at least four general approaches in current use. A first and very common one involves a simple *listing* of factors that have shown an effect on a dependent variable in at least one of a group of studies. Such lists are usually long, and often do not distinguish between those factors which were found important in many studies versus those singled out only once or twice.

A second approach effectively amounts to the opposite of the first. In this case, a researcher essentially chooses a single favorite study from a set. He thus *excludes* the findings of all studies except one or two, and thereby creates consistency. Unfortunately, the consistency will be artificial unless all of the rejected studies are in fact valueless.

The third and fourth approaches are somewhat more systematic. The third consists of computing overall *averages* for relevant statistics across a complete set of studies. Often the summary measure chosen is not a mean, but rather a median or some other measure which offers some protection against extreme values. For example, a researcher might take five values of the simple correlation between a student's family income and his college aspirations, found in five different studies, and report the median value.[3] While this is a first attempt at

---

[3] For an example of an effort to combine studies using the median as a summary measure, see Fred E. Fiedler, "Validation and Extension of the Contingency Model of Leadership Effectiveness: A Review of Empirical Findings," *Psychological Bulletin*, 75 (August 1971), pp. 128-148. In several tables in this analysis, a median of a group of correlation coefficients is given, where

quantification, a purpose of this essay will be to show that such estimates throw away precisely the information we most want.

The fourth approach to combining studies is the best and most systematic of the lot. Perhaps that is why it is being used more and more frequently. Because it is a bit more elaborate than the other procedures, we will discuss it in greater detail. This method can be described as *taking a vote*. All studies which have data on a dependent variable and a specific independent variable of interest are examined. Three possible outcomes are defined. The relationship between the independent variable and the dependent variable is either significantly positive, significantly negative, or there is no significant relationship in either direction. The number of studies falling into each of these three categories is then simply tallied. If a plurality of studies falls into any one of these three categories, with fewer falling into the other two, the modal category is declared the winner. This modal categorization is then assumed to give the best estimate of the direction of the true relationship between the independent and dependent variable.

One example of "taking a vote" is the work of Murray.[4] He reviewed the results of 44 studies relating children's anxiety to other variables. Both younger and older children were studied. This review examined the relationship of anxiety to one or more of the verbal productivity variables common in the psychological literature. A second example is the paper by Luborsky, Chandler, Auerbach, Cohen, and Bachrach, reviewing 166 studies concerning factors influencing the outcome of psychotherapy.[5] Both of these reviews aim toward a desirable scientific compendium of different studies. However, while the methods used by these authors in their attempt to combine studies are more systematic than ordinary reviews of literature, they are unfortunately still not likely to yield rich inferences.

Let the following example from the review of psychotherapeutic outcomes illustrate a weakness. Five of the 166 studies included social class of a patient as an independent variable. In two of these studies, the relationship between social class and beneficial outcome was positive. In two, no significant relationship was

---

about half of the original correlations are positive and half are negative. Sometimes the median is relatively far from zero, despite the nearly even positive-negative split in the original coefficients.

[4] David C. Murray, "Talk, Silence, and Anxiety," *Psychological Bulletin*, 75 (April 1971), pp. 244-260.

[5] Lester Luborsky, Michael Chandler, Arthur H. Auerbach, Jacob Cohen, and Henry M. Bachrach, "Factors Influencing the Outcomes of Psychotherapy: A Review of Quantitative Research," *Psychological Bulletin*, 75 (March 1971). pp. 145-185.

found. In one, the relationship was negative. By taking a vote, Luborsky *et al.* conclude, "In general, patients with higher social achievements are better suited for psychotherapy." Note that this conclusion is based on a two-to-one vote, with two recorded abstentions, and with 161 data points recorded as not voting.

The weakness of the method in this example should be obvious. A hidden assumption in the taking-a-vote process is that the less frequent outcome is due either to chance alone or to an undetected experimental error. But notice that we could just as reasonably conclude that the relationship between the patient's social class and the benefits of therapy varies from therapist to therapist. This alternate conclusion also could follow from the data. The ambiguity is, in the first instance, a methodological problem. However, it may lead to an error of inference. Wrong inferences are one of the costs of combining studies incorrectly. We now discuss such costs.

Costs of Combining Studies Incorrectly

There are three losses which may be incurred if studies are combined incorrectly. Each of the three is illustrated below with an example from the "taking-a-vote" procedure.

Weakened inferences

We only choose to combine studies when we have no one study available (from a known population) which is sufficiently large and sufficiently comprehensive. When we combine several studies, we do so to increase the overall effective sample size, or to increase the comprehensiveness of the measures available to us on at least some part of the sample. An inappropriate approach to combining studies can cost us one or both of these objectives.

The statistical significance of a relationship between two variables in any study depends upon the sample size used. Thus, the "structure" of the relationship between two variables may be identical in two studies, and yet this structure may be identified as statistically significant for a large study, while not being statistically significant for a smaller one. The "taking-a-vote" procedure does not incorporate sample size into the vote. Thus, in this procedure a large study has the same weight as a small study. They both have one vote. For example, suppose we had available ten studies, each with ten subjects. Suppose further that only one of the ten studies showed a significant treatment effect. We would probably conclude, using a voting procedure and examining all ten studies, that the treatment was ineffective.[6] However, it is quite possible that if all 100 subjects were "pooled" into the equivalent of a single large study, a highly significant treatment effect would emerge. Therefore, by failing to pool, we lose the advantage of having the hundred cases from all the studies.

Under what circumstances might we lose the value of a comprehensive selection of measures? This happens whenever any method of combining studies ignores the fact that a subset of studies which includes additional independent variables deserves special recognition. For example, the "taking-a-vote" procedure ignores the possibility that those studies which include a particular independent variable of interest may not be representative of all studies to be reviewed. There may be important qualitative differences among subsets of studies. It would be throwing away potentially valuable data to restrict our conclusions to only those independent variables which were measured in all studies. But to have confidence in a conclusion taken from a small subset of studies, we should use a procedure which has the capacity to detect whether those studies were exceptional in other respects. For example, in the review of psychotherapy, we would like to know whether the five studies which measured patient's social class differed among themselves, or from the other 161 studies, in the relation-

---

[6] What would such a conclusion assume? In essence, it assumes that the one significant result was a false positive. If each study was carried out at the .05 level of significance, then of course we would expect to find on the average approximately one out of twenty falsely significant treatment effects when none really existed. In the text example we found one out of ten, which is not so different from one out of twenty. What, then, is the danger of accepting a nine to one vote that the treatment is ineffective? There are two dangers. The first danger is that when the treatment effect is small but real, and the sample sizes are small, as in our example, then significant treatment effects will not be detected much more than one time in twenty. That is because with small samples the power of statistical tests is relatively low. (For a detailed discussion of this point, see Jacob Cohen, *Statistical Power Analysis for the Behavioral Sciences* [New York: Academic Press, 1969].) A primary purpose of enlarging sample size by pooling data is to increase the power of statistical tests. This is reflected in our inferences in that we will prefer the decision from the larger pooled sample to a "vote" taken among its smaller components. The second danger is not related to experimental statistics. Rather, it comes from the fact that educational studies are often not random samples. In fact, they are often not samples at all. For example, complete sets of school records form the basis for evaluations of programs such as Title I. When the data is a complete census, significance computations have no meaning. Whatever is observed in one study is the fact for that study. If 60 percent of the studies show girls reading earlier than boys, while 40 percent show the reverse, then a proper description of the "general finding" must reflect all that detail. Thus, we do not conclude by a 3 to 2 vote that girls read earlier than boys; rather, we simply conclude that girls read earlier than boys in approximately 60 percent of the school systems studied. Finally, if data are a set of complete censuses, and display differences, we cannot simply pool all the data into the equivalent of a single large study. Rather we must first represent and adjust for whatever differences have been observed among studies. Strategies for representing such differences are discussed later in this paper.

ship between, say, client's age and therapeutic outcome. Taking a vote, by dealing with only a single relationship at a time, ignores this information.

Overlooked inferences

An inference can be overlooked when a systematic pattern in some data is ignored. This happens most frequently when we fail to examine all the ways data can vary from study to study. We might, for example, search only for mean differences among studies when other kinds of differences would be even more important. To illustrate, suppose we chose to "take a vote" on five different investigations of the effects of tracking on initially low-achieving children. Each of these five studies compared test scores of such children assigned to low-track (homogeneous) classrooms versus scores for other such children who had been assigned to untracked (heterogeneous) classrooms. Assume the mean performance of the two groups never differed significantly. We therefore would conclude, by a five to nothing vote, that tracking has no effect on initially low-achieving children. But suppose that by focusing on means it was overlooked that the *variation* in final scores was larger for initially low-achieving children in heterogeneous classrooms than for such children in homogeneous classrooms. Tracking, then, might have the effect of decreasing variation among children's test scores, rather than increasing or decreasing a group's mean score. By examining only the means, an important effect of tracking would be overlooked.

Any procedure that combines studies can overlook an inference available from the data. It is just that taking a vote is particularly susceptible to this cost because it concentrates on only those statistics for which significance levels were computed in the original studies. Thus, if the investigators for the original studies did not compute an important statistic, this information will not appear in the summary produced by taking a vote. When combining studies, our goal is to condense a large mass of information about relationships into a few primary conclusions. The process used to make this condensation must not over simplify these relationships and thereby overlook important aspects of them.

Wrong inferences

The worst of all possible consequences of combining a set of studies incorrectly is coming out with the *wrong* inference. We define a wrong inference as the case when available data provides evidence for a correct conclusion, but our method of combining the data throws that evidence away, leading to an incorrect conclusion. In complex settings drastic errors of inference are possible. Here, however, we will give just a brief example. Suppose, hypothetically, that a new review of psychotherapeutic outcomes found some studies showing age of patient negatively related to outcome, and other studies showing age of therapist also negatively related to outcome. We would probably conclude from these two sets of data that the most optimistic prognosis occurs when a young psychotherapist treats a young patient. But suppose only one study actually tried the combination of young therapist with young patient. Further, assume that its outcome was uniformly poor. This unexpected finding would be an instance of an interaction effect, because while overall youth of patients and youth of therapists lead to favorable prognoses, the specific combination of young therapist and young patient was unfavorable. Any method of combining studies which does not allow for effects such as interactions can lead to incorrect inferences.

The "taking-a-vote" procedure is particularly open to wrong inferences of this kind. It almost invariably focuses upon the main effect of each variable in isolation from any other potentially interactive factors. Unless the original studies specifically computed significance levels for individual interactions, and reported them, taking a vote can never find such interactions on its own. No procedure can detect a relationship it cannot represent.

Illustrations from the Educational Literature

Four examples, taken from the educational research literature, illustrate the difficulties and contradictions which may arise when studies are combined in order to assess the value of an educational practice. Our four examples deal with controversial issues in education: ability grouping, school resources, compensatory programs, and school integration.

Example 1—Ability Grouping

There is no shortage of studies of the effects of ability grouping on academic achievement. A number of summaries of this literature are available. One of the best of these is the United States Department of Health, Education and Welfare's survey.[7] Their summary of the condition of the field seems to be a fair one. They say:

---

[7] Jane Franseth and Rose Koury, *Survey of Research on Grouping as Related to Pupil Learning* (Washington, D. C.: U. S. Government Printing Office, 1966), p. 2. Other reviews of this same issue are, Miriam L. Goldberg, A. Harry Passow, and Joseph Justman, *The Effects of Ability Grouping* (New York: Teachers College Press, Columbia University, 1966); and War-

Many studies throughout the years have compared academic progress of children grouped according to ability with progress made when grouped heterogeneously. Conclusive and definite answers to questions commonly asked are difficult to get. Some studies show gains favoring ability grouping, some favoring heterogeneous grouping. Others show little or no significant difference in pupil gains between procedures used. The evidence against or in favor of ability grouping remains vague in spite of a rather persistent belief that learning problems would be greatly alleviated if children on similar levels of ability or achievement could be grouped together for instructional purposes. Olson tells us that: 'Surveys of achievement demonstrate that no matter how children are grouped, they still learn in accordance with their individual abilities.'

However, the problem of securing optimal working groups continues, and as Wilhelms says, ". . . many good minds have worked at it in various ways, and a satisfying solution has not yet been found."

The authors deal with the problem of conflicting studies by examining each member of the conflicting group, and selecting one upon which to place their trust. The conclusions of this "best" study are then adopted. This may be an excellent strategy if only one among the many studies is qualitatively acceptable. However, it is rare that only a single study is well done. Even after untrustworthy studies have been eliminated, contradictory conclusions may remain among the contenders. If the elimination process is continued until only one study is left, then an equivalent of the "taking-a-vote" procedure has been carried to an extreme. The eligible votes (the studies under review) have been reduced to one, and we agree to abide by its decision. *To be satisfied with this approach is tacitly to assume that genuinely contradictory results can never be a valid description of reality.* Would we really be so surprised to find that one kind of ability grouping benefited children in one school, but that a similar program failed to benefit comparable children in a different school? Nature may be consistent, but to assume that her consistency has been captured exactly in current research is a rather strong assumption.[8] As we argue later, it is not a particularly credible one.

---

ren G. Findlay and Miriam M. Bryan, *Ability Grouping* (Athens: Center for Educational Development, University of Georgia, 1970).

[8] We leave to philosophers of science the question of whether laws of nature can ever be self-contradictory. But in social science research we never directly observe laws of nature. The conceptual objects in which we try to capture a description of empirical or observed evidence are theories. These theories are the creation of men. When an educational research effort is mounted in Yonkers, its conclusions may well be a parsimonious description of the data from Yonkers. A different study in Hackensack, encountering a new set of data, may summarize that data

Example 2—School Resources

In the second example, the compilers of research results took a rather different approach. Prior to the Equal Educational Opportunity (E.E.O.) survey reported in 1966, the conventional wisdom among both educators and laymen was that the amount of school resources was highly related to students' achievement. The E.E.O. survey suggested the contrary.[9] In an extensive re-analysis of the E.E.O. data and data from other surveys, researchers at the Center for Educational Policy Research (C.E.P.R.) at Harvard confronted the contradictions head on.[10] Their report stated:

One of us (Michelson) believes he has found evidence that certain school resources have a significant effect on achievement. The rest of us are unconvinced by his evidence and convinced by other evidence that the contrary is the case.

The basis for our skepticism is *not* our inability to find "statistically significant" relationships between selected school resources and student achievement. Such relationships can be found, and a few of them persist even after the background of the students has been controlled. Rather, our skepticism arises from the fact that the school resources which have a non-random relationship to achievement are never the same from one survey to another, from one group of schools to another, from one method of analysis to another, or

---

with a *different* parsimonious description. The likeliest explanation for any contradiction is *not* that laws of nature change when the Hudson River is crossed. But neither is it that *nothing* changes when the River is crossed, and that one of the two studies is merely a statistical quirk. Rather the most likely explanation begins with the assumption that some independent variables are different in Yonkers and Hackensack. The extreme case would be where some variable (e.g., the degree of bureaucratization of the central school administration) was constant within each city, but differed sharply between the two cities. If such a variable interacted with others in determining the dependent variable, the conclusions from the two research studies are *too* parsimonious. Since a key variable was constant within each of the two studies, a description of each school system, developed separately, would have ignored it. Thus, both descriptions would have been wrong. What are the implications of this situation for the combining of studies? First, any method which tries to choose one of the two studies as being the correct one is merely choosing which of two mistakes to make. Second, any method which tries to stitch together the two conclusions without confronting the discrepancy is in some respects even worse. Errors of theory are different from errors of measurement in that averaging many of these will not, in general, lead to "cancelling out." The cost of such averaging is not only that the resulting theory is incorrect; it is that the one opportunity to detect the omissions in the original "parsimonious" descriptions has been thrown away. Only by returning to the two original sets of data and looking for explanations for differences between them is there any hope of discovering the presence of an important and omitted variable.

[9] James S. Coleman, *et al., Equality of Educational Opportunity* (Washington, D. C.: U. S. Government Printing Office, 1966).

[10] Christopher Jencks, *et al., Education and Inequality: A Preliminary Report to the Carnegie Corporation of New York* (Cambridge, Mass.: Center for Educational Policy Research, Harvard University, 1970), pp. 52-53.

from one type of student to another. While it is always possible to invent explanations of these differences after the fact, the necessary explanations become progressively more far-fetched.

These findings are subject to several possible interpretations. One interpretation is that resources have important effects on achievement, but that the nature of these effects varies according to the type of student, the type of school, the type of community, the other resources available, and many other unknown factors. The other interpretation is that resources are allocated in different ways in different communities, that these allocation processes have a non-random relationship to achievement, and that this creates a spurious impression that resources are affecting achievement in some instances. Because resource allocation varies according to all kinds of local and regional considerations, no consistent pattern emerges.

Thus, rather than selecting a "favorite study," the C.E.P.R. Report allowed for the possibility of real variation in how schools work from place to place. If one wanted to pursue the nature of this variation further, the cluster approach suggested later in this paper provides a vehicle.

Example 3—Compensatory Education

In 1965, Congress passed Title I of the Elementary and Secondary Education Act. Its purpose was to distribute funds to school systems for the special educational needs of disadvantaged children. Not surprisingly, a number of evaluations of the effects of Title I have been undertaken. What, then, has been the overall impact of Title I? Has it "worked"? Cohen, in his critical review of these evaluations, quotes the following passage from an Office of Education study of pre- and post-test scores in big-city Title I programs[11]:

For the total 189 observations (each observation was one classroom in a Title I program), there were 108 significant changes (exceed 2 s. e.).[12] Of these 58 were gains and 50 were losses. In 81 cases the change did not appear to be significant. As the data in Appendix D show, success and failure seem to be random outcomes, determined neither clearly nor consistently by the factors of program design, city or state, area or grade level.

In fact, do such results seem to be "random outcomes"? Has Title I no effects except those attributable to natural sampling variability? Accepting the summary of the 189 studies given above, the answer is that Title I has pronounced

[11] David K. Cohen, "The Politics of Evaluation," in *Review of Educational Research*, 40 (April 1970), p. 224.
[12] A standard error is the standard deviation of the sampling distribution of the relevant statistic.

TABLE 1

Review of Effects of Integration on School Performance Taken from Summaries of 22 Studies

| | | EXPERIMENTAL CONDITIONS OR DESIGN | | | | | | | | OUTCOMES | | |
| | | | Control Group Comparison | | Matching Comparison | | Control for Covariates | | | Gains Favoring Integrated Schools | | |
City	State	Survey	Non-Random Design	Random Design	Matching Comparison Pairs	SIBS	Pretest	SES	Others	Verbal	Reading	Math
Boston (a)	Mass.	✓			✓					o		+
Boston (b)	Mass.						✓			+	o	o
Hartford	Conn.			✓			✓			o		o
Cheshire	Conn.			✓			✓			+	+	
Riverside	Calif.	✓	✓				✓			o		o
	Miss.	✓	✓							+	o	+
	Calif.									+	o	+
Pittsburgh	Pa.		✓				✓	✓	✓	+	o	+
Ann Arbor	Mich.		✓				✓	✓	✓	o	o	o
Springfield	Mass.		✓		✓		✓			o	−	
Chapel Hill	N.C.		✓							+		−
Oklahoma City	Okla.		✓			✓	✓	✓	✓	+		+
(Tennessee)							✓	✓	✓	+		+
New Rochelle	N.Y.		✓				✓			o		o
White Plains	N.Y.			✓						+		o
Rochester	N.Y.		✓				✓	✓	✓	o		+
Syracuse	N.Y.		✓				✓	✓	✓	+	+	
Buffalo	N.Y.		✓		✓					o		o
Philadelphia	Pa.		✓							+		+
Berkeley	Calif.						✓	✓	✓	o	+	o
New York City	N.Y.		✓		✓		✓	✓	✓	+	+	o
Richmond	Calif.				✓		✓			o		o

effects. A "random outcomes" explanation is incorrect. If in fact Title I programs consistently have no effect, then random samples evaluating these programs would show a false positive result two and a half percent of the time, and a false negative result two and a half percent of the time. Thus, if Title I had no effect, out of 189 evaluations we would expect about 5 significant gains and about 5 significant losses using the 2 standard error criterion given in the original study.

Instead, 58 significant gains and 50 significant losses were found. The abundance of significant results in both directions exceeds that expected from sampling variability by an overwhelming amount. Thus, the assumption that Title I consistently has no effects is wrong. Further, the assumption that Title I programs have any *single* effect, positive or negative, would be equally wrong. The only reasonable interpretation of the 189 evaluations is that the effects of Title I programs differ, and they differ systematically from school system to school system. The purpose of combining many studies is to secure an amount and kind of information that would not be available from any one study. Approaching this task with the point of view that there is a single truth (e.g., a single effect of Title I), surrounded only by sampling variability, is not productive. Our conclusion from the data above is that there are several truths. Title I programs vary in their effects; some help, some hurt, and some make no difference at all.[13]

Example 4—School Integration

Another area where the conclusions of various studies conflict is the effect of school integration on the achievement of Black children. We examined the studies reported in two recent reviews of this literature in order to determine whether any results consistently emerged.[14] We believe the reader can share something of our experience by looking through Table 1. Table 1 gives a condensed summary of some features of all the studies found in the two reviews.

Each study was confined to a single city. Each row gives information about one

[13] For the case of Title I, it is clear that there is no such thing as a "standard" Title I program. The programs vary among states, and among school systems within a state. Thus, the 189 programs were probably not directly comparable in the first place, as they involved the manipulation of different sets of independent variables. Our discussion assumed, for the sake of illustration, that the programs were comparable in both their goals and instrumentation. Cohen, *op. cit.*, indicates clearly that Title I does not meet this assumption.

[14] Nancy H. St. John, "Desegregation and Minority Group Performance," *Review of Educational Research*, 40 (February 1970); and Robert P. O'Reilly, ed., *Racial and Social Class Isolation in the Schools* (New York: Praeger, 1970).

study. A check in any column indicates the presence, for that study, of the feature of experimental design which labels that column. The columns for the dependent variables are coded plus or minus for significantly positive or negative results respectively; zero for non-significant results; and a blank where no finding was reported. The variety of experimental techniques used and measures taken over the 22 studies was enormous.

Is there anything one can conclude from Table 1 about the effects of integration upon the school performance of Black children? Perhaps the one conclusion to which we are led is that the contradictions among the studies are more striking than the similarities. The two studies from Boston, for example, examined the same bussing program. One found significant gains for mathematics achievement, but not for verbal achievement. The other found significant gains for verbal achievement, but not for mathematics achievement. In two neighboring towns in Connecticut, rather similar sophisticated experimental designs again led to opposing conclusions. In one, significant gains in reading and mathematics were reported. The other found no such gains. The reader can surely find other contradictions in Table 1.

The lesson that we believe flows from this and our three previous examples is that little headway can be made by pooling the *words in the conclusions* of a set of studies. Rather, progress will only come when we are able to pool, in a systematic manner, the original data from the studies.

What Makes Educational Research Special

From one point of view, there should be no difficulty in combining the original data from a series of education studies. A broad repertoire of classical statistical procedures is available. However, classical statistical procedures have not yet been fully adapted to the world we encounter when we enter the nation's classrooms.

Oversimplifying a bit, it is worth recalling that classical statistical procedures grew out of research conducted in the field of agronomy. But the processes of growth of plants have some special features which are obviously different from and often simpler than the processes of growth of children. Three examples will serve to contrast the agricultural processes, which are represented in statistical models, with the educational processes which are not.

First, when combining studies in educational research, we must allow for an extensive battery of treatment-by-subject interactions that could be safely ignored in agricultural research. A treatment, when applied in an agricultural setting, can usually be evenly distributed over the plants. For example, when fertilizer is added to a field, we can generally assume that the individual nitrates will not decide to lurk about the roots of selected pea plants in preference to others.

A similar asumption cannot be made about teachers. Individual teachers in a classroom may well, choose to spend somewhat more time with certain children than with other children. Such variations in teachers' behavior towards several children may reflect an educational philosophy, a personal philosophy, or the nature of a curriculum being tested. But the main point here is that the teacher is a human being: he or she has the ability to gather information about members of a group, and to differentiate among the members through actions based on that information. This ability of the "treatment" (assuming here that a teacher is a "treatment") to have or to gain as much information about the subjects as the researchers can gain is a special feature of the educational setting.

Second, in educational research, each specific site (e.g., a classroom) may have systematic (and in part unmeasured) differences from neighboring sites. In agricultural experimentation, one small and randomly selected patch of earth near another usually has characteristics that closely resemble those of its neighbor. The change in the composition of the soil chemicals with distance from a certain point is generally slow, and it is rare that a cloud rains heavily on a randomly selected square foot of land without getting its neighbors a bit wet. In educational research, however, two adjacent classrooms in a single school may differ from one another extensively, and in ways that are often difficult to measure. Two adjacent classrooms in the same school may well resemble classrooms located elsewhere in the nation much more closely than they resemble each other.

A third contrast between agricultural and educational research settings involves the importance of contextual effects. It is rather straightforward to deal with the fact that each plant grows in a context of other plants. Experimenters sometimes take note of the fact that planting density may affect crop yield, or that combinations of two or three plants grown in parallel rows are particularly effective, but these are rather simple concerns in agronomy. In contrast, educational researchers generally need to elevate the composition of a classroom into a variable of primary concern. Two common examples of compositional variables are the degree of racial integration of classrooms within a school, and the "characteristic academic or vocational milieu of a school." Thus, when combining educational studies, we must allow for the presence of a rather complex sort of interaction. A treatment value for a specific child may be related to the numbers or proportions of other types of children present in a classroom.

The Cluster Approach: A Perspective for Combining Studies

We have just pointed out that there are broad distinctions between processes at work in a classroom and in a cornfield. In view of these differences, we now will develop a perspective tailored specifically to educational settings that strengthens our ability to draw rich inferences from a set of educational studies.[15]

The argument will proceed in four stages. First, we describe a cluster sample, which is a direct outgrowth of standard sampling theory. Second, we re-interpret the idea of a "cluster" for specific use in educational settings.[16] Third, we develop a small illustrative example of a set of preschool studies that we draw upon throughout this section. Fourth, we outline the major ways in which clusters can differ from one another. The thrust of the analysis we offer is towards what John Tukey calls "exploratory data analysis." We mean to search out candidate explanations for the results observed in a set of existing studies.

We remind the reader that the purpose of everything that follows is not only to represent educational processes more accurately; the purpose is also to help resolve seeming contradictions among several studies. The ideas presented in this section will illustrate that different studies may well reach opposing conclusions without logically contradicting each other. It will thus be possible to draw from a set of seemingly conflicting studies inferences of a kind otherwise unavailable to us.

Generalizing an Approach from Cluster Sampling

The conventional idea of combining studies is rooted in a simple assumption. This assumption is that each study can be viewed as a random sample taken from a common population. Thus, the set of studies are viewed as several differ-

---

[15] The general issue of combining studies can occur in two broad settings. We have already discussed one of them: combining a number of different studies, frequently done by different researchers, at different places, at different times. A situation which is often viewed as different, but which we believe is substantively the same, can be described as "multi-local" studies. A multi-local study occurs when a single team of researchers collects similar data from a number of different sampling units, or clusters, where, for example, clusters are schools. The procedures we outline in the remainder of this paper apply to both multiple and multi-local studies.

[16] In what follows, the term "cluster approach" will appear often. We use it because the procedures we present are adaptations from cluster sampling. Perhaps a more appropriate term might be *latitudinal approach*. Since longitudinal analysis refers to repeated measurements on some phenomena over time *within* a study, a symmetric interpretation of latitudinal analysis would refer to the investigation of some phenomena *across* a set of various studies. Further, the latitudinal approach will allow for several kinds of differences among the various studies, which standard cross-sectional procedures do not.

ent random samples from the same population. Statisticians, however, have developed a slightly different approach called cluster sampling. This approach stems from a pragmatic insight: that many populations can be broken down into small, identifiable sub-populations which are called clusters. These clusters are not random samples from a population; rather, they are *natural aggregations* within the population, and they usually differ in broad and systematic ways. For example, suppose we wanted to estimate mean family income in the United States. We could then assume in advance that incomes of neighbors living on the same block would tend to be more similar than would incomes of two people selected at random from the population as a whole. A cluster sampling design would thus define a neighborhood as a cluster, and would allow for systematic differences in mean income among neighborhoods.[17]

For survey researchers, the primary virtue of cluster sampling is that it allows data collection to be concentrated in a few conveniently "compact" regions, such as neighborhoods. The cost of data collection is therefore reduced. An almost incidental feature of cluster sampling is that clusters are assumed to differ one from another in ways that are not reflected in the variations within any one cluster. Conversely, variations within clusters need not be reflected in variation among them. We now capitalize on this view of clustering to develop a framework for combining sets of studies.

Suppose we have a set of educational studies. Where do we find the clusters? We should take as a cluster the smallest natural unit of the educational process which is available in the data. The choice of a natural unit will depend upon the research questions at issue. Very broad studies might settle for an entire school as their clustering unit. Other studies might require classrooms, or even reading groups within classrooms, to be taken as clusters.

For example, when research questions are directed towards the effects of tracking, each individual tracked classroom can be taken as an independent cluster. On the other hand, when early reading instruction is the focus of research, the reading groups within classrooms are the logical choice for a clustering unit. The crucial point is that whatever unit is chosen to be a cluster, it should be the

---

[17] The statistical theory underlying cluster sampling has been developed extensively. For two detailed treatments of this topic, see W. G. Cochran, *Sampling Techniques,* second edition (New York: John Wiley and Sons, 1963); also, Leslie Kish, *Survey Sampling* (New York: McGraw Hill, 1965

natural focal point or molar unit of whatever educational process we are investigating.[18]

A cluster is, therefore, often not a complete study. Generally, each study in a set to be combined will contain several individual clusters, such as several classrooms. Notice how this differs from the procedures we discussed earlier, such as "taking a vote," where a complete study was the unit of analysis. Now, when there is more than one treatment per study, the set of treatments compose our set of clusters. Thus, a study will often contain several clusters, and the cluster is the unit of analysis.

An Illustrative Example

Throughout the rest of this paper we will develop a perspective for combining studies which grows from the concept of a cluster sample. Doing this will require the illustration of many specific points. For simplicity, we will use a single hypothetical example throughout.[19]

Assume we are interested in helping to develop "reading readiness" among preschool children. We wish to focus on the effects on reading readiness of four different kinds of programs:

1. day care centers;
2. Head Start centers;
3. Montessori programs;
4. pre-kindergartens.

---

[18] The question may arise whether a single child can be considered a cluster. In a logical sense, the answer should be yes, as an individual child may be the specific focal point of an educational program. Here, we will generally not consider an individual child as a cluster because of a methodological limitation: within-cluster variance must be estimated, and with a single child this cannot be done. Fortunately, even when a specific child is the focus of a research effort, there are many questions that can be asked without defining a child as a cluster. For example, in a case where teachers differentiate among children in a classroom, we can still ask whether the kind and extent of the differentiation is similar among many classrooms. The natural focal point for this educational process (differentiated instruction) is the classroom.

[19] In the earlier discussion we mentioned that one difficulty in combining studies may be that all studies in a set did not measure the same independent variables. In our hypothetical illustration, we will assume that all studies, and all clusters within each study, have comparable data. In practice, when studies do not have comparable data, the approach we recommend must be carried out in two steps. The first step involves comparing those clusters which have similar measurements. The second step is to compare measures which were similar among sets of studies that also contained non-comparable measures.

(Assume all preschool programs have been classified into one of these four categories. Variations within each type will be considered in detail later.) Suppose there exist in the literature five studies. Altogether, the five studies contain twelve sites. A breakdown of which studies contain which sites is given in Figure 1. Here we define a cluster as an individual site.[20] Thus, the cluster perspective focuses our attention on the twelve preschools rather than the five studies.

Each of the twelve sites contains a group of children. For each child at each site, we have a measurement on the dependent variable: reading readiness. Further, for each child we have data on two continuous independent variables: a count of children's books in his home, and a pretest score. We also know each child's sex. We have, then, data on four variables.

The cluster approach requires access to the original data from these studies. Assuming the data are available, the first step is to group this information into the twelve "clusters." Thus, at the inception of our analysis, there would be four measures on each child assembled into twelve separate groups. Notice an important point: we cannot assume the data we are analyzing came from a true experiment. In a true experiment, all the children would have been assembled into a single large group, pretested, and then randomly assigned among the twelve sites.[21] In the real world, however, when the results of disparate studies are to be combined, we know that no such group was assembled in advance, and that no such randomization took place. In a realistic case, also, there would have been one more preliminary step. The *quality* of the available studies from the literature (e.g., our five preschool studies) would have been reviewed. The studies accepted for further analysis would be only those which met the following three standards:

a) All subjects in the study must have been selected from a known and precisely definable population.

[20] What we have done, in our preschool example, in choosing to identify the site as a cluster, is a consequence of our previous discussion that educational research often involves locales that can differ from one another substantially, even if they are close in space. Thus the fact that several centers from our preschool studies were initially designated as a certain type of preschool can be overridden by the assumption that they may differ in important ways.

[21] As we have indicated, the cluster approach grows out of the basic concepts of cluster sampling. However, the analogy is not perfect. In cluster sampling, one assumes that the selected clusters constitute a random sample from a population of similar clusters. Here, we *know* that the clusters taken from the several studies are *not* a random sample. Thus, the statistical procedures we later recommend are not based on the probability model underlying cluster sampling. That model would have led to using procedures such as random effects ANOVAs. Instead, the procedures we discuss will be primarily fixed effects ANOVAs and multiple regressions which presume arbitrary values for the independent variables or their categorizations.

		Study Number			
	1	2	3	4	5
Head Start	A	B	C		
Day care	A	B			C
Preschool type					
Montessori			A	B,C,D	
Pre-kindergarten			A		B

FIGURE 1.

Location of the Twelve Preschools in the Five Studies for Illustrative Example

b) A study's dependent variables and those independent variables which are measured must be measured in the same way as, or in a way subject to a conversion into, those employed in the rest of the studies.

c) Overall, the instrumentation and quality of the experimental work in a study must be generally comparable to that in all the rest of the studies.[22]

What Research Questions Can Be Asked?

In the preschool example, the standard research strategy would lead to the question: "Which of the four types of preschool programs offers the greatest improvement in children's reading readiness?" The cluster formulation permits a much richer analysis.

Twelve clusters have been identified. These twelve clusters can differ in a variety of ways. Our research question now takes the form, "In what ways do these twelve clusters differ from one another, and of the ways in which they do differ, which can be identified with differences among the four types of preschool?" The essence of the cluster approach is to turn the first research question

---

[22] There is always a question when studies differ as to whether the differences are due primarily to genuine phenomena or merely to "instrumentation." For example, studies done by different experimenters may show clear "experimenter effects." There is no a priori way to assign such effects either to the category of instrumental differences or to the category of real cluster to cluster differences. This assignment will depend largely upon the judgment of the person combining studies. If he believes that some experimenters committed errors which invalidate their data, then he will discard their studies as instances of instrumental errors. A different researcher may be willing and even eager to accept data from different studies which he knows reflect experimenter effects. From this latter perspective, differences attributable to the specific investigator in each cluster have a status identical to differences attributable to primary phenomena, such as different teachers in classrooms, or different mean levels of attention as measured in several preschools.

into the second. By converting the research question, we can gain new insights into whatever educational processes are at work, and can avoid being tied down to the relatively weak results of a simple tally of significance tests.

What additional questions might a researcher wish to ask, given these data? One might be, "Were the children selectively assigned, or attracted, to the different sites in the first place?" A second might be, "Is the relationship between pre- and post-test scores identical in all twelve sites?" A third and more sophisticated question might be, "Are the variations in the differences between boys' and girls' reading readiness from site to site associated with the four program types?"

There are many other research questions one may wish to ask. A general format is needed to summarize the comparisons implied by such questions. Further, we want a format where apparent contradictions in the conclusions of the five original studies can be examined, and perhaps resolved. The necessary next step, then, is to classify the ways clusters can differ systematically.

How Clusters Can Differ

A group of clusters can differ in at least the following five ways: they can differ in the means of their variables, in the variances of their variables, in the relations between the independent and dependent variables, in the child by treatment interactions, and in a more complex manner where each child is affected by the composition of his or her group. These five kinds of differences are not mutually exclusive. A set of clusters (such as the twelve preschools) may differ on any or all of these.

In the following sections we discuss the five kinds of differences in turn. After defining and illustrating each difference with an example, we discuss what action can be taken, or conclusion drawn, from statistical evidence about these differences. But there is a degree of asymmetry in the way the presence versus absence of differences is handled. If any one of the five types of differences is found, it follows that the clusters are not all alike, and therefore cannot be directly combined. On the other hand, finding that clusters do not differ in any one respect does not lead to the conclusion that they are alike until *all five* of the ways in which clusters can differ have been examined. Further, even if clusters are found to differ in, say, means, one must still search out other possible differences if only to explain the variation among means. We deal with this point in more detail shortly. Let us now examine the five ways clusters can differ.

1. *Means*

The simplest way clusters can differ is in the means of variables. But why are such differences important? They are important because the nature of any differences will play a large part in determining how our data is analyzed and combined. For example, if the twelve reading readiness pretest means differ, we are not able to make direct comparisons among the four types of preschools. On the other hand, such differences may be worth studying in their own right if they suggest that different types of children are being attracted to different types of programs. These are called selection effects.

Suppose on the other hand the twelve pretest means do not differ. Then there is no direct evidence for selection effects. If no substantial differences are observed among the final reading readiness scores, at least within each of the four preschool types, then we can combine the clusters which make up each preschool type.

What do we gain by being able to combine clusters? As indicated earlier, we gain the advantages of a much larger overall sample size, which leads to greater power in comparing the four preschool types. This increase in power is the ultimate purpose of any method for combining studies. There are two advantages of reaching this point by way of the cluster approach. First, we would have detected any selection effects that might have invalidated a comparison among the four programs. *Second, and even more important, we will have tested the validity of the classification of all twelve preschools into the four program types.* Had differences been found among the final readiness means of, say, the four Montessori centers, we would not have combined the data from these four centers. Rather, we would have sought an explanation for the differences in performance among the Montessori centers. Conventional approaches for combining studies do not include such an examination of the validity of the classifications employed.[23]

---

[23] This last point deserves a bit of amplification. A primary problem we are discussing in this paper is the different results which replicated studies can display. An alternative way of saying a replicated study has failed is to say that the supposedly identical treatment, applied twice, had different consequences for the children each time. We are building into the cluster perspective an opportunity to examine whether or not supposedly similar "treatments" (that is, clusters which are supposedly exposed to identical conditions) do in fact have similar effects on the children. A method which combines studies by using a procedure that assumes treatments thought to be similar are in fact similar would obviously fail to detect unexpected differences among supposedly comparable treatments.

Let us mention briefly the specific procedures used to carry out the search for differences among cluster means. The standard procedure for comparing a group of cluster means is the F test from the traditional one-way analysis of variance.[24] This test assumes that the variation in readiness scores within each cluster is the natural measure for variation due to chance alone. There is good reason for confidence in this assumption when working with a true experimental design. However, as pointed out earlier, our children from the five studies were not assigned to the twelve preschools at random. Thus, chance is only one among several competing explanations for the variation within each preschool. This remains true even if no selection effects are detected.

2. Variances.

A second way that clusters can differ is by having different within-cluster variances for some variables. Researchers naturally tend to look first for differences among means. However, even when means are alike, other important differences may exist. Suppose, for example, two particular preschool programs produced similar mean reading readiness for groups of children that were originally similar. Imagine, however, that one program enlarged the variation among its children, while the other did not. From a policy point of view, then, the two programs are clearly not interchangeable.

Finding that clusters have different variances thus may be important in its own right. If such differences are found, can we combine clusters? The answer may be yes, but only if a tenable explanation for the differing variances can be identified. (When an explanation for the differences is found, statistical adjustments can be made that will equate the clusters.) What are some possible explanations for differing variances among clusters? We give three here. Readers may easily add to this list.

a. *Initial selection decisions.* Children entering the different preschool programs may have been differentially attracted or selected. Differences among pre-

[24] An alternative procedure is available for comparing cluster means. That alternative is the computation of the intracluster correlation coefficient. Computational details for the general case where cluster sizes differ are given in M. G. Kendall and A. Stuart, *The Advanced Theory of Statistics* (New York: Hafner, 1967). While the intracluster correlation is generally less well known than the standard F test, it provides a useful index. The index describes how the variation among data can be partitioned within and between clusters. Its virtue is that it describes the structure of this partition without being affected by absolute sample sizes. For example, if day care centers were generally large, while Head Start centers were small, F ratios might differ if computed separately for the two groups. This would be true even if the partition of variance was identical for the two program types. The two corresponding intracluster correlation coefficients would be identical.

schools in their selectivity often take the form of more selective preschools having higher initial cutoff points for admission.[25] Under this form of selection, the more selective preschools will have higher means and smaller variances in reading readiness scores. Other forms of selection can also lead to differing variances.

b. *The effect of cumulative learning.* Many forms of learning are cumulative. What is learned at one moment may depend upon the amount a child has already learned. A rather simple form of such a cumulative learning process acts as an amplifier for original differences among individual children. Two children enter a program with different amounts of initial knowledge. What each child learns is proportionate to what he already knows. The result will be to increase the absolute difference in knowledge between the two children. On the whole, then, all children in such a program will be spread further apart at the end of the program than when they first entered. Thus, the variance in final scores is larger than the variance in initial scores. The increase in variance is related to the proportion by which each child's initial score has been amplified. Preschool programs may differ in the degree to which their curricula depend upon amplifiers. A highly cumulative curriculum will tend to produce large amplification. These differences in amplifications are reflected in differences in variance.

c. *Differential sensitization of children by programs.* Some preschool programs may increase the sensitivity of children to out-of-school differences in their lives. Their reactions may well be reflected in their school performances. For example, all children do not have the same number of books to read in their homes. In a program that depends heavily on outside reading materials, the more of these a child has the better he does. Thus, such programs sensitize children to differences in reading materials in their homes. A program in another preschool may not have a strong linkage between a child's home reading materials and his final reading readiness. This second program, instead of sensitizing children to differences in home reading materials, might lead to roughly comparable gains in reading readiness for all children. The first program, then, increases the variance in performance by tying a child's final performance back to an outside source of variation, such as home reading materials. The second program, that does not sensitize children, does not increase the variance in their final performances. Thus, if different preschool programs differ in the degree to which they sensitize

---

[25] Some preschools have rather formal admissions procedures which involve readiness tests, or some sort of scaled judgments. But a simpler and more widespread admission selector, or criterion, is the amount of tuition charged.

children, that fact may appear in our data as differing reading readiness variances.

Choosing among explanations such as these remains the job of a clinical investigator. *The crucial point here is that the cluster approach at least allows us to detect the fact that there is something to explain.* If we found, for example, that four Montessori centers differed in their selectivity, or their dependence on amplification or sensitization, our conclusion would be that they should not be lumped together as a single program type. They differ in important ways. Adopting the cluster perspective has allowed us to verify the consistency of the program classifications, which other methods of combining data can only assume.[26]

To test statistically whether variances differ, a well-known procedure called Bartlett's Test is available. It examines the null hypothesis of equal variances for any number of clusters. As in the rest of this paper, we will omit here the statistical and computational details in order to concentrate on the fundamental concepts that guide the testing.[27]

To conclude, let us review what we have gained by using the procedures discussed so far. First, we have been forced to examine whether similarly "titled" programs (e.g., Head Start, or Montessori preschools) really work the same way. Second, if they are the same, we can combine their data with some confidence that we are not burying contradictions in our conclusions. If they differ, we are led to ask fundamental theoretical questions about why they differ.[28] These

[26] It should be pointed out here that while the cluster approach may permit the combining of several sites into the equivalent of a single large site, this combining should only be done within a single program type. Thus, the data from four Montessori schools can be combined, but the four Montessori schools should not yet be combined with, say, the three Head Start centers, even if no differences among the two sets of clusters are found. Only after different sites within a single typology are combined can this complete typology be compared to another complete typology. If the pooled data from the two typologies is again found to be operationally equivalent, it would be reasonable to combine them. Notice that this leads to an ordered set of tests which locate the existence of differences within a hierarchical framework.

[27] The details of Bartlett's test are given in B. J. Winer, *Statistical Principles in Experimental Design* (New York: McGraw Hill, 1962). It is worth remembering that non-significant results do not "prove" that clusters are alike. They merely indicate that sample sizes were too small to detect whatever differences may exist. Many other procedures discussed here also have "reversed hypotheses." They are "reversed" in the sense that "accepting" a null hypothesis does not *prove* the consistency of a typology (a grouping of clusters as similar).

[28] The hope of course is that we will find a theoretically satisfying explanation of why cluster variances differ. If such an explanation is found, it will usually lead to an adjustment that will remove the differences from the data. Such adjustments are often either transformations of the data, or covariate adjustments within each cluster. We *must* remove differences among clusters in order to use procedures such as the analysis of variance to make overall comparisons among preschool types. Why, if these differences are left intact, can't the standard analysis of variance

questions might not have occurred to us in advance. Third, because each cluster is isolated and examined separately, the procedures not only detect effects; they also display the scope of those effects. For example, if a relationship between means and variances of clusters appears, one can immediately see whether it holds for all clusters, or only for specific program types.

3. *Introducing Covariates.*

A third way that clusters can differ is in the relationship between a dependent variable (e.g., reading readiness score) and one or more covariates. A covariate is an independent, "auxiliary" variable which is related to the dependent variable. For example, the number of books in a child's home might be related to his reading readiness. In educational research, two assumptions about covariates are generally made. First, the relationship between a covariate and the dependent variable is assumed to be linear. Second, this relationship is assumed to be the same in every study, or treatment group. Combining a set of studies using the cluster approach allows a questioning of the second assumption. It allows for differences in the relationship between the covariates and dependent variables from cluster to cluster. Thus, in the preschool example, reading readiness might be highly related to home book counts in some clusters, and less so in others. Previously we have characterized this phenomenon as "differential sensitization."

Let us pursue this example in a bit more detail. The data in Figure 2 illustrate the linear relations we might find when children's reading readiness is related to their home book count for the four Montessori centers and the two pre-kindergartens. Notice that the four equations for the Montessori schools differ slightly one from another, but are essentially similar. The equations for the two pre-kindergartens also resemble one another. The two sets of equations, however, are quite different.[29] (We remind the reader the data in Figure 2 is hypothetical. We do not know what relationships exist in real preschools at this time.)

---

be used? First, the analysis of variance depends upon having a "clean" source of chance variation against which to compare differences among overall means. If additional variation is confounded with the "clean" variance, the power of the ANOVA will be reduced, possibly to the point where real differences between programs go unobserved. Second, the ANOVA assumes that being in a program has the effect of changing each child's score by a fixed amount. But the unadjusted source of variation cannot be a uniform constant. The addition of a constant never changes the variance of a set of scores. Thus, the presence of the unaccountable source of variance fundamentally contradicts the model of effects assumed by the standard additive ANOVA.

[29] The standard computations and statistical tests for the analysis of covariance are given in Maurice M Tatsuoka, *Multivariate Analysis: Techniques for Educational and Psychological*

	Montessori Schools		Pre-kindergartens
A:	Y = 60 + 2.4X	A:	Y = 36 + 5.1X
B:	Y = 58 + 2.3X	B:	Y = 35 + 5.3X
C:	Y = 61 + 2.5X		
D:	Y = 62 + 2.3X		

In the above six equations, X represents home book count and Y represents final reading readiness.

FIGURE 2.

Illustration of Use of Covariates

What do the six equations indicate? The Montessori preschools have multipliers (b coefficients) which are half the size of those for the pre-kindergartens. This indicates that the two kinds of programs differ in the extent to which they are "converting" a child's home library into reading readiness. The size of a child's library plays a greater role in the pre-kindergartens than in the Montessori schools. Thus, the pre-kindergartens are "sensitizing" their children to differences in this home resource far more than are the Montessori preschools.

Research (New York: John Wiley and Sons, 1971), Chapter 3. An alternative approach, suggested by D. Gujarati, "Use of Dummy Variables in Testing for Equality between Sets of Coefficients in Two Linear Regressions: A Note," *The American Statistician*, 24 (February 1970), pp. 50-52, allows us to use dummy variables and a standard regression program to make an equivalent test. Extensions to more than one covariate and two groups are given by Gujarati in "Use of Dummy Variables between Sets of Coefficients in Linear Regression: A Generalization," *The American Statistician*, 24, (December 1970). We outline the procedure for the case of a single covariate and k clusters. Assume a standard regression program is available. Let y_{ij} and x_{ij} be the dependent variable and the covariate value respectively for the ith child in the jth cluster. One cluster is selected, arbitrarily if necessary, to set as a baseline. Call that the kth cluster. The Gujarati procedure tests whether any of the other k-1 clusters have regression lines which differ from that in the kth cluster. For each child, k-1 dummy variables are coded; d_{iju} representing the uth dummy variable for the ith child in the jth cluster. This dummy variable is one when u = j; otherwise $d_{iju} = 0$. Thus all children in the baseline cluster will have all their d's equalling zero; all children in other clusters will have exactly one d equalling one. Similarly for each child define c_{iju} where $c_{iju} = x_{ij} \, d_{iju}$. These variables are zero except for the one which corresponds to the cluster in which any child is located, when the variable equals the covariate measurement for that child. Children in the baseline cluster have all their $c_{iju} = 0$. We thus have 2k independent variables; a constant, the covariate x_{ij}, k-1 d_{iju}'s, and k-1 c_{iju}'s. The standard regression of y_{ij} on these 2k variables is now run, and t values for the significantly nonzero coefficients are computed. We conclude that the covariate relationship in the uth cluster differs from that in the baseline cluster if either of the corresponding d_{iju} or c_{iju} is significant. A difficulty with this procedure is interpreting differences from an arbitrary baseline. A remedy might be to create a standard baseline by taking a random sample from all children in all clusters. That sample might be simple, stratified, or weighted to reflect the original population. We treat this sample just as if it was a cluster in its own right. This sample provides a baseline regression equivalent to the regression that would be estimated from the complete set of data. Thus, the subsequent tests investigate whether the regression in any cluster departs from the "complete" regression.

The differences among the six equations in Figure 2 occur primarily between the two types of preschools, rather than within each type. Since the four Montessori clusters have similar covariate relationships, we can pool these clusters into the equivalent of a single large study (although they originally came from different studies). We can similarly pool the two pre-kindergartens into the equivalent of a single large study. The next step, substantively, would be to identify those differences in learning environments and curriculum content which brought about the differential sensitization of children in the two kinds of preschools.[30]

Note, finally, that adopting the cluster approach here has led to a clear policy implication. If a goal of public policy is to develop a preschool program specifically targeted toward disadvantaged children, then in our hypothetical example the Montessori approach has the virtue of less dependence than a pre-kindergarten on a home resource those children may lack. (This assumes poorer families have less discretionary income to spare for the purchase of children's books.) If, on the other hand, for some reason we must institute pre-kindergartens, valuable information has still been gained. The analysis suggests the potential value of augmenting the school program with supplementary books for children to take home.

With covariate relationships as they are in our example, it is possible that the relationship of reading readiness to books in a home could have been statistically significant in the two pre-kindergartens but not in the four Montessori centers. (Had the standard errors of all the b coefficients in Figure 2 been approximately 2.0, just such a pattern of significance and lack of significance would be observed.) Thus, if the original data were combined by the "taking-a-vote" procedure,

---

[30] Once we have concluded that the covariate relationship differs among clusters, we know how to adjust for such differences. If we subtract from the final reading readiness scores the values predicted by their individual covariates, we have removed the covariates' effect on the cluster means and variances. When similar adjustments are made for all sections of the original data, we will have increased the power of statistical tests. The power will increase because the within cluster variance has been reduced, and that value is our measure of chance variation. This handling of covariates illustrates the essence of the pooling strategy. We use the cluster approach to identify differences among clusters in the relationship between a covariate and the dependent variable. When we explain those differences, we remove them. Had we made the conventional assumption of an identical relationship between the covariate and dependent variable for all clusters, we would have estimated a regression coefficient of approximately 3.5. As a result, we would have inaccurately adjusted the reading readiness scores for all six centers, and left a considerable amount of within cluster residual variation unexplained. That unexplained variance is not due to chance; it is due to the failure to make a correct adjustment. Further, that extra variance cannot be removed by any subsequent adjustment. Thus, it will remain as within-cluster variation, reducing the power of our statistical tests.

books would have been voted down four to two. That decision simply would not provide the kind of information from which public policy could benefit.

4. Subject-by-Treatment Interactions.

A fourth way that clusters can differ is in their subject-by-treatment interactions. Normally the term "treatment" would refer to a program type. In our illustration, for example, it might refer to Head Start. From the cluster perspective, however, several different versions of the same program cannot be assumed to offer identical "treatments" to all children in the different centers. Therefore, we begin by assuming that each individual cluster is a treatment in its own right.

Using this interpretation of "treatment," the idea of a subject-by-treatment interaction is easily explained. Subjects (children within preschool sites in our example) differ from one another in many identifiable ways. If the effect of a treatment (being in a cluster) depends upon one or more of the ways subjects differ, there exists a subject-by-treatment interaction.[31] To illustrate, suppose that the effect on a child's reading readiness of being in a particular day care center depended upon his or her sex. For example, suppose that being in day care "A" was relatively more advantageous for boys than for girls, while in day care "B," the relative advantages were reversed. This would be a subject (sex)-by-treatment (cluster) interaction.

If subject-by-treatment interactions are overlooked, studies may lead to apparently contradictory conclusions, particularly from the point of view of public policy decisions. The preschool example can be used to illustrate this point.

Recall from Figure 1 that Studies No. 1 and 2 each compared a day care center to a Head Start center. Figure 3 shows the number of children and their final reading readiness means for each of these four centers. The final column in Figure 3 gives the overall means, for boys and girls combined, for each center. In Study No. 1, Head Start outperforms day care. In Study No. 2, the conclusion is reversed. Finding these two studies reported in the literature might lead only into confusion.

[31] The overall test for the presence of subject by treatment interactions is derived from the standard two-way fixed effects ANOVA. The categories into which children are classified constitute one factor. The clusters are the other factor. While the F test for interaction can establish the presence of such effects, it does not by itself isolate which clusters "work" the same way and which "work" differently. Fortunately, a paper by Leon Harter, "Multiple Comparison Procedures for Interaction," *The American Statistician*, 24 (December 1970), pp. 30-32, presents a method, similar conceptually to multiple contrast procedures, which allows the interactions to be examined in detail.

	Girls	Boys	Overall
STUDY #1			
Head Start A			
Means	71	69	70
No. of Children	(20)	(20)	(40)
Day Care A			
Means	63	80	68
No. of Children	(25)	(10)	(35)
STUDY #2			
Head Start B			
Means	72	66	69
No. of Children	(15)	(15)	(30)
Day Care B			
Means	78	66	74
No. of Children	(30)	(15)	(45)

FIGURE 3.

Mean Achievement Scores, Separately by Sex, for Studies 1 and 2

Using the cluster approach, and searching for the subject-by-treatment inter-actions discussed in this section, the contradiction can be resolved. The means for boys and girls are given separately in Figure 3. First, examine the means for the two Head Start centers. We find that girls slightly outperform boys and that the relationship is the same in both centers. Thus, while there is a slight sex dif-ference, there is no sex-by-center interaction. Second, examine the means for the two day care centers. Here the situation is very different. In day care "A," boys outperform girls. In day care "B," girls outperform boys. Thus, the day care centers exhibit a subject-by-treatment interaction.

Does the presence of this interaction explain the contradiction between the two original studies? It does, because when subject-by-treatment interactions are present, simple overall comparisons between means are insufficient by themselves for drawing useful inferences. Notice that for the two day care centers the final overall mean depends heavily upon the proportions of boys and girls in each center. If day care "A" had contained a higher proportion of boys, the conclusion of Study No. 1 would have been reversed; the day care center would have out-performed the Head Start center. The conclusion of Study No. 2, similarly, could have been reversed if more boys had been in the day care center. In fact, the con-clusions from the two studies are almost entirely an artifact of the number of boys and girls who happened to be assigned to the two day care centers.

For policy purposes, we see now that we would be in a good position if it were somehow possible to combine the best features of each of the two day care centers. Such a new kind of center, with expected readiness means of 78 for girls and 80 for boys, would clearly be preferable to Head Start. If, on the other hand, such a center could not be developed, public policy faces a difficult choice. The highest scores would be achieved only by assigning boys and girls to separate day care centers. If this is socially and ethically unacceptable, however, all children should be assigned to Head Start centers, where sexual differentiation will be minimized at the cost of lower scores. Combining data within the cluster perspective cannot answer definitively such policy questions, but at least it lets us know that we have to ask them.

5. Contextual Effects.

The fifth way that clusters can differ is in shared features which are uniform for all children within any cluster. The impact of such uniform features are called contextual effects. For example, the per-pupil expenditure in a preschool center is the same for every child in that center. So is the sex of the teacher. Measures that reflect the composition of the entire group of children in each cluster are also common contextual variables. Examples of these would be the size of the class, or the proportion who are male.

Since the clusters in the original studies have been separated, the data can be examined to see if changes in the dependent variable (i.e., reading readiness) parallel differences in the contextual features of centers. For example, the preschool data from Figure 1 might be examined to see whether differences in per-pupil expenditures were reflected in reading readiness.

Why search for the impact of contextual features? One reason is that clusters cannot be combined before we have identified and adjusted for any real consequences that contextual features have had. Second, such features are usually the program components most subject to policy manipulation. Examples of such components are the extent to which a teacher reads aloud to a preschool class, or the presence or absence of programmed instructional materials.

The search for contextual differences among clusters is substantially different from the procedures discussed in the preceding four sections. Previously, each cluster was examined separately. The analysis of any one cluster did not depend upon the data from another. With contextual variables we are forced to proceed differently. The only way the influence of a contextual variable can be estimated is by looking at a *group* of clusters. This is because a contextual variable is defi·

as having the identical value for each child in a cluster. With no variation of a contextual variable, we cannot estimate its relationship to a dependent variable within any cluster. The inability to examine separately, within each cluster, the impact of a contextual variable is a limitation of the cluster approach. After all, a contextual variable such as a teacher's reading to children might be important, but its importance as well as its amount may vary from preschool to preschool. Since its importance cannot be established within each cluster separately, the effect of a contextual variable may be overlooked or evaluated incorrectly.

Limitations of the Cluster Approach

We have just mentioned one limitation of the cluster approach when combining a set of studies: that contextual effects cannot be examined separately within each cluster. We now discuss this limitation as well as a second limitation of the cluster approach: the inability to handle unmeasured variables, and interactions between unmeasured variables and measured variables. This latter problem may seem to be a tautology. No standard technique can incorporate the effects of unmeasured variables in a set of studies. We raise this issue here, however, because it leads to a substantive point worth discussing.

A question that always faces a researcher is what to do when he runs up against limitations of statistical procedures. In one sense, such limitations are impassable, and the best available solution is simply to be aware of them. But in practical evaluation work, although such problems cannot be avoided, rough or approximate procedures can sometimes provide a bit of protection against the problem. For the two limitations of the cluster approach—contextual effects whose importance differs among clusters, and the possible effects of important unmeasured variables—such approximate procedures are available.

First, what about the contextual effects problem? Recall the earlier discussion about checking the "uniformity" of a program type by examining the way it worked at several different sites (clusters). "Program type" itself is, after all, an example of a contextual variable. We can investigate the uniformity of the effects of other contextual variables in the same way that program type was investigated. Suppose for example there were several clusters in which the teacher read to children roughly one hour each day. After isolating this subset of clusters, which may come from a number of different studies, we could test them for differences among means, variances, or any of the other potential differences that have been mentioned. If no differences are found, then we are in a better position to assume that contextual effects are uniform. If differences are found, we know that the uniformity of the effect of teachers' reading to children cannot be assumed.[32]

Second, what can be done about the potential presence of unmeasured variables? The first step is to get the effects of the measured variables out of the way. In previous sections we indicated that when differences were found among clusters, statistical adjustments were available to remove them. After all such adjustments have been made, what remains in the data? Two things: chance or "natural" variation, and the systematic effects of unmeasured variables. Both natural variation and any unsystematic effects of unmeasured variables should be distributed about the same way in every cluster. Further, the systematic effects of the unmeasured variables of concern are those that affect some clusters differently from others. This is the pivot of the approximate method for detecting their presence. The approximate method consists simply of repeating the test for differences in variance among clusters, except now applying the test to the adjusted data. If differences are found among the variances, there is good reason to suspect the presence of unmeasured variables whose effects differ systematically among clusters.

Note that this approximate procedure does not name the unmeasured variable, nor does it tell us which clusters were affected by it. But something valuable has been learned. An important unmeasured variable is "there." A signal has been flashed; future studies should search for the identity of this variable. Finally, when we find that an unmeasured variable has been at work, we should not be disheartened if unreconciled conflicts remain in the results of the original studies.

---

[32] Suppose we approach this problem in the following way. Consider the set of preschools where teachers read to students one hour per day. We can think of each preschool as one level of a treatment factor. If school-to-school differences in mean level of reading readiness differ more than expected from chance variation alone, what would we conclude? We would not conclude that our findings on the effects of teachers' reading to children are ambiguous. Rather, we would begin to search for some other source of school-to-school variation in reading readiness. If we find this unknown factor, it may either interact with the extent of teacher's reading, or operate independently of it. For example, the effect of teacher's reading may depend upon the character of the administration of any particular preschool. This would be an interactive effect. We must therefore not throw up our hands in despair when replications of studies lead to contradictory results. The equivalent of "throwing up our hands" is to attribute the observed variations to inexplicable factors or to normal sampling error. Assuming the several studies were qualitatively well conducted, we must conclude that the disparate results from the several replications are due either to the direct effects of an unmeasured variable, or to the interaction of an unmeasured variable with one of the measured variables. We then follow the same procedure as in any post hoc research: search through the data for the most likely explanation of observed differences among sites or centers.

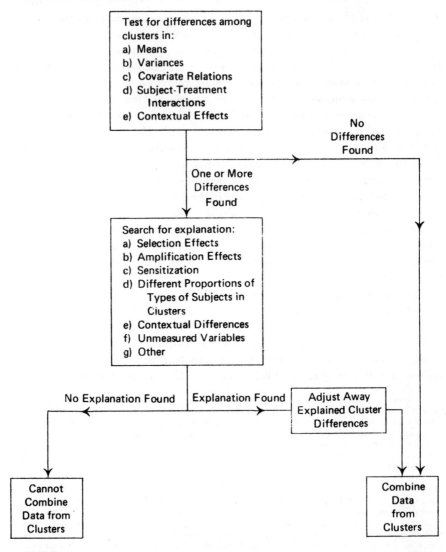

FIGURE 4.

Overview of the Cluster Approach

At least we know why the conflicts exist, and we may even have hit upon some idea of where to seek their resolution.

This concludes our discussion of the ways clusters can differ, and some strengths and weaknesses of the cluster approach. Figure 4 gives an abbreviated overview of the basic logic of that approach. The first block in Figure 4 gives the five kinds of cluster differences for which one tests. As the Figure indicates, when all five tests fail to find differences, data from the several clusters can be combined. When one or more of the tests indicates a difference, and an explanation for that difference is found, the data can still be combined after the differences are adjusted away. When differences exist but no explanation is found, the data cannot be combined.

Where the Cluster Perspective May Lead Us

Until now the development of the cluster approach has been pitched specifically towards the goal of combining studies. Thus, an analysis of the five ways clusters can differ throws some light on the question of when data can be combined. But the original purpose of combining studies was to gain insights into educational processes. To what kind of inferences, in general, does the cluster perspective lead? There is no way to summarize all inferences that grow from a point of view. We offer here, however, two examples of the type of thinking which might flow from the cluster perspective. The first is a resolution of a contradiction that arises from two different analyses of the same data. The second example identifies a fundamental relationship among several different ways in which an educational program can operate.

Example 1—Contradictory Results from the Same Data

Suppose a survey collected achievement scores for children in a sample of 100 classrooms. In addition, the number of years of experience for each teacher was recorded. One researcher wanted to know whether the variation among the 100 classroom means was more than might be expected due to "chance." To do this, he carried out a standard one-way analysis of variance; the resulting F ratio was not significant. This researcher therefore decided that the classroom means did not differ among themselves by more than would be expected from "chance." A second researcher approached the data from a different perspective. He was interested in whether differences among the classroom means were related to differences in teachers' experience, beyond the level of chance. He computed the ordinary product moment correlation coefficient for the 100 pairs of data points. He found a high, positive, statistically significant correlation between mean achievement and teacher's experience.

When the two researchers discussed their results, they found they had a paradox. Apparently, the mean differences among the 100 classrooms both do and do not differ by more than chance. How can this paradox occur? It occurs because the F-test treats variation within classrooms as its measure of chance variation.[33] But this is simply an assumption. Further, this assumption is wrong whenever there is some source of within-classroom differentiation among children which does not affect the classroom mean (e.g., recall the tracking illustration earlier where tracking worked in this fashion: enlarging the variance within clusters without affecting the mean of the clusters). Whenever this assumption of only chance variation is wrong, a researcher is likely to encounter just the paradox described above.

Is there a resolution? Without advancing the details of a statistical argument, the simplest resolution of the paradox is to admit a distinct preference for explanations that presume structure rather than chance. In this example, the preference is given to the correlation analysis that related classroom means to teachers' experience, rather than to the analysis of variance that related classroom means only to chance.

How does the paradox, and our preference for structural rather than chance explanations, relate back to the cluster perspective? The cluster perspective allows for processes which can occur separately within any classroom. Suppose, for example, there was intense academic competition among the children in each classroom. The competition took a form that led to an increase in variation within each classroom while leaving its mean unaffected. This could be the kind of competition often described as a "zero-sum game." The variation thus induced could lead a standard analysis of variance to overlook the systematic impact of teachers' experience on classroom performance.[34]

[33] Two alternative explanations can be ruled out. First, two statistics can come to different conclusions from the same data if the relative *power* of the two statistics differs. That argument does not apply here because we can assume enough cases to make both F-tests and correlations reasonably powerful. Second, the paradox cannot be attributed to inherent contradictions in the assumptions of the two tests. Had our results been reversed, with a significant F and an insignificant correlation, we would have simply interpreted the situation as one where "while there are significant differences among the classroom means, those differences are unrelated to the teachers' experience."

[34] Our resolution of the paradox *depends essentially* on the fact that the cluster approach allows for the existence of differences located *within* each cluster, such as the zero-sum academic

The problem initially motivating this essay was the presence of contradictions among the conclusions of different studies. The cluster perspective has been proposed as a useful approach. It also yields an unexpected gain; it may provide an explanation when two different analyses of the *same* data lead to contradictory results.

Example 2—Catalytic and Stereotypic Operating Programs

The second example is an attempt to see whether the cluster perspective leads to explanations of events in a classroom that a teacher would recognize. We suspect that many practitioners adopt an informal version of the cluster perspective in their own thinking about educational programs. Below are two "explanations of how a program works" that fit directly into the cluster perspective.

Recall that in the section on variances, two possible "outcomes" of a preschool's operation were defined as the amplification of prior learning and the differential sensitization of students. Both of these processes are instances of a more general type of program operation. These operations can be called "catalytic." The program, acting as a catalyst, facilitates the conversion of some characteristic of a child into a performance gain. In the case of an amplifier process, the "input" being converted into final performance is a child's prior learning. For differential sensitization, it is some other aspect of a child's background, such as reading materials in his home. We have seen earlier how the cluster approach enables us to search for such catalytic phenomena. The approach also enables us to represent the more general case where the *degree* of catalytic action varies from site to site in a program, or between different types of program. Such flexibility is not a luxury. Without the flexibility built into the cluster approach, we are likely to be trapped into such misleading absolutes as: "the child's performance depends upon his home background," and thereby overlook the possibility of the brief but crucial modifier: "but the dependence is greater for some kinds of programs than for others."

Catalytic programs are at one end of a spectrum. At the other end are programs that operate stereotypically. A stereotypic program can be defined as one that

---

competition described. It does more than just allow for them; it can sometimes lead to a test for the existence of such within-cluster processes *even though they cannot be directly measured.* In our example, we need merely to adjust the original scores for the effects of variations in the teachers' experience, and then retest for a significantly *smaller* F-ratio than would be expected due to chance. If this was found, we would have reason to suspect the existence of something like the zero-sum academic competition process. This suspicion would be strongly supported if the F-ratio of the pretest scores was *not* significantly small.

does not reflect any one feature of a child's background or achievement, but rather as a program that ties a child's future performance to a general average taken across many of the child's characteristics. Such programs deal with the "whole child" in a very special sense. Essentially a large number of a child's characteristics are noted and then reduced to a single "picture" of who that child is: a stereotype. Thereafter, such programs teach to the stereotype; and the child's final performance typically comes to reflect the initial impression of him formed when he entered the program.

Educators often see stereotypic phenomena. Nearly every teacher has encountered a child who was characterized as "average," despite one or two unique abilities. A poor child is sometimes labeled "disadvantaged," despite strong emotional support from his home. Notice that stereotypic programs operate differently from catalytic programs. Both kinds of programs tie a child's final performance to some initial feature of his background or abilities. But catalytic programs tie a child's progress to *one* or a *few* of his specific characteristics, while stereotypic programs tie a child's progress to the *general tenor* of his characteristics, and ignore any isolated advantages or disadvantages he may have.

Let us use another preschool example to contrast the two kinds of programs. Suppose there exist two preschools, and that both include cultural enrichment in the form of some sessions of listening to a classical pianist. Imagine further that both preschools decide only those children who "show enough ability" to benefit from these sessions should attend them. In the first preschool, let the selection take a catalytic form. The teacher asks each child to sing along with her as she plays a simple tune on a piano. Those children whose parents have pianos at home will probably tend to be more comfortable in this exercise, and will be selected. It is also probably true that, on the average, the selected children will come from wealthier homes than the unselected children. What characterizes this program as catalytic, however, is the fact that selection depends specifically upon the presence or absence of a piano in the home, and not on "middle class status" in general. Thus, a middle class child without a piano probably will not be selected, while a poorer child with a piano probably will be.

Contrast this to a second preschool where the teacher chooses stereotypically. She may feel that wealthier children will be comfortable with classical music, while poorer children will not be. She may therefore select those children who, she believes, come from prosperous homes. But her impression of prosperity is not tied to any one characteristic of a family's economic status, such as the presence or absence of a piano in the home. Rather, her impression is a melange of many characteristics, such as the child's dress, manner, neighborhood, and whatever snippets of family information she may have. In striking a sort of average over these many characteristics, the teacher will give little weight to those which run counter to her general stereotype. Some children she views as wealthy will have pianos in their homes. Many, however, will not. A child who is driven to school in a nice car, whose mother dresses well, and who comes from a desirable neighborhood will be selected for classical music whether or not he has a piano in his home. On the other hand, a child who walks to school in ragged sneakers, whose mother dresses poorly, and who comes from a poor neighborhood will not be selected even if he has a Steinway in his parlor.

Obviously it is important that statistical procedures detect whether a program operates catalytically or stereotypically if we are to understand its effects on children. The problem, however, is that while conventional analyses may work well on data from catalytic programs, they fall down badly when used to analyze stereotypic programs. A statistical technique is available to identify the importance of individual characteristics of children in determining their achievement. This technique assesses the "unique" contributions of individual characteristics, "controlling" for the other aspects of a child's measured background.[35] But if a program is stereotypic, no unique contributions from individual characteristics will appear. Insofar as one characteristic of a child departs from the general trend of all his characteristics, the stereotypic program ignores it.

There are, however, certain variables in stereotypic programs that conventional analyses will identify as important. Such variables are summary averages across many characteristics (such as social class and measured IQ). It will require further discussion to make clear how standard analyses respond to data from stereotypic programs, and why they exaggerate the importance of summary variables.

Returning to the music enrichment example will provide the needed illustration. Both preschools will send some children to the music sessions. For the catalytic program, we will be able to pin down the determining factor of who gets to go as the presence or absence of a piano in the home. If we later found that

[35] The technique for assessing unique contributions of independent variables is generally some form of a step-down regression procedure. Details on this can be found in A. Mood, "Partitioning Variance in Multiple Regression Analyses as a Tool for Developing Learning Models," *American Educational Research Journal*, 8 (March 1971), pp. 191-202. Also, see C. E. Werts, "Partitioning of Variance in School Effects Studies," *American Educational Research Journal*, 7 (January 1970), pp. 127-132.

wealthier children had a greater familiarity with Chopin, we would be able to identify specifically how the program operated to bring out this result. Thus, we would learn, correctly, that the *selection* rules in that preschool accounted for the wealthier children's greater familiarity with Chopin. Standard statistical techniques for locating the important covariates of a child's performance fit the catalytic program well.

Contrast this with what happens in the stereotypic preschool. Here, standard statistical procedures may throw us completely off the track. Those procedures cannot link the wealthier children's greater familiarity with Chopin to any single characteristic of the children's background. A data analysis will show that after controlling for family car, mother's clothing, and neighborhood, pianos in the home are unimportant predictors of knowledge of Chopin. Similarly, after controlling for mother's clothes, neighborhood, and piano in the home, the family car will have little to do with knowledge of Chopin. Yet a general index of family wealth, such as socioeconomic status, will be highly correlated with a child's knowledge of Chopin.

We know that in our example of a stereotypic program this correlation exists because the teacher selected children in accordance with her intuitive equivalent of the summary variable, "socioeconomic status." Thus, knowing the details of what happened in this preschool explains the correlation. But suppose we did not know the real details of how this preschool worked. Suppose, rather, we were faced only with published data from someone else's study of this preschool. What would we be likely to conclude? Since we cannot pin down the educational process to one particular independent variable, we might well decide that the "general cultural milieu" of the wealthy home leads to a familiarity with Chopin. Further, we would be unable to perceive any specific role that the preschool played in the process. Thus, we might incorrectly conclude that, "preschools have no effect, it's all social class." *This is one of the most dangerous errors that can be made. We will have misidentified the active agency in the children's development. A school effect will have been mistaken for a home effect.* Educational programs which operate stereotypically may artificially inflate, in a data analysis, the importance of summary variables such as socioeconomic status, and a child's measured IQ.[36]

---

[36] Ever since the Coleman study *op cit.*, a number of evaluations of both schools in general and particular compensatory education programs have indicated that school resource variables are much less important than social background variables of children and their peers in explaining variation in children's achievement. For example, see Jencks, *et al.*, *op cit.* We do not know how

How can this problem be avoided? Adopting the cluster approach offers some help. Imagine we had set out to combine the data from the two preschools using the cluster approach. What would we have found? While knowledge of Chopin would be correlated with socioeconomic status in both clusters, we would have detected the presence of a specific link to owning a piano in the catalytic program, and the absence of that link in the stereotypic one. Further, we would realize that when the linkage between family wealth and a child's knowledge of Chopin varies from preschool to preschool (cluster to cluster), the cultural milieu of the home can hardly be the immediate agency for a child's musical knowledge. *By discovering that the linkage differs among preschools, we would know that preschool operations must mediate a child's musical learning.*

Thus, the cluster approach can help to decipher school effects, even when programs operate stereotypically. It offers some protection against misjudging the way educational programs operate.

Conclusion

To be powerful, a research method must be tailored to the problems it is intended to solve. The cluster approach is the adaptation of common statistical procedures to educational settings. Its chief adaptation is to center attention on specific educational locales. The assumption that whatever happens in one locale happens in all others is abandoned. Thus, the cluster approach enables us to pool data from conflicting studies by resolving their contradictions into represented differences among clusters.

The cluster approach will often be more powerful, and should never be worse, than other available procedures for combining studies. That virtue flows from the following logic. Suppose upon examination all differences among clusters prove to be insignificant. Then the cluster approach will lead us to conclude that all data from the studies can be combined into the equivalent of a single large study. But that is the assumption with which most other procedures begin. Therefore, the cluster approach enables us to test an important assumption which alternatives leave unexamined. If the assumption is true, we will be aware of its truth. If it is false, we will be in a position to proceed without it.

The cluster approach grew out of the problems encountered in combining

many, or which, educational programs operate in a stereotypic fashion. But as the standard statistical procedure in these analyses is to search for the "unique contribution" of each independent variable in explaining variation for the dependent variable, the school effects of stereotypic programs may be somewhat underestimated.

different studies. However, it is equally applicable for a single large·study, where one team of researchers collects data f.om many sites. After all, the issue is the same in either case; whether or not an educational process is uniform among all sites. The cluster approach confronts this question head on.

What is the payoff to educational policy in adopting this approach? Seeking out differences among clusters leads to two different kinds of information, both of which help in choosing among policy alternatives. The first kind of information we need is to know precisely what policy alternatives are available. Seeking out differences among clusters enables us to generate a list of the program versions which currently exist. Thus, the alternatives will be operationally defined, and the danger of instituting a program with enormous and uncontrollable variations from site to site will be minimized.

The second kind of information we may gain is a specific identification of commonalities among sites. Some features of educational programs may have similar effects on all children. Features which work in this way are often masked by other aspects of educational settings which vary from site to site. By stripping away the variations, the cluster approach both isolates the commonalities and marshals the statistical power needed to detect them.

The generality of the cluster approach is its premise; it represents a broad range of variations in educational processes. Its flexibility may lead us around current barriers to the accumulation of evidence in education.

12

CONFIDENTIALITY-PRESERVING MODES OF ACCESS TO FILES AND TO INTERFILE EXCHANGE FOR USEFUL STATISTICAL ANALYSIS

By
**DONALD T. CAMPBELL, ROBERT F. BORUCH,
RICHARD D. SCHWARTZ, and JOSEPH STEINBERG**

In releasing individual data for statistical analysis by outsiders, deletion of direct personal identifiers is sometimes insufficient to preserve confidentiality. Restrictions on the release of data that are publicly listed elsewhere or error innoculation of these variables may be required. Microaggregated release is safe, but statistically costly. In-file capacity to run outsiders' analyses, with randomized rounding of frequency tallies, is best. Interfile linkage of confidential data in statistical analyses is of great potential value for program evaluation and can be achieved without the release of individually identified data from either file by the "mutually insulated file linkage" procedure described. Link file brokerage is unacceptable on confidentiality grounds, and microaggregation and synthetic linking by matching are unacceptable on statistical grounds. For both types of use, it would be beneficial for governmental program evaluation to fund internal statistical analysis capability in important administrative archives, including those in the private sector such as health and automobile insurance.

From Donald T. Campbell et al., "Confidentiality-Preserving Modes of Access to Files and to Interfile Exchange for Useful Statistical Analysis." *Evaluation Quarterly*, 1977, *1*(2), 269-300.

*A*t present, there is great concern about invasion of privacy and confidentiality and about the threat to individual freedom represented by data banks. Such concerns are currently much stronger than are demands for increased objectivity in the evaluation of governmental programs. It is our belief, detailed in this paper, that both concerns can be reconciled—that data archive use for program evaluation can be achieved without increasing the dangers of invasion of

AUTHORS' NOTE: *This paper constituted Appendix A of the 1975 final report of the NAS-NRC Committee on Federal Agency Evaluation Research, Protecting Individual Privacy in Evaluation Research,* A. M. Rivlin, Chair. The efforts of Donald T. Campbell privacy. But we also believe that the means of such reconciliation are too little recognized and that there is a real danger of ill-considered solutions to the privacy problem that would needlessly preclude the use of archives in program evaluation. At its worst, the privacy issue becomes a rationalization for evading meaningful program evaluation.

The present analysis starts out by assuming the existence of administrative records and of archived statistical research data and then asks how both of these can be further used to generate nonindividual statistical products without increasing the risks to individuals that are already implicit in these existing files. Such a focus is tangential to many of the main concerns in the discussion of the threats of data banks. While we favor a number of the current proposals for the reform of government data archiving, both present practice and these reforms are compatible with the recommendations in this paper.

Thus, although not the focus of this paper, we join others in a number of recommendations on the management of data archives.

(1) Administrative data collectors and evaluation researchers should refrain from collecting sensitive personal data not directly relevant to the government's legitimate concerns appropriate to the transaction at hand.

(2) Identifying information should not be collected at all; that is, respondents should be kept anonymous from the beginning where this is compatible with the purposes of the evaluation.

(3) For the purposes here represented, there would be no loss and perhaps some gain if individuals were given a copy of their own data at the time it is filed, with the opportunity to correct it if necessary, and with the right to future access. (Much of this is already achieved for Social Security Administration and Internal Revenue Service files.)

and Robert F. Boruch have been supported in part by grants from the Russell Sage Foundation, by National Science Foundation Grant GSOC-7103704, and by National Institute of Education Grant NIE-C-74-0115. The authors are indebted to Professor Tore Dalenius for a careful review of an earlier draft of this manuscript. Portions of an earlier draft of this report have been used by Boruch and Campbell as a basis for pages 261-269 of H. W. Riecken, R. F. Boruch, D. T. Campbell, T. K. Glennan, J. Pratt, A. Rees, and W. Williams, Social Experimentation: A method for planning and evaluating social intervention *(New York: Academic Press, 1974). The resulting duplication is retained with the permission of Academic Press.*

(4) In regard to the desirability of restricting the uses of data to those which the individual anticipated and was agreeable to when providing the data, it would probably be desirable if the forms used for data collection (e.g., income tax returns) announced that the data would also be used for statistical summaries in which the individual would be unidentifiable.

(5) Restrictions would be desirable to prevent any secondary use of archived data for "intelligence" or investigatory purposes, that is, for actions or descriptions targeted on the individual; all secondary uses of data would be restricted to statistical products in which individuals were unidentifiable.

(6) For statistical research data files, individual identifiers should be replaced with code numbers for data processing and computer storage, and the code key kept under tight security. For administrative data files this may not always be feasible, but certainly should be required for any computer memory storage on a time-sharing basis.

(7) Formal rules and guidelines should be promulgated to guarantee high standards of confidentiality and security management on the part of all data file staff.

(8) For the data uses we advocate, a unified national data bank is not required. Such a data bank is feared because it multiplies the power of a corrupt employee to blackmail, or of the government to police, the individuals on whom data are recorded.

On the other hand, there are some recommended reforms of public recordkeeping that would preclude the uses here advocated and that we regard as both needless and contrary to the public interest.

(1) Abolition of the use of Social Security numbers for all but Social Security Administration files. Our recommendation is quite the opposite, namely, that Social Security numbers be recorded where possible. The abolition recommendation was designed to preclude merging files into larger data banks. Through the "mutually insulated file linkage" described in this paper, some types of file linkage can be achieved *without* merging, i.e., in a manner that prevents either file from acquiring identifiable individual information from the other file. This procedure does require, however, that common identifiers, such as names and Social Security numbers, exist in each file. We believe that were this procedure adopted, the reasons for the suggested prohibition on Social Security numbers would be eliminated.

(2) The destruction of personal data files after a specified period, say five or ten years. Many social innovations call for longer-term statistical follow-ups that would be precluded by such a rule.

(3) The requirement of a specific, separate permission statement and explicit informed consent for each separate statistical *research* use of an administrative file. We regard this recommendation as contrary to the public interest as well as needless

when no individually identifiable data are being released from the file, as in procedures described below.

(4) Elimination of all individually identified files in any form. Needless to say, we regard this as impossible for administrative files in their administrative use, unneeded for protection of individuals since this can adequately be done in other ways, and seriously detrimental to our capacity for program evaluation.

The requirements for safeguarding confidentiality are, of course, the responsibility of the administrators of each specific data file. The precautions and procedures necessary will vary from setting to setting. This paper focuses on the most cautious and conservative approaches, not to recommend that they be required in all settings, but rather to emphasize that, for even the most sensitive settings, there are safe modes of access that will permit important statistical analyses. These conservative approaches do set limits to the degree of refinement possible in the statistical analyses, and, to avoid such costs, one should not use a more conservative approach than is called for by the requirements of the situation.

The major sections of this paper discuss specific procedures under two main headings. The first is designated *intrafile analysis by outsiders*. In this category, all of the statistical analyses under consideration are to be done within a single data file. This category is exemplified by the U.S. Census Bureau's Decennial Census public use 1% and 0.1% samples which are released for social science research purposes, or by the Social Security Administration's 1% Continuous Work History Sample (CWHS). In the experience of the Office of Economic Opportunity (OEO), such uses are encountered in the release of data for reanalysis from the evaluations of Head Start, Performance Contracting, and the New Jersey Negative Income Tax Experiment (NJNITE; Watts and Rees, 1973; Kershaw, 1972, 1975; and the Spring 1974 issue of the *Journal of Human Resources*). Six classes of procedures are considered for intrafile analysis by outsiders, concluding with the following recommendations.

Deletion of known identifiers (name, Social Security number) is insufficient unless also accompanied by restrictions in number and refinement of data on variables that are publicly available elsewhere, or unless accompanied by error inoculation on public variables, especially by additive normal error.

Microaggregated release is acceptable, albeit statistically costly.

Best of all is in-file capacity as a public utility to run outsiders' statistical analyses, accompanied by randomized rounding of frequency tabulations to prevent disclosure through comparisons of sets of results.

The secondary category of utilization considered is *interfile linkage of confidential data*, where one or both files are confidential and the objective is to relate variables across files in statistical analyses. (Most conservatively, such exchanges can be done without merging files, i.e., with neither file acquiring the other's confidential data.) Examples of this occur when Social Security Administration data are used to evaluate Job Corps training programs, when the Census Current Population Survey data are related to IRS Statistics of Income data derived from income tax reports, or, conjecturally, if NJNITE interview data were to be related to withholding tax information or to FICA earnings. For such purposes, this paper emphasizes the most conservative of several procedures: mutually insulated file linkage with random deletion of one respondent from each list. Link file brokerage, a widely discussed procedure, is considerably less conservative, but may be a useful strategy if adequate protection for confidentiality can be assured. There are also settings with confidentiality safeguards and legal protection from subpoena in which the still less conservative approach of direct file merging provides reasonable safeguards. Full merging has the advantage of preserving full statistical information on all relationships among all variables for any analysis or reanalysis. Where this approach is used, it would be very important for the merged file to have in-file capacity to run outsiders' statistical analyses (as discussed more extensively in the next section).

INTRAFILE ANALYSIS BY OUTSIDERS

DELETION OF IDENTIFIERS

It is customary in releasing data for reanalysis to delete names, Social Security numbers, and addresses from the data on individuals. In some settings this may provide sufficient protection in that it may not increase the respondent's loss of privacy or increase the risks of breach of confidentiality. In other settings, deletion of identifiers is an insufficient safeguard. Two features seem crucial: the number of items of information on each person and the availability of those items on public lists with names attached. For example, deletion of identifiers might be sufficient for a 0.1% sample of the 1970 Census because of the extremely scattered nature of the sample and the absence of parallel lists. However, even in this case, if census tract, age, and specialty are given for a low-frequency, visibly listed profession, such as M.D., individual identification could frequently be made and the other information on the record thereby identified with a specific person, thus making it possible for a corrupt user to infringe upon the M.D.'s privacy (Hansen, 1971).

Where the research population is compact and where some of the variables are conveniently recorded with names on public or semipublic lists (here designated as *public variables*), the deletion of identifiers is less adequate. Thus, for a study conducted within a single school, even the date and place of birth are usually sufficient to reveal names. (Specific birth date in combination with birth place probably should always be treated as a personal identifier.)

In the case of the NJNITE, data tapes are now being released to outside users through the Data Center of the Institute for Research on Poverty of the University of Wisconsin. It was decided in this case that a thorough deletion of identifiers provided adequate protection. This deletion covered names, addresses, exact birth places and birth dates, Social Security numbers, and, in addition, the names of doctors, teachers, and the like. These data have been deleted not only from the released tapes, but also from the original interviews preserved in microfilm.

CRUDE REPORT CATEGORIES FOR, AND RESTRICTION OF, PUBLIC VARIABLES

For public variables in the confidential file (variables that are readily available elsewhere with names attached), cruder report categories should be used in the data released, to the level needed to prevent disclosure: e.g., county rather than census tract, year of birth rather than day or month, profession but not specialty within profession, and so on. For variables unique to the research project (unique variables), which therefore do not exist on other lists with names attached, this precaution is not necessary. Thus, for a multi-item attitude test or for an achievement test, individual item responses and exact total scores can be made available without jeopardizing confidentiality. (Such data probably should be made available because of their relevance to the estimation of error for use in generating alternate statistical adjustments, an issue of ever-increasing concern.)

Even with crude report categories on such public variables as geographic areas, places and years of schooling, age, profession, and so on, if there are enough such variables, combinations emerge in which only one or two persons occur and discovery of individual identity becomes possible. Thus, there should be a minimum lower bound restriction on the cell sizes of the full combination of public variables. For example, the rule might be adopted that there should be no combination of public variables yielding a frequency less than three persons (Fellegi and Phillips, 1974; Hansen, 1971; Hoffman and Miller, 1970). Recoding of variables using still cruder report categories, or complete deletion of some public variables, should be done until the chosen criterion is achieved. Before a criterion is chosen, tests of the anonymity-breaking potentials of various criteria should be tried out using actual bodies of data and publicly available lists.

These restrictions are obviously at the cost of some potential statistical analyses, particularly if some public variables have to be eliminated entirely. It might be thought that this could be avoided by releasing to each given user only some of the public variables, permitting the user to specify which public variables were of highest priority to the particular work. This strategy would suffice if there were only one user on one occasion or if users could be kept from sharing their data sets. But this seems impossible to guarantee, and such sharing would permit discovery of identity. For example, if user Alpha received public variables P_1 and P_2 plus all unique variables U_1 through U_n, while user Beta received public variables P_3 and P_4 plus all unique variables U_1 through U_n, they could easily employ the shared unique variables to achieve perfect matches and thus generate a complete, merged deck with P_1, P_2, P_3, and P_4 on each person. This full set of public variables might then be sufficient to identify individuals with the help of public lists.

RANDOM SUBSAMPLE RELEASE

The last-mentioned problem of multiple users sharing differentially deleted data sets and thereby gaining increased ability to disclose individual identities can be greatly attenuated by providing each user with a different randomly selected subset of the data. This approach is obviously most usable for files containing a large number of individuals. It provides most protection where the sample is a small portion of the total available population and when the public and unique variables are few enough in number and crude enough in categories so that many persons end up with identical patterns and individual identification is precluded.

MICROAGGREGATION

Feige and Watts (1970; Watts, 1972) have developed a technique of microaggregation for the release of census data on firms, as a substitute for the release of individual data. This approach has been recommended as a general approach to the release of confidential data. The idea of microaggregation is to create many synthetic average persons and to release the data on these rather than on individuals. Thus, instead of releasing individual data on the 1,200 participants of the NJNITE, as has been done, hypothetically one might group the data into 240 sets of five each and release average data on every variable for each set (probably with within-set variance as well as mean). Outside users could then do all of their secondary analyses on these 240 synthetic persons.

Feige, Watts, and their colleagues have done such analyses on Federal Reserve Board data on banks and have been able to compare microaggregate analyses with individual data analyses. Their conclusion is clear that such microaggregation is much more useful than no release of data at all. It results in a loss of statistical efficiency, but does not necessarily bias the statistical estimates. For most conceivable grouping variables, anonymity and confidentiality are preserved at the individual level.

The actual acceptable basis for microaggregation must be thought through in detail for every specific body of data. The following preliminary suggestions hypothetically illustrate the problem for the

NJNITE. For most purposes, aggregation should probably keep intact the experimental design, that is, aggregation should be done within treatments and in comparability across treatments. (There would be many more such aggregates in the 640-person control group than in one of the experimental groups that average around 80 persons, but each one of the experimental group aggregates should be identifiable as parallel to certain control aggregates, and so on.) In the Feige and Watts discussion, local region is a preferred basis of aggregation. In the NJNITE, cities differ considerably in time of initiation of the experiment and in attrition rates. Therefore, city should be used as a basis for aggregation, and possibly region within city. Ethnicity would be wanted for some uses, but with an initial sampling model assigning as few as 16 cases per experimental treatment per city, comparability would be hard to maintain for any variable not blocked on initially. (Aggregating by initial blocking seems a reasonable rule in most social experiments.) If complete data cases are aggregated separately from those lost through attrition, comparability is jeopardized, because the attrition in the NJNITE is differential, being greatest in the control and low payment treatments. Possibly, attrition could be handled by reading out for each variable not only mean and variance, but also the number of persons on which data were computed, basing the mean on those cases providing data.

The variables used as a basis for aggregation must be independent of sampling variation to assure that an estimator (of slope, say, in a linear function) based on aggregated data is unbiased. Since the dependent variable is a function of that error, aggregation in the NJNITE data, for example, could not be based on number of hours worked by members of treatment and control groups. Similarly, any other outcome variable, such as attrition rate, could not be used as a basis for aggregation since its correlation with sampling variation would induce bias in estimators.

The possible basis for aggregation in the NJNITE data include experimental treatment, city, and ethnicity. For the purposes of relating any of these aggregation variables to each other or to any of the nonaggregation variables, there is essentially no loss of information or precision except from the crudeness of the categories of aggregation (e.g., using three categories of ethnicity rather than 30) if variances and cell ns are provided and distributional assumptions and assumptions about relations among variables are approximated. For relating the unique variables to each other, however, there is certain to be a loss of efficiency. In many cases, there will be no bias accompanying this loss of efficiency, given proper adjustments for the known parameters of aggregation. However, both suppressions of relationships and pseudo-relationships are possible in a complex body of data (multifactored in the factor-analysis sense). Consider an extreme example: if variables U_1 and U_2 each were to correlate zero with the variables of aggregation and if a large number of individuals were in each aggregate, then all aggregates would tend to have identical scores on U_1 and identical scores on U_2, and any true relationship between U_1 and U_2 would be suppressed. At the other extreme, if in fact U_1 and U_2 were totally uncorrelated, but if each correlated strongly with some of the variables of aggregation, then an artificial correlation would be generated between them. Obviously, such biases are less the smaller the number of individuals per aggregate, disappearing as this aproaches one. Such biases are also less insofar as the variables of aggregation result in a high, all-purpose similarity among the individuals aggregated.

For reasons such as the above, Feige and Watts recommend flexible microaggregation, tailoring the biases used for aggregation so that the efficiency and lack of bias are optimal for the user's needs. Such flexible microaggregation requires that the archiving file have some statistical reanalysis capacity, probably very nearly as much as would be required for doing the customer's analyses internally, releasing only statistical indices (see below). If a user were to sequentially request different microaggregations of the same data, it might be possible to deduce individual data. As discussed more fully below, random deletions of individuals from each microaggregate would protect against this.

ERROR INOCULATION OF INDIVIDUAL DATA

Boruch (1969, 1971) and others have suggested error inoculation as a means of rendering incriminating responses immune from subpoena. Like the randomized response method (Warner, 1965; Greenberg et al., 1969, 1970), this was initially proposed for sensitive unique variables, such as drug use or abortion, rather than for public variables usable in decoding individual identity. The present suggested usage is different and has different requirements. (For example, damage from gossip and the threat of blackmail may result from randomly produced misinformation as well as from valid confidential information.) Prior to error inoculation in the release of files for reanalysis, identifiers should of course be eliminated. Most or all public variables should be error inoculated and with enough error so that each individual record contains some imperfection on at least one of the public variables. That is, a potential code-breaker armed with a complete list of all names and public variables should not be able to make any exact matches. Under these conditions, unique variables, even those with sensitive or incriminating information, could be spared error inoculation. All users should be informed of the error inoculation and of its parameters.

Two types of error inoculation can be considered: (a) adding random error, and (b) random score substitution. For a continuous-dimension public variable, such as age, years of education, income (public for some institutions, such as corporations and banks, government employees in some states, as reported for state income tax payments in Wisconsin, and so on), purchase cost of house, mean rental level of residence block, geographic location by latitude and longitude or miles from center of city, and the like, a random error of relatively small variance and a mean of zero can be added to each individual score. This increases the overall variance a predictable degree and attenuates all nonzero relationships (correlation coefficients, regression coefficients, slopes, t-ratios, F-ratios, and so on) a predictable amount for those relationships where the ordinary linear statistical model holds. The variance of the inoculated error can be kept small relative to the variance of the original data, thus minimally attenuating relationships, while effectively maintaining disguise since almost every score is changed to some degree (except for those very few who by chance draw a normal random number of exactly zero). This procedure affects the error of estimation, but *not* the degrees of freedom. It does tend to dampen curvilinear relationships, biasing the statistical decision in favor of linear ones. For all public variables whose statistically useful aspects can be converted into continuous form, this is the recommended procedure.

In many data sets, the procedure could be used for most public variables, leaving the remainder with such large cell size (see the discussion of crude report categories for public variables, above) that they could be left without error inoculation. Place of residence and place of birth, for example, could each be replaced by a number of related continuous variables: degree and minutes of longitude and latitude, population per square mile of census tract, percent black of census tract, mean residential rental value of census tract, and the like. To each of these variables could be added normal random error (e.g., adding 5% or 10% to the variance). If this were done, it might then be unnecessary to add error to high frequency categories, such as sex and race. For low frequency variables that are visibly listed, such as some professions or specialties, a second kind of error inoculation might be necessary.

The second form of error inoculation, random score substitution, is the appropriate procedure for dichotomous variables and for category systems that cannot be converted into continuous dimensions. For example, suppose a sample of doctors contained 30% general practitioners, 25% internists, 20% surgeons, 10% gynecologists, 10% psychiatrists, and 5% other medical specialties. Two randomizations would be involved: first, for each person, a simple random number would be drawn to determine if her or his data were to be left as is or were to be substituted. For example, if a 5% error rate were the aim, all those assigned random numbers from 00 through 04 would be selected for response substitution. For each of these, a second two-digit random number would be selected to determine the substitute response, and this response would be so chosen that the original overall distribution would be maintained. Thus, if the second two-digit random number were between 00 and 29, general practitioner would be assigned; if 30-54, internist; if 55-74, surgeon; and so on. (By chance, the substitute specialty would sometimes be the same as the original.)

This method can also be used for continuous variables, but it would be much less desirable than error addition. For tolerable levels of error inoculation, most scores remain exactly the same under random score substitution, making presumptive identification from public variables possible; under the random error addition, most scores are changed to some degree. Under error substitution the substitute response has no similarity to the correct response, while under normal random error addition the response is still similar to the original data, big errors are much less frequent than small ones, and thus much information is still retained. Even so, the general effect of the error inoculation by response substitution on summary statistics of association is calculable, although statistical power is inevitably reduced. (For error inoculation of statistical products rather than individual data, see below.)

In summary, error inoculation of individual data on public variables, while costly as far as statistical efficiency is concerned, is an acceptable safeguard that still permits many valuable reanalyses to be done.

IN-FILE CAPACITY TO RUN OUTSIDERS' STATISTICAL ANALYSES

It is already the practice of some archives of research data to provide for reanalysis of their data, not by releasing the raw data, but instead by performing on their data the statistical analyses requested by an outsider, who is charged for the costs involved. Project Talent, the American Council on Education, the Bureau of the Census, the STATPAK service of Statistics Canada, and other repositories provide such services. One of the obviously desirable features of maximally useful federal data archives would be that each be provided with such statistical analysis capacity. It is also in the interest of increasing our capacity to evaluate federal programs that nongovernmental archives with large relevant record sets be funded with federal evaluation research funds. Blue Cross/Blue Shield and other carriers of medical insurance, automobile and life insurance companies, and the like all could be made accessible by funding each major record center with a statistician and a computer programmer for this purpose.

Where the requested outputs are summary statistics, such as means, standard deviations, correlation coefficients, regression weights, slopes, rates, and so forth, summarized over large populations, few if any threats to individual privacy are involved. For sample surveys, the lists of participants can and should be kept confidential, precluding most conceivable code-breaking efforts. Where the data represent a complete census of some small population and where an outsider user is able to request repeatedly separate analyses, he or she might be able to decode data on a single person by using knowledge of public variables to move that person from one cell to another in two subsequent analyses, keeping the other people intact, and thus learn that one person's data by subtraction. If this is a hazard, the precaution of deleting one or more persons at random from each cell (deleting different persons for each reanalysis) will preclude such a subtractive code-breaking.

Where the output requested involves frequency counts and where, as in complete census, knowledge of who is in the file is available, the anonymity-breaking possibilities are much greater. The problem is the same as is met with in the publication of detailed tabulations. Hansen (1971) describes as "random modification" an approach to altering exact count data prior to publication. To adjust counts within categories, one simply multiplies the count by a random factor whose range is, say, 0.5-1.5 and whose properties are known. The long-run average count will be accurate if the random number is drawn from a uniform distribution, but the variance of the published estimators will be large relative to unadulterated counts. The method differs from error inoculation in that modification is limited to published count data and is not introduced at the individual data level. Where the outside analyst has no access to individual records, but does have access to tabulated statistical data, the Hansen variant appears to be more desirable than error inoculation of individual data.

Members of the Statistics Canada staff have recommended "random rounding" for the preservation of privacy in the publication of tabular material and in performing customer-specified analyses. Felligi and Phillips (1974) provide a convenient introduction to the papers that various members of this group have published. Even if small cell frequencies—say, below three—are not reported, these can usually be reconstructed from marginal frequencies and from considering several tables jointly. Collapsing categories into cruder ones must be applied to all tables involving that dimension if reconstruction of small cell frequencies is to be precluded, and thus has a greater informational cost than random rounding. Ordinary rounding is biased through a preponderance of rounding down and, because of its fixed rules, also often permits reconstruction of the real frequencies.

In random rounding all cell frequencies are rounded, either up or down depending on the random number drawn. Were the true frequency exactly half-way between the rounded values (e.g., ending in a five), then the chances of rounding up or down would be 50-50. In their system, as the true frequency is nearer the rounding up value, the chances of drawing a rounding up are increased so that an average of many roundings will give the true value. Marginals and total are rounded independently of cell roundings. Corresponding sums and averages are computed so as to be consistent both with the rounded frequencies and with the actual average per unit values computed on the unrounded data. Fellegi and Phillips report minimal bias or information loss once cell frequencies rise above 10 or 15 persons.

INTERFILE LINKAGE
OF CONFIDENTIAL DATA

The second major category of use to be considered is that in which statistical relations are sought between the data contained in two confidential files. In accordance with this paper's objective of providing very conservative but usable procedures, this can be achieved without increasing the number of file personnel or users who have access to confidential information about individuals. That is, if File A is being related to File B, the custodians of File A need not end up with confidential information from File B, or vice versa. Neither file need expand in the amount of confidential information it contains.

Even under these restrictions, interfile exchange is an extremely valuable tool in federal agency evaluation research. Once the major administrative archives of government, insurance companies, hospitals, and the like are organized and staffed for such research, the amount of interpretable outcome data on ameliorative programs can be increased tenfold.

For example, Fischer (1972) reports on the use of income tax data in a follow-up on the effectiveness of manpower training programs. While these data are not perfect or complete for the evaluation of such a training program, they are highly relevant. Claims on unemployment compensation and welfare payments would also be relevant. Cost is an important advantage. Using a different approach, Heller (1972) reports retrieval costs of $1 per person for a study of several thousand trainees. Even if $10 were more realistic, these costs are to be compared with costs of $100 or more per interview in individual follow-up interviews with ex-trainees. Rate of retrieval is another potential advantage. Follow-up interviews in urban manpower training programs have failed to locate as many as 50% of the population, and 30% loss rates would be common. Differential loss rates for experimental and control groups are also common, with the control groups less motivated to continue. In the NJNITE, over three years, 25.3% of the controls were lost, compared with a loss of only 6.5% of those in the most remunerative experimental condition. While retrieval rates overall might be no higher for withholding tax records, the differential bias in cooperation would probably be avoided, and the absence of data could be interpreted, with caution, as the absence of such earnings.

In many settings where programs are focused on special needs and where there are more eligible applicants than there are spaces for them, access to government records can enable program administrators to use experimental evaluation designs at minimal costs. With an excess of eligible applicants, there are several strategies available. An administrator can randomly select trainees from the pool of eligibles or from a pool of those at the borderline of eligibility, keeping records on those randomly rejected as a control group. Or the administrator can quantify the grounds of eligibility, or some component of it, admitting those who are most eligible according to this quantitative criterion, and keeping records on those above and below the cut-off point as categorized by their eligiblity scores. Access to appropriate administrative file records for subsequent outcome studies then provides a low-cost estimate of program effects. Such results might be used to justify an expensive follow-up by individual interviews.

The requirements for achieving such linkage are more complicated than for intrafile reanalysis. But it can and has been done with adequate guards to confidentiality (e.g., Schwartz and Orleans, 1967; Fischer, 1972). Even though such use requires special restrictions and rituals, its potential value justifies an investment in making these procedures routinely available. In what follows, four procedures are discussed: (1) microaggregation, (2) synthetic linkage by matching, (3) link file brokerage, and (4) mutually insulated file linkage. We provide no discussion of the procedures for file merging because the number of situations in which full confidentiality protection of all data from subpoena or the like is presently available to both of the federal agencies that might be involved in a file merger is extremely rare. If two agencies do have such full protection, adequate within-agency procedures would be available to protect merged files, including a need-to-know access limitation for agency employees.

MICROAGGREGATION

While the focus of the Feige and Watts (1970) paper is on single file analyses (albeit for a unified confidential federal statistical data center), their paper suggests that files be linked after microaggregation by parallel use of the same aggregation criteria, for example, one based on geographical units—a "micro zip-code system" (Feige and Watts, 1970: 270). For administrative files, this would certainly be of great use. For example, to have average income data available on pseudo-census tracts or block statistics (subject to limitations on the minimum number of individuals within aggregates) would greatly expand our capacity for social reality testing. If social experiments in community services or urban renewal could be allocated by census tract or block, microaggregated administrative data would be available for program evaluation.

Such a system could not be used to link NJNITE data to census or income tax records, for example, since the treatment was not assigned by microregion. It would be usable only for those social experiments where the experimental units corresponded to census tracts, blocks, zip codes, or other compact aggregation bases in use by other files. Moreover, even in such cases, the treatment would have to saturate the area, being applied to most persons in the aggregation unit rather than just to a few selected ones. Such experiments will occur, and this method should be kept in mind. But for most federal agency evaluation research, useful interfile linkage will have to be achieved through individual identifiers.

SYNTHETIC LINKAGE BY MATCHING

This title will be used to designate a technique used by Budd and Radner (1969), Okner (1972, 1974), and others (Ruggles and Ruggles, 1974; Alter, 1974) to link the data in two files from which individual identifiers have been removed or which contain only similar individuals, not necessarily the same individuals. If there are a number of variables shared by both files, these can be used for a one-to-one matching of individual cases from which a composite individual file can be made combining the unique data of the two files. These extended files can then be analyzed as though all of the data came from the same person.

Let us call the shared variables $X_1, X_2, \ldots X_n$, the variables unique to the first file $Y_1, Y_2, \ldots Y_n$, and those unique to the second file $Z_1, Z_2, \ldots Z_n$. A typical analytic goal is to determine relationships between Y and Z variables. If the X and Y variables and/or the X and Z variables are entirely independent, any Y and Z relationships will be lost, inasmuch as an essentially random matching will have been achieved. Consideration of the effect of error and other unique variance in variables would seem to predict that even with strong X-Y and X-Z relationships, the Y-Z correlations will be underestimated since they will be attenuated not only with the unique variance of the Y and Z variables (as in a direct study) but also by the unique variance in the X variables used for matching. The extent of such underestimation will be a function of the exactness of the matching and of the two multiple correlations between the matching X variables as independent variables and the specific Y and Z variables as dependent variables. It is possible that the extent of such attenuation can be estimated.

Where the two files differ widely on the means of the X variables—as where, for example, a survey of unemployed youth were to be linked with census data or, as in an example mentioned by Okner (1974), where homeowners were matched with nonhomeowners, both from IRS files—the matching process will systematically undermatch for the latent variables (as per considerations of the theory of error in variables and the experience with regression artifacts). Even with no file population mean differences to begin with (as he had two sample surveys of the same population), Alter (1974) found that inexact matches were necessary and that those cumulated to produce significant differences, even on the X variables used in matching (for other criticisms, see Sims, 1972, 1974). The technique is still under valuation. Its practitioners are properly self-critical. We may soon expect trial runs where all variables, X, Y, and Z, exist in the same file so that the Y-Z relationship produced by matching linkage can be compared with the true values. For the present, we judge the technique inferior to linkage procedures (such as the mutually insulated file linkage discussed below) based on individual identity and using individual identifiers, if these are available.

Synthetic linkage by matching would not seem feasible for the specific purpose of using administrative archives for follow-up measures in the evaluation of the effects of experimental programs.

LINK FILE BROKERAGE

Manniche and Hayes (1957), Astin and Boruch (1970), and others have proposed that a responsible broker, located perhaps in another country, provide the linkage. Domestically, we can visualize this done in an agency like the Census Bureau, where records are immune from subpoena. Each file would prepare a list of names or other individual identifiers and corresponding file-specific code numbers, which would be turned over to the linkage broker. Using the individual identifiers common to the two files, the broker would prepare a list, deck, or tape linking the two file-specific codes from which the names and other individual identifiers would be removed. Subsequently, the files would provide data sets to the broker identified only by file-specific codes. The broker could then merge such decks from the two files and turn the merged deck over to either of the files, with both file-specific codes now deleted.

This suggestion comes out of a well-justified policy of keeping the data of a research project separated, insofar as possible, from the names and addresses of the respondents during data analysis. But it also assumes that deletion of identifiers provides adequate protection of confidentiality. As we have seen, this is not always sufficient. In addition, the broker represents a new file that has access to identified confidential information (unless it can be assured that the two lists linking public identifiers to the file-specific code information were destroyed immediately after use).

As originally proposed, link file brokerage also permits personal identifiers to be reconnected easily with the total merged data set if either of the original files still has its original data with personal identifiers. The replication of the unique variables on both the original data and on the new composite deck will usually provide a basis for exact matching, making the reinstatement of personal identifiers on the merged deck a simple process and thus giving one file access to the confidential information of the other file.

To avoid these difficulties, the link file brokerage device must be modified in one or more directions. In some settings it might be possible for each original file to destroy all records of names and other public identifiers after having transmitted the linking list to the broker. This would be hard to police, and particularly hard for one file to insure on the part of the other file, as would be necessary in settings where a custodian of confidential data has assumed responsibility for restricting the dissemination of the data in individually identifiable form. Where the broker is isolated from opportunities and temptations to misuse data, or if ways can be developed to guarantee the broker's destruction of the intermediate lists containing identifiers, it would be desirable for the broker to do the analyses on the merged deck, operating as a public utility data archive, as described in a preceding section. (Such analyses could be done without the broker knowing the meaning of the variables being analyzed, although later publication could reveal variable names.) Under such conditions, the merged deck would never get back to the original files. If the merged deck is to be shared with an originating file, sufficient error inoculation of the unique variables could preclude the exact matching that would reinstate identifiers.

The use of a link file broker may be of some value in protecting against subpoena if the broker is located beyond the reach of subpoena or protected from subpoena by statute. But, for the goal of restricting identifiable data to the files for which permission has been given, this system has serious weaknesses unless much modified.

(The linking of research files by remembered or regenerated codes retained by the respondent so that longitudinal studies are made possible while files have no individual identifiers is a separate technique needing a review and analysis. Where one of the files is a government record, this does not seem feasible.)

MUTUALLY INSULATED FILE LINKAGE

This phrase is used to cover a group of similar devices for linking files without merging, preserving confidentiality. The essential notions involved have no doubt been hit upon independently on many occasions, particularly in statistical research with government records. Of published discussions, probably the first and certainly the most cited is by Schwartz and Orleans (1967), in a study linking public opinion survey responses to income tax returns. But it is clear from Fischer (1972) that similar processes have been in use in a number of government agencies.

It seems well to start with a concrete exposition of the full model in its most conservative version, and subsequently to discuss alternatives and abbreviations. The hypothetical problem in Figure 1 is to relate a local Job Corps experimental program to Social Security Administration records on earnings subject to FICA deductions. It is assumed that both files are to be kept confidential from each other. The experimental trainees and the control trainees would have been grouped by socioeconomic level, chosen as a useful dimension of analysis. Where there are a sufficient number of trainees within a given level, two or more lists would have been formed. The resulting 26 lists would then have been assigned list names from A to Z on a random basis.

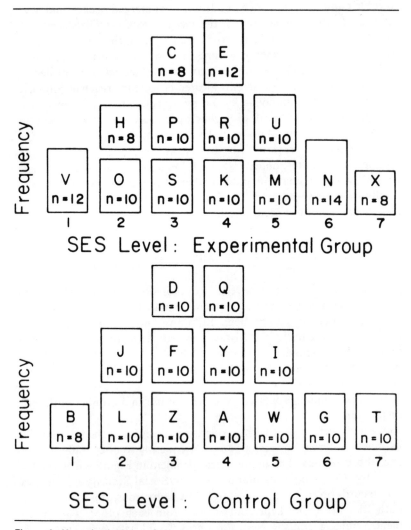

Figure 1: Hypothetical data from two treatment groups in a social experiment, grouped by SES level and given coded list designators A through Z.

Each list itself would consist solely of person identifiers useful in SSA's retrieval operation, such as name and Social Security number. SSA would delete one person at random from each list, locate the data on all variables of interest for the remainder, compute for each variable a mean, variance, and frequency for the persons on the list for whom FICA deductions were on record, and send back these summary statistics, identified with their unique list designators. The Job Corps project evaluators would then reassemble these cell-by-cell data into their meaningful dimensional order and compute summary statistics. While the SSA file would get individual identifiers, they would get no interpretable data about these individuals. In return, they would send back no information about individuals, but only summary statistics about a group, which the evaluators would decode as a data cell in a statistical grid. The returned data would be microaggregated, but by an aggregation scheme unrevealed to and undecodable by the SSA. It should be emphasized that the researching agency receiving the microaggregated data (in this example, the Job Corps) must not in its published report provide results for any single list, but must further aggregate the dependent-variable information received from the furnishing agency (SSA) in such a manner as to conceal the confidential characteristics of the individuals for whom the information might be sought. Otherwise, publication of the furnished information by the researching agency could provide the furnishing agency with the ability to identify the individuals in terms of the independent variables by which they are characterized.

In Figure 1, the vertical dimension represents frequency, but it could represent cross-classification on any other dimensional score. Note that adjacent (and even identical) scale values are assigned haphazardly nonadjacent list codes. Not only are the names of the variables disguised from the second file, but also the ordering of respondents on these variables. When the cell means and variances have been returned to the initiating file, they can be reassembled to provide publishable group means, standard deviations, t-ratios, F-ratios, covariances, correlations, regression weights, slopes, and so on. Frequency distributions, cross tabulations, and cell means would often reveal to the second file (SSA) first file (Job Corps) information, although this might be precluded by adding random values as discussed by Hansen (1971) and above.

It probably would have been of both scientific and public policy value to have the results of the NJNITE cross-validated with SSA income data, ideally using years prior to, during, and subsequent to the three years of the experiment. As a hypothetical exercise, consideration of such a study will serve to develop a number of points. While not all income would be picked up in this manner, the results would still be very useful. The effects of attrition, and especially differential attrition, would be minimized, since many noncooperators in the periodic interviews would still have employers sending in reports to the SSA on earnings subject to FICA. For such a study to be done, lists would be prepared subject to the same considerations discussed under the first presentation of microaggregation above. Thus, each of the eight experimental payment plans in each of the five cities would provide 40 lists of varying size, averaging some 16 persons per list. The control subjects in each of the five cities could be randomly assigned to eight lists per city. The resulting 80 lists of names would be randomly assigned list designations and then sent to the SSA.

With these uses and procedures in mind, some more detailed problems and questions can be considered.

1. The random deletion of one individual from each list is to prevent detection of identified individual data through repeated negotiations. For example, without that precaution File A could group an individual in one list on one negotiation and delete that individual from the list on a second negotiation, keeping all of the other individuals on the list intact. The difference between the two means would then represent this individual's score. The random deletion process prevents this possibility and would, of course, be done anew for each negotiation.

In place of random deletion, the addition of a random normal error to each set of scores for each list could be substituted. In the case of longitudinal data, this would seem to be more damaging to the analysis than the loss of one randomly selected case per list.

2. In the Schwartz and Orleans study (1967), individual scores were provided, rather than means and variances. This was adequate safeguard in that instance, but where repeated negotiation between files has to be anticipated, it would usually permit disclosure of individual data by the device of moving a person from one list to another list on successive negotiations. A random deletion from each list would not usually protect against this.

If the general normal linear additive model is being assumed in the analysis, the cell means and variances are as useful as the individual scores, although new computational versions of standard formulas are needed. Other summary statistics, higher order moments, indices of skewness, and so on could be added to the mean and variance data.

An intermediate degree of disguise can be considered, in which the originating file turns over its variables with code names for the variables (rather than, as here suggested, unique and scrambled codes for each category on each variable). This probably makes the discovery of the variable more likely and makes it definitely possible once the results are published, if the second file has kept the records of the transaction. In contrast, under mutually insulated file linkage as first presented above, the published analyses of the data by the initiating file would provide summary statistics for the whole sample, pooling the information from numerous lists, so that the second file would not be able to identify values on the variables reported in the published articles for any lists they might retain.

4. Lower limits on the number of persons in any list need to be established by practical exercises in identity breaking. Heller (1972) says only "small cells have to be withheld." Fischer (1972) suggests a three-person minimum. The random deletion of one person per cell gets very costly at this cell size. In the illustrations above, a minimum of eight has been used.

5. The requirement of minimal cell size will set limits on the number of variables or dimensions from the originating file that can be employed. One, two, or three may be common maximums. (There is no limit, however, on the number of variables from the second file.) More first-file variables can be handled by repeated negotiations. If, as for a factor analysis, one wanted to relate 20 variables from the first file with 20 from the second, one might do this in seven negotiations, each using two or three variables from File 1 and all 20 from File 2, to get the 400 cross-file correlations. The 90 intra-File 1 and the 90 intra-File 2 correlations would best be done within each file, but for the linked cases pooled from all lists. (For File 1 to do the File 2 intrafile correlations from the list aggregates it has received would potentially bias these correlations as described under microaggregation above.) The matrix of correlations would have the defect of being biased upon differing numbers of cases, but with substantial numbers this should not render a factor analysis inconsistent.

6. Because of some confusion in previous discussions of the method, it must be emphasized that the file linkage achieved is strictly limited and that file merging does not result. File 2 gets no addition at all. File 1 has access to File 2 variables for further analyses only in a micro-aggregated form. File 1 could microaggregate other File 1 variables by the lists used in a prior negotiation and could relate these means to the means on the File 2 variables received in that prior negotiation. These indirectly estimated relations would not be ascertained with the precision of those involving variables used in the initial negotiations, but rather in the form described for the relationships among unique variables ascertained fro microaggregate data, as described in the first section above.

7. In the hypothetical illustration involving the NJNITE, SSA rather than IRS files were used because consideration of the latter raises several unique issues that would unduly complicate the general model. First, there are some interfile exchange settings where it is a loss of privacy and a breach of confidentiality for one file to even inform another file that a person exists. If the NJNITE were to send its lists to the IRS, this might make the IRS aware of nonfilers who should have been filing income tax returns. To avoid this, the NJNITE would need to access the IRS index files, identify the tax return document locator numbers for those who had filed returns, and negotiate only for summary information for filers (Steinberg and Pritzker, 1969). This is probably not a realistic worry for the NJNITE, because most of its respondents were probably motivated to file tax returns in order to obtain refunds of withheld taxes. However, even if any exposed delinquent cases would likely be cases in which the IRS owed the wage earner money rather than vice versa, the best approach would still be to have the NJNITE access the IRS index files. In many studies there would be a real jeopardy, and however the researcher felt about delinquent taxpayers, she or he would realize that it was not a part of the research role to bring them to justice and would therefore arrange for screening by her or his own staff so that negotiations with the IRS would be limited to known tax filers.

Schwartz and Orleans (1967), working with prosperous respondents, avoided this problem by a three-stage negotiation. First, the IRS provided them with a regionally concentrated list of names and addresses of taxpayers who itemized their deductions and filled out their own income tax forms. Four groups to receive four different types of interview were randomly chosen. These were further subclassified by the attitudes they expressed, and formed into lists that were sent to IRS in the second stage. In the third stage, the IRS turned back to Schwartz and Orleans' unidentified data in scrambled order within lists. In that instance they published data that identified only the treatment groups. If, however, they had published information concerning attitudes or behavior, the protection of privacy would have required further aggregation, as mentioned above. The first stage could also be done by asking respondents whether or not they filed income tax returns or by ascertaining withholding tax status by knowing their place of work and so on. In the three-way linkage study discussed by Steinberg and Pritzker (1969), the IRS allowed a Census Bureau representative to examine the IRS taxpayer index to find out if there were tax records on certain respondents, but the representative was not allowed to see the content of the records. Only for those Census Bureau cases certified to exist in IRS files were tax data requested. Use of this device, or the stage one of Schwartz and Orleans, depends upon the relative sensitivity of the knowledge of presence or absence of persons in each of the files; this must be evaluated separately for each study.

8. Considering a hypothetical NJNITE-IRS exchange also raises the possibility that in some cases co-occurrence on a File 1 list might provide meaningful incriminating evidence to File 2. For example, suppose that NJNITE income supplement recipients were supposed to report this experimental income on their tax forms and that most of them had done so. The IRS's general knowledge of the experiment, plus their observation that on certain lists many persons were reporting such income, could have led them to suspect that the others on such lists should also have done so.

Such possibilities occur when the second file has partial information on a variable being used in the negotiation by the first file. Such information leads the second file to deduce a dimension of homogeneity for the list (lists must be homogeneous for the system to work). This deduction then justifies the deduction that the remaining persons on the list should also have the same value on this variable. In general, this is a very unlikely set of circumstances and would not stand in the way of most interfile exchanges. But it is an appropriate worry in this concrete case, and it should be checked. Consideration should be given to a procedure that has been used which requires embedding the File 1 population in a larger one. Random subsets would include one or more non-File 1 population members in each microaggregated list. Other lists would contain small numbers of the File 1 population and the largest portion from the larger population. This, while more expensive, creates the desired heterogeneity. In carrying out analyses using File 2 data, File 1 could discard lists primarily from the larger population. Occasionally, concerns about list homogeneity will lead one to forego a dimension of analysis. One might decide not to use lists grouped on criminal record, or grouped on having committed a given crime, because of the danger that colisting will convey incriminating information.

For most of the wide range of federal agency evaluation research uses, such incriminating categories will not be involved. Classifying Job Corps trainees by number of months of training will produce no colisting jeopardy with either the IRS or the SSA. If family income provides jeopardy when negotiating for IRS or welfare agency records, this variable can be sacrificed and some effects of the training still ascertained, providing that there has been a good experimental or quasi-experimental scheduling of admission.

SUMMARY

Realistic testing of the effects of federal programs designed to ameliorate social problems can be greatly improved by making available administrative records on unemployment, earnings, educational attainment, medical insurance usage, and the like. Research data evaluating social experiments need to be open to critical reanalysis. Both types of use of records and files must be done in ways that avoid violating the confidentiality of the data provided by respondents or increasing the risk of gossip, blackmail, or arrest. Confidentiality-preserving modes of access to files and to interfile exchange for statistical analysis exist. It is in the public interest that facilities for using these modes of access be made readily available. Where maximal protection of confidentiality is required, the present analysis of the problem results in the following conclusions.

(1) The major sets of administrative and research records on individuals can be kept separate, rather than being merged into combined data banks, and still permit useful statistical linkage.

(2) It would be desirable that data archives relevant to federal agency program evaluation be funded to do statistical analyses on their own data. Data files relevant to federal program evaluation include not only governmental records such as Census Bureau, Social Security, Internal Revenue, crime, and welfare, but also record files in the private sector such as medical and automobile insurance.

(3) In order for statistical analyses to be done that link data from different files, all files should record common person identifiers, such as name, birth date, birth place, and Social Security number. In the mode of mutually insulated interfile linkage described here, the presence of such shared identifiers does *not* jeopardize confidentiality. The confidential information linked with each personal identifier remains limited to the original file.

(4) For the statistical reanalysis of data from a single file, it is usually not a complete safeguard to release the data with personal identification deleted. If, in the data released, there are items of information that are also available publicly, then additional precautions are required, such as restrictions on the number and refinement of these public variables in the data released or error inoculation of the public variables. Microaggregated release is acceptable. The optimal procedure is for the file in question to have the capacity to do the required reanalyses itself, using randomized rounding where frequency data are released.

(5) For the interfile exchange of confidential data, where one or both of the files are confidential, analysts should actively consider use of mutually insulated file linkage with random deletions of one person per list. It would be desirable that all relevant files be staffed with the minimum retrieval and statistical analysis capacities required to cooperate in any such linkage.

REFERENCES

ALTER, H. E. (1974) "Creation of a synthetic data set by linking records of the Canadian Survey of Consumer Finances with the Family Expenditure Survey 1970." Annals of Econ. and Social Measurement 3: 373-394.

ASTIN, A. W. and R. G. BORUCH (1970) "A link file system for assuring confidentiality in longitudinal studies." Amer. Educ. Research J. 1: 615-624.

BAUMAN, R. A., M. H. DAVID, and R. F. MILLER (1970) "Working with complex data files: II. The Wisconsin assets and income studies archive," pp. 112-136 in R. L. Bisco (ed.) Data Bases, Computers, and the Social Sciences. New York: Wiley-Interscience.

BORUCH, R. F. (1972a) "Strategies for eliciting and merging confidential social research data." Policy Sciences 3: 275-297.

——— (1972b) "Relations among statistical methods for assuring confidentiality of data." Social Sci. Research 1: 403-414.

——— (1971) "Maintaining confidentiality in educational research: a systematic analysis." Amer. Psychologist 26: 413-430.

——— (1969) "Educational research and the confidentiality of data: a case study." ACE Research Reports 4. Washington, D.C.: American Council on Education.

BRYANT, E. C. and M. H. HANSEN (1975) "Invasion of privacy and surveys: a growing dilemma." Paper presented at the Smithsonian-Navy Conference on Survey Alternatives, Santa Fe, New Mexico, April 22-24.

BUDD, E. C. and D. B. RADNER (1969) The O. B. E. size distribution series: methods and tentative results for 1964." Amer. Econ. Rev. 59: 435-449.

DUNN, E. S., Jr. (1974) Social Information Processing and Statistical Systems: Change and Reform. New York: Wiley-Interscience.

FEIGE, E. L. and H. W. WATTS (1970) "Protection of privacy through microaggregation," in R. L. Bisco (ed.) Data Bases, Computers, and the Social Sciences. New York: Wiley-Interscience.

FELLEGI, I. P. (1972) "On the question of statistical confidentiality." J. of the Amer. Stat. Assn. 67: 7-18.

——— and J. L. PHILLIPS (1974) "Statistical confidentiality: some theory and applications to data dissemination." Annals of Econ. and Social Measurement 3: 399-409.

FISCHER, J. L. (1972) "The uses of Internal Revenue Service data," pp. 177-180 in M. E. Borus (ed.) Evaluating the Impact of Manpower Programs. Lexington, MA: D. C. Heath.

GOSLIN, D. A. (1971) "Ethical and legal aspects of the collection and use of educational information," pp. 149-159 in G. V. Glass (ed.) Proceedings of the 1970 invitational Conference on Testing Problems. Princeton, NJ: Educational Testing Service.

GREENBERG, B. G., J. R. ABERNATHY, and D. G. HORVITZ (1970) "A new survey technique and its application in the field of public health." Milbank Memorial Fund Q. 68: 39-55.

GREENBERG, B. G., A. A. ABUL-ELA, W. R. SIMON, and D. G. HORVITZ (1969) "The unrelated question randomized response model: theoretical framework." J. of the Amer. Stat. Assn. 64: 520-539.

HANSEN, M. H. (1971) "Insuring confidentiality of individual records in data storage and retrieval for statistical purposes," pp. 48-61 in Federal Statistics, Vol. II: Report of the President's Commission (No. 4000-0269). Washington, D.C.: Government Printing Office.

HELLER, R. N. (1972) "The uses of social security administration data," pp. 197-201 in M. E. Borus (ed.) Evaluating the Impact of Manpower Programs. Lexington, MA: D. C. Heath.

HOFFMAN, L. J. [ed.] (1973) Security and Privacy in Computer Systems. Los Angeles: Melville (Wiley).

——— and W. F. MILLER (1970) "How to obtain a personal dossier from a data bank." Datamation 16: 75-76.

KERSHAW, D. N. (1975) "The New Jersey negative income tax experiment: a summary of the design, operations and results of the first large-scale social science experiment," pp. 87-116 in G. M. Lyons (ed.) Social Research and Public Policies. Hanover, NH: Dartmouth College Public Affairs Center.

——— (1972) "A negative income tax experiment." Scientific Amer. 227: 19-25.

MANNICHE, E., and D. P. HAYES (1957) "Respondent anonymity and data matching." Public Opinion Q. 21: 384-388.

MILLER, A. R. (1971) The Assault on Privacy. Ann Arbor: Univ. of Michigan Press.

OKNER, B. A. (1974) "Data matching and merging: an overview." Annals of Econ. and Social Measurement 3: 347-352.

——— (1972) "Constructing a new data base from existing microdata sets: the 1966 merge file." Annals of Econ. and Social Measurement 1: 325-342.

RIECKEN, H. W., R. F. BORUCH, D. T. CAMPBELL, N. CAPLAN, T. K. GLENNAN, J. PRATT, A. REES, and W. WILLIAMS (1974) Social Experimentation: A Method for Planning and Evaluating Social Intervention. New York: Academic Press.

RUEBHAUSEN, O. M. and O. G. BRIM, Jr. (1965) "Privacy and behavioral research." Columbia Law Rev. 65: 1184-1211.

RUGGLES, N. and R. RUGGLES (1974) "A strategy for merging and matching microdata sets." Annals of Econ. and Social Measurement 3: 353-371.

Russell Sage Foundation (1970) Guidelines for the Collection, Maintenance and Dissemination of Pupil Records. New York: Russell Sage Foundation.

SAWYER, J. and H. SCHECHTER (1968) "Computers, privacy and the National Data Center: the responsibility of social scientists." Amer. Psychologist 23: 810-818.

SCHEUREN, F., B. BRIDGES, and B. KILSS (1973) "Subsampling the current population survey: 1963 pilot link study. Report No. 1: Studies from interagency data linkages." (DHEW Pub. No. (SSA) 74-11750.) Washington, D.C.: Department of Health, Education and Welfare, Social Security Administration, Office of Research and Statistics (August).

SCHWARTZ, R. D. and S. ORLEANS (1967) "On legal sanctions." Univ. of Chicago Law Rev. 34: 274-300.

SIMS, C. A. (1974) "Comment: January 17, 1974." Annals of Econ. and Social Measurement 3: 395-397.

——— (1972) " 'Comments' to Okner's 1966 merge file." Annals of Econ. and Social Measurement 1: 343-345.

STEINBERG, J. (1973) "Some observations on linkage of survey and administrative record data," in Studies from Interagency Data Linkages. (DHEW Pub. No. (SSA) 74-11750.) Washington, D.C.: Department of Health, Education and Welfare, Social Security Administration, Office of Research and Statistics (August).

——— (1967) "Interacting data systems and the measurement of income size distributions." Paper presented to the Conference on Research in Income and Wealth: The Size Distribution of Income and Wealth, University of Pennsylvania, March.

——— and L. PRITZKER (1969) "Some experiences with the reflections on data linkage in the United States." Bull. of the Int. Stat. Inst. 42: 786-805.

TURN, R. (1973) Privacy Transformations for Data Bank Systems. Rand Research Report P-4955. Santa Monica, CA: Rand Corporation.

WARE, W. H. [chair] (1973) Records, Computers, and the Rights of Citizens. Report of the Secretary's Advisory Committee on Automated Personal Data Systems, Department of Health, Education and Welfare, July. No. 1700-00116. Washington, D.C.: Government Printing Office.

WARNER, S. L. (1965) "Randomized response: a survey technique for eliminating evasive answer bias." J. of the Amer. Stat. Assn. 60: 63-69.

WATTS, H. W. (1972) "Microdata: lessons from the SEO and the Graduated Work Incentive Experiment." Econ. and Social Measurement 1: 183-192.

——— and A. REES [eds.] (1973) Final Report of the New Jersey Graduated Work Incentive Experiment. Volume I: An Overview of the Labor Supply Results and of Central Labor-Supply Results. Volume II: Studies Relating to the Validity and Generalizability of the Results. Volume III: Response With Respect to Expenditure, Health, and Social Behavior and Technical Notes. Madison: University of Wisconsin Institute for Research on Poverty. (duplicated paper)

WESTIN, A. F. (1972) Data Banks in a Free Society. New York: Quadrangle.

——— [ed.] (1971) Information Technology in a Democracy. Cambridge, MA: Harvard Univ. Press.

——— (1967) Privacy and Freedom. New York: Antheum.

WHEELER, S. [ed.] (1969) Files and Dossiers in American Life. New York: Russell Sage Foundation.

13

SCHOOLS OR STUDENTS: AGGREGATION PROBLEMS IN THE STUDY OF STUDENT ACHIEVEMENT

By

LAURA IRWIN LANGBEIN

Laura Irwin Langbein's investigation illustrates significant disparities between identical models of student achievement estimated for both students and schools. She shows that standardized aggregate measures of the influence of race and status on achievement are really inflated versions of their individual level counterparts. Moreover, she shows that reliance on unstandardized estimates can be equally invalid. The author states further that exclusive reliance on less costly aggregated data may produce misleading and ultimately more costly results. Therefore she recommends analysis of both individual and aggregate data in the process of evaluation.

From Laura Irwin Langbein, "Schools or Students: Aggregation Problems in the Study of Student Achievement." Unpublished paper, 1977.

ABSTRACT: *Studies of student achievement have disclosed little agreement about whether schools or students are the most appropriate unit of analysis. This investigation demonstrates significant disparities in identical models of student achievement estimated for students and schools. The study indicates that standardized aggregate measures of the influence of race and status on achievement are inflated versions of their individual level counterparts. Relying on unstandardized estimates can be equally hazardous. First, it is impossible to estimate uniquely the impact of two contextual variables—the ability and status of a student's peers— on individual behavior from aggregate data. Since contextual properties are manipulable whereas individual properties are not, unique estimates of their impact are crucial if educational research is to be policy relevant. Second, simultaneous analysis of individual as well as aggregate data indicates whether aggregate estimates are more biased than those from individual level data. Even if aggregation does not increase bias, the importance of estimating contextual effects makes exclusive analysis of less costly aggregate data potentially misleading and ultimately more expensive.*

After countless reanalyses and replications two fundamental conclusions of the Coleman report (1966) remain widely accepted. Even staunch critics of the report concede both the crucial importance of family background for student achievement and the relative insignificance of such contextual properties of a student's environment as the characteristics of peers and the quality of teachers and school facilities.[1] Since contextual properties can be manipulated, whereas the family background of individual students cannot, these conclusions have disturbed and frustrated those charged with shaping educational policy. If Coleman's findings are correct, such traditional educational reforms as improving school facilities, reassigning students, and upgrading the quality of teachers are likely to have little or no effect on the cognitive development of students.

AUTHOR'S NOTE: The research reported herein was performed pursuant to a grant contract with the National Institute of Education, U.S. Department of Health, Education, and Welfare. Contractors undertaking such projects under Government sponsorship are encouraged to express freely their professional judgment in the conduct of the project. Points of view or opinions stated do not, therefore, necessarily represent official National Institute of Education position or policy.

Accurate empirical estimates of the impact of individual and contextual properties, however, depend critically on whether schools or students constitute the unit of analysis. Yet replications and reanalyses of the Coleman report disclose little agreement about the unit of analysis most appropriate for the study of student achievement.[2] These inconsistencies in the choice of units can have important substantive implications. Previous work in social statistics has firmly established that changes in the unit of analysis may generate substantial changes in the results of quantitative analysis. This investigation, a reanalysis of Coleman's data, demonstrates significant disparities in identical models of student achievement estimated for students and schools. First, standardized measures like correlations and beta weights are particularly sensitive to changes in units of analysis. The correlation between family background and achievement increases considerably when schools rather than students constitute the unit on which data are measured. Family background is a good predictor of student achievement only when schools are the unit of analysis. Its poor performance when students are the unit of analysis suggests that very little is known about cognitive development (Hanushek and Kain, 1972: 130). Moreover, as measured by standardized regression coefficients, the impact of family background variables on achievement appears to be very large when schools are the unit of measurement. Yet much of this impact is an artifact of the grouping process and has no causal significance.

Second, when schools are the unit of analysis, quantitative techniques may be unable to separate the influence of contextual from individual variables, even if the estimating equation is properly specified. The ability to distinguish between the effects of individual and contextual properties depends on the contextual characteristics that influence a particular situation. Previous research has not centered specifically on the problem of decomposing different kinds of contextual properties in the absence of individual data. Hannan, Freeman, and Meyer (1976), for example, consider problems of cross-level inference for several kinds of contextual properties. Their treatment, however, does not concern the decomposition of aggregate estimates into contextual and individual effects. Sprague (1976), in contrast, focuses on problems of identification in contextual models, but not on problems of aggregation. Finally, Alwin (1976) considers problems of both identification and aggregation, but only for one type of contextual characteristic. Yet this study identifies six such characteristics, three of which require the use of individual level data to isolate their unique impact on achievement. Of these, two appear to be effective determinants of student achievement: the family background and cognitive ability of a student's peers. When investigators analyze schools rather than students, they are likely to attribute erroneously the contribution of these variables to the students themselves rather than to their environment. Manipulable properties of a student's environment, although important influences on student achievement, may be obscured by the analysis of aggregate data. Only by using students rather than schools as the unit of analysis can investigators avoid such faulty and misleading inferences.

Finally, the study shows that, under certain circumstances, using both individual and aggregate level data to estimate identical models also establishes a partial test for the adequate specification of the individual level model. Adequate specification assures investigators that estimates of the impact of independent variables are unbiased. At best, the test eliminates several sources of misspecification. At worst, it assures investigators that estimates from less costly grouped data are no worse than those from more costly data on individuals. For educational policy research, testing models of achievement using both students and schools can help assess the validity of estimates of the impact of nonmanipulable contextual properties. Although this test demands costly data on students, it significantly reduces the likelihood of misleading, and therefore even more costly, estimates.

THE EFFECTS OF GROUPING:
STANDARDIZED MEASURES, CONTEXTUAL EFFECTS,
AND THE SPECIFICATION OF MODELS

Ever since Robinson's (1950) seminal article on the "ecological fallacy," the dangers of using aggregate data to make inferences about individuals have been well known. In particular, investigators have determined that the magnitude of correlations and other standardized measures of association like beta weights and partial correlation coefficients usually increases with increasing levels of aggregation. The grouping process itself generates this result. The effects of grouping on standardized measures of association can best be understood in the context of a specific model of student achievement.

Suppose, for example, that a student's achievement (Y) is affected by his race (X_1) and by his socioeconomic status (X_2). Suppose also that the error term in the following regression equation is uncorrelated with X_1 and X_2:[3]

$$Y = b_1^* X_1 + b_2^* X_2 + e. \qquad [1]$$

In this equation, b_1^* and b_2^* are beta weights. In lieu of data regarding the achievement, race, and socioeconomic status of individual students, schoolwide means may be used. Instead of equation [1], the equation:

$$Y = b_1^* X_1 + b_2^* X_2 + e \qquad [2]$$

is used.

The magnitude of standardized measures associated with equation [2] relative to those associated with equation [1] depends on the grouping process. Several grouping processes could determine how students are allotted to schools. At one extreme, a student's race and socioeconomic status could dictate school attendance. Each school would then be more homogeneous with respect to race and status than the population of students in the district. Such an assignment procedure groups students according to their values on the two independent variables in equation [1]. At the other extreme, a student's achievement score could determine which school he attends. In this case, high achievers attend schools with other high achievers; low achievers attend with other low achievers. Empirically, school asignment is more likely to approximate the first rather than the second extreme.[4] Thus, examination of the behavior of standardized measures of association when data have been grouped by values of X_1 and X_2 is instructive.

If students are grouped into schools according to their race and status, the magnitude of standardized measures of association increases. Grouping by these variables increases their variance relative to the variance in the dependent variable, so that $R^2_{\bar{y}.\bar{x}_1\bar{x}_2} > R^2_{y.x_1x_2}$.[5] In other words, the school-to-school variance in achievement explained by race and status exceeds the student-to-student variance explained by the same variables. Aggregate analysis may therefore suggest that more is known about the determinants of student achievement than individual analysis would warrant.

In addition, grouping by race and status increases the magnitude of beta weights, so that the absolute value of $\bar{b}^*_1$ and $\bar{b}^*_2$ will be larger than b^*_1 and b^*_2 respectively.[6] Thus, as long as equation [1] is properly specified, and as long as schools are relatively homogeneous with respect to X_1 and X_2, the standardized influence of race and status on achievement will appear larger when data are measured on schools instead of students. In contrast, under these same conditions, the unstandardized regression coefficients are stable from one unit of analysis to another.[7] Analyses of student achievement that rely on aggregate data to compute standardized measures of influence are therefore likely to overestimate the effects of individual level variables like race and status.

Nevertheless, even if the aggregate model is properly specified, estimating unstandardized rather than standardized coefficients from aggregate level data is likely to remain unsatisfactory for the measurement of contextual effects. Specifically, aggregate data alone are insufficient to isolate the impact of some types of contextual variables. The source and impact of contextual variables determines whether they are amenable to aggregate level analysis. The source of a contextual variable specifies how it is related to individual level independent variables. Its impact specifies how it influences the individual level dependent variable.

There are three sources of contextual effects. First, a contextual variable can be a function of an independent variable included in an individual level relation. For example, $\bar{X}_2$ defines the socioeconomic status of those with whom a student attends school; $\overline{X}_2$ is a function of X_2, the status of individual students. Second, a contextual variable can be a function of the dependent variable included in an individual level relation. The achievement level of a student's peers, $\overline{Y}$, is such a contextual variable. In fact, school policies based on tracking presuppose that the achievement of peers has an independent impact on the achievement of individual students. Finally, the definition of many contextual variables is unrelated to any of the variables included in the individual level relation. Variables like the quality of the teachers and the school's facilities typify this type of contextual variable, denoted by $\overline{Z}$.[8]

Contextual variables can also affect behavior in two ways. First, they can affect behavior directly.[9] Thus, the socioeconomic status of those with whom a student attends school could have a direct effect on his own achievement. Contextual variables can also have interactive effects.[10] For example, attending school with students of higher status can reinforce the effects of a student's own race or status on his ability. If a high status student has high achievement, that impact may be magnified if the student attends school with other high status students. Alternatively, the impact may be lessened if he attends school with lower status students. With regard to school quality, the impact of low status may be reduced if low status students attend schools with good facilities and high calibre teachers. In fact mitigating the effects of race and status by improving quality was an early goal of Title I of the Elementary and Education Act of 1965 (McLaughlin, 1975: 34).

Aggregate estimates of the independent impact of contextual variables, however, are often underidentified, even when the aggregate equations are perfectly specified. Consider first contextual variables that arise from independent variables included in the individual level relation, such as the socioeconomic status of a student's peers. Coleman (1966: 304-310) showed clearly that low status students benefit from daily contact in school with higher status students. As the status of their peers increases, low status students are more likely to score higher on standardized verbal achievement tests. At the individual level, peer effects like these could operate in one of two ways. First, they could affect achievement directly:

$$\overline{Y} = \overline{b}_1 \overline{X}_1 + b_2 \overline{X}_2 + \overline{b}_3 \overline{X}_2 + e, \qquad [3]$$

where each variable was previously defined but the regression coefficients are now unstandardized rather than standardized.[11]

Peer effects could also interact multiplicatively with race. Attending school with high status peers may mitigate the effects of race on achievement.[12] In other words, the achievement differences between blacks and whites in high status school may be less than the differences in a low status school. Such a model can be formalized by a regression:

$$Y = b_1 X_1 + b_2 X_2 + e, \qquad [4]$$

where $b_1 = (b_3 + b_4\overline{X}_2)$, so that the resultant equation is:

$$Y = b_3X_1 + b_4X_1\overline{X}_2 + b_2X_2 + e. \qquad [5]$$

Peer effects could also interact with an individual student's socioeconomic status. In other words, a student's own status may have less impact on his achievement when he attends school with high status peers than when he attends with low status peers. In this case, b_2 in equation [4] is a function of the mean status of those with whom a student attends school:

$$b_2 = (b_3 + b_4\overline{X}_2).$$

By substitution, the appropriate model becomes:

$$Y = b_1X_1 + b_3X_2 + b_4X_2\overline{X}_2 + e. \qquad [6]$$

A significant value for b_4 would indicate that a student's own status has differential effects on his achievement, depending on the status of his peers.[13]

Thus, the socioeconomic background of peers constitutes a contextual variable that could affect a student's achievement in three different ways, represented by equations [3], [5], and [6].[14] Each individual level model has a corresponding aggregate model whose variables are measured on schools to make inferences about students. School means therefore replace individual values.

If the effects of contextual variables derived from independent variables included in the individual level relation are direct, the corresponding aggregate model makes it impossible to separate the effects of contextual from individual variables. For example, equation [3] uses data on students to isolate the effects of individual and peer socioeconomic status. Reliance on aggregate data makes it impossible to estimate the unique contribution of those variables, as equation [7] illustrates:[15]

$$\overline{Y} = b_1\overline{X}_1 + b_2\overline{X}_2 + b_3\overline{X}_2 + e = b_1\overline{X}_1 + (b_2 + b_3)\overline{X}_2 + e. \qquad [7]$$

In this equation, as well as in equation [3], b_2 represents the coefficient of individual status effects, while b_3 represents the coefficient of contextual status effects. In equation [3], however, each coefficient can be uniquely estimated; equation [3] has three unknown and three known values. Equation [7], in contrast, has only two known values. A unique estimate of contextual effects, represented by b_3, cannot be obtained unless some a priori value is assumed for b_2, the coefficient of individual effects. Until more is known about the impact of status on achievement to warrant any such assumptions, all that can be estimated is the total effect on both peer and individual status on achievement.

Thus, if contextual effects derived from an individual level variable included in the individual level equation are direct, unique estimates of their effects cannot be obtained from aggregate data alone. Bereft of individual level data, an investigator cannot distinguish between a model that includes only individual level effects and one that includes both individual and contextual effects. At the individual level, a model that includes only the effect of a student's own race and status is:

$$Y = b_1 X_1 + b_2 X_2 + e. \qquad [8]$$

In the absence of data on students, equation [8] becomes:

$$\overline{Y} = b_1 \overline{X}_1 + b_2 \overline{X}_2 + e. \qquad [9]$$

Equation [9] is indistinguishable from equation [7], even though [9] omits contextual effects while [7] includes them. An analyst investigating the impact of pupil assignment and selection procedures based on grouping students by status would be stymied if he had to rely on information collected at the school level.[16]

In contrast, unique estimates of interactive contextual effects can be obtained from aggregate data when the effects arise from individual level variables included in the individual level relation. At the aggregate level, equation [5] produces unique estimates:

$$\overline{Y} = b_3 \overline{X}_1 + b_4 \overline{X}_1 \overline{X}_2 + b_2 \overline{X}_2 + e \qquad [10]$$

and equation [6] does also:

$$\overline{Y} = b_1 \overline{X}_1 + b_3 \overline{X}_2 + b_4 \overline{X}_2^2 + e. \qquad [11]$$

To summarize, when contextual effects originate from individual level variables included in the individual level model, aggregate data cannot always yield unique estimates of those effects. Only if the effects are known to be interactive will aggregate data produce unique estimates. However, the investigator's most likely task is to determine whether contextual effects are interactive, direct, or nonexistent. For that task, aggregate data are inadequate.

In contrast, aggregate data provide unique estimates for variables defined independently of variables included in the individual level relation.[17] Consider, for instance, the effects of variables like the quality of teachers or school facilities, denoted by $\overline{Z}$. If $\overline{Z}$ has direct effects on student achievement, apart from the effects of race and socioeconomic status, then:

$$Y = b_1 X_1 + b_2 X_2 + b_3 \overline{Z} + e \qquad [12]$$

is an appropriate individual level model. At the aggregate level, the model still has three knowns and three unknowns:

$$\overline{Y} = b_1\overline{X}_1 + b_2\overline{X}_2 + b_3\overline{Z} + e. \qquad [13]$$

Even if the effects of $\overline{Z}$ are interactive, an investigator can rely on aggregate data to secure unique estimates. Suppose that high quality school facilities mitigate the effects of race on achievement. Interracial achievement differentials, measured by b_1, will therefore be less in schools with good facilities. Such a model is represented by:

$$Y = b_1X_1 + b_2X_2 + e,$$

where $b_1 = (b_3 + b_4\overline{Z})$, so that the full equation is:

$$Y = b_3X_1 + b_4X_1\overline{Z} + b_2X_2 + e. \qquad [14]$$

The corresponding aggregate equation has identical form:

$$\overline{Y} = b_3\overline{X}_1 + b_4\overline{X}_1\overline{Z} + b_2\overline{X}_2 + e. \qquad [15]$$

Thus, aggregate data alone are sufficient to estimate all three coefficients uniquely.

Aggregate data can also generate unique estimates if school facilities interact with socioeconomic status. Attempts to upgrade school facilities imply that the link between status and achievement can be diminished. Status differentials should therefore be reduced in high quality schools. This expectation is represented by:

$$Y = b_1X_1 + b_2X_2 + e,$$

where $b_2 = (b_3 + b_4\overline{Z})$, yielding a full model:

$$Y = b_1X_1 + b_3X_2 + b_4X_2\overline{Z} + e. \qquad [16]$$

The aggregate version of this model has the same number of knowns as unknowns:

$$\overline{Y} = b_1\overline{X}_1 + b_3\overline{X}_2 + b_4\overline{X}_2\overline{Z} + e. \qquad [17]$$

Thus, aggregate level data are sufficient to analyze direct as well as interactive contextual effects defined independently of individual level variables.[18]

In sharp contrast, when contextual effects depend on values of the individual level dependent variable, unique estimation from aggregate data is impossible, no matter whether the effects are direct or interactive. Determining how the achievement of peers affects the achievement of individual students is crucial for the evaluation of policies based on tracking or ability grouping. Relying on aggregate data for such an evaluation, however, is likely to produce misleading conclusions.

First, suppose that peer achievement, represented by $\overline{Y}$, has direct effects on the achievement of individual students, apart from the effects of race and status:

$$Y = b_1X_1 + b_2X_2 + b_3\overline{Y} + e. \tag{18}$$

In the absence of data on students, the corresponding school level model becomes:

$$\overline{Y} = b_1\overline{X}_1 + b_2\overline{X}_2 + b_3\overline{Y} + e \tag{19}$$

$$= \frac{b_1}{(1-b_3)}\overline{X}_1 + \frac{b_2}{(1-b_3)}\overline{X}_2 + e'.$$

Equation [19] has more unknowns than knowns.[19] Unless some a priori value is assigned to b_2, the coefficient for status, unique estimation of b_3, the coefficient for peer ability, is impossible. Thus, using data on schools renders estimates of the effects of peer ability on individual achievement moot. Moreover, equation [19] is indistinguishable from both equation [7], which represents the direct effects of peer status, and equation [9], which represents the absence of all contextual effects. Thus, using aggregate data impedes evaluation of the alternative explanations of achievement that each of these equations depict.

If peer ability has interactive effects on achievement, aggregate data make analysis nearly intractable. Suppose, for instance, that the difference between the achievement scores of black and white students diminishes as the proportion of high achievers in their school increases. Controlling for race and socioeconomic status, such a relation is represented by:

$$Y = b_1X_1 + b_2X_2 + e$$

where $b_1 = (b_3 + b_4\overline{Y})$. By substitution, the full model becomes:

$$Y = b_3X_1 + b_4X_1\overline{Y} + b_2X_2 + e. \tag{20}$$

In the absence of data on students, the equivalent regression is:

$$\overline{Y} = b_3\overline{X}_1 + b_4\overline{X}_1\overline{Y} + b_2\overline{X}_2 + e$$

$$= \frac{b_3\overline{X}_1}{(1-b_4\overline{X}_1)} + \frac{b_2\overline{X}_2}{(1-b_4\overline{X}_1)} + e' \tag{21}$$

Equation [21] is not linear in its parameters. Therefore, conventional regression techniques yield no solution. In additional assumptions about the value of either

b_2 or b_3, only indirect estimation procedures could produce unique estimates of b_4, the parameter representing the effects of peer ability on individual achievement.[20] In summary, relying on aggregate data makes unique estimation very difficult if peer ability has direct or interactive effects on individual achievement.

However, even if contextual properties posed no aggregation problems for educational research, the use of aggregate data to study students could still be unwise. Aggregate data produce unbiased estimates of individual behavior only when the aggregate level equations are properly specified (Irwin and Lichtman, 1976; Hanushek, Jackson, and Kain, 1974). Proper specification of aggregate equations assures investigators that parameters are not systematically over- or underestimated. Whether the aggregate models of contextual effects outlined above are properly specified depends largely on theoretical criteria. At the aggregate level, however, specification also depends on how the data are grouped (Irwin and Lichtman, 1976). Some grouping procedures alter the specification of otherwise well-specified individual level models, while others do not. If attendance at a given school is largely determined by a student's race and socioeconomic status, then school level data approximate data grouped by the independent variable. Grouping by the independent variable does not alter the specification of the individual level equation. If the individual level model is properly specified, regression parameters estimated using data on students will be close to parameters estimated from data on schools (Irwin and Lichtman, 1976).

Even if the individual model is not properly specified, aggregate and individual regression estimates may also approximate each other when data are grouped according to values of independent variables included in the regression. If the individual level model is misspecified by the omission of an independent variable related to both the dependent variable and to one or more included independent variables, then the expected value of estimates from grouped and ungrouped data will be equal. (See Irwin and Lichtman, 1976, for a detailed explication.)

Thus, similar regression estimates from identical individual and aggregate equations have several implications. In the case of a model estimating the influence of race and status on achievement, similar estimates indicate that data grouped by school approximate data that have been grouped by the included independent variables. In effect, similar estimates indicate that attendance at a given school is largely determined by a student's race and status. However, it is not possible to determine whether the regression model omits a variable related to the dependent variable and to one or more included independent variables. Nevertheless, when individual and aggregate estimates are similar, the omitted variable will have no direct relation with the grouping variable, school. Most importantly, however, convergence assures an investigator that aggregate estimates are free of aggregation bias. Aggregation bias is simply the difference between the expected values of aggregate and individual parameter estimates.

Grouping data by independent variables produces no aggregation bias. If school level data approximate grouping according to the values of independent variables, then investigators of student achievement can be certain that estimates from less costly data on schools contain no more bias than estimates from more costly data on students.[21]

To illustrate, Figure 1 shows, for the bivariate case, the two causal models that produce similar individual and aggregate regression estimates.[22] In Figure 1a, grouping data by school approximates grouping according to the independent variable in a properly specified regression. In Figure 1b, data are also grouped according to the independent variable. However, the regression is misspecified by the omission of Z. The omitted variable is related directly to both X and Y. It must, however, be either independent of the grouping variable, school, or indirectly related to it. In Figure 1a, aggregate estimates would be free of both aggregation and specification bias. In Figure 1b, aggregate estimates would be free of aggregation bias alone.

In sum, comparing individual and aggregate estimates of student achievement enables the investigator to determine whether the use of less costly data on schools produces estimates that are as good as estimates obtained from more costly data concerning individual students. In addition, if the cross-level estimates are equivalent, an investigator can identify potential sources of misspecification as attributable to variables that have no direct relation to the grouping variable, school.

Suppose, in contrast, that the individual and aggregate estimates are not equivalent. Under these circumstances, the investigator can be certain that the aggregate estimates are biased. The process of aggregation alone could account for bias at the aggregate level. However, bias could also be attributable to the omission of theoretically relevant variables. Regardless of the source of bias, the inequality of aggregate and individual estimates indicates that aggregate estimates are the more biased.

The following results indicate that a model in which student achievement is determined by race and socioeconomic status and which incorporates peer status as a direct contextual effect yields equivalent estimates. Predictably, equivalence is only observed when unstandardized rather than standardized measures are used. According to the foregoing logic, this model is free of aggre-

(a)

School→X→Y

(b)

Z
School→X→Y

Z
School→X→Y

Figure 1: Models that produce equivalent individual and aggregate regression estimates of b_{yx}.

gation bias. School level data that approximate aggregation by race and socio-economic status apparently produce estimates that are no more biased than estimates from data on students. In addition, if in fact the aggregate estimates are biased, the error is attributable to omitting a variable that has no direct relation to the grouping variable, school.

If unbiased estimation were the only desiderata for policy relevant educational research, use of school level data to study students would clearly be advisable. Equally unbiased estimation could be obtained at much less cost. However, policy research must be judged by its evaluative capacity. Unfortunately, the model containing no aggregation bias also includes a direct contextual property that is defined in terms of an independent variable included in the individual level equation. Using aggregate data makes it impossible to obtain unique estimates of the impact of this type of contextual property. Yet analyzing the effects of changes in the socioeconomic status of those with whom a student attends school is of critical importance to educational policy. Therefore, even though aggregate and individual data appear to yield equivalent estimates, the failure of aggregate data to produce unique estimates of contextual effects jeopardizes their utility for educational policy research.

DATA SOURCE AND MEASUREMENT

The data for the analysis come from the 12th grade portion of Coleman's Equal Educational Opportunity Survey, completed in 1964.[23] Of the 97,654 12th graders in Coleman's sample, a 10% random sample was selected for this analysis.[24] The variables measuring student characteristics, teacher quality, and school facilities came from the 12th grade student, teacher, and principal questionnaires, respectively. Other measures of school characteristics were specially constructed for this analysis by aggregating the relevant properties of students attending the same school. The school level analysis has the same effective number of observations as the student level analysis. In other words, it weights each school by the number of students in the school.[25]

Since the purpose of this study is to investigate identical models at two different levels of analysis, each variable is comparably measured at each level. For students, verbal achievement is the difference between the number of correct and incorrect answers as a proportion of the total number of answers. In other words, it measures the relative predominance of right over wrong, or wrong over right, answers. Its value ranges from −1.00 to +1.00. For schools, verbal achievement is a function of the average number of correct, incorrect, and total answers given by 12th grade students attending the same high school. The aggregate measure of achievement also ranges from −1.00 to +1.00, and reflects the relative predominance of the average number of right to wrong answers within a school.

At the individual level, race is a dummy variable, where whites are scored 1 and nonwhites 0. At the school level, race is the proportion of students who are white.[26] The indicator of socioeconomic status is parental education. For students, the measure of parental education averages the mother's and father's education. At the school level, the measure weights the educational level of each parent by the proportion of students whose parent has attained that level, sums the weighted score for each parent, and then averages the score of each parent.[27] Thus, changes in the level of analysis do not change the scales of measurement for these variables. Regardless of whether the variable is measured for students or schools, a unit change has the same meaning.

The meaning of school facilities is more reflective of diversity and quantity than quality. The principal questionnaire included data on the number of books in the school library, the availability of science laboratories, the presence of guidance counselors, and the existence of a large variety of curricular offerings. Scores on these indicators were combined to produce a single index that reflects the variety of facilities potentially available to students in each school.

Like school facilities, teacher quality is a contextual variable defined without reference to variables included in the individual level model. In this study, teacher quality is measured by the average number of right over wrong answers as a proportion of the average number of all answers given by teachers on a verbal achievement test. Since it was impossible to match students to teachers, only schoolwide averages could be computed.[28]

Each of these indicators is simple. Single indicators and additive indexes were chosen instead of the multiple indicators and complex indexes frequently used in other analyses of the Coleman data.[29] For the particular purpose of this analysis, neither of the latter approaches is satisfactory. Using multiple indicators in a regression eqution often results in very small partial coefficients, because indicators of the same concept tend to be highly correlated. Artificially small partials can be avoided by using multiple partial correlation coefficients (Sullivan, 1971). However, this analysis depends on standardized (beta) and unstandardized (b) regression coefficients. Unfortunately, no easily interpretable multiple partial analogues of these measures exist. Finally, the use of complex indices raises another issue of aggregation that should be considered separately from those considered in this study. It is unclear whether each indicator should be combined into a single index before or after aggregation over students. In addition, the use of multiple partial analogues as well as complex index construction techniques like factor analysis makes interpretation of unstandardized regression coefficients unclear, particulary for policy analysis. It is meaningful to state that a percentage increase in an independent variable is associated with some percentage increase in the dependent variable. To claim that a unit increase in a factor score or composite variable is associated with change in the dependent variable has dubious meaning in policy research, because only variables and not factors are manipulable.

TABLE 1. REGRESSION OF ACHIEVEMENT ON RACE AND EDUCATION: STUDENTS VERSUS SCHOOLS

	Student		School	
	Race (X_1)	Education (X_2)	Race (X_1)	Education (X_2)
b	.004	.09	.004	.21
Standard error	.0002	.01	.0006	.003
Beta	.35	.31	.53	.56
R^2		.26		.83

RESULTS

Table 1 shows the standardized (Beta) and unstandardized regression coefficients obtained from the regression of verbal achievement on race and parental education at the student and school level. At the individual level, family background factors explain only 26% of the variance in achievement. In contrast, at the aggregate level, these same factors explain 83% of the between-school variance in achievement. Analyses that rely on individual data thus suggest how little we know about the determinants of educational achievement. In contrast, analyses that rely on aggregate data attest to the importance of family background.

Such an inference from aggregate data is, however, an artifact. First, the variance of achievement is greater within than between schools, as others have noted (Hanushek and Kain, 1972: 129). Consequently, there is less variance to be explained at the aggregate than at the individual level. Second, evidence presented subsequently suggests that school level data approximate data grouped by both independent variables. Grouping by independent variables maximizes their variance. The high aggregate R^2 is attributable, then, to less variance in Y and greater variance in X_1 and X_2 than at the individual level. In short, although family background factors explain a high proportion of the variance in achievement between schools, the high aggregate R_2 is no evidence that an individual student's achievement depends on his family background. Instead, it

TABLE 2. REGRESSION OF ACHIEVEMENT ON RACE, PARENTAL EDUCATION, AND PEER PARENTAL EDUCATION: STUDENTS VERSUS SCHOOLS

	Student		Peer Education	School	
	Race (X_1)	Education (X_2)	(X_2)	Race (X_1)	Education (X_2)
b	.003	.08	.09	.004	.21
Standard error	.0002	.005	.01	.0006	.003
Beta	.33	.29	.13	.53	.56
R^2		.27			.83

TABLE 3. REGRESSION OF ACHIEVEMENT ON RACE, PARENTAL EDUCATION, AND
PARENTAL EDUCATION TIMES RACE: STUDENTS VERSUS SCHOOLS

	Students			Schools		
	Race (X_1)	Education (X_2)	Education x Race (X_2X_1)	Race (X_1)	Education (X_2)	Education x Race (X_1X_1)
b	.006	.09	.0006	.003	.19	.0001
Standard error	.0008	.005	.0003	.0003	.008	.0001
Beta	.54	.31	.19	.49	.55	.05
R^2		.26			.83	

suggests that students who have similar racial and socioeconomic characteristics
are likely to attend the same school.

Evidence in Table 1 is also consistent with the argument that school level data
are grouped by family background characteristics. Because grouping by independent variables maximizes their variance, standardized measures of association like r and Beta should increase with increasing levels of aggregation. We
have already shown that the coefficient of multiple determination (R^2) increases.
The simple correlations do also. At the individual level, the Pearson product-
moment correlation between parental education and achievement is .37; at the
aggregate level, it is .77. The individual level correlation between race and
achievement is .40; the aggregate correlation is .75. The correlation between the
two independent variables also increases, but not dramatically enough to make
collinearity a threat to the aggregate level multiple regression equation. The
correlation between students' race and parental education is .16; for schools, the
correlation is .38.

Table 1 also shows that, as measured by standardized partial regression
coefficients (Betas), the influence of race and parental education on achievement
appears about 60% greater at the aggregate than at the individual level. This
effect is consistent with the hypothesis that data on schools constitute data
grouped by family background.

TABLE 4. REGRESSION OF ACHIEVEMENT ON RACE, PARENTAL EDUCATION, AND
PARENTAL EDUCATION SQUARED: STUDENTS VERSUS SCHOOLS

	Students			Schools		
	Race (X_1)	Education (X_2)	Education x Race (X_2X_2)	Race (X_1)	Education (X_2)	Education x Race (X_2X_2)
b	.003	.01	.02	.004	−.20	.06
Standard error	.0002	.01	.003	.00006	.02	.003
Beta	.33	.04	.30	.55	−.59	1.15
R^2		.27			.85	

Moreover, if data are grouped by independent variables, unstandardized regression coefficients should remain unchanged. Table 1 shows that the coefficient for race is stable; the education coefficient, however, is larger at the aggregate than the disaggregate level.[30]

Rather than reject the hypothesis that school level data are grouped by family background, respecification of the student level equation may yield better results. Inclusion of the parental education of students' peers, represented by equation [3], does indeed yield equivalent individual and aggregate regression weights (see Table 2). In the absence of individual data, the aggregate version of such a model, represented by equation [7], is indistinguishable from equation [9], the aggregate version of a model that omits the family background of a student's peers. However, equation [7] shows that the individual level coefficient associated with a student's own parents' education plus the coefficients associated with his peers' parental education should equal the single aggregate level coefficient associated with parental education.

Table 2 shows that the empirical results very nearly approximate theoretical expectations. The sum of the two parental education coefficients estimated from individual level data (.08 + .09 = .17) is very close to the single education coefficient estimated from aggregate level data (.21).

In sum, the stability of the regression coefficients in Table 2 indicates that school level data approximate data grouped by family background and not by achievement. As a result, using aggregate data generates no aggregation bias. However, the apparent cost-effectiveness of aggregate data to study student achievement is specious in this case. The model includes a contextual variable that has direct effects on achievement and is a linear function of an individual level independent variable. Under these circumstances, use of aggregate data cannot reveal the separate impact of contextual and individual factors.

Specifically, only individual level data disclose that the effects of peer and individual parental education are about equal, as measured by unstandardized partial regression coefficients.[31] Increasing the average educational level of the parents of those with whom the average student attends school will increase his

TABLE 5. REGRESSION OF ACHIEVEMENT ON RACE, PARENTAL EDUCATION, PEER PARENTAL EDUCATION, AND FACILITIES: STUDENTS VERSUS SCHOOLS

	Students				Schools		
	Race (X_1)	Education (X_2)	Peer Education (X_2)	Facilities (Z)	Race (X_1)	Education (X_2)	Facilities (Z)
b	.003	.08	.09	.001	.003	.20	.003
Standard error	.0002	.005	.01	.002	.00006	.003	.0004
Beta	.32	.29	.13	.01	.52	.56	.06
R^2			.27			.84	

verbal achievement by 9%, according to Table 2.[32] Reliance on aggregate level data makes it impossible to tell what portion of the single aggregate level coefficient is attributable to individual factors and what portion is attributable to contextual factors. In addition, reliance on aggregate data makes it impossible even to distinguish between a model which includes contextual variables of this sort and one which does not.

A better specified model, of course, might show that peer socioeconomic status has interactive rather than direct effects. (See equations [5] and [6].) If so, then using aggregate data could be a cost-effective strategy for studying achievement because interactive models do not preclude using aggregate data to estimate contextual effects. However, the instability of the regression coefficients estimated from student and school level data suggests that aggregation produces biased estimates. Tables 3 and 4 indicate that only the coefficients for race are stable from one unit of analysis to another.[33] Moreover, since the results from the direct effects model suggested that the school level data produce no aggregation bias, the use of school level data should produce no aggregation bias in the interactive model. It seems more likely that poor specification accounts for the inequality of aggregate and individual estimates. In short, hypotheses that peer status has interactive effects on achievement are probably inferior to those hypothesizing direct effects.

Although the parental education of peers seems to have direct contextual effects on achievement, school facilities appear to have no effects. In fact, Tables 5, 6, and 7 are consistent with previous statements about the seeming irrelevance of gross measures of the quality of school facilities for student achievement. No matter whether school facilities are hypothesized to have direct or interactive effects, adding the indicator of facilities to the basic model reveals the inefficacy of hardware. The unstandardized regression coefficients and the small Betas associated with the measure of facilities support such a conclusion. Table 5 shows that adding facilities to a model that includes peer parental education does not alter its specification. The stable regression coefficients indicate that an aggregate model which includes both peer status and facilities as direct con-

TABLE 6. REGRESSION OF ACHIEVEMENT ON RACE, PARENTAL EDUCATION, PEER PARENTAL EDUCATION, AND FACILITIES TIMES RACE: STUDENTS VERSUS SCHOOLS

	Students				Schools		
	Race (X_1)	Education (X_2)	Peer Education (X_2)	Facilities x Race $(X_1 Z)$	Race (X_1)	Education (X_2)	Facilities x Race $(X_1 Z)$
b	.004	.08	.09	.001	.003	.20	.00003
Standard error	.0009	.005	.01	.003	.0002	.003	.00001
Beta	.34	.29	.13	.02	.40	.57	.14
R^2			.27			.84	

TABLE 7. REGRESSION OF ACHIEVEMENT ON RACE, PARENTAL EDUCATION,
PEER PARENTAL EDUCATION, AND FACILITIES TIMES PARENTAL
EDUCATION: STUDENTS VERSUS SCHOOLS

	Students				Schools		
	Race (X_1)	Education (X_2)	Peer Education (X_2)	Facilities x Education (ZX_2)	Race (X_1)	Education (X_2)	Facilities x Education (ZX_2)
b	.003	.08	.09	.0002	.003	.18	.0006
Standard error	.0002	.01	.01	.0004	.00006	.005	.0001
Beta	.33	.27	.13	.02	.53	.51	.07
R^2			.26				.84

textual effects is free of aggregation bias. Consequently, in the case of contextual
variables like facilities which are defined independently of other variables,
conclusions reached from aggregate and disaggregate data will be similar.
Regardless of the unit of analysis, school facilities appear to have no impact on
achievement.

Investigators have also hypothesized that the teacher's verbal ability has an
important impact on the ability of the students he teaches. Table 8 discloses that
the teacher's verbal ability has only a small direct effect. Adding that variable to
the basic regression which includes race, parental education, and peer parental
education does not significantly increase the explained variance. In addition,
the unstandardized partial regression coefficient has weak statistical and
substantive significance. A unit increase in the teacher's score is associated with
an increase in the average students' verbal score of .14 units. At the aggregate
level, the corresponding coefficient is larger. While this might indicate that the
aggregate estimates are biased, no final conclusion seems warranted in this case.
Failure to measure the verbal ability of the teacher in each of the student's
classes could introduce significant error into the analysis. Moreover, at the

TABLE 8. REGRESSION OF ACHIEVEMENT ON RACE, PARENTAL EDUCATION,
PEER PARENTAL EDUCATION, AND TEACHER SCORE:
STUDENTS VERSUS SCHOOLS

	Students				Schools		
	Race (X_1)	Education (X_2)	Peer Education (X_2)	Teacher Score (Z)	Race (X_1)	Education (X_2)	Teacher Score (Z)
b.	.003	.08	.08	.14	.003	.17	.35
Standard error	.0002	.005	.01	.07	.00007	.003	.02
Beta	.32	.28	.11	.05	.41	.50	.23
R^2			.27				.86

TABLE 9. REGRESSION OF ACHIEVEMENT ON RACE, PARENTAL EDUCATION,
PEER PARENTAL EDUCATION, AND TEACHER SCORE TIMES RACE:
STUDENTS VERSUS SCHOOLS

	Students				Schools		
	Race (X_1)	Education (X_2)	Peer Education (X_2)	Teacher Score x Race (ZX_1)	Race (X_1)	Education (X_2)	Teacher Score x Race (ZX_1)
b	.005	.08	.08	.23	.001	.18	.004
Standard error	.0006	.005	.01	.08	.0002	.003	.0003
Beta	.46	.28	.12	.14	.11	.52	.46
R^2			.28				.85

aggregate level, the correlation between race and the teacher's score is .64; unstable estimates could, in this instance, result from collinearity.

If the direct effects model of teacher ability seems inconclusive at best, an indirect effects model appears unwarranted. The unstable coefficients in Tables 9 and 10 suggest that including the multiplicative terms unfavorably alters the specification of the rest of the model. The coefficients associated with race are unstable in Table 9. In Table 10, the sum of the two education coefficients for the student model do not sum to the coefficient for education in the aggregate model. Yet previously these coefficients were relatively constant from one unit of analysis to another.

Overall, inclusion of contextual variables that are defined independently of variables in the individual level relation does not preclude using data to obtain unique estimates of contextual effects. Of these kinds of contextual variables, only the teacher's verbal ability appears to have any impact on student achievement. In contrast, it is clear that peer parental education, a contextual property derived directly from an independent variable included in the individual level

TABLE 10. REGRESSION OF ACHIEVEMENT ON RACE, PARENTAL EDUCATION,
PEER PARENTAL EDUCATION, AND TEACHER SCORE TIMES
EDUCATION: STUDENTS VERSUS SCHOOLS

	Students				Schools		
	Race (X_1)	Education (X_2)	Peer Education (X_2)	Teacher Score x Education (ZX_2)	Race (X_1)	Education (X_2)	Teacher Score x Education (ZX_2)
b	.003	.06	.08	.04	.003	.08	.13
Standard error	.002	.01	.01	.02	.0001	.005	.005
Beta	.32	.19	.11	.11	.40	.22	.45
R^2			.28				.87

TABLE 11. REGRESSION OF ACHIEVEMENT ON RACE, PARENTAL EDUCATION,
PEER PARENTAL EDUCATION, AND PEER ABILITY: STUDENTS
VERSUS SCHOOLS

	Students				Schools	
	Race (X_1)	Education (X_2)	Peer Education (X_2)	Peer Ability (Y)	Race (X_1)	Education (X_2)
b	.003	.08	.002	.36	.004	.20
Standard error	.0002	.005	.02	.06	.00006	.003
Beta	.28	.28	.002	.18	.53	.53
R^2			.28			.83

model, has a direct effect on achievement. Unique estimation of this effect is impossible without data on individuals.

Finally, the ability of peers is a contextual property derived directly from the dependent variable in the individual level model. Any impact that it might have on achievement could only be detected with individual level data. Unfortunately, problems of collinearity as well as problems of aggregation make it impossible to estimate its impact with clarity. If peer ability has direct effects on individual ability, Table 11 shows that its impact is both statistically and substantively significant. A unit increase in the achievement scores of peers increases the score of the average student by .36 units, if the evidence is plausible. Oddly, however, the effect of peers' parental education is sizeably reduced from its estimated coefficient of .09 in Table 2. In Table 11, it is not even statistically significant. This result, however, simply reflects the very high correlation of .77 between peer ability and peer parental education. The presence of such high collinearity makes reliable estimation impossible.

Aggregate level data in this case are no help. The school level estimates in Table 11 are identical to those in Tables 1 and 2. In other words, a model based on direct effects of peer ability is indistinguishable from one in which peer parental education has direct effects as well as from one in which there are no

TABLE 12. REGRESSION OF ACHIEVEMENT ON RACE, PARENTAL EDUCATION,
PEER PARENTAL EDUCATION, AND RACE TIMES PEER ABILITY:
STUDENTS VERSUS SCHOOLS

	Students				Schools
	Race (X_1)	Education (X_2)	Peer Education (X_2)	Ability x Race (YX_1)	
b	.003	.08	.08	.17	
Standard error	.0002	.005	.01	.08	No estimates possible
Beta	.32	.29	.11	.04	
R^2			.27		

TABLE 13. REGRESSION OF ACHIEVEMENT ON RACE, PARENTAL EDUCATION, PEER PARENTAL EDUCATION, AND EDUCATION TIMES PEER ABILITY: STUDENTS VERSUS SCHOOLS

	Students				Schools
	Race (X_1)	Education (X_2)	Peer Education (X_2)	Ability x Education (YX_2)	
b	.003	.08	.02	.07	
Standard error	.0002	.006	.02	.01	No estimates possible
Beta	.30	.25	.03	.15	
R^2			.28		

contextual effects at all. The partial regression coefficient of .20 associated with education in the aggregate model cannot be decomposed. It is impossible to tell whether its value reflects the combined effects of contextual and individual parental education, the impact of individual background weighted by the contextual effects of peer ability, some combination of these, or perhaps none of these at all.

Finally, no aggregate level model can be estimated at all if peer effects are indirect, as equation [18] demonstrates. The coefficients associated with the individual level multiplicative term in Tables 12 and 13 are statistically significant. Moreover, the R^2's are similar to those computed for a direct effects model.

In Table 13, the regression coefficient associated with peer parental education is not significant, in contrast to Table 12. However, this is an artifact of multicollinearity, since the correlation between peer parental education and the multiplicative term is .72. In short, analysis of individual level data suggests that peer ability ineracts wih a student's race and status to affect his achievement. Simple regression analysis with aggregate data would fail to disclose these effects.

SUMMARY AND IMPLICATIONS

The study of student achievement is critical to the development of educational policy. Determining whether improvements in school facilities, upgrading teacher quality, or reassigning students has a direct impact on the performance of students is necessary if funds for education are to be wisely allocated. Such a determination requires the impact of these policy alternatives to be evaluated apart from the effects of characteristics of students that policy cannot affect. Analysts concerned with empirically estimating the independent impact of manipulable variables must choose between using students or schools as the unit of analysis. Gathering data on students, however, is very costly. Moreover, both parents and school administrators are increasingly unwilling to collect information from students. If they are willing to collect information, they are increasingly unwilling to release it. In contrast, gathering data on schools is cheaper and easier to obtain. It is therefore important to consider the implications of using data on schools to evaluate how potential policy changes affect students.

The findings disclose that reliance on standardized measures estimated from aggregate data can be hazardous. More specifically, aggregate correlations and beta weights were inflated. Beta weights obtained from aggregate data tend to exceed weights obtained from individual level data. Moreover, the inflation is greatest for coefficients associated with variables on which the individual level data have been grouped. Students appear to be grouped into schools on the basis of their race and socioeconomic status. Grouping, in effect, maximizes the variance of race and status. Standardized measures of association and influence are sensitive to changes in relative variance produced by grouping. Consequently, school level estimates of the standardized influence of race and status on achievement are much larger than similar estimates based on student level data. In short, the importance attributed to family background may be exaggerated when standardized estimates from aggregate data are the source of information.

Unfortunately, substituting unstandardized for standardized aggregate estimates is often an unsatisfactory solution. Under certain circumstances, it is impossible to obtain unique estimates of the effects of contextual variables from aggregate data. Of six types of contextual properties identified in the analysis, three cannot be assessed from aggregate data. This dilemma would be academic if individual level analysis revealed that these properties were unimportant. However, individual level analysis discloses that the socioeconomic status and ability of peers have direct effects on the achievement of students. The former is a contextual property derived from an independent variable included in the individual level relation. The latter is derived from the dependent variable in the individual level relation. Unfortunately, using aggregate data makes it impossible to estimate uniquely the effects of these types of contextual properties. Unique estimates must be obtained from data on students. Even though data on students are costly, unique estimates are essential for educational research to have policy relevance.

In addition to being unique, aggregate estimates of the impact of contextual variables should also be unbiased. Simultaneous analysis of individual and grouped data can help to assess whether aggregate estimates are biased. The divergence of individual from group level estimates is an indicator of bias in group level estimates. Their convergence, in contrast, suggests either that both models are properly specified or that the omitted variable has no direct relation to the grouping variable. Most importantly, equivalence quarantees that estimates from less costly aggregate data contain no more bias than estimates from data on individuals.

Analysis of student achievement using data on both schools and students revealed one model that exhibited convergent coefficients. When race, parental education, and peer parental education are included as independent variables, aggregate estimates appeared to be free of aggregation bias. Nonetheless, use of aggregate data to estimate the unique impact of peer parental education on student achievement is futile. Even though aggregation may yield estimates that are no more biased than those from more costly individual level data, the savings come only at the expense of policy relevance.

Finally, the analysis also indicates the utility of individual level data even for investigations of between-school variations in achievement. The regression of average achievement on average parental education can be decomposed into a contextual and individual component, offering a policymaker alternative means to increase average achievement levels. He can seek to alter either the context of behavior or the properties of individuals. Only the former, of course, is potentially feasible. Yet without individual data the analyst would not know the extent to which an observed effect was attributable to changes in individual or contextual variables. Thus, exclusive reliance on aggregate data precludes an understanding of whether manipulable variables affect average as well as individual achievement levels. Despite additional costs, obtaining data on students is critically important if research on educational achievement is to be relevant to educational policy.

NOTES

1. Reanalyses of Coleman's data substantially reach these conclusions. See, for example, Smith, 1972; Armor, 1972; Jencks, 1972; and Mayeske, 1972. Analyses using different data also replicate these findings, as Averch et al., 1974, report.

2. For example, the Rand Corporation selected for careful evaluation 21 studies that both investigated the impact of school resources on cognitive abilities and contained no egregious statistical errors. Among these, nine use the student as a unit of analysis; the remainder use the school or even the school district (Averch et al., 1974). In addition, some reanalysis of Coleman's own data use the student as a unit of analysis (Smith, 1972); others use the school (Armor, 1972; Mayeske, 1972).

However, deciding whether to analyze students or schools is not entirely methodological. Miller (1977) points out, in fact, that methodological choices have normative implications. Specifically, if the goal of educational policy is to reduce inequalities among groups, then analysis of individual level data can produce misleading results. In contrast, if the goal of policy is to reduce inequalities among individuals, then analysis of group level data can be misleading. Thus, by considering the analysis of individual level behavior, this study is relevant primarily for the evaluation of inequality among individuals rather than groups.

3. Independence between the error term and the included independent variables is necessary for proper specification.

4. The data analysis below, based on Coleman's 1966 Equal Educational Opportunity Survey, strongly suggests this possibility. While busing may have reduced the amount of racial grouping, it is unlikely to have reduced socioeconomic grouping. The conclusions that follow are also true if students are grouped into schools according to status alone.

5. To sketch the algebraic derivation, let $R^2_{y.x_1,x_2} = R^2_{y.12}$. By definition, and then by substitution:

$$R^2_{y.12} = r^2_{y1} + r^2_{y2.1}\,(1 - r^2_{y1}) = (b_{y1}\frac{S_1}{S_y})^2 + b_{y2.1}b_{2y.1}\left[1 - (b_{y1}\frac{S_1}{S_y})^2\right]$$

$\bar{R}^2_{y.12}$ can be similarly expressed in terms of aggregate level regression coefficients and standard deviations. Since we assume that $E\,(X_1,e) = E(X_2,e) = 0$ and that the data are grouped by X_1 and X_2 alone, it follows that $E(\bar{b}_{y1}) = E(b_{y1})$; $\bar{S}_1/\bar{S}_y > S_1/S_y$; $E(\bar{b}_{y2.1}) = E(\bar{b}_{y2.1})$; and $|\,E(\bar{b}_{2y.1})\,| > |\,E\,(b_{2y.1})\,|$. (See Cramer, 1964, and Irwin and Lichtman, 1976, for these derivations.) Therefore, $\bar{R}^2_{y.12} > R^2_{y.12}$.

6. The explanation is straightforward. By definition

$$b^*_1 = b_{yx_1.x_2}\frac{S_{x_1}}{S_y}\quad\text{and}\quad \bar{b}^*_1 = \bar{b}_{yx_1.x_2}\frac{S_{x_1}}{S_{\bar{y}}}$$

If equation [1] is properly specified and if data are grouped by the independent variables, then $b_{yx_1.x_2} = \bar{b}_{yx_1.x_2}$ but $S_{\bar{x}/}_1\,S_y > S_{x_1}/S_y$. The behavior of b^*_2 relative to b^*_2 is identical. Hannan, Freeman, and Meyer (1976) make the same point.

7. Unstandardized coefficients are stable because grouping by independent variables will not confound the error term with the independent variables. Values of the error term will not be systematically grouped with values of the independent variables as long as these values are uncorrelated at the individual level. Proper specification guarantees that they will be uncorrelated. For a fuller discussion, see Cramer, 1964, and Irwin and Lichtman, 1976.

8. The conceptualization of contextual effects is based on Przeworski (1974). The literature on contextual or "structural" effects has taken several different directions since the difficulty of distinguishing between contextual and individual effects was first addressed by Blau (1960), Davis, Spaeth, and Huson (1961), and Tannenbaum and Bachman (1964). Building on this tradition, Przeworski (1974) develops some considerably more complex contextual models. The task of separating contextual from individual effects in the absence of individual level data is addressed by Goodman (1959), Valkonen (1969), Scheuch (1969), and Hannan (1970: 96-106). More recently, a controversy over the very meaning of contextual variables has developed in the sociological literature. Some aver that contextual variables affect individual behavior only through the perceptual processes of individuals within the context; contextual variables are therefore no different from individual level variables. Others respond that contextual properties exist apart from individual perceptions and therefore should be measured directly. Barton (1968) and Farkas (1974) take the latter position, while Hauser (1974) advocates the former. Since much of this argument appears epistemological rather than theoretical or empirical, it is more useful simply to assume that contextual properties exist independent of how individuals perceive them. Even if this assumption were incorrect, no one has developed operational procedures for translating contextual effects into individual perceptions.

9. The individual level "direct effects" models that follow have two general properties: they are linear and additive in their variables, and they presume that the effects of individual level independent variables on individual behavior are constant across schools.

10. In these examples, all of the interactions are presumed to be multiplicative. Other forms of interaction, however, have similar methodological consequences. The following multiplicative models presume that the influence of individual level characteristics on individual level behavior varies with school context.

11. Equation [3] is identical to Alwin's model of contextual effects, except that Alwin omits X_1. See Alwin, 1976: 298.

12. Attending school with high status peers could also augment the relation between race and achievement. However, this outcome is theoretically less likely. In this and following examples, the illustrative outcomes are those predicted by theory.

13 The values of b_1 and b_2 in these and other models of interactive contextual effects can be solved for after b_3 and b_4 have been estimated. In these interactive models, b_1 and b_2 are variable coefficients whose values depend on the constants b_3 and b_4 and on the particular value of the contextual variable.

14. The racial characteristics of peers is another contextual variable that can have direct effects on individual achievement. It can also interact with race or status. However, these models will not be investigated since the problems of using aggregate data to estimate the contextual effects of race are identical to the problems that arise with estimating the contextual effects of status.

15. Alwin (1976: 298) gives the proof that equation [7] is the aggregate level equivalent of equation [3]. The quantity $(b_2 + b_3)$ in equation [7] equals his $b_{y\bar{x}} = b_{yx} + b_{y\bar{x}}$, where $b_{yx} = b_2$ and $b_{y\bar{x}} = b_3$ in equations [3] and [7]. The reader is referred to Alwin's article for the specific proof.

16. In terms of Note 15, it is impossible to determine whether $b_3 = 0$ in the absence of individual level data.

17. We continue to assume that the independent variables included in aggregate level models are uncorrelated with the error term. The problem of bias will be considered subsequently.

18. Even though unique estimation is possible when aggregate data are used to study contextual effects defined independently of individual level variables, problems of multicollinearity are likely to be considerably more severe at the aggregate than at the individual level. For example, the aggregate level correlation between student race and the verbal ability score of teachers is .64., which is high enough to produce large standard errors in regression estimates. Yet the individual level correlation is only .33.

19. Ordinary least squares estimates of the coefficients in equation [19] would also be biased, since $e' = e/(1-b_3)$.

20. Both equations [19] and [21] can be redefined in terms of their error sum of squares $(\Sigma \hat{e}_i^2)$. It is then possible to partially differentiate each equation in terms of their three unknowns, and to set each derivative equal to zero. For each equation, this produces three equations in three unknowns. Iterative methods may then yield numerical solutions for the unknowns.

21. This study presumes that aggregate estimates are ordinarily more biased than individual level estimates. Under certain circumstances, however, aggregate estimates can be less biased than individual level estimates. In this case, there will be an aggregation gain. Aggregation gain, however, is unlikely in studies of student achievement. Consider, for instance, a model of student achievement that includes race, parental education, and one or more contextual properties as independent variables. Income is potentially an omitted variable. An aggregation gain results when grouping reduces the correlation between included and excluded independent variables. (See Irwin and Lichtman, 1976, for a proof). Grouping students by school, however, will increase the correlation between the included and excluded variables, resulting in aggregate estimates that are more biased than individual level estimates.

22. The bivariate case is perfectly general, but simpler to illustrate.

23. The National Center for Educational Statistics provided the tapes.

24. A sample of Coleman's original sample was used simply to reduce computer time.

25. Coleman's survey oversampled schools with predominant minority proportions. However, it proved impossible to reconstruct these weights from publicly available information Armor (1972: 183) reports that his weighted and unweighted analyses produced very similar estimates of racial differences. Although means differed, differences between means did not. This analysis concerns only the latter; absolute mean values are not crucial to the study.

26. The regression coefficient associated with a dummy variable can be interpreted as the proportionate difference in achievement between whites and nonwhites. Thus, even though the

individual level indicator for race is dichotomous and the school level indicator is interval, their regression coefficients have identical interpretations.

27. The values of education ranged from 1 (some grade school) to 8 (attended graduate school). For the i-th student, education was $X_{ij} = (X_{mij} + X_{fij})/2$, where X_{mij} = educational level of mother of i-th student and X_{fij} = educational level of father i-th student. For the j-th school, education was $\overline{X}_j = (\Sigma X_{mij} P_{ij} + \Sigma_{fij} P_{ij})/2$ where p_{ij} = proportion of students whose parents had educational level X_{mij} or X_{fij}. Missing values were eliminated from all computations.

28. Equations including multiple measures of teacher quality were originally estimated. Included as indicators were the percent of teachers who were white, the pupil-teacher ratio, the percent of teachers with a masters' degree or better, the percent of teachers whose parents had college degrees, full-time years of teaching, and the percent who were certified. Of these, only the teachers' verbal ability and the percent white had any significant impact on student achievement, regardless of the unit of analysis. The racial composition of teachers and their verbal ability are highly interrelated. Since both variables could not be included in a single equation, only verbal ability was retained due to its theoretical importance and policy significance.

Measuring verbal ability of teachers at the school rather than classroom level undoubtedly reduces its variance. The analysis to follow therefore probably underestimates the amount of variance shared between achievement and teacher quality.

29. Mayeske (1972), for example, used factor analysis to construct indexes of underlying concepts, while Coleman's original analysis employed numerous but uncombined indicators of each concept.

30. This implication reinforces Cain and Watt's argument for the use of unstandardized rather than standardized coefficients. Standardized coefficients are not stable across units of measurement, but unstandardized coefficients are. See Cain and Watts, 1970.

31. The addition of peer parental education to the original model does not increase explained variance. The R^2 would probably have increased more had it been possible to match students to other students with whom they attend class rather than school. In other words, a better model would have measured peer parental education at the class rather than at the school level. (See Averch et al., 1974: 45.) Moreover, the standardized (Beta) coefficients show that X_2 has greater impact than $\overline{X}_2$. This is an artifact, since the variance of X_2 is total variance and that of $\overline{X}_2$ is between variance. Total variance is always greater than or equal to between variance. All other things equal, the greater the variance, the larger the Beta. Thus, in this situation, reliance on standardized coefficients is misleading.

32. Recall that achievement is measured as a proportion. Thus a proportionate change of .09 is equal to a percentage change of 9%. More generally, if $Y' = 100Y$, $b'_{yx} = 100b_{yx}$.

33. The coefficients of the interactive terms in Tables 3 and 4 as well as in many subsequent tables have signs opposite from those predicted by theory. In addition to the unstable coefficients, these sign reversals also suggest the relative superiority of the direct effects model. The negative sign for $\overline{X}_2$ in Table 4 is due to multicollinearity between $\overline{X}_2$ and $\overline{X}_2^2$; their intercorrelation is .99. Sprague (1976) suggests that multicollinearity will frequently be a problem in aggregate models of this form.

REFERENCES

ALWIN, D.F. (1976). "Assessing school effects: Some identities," Sociology of Education, 49 (October): 294-303.

ARMOR, D.J. (1972). "Equality of educational opportunity: The basic findings reconsidered." Ch. 5 in F. Mosteller and D.P. Moynihan (eds.), On equality of educational opportunity. New York: Random House.

AVERCH, H., CARROLL, S.J., DONALDSON, T.S., KIESLING, H.J., and PINCUS, J. (1974. How effective is schooling: A critical review of research. Englewood Cliffs, N.J.: Educational Technology Publications.

BARTON, A.H. (1968). "Bringing society back in: Survey research and macro-methodology." American Behavioral Scientist, 12: 1-9.

BLAU, P.M. (1960). "Structural effects." American Sociological Review, 25: 178-193.

CAIN G.G. and WATTS, H.W. (1970). "Problems in making policy inferences from the Coleman Report." American Sociological Review, 35: 228-242.

COLEMAN, J.S., CAMPBELL, E.Q., HOBSON, C.J., McPARTLAND, J., MOOD, A.M., WEINFELD F.D., and YORK R.L. (1966). Equality of educational opportunity. Washington, D.C.: U.S. Government Printing Office.

CRAMER J.S. (1964). "Efficient grouping: Regression and correlation in Engel curve analysis." Journal of the American Statistical Association, 59 (March): 233-250.

DAVIS, J.A., SPAETH, J.L.,and HUSON, C. (1961). "A technique for analyzing the effects of group composition." American Sociological Review, 26: 215-226.

FARKAS, G.(1974). "Specification, residuals and contextual effects." Sociological Methods and Research, 2 (February): 333-363.

GOODMAN, L.A. (1959). "Some alternatives to egological correlation." American Journal of Sociology, 64 (May): 610-625.

HANNAN, M.T. (1970). Problems of aggregation and disaggregation in sociological research. Institute for Research in Social Science Working Papers in Methodology no. 4. Chapel Hill: University of North Carolina.

HANNAN, M.T., FREEMAN, J.H., and MEYER, J.W. (1976). "Specification of models for organizational effectiveness: A comment on Bidwell and Kasarda." American Sociological Review, 41 (February): 136-143.

HANUSHEK, E.A., JACKSON, J.E., and KAIN, J.F. (1974). "Model specification, use of aggregate data, and the ecological correlation fallacy." Political Methodology, 2: 87-106.

HANUSHEK, E.A. and KAIN, J.F. (1972). "On the value of 'Equality of Educational Opportunity' as a guide to public policy." Ch. 3 in F. Mosteller and D.P. Moynihan (eds.), On equality of educational opportunity. New York: Random House.

HAUSER, R.M. (1974). "Contextual analysis revisited." Sociological Methods and Research, 2 (February): 365-375.

IRWIN, L. and LICHTMAN, A.J. (1976). "Across the Great Divide: Inferring individual level behavior from aggregate data." Political Methodology (Fall): 411-439.

JENCKS, C.S. (1972). "The Coleman Report and the conventional wisdom." Ch. 2 in F. Mosteller and D.P. Moynihan (eds.), On equality of educational opportunity. New York: Random House.

MAYESKE, G.W. (1972). A study of our nation's schools. U.S. Department of Health, Education and Welfare: Publication no. OE 72-142.

McLAUGHLIN, M.W.(1975). Evaluation and reform: The Elementary and Secondary Education Act of 1965, Title I. Cambridge: Ballinger.

MILLER, T.C. (1977). "Toward the use of articulate statistics." Evaluation Studies Review Annual 2 (1977). Bevery Hills, Calif.: Sage.

PRZEWORSKI,A. (1974). "Contextual models of political behavior." Political Methodology, 1 (Winter): 27-60.

ROBINSON, W.S. (1950). "Ecological correlations and the behavior of individuals." American Sociological Review, 15: 351-357.

SCHEUCH,E.K. (1969). "Social context and individual behavior." Pp. 133-155 in M. Dogan and S. Rokkan (eds.), Quantitative ecological analysis. Cambridge: Massachusetts Institute of Technology Press.

SMITH,M.S. (1972). "Equality of educational opportunity: The basic findings reconsidered." Ch. 6 in F. Mosteller and D.P. Moynihan (eds.), On equality of educational opportunity. New York: Random House.

SPRAGUE, J. (1976). "Estimating a Boudon type contextual model: Some practical and theoretical problems of measurement." Political Methodology, 3 (3): 333-353.

SULLIVAN, J. (1971). "Multiple indicators and complex causal models." Ch. 18 in H.B. Blalock, Jr. (ed.), Causal models in the social sciences. Chicago: Aldine-Atherton.
TANNENBAUM, A.S. and BACHMAN, J. (1964). "Structural versus individual effects." American Journal of Sociology, 69: 585-595.
VALKONEN, T. (1969). "Secondary analysis of survey data with ecological variables." Social Science Information, 8 (December): 33-36.

PART 3
EVALUATION INTO POLICY

14

DOES IT WORK WHEN IT HAS BEEN TRIED?
AND
HALF FULL OR HALF EMPTY?

By

LOIS-ELLIN DATTA

Efficiency and accountability in delivery of service is particularly important with the increase in number of career education programs. Lois-ellin Datta, in a refreshing article, claims that using inferential data in program implementation rather than summative data would help us answer pressing questions concerning the effectiveness of implemented programs in career education. Aware that the more informative the data the better the chance for utilization of the study, she is particularly concerned with the format of data presentation. The author also makes various recommendations for the presentation of evaluation results so that decision makers can use them effectively in future planning.

From Lois-ellin Datta, "Does It Work When It Has Been Tried? and Half Full or Half Empty?" *Journal of Career Education*, 1976, *2*(3), 38-55.

...experimentation occurs in an intellectual environment marked by diverse, competing and non-comparable
theoretical traditions. Consequently there is only
weak guidance for inquiry: it is difficult to decide
when treatments have been either implemented or successful, for there are no solid theoretical or empirical
anchors for measures of either. (Cohen, 1975, p. 166).

DOES IT WORK WHEN IT HAS BEEN TRIED?

On my desk is a thick set of final reports on a career education

program. The first section presents summative findings; no effects on

academic achievement, no effects on occupational knowledge, statistically

reliable gains in attitudes related to career maturity, and more positive

attitudes toward school. Students, parents, and community participants

a ree that the program is beneficial. The second section reports forma-

tive results such as student folder completeness, drop-outs and attendance,

and how academic credit was assigned. All findings are interpreted as

evidence that the program was implemented as planned. A third report,

an ethnographic evaluation, presents a more complex picture of the

students, the program, and the setting. As one example, many students

spent much of their time when they were in the alternative school socializ-

ing. They rarely participated in the counseling seminars and other

planned program activities. These tended to become empty structures.

---

[1]Dr. Datta is Associate Driector of the Education and Work
Program, National Institute of Education.

*(Opinions expressed are those of the author. Endorsement by
the National Institute of Education should not be inferred. My thanks to
Ronald Bucknam, Michael Langsdorf, Garry McDaniels and David Tiedemann for
their helpful criticisms of an earlier version, and to Andrew Porter for
the Chamberlin and Platt references).

The ethnographic report suggests the operating program and the idealized program diverged at many points. Whether enough of the program on paper was implemented to be a fair test of the model is not explicitly addressed by the evaluators, ethnographers or developers.

Such findings cry for analysis relating what was happening to what happened. What an integration might show is uncertain. The data in the three reports slip past each other. For example, one can not tell if students who did participate in activities intended to develop occupational knowledge gained as much as expected. Perhaps it was only the non-participants in these activities whose occupational knowledge grew slowly.

This series of reports is not atypical. Few career education evaluation studies integrate implementation and outcome data. Examples of such practice from other educational areas are scant. In addition, there is little discussion of whether implementation will influence the magnitude, durability or selectivity of effects, and whether the outcomes are related to degree of implementation in a discontinuous or continuous fashion.

The idea that evaluations should examine implementation as well as outcomes has been discussed for over a decade. There are at least two reasons for such examination. First, suppose the results are disappointing. Implementation data can help disentangle (a) an idea that has been fairly tried but doesn't work, (b) an idea that works when it has been tried and (c) an idea that might work, but hasn't been tried. Second, recent studies have shown the influence of institutional variables on implementation. Whether the idea was imported or locally originated, teachers' participation in program development, leadership stability, the presence or absence of an advocacy group and so on affect the resemblance of idealized and actualized educational innovations. An innovation is not an innovation, however. Some innovations seem robust in the presence of situational variations. Other adapt chameleon-like as the background changes, varying in appearance but not function. Both appearance and outcomes of others may shift markedly as settings change. Understanding these relationships may improve generalizability, precision, and sensitivity of evaluations (Nachtigal, 1972; McLaughlin et al., 1975).

But all this has been said before. What seems to be less examined is *how* to relate implementation and outcome data, in ways perhaps more useful than parallel reports.

The next sections examine some ways of relating implementation and outcome data, and some assumptions underlying these models. With two exceptions such analyses might be part of many evaluation studies. These exceptions are instances (a) where implementation is perfect and thus homogeneous, and (b) where implementation, while imperfect, shows almost no variation by students, program components, or across educational units.

WHAT KIND OF IMPLEMENTATION?

Lukas, searching for a fully specified treatment in her study of implementation in compensatory education, concludes that "Failure to have well-defined models (in Head Start Planned Variation) is the result of the state of the art of educational theory (1975, p. 119)".

Full specification of career education models seems equally elusive. In the report on my desk, for example, the first implementation question is completeness of information in a student folder. The evaluators state that "almost every item specified in a student folder checklist" was found. Missing items (transcripts, career guides, student evaluation forms, site visit reports) are explained away as being "possibly of limited value." The evaluators end, however, "There was no consensus as to what must be in a student folder."

Such uncertainty about what constitutes implementation of a career education program is neither unusual nor unreasonable. In a new field, most programs are educated guesses. The field is learning what combination of experiences may influence outcomes. Drawing from career development theory and diverse educational traditions, career education is gradually evolving its conceptual base and practical applications. Guidelines for judging completeness of career education implementation have been suggested by the U.S. Office of Education (Hoyt, 1975). In the field, however, considerable latitude seems to be given in setting standards for how much or what quality of experiences is necessary for a career education program to be considered implemented.

Career education at present may be more defined by its objectives than by its procedures. Happily, from the perspective of evaluation, a carefully developed consensus on measurable objectives seems to be emerging (Arterbury et al., 1975; Hoyt, 1975). Also, tested curricula, materials and training programs are increasingly available. These, and cumulative experience with career education may contribute to operational stability and to the fuller specification of treatments.

Taking these uncertainties into account, there are at least five types of programs with regard to implementation:

Type 1: This program can be specified in sufficient detail to permit measurement of completeness and quality of implementation. Full implementation can be defined at least by components.

Type 2: Some components can be specified. Others can be sketched. Still others may become specified during implementation. Full implementation can be defined at least by components.

Type 3: The evaluator may be given some guidelines on what to look for, but the program developer can not (or in some instances will not) specify criteria permitting judgments of completeness or quality.

Type 4: The program developer may be willing or able only to indicate whether observed experiences are consistent with intended treatments and whether observed practice is compatible with program philosophy.

Type 5: A fifth possibility places the program more in the realm of research than evaluation: the developer would consider almost anything that works as consistent with the treatment and would judge implementation by outcomes. Type 5 may predominate in replication or adaptation situations where a career education model developed elsewhere is intended as a starting point rather than a template.

Caution may be needed in distinguishing among these types (Wholey, 1975; Young and Schuh, 1975). Some programs can furnish head counts on field trips for two years, the total class minutes spent on careers or the hours of teacher training. Project directors may be unable or unwilling to judge, however, what levels of such data represent incomplete, adequate, or full implementation of a career education program. Enumeration data permit romps through meadows of factor analyses and fields of correlation but have more to do with evaluative research than summative evaluation.

Somewhere, in order to measure implementation, standards must be set. As Lukas notes,

...there must be limits to variation. There must be some guage of the amount of variation that can exist in a fully implemented model, as well as some point at which the variation becomes so great that the implementation becomes partial and another point at which implementation becomes so minimal that there is no evidence of the model (1975, p. 123).

MODELS RELATING IMPLEMENTATION AND OUTCOMES

Three analytic models have been applied in relating implementation to outcomes: selection, blocking and regression.

Selection: The evaluative question in this model is, "When the
program has been implemented, how well does it work?" Type I implementation data are used to select those educational units (lessons, teachers,
students, schools) where the treatment was implemented as intended
(Lukas, 1975, p. 123). Outcome data are reported only for these well-
implemented units in contrast to data (control, comparison, trend)
offered to estimate outcomes if the program had not been available.

There are at least three limitations to selection. First,
selection requires Type I data for assurance of implementation: there
must be some guage of the limits of variation below which the model is
not fully implemented. Second, selection may decrease sensitivity of
evaluation if the cut-off point is set too low, including partially as
well as fully implemented units. Third, generalizability of results may
be questioned if a large proportion of the total sample is discarded due
to inadequate implementation.

On the other hand, selection may increase sensitivity of evaluation to the true effects of a possibly beneficial program. If implementation is reduced for reasons unrelated to the treatment (e.g.,
natural or political upheavals), selection may permit a more informed
decision about whether to continue or expand a possibly costly program.
Lastly, selection may be the fairest evaluation of a generally well-
implemented program having a few outlier classes or units with poor
implementation.

As examples, selection of well-implemented classes only was
used in presenting the U-Sail evaluation to the Joint Dissemination Review Panel in 1975 and in comparisons among early childhood programs in
Head Start Planned Variation (Stanford Research Institute, 1972). An
example for a career education evaluation was not found.

Blocking: Blocking involves comparison of educational units
representing different types or degrees of implementation. Two approaches
to blocking may be identified: (a) theory-based using natural or planned
variations (b) by quantity or quality of implementation. The question
asked is, "Does the nature or degree of implementation make a difference
in outcomes?"

Blocking requires Type 1 or Type 2 specification of treatment and implementation. In addition, application requires control or comparison data to avoid the unjustified conclusion that failure to find differences of degree means failure of the treatment itself. It may also be a costly approach, since a large sample of educational units may be needed for adequate sensitivity to true effects.

Blocking can, however, retain all units so no data are lost. It may be most sensitive also to the frequently reported "specificity of effects" findings.

An example of Type (a) blocking is the 1972 Stanford Research Institute evaluation of Head Start Planned Variation. SRI compared eight different educational programs grouped theoretically as "preacademic", "cognitive-discovery", "discovery" and "parent education." Analyses showed a specificity of effect that would have been cancelled out in comparisons of pooled experimental and comparison classes.

As another example of Type (a) blocking, comparison of program effects across cohorts in programs under development sometimes show an increase in magnitude of gains, Langsdorf et al. (1976) are finding sensitivity of outcome data to program changes in a three cohort, true experimental and control study of a career education program. Interpretation of cohort data is delicate, however. The presumably increasing benefits of an improved program are often balanced against the attitudinal cycle of enthusiasm, disenchantment, and consolidation or dissolution in educational change.

An example of Type (b) blocking in a career education program is found in the Behavioral Research Associates evaluation of the Cochise County Career Education Project (cited in Arterbury et al., 1975a). Outcome measures were selected from dimensions related to the Arizona Career Education Matrix: knowledge of skills requirements, common threads in jobs, economic awareness, awareness of career mobility, decision-making, appreciations and attitudes, and employability skills. Students who had been exposed to lower levels of career education process variables. On all the measures reported, the high exposure sample had scores that seemed substantially higher as well as statistically reliable.

The blocking design is also recommended by Young and Schuh in their *Guide to evaluating Career Education:*

> *...it is important that information on program design activities be related to estimates of program impact. For example, even in the absence of a group of students who*

had not been exposed in some manner to the program (i.e.,
no control group) it is generally possible to identify the
level or amount of program exposure for each student or
class, and treat those with the lowest exposure level as
a comparison group relative to those with the highest
exposure level. Comparison between the gains made by the
high group and those made by the low group would then
provide the basic data needed for assessing whether the
program had had any impact on outcome measures, providing
there are meaningful differences between activities en-
gaged in by the two groups. If the activities are quanti-
fiable on a fairly fine scale, such as number of hours,
the 'high' group might consist of the 25% of the students
who had the greatest number of hours and the 'low' group
might consist of the 25% of the students who had the fewest
hours of exposure. (1975, p. 64).

Regression: The assumption underlying regression analysis is
that more of some aspect of the program is associated with greater impact
than less exposure to this aspect. The question asked is, "How much
variation in the outcomes is predictable from variation in implementation?"
Multiple regression and canonical correlations would permit tests of
various combinations of both treatments and outcome events. Lukas (1975)
also suggested "...using implementation as a covariate or an independent
variable in a regression equation to control for the variation in effect
that result from differences in implementation (p. 123)".

The applicability of regression may be limited in several ways.
Most regressions assume linear relationships (in addition to other often
difficult-to-meet requirements). Caution is needed in checking scatter
plots for discontinuous or non-linear patterns. Also, the range of
variation may be too limited or samples may be too small at the extremes
to be sensitive to variation in impact with amount of treatment. Furthermore, the greatest educational effects seem to be found for treatment vs
no treatment comparisons. Thus a fair test of program impact requires
measures for a unit at or near the zero treatment level. Lastly,
scales measuring implementation must be anchored, so criteria for full
implementation are explicit and the problems of partial implementation
resolved (Lukas, 1975, pp. 123-124).

Regression may be most appropriate for instances where summative
data are needed before programs are well-developed (Type 3, 4 or 5 programs
assuming the scales can at least be anchored at head and foot). In a
addition, statistical models are available to test the impact of clusters
of treatment conditions. This may be more sensitive to a critical mass
of events that are both necessary and sufficient to influence outcomes

than are blocking or selection approaches.

Applications of regression analyses relating implementation and outcomes are fairly plentiful in compensatory education evaluation and studies of what teacher behavior influences what learner outcomes. Two examples are Stallings' (1975) and Soars' (1974) elegant analysis of what happened in Follow Through classrooms in terms of type and magnitude of learner outcomes.

One instance of a correlational technique was found for career education. Christensen, Spotts and Evenson (1975) correlated student participation in various features of an individualized career education program with student characteristics and with outcome variables. The factor analyses focused on relating student characteristics to choice of program features, however, rather than identifying outcomes associated with high and low degrees of program utilization. As examples of the findings: "Those students with previous paid work experience are among the most satisfied with their progress in basic and academic skills and with their one-to-one experience with learning coordinators; and "Students from less affluent and higher minority schools seek help especially in language skills, writing and reading, and feel their major benefit... is assistance in preparation for college (pp. 99-100)".

An example using implementation as a co-variate control or as an independent variable in a regression equation in a career education study was not found. It is this application, rather than correlations among implementation and outcomes that would distinguish the third model.

Some Issues:

At least three issues are troublesome in analyses relating implementation and outcomes. First, almost nothing is known about whether degree of implementation is most likely to influence the magnitude of results, the durability of results, the specificity versus breadth of results, or the generalizability of results. Full implementation may affect only how many students will benefit, only the size of the benefit for the same kind of student, only the durability of benefits, or only whether a few or all of the predicted objectives are achieved. The examples found have related implementation only to magnitude of results. *A priori* prediction using the research literature could help select the most promising spots (magnitude, durability, spread or generalizability) in which to dig for the effects of implementation.

Second, little is known about the shape of the relation between implementation and effects. Most analyses assume continuous, linear relationships between implementation and outcomes. Yet recent educational research suggests the prevalence of discontinuities. Again, *a priori* prediction based on the research literature could supplement *posteriori* scatter plots.

The third issue is whether program implementation should be considered as a whole in these analyses. This would imply that a total implementation score across all components would be used for selection, blocking or regression. An alternative approach would be to begin, as Young and Schuh (1975) recommend, with an evaluation scheme showing what activities are intended to influence what outcomes. This would imply that only the implementation score for the set of activities intended to influence the dependent variable under analysis would be used for selection, blocking or regression. The first approach makes theoretical sense where the career education program is conceived wholistically, as being greater than the sum of its parts, as a Gestalt. The second approach makes theoretical sense where the program is regarded more as an aggregation of activity sets, each intended to achieve specific outcomes, and where the analyses are intended to fine-tune the program. Young and Schuh's *Guide* provides many instances of this second approach.

In summary, evaluating whether an idea works when it's been tried is relatively infrequent in career education evaluation. Among the arguments in favor of relating implementation and effects is that some implementation data usually are collected as part of summative evaluation. These data are often treated descriptively. They could be treated inferentially. Implementation data used inferentially could add precision with little additional data collection effort.

Career education is likely soon to be held accountable for substantial effects, although the objectives and treatments have barely been formulated in measurable terms. An increase in sensitivity to true effects for the cost of a few minutes more on the computer and, admittedly, rather a lot more thinking about the nature of a good career education program may be worth trying. More and more career education programs are in operation. A fairly large number of evaluation reports are accumulating. The ability to distinguish clearly the impact of well-implemented programs from the results of those where the idea has not really been tried may be pivotal to public judgment about the cumulative value of career education.

HALF FULL OR HALF EMPTY: INTERPRETING MIXED RESULTS

The report on my desk is summative. After three years of effort, the developer wants to disseminate the career education program and is providing potential adoptors with evidence of its effects. The developer has chosen four student outcome criteria: academic growth will not be slowed by this alternative career education program, career competence will be enhanced, career planning will improve, and attitudes toward school will become more favorable. In addition, parent, student and community satisfaction with the program were assessed, and graduates followed up.

All told, there are 101 findings. Of these, 42 show greater gains for participants than comparisons, 17 show greater gains for comparisons or are non-significant where gain is predicted, and 52 seem neutral, descriptive, or uninterpretable. With regard to achievement of program objectives, results could be considered mixed.

If there was only one outcome measure, deciding whether or not the program succeeded would suffer only three hazards: (a) data slippage, (b) presenting only the most favorable (or unfavorable) interpretations, and (c) considering statistical significance without regard to educational significance (and vice versa).

The educational evaluation with one criterion measure is slightly rarer than the unicorn, however. Almost every educational program apparently expects to change many of the cognitive and affective outcomes in the Great Taxonomy. Since few seem to achieve unequivocal success on all criteria, the evaluator faces post-analysis trauma: what does it all mean? Thus, two more hazards are added: (d) placing greater weight on measures most likely to be favorable (and vice versa) and (e) basing conclusions on the most favorable (or unfavorable) results without presenting conclusions based on alternative interpretations of the same data or on alternative constellations of different data from the same universe.

Is this really a problem? One reviewer of an earlier draft wrote:

> ...maybe the question itself is too simplistic. The more evaluation I do, the more I'm struck with a notion that maybe we can't ever say whether or not a program has succeeded. Maybe all we can say is that a given program attained x number of outcomes, that these outcomes were either positive or negative, anticipated or unanticipated or unanticipated, and let the reader judge for himself or herself whether or not the program was successful.

In my opinion, mixed results are a problem. Evaluators ought to contribute to decisions, if the findings seem reliable and valid. Many decisions are simplistic: yes, continue the program or no, don't; yes, continue to this degree or in this way. The evidence contributing to these decisions need not be simplistic or simplistically presented. It may need, however, to be organized in terms of arguments supporting one decision or another. And this organization requires judgments on the part of the organizer, presumably based on some standards or criteria for program achievement, rather than neutral lists of outcomes and their direction.

Scriven (1974) comments,

> ...within minutes of the initial discussion, what the negotiator or the liaison person from the evaluation outfit has identified--whether this is conscious or unconscious is irrelevant--is what outcome the agency that's going to pay the bill would like to see. If the agency happens to be a developing agency, then it's obvious they'd like to see a favorable report...There are also those interesting cases where personnel in the agency have switched and someone would like nothing better than to knife a project in the neck and get the money released for some of his or her own favored children. With the best will in the world, you can't act like you're completely independent of this type of bias when you've found out what result would be liked and when it's within your economic self-interest to produce a result that is liked (p. 13).

STICKING TO THE DATA

Sometimes one thing is reported in the text, summary and recommendations when the data are uninterpretable or show something different. Checking each statement against the data displays can catch such instances of data slippage in full reports. Checking requires more labor, however, than most readers can devote to evaluations. Misstatements tend to glide uncorrected into the citations of evaluation studies and the folklore of evaluation.

As an example, the report on my desk stated, "The third hypothesis was that experimental students will acquire positive attitudes toward their learning environment...Table 8 presents the means and standard deviations for the post-test (attitude) subscores...Hypothesis #3 was not rejected...students did acquire positive attitudes."

The data are post-only scores on a Likert-type measure. The average scores in Table 8 are between neutral (3) and favorable (4) on a

five point scale. It seems fair to say that these attitudes are favorable. But there are no data on initial attitudes toward education for
these students. It is as tenable (and unjustified) to conclude that
student attitudes have been unchanged or have deteriorated as it is to
conclude the students acquired a favorable attitude.

PRESENTING ON THE MOST FAVORABLE (OR UNFAVORABLE) INTERPRETATION OF THE DATA

Suppose an hypothesis isn't confirmed or the effect is weak.
There are several favorable interpretations: (1) consider the measures as
being unreliable, insensitive or inappropriate; (2) attribute the lack of
statistical significance to the small N and a few outlier subjects;
(3) suggest implementation was inadequate due to lack of time, program
complexity, lack of funds, etc.; (4) present the findings leaving conclusions to the reader; and (5) reverse the hypothesis, claiming the
results actually indicate program effectiveness.

Several unfavorable interpretations are possible: (6) consider
only the conclusion that the program is either unproven or a failure; and
(7) conclude that because this particular example has failed to demonstrate success, the basic idea underlying the program is guilty by
association.

As an example, a formative evaluation question concerned criteria for assigning academic credit to students' products. According to
the evaluators, "credit and grading procedures appeared to incorporate
the guidelines presented in the Basic Procedures Manual, but seem to be
somewhat subjective in nature. Nevertheless it seems they should all
be taken into consideration in the grading process."

Put in different terms, the Basic Procedures Manual guidelines
for assigning academic credit were not being used. Credit was being
assigned by subjective ratings developed by those directly responsible
for each student's records. The evaluators conclude this is good.
Alternative interpretations might be that the original guidelines should
be revised, that the learning coordinators should receive training in
using the established guidelines, or both. The trade-offs between
possible abuses of subjective guidelines and possible inapplicability of
the original guidelines might be probed.

CONSIDERING ONLY STATISTICAL OR EDUCATIONAL SIGNIFICANCE

One common interpretational problem is the confusion of statistical and educational significance. A p value of well beyond the .001 level for an average IQ difference of one point means that a difference between the two groups as large as one IQ point would be unlikely to occur if only chance were operating. Whether or not a one point IQ difference is worth whatever the educational treatment costs or would compensate for possible negative side effects, the t value doesn't say.

On the other hand, the magnitude of a difference and its apparent educational significance have sometimes been reported as if the question of the reliability of the difference or the effort involved to achieve it were irrelevant.

As an example, "The ninth hypothesis was that the experimental subjects will acquire increased career maturity." The pre-test mean score was 35; the post test, 38, on a 50 item scale. The scale is labelled by the test constructor as an "attitude scale" and said to measure "involvement in the career choice process, orientation to work, independence in decision-making, preference for career choice factors, and conceptions of the career choice process." The attitude scale is one of the six parts of the Career Maturity Inventory. The experimental sutdents answered three times more positively, on the average. The evaluators conclude, "The ninth hypothesis is not rejected. The students acquired increased career maturity."

There are several considerations here: (1) career attitudes are not synonymous with career maturity according to the test developer; (2) on the five other subtests, no differences in favor of the experimental group were found; (3) the magnitude of the gain is 3 points of a 50 item scale; (4) the program is not a minor addition to a regular curriculum but an alternative school; and (5) no other evidence of increased career maturity is offered.

An example of greater caution is found in McKinney and Golden's (1973) evaluation of a career awareness program. They write,

> ...the differences between groups were not great and did not exceed .3 of a year as measured by grade equivalent scores...although the group differences reported above (favoring the experimental groups) are reliable in a statistical sense, it is doubtful whether they are educationally important (p. 26).

PLACING THE GREATEST WEIGHT ON ATTITUDES

How much weight should be given to consumer satisfaction? One
of the puzzles of educational research is the tendency for consumers to
be positive and often enthusiastic when almost every other indicator is
neutral or negative. Positive response sets on attitude scales, semantic
differentials and questionnaires may contribute something to this tendency. Where participation in the program is involuntary, positive
response set problems can be in part reduced through scaling devices.
Where participation is voluntary, presumably only those who are reasonably satisfied with the program remain in it. Where the program is in
addition experimental, remaining participants tend to become advocates.
Here caution would suggest attention to the effort required for recruiting,
the application rate, and examination of the attitudes of applicants who
never attended or dropped out.

On the other hand, the opinion of participants is often an outcome in its own right, particularly where attitudes toward schools may be
unfavorable initially. The temptation to give twice as much space to
endorsements as to negative or marginal learner outcomes seems hard to
resist, however. Rarely are possibly more objective attitudinal indicators (e.g., absenteeism, truancy, vandalism, or disruptive behavior)
given precedence over semantic differentials.

As an example, in one study, the three conclusions of the
summative evaluators were that the program was very successful since it
was actually operating to serve students; that it was transportable since
it had been used in one other site; and that it "was demonstrated to be
an enjoyable experience since it was positively received by students,
employers, parents and former students." The relatively modest learner
outcomes aren't mentioned in the conclusions.

SELECTING THE MOST FAVORABLE (OR UNFAVORABLE) FINDINGS

Without established standards of success, selection and weighing
of mixed findings seems susceptible to non-experimental factors (Cohen,
1975; Scriven, 1975). In the 101 finding report on my desk, for example,
40% of the summative findings seem positive in the text, 15% seem negative, and 47% seem neutral, descriptive or uninterpretable. In the
summary chapter, of the 49 findings reported, 60% are positive, 28%
were negative, and 12% are neutral. In the conclusion, three positive

statements are made. The proportion of positive findings has increased from 30% in the text and tables, to 60% in the summary, to 100% in the conclusions and recommendations chapter. The mixture gets more positive as it goes along until the two-thirds empty jug is 100% full of good news about the program.

WHAT CAN BE DONE?

Several approaches to the half-full or half-empty quandry have been suggested or tried. Among these are:

1. *Emphasize analysis of the reasons in the program for the mixed results, somewhat transforming the evaluation into a formative activity (Young and Schuh, 1975).*

2. *Forensic evaluation, in which the effort of the evaluator to make the best (or worst) possible case is overt (Rivlin, 1974).*

3. *Adversarial evaluation, in which the same data are interpreted with equal time for researchers who are in favor of or skeptical about the educational innovation (Arnstein, 1975; Levine, 1974; Owens, 1973; Wolf, 1975)*

4. *Reviews by researchers of different persuasions are bound in with the original report (Merrow, 1975).*

5. *Having the evaluation text and appendices prepared by on set of evaluators and the conclusions by an eminent, neutral and broad spectrum policy analyst.*

6. *Reporting on the findings, leaving consolidation to the reader (Gartner, 1975).*

7. *Improving quality through evaluation audits (Montana State Department of Public Instruction, 1973; Norton and and Waltley, 1972).*

Perhaps, however, the problem is more one of an experimenting attitude than of technological fixes. The problem of bias in interpreting results has been recognized at least since 1890. Chamberlin (1890, reprinted in 1965) write then:

> *The moment one has offered an original explanation for a phenomenon which seems satisfactory, that moment affection for his intellectual child springs into existence. The mind lingers with pleasure upon the facts that fall happily into the embrace of the theory and feels a natural coldness toward those that seem refractory...The remedy lies, indeed, partly in clarity, but more largely in correct intellectual habits, in a predominant, ever-present disposition to see things as they are, and to judge them in the full light of an unbiased weighing accompanied by the withholding of judgment when the evidence is insufficient to justify conclusions (p. 759).*

Platt, in 1964, joined Chamerlin in urging a return to the method of strong inference, arguing that advances in fields such as molecular biology could be attributed to explicit formulation of multiple working hypotheses.

> *Of course it is easy---and all too common--for one scientist to call others unscientific. My point is not that my particular conclusions here are necessarily correct, but that we have long needed some absolute standard of scientific effectiveness by which to measure how well we are succeeding in various areas...I will mention one severe but useful private test...I call it 'The Question'. Obviously, it should be applied as much to one's own thinking as to others. It consists in asking in your mind, on hearing any scientific explanation or on hearing a scientific experiment described, "But, sir, what hypothesis does your experiment disprove? (p. 352)"*

Correct intellectual habits seem difficult of attainment. Few have been trained in rigorous application of the method of multiple working hypotheses. The stakes of program expansion, continuation, or phase-out may be too high to achieve dispassionate interest in multiple hypotheses. Perhaps, too, the intellectual style of our time is more partisan than impartial. Some will give the benefit of almost every doubt to the programs; others will scarcely grant an inch of the cloak of a favorable interpretation.

For a while, then, we may need to fall back on technological fixes. None of the approaches suggested above are perfect. There are no estimates of the increment in educational knowledge gained by the extra effort involved in each. The public interest may be better served, however, through adopting at least one of these approaches than by perpetuating the present reliance on the objectivity of evaluators in an area where judgment in dealing with the often mixed results plays so prominent a role.

REFERENCES

Arnstein, George E., "Trial by Jury: A New Evaluation Method. II. The outcome." *Phi Delta Kappan*, 1975, 57 (3), 188-191.

Arterbury, Elbis J.; Collie, John; Jones, David A.; and Morrell, Jayne, *The Efficacy of Career Education: Career Awareness*. A report presented to the National Advisory Council on Career Education, U. S. Office of Education, 1975 (a).

Behavioral Research Associates. *Careers: Career Awareness and Readiness, an Educational Evaluation Research Survey*. Arizona: 1975.

Bliss, Sam W. and Foster, Scott. *Pilot Test of Career Education Instruc-*

tional Units. Final Report. Northern Arizona University, Flagstaff, Arizona, 1973 (ED 080 878/CE000095).

Chamberlin, Thomas C., "The Method of Multiple Working Hypotheses". *Science*, 1965, 148, 754-759.

Christensen, Paul; Spotts, Robert and Evenson, Jill, *Experience Based Career Education*. Final Evaluation Report, FY1975. Far West Laboratory for Educational Research and Development. *Differential Effects on Students (IV)* 147-176, 1975.

Cohen, David K., "The Value of Social Experiments". In Alice M. Rivlin and P. Michael Timpane, (eds.), *Planned Variation in Education*. Washington, D. C.: Brookings Institution, 1975, 147-176.

Hoyt, Kenneth, "An Introduction to Career Education: A Policy Paper of the U. S. Office of Education". Washington, D. C.: U. S. Office of Education, Department of Health, Education and Welfare, 1975.

Levine, Murray, "Scientific Method and the Adversary Mode". *American Psychologist*, 1974, 666-677.

Lukas, Carol Van Deusen, "Problems in Implementing Head Start Planned Variation Models." In Alice M. Rivlin and P. Michael Timpane (eds.), *Planned Variation in Education*. Washington, D. C.: Brookings Institution, 1975, 113-126.

Langsdorf, Michael A., Gibboney, Richard, and Weiler, James. *Report on The Career Internship Program*. Philadelphia, Pa.: Gibboney Associates in process, 1976.

McLaughlin, Milbrey et al., *Federal Programs Supporting Educational Change: Vol. I, A Model of Educational Change, Vol. II, Factors Affecting Change Agent Projects, Vol. III, The Process of Change Vol. IV, The Findings in Review*. Santa Monica, Ca: Rand Corporation, 1975.

McKinney, James D. and Golden, Loretta. *Evaluation of an Occupational Education Model for Primary Grades*. Chapel Hill, N.C.: Frank Porter Graham Child Development Center, 1973.

Merrow, John G., *Politics of Competence: A Review of Competency Based Teacher Education*. National Institute of Education, 1975.

Montana State Department of Public Instruction. *Audit Report: Research and Development Project in Career Education*. Vol. III. Missoula, Montana, August 1973. (ED 089120/EC D01176)

Nachtigal, Paul, *A Foundation Goes to School: The Ford Foundation Comprehensive School Improvement Program*. New York: The Ford Foundation, 1972.

Norton, Daniel and Waltley, Donovan J. *The Efficiency and Efficacy of Evaluation Practices of the Illinois Division of Vocational and Technical Education*. Evanston, Illinois: Educational Testing Service, December, 1972.

Owens, Thomas, "Educational Evaluation by Adversary Proceeding". In Ernest House, (ed.), *School Evaluation: The Politics and Process*. Berkeley, Ca: McCutcheon, 1973.

Platt, John R., "Strong Inference". *Science*, Vol. 147, October 16, 1974, 347-353.

Scriven, Michael, "Exploring Goal Free Evaluation: An Interview."
   Evaluation, Vol. 2, No. 1, 1974, 9-16.

Statford Research Institute. *Interim Report: First Year of Evaluation:
   Implementation of Planned Variation in Head Start. Preliminary
   Evaluations of Planned Variation in Head Start According to
   Follow Through Approaches. (1969-1970).* Menlo Park, Ca.: 1972.

Stallings, Jane and Kaskowitz, D., *Follow Through Classroom Observation
   Evaluation, 1972-1973.* Menlo Park, Ca.: Stanford Research
   Institute, 1974.

Soar, Robert, *Follow Through Classroom Process Measurement and Pupil
   Growth (1970-71).* Final Report. Gainesville, Florida:
   University of Florida, June 1973.

Tuckman, Bruce W. and Carducci, Joseph A., *Evaluating Career Education:
   A Review and a Model.* Mimeo, 1974.

Wholey, Joseph S. et al., "Evaluation: When Is It Really Needed?"
   Evaluation, Vol. 2, No. 2, 1975, 89-93.

Wolf, Robert L. "Trial by Jury: A New Evaluation Method. I, The Process."
   Phi Delta Kappan, Vol. 57, No. 3, 1975, 185-188.

Young, Malcolm B. and Schuh, Russell G., *Evaluation and Education
   Decision-Making: A Functional Guide to Evaluating Career
   Education.* Washington, D. C.: Development Associates, Inc.,
   September 1975.

15

APPLIED SOCIAL RESEARCH:
IN COMBAT WITH WASTE AND SUFFERING

By

HOWARD R. DAVIS and SUSAN E. SALASIN

Growing interest in the utilization of social research by policymakers is an encouraging sign for the more skeptical among researchers. Increasing cooperation between social researchers and policymakers indicates that the gap between evaluation research and policymaking is being bridged. According to Howard R. Davis and Susan E. Salasin, evaluators should therefore become more concerned with the improvement of their search for knowledge in order to make it relevant to the needs of policymakers. The authors conclude by making five recommendations which they consider critical for improvement of the quality of knowledge in evaluation research.

From Howard R. Davis and Susan E. Salasin, "Applied Social Research: In Combat with Waste and Suffering." *International Journal of Comparative Sociology,* Spring 1977.

In response to a dramatically rising concern among federal policymakers concerning our national performance in delivering human services, *Evaluation* magazine dedicated a special issue (1974) to the frustrating problem of the shortfall in human services. American leaders—Jimmy Carter, Amitai Etzioni, Henry Ford II, Walter Heller, Elliot Richardson, James Tobin, Martha Griffiths, among others— deplored the disappointed hopes of millions of suffering people who were intended to be, but who were not, rescued by vast human service programs. Not always was or is cost the culprit. The resistances to the policies established, inefficient administrative systems, changing circumstances, and time itself all played a part. But the conclusion of Lynn (1974:43) is compelling: "Our only realistic hope, as far as a strategy is concerned, lies in . . . doing the hard work of *researching, evaluating, experimenting, advocating,* and *negotiating,* but doing it as well and as thoroughly as we can" (italics ours).

Social research can indeed serve as a combatant against policy failure, waste, and the consequent unmet needs. For the myriad shortfalls of social policy at local, national, and international levels, social research has significant help to offer in rendering murky waters clearer to allow accurate analysis. It can provide if-then foresights to reduce the risk attendant in alternative policy decisions. The harvest of knowledge contributions from social research mounts increasingly. Like a phalanx of soldiers, the long line of journals on library shelves grows steadily. We estimate that some 2,000 abstracts are added to retrieval systems each month, many of them representing sound researches.

Unfortunately, the existence alone of relevant knowledge seems to have unspectacular impact. Mackie and Christenson (1967) have documented the poor utilization performance of research information in the field of education. The Battelle Columbus Laboratories (National Science Foundation, 1973) documented the amount of time required for knowledge to reach utilization. For example, the technology for input-output economic analysis required some 28 years between the first year of conception and its realization. Four years have passed since the results of the New Jersey Graduated Work Incentive Experiment laid to rest the fear that primary wage earners would significantly reduce work effort if they were generally eligible for cash assistance. Yet, as Lynn (1975) has documented, incrementalism persists rather than needed overhaul—which could be guided by the New Jersey experiment—in welfare reform.

In our evaluations of the impact of applied research results in mental health, an earlier analysis revealed that for barely one result in ten could any utilization be identified a year after project completion. On the other side of the ledger, there is at least hope that better effort can relieve the often poor showing of research impact. Due to application of various change technologies, there has been an eightfold increase over the initial utilization rate of "one result in ten" for applied mental health research projects. In addition, Caplan, Morrison, and Stambaugh (1975) found evidence that top federal policymakers could name, on the average, approximately two uses that had been made of research-based knowledge in reaching decisions. And Rich (1975) reports encouraging experiences with knowledge transfer efforts associated with the Continuing National Survey Operation.

Though we hardly have a wellspring of hope about improving the utilization of social research knowledge as yet, there is enough encouragement to warrant moving forward with deliberateness toward giving more appropriate speed and soundness to the transfer of social research knowledge into policy and practice formulation. Glaser in the volume *Putting Knowledge to Use* (1976:1) has paraphrased H.G. Wells's well-known reference to the importance of education in alerting us to the fact that "civilization is a race between knowledge utilization and catastrophe." One is hard pressed to think of any field in which knowledge utilization is so urgently needed as that of social research, and hardly is there another field that possesses the talent and tools to forge effective practices to facilitate the transfer of appropriate knowledge into action.

Though the rewards of greater concentration on fostering the contributions of social research to society could be significant for the field itself, the National Science Foundation's review—*Report of the National Science Board* (1975)—of federal investments in research and development reported that only 11% went to areas that could be considered social research (including education and economics). The proportion of university faculty members performing research through federal funds for all fields in 1974 was 56%, nearly the lowest. Our point is that as awareness grows of the gains to be made by the effective infusion of social research contributions to social policy so should investments in this research enterprise. Perhaps there was a message about attitudes behind President Lyndon Johnson's reference to "sociologists and kooks." (At least he didn't say " . . . and other kooks.") But a far greater reward would seem to be the contribution to the reduction of the frequency of ineffectual policy decisions and shortfall in quality-of-life advances. With these experiences and observations in mind, two matters, it seems to us, must be addressed and systematically developed for the realization of optimum benefits from social research to social policy.

1. Binding the Interface Between Researchers and Policymakers

It is a wry observation to note that not all persons on either side of the interface are reaching out their hands for assistance from the other group. Anti-utilitarianism still seems to influence the value of many researchers. One of the country's most eminent social psychologists once challenged us to name one research contribution that had been insufficiently used. Research in the area of early childhood stimulation was proposed. "Oh," he retorted, "those findings are nowhere near being safe to release yet." To be sure, refining research findings should progress as with the Head Start program. Yet, since the classical Skeels and Skodak Iowa studies on that topic in the late 1930s, there has been no major alteration of their early conclusions. One wonders "How long, O Lord, till the scientists will deign to cast their pearls?"

After some 18 years in research management, we continue to detect a pervasive fear among researchers that once a topic of study is utilized, support for further research will cease. Not so. To the contrary, research activities seem more often to accelerate when usage commences, as is the case in the field of evaluation research. The strongest reinforcement to researchers remains the publication of their findings, not involvement with social utilization. Research grants or academic promotions are not gained on the basis of "utilization events." The incentive system needs to be changed, and there are a few instances where it is changing (notable only due to the isolated nature of their occurrence). Archibald (1968) has confirmed another cost of the researcher becoming a policy contributor: when a scientist begins to even talk about utilization, she or he loses status among peers. So these are all issues to be considered in narrowing the distance between researchers and policymakers.

There are signs that the values are being changed, at least by leaders in social research. When Amitai Etzioni writes presidential papers, when Peter Rossi telephones a cabinet member, when Clark Abt launches a new professional organization for applied social researchers, "modeling behavior," as the psychologists say, is set into motion. To be sure, persons of that ilk can afford the risk, but they will also make it "safer" for others to follow and venture into the "hurly-burly political worlds" as Carol Weiss (1973) puts it.

On the side of policymakers, the huzzas are hardly resounding to the approach of researchers bearing gifts. In 1968 the Institute of Community Studies arranged what was to be a potlatch between social scientists and top policy people representing social agencies in the Kansas City area, with change consultants helping to pass the gifts back and forth. By noon of the first day, the policy people began—ever so politely and with a touch on the arm and a whispered apology—to slip "back to the office." "Enjoy it, hope to be back right after lunch." But for the next two days the scientists and consultants had everything all to themselves. Don Tiffany (Tiffany, Tiffany, and Cowan, 1969) had administered a semantic differential rating form. It asked for self- and other-views according to an array of opposite adjectives for researchers versus administrators. Stereotypes were confirmed. Scientists and administrators really are of "two solitudes."

On this side of the interface between the "two solitudes" the light is showing through. Caplan and coworkers (1975) report that 86% of the top federal policy people surveyed feel more use should be made of social science. A host of writers has contemplated the chasm between researchers and policy-practice people. Others have advocated the change agent role, as a bridge. You may wish to see a full discussion as presented in *Putting Knowledge to Use* (1976:47-63). Experimentation in this area is vitally needed to determine what techniques should be employed and with what effectiveness.

2. Researching the Applied Research into Social Policy Process Itself

It sounds like the wearisome windup of a graduate research report to say "further research is needed on . . . ," but that is precisely our plea; optimum transfer of social research into action indeed *should* be a deliberate subject of social research, paralleling the dictum "physician heal thyself."

But before instituting "standards of practice" for guiding this process, sounder knowledge appears needed on at least five decision stations along the road:

1. *Knowledge regarding the design, conduct, and other policy-tropic attributes of applied social research.* Some research, even after running the gauntlet of journal referees, is so poor that it is merciful that use of it by policy planners has not occurred. For example, Wilner (1976) found that a mere 3% of articles published in mental health journals met sound standards of research analysis. (Not all articles were research reports, as such.) At the other extreme, Cronbach (1977) warns, "excellent data can lead to wrong social actions if they report on a specially controlled treatment that cannot be duplicated when the program is disseminated." Further refinement of fresher approaches, such as decision theory employing Bayesian statistics, is advocated by Guttentag (1974). Glazer and Taylor (1969) discovered an array of practices, seldom considered consciously in the conduct of applied research, that make an immense difference in the quality of findings. Too often refereed selection for publication of research findings is decided by tightness of research design only. Our own studies of decision determinants employed by scientist review panels on applied research clearly reveal that tightness of research design is the primary criterion for approval and funding. It is not enough.

2. *Knowledge regarding methods of measuring research impact on policy planning.* At this point in time, methods of assessing what assimilation of social research in policy planning actually occurs do not exist. If the dependent variable (impact) cannot be measured, then all the noble manipulations of independent variables (factors that might influence utilization) represent only stabs in the dark.

3. *Knowledge regarding methods for assessing needs for specific policy-relevant researches.* Referring to the "great American gun war" between the gun controllers and the gun lobby, Bruce-Briggs (1976:37) states, "Yet it is startling to note that no policy research worthy of the name has been on the issue of gun control." Why? How did research scientists miss this one? When mass violence erupted in Detroit, the senior author of this paper *then* hustled to Wayne State University to help design a research project—and in one weekend! But why only then? Mea Culpa! J. Salasin (1977) has experimented with a modified Delphi method to assess forthcoming needs for research on children's mental health with edifying results. But will the same procedure be fruitful or even experimented with in the arena of social problems?

4. *Knowledge regarding the "anatomy and physiology" of policymaking.* Policy evolvement seems as often to flow in rivers underground as aboveground. President

Carter has mandated that "the person who writes Federal regulations, converting legislation into explicit policy, will affix her or his signature." Of course, one official will take responsibility and sign. But in the development of such guidelines for evaluation by federally funded community mental health centers, no fewer than 100 people were involved in varying capacities. Who decided what? How do we know the point at which social research findings should be offered? And how should they be offered? Or, even, where?

In contributing to welfare reform, as another example, whom does one approach? The programs are shaped by "at least 21 committees of the Congress and by 50 state legislators, by 6 Cabinet departments and 3 federal agencies, by 54 state and territorial welfare agencies and by more than 1,500 county welfare departments, by the U.S. Supreme Court and by many lesser courts" (Fraser, 1977). The problem has been likened to Rabindranath Tagore's story of the holy man who wandered the roads, searching for the touchstone of truth. As he began, he examined each pebble with care, then in a more perfunctory way as the years passed by, he would pick up a pebble, touch it to his waist-chain, and discard it without a glance. One day in gazing at his chain he was astonished that it finally had turned to gold. So he must have held the touchstone in his hand, but when and where he knew not.

5. *Knowledge regarding actual practices of fostering diffusion and utilization of social research.* An extensive literature has accumulated on the use of knowledge in bringing about needed change (*Putting Knowlege to Use,* 1976). But the vast majority of it deals with the adoption of new *practices,* not *policies.* Policies govern, practices do not. That difference may mean that the phenomenon of policy impact of research represents an entirely new arena. The cast is greater and more complex, the stakes higher, and the power plays more strident. What has been found to be effective in the adoption of knowledge in practices may not be generalizable in the policy world. One impressive study on the results of insinuating social research findings into the policy process was reported by Rich (1975). Through the Continuous National Survey Experiment data were provided to policymakers. As one example of Rich's findings, it turned out that those who were involved in the decisions concerning what information should be collected were more likely to make use of the data than policymakers who were not. There can be no question that case studies, surveys, and process analyses will lead to understanding of how social research may become more beneficial to policymaking. But the ultimate answer will come from experiments on approaches toward a deliberate and systematic introduction of findings into policy machinery.

As a final observation, there is a line from one of Yevtushenko's poems that goes "There is such security in small hope." The heroes of applied social research may be those who risk that security by reifying the very great hope that research may indeed serve as a latchkey that will open the door to fuller effectiveness of social policies in meeting the needs of the world's people.

REFERENCES

ARCHIBALD, K. (1968). The utilization of social research and policy analysis. Doctoral dissertation. Washington University.

BRUCE-BRIGGS, B. (1976). "The great American gun war." Public Interest, 45:37-62.

CAPLAN, N. (1975). A minimal set of conditions necessary for the utilization of social science knowledge in policy formation at the national level. Paper presented at the Conference of the International Sociological Association, Warsaw, Poland.

CAPLAN, N., MORRISON, A., and STAMBAUGH, R.J. (1975). The use of social science knowledge in policy decisions at the national level. Ann Arbor: University of Michigan.

CRONBACH, L. (1977). "Remarks to the new society." Evaluation Research Society Newsletter, 1(1).

FRASER, D.M. (1977). "Streamlining welfare programs." Washington Post, January 9, C3.

GLASER, E.M., and TAYLOR, S. (1969). Factors influencing the success of applied research. Final report on contract no. 43-67-1365, National Institute of Mental Health. Washington, D.C.: Department of Health, Education, and Welfare.

GUTTENTAG, M. (1974). "Subjectivity and its use in evaluation research. Evaluation. Minneapolis: Minneapolis Medical Research Foundation.

JOLY, J-M. (1967). Research and innovation: Two solitudes? Canadian Education and Research Digest, 2:184-194.

LYNN, L.E., Jr. (1975). "A decade of policy developments in the income maintenance system." Discussion Paper 33 D, Kennedy School of Government, Cambridge, Mass.: Harvard University.

——— (1974). "Gasoline shortages and human services shortages: What is the difference?" Evaluation, (spring):38-45.

MACKIE, R.R., and CHRISTENSON, P.R. (1967). Translation and application of psychological research. Technical report 716-1. Goleta, Calif.: Santa Barbara Research Park Human Factors Research.

National Science Foundation (1975). "Science indicators 1974." Report of the National Science Board. Washington, D.C.: Author.

——— (1973). Science, Technology, and Innovations. Report on contract no. NSF-667. Columbus, Ohio: Battelle Columbus Laboratories.

Putting Knowledge to Use: A distillation of the literature regarding knowledge transfer and change (1976). Washington, D.C. Human Interaction Research Institute, National Institute of Mental Health.

RICH, K.F. (1975). "Selective utilization of social science related info by federal policy-makers." Inquiry, 13(3).

SALASIN, J.J. (1977). Challenges for children's mental health services. McLean, Va.: Metrek Division, Mitre Corporation.

TIFFANY, D.W., TIFFANY, P.M., and COWAN, J.C. (1969). "Source of problems between social science knowledge and practice." Journal of Human Relations, 19:239-250.

WEISS, C. (1973). "Where politics and evaluation research meet." Evaluation, 1(3):37-45.

WILNER, P. (1976). Personal communication. University of California, Los Angeles.

16

WHY IS EVALUATION RESEARCH NOT UTILIZED?

By

REHKA AGARWALA-ROGERS

In this study, Rehka Agarwala-Rogers presents us with what she believes to be the underlying reasons responsible for the underutilization of evaluation research. According to the author, evaluation research can be better utilized if program officials participate in the evaluation process. Furthermore, by appointing evaluators who are insiders in the organization, the anxiety associated with evaluation is reduced; consequently, the likelihood that evaluation research will be utilized increases.

From Rehka Agarwala-Rogers, "Why is Evaluation Research Not Utilized?" Unpublished manuscript, 1977.

[327]

Evaluation research is a means to determine the effectiveness of present programs, and to assess the relative advantage of new alternatives that might be tried. But there is a rather small amount of attention devoted to evaluation in many fields.[1] One of the main reasons for conducting evaluation research is to obtain information that will improve program operations. By itself, evaluation research is of little importance, unless and until its results are put into use.

Research utilization is the process by which research results are produced to answer practitioner needs, and communicated to practitioners for their use. Three essential elements in the research utilization process include: (1) *the research system,* which creates and develops research results or innovations, (2) *the linking system,* which performs the functions of translating practitioner needs to researchers and of diffusing research results to practitioners, and (3) *the practitioner system,* which recognizes user needs for research and thus leads to its initiation and which later uses the research results. Figure 1 shows these three systems and the function of each in the research utilization process.

In every field there is a large body of research-based knowledge that has not been put to use; as a result, current practice lags far behind contemporary knowledge. A great deal of evaluation research is underutilized: it is not adequately put into actual practice. Why?

One reason for this unfortunate state of the evaluation research is due to deficiencies of evaluation research in general. *The field of evaluation is not academically respectable in most nations;* the number of individuals who have been trained to design and conduct evaluation research is relatively small. Evaluation is a more applied type of research, and most university scholars and students avoid it. As a result: "What passes for evaluative research is indeed a mixed bag at best and chaos at worst" (Cottrell, 1967:vii). Needed is "not only more evaluation, but more imaginative and skillful evaluation, well conceived, multidimensional, relevant to the issues, and meshed into policy-making and planning processes" (Weiss, 1972:xii).

Even considering this inadequate base *of general evaluation techniques, relatively little of these understandings have been utilized.* For instance, although most evaluation experts agree that the field experiment is one of the most powerful and appropriate evaluative designs, on few occasions has an experimental design been used in the family planning field. And these field experiments have usually been of low quality, without the random assignment of treatments to subjects and often without a control group. These field studies in family planning have usually been

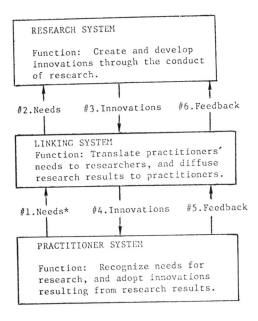

*The communication flows numbered in this paradigm may be identified as follows:

#1. Flow of user needs (for new information) to linkers.

#2. After interpretation and clarification, these needs are transferred to the research system.

#3. Researchers attempt to provide needed information for practitioners' needs, either from accumulated knowledge or via newly originated research.

#4. Linkers distill and interpret this new information (innovations) for practitioners.

#5. Feedback from practitioners to linkers on the adequacy of the new information in meeting their needs.

#6. Linkers convey practitioners' feedback to researchers, perhaps leading to further practitioner needs and recycling of the entire process.

Figure 1: PARADIGM OF THE RESEARCH UTILIZATION PROCESS

quasi-experiments rather than "true" experiments. So the results from such evaluation research have often been vague and imprecise.

The reasons for underutilization of the evaluation research results may lie in the following factors:

(1) Lack of administrator's participation and involvement in the evaluation process.

(2) Conflicting interests of program officials and evaluators of the program.

(3) Lack of mutually agreed upon "problem" definition and "needs" delineation between evaluators and users of the research findings.

(4) Lack of specialists who are trained to act as liaison between the program administrators and evaluation researchers.

(5) Lack of emphasis on providing solution to problems, rather than accurate description of events and activities only.

(6) Over emphasis on negative aspects of programs in the evaluation reports have led to the lack of utilization of evaluative research findings.

(7) Need of the program official for the research findings and the evaluator's ability to deliver results within that time frame creates problems of feedback and timeliness of evaluation results.

Yet another reason for the lack of adequate evaluation *may lie in the threat of evaluation.* For most program officials there is a certain comfortableness in continuing to follow existing practice. Evaluation has the potential of destroying this comfort, of forcing the program official to give up his customary procedures and consider new alternatives. Negative results from evaluation research are particularly threatening: "The very reasonable expectation that a good study will show no effect [of a programme] is itself a major reason why administrators fear hard-headed evaluation. . . . It is a very reasonable fear because a null effect is going to be interpreted as the administrator's failure or an error in his advocacy of the programme" (Donald T. Campbell in Salasin, 1973).

Evaluation may be especially fearful when the evaluation researcher is an outsider to the organization. Being an outsider ensures that the evaluator comes to his task with fresh ideas and a wide perspective, and that the evaluation results will be perceived as having relatively higher credibility than if the evaluator were an insider. But along with these advantages of outsider evaluation comes inevitable pressures toward negative results. The evaluation researcher, because he comes from outside the organization, feels that in order to justify his worth to the agency he should recommend important changes in the organization's present operations. Thus it is expected that outside evaluators are more likely to "find" and report negative results. And naturally such negative feedback is resisted and feared.

Not only does the threatening nature of evaluation explain why we have so few examples of adequate evaluation studies in many fields, but this inherent threat also explains why the results of evaluation research are so seldom utilized by program officials. "Organizations are comfortable in the status quo. When presented with negative results, their prestige, ideology, and even resources are threatened. They frequently react by rejecting the results" (Weiss, 1972:27). So *evaluation research results are more likely to be utilized (1) when the evaluator is an insider to the organization, and (2) when program officials are involved throughout the evaluation process.*

Often the conditions that lead to evaluation research are inherently threatening: An obvious failure, a shortage of funds, competing needs, disorders, or the approaching renewal of financial support.

Evaluation can also be threatening to the evaluator. If an evaluation finds a program successful, it will be attacked by the program's detractors. If the evaluation finds the program unsuccessful, it will be denounced by its advocates. "No good evaluation goes unpunished" (Rossi, 1973). Perhaps the perceived threat of evaluation, and the threat to the evaluator, are both reasons why more programs are not evaluated.

HOW CAN EVALUATION RESEARCH BE UTILIZED?

Experience in other fields shows that *some type of linkers is essential if research is to be effectively utilized.* Prior experience with linkers in agriculture, public technology, and education indicates that it is essential to create such a role if research results are to be implemented effectively. Thus, *providing liaison individuals or linking institutions to translate needs into evaluation research, and evaluation research into practice,* is important for utilization of evaluation research results.

A linker is an individual who acts as a liaison between two or more subsystems in a communication system. An effective research utilization system requires linkers to act as an intermediary between researchers and practitioners. Linkers are the bridges that make research results available to practitioners. Linking is a role that may be performed by full-time or part-time personnel. As Figure 1 shows, linkers are also important in inputting practitioners' needs to the research system.

In agriculture, extension agents perform the function of an intermediary between the agriculture experiment stations and farmers. The agricultural extension services are one of the earliest example of intermediaries to translate research results to the ultimate users. In the field of education and public technology there is a growing realization of the need for such a linker role. Public Technology, Inc., headquartered in Washington, D.C., and partly funded by the National Science Foundation (at $4.2 million for three years), established the role of technology agents in 1974. They transfer research knowledge to such users as urban governments, agencies, and organizations which seek to use technology to solve urban problems. A PTI technology agent is located in each of 27 cities in the United States, usually attached to the mayor's or city manager's office.

The National Diffusion Network Project is aimed at the utilization of knowledge by primary and secondary schools in the United States. Facilitators disseminate utilizable research results to local schools especially through the diffusion strategy of local school demonstrations of these innovations. The National Diffusion Network is funded by the U.S. Office of Education and presently involves 75 facilitators, working with about 150 innovations. Since this program began in 1974, there have been about 1,500 adopters of these innovations.

So in agriculture, public technology, and education, a linking system is provided between the research system and the practitioners.

Linkers essentially perform the following roles in the research utilization process:

(1) They gauge the needs of the users and convey these to the research system.

(2) They select the most relevant information from the mass of existing knowledge that bears on a user's problem, thus acting as gatekeepers.

(3) They are aware of the different needs of the users, so they custom-make packets of relevant information to meet these needs.

(4) They translate the language of research into the language of practice.

(5) They assist adopters in the implementation of the innovation.

In addition there are a number of ways and means available to increase the likelihood that results of evaluation research on programs will be utilized. Some selected ways are following:

(1) *Evaluation as built-in and interrelated component of program evaluation.* Evaluation is ongoing and continuous. Evaluation should be a state of mind on the part of all program officials, even though it may be conducted by certain individuals called "evaluators"; it should have its own budget, and be represented by a separate unit in a program. *Evaluation should be involved in every stage in the operation of a program, not just at the end of a program, project, or activity.* Design and process evaluation results are less threatening, and, hence, more likely to be utilized.

(2) *Both formative and summative evaluation need to be conducted by "insiders" as well as "outsiders."* Evaluation results by "insiders" are more likely to be utilized by the program's administrators. Evaluation research by "outsiders" would bring more objectivity and perhaps consensus which program officials do appreciate.

(3) *Evaluation research results should be fed back at time schedule of the program officials and not that of the evaluators'.* The shorter the time lag between a program official's registration of a problem needing evaluation and providing him with results, the more they are to be utilized.

(4) *Evaluative efforts should not interfere with the operations of an ongoing program.*

(5) *Evaluation research results should be presented in a manner understandable to the administrators.* Readability and the relevance of the reports would facilitate greater use of the results by administrators who typically are overworked, thus, do not read many research reports.

(6) *Multiple channels of communication to deliver results to administrators in addition to the written report.* Periodic oral presentations, short written reports and films ought to be used. Statistics tables should be accompanied with short explanation and text. Thus, the heavy emphasis on "receiver-orientation" when results of evaluation are communicated.

Finally, we do not maintain that all evaluation is good, nor recommend that every program should necessarily be evaluated. An evaluation should only be undertaken if it is expected to be worth the cost. We are convinced that much more and better evaluation research is needed in many fields today.

NOTE

1. Certain ideas are taken from Rogers and Agarwala-Rogers (eds.), *Evaluation Research on Family Planning Communication,* Paris, UNESCO, Population Communication: Technical Documentation no. 4, 1976.

REFERENCES

COTTRELL, L.S., Jr. (1967). "Forward." In E.A. Schwan, Evaluative research: Principles and practices in public service and social action programs. New York: Russell Sage.
ROSSI, P.H. (1973). "Testing for success and failure in social action." In P.H. Rossi and W. Williams (eds.), Evaluating social programmes: Theory, practice, and policy. New York: Seminar Press.
SALASIN, S. (1973). "Experimentation revisited: A conversation with Donald T. Campbell." Evaluation, 1:7-13.
WEISS, C.H. (ed., 1972). Evaluating action programmes: Readings in social action and education. Boston: Allyn and Bacon.

17

CONCEPTUALIZING INEQUALITY

By

TRUDI C. MILLER

For Trudi C. Miller the issue of equal opportunity is still alive. She attempts to reassess our past thinking and confusion over this subject in her concise but thoughtful article. Thus she makes an important contribution to the now vast literature on the subject. According to the author our confusion originated with evaluators themselves who inappropriately used individualized inequality in generalizing their findings. Her study explains how each political position on reform has used a distinctive statistical methodology. She concludes that to evaluate programs effectively social scientists must directly confront the effects of programs on various aspects of inequality.

From Trudi C. Miller, "Conceptualizing Inequality." Unpublished paper, 1977.

INTRODUCTION

Equal outcomes and opportunities are important goals of many social programs. But studies of equality and equal opportunity in the 1960s and early 1970s caused so much confusion that the subject seems to have passed from fashion. The importance of inequality as a social problem has not declined, despite inattention from research funders and academics. Evaluators must develop a credible capability to assess program effects on inequality among individuals and groups.

If social scientists are to improve their record, they will have to become more precise in their definition of reform goals and measures of inequality. Conceptual sloppiness has characterized past efforts to evaluate inequality. Although criticism is not a major purpose of this article, we will try to explain why reformers found the Coleman Report, Jenck's *Inequality,* and Jensen's early studies of racial differences in IQ so confusing.

More important, we will attempt to capture diverse reform perspectives on "inequality" with statistical indicators. Our five definitions of reform are (1) more equal access to inputs, (2) more equal recognition of merit, (3) more equal outcomes for advantaged and disadvantaged groups, (4) elimination of the extremes of deprivation and privilege, and (5) reducing individual differences in outcomes. In the first section, each goal is explained and presented graphically as a problem statement (inequality) and a reform statement (less inequality). In the second section, we review the literature, given these graphs, to show contrasts in findings. We are not "lying with statistics" when we shift political perspectives, statistical models, and therefore conclusions. Rather, we are simply capturing some of the diverse interests implied in the general idea of social inequality. Our goal is a precise expression of political positions on reform in terms of slopes, means, dispersions, and other standard statistics.

PERSPECTIVES ON EQUALITY

Equality I: More Equal Inputs

The equality framework used here focuses exclusively on equalizing access to resources required for achievement. While the ultimate intent is to equalize

AUTHOR'S NOTE: The author is employed by the National Science Foundation, Research Applied to National Needs. The opinions expressed in this paper are those of the author and do not represent policies or positions of NSF.

achievement, equalization of outcomes is restricted to that resulting from more equal inputs.

Equality I is usually applied to groups, calling for more equal opportunities regardless of race, color, creed, national origin, income, etc. This group version of Equality I permits individual differences in the consumption of resources like education, political participation, job opportunities, and health care within groups.[1] Equality I.A for groups is shown graphically in Figure 1.

One statistical indicator of equality implied by this framework is a correlation coefficient between race (or other grouping) and consumption of the resource. The greater the correlation, the greater the inequality. The absolute level of consumption indicated by the means (or more appropriate measures of central tendency) is also of interest.

Equality I could also be applied to individuals, regardless of the group classification. For individual equality, the key statistic is a measure of dispersion appropriate to the shape of the distribution. The greater the range of resources consumed, the greater the inequality.

Equality II: More Equal Recognition of Merit

Equality II captures much of traditional American liberalism. It is sometimes labeled conservatism, because advocates deeply value inequality, and wish to distribute rewards and many opportunities according to merit. Indicators of merit include willingness to work, basic intelligence, and personality characteristics that foster productivity.

While favoring inequality, advocates also believe in equitable procedures for identifying individual merit, regardless of social status. Thus, supporters of II endorse the status quo when existing inequalities seem to reflect real differences in talent and effort, but become reformers when they believe the distribution of

$\overline{X}_1$ = Black average consumption of R

$\overline{X}_2$ = White average consumption of R

R = Resource, which could be a measure of teacher quality, voting, registration, nutrition, or anything else considered to contribute importantly to success.

Problem Statement   Reform Goal

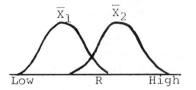
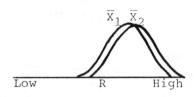

Figure 1: EQUALITY I.A. MORE EQUAL INPUTS FOR GROUPS[2]

$\overline{X}$ = grand mean or other measure of central tendency

R = Resource or "input" deemed important for success
and achievement. Inputs are often called
"opportunities".

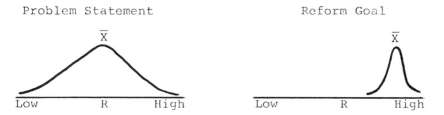

Figure 2: EQUALITY I.B. MORE EQUAL OPPORTUNITIES FOR INDIVIDUALS[3]

benefits only partly reflects merit and is serving to perpetuate elite privileges. Because their support for reform is conditional on beliefs about present practice in rewarding merit, it is imperative that advocates of II have accurate information about factors governing upward and downward mobility.[4]

The problem statement tells us that low status individuals will achieve lower levels of attainment than higher status individuals, even if levels of merit are identical. The graph shows two inequities, independent of merit, which hamper low status individuals during the attainment process. One is differences in intercepts (upper status lines cut the attainment axis at higher points). The other is differences in the slopes (upper status slopes are steeper). The reader can see how these intercept and slope differences "explain" attainment differentials by imagining two individuals starting out at medium merit. The first individual is from humble origins, so the problem statement predicts his attainment by running up to the medium point on the S_4 slope and then to the left to strike a low attainment level. The second individual is from an advantaged social class, so the problem statement predicts his attainment by running up to S_1 and over to a high position of attainment. Accordingly, if S_1 and S_4 groups started out with the same initial distributions of meritorious individual characteristics, we would expect the resultant distribution of attainment for S_4 to be lower (and less diverse) than the distribution for S_1.

Intercept differences reflect conditions which affect all low status individuals adversely, regardless of their abilities. Opportunities like access to good nutrition, health care, decent housing are examples, as are decisions to tie salary and promotion policies to education (a status indicator). Slope differentials reflect insensitivity to individual differences among individuals of lower status. Stereotyping by teachers and employers is one example, another might be relatively poor measurement of the learning ability of blacks with IQ tests. Slope differences express the observation that very able individuals suffer most from deprivation and discrimination.

S_1 = Highest Status Group

S_4 = Lowest Status Group

M = Merit measured by constructive attitudes, personality traits or mental abilities or other assets for performance.

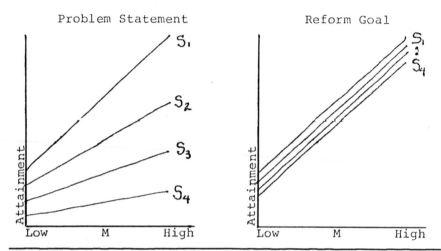

Figure 3: EQUALITY II. MORE EQUAL RECOGNITION OF MERIT[5]

The reform statement for II makes lower status slopes steeper and removes most of the intercept differences. In doing the former, it introduces greater competition for material rewards and status into the lives of lower status individuals. This is required if institutions are to identify talent regardless of social status of the individual. Implied also is a lessening of the dispersion and skewness of the attainment distribution.

Equality III: More Equal Outcomes for Advantaged and Disadvantaged Groups

This goal is popular with contemporary reformers. In contrast to Equality I.A, which it resembles in graphic form, Equality III focuses on outcomes or attainment levels. As Mosteller and Moynihan put it:

> The nation has acquired a goal, or, if it has not, we think we should accept it—equal educational opportunity defined as approximately equal distributions of achievement (but not just for cognitive skills) for the different ethnic/racial groups.[6]

Equality III is presented graphically in Figure 4.

$\overline{X}_1$ = Low SES (Bottom 25%) Average

$\overline{X}_4$ = Top SES (Top 25%) Average

A = Achievement or Attainment

Problem Statement

Reform Goal

$\overline{X}_1$ $\overline{X}_2$ $\overline{X}_3$ $\overline{X}_4$

$\overline{X}_1..\overline{X}_2$

Low   A   High   Low   A   High

Figure 4: EQUALITY III. MORE EQUAL OUTCOMES FOR ADVANTAGED AND DISADVANTAGED GROUPS[7]

Equality III is silent on the subject of individual differences in achievement within groups. This could imply respect for individual differences, which are assumed to be caused by merit. For example, Mosteller and Moynihan say of variation within schools:

> Why would most of the variation lie within the school? The readers' own school experience tells him that there is considerable variation in ability in the same schoolroom, and additional variation from room to room. Much of this variation comes from differences in intelligence within the same family ... part of the point of these remarks is to note that much of the variation within schools is probably not the sort of thing a school can do much about as long as it tries to improve all equally.[8]

Reflecting the authors' apparent respect for individual differences, our illustration of Equality III carries present group standard deviations into the reform state.

Equality IV: Eliminating Extremes of Privilege and Deprivation

Equality IV focuses on the extremes of affluence and poverty.[9] It is represented graphically in Figure 5.[10]

Reformers do not necessarily assault both ends of the status distribution simultaneously. Some educational reformers, for example, would guarantee a minimum level of education without reducing excellence in educational achievement at the top of the distribution.[11] Likewise, some American reformers are primarily interested in cropping the long tail of present distributions of wealth and income. Populists, for example, talk about breaking up concentrations of money and monopoly power in order to lessen exploitations of the vast majority of citizens.[12]

Equality IV's focus on extremes and its sharp cutoffs make it at least

A = Achievement or attainment - especially

wealth and income.

Problem Statement   Reform Goal

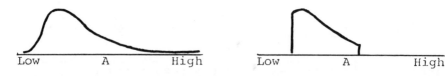

Figure 5: EQUALITY IV. ELIMINATING EXTREMES OF PRIVILEGE AND DEPRIVATION

superficially incompatible with the other reform goals. To implement the goal of assuring a minimum level of education, for example, society would have to spend most resources on the least promising students, because they have so much to learn. This willingness to dedicate most resources to the most disadvantaged contrasts sharply with Equality II, which would discriminate within groups in favor of the most talented individuals. Equality IV also differs from III, which does not tinker with pecking orders within disadvantaged groups.

Equality V: Reducing Individual Differences in Attainment

Equality V is the most radical of the goals because it is the least qualified.[13] Unlike Equality II, it does not see success differences associated with humble and privileged social origins as morally offensive. Unlike Equality I, it does not limit attainment equalization to that which would result from offering equal opportunities. Unlike Equality II, it places no positive value on inequality that reflects merit. Unlike Equality IV, which it resembles rhetorically, Equality IV does not focus on extreme differences in attainment. Equality V simply expresses a categorical and unqualified distaste for inequality (see Figure 6).[14]

Because Equality V is the least conditional of the goals, it is the most comprehensive. All of the more specific reforms would be classified as progress from the perspective of V. On the other hand, lack of qualification is probably responsible for the political unpopularity of Equality V. A recent survey of American elites shows that all sectors overwhelmingly choose equal opportunity (equal access to changes to develop ability) over "giving each person a relatively equal income regardless of his or her education and ability."[15]

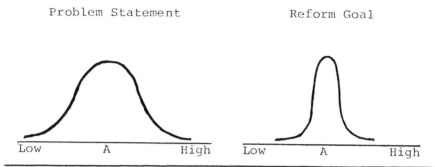

A = Achievement or Attainment

Problem Statement   Reform Goal

Low   A   High   Low   A   High

Figure 6: EQUALITY V. REDUCING INDIVIDUAL DIFFERENCES IN ATTAINMENT

STUDIES OF INEQUALITY

In this section we briefly link each perspective on inequality with appropriate methods and findings from studies using that method. We also show that it is incorrect to generalize findings from one perspective to others. We use Equality V to illustrate problems of generalization because the method congruent with this unpopular perspective dominates policy studies of inequality.

Equality V: Reducing Individual Differences in Attainment

Individual difference in outcomes are usually explained using statistics which apportion variance. The relative importance of variables in producing individual attainment is measured by partial correlations (often squared to estimate variance explained uniquely) and beta weights or path coefficients. Coefficients of multiple correlation (R^2) measure the proportion of variance explained by clusters of variables. Table 1[16] shows typical empirical results. Proportions have been changed to percents in this table.

Table 1 tells us that environment factors are not very important in explaining individual differences in scholastic achievement, but they are somewhat more important for blacks than for whites. Also "family," representing a set of home background variables like parents' education, is clearly more powerful than factors representing school characteristics (facilities, teachers, and student body). Indeed, measures of school quality appear to be almost negligible as causes of difference in achievement.

The null effect of schools and environmental factors is the primary finding of the literature on school effectiveness reviewed by Averch.[17] It is also the major conclusion of three well known studies: The "Coleman Report" or *Equality of Educational Opportunity*,[18] Jencks' *Inequality*,[19] and Arthur Jensen's many writings on racial differences in IQ.[20] These three major studies and the bulk of

TABLE 1. PERCENT VARIANCE EXPLAINED WITHIN RACE

Input Factor	Black		White	
	North	South	North	South
Family	7	12	14	17
Facilities	1	3	1	0
Teachers	2	2	1	1
Student body	3	5	1	1
% Explained	13	22	17	19

Table adapted from Coleman (see Note 16).

other studies of school effectiveness are primarily explanations of individual variance in outcomes.

Equality III: More Equal Outcomes for Advantaged and Disadvantaged Groups

None of the authors referred to above can be accused of inappropriately generalizing conclusions from individuals to groups. Few social scientists—let alone these very capable scholars—can be so charged. In fact, they provide some of the clearest discussions of the fallacy. For example, Jencks, in his introduction to *Inequality,* warns readers about the dangers of generalization.

> The reader should also be warned that we are primarily concerned with the inequality between individuals, not inequality between groups. This accounts for much of the discrepancy between our conclusions and those of others who have examined the same data. There is always far more inequality between individuals than between groups. It follows that when we compare the degree of inequality between groups to the degree of inequality between individuals, inequality between groups often seems relatively unimportant. . . . Our decision to emphasize individual rather than group differences was made on political grounds. We would, of course, like to see a society in which everyone's opportunities for advancement were equal. But we are far more interested in a society where the extremes of wealth and poverty are entirely eliminated than in a society where they are merely uncorrelated with skin color, economic origins, sex, and other such traits.[21]

Thus Jencks not only tells readers that group differences (and by implication their causes) pale in the context of describing individual inequalities, but also goes on to identify the political perspective he associates with his dominant statistical model.

Jensen is also clear about the impropriety of generalizing from individual differences to group differences.[22] Coleman and most scholars who re-evaluated Equality of Educational Opportunity (EEOS) data are not overt in saying their conclusions do not explain achievement gaps between blacks and whites.[23] However, they do not draw inappropriate inferences.

Despite clear warnings and careful language, reformers and others seem to believe that findings for individuals are categorically true and can be generalized.

Thus many infer from data like that displayed in Table 1 that most group differences in IQ and scholastic achievement cannot be explained by environmental factors.[24] They make this inference because the data seem to "prove" that environmental factors, especially schools, cannot explain achievement.

But regression studies designed to explain group differences in scholastic achievement and IQ come to altogether different conclusions about the total and relative effects of environmental factors. The regression technique is straight forward and recommended by econometricians for between-group analysis.[25] Coleman initially intended to use the regression approach, and his words describe it below.

> ... regression coefficients were to be used as weights for the various inputs, so that by replacing in the regression equation the levels of input resources for the average black in the region with those of the average white in the same region, the predicted level of achievement would be changed.

> This would produce two results: first a measure of effective inequality of opportunity would result as the increment in achievement that would be expected for the average black if all the input resources of schools and student bodies were at the level of those for the average white in the region; second, by selectively changing in the equation some of the input resource levels to those held by whites, while keeping others at the levels held by blacks, one could see which input inequalities were the effective ones, thus indicating which input resources would be expected to produce the largest effect if the input inequality for that resource were eliminated.[26]

McPartland and Sprehe reanalyzed the EEOS data using Coleman's initially preferred regression method, simple correlation coefficients from the Appendix to study report, and the same variables which generated Table 1. Table 2 summarizes the results.

Unfortunately, only results for school characteristics are reported. Numbers in the top four rows of the table are standard deviation shifts in achievement resulting from swapping resources between the races, holding everything else constant. For example, .03 represents a prediction that 3% of a standard deviation change in achievement will result from black students in the North acquiring the same facilities as white students in the North. "Gap" is the average difference between

TABLE 2. AVERAGE CONTRIBUTION TO BETWEEN-RACE ACHIEVEMENT GAP[27]

Input Factor	Black		White	
	North	South	North	South
Facilities	.03	−.02	.00	.00
Teachers	.05	.16	−.24	−.47
Student body	.13	.15	−.10	−.07
Total school	.21	.29	−.34	−.55
Gap	1.17	1.40	1.05	1.18
% Explained	18%	21%	−32%	−47%

Table adapted from McPartland and Sprehe (see Note 27).

black and white achievement scores within a region, expressed in standardized units for the group indicated. Percent gap explained is the predicted change from swapping all school resources over the gap (times 100). It is the percent of the achievement gap which is predicted to disappear as a result of equalizing schools for blacks and whites in the region.

We see from the table based on the regression approach that explanations of between-race achievement gaps bear little resemblance to explanations of achievement within the races. First, schools are far more important between the races than within. Second, whites, not blacks, show the greatest sensitivity to the prospect of a swap in school resources. Third, except for blacks in the North, teacher characteristics are more important between the races than are student body characteristics—overwhelmingly so for whites. Finally, even without home background included in the total, environmental factors explain a substantial proportion of the achievement gap. Remembering that school variables are measured at the aggregate not the individual level, it is clear that we cannot neglect schools as an important explanation of scholastic achievement differences between the races. Analysis in progress, using nonverbal ability as the dependent variable, suggests that schools are also responsible for the bulk of IQ differences between blacks and whites at the national level.[28]

Equality I: More Equal Inputs

The appropriate analysis from the perspective of I.A (equal inputs for groups) is a simple description of the distribution of inputs by race. A good example is contained in the "Coleman Report."[29] However, advocates of equalizing inputs were somewhat undercut politically by inferences that schools do not explain racial gaps in achievement. Moynihan describes the reformer's impression of the report's findings on school effects.

> With but a few exceptions (e.g., pupil-teacher ratio), Coleman found that the effects of what might be termed school input on output were in the direction that almost everyone had assumed. However, he found the strength of these relationships to be not nearly so great as had also been assumed. The relationship appeared to be of such different magnitude as to recede from a primary to a secondary, even tertiary category.[30]

Another problem for both Equality I.A and I.B is that most analyses of individual differences measure school inputs at the school level. Thus, despite the fact that high achievers and higher status students are more likely to be exposed to the best teachers and other inputs, all students in a school get the same school quality indicators.[31] This error for schools, relative to variables which are measured at the individual level, should lead to an absolute and relative downward bias in estimates of the importance of school inputs.

Equality II: More Equal Recognition of Merit

So far, we have used only additive models to explain inequality between groups. The operationalization of Equality II captures the additive effect of inputs, but also includes nonadditive effects or slope differences indicating unequal recognition of ability. For example, whites may have more influential friends than blacks who have the same education, IQ, and apparent social background. If so, equations predicting employment from education, IQ, and social status will be different in white populations and in black populations. For blacks, regression coefficients which estimate the contribution each variable makes to achievement will be lower. These low slopes or regression coefficients tell us that conventional indicators of ability are more useful to whites than they are to blacks.

The literature on status mobility in America shows ample evidence that lower status groups—especially blacks—are not as able as whites to convert personal assets into educational, occupational, and income achievements. Otis Dudley Duncan describes the double (additive and interactive) disadvantage blacks face.

> The Negro handicap, therefore, is a double handicap. First, the Negro begins the life cycle (typically) with characteristics that would be a disadvantage to anyone, white or Negro—specifically, in the present model, low levels of parental socioeconomic status. Second, achievements at subsequent stages of the life cycle, already lowered by the initial circumstances (to the extent that they exist), cannot be capitalized on as readily.[32]

Many other studies find interactions between conventional measures of merit and measures of status throughout the attainment process. For example, students of low economic status and high IQ are less likely to go to college than are high status students with the same IQ.[33] Enrollment in a quality college, attendance and progress in graduate school, and appropriate occupational attainment after school are also less probable for high ability students of low social origins.[34] IQ (and rank in high school class) predict differences in incomes for students who attain high status through a college education, but provide no advantage to students who stop at high school.[35] Age, which is at least a measure of experience, predicts greater increases in income for members of high status occupations than for members of low status occupations.[36] Age also predicts greater income for whites than for blacks, after controls for education.[37] Income returns to education are less for blacks and lower status individuals.[38] Finally, high aspirations and conventional desires for success do not predict achievement as well for blacks as they do for whites.[39]

Studies of individual differences in achievement appropriate to Equality V come to conclusions which are grossly misleading from the perspective of Equality II. For the additive portion of the model, the absolute and relative importance of inputs like schools and home background are incorrectly estimated, as they were for Equality III. In addition, interactions with socioeconomic status and race are often neglected and are almost invariably obfuscated by statistics like correlation coefficients and beta weights.[40] Indeed, most quantitative studies assume away the portion of the liberal problem statement which postulates unequal recognition of measurable ability (i.e., unequal slopes). In effect, the statistical model assumes that much reform (slope equalization) has occurred.

Equality IV: Eliminate Extremes of Privilege and Deprivation

Advocates of Equality IV are distinguished by their concern with the shape of the distribution of outcomes like wealth, income power, and even educational attainment. Skew is a sign of social problems. The long thin tail at the favored end of the distribution indicates that a few people control the bulk of society's resources. The bunching of the majority relatively near poverty reflects this concentration of elite control. The wealthy satisfy their own felt needs for goods and services before doling out leftovers to the majority. Residuals are not sufficient to reward individuals for productivity, and the masses are undifferentiated in their levels of wealth and self-actualization.

Advocates of IV would be greatly misled if they believed findings on inequality generated by studies of individual variation. Analysis of variance within a population requires the assumption of a normal distribution of outcomes. The frequent employment of the normality assumption at all stages of the attainment process is particularly problematic. By fiat, distributions of outcomes do not become increasingly skewed over time and must reflect the distribution of innate ability, which is assumed to be normal. Employment of such simplifying statistical assumptions must result in a serious underestimation of inequality and of causes of inequality which do not reflect innate ability. We know that distributions of outcomes are skewed, and that they become progressively more skewed over time.[41] Assuming away this information, which is critical in some ideological perspectives on inequality, creates a persistent conservative bias in assessments of inequality.

CONCLUSION

Most American reformers have limited political goals; for example, more equal recognition of ability and more equal outcomes for advantaged and disadvantaged social groups. Most statistical analyses of inequality are of individual differences in outcomes. Results from studies of individual inequality reflect the extraordinary ambition of the implied reform—eliminating individual differences in attainment. Environmental variables, such as school quality, do in fact have little leverage over individual differences in outcomes. But the same data show that the same environmental factors are important explanations of group differences in outcomes. The data also show serious policy relevant departures from assumptions of normality and additivity, which are common in studies of individual variance. When findings from studies of individual inequality are inappropriately generalized to explain inequality from other political reform perspectives, confusion and conservatism result.

If the effects of programs on social equality are to be reliably evaluated, researchers must conceptualize the problem and reform goals more precisely. When they do, they will discover many different empirical questions contained in the general query: How much inequality is there, and what are its causes? We have captured five of these meanings and have shown that each produces different findings when it is operationalized statistically. Therefore, any attempt to give a single answer to questions about inequality using a single method is bound to be politically biased. Objectivity in evaluations of inequality can only be achieved in the traditional manner—by looking at all sides of the problem.

NOTES

1. See James S. Coleman, "The Concept of Equality of Educational Opportunity," in *Equal Educational Opportunity* (Cambridge, Mass.: Harvard University Press, 1969), pp. 18-20, for a discussion of the policy goal and its supporters.

2. See James S. Coleman et al., *Equality of Educational Opportunity* (Washington, D.C.: U.S. Government Printing Office, 1966), Chapter 2, for a completely appropriate study from the perspective of Equality I.A.

3. There are very few opportunities for which complete equality in treatment is expected, but these are important. For example, everyone should have the right to vote and to express themselves freely.

4. For a statement of meritocratic values and a reaction to recent studies and developments, see Daniel Bell, "On Meritocracy and Equality," in *The Public Interest* (Fall 1972), pp. 26-68.

5. Otis Dudley Duncan has developed a model of the socioeconomic life cycle which identifies both additive input and multiplicative components of disadvantage. See Otis Dudley Duncan, "Inheritance of Poverty or Inheritance of Race," in Daniel P. Moynihan, ed., *On Understanding Poverty* (New York: Basic Books, 1969), pp. 85-110; and Otis Dudley Duncan, "Discrimination Against Negroes," *Annals of the American Academy of Political and Social Science,* 171 (May 1967), 85-103. Our statistical treatment of the reform goal is borrowed almost completely from Duncan.

6. Frederick Mosteller and Daniel P. Moynihan, "A Path-Breaking Report," in Frederick Mosteller and Daniel P. Moynihan, eds., *On Equality of Educational Opportunity* (New York: Vintage Books, 1972), p. 45. The authors credit James Coleman and *Equality of Educational Opportunity* for establishing this goal.

7. There are at least two approaches to studying variance between groups. One is path analysis which explains the correlation between status and the outcome variable in terms of paths. See Otis Dudley Duncan, *Introduction to Structural Equation Models* (New York: Academic Press, 1975). Another more ambiguous approach is communality analysis, which describes the overlap of factors in explaining the outcome variable. Alexander M. Mood is credited with the development of this technique, which is used and described in George Mayeske et al., *A Study of Our Nation's Schools* (Washington, D.C.: Office of Education Working Paper, c. 1970). A regression approach, which is preferred, is described by James S. Coleman, "The Evaluation of Equality of Educational Opportunity" in Mosteller and Moynihan, eds., *On Equality of Opportunity,* pp. 153-156.

8. Mosteller and Moynihan, "A Pathbreaking Report," pp. 17-19.

9. We may have lumped two political perspectives together in Equality IV. The first is radical—characteristic of Marxists and extreme Populists—the second is moderate. Marxists and Populists worry about the long tail of the distribution of wealth and power because they think concentration leads to collaboration among the elites and exploitation of the majority. Classically, Marxists call for complete equality, not just surgery on the tails, which we represent in our model. By contrast, many moderate American reformers do think in terms of taxing the wealthy to, at a minimum, put a floor under the incomes of the poor. Unlike the Marxists and the Populists, the moderate reformers seem more concerned with helping the poor than with busting up concentrations of wealth and power. An example of the Marxist concern is William Dumhoff, *Who Rules America?* (Englewood Cliffs, N.J.: Prentice-Hall, 1967). The more

moderate reform tradition is represented by Herbert J. Gans, *More Equality* (New York: Pantheon Books, 1968).

10. Studies appropriate to IV have to take skew in the distribution of attainment and increases in skew into account. Very few studies of the attainment process do this. Major exceptions are found in the work of Lester C. Thurow, for example "Education and Economic Equality," *The Public Interest* (Summer, 1972), 66-81; and Gary S. Becker, *Human Capital* (New York: Columbia University Press, 1964). The tax simulation studies at the Brookings Institution provide excellent examples of policy studies. For a recent use see George F. Break and Joseph A. Peckman, *Federal Tax Reform* (Washington, D.C.: The Brookings Institution, 1975).

11. Edmund W. Gordon, "Defining Equal Opportunity," in Mosteller and Moynihan, eds., *On Equal Educational Opportunity*, pp. 431-434.

12. For a recent example, see Jack Newfield and Jeff Greenfield, *A Populist Manifesto* (New York: Praeger, 1972).

13. The political goal of equalizing outcomes regardless of merit is not popular, especially in the area of educational achievement. See Harold L. Wilensky, *The Welfare State and Equality* (Berkeley, Calif.: University of California Press, 1975), p. 7; or more recently results of the Post-Harvard study, *The Washington Post* (September 26, 1976), p. A8. However, some academics seem to accept the goal. The "new left" diffuse dislike of inequality and hierarchy probably captures the feeling. For an overview of the new left position and bibliography, see Chapter 8, "The New Left" in Kenneth M. Dolbeare and Patricia Dolbeare, *American Ideologies* (Chicago: Markham, 1973), pp. 188-216. Jencks is one analyst who argues for greater individual equality, thus his use of the standard statistical model is appropriate. See Christopher Jencks et al., *Inequality: A Reassessment of the Effect of Family and Schooling in America* (New York: Basic Books, 1972).

14. Explaining individual variance in achievement is a standard statistical approach. Jencks used it in *Inequality*, Coleman used it in *Equality of Educational Opportunity*. Most large quantitative studies of school effectiveness explain individual differences in achievement. For a review see Harvey A. Averch et al., *How Effective is Schooling?* (Santa Monica, Calif.: Rand, 1972).

15. *The Washington Post*, September 26, 1976, p. A8.

16. The data are from Coleman, "The Evaluation of Equality of Educational Opportunity," p. 160. The table title reads: "Unique contributions to variance in verbal achievement (scaled up to sum to R^2 in each regression) as measures of the importance of each of four clusters of variables: family background (6 variables), school facilities and curriculum (11 variables), teacher characteristics (7 variables), and student body characteristics (5 variables). Blacks and whites in North and South, grades 12, 9, 6." We converted the proportions in the original table to percentages and averaged across the grades to produce the simple table that appears in the text.

17. Averch et al., *How Effective is Schooling?* (Educational Technology Publications, 1974).

18. Coleman et al., *Equality of Educational Opportunity*. The authors do discuss the implications of average differences in input variables between the races. However, statistical analysis is executed within each racial group, and variance explained is the only result reported.

19. Jencks et al., *Inequality*. Jencks also uses his regression equations to explain group differences in ability. However, probably because it is not his major interest (p. 14), he does not cumulate the effects of independent variables between groups.

20. Much of Jensen's argument is contained in Arthur R. Jensen, *Educability and Group Differences* (London: Methuen, 1973). Jensen works almost exclusively with measures of heritability, which are based on variance explained within groups. He argues that if heritability of IQ within groups is as high as studies of twins indicate, then it is highly improbable that nongenetic factors can explain differences in IQ between the races.

21. Jencks et al., *Inequality*, p. 14. Actually, Jencks' study is not of extremes as we define

them for Equality IV. Indeed, given the degree of skew in the distributions of educational attainment and income, and interactions between ability and status variables discussed for IV, it is hard to see how any study of population statistics for individuals could produce valid discussions of "extremes."

22. For example, see Jensen, *Educability and Group Differences*, pp. 355-356.

23. The issue of explaining individual as compared to group differences in achievement was not important in most of the reanalysis. See *Equal Educational Opportunity, On Equality of Educational Opportunity*, and Gerald Grant, "Essay Review," *Harvard Educational Review* (February 1972).

24. In *Educability and Group Differences*, Jensen makes strong inferences from the null effects of environment. He says to critics who argue that he has encouraged acceptance of genetic explanations of racial differences in intelligence:

> The interesting point is that I have *not* urged acceptance of an hypothesis on the basis of insufficient evidence, but have tried to show that the evidence we have does not support the environmentalist theory which, until quite recently, has been clearly promulgated as scientifically established. [p. 19]

Jensen quotes the literature on school effectiveness, especially the Coleman report, to support his conjecture that environment cannot explain racial differences in scholastic achievement and IQ.

25. Eric A. Hanushek and John F. Kain, "On the Value of Equality of Educational Opportunity as a Guide to Public Policy," in Mosteller and Moynihan, *On Equality of Educational Opportunity*, p. 136. The authors argue that a variance based statistic—including the beta weight per se—"gives little indication of the extent of policy leverage provided by different variables." They prefer parameter estimates—that is, the raw regression coefficients.

26. James S. Coleman, "The Evaluation of Equality of Educational Opportunity," in Mosteller and Moynihan, *On Equality of Educational Opportunity*, pp. 153-158.

27. Table from James McPartland and J. Timothy Sprehe, "Racial and Regional Inequalities in School Resources Relative to Their Educational Outcomes," in *Social Science Research*, 2 (December 1973), 326. Data from original have been averaged over grades 6, 9, and 12. McPartland and Sprehe deliberately employed the same equation which was used in most of the EEOS. Family background variables were in the equation, although results for school factors alone are reported. See Note 16 for more description of the equation.

28. Following McPartland and Sprehe, we use the simple correlations provided in the *Supplemental Appendix* to Coleman et al., *Equality of Educational Opportunity*. Family background and school factors explain an average of about 80% of the IQ gap between blacks and whites, when environments faced by blacks are substituted into equations calibrated for whites. As implied by Table 2, results are not as dramatic when white environments are substituted into equations calculated for black students. Swapping school environments between the races generally has a more important effect than swapping advantages in the home.

29. Coleman et al., *Equality of Educational Opportunity*, Chapter 2.

30. Daniel P. Moynihan, "Sources of Resistance to the Coleman Report," in *Equal Educational Opportunity*, p. 29.

31. In the mid-1960s, about 75% of both blacks and whites attended secondary schools which used tracking. The figure in elementary school was about 40%. Coleman et al., pp. 13-15. These figures have undoubtedly changed, but the point is still valid. For more discussion, see Hanushek and Kain, "On the Value of Equality of Opportunity . . . ," pp. 130-133.

32. Duncan, "Inheritance of Poverty or Inheritance of Race," p. 96.

33. The data are from Project Talent. See Robert H. Berls, "Higher Education Opportunity and Achievement in the United States," in U.S. Congress, Joint Economic Committee, *The Economics and Financing of Higher Education* (Washington, D.C.: U.S. Government Printing Office, 1969), p. 150.

34. For a review of the literature, see Murry Milner, Jr., *The Illusion of Equality* (San Francisco: Jossey-Bass, 1972), pp. 46-58.

35. Several studies reported by Gary S. Becker, *Human Capital: A Theoretical and Empirical Analysis with Special Reference to Education* (New York: Columbia University Press, 1964), show this pattern. More recently John C. House, "Earning Profile: Ability and Schooling," *Journal of Political Economy,* 80 (May/June 1972), 5108-5138, finds interaction between years of school and a measure of IQ. For low levels of schooling (below a high school graduate) ability differences are of negligible importance in predicting earnings differences. For high levels of education, ability is strongly related to earnings, and this increases with age.

36. Becker, *Human Capital,* p. 141, reports this effect. Valerie Kincade Oppenheimer, "The Life-Cycle Squeeze: The Interactions of Men's Occupation and Family Life Cycles," *Demography,* 2 (May 1974), 237, provides a graphic display for 1959. Ross M. Stolzenberg, "Occupations, Labor Markets and the Process of Wage Attainment," *American Sociological Review,* (October 1975), 645-665, argues more generally that processes governing wage attainment are fragmented along occupational lines. He notes that wages peak later for upper status professions and that the differentiation in earnings is greater.

37. Gary S. Becker, *The Economics of Discrimination* (Chicago: University of Chicago Press, 1957), p. 92, provides a table with 1939 data arrayed by age and education level. Blacks fall increasingly behind whites as both groups become more educated.

38. For a review of the literature on returns to education for blacks, see Seymour Martin Lipset, "Social Mobility and Equal Opportunity," *The Public Interest,* (Fall 1972), 96-98. He says the gap in returns narrowed somewhat in the 1960s. The classic study is Becker, *Human Capital,* which contains evidence of lower returns to education for rural, female, and black persons. Gloria Hanock, "An Economic Analysis of Earnings and Schooling," *Journal of Human Resources,* 2 (Summer 1967), 310-329, finds little evidence of a strong income/ schooling relationship for blacks.

39. For a review of the literature on motivation and educational attainment, see Harold Proshansky and Peggy Newton, "The Nature and Meaning of Negro Self-Identity," in Martin Deutsch, Irwin Katz, and Arthur Jensen, eds., *Social Class, Race and Psychological Development* (New York: Holt, Rinehart and Winston, 1967). Data from *Equality of Educational Opportunity* show blacks have a strong interest in learning and favorable images of their ability to learn. However, they differ from whites in optimism that the system rewards hard work and grants success to people like themselves. They also are less likely to have read a college catalog. See Coleman et al., p. 24. There also does not seem to be much difference between black and white enthusiasm for education in the home. Coleman et al., 186-189.

40. Many analysts argue against the use of variance based statistics in policy or theoretical studies. See, for example, Duncan, *Introduction to Structural Equation Models,* p. 51. For a strong assessment, see Hanushek and Kain, "On the Value of Equality of Educational Opportunity as a Guide to Policy," pp. 135-136. The problem is that statistics like beta weights and correlation coefficients combine variation within the population and effects (regression coefficients) to estimate importance.

41. Curves may be constructed from U.S. Bureau of Census, *Statistical Abstract of the United States, 1921-* (Washington, D.C.: U.S. Government Printing Office, 1921-). Thurow, "Education and Economic Inequality," is an example of a study trying to explain increasing skew, as is Becker, *Human Capital.*

18

SOCIAL RESEARCH AND NATIONAL POLICY:
WHAT GETS USED, BY WHOM, FOR WHAT PURPOSES,
AND WITH WHAT EFFECTS

By

NATHAN CAPLAN

"What information is used by whom; for what purpose; and with what effects?" are the major questions which Nathan Caplan addresses in his frequently quoted study. Applying relevant information to policy issues is complicated; however, his findings give us hope that the situation is not totally gloomy.

From Nathan Caplan, "Social Research and National Policy: What Gets Used, By Whom, For What Purposes, and With What Effects?" *International Social Science Journal*, Vol. XXVIII: 1, ©UNESCO, 1976. Reprinted by permission of UNESCO.

The use of social science information in important matters of government has been the subject of increasing interest over the last several years. However, tested information on the subject is very limited. Furthermore, social science utilization in policy-making is complex and not a subject on which *a priori* assumptions can be expected to shed much light. In consequence, we know very little about what information gets used, by whom, for what purposes and with what, if any, impact. The research reviewed here was undertaken to reduce some of these uncertainties.

Brief description of the study

During the period October 1973 to March 1974, 204 interviews on social science research utilization and policy formation were conducted with persons holding important positions in various departments, major agencies and commissions of the executive branch of the United States Government. Within the governmental hierarchy, almost all of the respondents were either political appointees immediately below cabinet rank or high-level civil servants. The mean income of the respondents was approximately $34,000 a year.

The majority of respondents were experienced persons. The average time in their job when interviewed was slightly over two years for political appointees and approximately six and a half years for civil servants. The respondents were chosen from agencies which represent the entire range of governmental activities, not simply those concerned with social policy, social programme implementation, social problems, or the like.

The interviews conducted by professional interviewers were carried out on a face-to-face basis. The average time required for each interview was about one and a half hours. The interviews were recorded on tape. During the course of each interview, the tape was used by the interviewer to help edit and complete the written narrative on the interview form. These tapes have also proved valuable for coding difficult open-ended items.

A few terms defined

The term 'policy-maker' is used here to refer to the upper-level decision-makers included in the study. It is not meant to imply that the respondents dictated policy, but rather to indicate that they were in policy-influencing positions. The conclusions pertain only to the influencing of policy at the upper level of the executive bureaucracy, since the utilization and application of social science information at lower levels of government were not examined.

'Social science knowledge' or 'social science information' refers primarily to information derived empirically from the following behavioural sciences: psychology, sociology, anthropology, political science and the multidisciplinary matings of fields (e.g. behavioural-economics, behavioural-geography, psychiatry). These terms have been defined as such in order to describe the limits of the inquiry, not to imply that there are not other fields within the social sciences.

In the literature dealing with utilization, certain important conceptual discriminations are ignored, and others are not made explicit, particularly differences between such terms as 'dissemination', 'utilization' and 'application'. In coding for utilization, attention was limited to

* Programme Director, Center for Research on Utilization of Scientific Knowledge, Institute for Social Research, University of Michigan, Ann Arbor.

instances of use where the decision-maker received policy-relevant social science information (i.e. by dissemination) and reported efforts to put that knowledge into use (i.e. by utilization) even if this effort to produce an impact (i.e. by application) was unsuccessful. Thus, 'utilization of knowledge' in the context of this study occurred when the respondent was familiar with at least one relevant research study and gave serious considerations to and attempted to apply that knowledge to some policy-relevant issue.

What is used?

Approximately one-third of the instances of use given by respondents involved research knowledge from staff summaries outside consultants and reviews of existing reports. Thus it was impossible to classify the knowledge from secondary sources in terms of the methodologies represented. The remaining two-thirds involved primary data sources; that is raw data or reports of data as they were originally compiled. The distribution of the instances of use for these information-gathering techniques is given in Table 1.

It is not possible to comment on all of the methodologies here. However, some comment on social statistics is appropriate because they constitute the most frequently used data among the policy-makers studied, accounting for about one-third of all social science data impacting upon policy decisions.

Social statistics as used here included information of the following types: demographic data, including the United States census information; rate and non-economic trend data, such as unemployment rates, crime rates, etc.; large-scale survey research data on public attitudes or direct behaviour measures in a variety of areas (e.g. health-related items such as insurance, medical needs). Thus, data that involved the monitoring or the assessment of rates or trends on large segments of the population or of the total population were classified as social statistics.

The following examples drawn from reports of respondents illustrate the diverse use of social statistics in policy-related matters:

Longitudinal surveys of the aged population were conducted to acquire information on how much was spent for medical care and what fraction was covered by private health insurance. These data were instrumental in shaping the Medicare programme.

Large-scale surveys were used to determine minority group ownership of business. In turn these data were used to plan policies to stimulate such ownership.

Long-term supply and demand for trained manpower and the planning of education programmes needed to train or retrain to meet demands for these skills were influenced by social statistics.

Finally, levels of voter participation by diverse registration procedures across different states were studied to determine if a national voter registration policy would increase participation.

Sponsorship of research used

Most of the production of social science information used in policy-related decision-making was sponsored by the using agency. The funding sources for 218 of the primary research reports were identifiable and are shown in Table 2.

Fifty-one per cent of the research in these instances of use was conducted in-house. Another 35 per cent was extramural, but funded by the using agency. Eight per cent of the instances of use

TABLE 1. Distribution of knowledge use by research methodologies[1]

Research methodologies	Percentages of instances of use
Social statistics	32
Programme evaluation	20
Survey research	9
Field experimentation	9
Cost benefit analysis	8
Organizational analysis	6
Laboratory experimentation	4
Participant observation	4
Clinical case histories	4
Psychological testing	3
Experimental games and simulations	1
	100

1. Based on 367 primary data sources.

TABLE 2. Distribution of knowledge use by funding source

Funding source	Percentages of instances of use
Using agency (conducted in-house)	51
Using agency (extramural funding)	35
Another governmental agency	8
Non-governmental agency	6
	100

involved research funded by government agencies other than the using agency, and 6 per cent involved research information sponsored by non-governmental agencies. Thus 94 per cent of all research activities represented in the instances of use was either funded by the government, conducted by the government, or both; and 86 per cent was funded or conducted by the using agency.

Other than research conducted in foreign countries on issues of international relations, probably no more than 2 per cent of the reported uses involved policy-relevant research conducted outside of the United States. Whether foreign research, such as that in the areas of health care and job development are known but deliberately not used, or whether such research is simply unknown, cannot be determined from our data. Contact with researchers outside of the United States would indicate that a considerable amount of research produced in the United States is used in social policy-related decisions in other countries. Many foreign social scientists are trained in the United States, while few United States scientists are trained abroad. It may well be that the United States social scientist community and those who provide information to policy-makers are not as conversant with relevant foreign research as their counterparts outside the United States. In any case, policy-relevant work is produced outside the United States, and why such research is either unknown or ignored is as interesting and important a question as the alleged underutilization of data produced domestically.

Sources of information used

Respondents were asked whether they obtained social science knowledge from each of the following sources: books, professional journals, newspapers

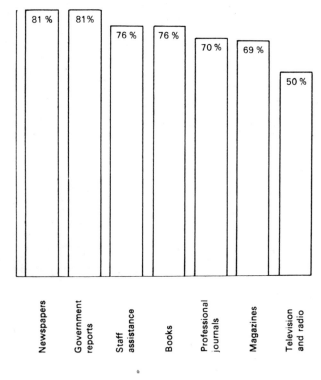

popular magazines, television and radio, and reports of government-sponsored research. In addition, they were asked whether they received assistance from their staffs in retrieving social science information and whether they consulted a social scientist for professional advice with respect to recommending a position on some policy issue. Figure 1 shows the percentage of respondents using various information sources.

There is little doubt that decision-makers are eclectic in their use of sources to retrieve and incorporate new knowledge into their perspectives, and to assimilate information that they deem relevant at any point in time, with or without an immediate anticipation of its use in influencing policy.

One gets the impression from the widespread use of informal knowledge channels that social science knowledge is used like the news. It allows users to feel that their awareness of social problems and concerns does not lag behind the rest of society or the professionals who deal with the policy-makers' fields. In addition, the use of informal channels of scientific knowledge suggests that, when decision-makers contribute to the formation of policy, they can see themselves moving from scientifically supported positions without becoming embroiled in the more esoteric deliberations required to substantiate the true scientific merit of such positions. This is not to say that decision-makers using knowledge from such sources are always heedless of the true scientific import of the social science information they use, but it is more often the case than in their use of formal sources of hard information.

Who uses social research?

There are very marked differences in the exten of knowledge use among the governmental officials studied even though they were similar in terms of their level of responsibility.

In order to learn something about individual differences in the extent of knowledge use among government policy-makers, a 'utilization score' was assigned to each of the 204 respondents. This score was determined by the number of instances of use provided by the respondent in six open-ended items, as well as by the specificity of the information given on the nature of the knowledge used and the policy situation to which the information was applied.

TABLE 3. Distribution of respondents by utilization score

Utiliz-ation level	Criteria for assigning utilization scores	Number of respondents	Percentage of respondents
1	5-10 instances of use with good supporting evidence	26	13
2	2-4 instances of use with good supporting evidence	124	61
3	1-7 instances of use with meagre supporting evidence	35	17
4	No instances of use	19	9
		204	100

On the basis of these utilization scores four levels of utilization were determined among the 204 respondents as shown in Table 3.

While the data show the relative differences in the extent of knowledge utilization, any interpretation of these differences must be made with the foregoing qualifications in mind. These data are simply too limited to determine with a high level of confidence whether knowledge input, the flow of knowledge, the absorption and translation of it into policy, and other related uses are unique or generically similar across the power hierarchies studied; or, across agencies and departments that vary so greatly in scope and purpose. None the less, at least one factor appeared to be of special importance in influencing the level of utilization.

Information-processing style

The ways in which policy-makers process information appear to have different consequences in determining the amount and kinds of knowledge used in arriving at a policy decision even after variables such as rank and department are controlled statistically.

Before describing these styles it is important to comment briefly on the kinds of information involved and their functions in decision-making. While scientific and extra-scientific are appropriate and proper labels for the issue under discussion, it will facilitate understanding if we think in functional terms: consider 'scientific' as referring to matters bearing on the internal logic of the policy issue, that is, pertaining to the gathering, processing, and analysis of the most objective information available to arrive at an unbiased diagnosis of the problem; and 'extra-scientific' as bearing on the external logic of the policy issue, that is, pertaining to the political, value-based, ideological, administrative and economic considerations involved.

The clinical orientation

The federal officials who expressed this style, approximately 20 per cent of those interviewed, were the most active users of scientific information. They combine two basic approaches to problem-solving. First they gather and process the best available information they can obtain to make an unbiased diagnosis of the policy issue. They use knowledge in this way to deal with the 'internal logic' of the problem. Next they gather information regarding the political and social ramifications of the policy issue to deal with the 'external logic' of the problem. To reach a policy decision, they finally weigh and reconcile the conflicting dictates of the information.

The academic orientation

The largest group of social science information users, approximately 30 per cent of those interviewed, processed information with an academic orientation. They are often experts in their fields and prefer to devote their major attention to the internal logic of the policy issue. They are much less willing, however, to cope with the external realities that confound this type of problem. Considerations of the external logic of the problem are likely viewed as a menace to the prestige and standing of their expertise. Consequently, they use scientific information in moderate amounts and in routine ways to formulate and evaluate policies largely on the basis of scientifically derived information.

The advocacy orientation

Comprising another 20 per cent of the federal officials, this group is much at home in the world of social, political and economic realities. Their use of social science information is limited, but when used, its use is almost exclusively dictated by extra-scientific forces to the extent that they will at times intentionally ignore valid information that does not fit the prevailing political climate. Their preoccupation is with the external logic of a policy issue and the function of scientific knowledge when used in that context is largely to rationalize a decision made on extra-scientific grounds.

Respondents with a particular educational background or training tended to show an information-processing style highly reflective of that particular type of educational background. For example, medical doctors tended to favour the clinical style of processing information; Ph.Ds favoured the academic style; and lawyers most frequently favoured the advocacy style. Similarly, this pattern of differences is reflected in the correlations (gamma) between educational backgrounds and level of knowledge use as represented by the utilization scores of the respondents from the three educational backgrounds: M.D. degree, $+.64$; Ph.D. degree (social as well as nonsocial sciences), $+.03$; and LL.B., LL.D., or J.D. degree, $-.36$. It should be kept in mind, however, that the data base for these generalizations about differences in information processing orientations is the analysis of data from 70 per cent of the respondents and therefore involves many more individuals than those who come from these particular backgrounds.

Purposes of knowledge use

The 575 instances of knowledge use were coded according to the policy issue, or decision-making area, represented. The distribution of knowledge use among these policy areas is shown in Table 4.

The social science knowledge uses represented in this table involve a broad spectrum of governmental agencies with quite diverse interests, diverse target or client populations, and diverse missions. This diversity of use is striking, both within and across governmental agencies and, even within the same methodology classifications as evidenced by examples of social statistics use reported earlier.

It is interesting to note that social research is most frequently used in policy decisions related to organizational management. Those items assigned to this particular policy area pertained

TABLE 4. Distribution of knowledge use by policy area[1]

Policy area	Percentage of instances of use
Organizational management	11
Education	8
Health	8
Crime	7
Communications	7
Public opinion management	7
Welfare	7
Military	6
Employment	6
Other	6
Civil rights and minority affairs	5
Environment	4
Housing	4
Transportation	4
International relations	3
Research methodology	3
Consumer affairs	2
Recreation	2
	100

1. Energy as a decision-making area is conspicuously absent because it was just emerging as a major policy area while the survey was being conducted. Those references by respondents to energy matters were coded under such categories as 'Public Opinion Management', 'International Relations', 'Transportation and Environment'.

directly to operational problems of running a governmental agency or office. Further, it is worth mentioning that the percentage of social science utilization for these types of policies may be considerably higher than that shown in Table 4. At least one-third of the instances coded as 'Education', for example, pertained to internal governmental policies, such as training etc., rather than issues which involve public education. Thus the 11 per cent of instances shown as Organizational Management involve the application of purely organizational development-type research to the in-house problems of operating the government; the actual percentage of utilization of all types of social science research for such purposes may be quite high, possibly as much as one-third. While the literature on the topic of social science utilization and national policy is primarily concer-

ned with application in matters of domestic policy, the prevalence and magnitude of organizational research applied to operating the government itself are simply too great to be ignored in addressing the 'Knowledge for what?' question: the predominant purpose of knowledge utilization is to improve bureaucratic efficiency.

Impact

An estimate of impact was derived from a coding of the 575 instances of knowledge used for (a) an estimate of the number of people affected by the related policy decision and (b) the relative importance of the policy decision in their lives. As is shown in Table 5 four levels of impact could be differentiated based on this coding scheme as follows:

At the lowest level, impact could be discerned in administrative reorganizations and other policy changes within an agency, and in decisions concerned with evaluating the agency's internal affairs that were of little immediate external consequence. Thirty-seven per cent of the instances of use were at this level.

At the next level, impact could be seen in decisions involving matters external to the agency, but not national in their consequences. Target populations affected by decisions of this type were small. Policy decisions categorized at this level involved such issues as changes in immigration quotas. Nine per cent of the instances of use were at this level.

TABLE 5. Policy impact by national significance of policy issue

Type of policy issue and national significance	Percentage of instances of use
Policy issues affecting the entire nation	13
Policy issues affecting large population segments	41
Policy issues affecting small population segments	9
Administrative issues affecting government personnel	37
	100

At the next highest level, impact involved large segments of the national population. Policy decisions categorized at this level included the changing of poverty level requirements and the establishment of compensatory educational programmes. Forty-one per cent of instances of use were at this level. At the highest level, impact could be discerned in important decisions involving the nation as a whole, such as national health insurance, a voluntary or conscripted army, and civil rights issues, such as cross-district bussing. Thirteen per cent of the instances of use were categorized at this highest level. While we have little basis for concluding that the 575 self-reported instances of social science utilization identified in this study represent a high or low amount of knowledge use in the absence of comparative data, these data on impact do show that many of these instances of utilization involved strategically important applications of policy-related social science and would suggest reasons for modest satisfaction rather than the despair and cynicism so prevalent in the literature on social science utilization and public policy. Over half the instances of use involved matters of considerable individual and social consequence that affect sizeable segments of the population or the nation as a whole.

Parochialism and utilization

The possibility that parochialism affects knowledge utilization was implied previously by the earlier findings which showed that policy-makers did not use relevant research produced outside of the United States and, also, that the knowledge used was most often produced within the using agency. This narrow tendency for policy-makers to rely on knowledge with which they are familiar or with knowledge over which they can exert the greatest control becomes even more evident when the relationships between impact, sponsorship, and acquisition are examined.

Table 6 combines the data shown earlier in Tables 2 and 5 to illustrate the relationship between control over knowledge retrieval, production and procurement processes and impact: the more important the policy issue, the greater the control over the scientific knowledge used. This is particularly evident if we examine impact measures in relation to the two types of knowledge sponsored by the using agency (i.e. in-house and extramural), which together accounted for 86 per cent of the primary research used.

By looking down the column labelled 'Nation as a whole' (i.e. the highest impact level), it can be seen that the research produced within the using agency tends to be overrepresented when

TABLE 6. Distribution of knowledge use by impact and sponsorship

Sponsorship	Impact				
	Government only	Small population segments	Sizeable population segments	Nation as a whole	Total
Using agency: in-house	37	6	42	12	97
	(53)[1]	(55)	(46)	(57)	(50)
Using agency: extramural	25	2	38	4	69
	(36)	(18)	(42)	(19)	(36)
Other government agencies	3	2	7	3	15
	(4)	(18)	(8)	(14)	(8)
Not funded by government	5	1	4	2	12
	(7)	(9)	(4)	(10)	(6)
TOTAL	70	11	91	21	193
	(100)	(100)	(100)	(100)	(100)

1. Figures in parentheses are percentages.

TABLE 7. Distribution of knowledge use by impact and acquisition

Aquisition	Impact				
	Government only	Small population segments	Sizeable population segments	Nation as a whole	Total
Information flow initiated by end-user	90	22	106	38	256
	(77)[1]	(79)	(80)	(83)	(79)
Information flow initiated by subordinates	26	6	26	8	66
	(23)	(21)	(20)	(17)	(21)
TOTAL	116	28	132	46	322
	(100)	(100)	(100)	(100)	(100)

1. Figures in parentheses are percentages.

compared with research contracted to an outside group by the using agency. While the percentage of in-house research shown for the highest impact level was slightly higher than the percentage of in-house research for all instances regardless of impact level (57 per cent versus 50 per cent), the percentage of use for extramural research in matters involving the most important policy issues was considerably lower than the percentage of extramural research for all utilization instances (19 per cent versus 36 per cent).

Parochialism, however, involves more than the control over information by the using agency. To a large degree the knowledge used in upper-level decision-making reflects informational needs as defined by the individual policy-maker. The data in Table 7 show that about 80 per cent of the knowledge used was ordered at the specific request of the policy-maker. Also, the figures show a slight, although statistically unreliable, tendency for knowledge initiated by policy-maker request to be utilized more often as the importance of the policy issue increased. Thus, it appears that utilization is a 'top-down' process and that the role of the policy-maker in this process is not a passive one. He does not simply filter through and selectively utilize the information fed to him by staff aids. He plays a very active role in utilization by prescribing the information he wants and will

ultimately use in reaching decisions on policy relevant matters. The rather narrow and instrumental-like, or parochial, use of knowledge in policy-making reported by the respondents studied appears to start with the policy-maker himself and then to evolve through a combination of organizational controls and information procurement procedures which progressively delimit the opportunity for new ideas and research findings to reach those who make decisions at the top levels of governmental power.

Concluding remarks

It was the purpose here to address a question of central importance to knowledge utilization, namely: What information is used by whom, for what purposes and with what effects? It should be kept in mind, however, that knowledge utilization of any kind does not occur in a vacuum. In policy-related situations even under the most ideal conditions, how knowledge is used, and what impact it may have are influenced by the content of the issues under consideration, the values and perspectives of the policy-makers, and the relevant political and administrative hierarchical networks in which they operate. The findings discussed here should be viewed in this context.

PART 4

EVALUATION IN EDUCATION

19

THE WHITE FLIGHT DEBATE

The impact of the Coleman study on "white flight" has not weakened with time. Claims, counterclaims, and various statistical reevaluations have been done to substantiate or refute Coleman's conclusions. In this study, Pettigrew and Green go beyond Coleman's data to the policy implications of his interpretations. They show how a variety of biases in the reporting of evaluation research findings may combine and lead to faulty public policy decisions. Public trust in social scientists' ability to find solutions for public problems may thus be undermined. With additional data, they offer an alternative interpretation of Coleman's findings. They stress that social science researchers must pay attention to the impact of their research on the media and on public opinion. They believe that this is particularly critical with politically sensitive issues.

Coleman does not remain silent to Pettigrew and Green's criticism. He, in turn, argues that there are flaws in their analysis which, he claims, are based on their biases. In addition to his statistical points, he insists that free inquiry and expression are essential prerequisites for solid social science research, and explains that his views arise from his findings.

Pettigrew and Green respond to Coleman by pointing out that he has addressed himself to only two of the many critical issues that they have raised. They argue that their sample is more realistic, and, therefore, that their analysis is more accurate. They also outline some of the issues in their original refutation to which Coleman did not respond. They did not question the researcher's right of free inquiry and expression. Instead, they insist that the researcher must take exceptional care to see that interpretations of findings not be tainted by bias since the policy effects of evaluative interpretations can be far-reaching.

By increasing the sample of cities and analyzing data over a longer time period, they show that "white flight" is less the result of desegregation policy than of long-term urban trends.

A.

In this article, Thomas Pettigrew and Robert Green closely examine sociologist James S. Coleman's research and public statements on the relationship between school desegregation and white school enrollment. Describing their own study and other studies whose findings diverge from Coleman's, they contend that Coleman's research is methodologically and conceptually faulty and that it provides no basis for his highly publicized conclusion that urban school desegregation leads to massive "white flight." Rather, they argue, his and others' research tends to support metropolitan solutions to school segregation. The authors criticize Coleman for failing to distinguish between his scientific findings and his personal beliefs and go on to comment more generally on the delicate relationship between social science and the mass media.

"A SCHOLAR WHO INSPIRED IT SAYS BUSING BACKFIRED," declared the June 7, 1975, headline in the *National Observer*. "COURT ORDERED INTEGRATION RAPPED BY SOCIOLOGIST WHO STARTED IT ALL," read a June 1, 1975, headline of the Lansing, Michigan, *State Journal*.

From Thomas F. Pettigrew and Robert L. Green, "School Desegregation in Large Cities: A Critique of the Coleman 'White Flight' Thesis." *Harvard Educational Review*, February 1976, *46*(1), 1-53. Copyright © 1976 by President and Fellows of Harvard College.

These and equally misleading headlines appearing in most of the nation's major newspapers were attempting to describe a series of press interviews held by James Coleman, professor of sociology at the University of Chicago. Coleman is best known as the chief author of the highly publicized study *Equality of Educational Opportunity,* published in 1966 and popularly called "the Coleman Report."[1] He is not, nor has he ever claimed to be, the "scholar who inspired . . . busing" or the "sociologist who started it all." The man who might more truly be said to have started it all, four decades ago in *Missouri ex rel. Gaines v. Canada,*[2] is the late Charles Hamilton Houston, then chief counsel of the National Association for the Advancement of Colored People (NAACP); the United States Supreme Court handed down its historic public-school–desegregation ruling in 1954, a dozen years before the appearance of the Coleman Report.

Nevertheless, Professor Coleman is a highly regarded sociologist whose work and opinions are influential and deserve careful review. But this review is necessarily complicated. The events we discuss began in April 1975 and extended through December. Coleman's research has included three completely different analyses, put forward at various times; his results have been described in five different versions of a paper and thirty-nine pages of errata. Over the months, Coleman has repeatedly granted mass-media interviews; authored several articles in popular magazines; made an hour-long television appearance in Boston; submitted three affidavits in Boston's school-desegregation case; testified before the United States Senate's Judiciary Committee; and addressed a national conference in Louisville, Kentucky, on alternatives to busing.

We are not discussing, then, a single research study and the policy interpretations to be drawn from its findings. Rather, we are reviewing an unprecedented campaign by a sociologist to influence public policy. Consequently, it is important to review exactly what Coleman has said about busing and desegregation, what his research has found, and how his opinions and research results lend themselves to contrasting policy interpretations.

Given the complexity of this episode, the reader will find the chronological guide in table 1 useful in following our discussion.

---

[1] James S. Coleman, Ernest Q. Campbell, Carol J. Hobson, James McPartland, Alexander M. Mood, Frederic D. Weinfeld, and Robert L. York, *Equality of Educational Opportunity* (Washington, D.C.: GPO, 1966).
[2] 305 U.S. 337 (1938).

TABLE 1
Chronological Guide

Date	Event	Referred to in Text as:
April 2	Coleman delivers initial paper to the American Educational Research Association, citing the findings from an analysis of the extended effect of urban school desegregation, 1968–1970, on decline in white enrollment, 1970–1973.	Paper I Analysis I
May–June	Coleman grants numerous media interviews.	
June 12	Coleman submits his first affidavit to the federal court on behalf of the anti-busing Boston Home and School Association.	Affidavit I
June 13	The NAACP holds a press conference in New York City to reply to Coleman.	
June 24	Kenneth Clark and seven other social scientists hold a press conference in New York City to reply to Coleman.	
July 3	Meyer Weinberg presents "A Critique of Coleman" to the National Education Association.	
July 11	The *New York Times* questions Coleman's Analysis I after discovering that none of the nineteen cities in question had had any court-ordered school desegregation during 1968 to 1970.	
July 14	Coleman participates in an hour-long, question-and-answer, commercial program on Boston's WNAC-TV.	
July 27	Coleman publishes an article in *Newsday* that refers to a new analysis and proposes an "entitlement" plan for limited metropolitan desegregation.	
July 28	Coleman issues a second paper. Analysis I is dropped, but a radically new analysis investigates the concurrent effect of school desegregation on the loss of white students for each year, 1968–1973. This paper provides analytic details to the social-science community for the first time.	Paper II Analysis II
August 4	A group of experts at The Urban Institute makes a private review of Coleman's Analysis II.	
August 15	Coleman issues a third paper with extensive revisions.	Paper III
August 15	A "Symposium on School Desegregation and White Flight" is held at the Brookings Institution. This second review of Coleman's research is open to the mass media and features a discussion of Reynolds Farley's research.	
August 27	Coleman submits his second affidavit for the Boston Home and School Association to the federal court.	Affidavit II
August– September	Coleman continues to grant numerous media interviews.	
August 30	The Urban Institute publishes the "final" version of Coleman's paper.	Paper IV

TABLE 1 — continued

Date	Event	Referred to in Text as:
	Along with Analysis II, this paper introduces a new analysis that consists of a set of "white flight" projections for segregated and desegregated urban school systems.	Analysis III
September 3	Christine Rossell presents research findings that contradict Coleman's in a paper delivered to the American Political Science Association.	
September 22	Coleman submits his third affidavit for the Boston Home and School Association to the federal court.	Affidavit III
October	Coleman publishes another popular article, in the *Phi Delta Kappan*, and agrees to be a defense witness in the crucial federal court case involving metropolitan school desegregation in Wilmington, Delaware.	
October 22	The Urban Institute issues a thirty-nine-page insert of errata for Paper IV.	Paper V
October 28	Coleman testifies before the United States Senate's Judiciary Committee hearings on proposed anti-busing amendments to the Constitution.	
December 5	Coleman speaks at a conference in Louisville, Kentucky, on alternatives to busing.	
December 8	Coleman presents another version of his paper to the United States Commission on Civil Rights in which he admits that it "is not clear . . . whether desegregation itself induces an increased movement of Whites from the desegregated district."	Paper VI

Since we shall analyze Coleman's research and policy recommendations, it may also help the reader to know in advance our major critical points.

(a) *There are serious methodological and conceptual problems in Coleman's work on so-called "white flight."* In particular, we challenge his principal conclusion: court-ordered, urban school desegregation is self-defeating because it *causes* massive white movement out of the public schools. Throughout our paper we shall refer to many problems in this research.

First, Coleman's research is conducted in a demographic vacuum. It ignores the fact that separation of the races between suburbs and central cities has been under way throughout this century and was a *fait accompli* well before court-ordered busing even began. Second, Coleman's projections of future "white flight" in northern cities are dubious on three grounds: the projections are based largely on data from desegregated southern cities; extreme conditions are posited to estimate average "effects" from misspecified models; and the projections assume stability in demographic factors. Third, Coleman's research involves purely aggregate data at the district level only; but interpretations about individual actions and "white flight" require either individual data or at least school-level data. Not one white parent was asked by Coleman if his or her child was removed from the public schools because of school desegregation, nor were any data by schools utilized. Thus the findings, even if they were valid on other grounds, would be open to a variety of interpretations.

We will explore two such interpretations. For one thing, parents who intend to leave the city for other reasons might hasten their move when school desegregation begins; thus, the accelerated decline in white enrollment in the first year of desegregation would be compensated by fewer white departures in later years. For another, some of what Coleman defines as "desegregation" very likely represents the temporary mixing of black and white children in schools located in areas undergoing residential shifts from white to black. In these instances, it may be that "white flight" leads to temporary school desegregation rather than that school desegregation leads to "white flight," as Coleman assumes.

Another objection to Coleman's investigation is that his findings depend heavily upon the cities he chose to study. "White flight" occurs in the very "largest" urban school districts, he suggests, and only slightly, if at all, in smaller urban districts. But a close examination of his data reveals that much of the "white flight" effect, even for the "largest" districts, is contributed by just two atypical cities in the deep South—Atlanta and Memphis. Moreover, Coleman inexplicably omitted from his sample a number of the truly largest urban school districts, such as Miami, Jacksonville, and Nashville. We shall demonstrate how including data from these omitted cities reduces the alleged effect of school desegregation upon the decline in white enrollment.

Not surprisingly, Coleman's "white flight" findings are not supported by other studies using similar data and a variety of methods. After describing these conflicting studies, we shall present our own analysis, which uses Coleman's data but yields very different results. We shall then try to resolve the apparent conflict.

(b) *There is only a tenuous connection between Coleman's research findings and his political opposition to school busing for racial desegregation.* Contrary to the impression conveyed by the mass media, Coleman's research has not been on busing, court orders for desegregation, student achievement, classroom disruptions, or the behavior of poor black children. We believe his opposition to court-ordered busing for school desegregation derives less from his research than from two beliefs which he has expressed publicly: changes in relationships between the races should flow from the will of the community and not from the federal courts; and only a small part of racial segregation in schools is a result of state action—most of it is caused by individual actions beyond the appropriate reach of the law. We shall critically consider these two beliefs.

(c) *The whole episode raises serious questions about the relationship between social science and the mass media.* First, the news media tended to confuse Coleman's research with his political preferences. All too often his views were presented as if they were results from a "second Coleman Report." Complicating the matter further, Coleman and The Urban Institute, under whose aegis the study was done, failed to provide the social-science community with any analytic or methodological details until four months after the initial paper was delivered. We shall emphasize the lack of fit between social science and the mass media, for it has led, in the Coleman episode and other instances, to a disservice to the American public and to the two institutions themselves.

Coleman's First Paper

The episode began on April 2, 1975, with Coleman's delivery of "Recent Trends in School Integration" (hereafter referred to as Paper I) at the American Educational Research Association's annual meeting.[3] Copies of the paper were labeled "Draft for discussion purposes only. Not to be quoted or cited." Although the paper provided little analysis, it was restrained in tone and content in contrast to what was to follow in Coleman's interviews with reporters.

The first paper's argument can be summarized in four points:

(1) Intra-district public-school desegregation increased markedly from 1968 to 1972, primarily in the South. Simultaneously, intra-district desegregation declined slightly in the New England and Middle Atlantic states. During this period, desegregation trends were negatively related to district size; school segregation was most intense in large northern districts.

(2) These trends, Coleman argued, were products of two often conflicting processes: the collective, formal process that can be shaped directly by government agencies; and the individual, informal process by which families remove their children from the public schools. Coleman called this latter process "white flight" and suggested that its rate may be accelerated by rapid school desegregation.[4]

---

[3] James S. Coleman, Sara D. Kelly, and John A. Moore, "Recent Trends in School Integration," paper presented at the Annual Meeting of the American Educational Research Association, Washington, D.C., 2 April 1975. Hereafter referred to as Paper I.

[4] There are two main forms of what is commonly called "white flight" from the schools: (1) white students being withdrawn from public schools undergoing desegregation and being enrolled in private or religious schools; and (2) white students being withdrawn from public schools as they

(3) Coleman calculated the effect on "white flight," as measured by the decline in white enrollment from 1970 to 1973, of three variables: the natural logarithm of district size, the district's 1970 proportion black of total enrollment, and the increase in school desegregation in the district from 1968 to 1970. Although he did not provide the regression equations, his results for the nineteen "largest" central-city districts showed that both the proportion black of total enrollment and the pace of desegregation were positively related to the net number of white children leaving the public schools. For the next fifty largest central-city districts, however, the results were sharply different: net losses of white pupils were related positively to the district's size and to the proportion black of total enrollment but *not* to desegregation.[5]

(4) Coleman derived two major conclusions from these findings. First, "insofar

---

and their families move from cities undergoing school desegregation to cities or suburbs not undergoing school desegregation. In both cases, "white flight" implies that the withdrawal is caused by school desegregation. The distinction is important because the two forms of educational "white flight" from the schools have very different relations to residential "white flight."

In Coleman's definition of "white flight" from the schools, it is not entirely clear whether he means the first form of the process, the second, or both. Nevertheless, his operational definition—percentage change in the absolute number of white students enrolled in public schools—includes both forms. Although it is important to distinguish between the two forms of educational "white flight," particularly when drawing inferences (as Coleman does) regarding residential segregation, throughout the remainder of this paper and in the literature reviewed operational definitions of educational "white flight" include both forms of the process.

[5] This first version of Coleman's paper did not list the cities that constituted his two categories of central cities. Four months later, this vital information was provided in Coleman's second paper. Only then was it known that both the exclusion of some of the nation's largest urban school districts (e.g., Miami-Dade, Fort Lauderdale-Broward) and the placement of the dividing line between the two categories were arbitrary. These decisions, as we shall subsequently review in detail, acted to enhance the association between school desegregation and the loss of white pupils. For this first paper, the nineteen "largest" central-city districts were New York, Los Angeles, Chicago, Philadelphia, Detroit, Houston, Baltimore, Dallas, Cleveland, Memphis, Milwaukee, San Diego, Columbus, Tampa-Hillsborough, St. Louis, New Orleans, Indianapolis, Boston, and Atlanta. The next largest, medium-sized urban districts, as categorized by Coleman, were Denver, Albuquerque, San Francisco, Charlotte-Mecklenburg, Newark, Cincinnati, Seattle, San Antonio, Tulsa, Pittsburgh, Portland (Oregon), Baton Rouge, Mobile, Oakland, Kansas City (Missouri), Buffalo, Long Beach, Omaha, Tucson, El Paso, Toledo, Minneapolis, Oklahoma City, Birmingham, Wichita, Greenville (South Carolina), Austin, Fresno, Akron, Shreveport, Dayton, Garden Grove (California), Louisville, Sacramento, Norfolk, St. Paul, Winston-Salem–Forsythe, Corpus Christi, Gary, Richmond (Virginia), Rochester, Fort Wayne, Des Moines, Rockford (Illinois), Jersey City, Anaheim, San Jose, Montgomery, and Colorado Springs. Richmond was later dropped from the analysis because of its extensive annexation of white suburbs, although other cities (e.g., Dallas, Denver, Houston, and Memphis) with similar annexation during these five years were retained in later analyses. Tucson was dropped in an October set of corrections due to reporting difficulties. Moreover, for the completely different analysis of the second, third, and fourth versions of the paper, Denver and San Francisco were shifted over to the "largest" district category—a shift which, as we shall later demonstrate, also acted to heighten the critical correlation between desegregation and white loss.

as one intended consequence of integration is an increase in achievement of black children, the intent is largely defeated."[6] Second,

> the courts are probably the worst instrument of social policy. Yet this does not answer the central questions, for the other agencies of government, which can initiate policies that excite fewer of the fears that ultimately defeat the policy, have often failed to initiate them. It is clear that if school desegregation policies are not to further separate blacks and whites in American society, far greater coordinated efforts on the part of different branches and levels of government are necessary than have taken place until now.[7]

The Media Interviews Begin

While at first the mass media gave Paper I only moderate coverage and comment, Coleman later granted numerous interviews to reporters. At this point the furor began. In contrast to the caution of the initial paper, Coleman now offered blunt and far-ranging opposition to federal court orders that required extensive urban school desegregation. To Muriel Cohen of the *Boston Globe* he argued that "a whole generation of young legal talent thinks it can transform the society by winning court cases. That's enormously subversive of the whole political process in the United States."[8]

Coleman continued his attack in an interview with Bryce Nelson of the *Los Angeles Times:* "When the imposition of school integration occurs, and doesn't flow out of the will of the community, then the response on the part of the whites, if they have the income to leave, is to leave." The courts should recognize, he said, that the "much greater commitment" to school integration during the 1960's has diminished, and that such integration is no longer "the first national priority."[9]

For the *New York Times,* Coleman broadened his attack to include social-class as well as racial considerations, although class was not a variable in his study. Reporter Paul Delaney quoted him as saying:

> If integration had been limited to racial integration, then the fear of incidents would have been much less, and the experience with integration would have been

---

6 Coleman et al., Paper I, p. 18.

7 Coleman et al., Paper I, p. 22.

8 "Desegregation's Architect Unhappy with Overall Results," *Boston Globe,* 18 May 1975, p. 8, cols. 1–8, and p. 9, cols. 5–7.

9 "Courts Scored as Going Too Far in School Integration," *Los Angeles Times,* 29 May 1975, Part I, p. 10, cols. 1–4, and p. 11, cols. 1–4.

much more positive. There has never been a case of lower-class ethnic integration in the schools, because schools historically were ethnically segregated by ethnic neighborhoods.[10]

Perhaps the most influential interview appeared in the *National Observer*.[11] After summarizing his research results, Coleman called the courts "the worst of all possible instruments for carrying out a very sensitive activity like integrating schools." Moreover, he said "the courts were wrong to consider the [Coleman] report in any way." He did not mention his own use of his earlier study when he served as an expert witness in desegregation cases in Washington, D.C., and Denver. Coleman also claimed that the courts are wrong when they attempt to eliminate all the racial segregation in a school system. "I think the courts constitutionally should limit their actions to undoing the effects of official discrimination. But the very large proportion of school segregation by race and by social class is due to individual action, and I think courts overstep their bounds when they try to counterbalance those individual actions."[12]

Beyond rendering these legal judgments, Coleman also speculated on the social-psychological difficulties of big-city schools. Desegregation seemed to cause "white flight" in only the largest central-city districts, he argued, because "there's a much greater feeling of inability to have any impact on the schools, a feeling that schools cannot maintain order and . . . protect the child." Much of this feeling, he believed, stems from the failure of big-city schools "to control lower class black children."[13]

When asked if metropolitan desegregation were not the answer to the problem he was raising, Coleman said he did not think so for two reasons. First, metropolitan districts would necessarily be even larger, and the problematic districts were already too large. Second, middle-class families would just move farther from the city.

Finally, when pressed for concrete policy recommendations, Coleman answered:

I think there has to be an incentive either in Government money and assistance or in attractive programs. . . . More generally, school desegregation is not the only way to promote social integration. Nor is it, I believe, the best way. For example, activi-

---

[10] "Long-Time Desegregation Proponent Attacks Busing as Harmful," *New York Times*, 7 June 1975, p. 25, cols. 4–8.
[11] Mark R. Arnold, "A Scholar Who Inspired It Says Busing Backfired," *National Observer*, 7 June 1975, p. 1, cols. 1–2, and p. 18, cols. 1–6.
[12] Arnold, p. 18.
[13] Arnold, p. 18.

ties that encourage racial intermarriage could be much more effective in creating stable forces for social integration.[14]

He did not specify what these "activities" might be.

These initial interviews met three of the mass media's major criteria as to what constitutes big news. They appeared to represent (1) a "surprising" reversal of position (2) by a publicly known authority (3) in a direction that fitted snugly with the prevailing national mood of retrenchment. Almost at once, newspapers throughout the country ran "Coleman" stories, and conservative editorialists had a field day. Rarely, if ever, had a sociologist's opinions been so sought after by the media. Earlier reluctant to deal with the media, Coleman granted dozens of separate interviews, many of them by telephone. In late June, *Newsweek* even sent two reporters to talk with Coleman at his remote vacation home in West Virginia.[15]

On June 12, while still vacationing, Coleman consented to give an affidavit to a lawyer for the anti-busing Boston Home and School Association. After outlining his research results, he concluded the affidavit by asserting that "when court-ordered remedies have gone beyond [the redress of specific state acts of segregation], they have exacerbated the very racial isolation they have attempted to overcome."[16] Coleman was apparently unaware of the fact that the court-imposed desegregation plan in Boston sought only to redress the consequences of the school committee's unconstitutional acts to promote segregation.[17] The appeals court later ruled that the affidavit was irrelevant.

In July, Coleman flew to troubled Boston and participated in an hour-long, commercially sponsored, question-and-answer television program on WNAC-TV. Entitled "Another Look at Busing," the program presented a large number of reporters firing often barbed queries at the sociologist. Coleman began by admitting that his "very appearance may be mischievous" in Boston, since the court ruling had already been handed down. Yet he continued to attack the federal courts for moving against segregation that he saw as caused by "individual action"; he described the important desegregation decision of the Supreme Court, *Swann v. Charlotte-Mecklenburg Board of Education*,[18] as the "wrong precedent"; and he stated flatly that the federal courts should not impose metropolitan desegrega-

14 Arnold, p. 18.

15 Merrill Sheils and Diane Camper, "Second Thoughts," *Newsweek*, 23 June 1975, p. 56.

16 Affidavit of James S. Coleman, Morgan v. Kerrigan, United States Court of Appeals for the First Circuit, C.A. No. 72-911-G, 12 June 1975, pp. 3–4. Hereafter referred to as Affidavit I.

17 Roger I. Abrams, "Not One Judge's Opinion: Morgan v. Hennigan and the Boston Schools," *Harvard Educational Review*, 45 (1975), 5–16.

18 402 U.S. 1 (1971).

tion. Coleman also accused his social-science critics of suffering from "motivated blindness," and, when pressed for a policy recommendation, said only, "I don't have a solution."

Coleman's sensitivity to his social-science critics may have been related to the fact that, during June, two press conferences had been held in New York City to rebut many of his contentions. The authors of this article, together with Roy Wilkins and Nathaniel Jones, executive director and chief legal counsel, respectively, of the NAACP, held the first press conference on June 13. Jones summed up a dominant reaction of black Americans to Coleman's unrelenting attack upon the federal judiciary:

> Less than a decade ago, white people were telling black people to get out of the streets, stop public protesting, and go use our constitutional safeguards through the courts. Now that we have followed that advice successfully in American cities, Coleman tells us to stop using the courts for they are an inappropriate source for remedies. Can black people seriously be expected to listen to him?[19]

In another press conference eleven days later, Kenneth Clark and seven other social scientists also countered many of Coleman's assertions. These initial criticisms received inside-page coverage in the *New York Times*[20] and were not widely reported in other newspapers and media. That a few "liberal social scientists" should "assail" the "new Coleman study" was not considered particularly newsworthy.

These first critiques of Coleman's position centered on three points. First, they stressed the complexity of the so-called "white flight" phenomenon and suggested the importance of variables that Coleman's work had not considered. Second, they questioned the scientific ethics of communicating opinions in the form of research results before any analysis was available for review by the social-science community. Third, they emphasized that even if Coleman's dire predictions of massive losses of white students were accurate, the appropriate policy response would be extensive metropolitan desegregation rather than the abandonment of constitutional protections.

Another early response to Coleman's research came on July 3 at the annual convention of the National Education Association. Meyer Weinberg, the editor of

---

[19] Comment made at a press conference held in New York City, 13 June 1975.

[20] Barbara Campbell, "Five-Year Study on Busing Scored: Finding That It Causes White Exodus Disputed," *New York Times*, 14 June 1975, p. 12, cols. 1–2; and Iver Peterson, "Clark Group Assails New Coleman Study," *New York Times*, 25 June 1975, p. 49, cols. 1–3.

Integrated Education, presented a paper which faulted Coleman's total neglect of relevant research and reviewed five earlier studies of "white flight" that had presented diverse findings.[21]

All of these early critiques noted that little or no court-ordered school desegregation had occurred in the nation's largest central-city districts between 1968 and 1970, the period that Coleman had used in his research. Robert Reinhold of the *New York Times* checked this point for himself by calling each of the twenty districts in question. His story, headlined "COLEMAN CONCEDES VIEWS EX-CEEDED NEW RACIAL DATA," appeared on the front page of the *Times:*

> The crux of his argument is that integration in the first two years, 1968–1970, led directly to a substantial exodus of white families in the following three years, 1970–1973, over and above the normal movement to the suburbs. However, a thorough check of all 20 cities—in which key officials were questioned by telephone—could find no court-ordered busing, rezoning or any other kind of coerced integration in any of the cities during the 1967–1970 period. Court suits were pending in many, but desegregation was limited to a few modest open enrollment plans, used mostly by blacks. If there was "massive and rapid" desegregation, as Dr. Coleman said, it could not have been due to court-imposed remedies.[22]

In response to these facts Coleman conceded, according to Reinhold, "that his public comments went beyond the scientific data he had gathered." "In answer to questions," wrote Reinhold, "he said that his study did not deal with busing, and that his arguments applied to trends in only two or three southern cities. Nonetheless, he maintained that the 'over-all implications' of his remarks were still valid. . . ."[23] Later, Coleman asserted that he had been misquoted.[24]

The New Analysis and Paper II

As the questioning of his initial analysis grew more widespread, Coleman and his colleagues at The Urban Institute undertook a second, more sophisticated, and sharply different analysis. The first public mention of the second analysis appeared

21 "A Critique of Coleman," paper presented at the Annual Meeting of the National Education Association, Los Angeles, Calif., 3 July 1975.

22 Robert Reinhold, "Coleman Concedes Views Exceeded New Racial Data," *New York Times,* 11 July 1975, p. 1, cols. 3–4, and p. 7, cols. 1–2.

23 Reinhold, p. 7.

24 Reply Affidavit of James S. Coleman, Morgan v. Kerrigan, 28 Aug. 1975. Hereafter referred to as Affidavit II.

in an article by Coleman in *Newsday*.[25] The article, which repeated the familiar argument that the courts should not correct *de facto* segregation, made little use of the new findings. Rather, Coleman placed a new emphasis on policy recommendations. Besides again suggesting interracial marriage, Coleman stressed a range of voluntary programs from specialized interracial schools and remedial programs in all-black schools to integrated summer camps. More significantly, for the first time he advocated a minimal metropolitan plan in which every central-city child would be entitled by the state to attend any public school in the metropolitan area, so long as racial segregation was not thereby increased. Suburban schools would be required to allot up to 20 percent of their enrollment capacity to out-of-district children.

The complete new analysis appeared in a sixty-seven–page document dated July 28, 1975, and entitled "Trends in School Segregation, 1968–73."[26] This second paper was distributed to a small group of social scientists invited to attend a one-day discussion with Coleman at The Urban Institute on August 4. This paper opened with a brief history of school-desegregation efforts and closed with a description of desegregation attempts in Wyandanch, New York. Both of these sections were largely irrelevant to the research; both came in for intense criticism at the Urban Institute meeting; and both were eliminated from later drafts and need not be discussed further. Again no mention was made of earlier research.

The new analysis attempted to ascertain the average effect of desegregation upon the loss of white students during each of the five school years from 1968 to 1973. In other words, unlike the initial analysis which looked at white-student loss from 1970 to 1973 *after* desegregation between 1968 and 1970, the new analysis examined the yearly relationship between concurrent changes in desegregation and white enrollment. Thus, reductions in segregation in 1968–1969 were related to white-student losses in 1968–1969, and so on for each of the five years in each of sixty-nine central cities. Each city/year combination was treated as a separate observation in the regression analysis, and consequently, no trends over time could be ascertained from this analysis. Once again the sample was split in two, roughly on the basis of system size (a somewhat arbitrary procedure which, as we shall later demonstrate, strengthens the "white flight" effect).

---

[25] James S. Coleman, "Another Look at Integration," *Newsday*, 27 July 1975, Ideas Sec., p. 1.
[26] James S. Coleman, Sara D. Kelly, and John A. Moore, "Trends in School Segregation, 1968–73," unpublished paper, The Urban Institute, Washington, D.C., 28 July 1975. Hereafter referred to as Paper II. Notice the shift in the title from "School Integration" in the first paper to "School Segregation" in this and all later versions.

The corrected results, which were not made available until October, are provided in table 2. The table presents the regression coefficients together with their standard errors in parentheses and the variance accounted for by the predictors. Notice that for six of the thirty-two coefficients for which standard errors are computed the standard errors are *larger* than the coefficients, and that many of the

TABLE 2

Coleman's Basic Regression Coefficients for Analyses of Decline in White Enrollment in Central-City Public Schools

	"Largest" 21	Next 46
Equation 1		
ΔR (desegregation)	.279 (.062)	.056 (.026)
Prop. black students	−.133 (.028)	−.090 (.01
ln N (system size)	.000 (.008)	−.042 (.010)
Constant	.013	.452
R^2	.29	.26
Number of observations	(105)	(226)

Including inter-district segregation in SMSA, and interaction term for desegregation with South:

	"Largest" 21	Next 46
Equation 2		
ΔR (desegregation)	.199 (.156)	−.148 (.137)
Prop. black students	−.044 (.039)	−.035 (.016)
ln N (system size)	.066 (.008)	−.041 (.010)
R SMSA	−.165 (.050)	−.110 (.021)
ΔR × SOUTH	.143 (.170)	.242 (.137)
Constant	−.059	.438
R^2	.36	.35

Including interactions of desegregation with proportion black and inter-district segregation, and also including South as a dummy variable:

	"Largest" 21	Next 46
Equation 3		
ΔR (desegregation)	−.459 (.184)	−.349 (.151)
Prop. black students	.051 (.037)	−.026 (.019)
ln N (system size)	.003 (.006)	−.039 (.009)
R SMSA	−.210 (.044)	−.102 (.025)
ΔR × SOUTH	.148 (.198)	.244 (.145)
ΔR × Prop. black	1.770 (.307)	.511 (.215)
ΔR × R SMSA	.561 (.494)	.894 (.314)
SOUTH	−.006 (.010)	−.002 (.006)
Constant	−.039	.414
R^2	.60	.40

Source: James S. Coleman, Sara D. Kelly, and John A. Moore, "Insert for Trends in School Segregation, 1968–73," The Urban Institute, Washington, D.C., Oct. 1975, textual revision for p. 59.

variables contribute little to the prediction. The two equation 1's use only three variables to predict white-student loss: the annual change in public-school desegregation (ΔR); the proportion of student enrollment that was black (Prop. black); and the natural logarithm of the total number of students (ln N). These three variables together explain about 29 percent of the variance in white-enrollment change for the largest cities and about 26 percent of the variance for the medium-sized cities.

The second set of equations does not substantially improve the prediction. Adding two more predictors—the degree of inter-district school segregation in the Standard Metropolitan Statistical Area (R SMSA), and an interaction term to allow for differential effects of desegregation in the South ($\Delta R \times$ SOUTH)—explains about 36 percent and 35 percent of the variance of annual white-enrollment changes in large and medium-sized cities, respectively.

A more interesting and dramatic increase in predictive power for the largest cities occurs in equation 3. Here three more variables have been added: a dummy (dichotomous) variable for the South (SOUTH) and interaction terms to allow the effect of desegregation to vary with inter-district metropolitan segregation ($\Delta R \times R$ SMSA) and with the proportion of students who are black ($\Delta R \times$ Prop. black). These eight variables explain 60 percent of the variance for large cities but only 40 percent for smaller cities. But note that this improvement derives largely from the interaction between annual desegregation changes in a school system *and* the system's proportion black of total enrollment.

This interaction suggests that so-called "white flight" is a function less of desegregation *per se* than of the conditional relationship between desegregation and the proportion black of school enrollment. Although this crucial finding of the second Coleman analysis has not yet received public attention, we believe that its policy implications—to the extent that any policy implications can be safely drawn from this work—are potentially important and contrast sharply with those now publicly identified with this research. In short, we feel this finding offers further support for metropolitan approaches to school desegregation.

Rather than consider the implications of equation 3, Coleman next chose to use the regression results to project average annual rates of loss of white students after desegregation. To do this, he posited a set of extreme conditions—a system with 50 percent of its enrollment black and a one-year reduction of 0.2 in the segregation index. These conditions were atypical, since in 1970 the median black enrollment in his 69 cities was only 28 percent and in only 20 of his 342 city/year observations was there a segregation reduction of 0.2 or more. Indeed, only 4 of his 342 observations actually met both of these conditions.[27]

Under these unrealistic assumptions, Coleman's equation 1 models predict that desegregation would result in a loss of white students 5.5 percent greater than expected on the basis of the other predictor variables in the large cities and 1.8 percent greater in the medium-sized cities. The equation 2 models show the projected effect of major desegregation to be far greater in the South than in the North. For the largest urban systems, the model predicts that desegregation would lead to an additional white-enrollment loss of 6.8 percent in the South and 3.9 percent in the North; for the medium-sized systems, the comparable figure for the South is 2.6 percent and for the North, 0.2 percent.

Still using equation 2, Coleman turned to inter-district segregation and demonstrated that the difference in proportion black of all students between central-city schools and schools in surrounding suburbs is positively related to the annual loss of central-city white students, even in the absence of intra-district desegregation. This finding, too, presents a powerful argument for those interested in furthering metropolitan, interracial education.

Coleman used the equation 3 models to illustrate the critical interaction between desegregation and the proportion of the school district's enrollment which is black. Under the extreme condition of a 0.2 reduction in the segregation index, the projected decline in white enrollment in the largest central-city districts varies by a factor of two to four as the proportion black of total enrollment varies from 25 percent to 75 percent.

Coleman next attempted to determine if the loss of white enrollment he attributed to desegregation continues beyond the first year of the process. Though his results on this point were inconsistent, he concluded that the presumed effect of desegregation is concentrated in the first year. Then, in partial answer to his critics who had stressed additional variables related to so-called "white flight," Coleman tried to control for factors unique to each city by introducing into the regression equations a dummy variable for each city. This procedure only slightly reduces the equation 1 effect of desegregation on changes in white enrollment in the large-city schools. It does not, however, remove the need for more independent variables. Joseph Wisenbaker of Michigan State University has noted that, when using dummy (dichotomous) variables to control for inter-city differences unrelated to school attendance, one must assume that all such differences remained

---

27 Coleman et al., Paper II, p. 51. The four times these rare circumstances occurred were in Memphis (1972–1973), Birmingham (1969–1970), and Richmond (1960–1970, 1970–1971); only the first two cities were employed in Coleman's second analysis.

constant over the five-year period—a stringent and probably unjustifiable assumption.[28]

Finally, Coleman carried out what he reported as a full analysis of covariance that considered not only the rate of desegregation and dummy variables for each city but also the possibility that the effect of desegregation could vary from city to city. Again assuming a large one-year reduction of 0.2 in the school-segregation index, he projected figures for white-enrollment decline in excess of what would have occurred without desegregation. Of those eight cities which had actually experienced substantial desegregation, two showed predicted *gains* in white enrollment; four others showed only modest predicted losses in white enrollment. The only cities for which "massive" loss was predicted were Memphis and Atlanta. The average estimated loss for the eight cities was only 5.2 percent, and without Memphis and Atlanta, the average was only 1.5 percent.[29] Again we see what a crucial role just two atypical southern cities played in Coleman's *public* argument against court-ordered urban school desegregation throughout the United States. His own conclusion is less specific: "They show that the estimated white loss does vary considerably from city to city, and that the average loss rate specified earlier obscures very different loss rates in different cities."[30] Unfortunately, Coleman has consistently failed to make this point forcefully in his court affidavits and his many public interviews.

The Urban Institute Meeting

The Urban Institute called a meeting at its offices in Washington, D.C., on August 4 to review in detail this second draft.[31] Coleman, his co-author Sara Kelly, and the president of the Institute, William Gorham, chaired the one-day session. Those in attendance included three economists, four sociologists, two demographers, one

---

[28] "A Critique of 'Trends in School Segregation, 1968–73,'" unpublished paper, College of Urban Development, Michigan State Univ., Lansing, Mich., Nov. 1975.

[29] James S. Coleman, Sara D. Kelly, and John A. Moore, "Insert for Trends in School Segregation, 1968–73," unpublished paper, The Urban Institute, Washington, D.C., Oct. 1975. Hereafter referred to as Paper V. Coleman stressed that his figures probably *underestimated* "white flight" in the cities listed because a number of them had annexed white areas during the years he studied. But he failed to mention in any of the various discussions of this table the fact that the extreme conditions posited for his calculations undoubtedly *overestimated* "white flight."

[30] Coleman et al., Paper II, p. 62.

[31] A partial, edited transcript of this meeting is available from The Urban Institute, 2100 M Street, N.W., Washington, D.C. 20037. References made to the meeting's discussion are taken from this transcript.

lawyer, and one social psychologist. The session was brisk, hard-working, direct, and friendly. The review panel's criticisms of the second paper centered on three issues: (1) the study's political context, (2) its demographic context, and (3) its methodology.

Coleman opened the meeting by asking participants to limit their comments to the research paper under discussion and to refrain from discussing the opinions he had expressed publicly. Many participants rejected this request on the grounds that Coleman's opinions had been advanced in the mass media as if they derived directly from his research and that both the study's design and its interpretation were heavily influenced by its author's opinions.

Panelists agreed that the research dealt with few of the subjects about which Coleman had expressed opinions in his interviews. The research was *not* about student achievement, classroom disruptions, or the behavior of poor black children; it was not about busing or court orders. Strictly speaking, it was not even about "white flight," a prejudicial label that implies a phenomenon prompted solely by desegregation. Rather, it concerned the relationship between school desegregation —achieved by any means—and changes in white-student enrollment in urban public-school systems.

The group advanced many policy interpretations that contrasted with Coleman's. In particular, many felt that Coleman's results seemed to speak for metropolitan approaches to desegregation. At base, Coleman's interpretations reflected a firm political belief that since only a relatively small part of segregation has been caused by "state action" in the Fourteenth Amendment sense, only a small part of it should be dealt with by the courts.

Even the study's design had political overtones. If one were to set out to formulate a complex causal model to predict changes in white-student enrollment, one would ask broad questions, utilize a variety of predictor variables, and place the problem in its full demographic context. Coleman instead chose to test the narrow question of whether the racial desegregation of urban schools leads to a loss of white students. In doing so, he virtually ignored the broader demographic context of the problem. Any study that considers only the period from 1968 to 1973, without noting the fifty-year trend towards concentration of Whites in the suburbs and Blacks in the central cities, is bound to be myopic and misleading.

As it stood, the study paid little attention to the possibility that central cities might have annexed white suburbs; it confounded race with social class; it ignored differences in residential segregation patterns among cities; and it did not control for differential birth rates by race.[32] Moreover, Coleman's projections erroneously assumed stability in demographic variables. For example, net black migration from the South to northern cities is now trickling to its end, and this will retard the increase of black enrollments in central-city schools. And in some metropolitan areas, Blacks are beginning to move into the suburbs in substantial numbers.

Moreover, torn from their demographic context, the effects of desegregation are difficult to assess from only district-wide aggregate data. Coleman interpreted any unusual decline in white enrollment in a year of desegregation as "white flight"—white families with school-age children fleeing from interracial schools to private or suburban schools. But not one white family was actually asked about its motivations for staying or leaving, nor were data available from individual schools. Coleman here committed a classic ecological fallacy, inferring individual motives from broad-gauged aggregate data.[33] Since Coleman based his policy arguments on assertions about individual actions, this defect seriously weakens his case.

These issues and the great inter-city variation in Coleman's data led the panel to recommend that case studies be undertaken. Norman Chachkin of the Lawyers Committee for Civil Rights under Law offered an example which underscored the utility of such case studies and the danger of the ecological fallacy. Prior to 1972, the average annual decline in white enrollment in the Harrisburg, Pennsylvania, public schools had been below 3 percent. But during the 1972–1973 school year, when widespread desegregation took place, the decline was approximately 10 percent. In 1973–1974, the decline returned to 2.9 percent. An analyst using Coleman's approach would have assumed that the increased decline was caused by desegregation. But a case study would have revealed that a serious flood in June 1972 had caused many white families to leave Harrisburg.

Panel members further questioned the research on a number of methodological grounds. First, they criticized Coleman's choice of independent variables, noting that many had large standard errors and explained little variance. They went on to suggest a wide range of alternative variables, such as those Gregg Jackson of

[32] The total number of white students fell during this period, in part because of a rapid decline in the white birth rate in the 1960's; the decrease in white migration *into* the central city; the changing white age structure; and the rise of non-educational urban problems that drove both white and black families out of the city.

[33] For a discussion of ecological fallacy, see Hanan C. Selvin, "Durkheim's *Suicide* and Problems of Empirical Research"; W. S. Robinson, "Ecological Correlations and the Behavior of Individuals"; and Herbert Menzel, "Comment on Robinson's 'Ecological Correlations and the Behavior of Individuals' "; all in *Sociology: Progress of a Decade*, ed. Seymour M. Lipset and Neil J. Smelser (Englewood Cliffs, N.J.: Prentice-Hall, 1961).

the United States Commission on Civil Rights had already demonstrated to be significant.[34] Employing Coleman's original research design and data, Jackson found four independent variables—population density, the 1960–1970 change in black population, median white income, and current per-pupil expenditures— each of which, in combination with the proportion black of student enrollment and school-system size, predicted decline in white enrollment *better* than did reduction of school segregation.

The panel also noted that the dependent variable, change in white enrollment, indicates the *net* effect of gains and losses and was not decomposed into its constituent parts. And many questioned the wisdom of using average effect estimates to predict future decline in white enrollment. Moreover, it is incorrect to interpret the positive correlation between desegregation and decline in white enrollment as necessarily indicating that the former causes the latter; decline in white enrollment often precedes desegregation, as it did in Detroit, Birmingham, Atlanta, and Memphis.

Perhaps the most serious issue raised by the review panel was the difference between Coleman's key results and the findings of previous research on the topic. For instance, Jane Mercer and Terrence Scout had earlier investigated twenty-three desegregating school districts in California and sixty-seven districts there which had not desegregated.[35] They found no significant differences between the two groups in direction or rate of change in the proportions of student enrollment that were black or Chicano.

Furthermore, Reynolds Farley, using the same national data source as Coleman, failed to uncover a significant relationship between school desegregation and decline in white enrollment in southern or northern cities.[36] We will later discuss at greater length Farley's research and two other important studies which fail to replicate Coleman's critical result.

Review of Coleman's work by social scientists and lawyers continued through

34 Gregg Jackson, "Recent Trends Critique: III. Reanalyses of Coleman's Data and Additional Data," unpublished paper, United States Commission on Civil Rights, Washington, D.C., July 1975. Jackson found each of these four variables predicted changes in white-student enrollment better than did degree of school desegregation.

35 Jane R. Mercer and Terrence M. Scout, "The Relationship between School Desegregation and Changes in the Racial Composition of California School Districts, 1963–73," unpublished paper, Sociology Department, Univ. of Calif., Riverside, 1974.

36 "Racial Integration in the Public Schools, 1967 to 1972: Assessing the Effects of Governmental Policies," *Sociological Focus*, 8 (1975), 3–26; and "School Integration and White Flight," paper presented at the Symposium on School Desegregation and White Flight, Brookings Institution, Washington, D.C., 15 Aug. 1975.

August. On August 15, 1975, the Center for National Policy Review of the Catholic University Law School and the Center for Civil Rights of Notre Dame University co-sponsored a "Symposium on School Desegregation and White Flight" at the Brookings Institution in Washington, D.C. Unlike the meeting at The Urban Institute, this one-day session was open to the press. It featured a presentation by Coleman, a panel discussion by three civil-rights lawyers on the legal significance of the controversy, and four papers by social scientists.

Coleman produced yet another draft of his paper (Paper III) for the occasion.[37] Paper III remained essentially the same as the earlier versions. Although the new version was longer, included references to a few previous studies, contained two additional appendices, and thanked members of the earlier review panel, it reflected little response to the panel's many criticisms.[38] The final paragraph avoided the loaded term "white flight" and interpreted the results somewhat more cautiously:

> All this leads to general conclusions consistent with those from earlier sections of this examination: that the emerging problem with regard to school desegregation is the problem of segregation between central city and suburbs; and in addition, that current means by which schools are being desegregated are intensifying that problem, rather than reducing it. The emerging problem of school segregation in large cities is a problem of metropolitan area residential segregation, black central cities, and white suburbs, brought about by a loss of whites from the central cities. This loss is intensified by extensive school desegregation in those central cities, but in cities with high proportion of blacks and predominantly white suburbs, it proceeds at a relatively rapid rate with or without desegregation.[39]

Most specialists would agree with the basic thrust of this conclusion. At issue is whether court-ordered desegregation within central cities significantly hastens the development of two separate Americas—black central cities and white suburbs. This formulation of the issue is far different from the simple "busing backfires" argument that Coleman's numerous press interviews led the nation to focus upon.

In his third paper, Coleman added one additional analysis that demonstrates—

---

[37] James S. Coleman, Sara D. Kelly, and John A. Moore, "Trends in School Segregation, 1968–73," unpublished paper, The Urban Institute, Washington, D.C., 15 Aug. 1975. Hereafter referred to as Paper III.

[38] For example, four citations of other research on "white flight" which had been provided Coleman at the August 4 meeting were now mentioned briefly in footnotes. Coleman et al., Paper III, pp. 46, 50.

[39] Coleman et al., Paper III, pp. 68–69. This conclusion was retained in the fourth version, Paper IV, pp. 79–80.

TABLE 3

Coleman's Prediction of Proportion Black in Years after Desegregation

	0	1	2	3	4	5	6	7	8	9	10
Equation 1											
With desegregation (.4)	.5	.54	.56	.58	.60	.61	.63	.65	.67	.69	.70
Without desegregation	.5	.51	.53	.55	.56	.58	.60	.61	.63	.65	.67
Equation 3											
With desegregation (.4)	.5	.58	.60	.62	.63	.65	.67	.69	.71	.73	.75
Without desegregation	.5	.51	.52	.54	.55	.56	.58	.59	.61	.63	.65

Source: James S. Coleman, Sara D. Kelly, and John A. Moore, *Trends in School Segregation, 1968–73*, (Washington, D.C.: The Urban Institute, Aug. 1975), p. 74.

even under extreme conditions—how trivial are the policy implications of his results. Even positing conditions so rare that they never occurred in his 342 observations—an enormous district (169,000 students)[40] with 50 percent black student enrollment and a huge one-year reduction of 0.4 in the segregation index—the model predicts minimal effects of desegregation on a school system's racial proportions (table 3).[41] On the basis of equation 1 (see table 2), the projected percentage black of total enrollment in cities with desegregated schools would exceed that in cities with no desegregation by only 3 percentage points in the first year and the same 3 percentage points in the tenth year. The next projections, using equation 3 (see table 2), are based on data from northern cities only and posit several further assumptions: suburbs are entirely white and equal in population to the central city; all white-student losses in the central city appear as gains in the suburbs; and there is no movement of Blacks to the suburbs. Although the omission of southern cities addresses one major criticism of the research, the latter two conditions are unrealistic and inflate the projected effect of within-city desegregation. Even under these assumptions, the equation 3 projections reveal a difference between desegregated and segregated cities of only 7 percentage points in the first year and a total of 10 by the tenth year after desegregation.

[40] There are only seven school districts in the nation that are this large or larger. The figure is an average of the sizes of the particular twenty-one urban districts Coleman chose as the "largest." But an average is a poor measure of central tendency for a highly skewed, small distribution, where New York alone has over a million students. The median figure for Coleman's twenty-one urban districts in 1972 is 128,000 (Milwaukee). James S. Coleman, Sara D. Kelly, and John A. Moore, *Trends in School Segregation, 1968–73* (Washington, D.C.: The Urban Institute, Aug. 1975), p. 5. Hereafter referred to as Paper IV.

[41] The only situation that even approaches these conditions is Memphis in 1972–1973; but in 1972 it had a total of 139,000 students, not 169,000.

Since Coleman's own successive analyses revealed smaller and smaller effects, it is hardly surprising that other investigators at the symposium reported results that belie the much-heralded warning that desegregation prompts "white flight." For example, Michael Giles of Florida Atlantic University reported on his detailed desegregation research in seven Florida school districts.[42] Since these districts were all county-wide, residential relocation was impractical and transfer to private schools offered the only mechanism of "white flight." Giles found that avoidance of desegregation among Whites was *unrelated* to racial prejudice or to "busing," was greatest among upper-status families, and was least among families whose children attended schools with less than 30 percent black enrollment.

Luther Munford presented his study of thirty Mississippi school districts that had been desegregated between 1968 and 1970. He demonstrated that, for his sample, "white flight" was explained by the "black/white ratio in the population as a whole rather than just the ratio in the schools."[43]

A third paper, by Gary Orfield, a political scientist at Brookings, provided the symposium with a political analysis of "white flight research." "Too often," he warned, "selective, half-digested reports of preliminary research findings are disseminated by the media and become weapons in the intense political and legal battle being fought in major cities."[44] Emphasizing the difficulty of sorting out the forces that accelerate suburbanization, he stated: "It is impossible now to demonstrate that school integration, in itself, causes substantial white flight."[45] His conclusion echoed a consensus among race-relations specialists: "There is no evidence that stopping school desegregation would stabilize central city racial patterns. If those patterns are to be significantly modified, positive, coordinated, and often metropolitan-wide desegregation efforts will probably be required."[46]

Reynolds Farley delivered the fourth paper at the symposium.[47] As noted ear-

[42] Michael W. Giles, Everett F. Cataldo, and Douglas S. Gatlin, "Desegregation and the Private School Alternative," paper presented at the Symposium on School Desegregation and White Flight, Brookings Institution, Washington, D.C., 15 Aug. 1975; also Everett F. Cataldo, Michael W. Giles, Douglas S. Gatlin, and Deborah Athos, "Desegregation and White Flight," *Integrated Education*, 13 (1975), 3–5.

[43] Luther Munford, "Schools that Quit 'Tipping' in Mississippi," paper presented at the Symposium on School Desegregation and White Flight, Brookings Institution, Washington, D.C., 15 Aug. 1975, p. 7. Also Munford, "White Flight from Desegregation in Mississippi," *Integrated Education*, 11 (1973), 12–26.

[44] "White Flight Research: Its Importance, Perplexities, and Possible Policy Implications," paper presented at the Symposium on School Desegregation and White Flight, Brookings Institution, Washington, D.C., 15 Aug. 1975, p. 1.

[45] Orfield, p. 2.

[46] Orfield, p. 21.

[47] Farley, "School Integration and White Flight."

lier, this paper presented evidence that from 1967 to 1972 there was no statistically significant relationship between racial desegregation and decline in white enrollment in large or medium-sized urban districts in the North or South (see figure 1). Though this material, unlike Coleman's, had been in print since January 1975, the news media first mentioned it in a story about the Brookings symposium in the Sunday *New York Times* of August 17, 1975.[48] But Farley's results were not publicized beyond the major newspapers.

Farley's research differed from Coleman's in five ways. First, Farley used a larger sample of cities, fifty in the South and seventy-five in the North. Rather than limit his sample, he considered all cities with a 1970 population of one hundred thousand or more and at least 3 percent black enrollment in their public schools. He also ran analyses using only the twenty largest cities of each region, as shown in figure 1. Second, Farley investigated the 1967 to 1972 period rather than the period 1968 to 1973. Third, rather than examine annual changes in the variables, Farley analyzed changes across the entire five-year span. Fourth, Farley employed only elementary-school data, while Coleman used data from all grades. (This difference should have been unimportant, since Coleman showed that the relationship he discerned appeared to exist about equally across the grades.) Finally, Farley used a different index of school segregation. Both his and Coleman's indices measure whether black and white students attend the same schools, and both are independent of the school districts' racial compositions. It has been shown, for a sample of 2,400 school districts, that the two indices are correlated at 0.88.[49]

Unable to show any systematic relationship between white loss and school desegregation for either his extensive urban sample or his subsamples of the largest cities, Farley concluded:

> To be sure, when the public schools are desegregated or when they become predominantly black, some white parents—perhaps many—hasten their move away from the central city. However, whites are moving out of central cities for many other reasons. We have shown that cities whose schools were integrated between 1967 and 1972 did not lose white students at a higher rate than cities whose schools remained segregated.[50]

Why should two studies with comparable data reach opposite conclusions? Cole-

[48] Edward R. Fiske, "Integration Role on Cities Assayed," *New York Times*, 17 Aug. 1975, p. 19, col. 1.

[49] Barbara Zolotch, "An Investigation of Alternative Measures of School Desegregation," *Institute for Research on Poverty Discussion Papers*, Univ. of Wisconsin, Madison, 1974.

[50] Farley, "School Integration and White Flight," p. 10.

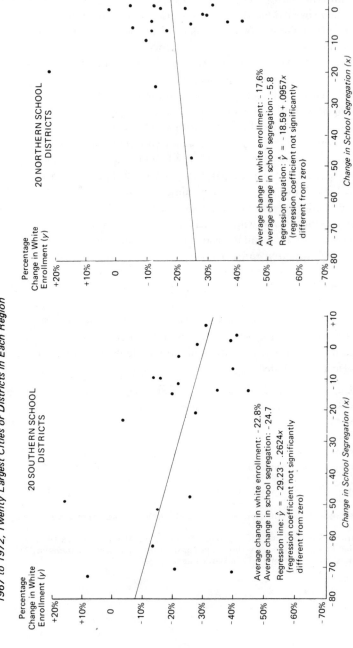

FIGURE 1

Percentage Change in White Enrollment Plotted Against Change in School Segregation, 1967 to 1972, Twenty Largest Cities or Districts in Each Region

Source: Reynolds Farley, "School Integration and White Flight," paper presented at the Symposium on School Desegregation and White Flight, Brookings Institution, Washington, D.C. 15 Aug. 1975; Figure 2.

man suggested that Farley failed to control fully for the proportion of students who were black. Farley did find that this variable was significantly related to the decline in white enrollment in the fifty southern cities but not in the seventy-five northern cities. Yet Farley also demonstrated that cities in both regions in which the 1967 percentage black of all pupils was high *and* schools were desegregated did not lose unusually high proportions of white enrollment.

Farley offered two other possible explanations for the difference in results. He suggested that the one-year effect Coleman found might represent only a hastening of migration by some Whites who were about to leave anyway and that, over a five-year span, this "hastening" effect disappears. Farley also noted

> . . . the great weight he [Coleman] placed upon observations for a few cities, par-
> ticularly Atlanta and Memphis. Most of his data describe the 1968 to 1972 span but
> for several cities he analyzed 1973 segregation data. In both Atlanta and Memphis
> integration orders went into effect between 1972 and 1973. Whites have been mi-
> grating out of Atlanta's central city at least since 1960 and white public school en-
> rollment dropped sharply prior to school integration. Undoubtedly the white
> out-migration continued between 1972 and 1973. Exclusively white freedom
> schools sprang up in southern cities in reaction to public school integration. How-
> ever, these are often short-lived as parents appreciate the tremendous costs of es-
> tablishing private school systems. Many Memphis parents enrolled their children
> in private schools in 1973 but it is probable that enrollment in such institutions
> will decline. In my view, it is inappropriate to draw overarching conclusions
> about school integration causing white flight from data for a few cities.[51]

White-enrollment figures in the Memphis public schools in the fall of 1975 bore out Farley's prediction that private-school attendance would decline.[52]

Coleman's Fourth Paper, Third Analysis

Two weeks after the Brookings symposium, Coleman produced a fourth version of his paper. Among other things, Paper IV included a third analysis which appeared to show enormous differences in "white flight" between central cities with desegregating schools and those with segregated schools.

By attempting to demonstrate that school desegregation does indeed accelerate "white flight," Analysis III responded to critics who had charged that Coleman's

---

51 Farley, "School Integration and White Flight," pp. 6, 9.
52 Task Force on Education of the L.Q.C. Lamar Society, "Public Schools in Memphis: Struggling but with Head Well Above Water," *Southern Journal,* 4 (1975), 3–4.

earlier analyses merely measured a long-term decline in white enrollment that was unrelated to school desegregation. In published form, the new analysis was described as "a rough test" and took up less than a page of discussion.[53] However, Coleman emphasized Analysis III in public statements after August 1975. He described it in an interview in the *New York Times Magazine*[54] and offered it as evidence in his second affidavit in the Boston desegregation case.

In Analysis III, Coleman used several subsets of what he called the "largest" central-city school districts (twenty-one districts in all) and predicted losses of white students for the years 1969–1973 from data for a single year, 1968–1969. Next, he grouped the districts into two sets: those that had a reduction of 0.1 or more on his school-desegregation index during 1968 to 1973 (ten districts) and those that did not (eleven districts). The predicted loss of white students from the eleven still-segregated systems (18 percent) was approximately what one would expect had desegregation not occurred (15 percent), but the desegregating systems had an average loss of about two and one half times that expected (26 percent instead of 10 percent). Inexplicably, in his public statements Coleman referred to a different version of this analysis based on the original subset of nineteen districts that omitted Denver and San Francisco. Using this sample, he found an average decline in white enrollment almost four times that expected (26 percent instead of 7 percent).

There are many serious problems with this much-publicized "rough test." First, the use of a single year as the base upon which to compute expectancies is a dubious practice at best. Second, the sample is small and unrepresentative: three of the ten desegregating districts, all in the deep South, provide most of the effect. When Memphis, Atlanta, and New Orleans are removed from the analysis, the remaining seven desegregating districts exhibit only an 18 percent decline instead of an expected 11 percent.

The third problem is the absence of controls for variables other than school desegregation that might be related to decline in white enrollment. Cities are divided into two categories (districts with more than 0.1 reduction in school segregation and those with less), with no control for other differences between them. Specifically, the lower expected rate of decline in the desegregating districts is in large part an artifact of regional differences. All eleven of the segregated urban districts are in the North, and six of the ten desegregating districts are in the South. Region

53 Coleman et al., Paper IV, pp. 70–71.
54 Walter Goodman, "Integration, Yes: Busing, No," *New York Times Magazine,* 24 Aug. 1975, pp. 10–11, 42, 46, 48.

in turn is a surrogate for such variables as suburbanization, in which the South lags a generation or more behind other regions. For the six southern desegregating systems (Atlanta, Dallas, Houston, New Orleans, Memphis, and Tampa), the average decline in white enrollment during the years from 1969 to 1973 was 29.5 percent compared with an expected decline of 7.5 percent. For the four northern desegregating systems (Denver, Indianapolis, St. Louis, and San Francisco), there was an average white loss during 1969 to 1973 of 21 percent compared with a predicted 15 percent. Yet Coleman generalized his basically southern results to Boston and other northern cities.

Despite Coleman's claim that this new analysis is "more stringent" because the 1968–1969 baseline projections cause each city to act as its own control, one cannot assume, as Coleman seems to, that all relevant variables in a given city will remain stable over a five-year period. For example, major highway construction or annexation of suburbs can cause great variability in student-attendance figures from year to year. A more detailed analysis of year-by-year data, which became available in early September, was to highlight further the inadequacies of Coleman's approach.

Christine Rossell's Analysis

Christine Rossell, a political scientist at Boston University, presented another analysis at the annual meeting of the American Political Science Association.[55] Her paper provided further evidence that conflicted both with Coleman's opinions about the political consequences of desegregation and with his findings about "white flight."

Rossell first considered the effects of public-school desegregation upon community politics. Her analysis of detailed time-series data on seventy urban school districts in the North from 1963 to 1973 revealed that school desegregation increased both voter turnout and dissent voting. Districts with highly educated voters most sharply displayed the increased turnout effect; low-education districts, the increased dissent effect. And while the increase in dissent voting was temporary and rarely halted the desegregation process, the increased turnout for school-board elections appeared to be stable over time. Rossell concluded from these re-

55 "The Political and Social Impact of School Desegregation Policy: A Preliminary Report," paper presented at the Annual Meeting of the American Political Science Association, San Francisco, Calif., 3 Sept. 1975. See also Rossell, "School Desegregation and White Flight," *Political Science Quarterly*, 90 (1975-1976), 675–95.

sults that "there is the possibility that in many [especially high-education] communities, school desegregation has more socially integrative characteristics than disintegrative with regard to voting behavior."[56]

Rossell next directed her analyses to the question of "white flight." She supplemented the HEW school-desegregation data used by Coleman and Farley with pre-1967 and case-history data, which she collected directly from each district. All told, Rossell assembled data on eighty-six northern and western districts. Twenty-six had undergone no desegregation, while sixty had experienced varying degrees of desegregation; but of the latter, only eleven were actually under court orders. This prodigious effort yielded an analysis of trends in pre- and post-desegregation white enrollment by district.

Pasadena and Pontiac, the two cities with the greatest proportion of school reassignments, showed significant white-enrollment decline over the first three and two years, respectively. But in Rossell's sample of sixty cities, these two were striking exceptions. In no other case was the implementation of a court-ordered plan followed by a significant increase in the decline of proportion white of total enrollment. Schools in South Bend, Indiana, for example, actually became significantly more white following a plan for minimal desegregation.[57]

Table 4 summarizes Rossell's data using five categories of districts: those with *Court Ordered* desegregation, those that reassigned over 10 percent of their pupils for desegregation (*High Desegregation*), those that reassigned between 5 percent and 20 percent (*Medium Desegregation*), those that reassigned less than 5 percent (*Low Desegregation*), and finally, a *Control Group* of districts that reassigned no children whatsoever for desegregation. The two right-hand columns in table 4 give the slopes of the pre- and post-desegregation trends in white enrollment. The "significance level" column indicates that there are no statistically significant differences either between the full pre-desegregation trend and the trend for the first year of desegregation or between the pre- and post-desegregation trends. Notice that there are no significant differences in the rate of decline in the proportion white between pre- and post-desegregation years for any of the four categories of desegregating districts. Furthermore, to whatever extent decline in the proportion white of total enrollment represents "white flight," there was not significantly more "white flight" in districts with court-ordered desegregation than in those without it, in districts with extensive desegregation than in those with

56 Rossell, "Political and Social Impact," abstract.
57 Rossell, "Political and Social Impact," table 10.

TABLE 4

Change in Percentage White for Four Desegregation Groups and a Control Group

	Change in % White										
Group	−4 Years	−3 Years	−2 Years	−1 Year	0 Years	1 Year	2 Years	3 Years	Signif. Level	Pre-Slope	Post-Slope
Court Ordered	−1.1	−1.8	−2.2	−1.0	−1.8	−2.1	−1.4		N.S.	.0	.2
High Desegregation (> 20%)	−1.5	−1.8	−1.8	−1.2	−2.4	−1.8	−.8		N.S.	.1	.8
Medium Desegregation (5–20%)	−1.1	− .7	− .9	− .9	−1.0	−1.0	−1.0		N.S.	.0	.1
Low Desegregation (< 5%)	−1.8	−1.8	−1.4	−1.5	−1.6	−1.6	−1.5	−1.7	N.S.	.1	−.1
Control Group (0%)		−1.5	−1.5	−1.9	−2.2	−1.8	−1.3	−1.2	N.S.	−.5	.3

Source: Christine H. Rossell, "The Political and Social Impact of School Desegregation Policy: A Preliminary Report," paper presented at the Annual Meeting of the American Political Science Association, San Francisco, Calif., 3 Sept. 1975; Table 10.

minimal desegregation, or in districts with desegregation than in districts without it. Especially noteworthy is the absence of a significant change in white-enrollment trends in districts which had court-ordered desegregation. Recall that Coleman had repeatedly attacked the federal judiciary and had alleged that their far-reaching desegregation orders resulted in "white flight"—without ever employing data on court orders like those used by Rossell.

Thus, in her extensive sample of northern urban districts, Rossell, like Farley, found no relationship between desegregation and "white flight." Why did Rossell and Coleman reach such different conclusions? Let us consider differences in their approaches and data.

Although both investigators based their work on the HEW data for 1968 to 1972, Rossell also included HEW's 1967 data (which Coleman ignored) and as much pre-1967 information as she could gather from individual districts. Rossell, then, could discern comparatively accurate and reliable pre-desegregation racial-enrollment trends. Coleman, as we noted earlier, based the trend calculations in his third analysis on the single base year of 1968–1969.

The two researchers also employed different samples of cities. Rossell limited her study to urban school districts in the North and West. Coleman did report a "white flight" effect for desegregation in large northern cities, but it was smaller than that reported in such southern cities as Atlanta and Memphis. Such an effect did not exist among the largest cities in Rossell's sample. As table 5 indicates, large

TABLE 5

Change in Percentage White for Three Desegregation Groups and a
Control Group by City Size

Group	-4 Years	-3 Years	-2 Years	-1 Year	0 Years	1 Year	2 Years	3 Years	Signif. Level	Pre-Slope	Post-Slope
Large Cities (> 500,000)											
High Desg.	-1.3	.7	-2.8	- .4	-2.3	-2.3	-1.4		N.S.	.1	.5
Med. Desg.	-4.0	-1.0	-1.1	- .9	-1.1	-1.1			a	a	a
Low Desg.		-1.5	-1.7	-3.6	- .8	- .9	- .4		N.S.	-1.1	.2
Control	-2.1	-1.3	-1.3	-1.9	-1.7	-1.6			a	.1	a
Medium Cities (100,000–500,000)											
High Desg.	-1.3	-1.6	- .3	-1.3	-2.0	-1.8	-2.2	- .8	N.S.	.1	.3
Med. Desg.	- .8	-1.3	- .6	-1.2	-1.2	-2.1	-1.1	-1.1	N.S.	- .1	.1
Low Desg.	-1.3	-2.5	-1.8	-1.3	-1.3	-1.6	-1.4	-1.3	N.S.	.1	.0
Control		-1.0	-2.0	-2.1	-2.4	-1.8	-1.3	-1.3	N.S.	- .6	.4
Small Cities (< 100,000)											
High Desg.	-2.2	-3.3	-4.8	-1.8	-3.6	-1.2	-1.1		N.S.	- .0	1.3
Med. Desg.	- .2	- .7	-1.2	- .2	- .9	- .3	- .9		N.S.	- .1	.0
Low Desg.			- .6	- .5	- .7	-1.5	-1.5		a	a	a
Control					-2.2	-1.9	-1.6	-1.2	a	a	a

aUnable to compute.

Source: Same as for Table 4.

northern cities with populations of over five hundred thousand showed no greater
desegregation effect than did smaller northern cities.

The most fundamental differences between the Rossell and Coleman studies
were their operational definitions of the two key concepts—"white flight" and "desegregation." Coleman defined "white flight" as the percentage decline in the
absolute number of white students in a district. But changes in the numbers of
white *and* black students are significantly and positively associated across urban
school districts, and black enrollments in some central-city systems are beginning
to decline. Consequently, Rossell defined "white flight" as the percentage decline
in the *proportion* white of total enrollment, a definition that considered both
black and white students.

These contrasting definitions can produce widely varying estimates of "white
flight." Consider the critical case of San Francisco. Coleman showed a 1971–1972
loss of 22.4 percent (7,534 out of 33,601) of the city's white public-school pupils
following San Francisco's major desegregation effort in 1971; in contrast, Rossell
showed that the white proportion declined by only 5.1 percent. The difference is

explained by the decline of black enrollment during these years. As Gary Orfield observed, "from September 1972 to September 1974, San Francisco's black enrollment declined by a ninth and its Latino enrollment by a twelfth."[58] In short, these two rival definitions of "white flight" will converge for cities where the number of black students is relatively stable and will diverge for cities with a rapidly changing number of black students.

Coleman and Rossell also differed in their operational definition of "desegregation." Coleman, as we have seen, regarded any reduction in his system-wide index of school racial segregation as evidence of desegregation, whether it resulted from governmental action, court orders, or demographic change. Rossell, on the other hand, measured desegregation in terms of governmental action, by the percentage of students reassigned to schools in order to further racial desegregation. She also distinguished between desegregation that was court-ordered and that which was not.

Coleman's operational definition of desegregation introduces a potentially major artifact into his analysis. As the review panel at The Urban Institute noted, much of the decline in his segregation index for particular cities may have resulted not from desegregation efforts but from neighborhood transition. Some cases of what Coleman labeled "white flight" caused by school desegregation were actually temporary instances of school desegregation caused by black movement into formerly white neighborhoods.

Rossell makes the point cogently:

> Although Coleman has claimed in television appearances and to journalists that he is conducting research on school desegregation policy, he is doing nothing of the sort. Indeed, there is no evidence he knows what school desegregation policy has been implemented in the school districts he is studying. . . . By simply measuring the changes in school segregation (which is much easier than tracking down the data on school segregation policy), Coleman cannot distinguish between ecological succession in neighborhood school attendance zones and an actual identifiable governmental policy resulting in the same thing—integration. In the case of ecological succession in school attendance zones, the integration will be temporary and the eventual re-segregation will look like white flight resulting from school desegregation. This confusion of two different phenomena means that his model is invalid for the case of governmental or court-ordered school desegregation policy.[59]

58 Orfield, p. 10.
59 Rossell, "Political and Social Impact," p. 55.

We have, then, three studies that have used basically the same HEW data base to investigate the same problem. Farley and Rossell report no relationship between school desegregation and "white flight"; Coleman reports a significant relationship. A number of factors have been cited as possible explanations for these differences. It is significant, however, that although Farley and Rossell differed in the scope of their samples, the years they studied, the research designs they employed, and their definitions of "white flight" and desegregation, both concluded, in contrast to Coleman, that school desegregation was related only weakly, if at all, to decline in white enrollment in urban schools.

Yet Another Analysis

We offer yet another analysis in an attempt to clarify this puzzle. We maintain that many of Coleman's results may stem from his choice of particular subsets of "largest" urban school systems.

Recall that in his first paper Coleman did not list the urban districts in his sample. Only four months and hundreds of headlines later was the list of the twenty "largest" urban school districts revealed: New York City, Los Angeles, Chicago, Philadelphia, Detroit, Houston, Baltimore, Dallas, Cleveland, Memphis, Milwaukee, San Diego, Columbus, Tampa, St. Louis, New Orleans, Indianapolis, Boston, Washington, D.C., and Atlanta. Washington was cited in this list, although it had been dropped during Analysis I due to its lack of white students.[60] This left only nineteen in the crucial subset of "largest" urban districts.

But these are *not* the nineteen largest urban school districts in the United States. Omitted and never mentioned in any of the four versions of Coleman's paper are Miami-Dade, Jacksonville-Duval, and Fort Lauderdale-Broward, all county-wide urban systems in Florida. Yet Tampa-Hillsborough, also a Florida metropolitan school district, was included, although it is smaller than the three omitted districts. Miami and Jacksonville, like Tampa, experienced widespread court-ordered school desegregation without a significant decline in white enrollment, while Fort Lauderdale's white enrollment *increased* by 39.2 percent from 1968 to 1972 during

---

60 We do not question the decision to drop Washington, D.C., because of its tiny percentage of white pupils, but we wonder why a comparable cutoff was not employed for districts with tiny percentages of black students. Thus, Coleman analyzed Garden Grove, Anaheim, and San Jose, all in California, though each had less than 2 percent black school enrollments. This is apparently another example of Coleman's exclusive concentration on white Americans.

an extensive school-desegregation program. Thus, Coleman's unexplained exclusion of these three huge districts may have contributed to his findings.

The problem of sample selection is yet more complicated. At times Coleman seemed to invoke criteria other than school-district size to designate his subset of "largest" urban school districts. For example, in his second analysis he included Denver and San Francisco, raising the number of cases to twenty-one, because they "were two of the few northern cities to undergo extensive desegregation during the period 1968–73. . . ." He excluded Albuquerque because it "is not among the first fifty [cities] in population,"[61] even though its school system is larger than that of San Francisco. No mention is made, however, of Nashville, which has a larger school system than San Francisco and ranks thirtieth in city population.

Nor did Coleman provide a rationale for cutting off his sample of "largest" urban school districts after San Francisco. This decision is particularly perplexing since it excluded Charlotte-Mecklenburg, North Carolina, the next largest urban school system and the district involved in the critical *Swann* decision. Under court order, this metropolitan school district experienced a larger drop in segregation, as measured by Coleman's segregation index, than any in his big-city sample save Tampa.

A less arbitrary procedure would have been to use Farley's method of choosing all urban school districts which enrolled a certain number of students in a given year. Employing Coleman's own rankings by 1972 enrollment, a sample of all urban school districts with more than seventy-five thousand students would have included not only Miami, Jacksonville, Fort Lauderdale, Denver, Nashville, Albuquerque, and San Francisco but also Charlotte, Newark, Cincinnati, and Seattle. All these cities except Albuquerque, Fort Lauderdale, and Charlotte are among the nation's fifty largest.

Our analysis uses both Coleman's sample and the one outlined above to show how Coleman's findings are influenced by his selection of urban school districts and his year-by-year procedure. We shall use Coleman's time period (1968 to 1973); his definitions of "white flight" and "desegregation"; his data as provided in Appendix 3 of the fourth version of his paper[62]; and his two principal control

---

61 Coleman et al., Paper IV, p. 56, n. 22. Coleman has since stated that he included San Francisco and Denver at our suggestion. He is mistaken. We suggested only that he rerun his analysis without Atlanta and Memphis so as to gauge the critical importance of these cities to his results. To the best of our knowledge, this suggestion has not been followed.

62 Coleman et al., Paper IV, pp. 99–121. We utilized the data for all school levels combined. Later Coleman discovered that major errors had been made in his analyses of elementary-school enrollments (Paper V), but these errors do not affect our present results. For the four cities omitted from

FIGURE 2
Scatter Diagram of Desegregation and White-Enrollment Losses, 1968–73

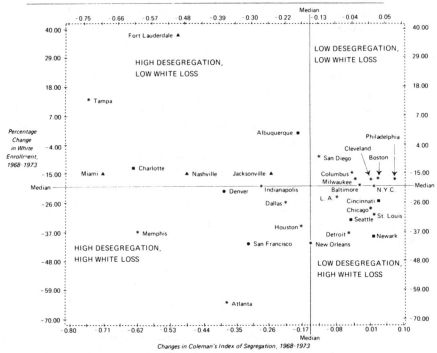

LEGEND
* Coleman's original sample of 19 urban school districts
● Cases which were added in Coleman's second analysis
▲ Cases which should have been included in sample of "largest" urban school districts
■ Cases which would be included if a standard cutoff of 75,000 district enrollment in 1972 were used

variables—the proportion of students who are black and the natural logarithm of the total size of each school system. However, in order to take into account factors like the "hastening effect" and residential transition, we shall use Farley's method of analyzing changes in the variables across the span of 1968 to 1973 rather than Coleman's year-by-year procedure.

Figure 2 presents our basic data and indicates the relationship between the amount of desegregation from 1968 to 1973 and the percentage change in white

Coleman's analyses and Appendix 3 (Miami, Fort Lauderdale, Jacksonville, and Nashville), enrollment data are from the HEW source utilized by Coleman; their desegregation estimates are taken from Farley's index for elementary desegregation, 1967–1972, which for other districts closely approximates Coleman's index for all grade levels, 1968–1973.

enrollment over these same years. If there were a strong positive relationship between desegregation and "white flight," we would expect the data points representing the thirty urban school districts to fall predominantly in the high-desegregation/high-loss and the low-desegregation/low-loss quadrants (lower-left to upper-right diagonal).

But figure 2 does not reveal this much-heralded relationship. Only a few of the thirty districts lie in the two predicted quadrants $(r = -0.30)$. This replicates Farley's earlier results for the districts shown in figure 1. Now notice the importance for Coleman's argument of the two extreme points in the lower-left quadrant. Not surprisingly, these points represent Memphis and Atlanta; figure 2 shows how unusual they are among the nation's thirty largest urban school systems. Finally, Denver and San Francisco, the two districts Coleman added as an afterthought in his second analysis, are also in the high-desegregation and high-loss quadrant.

Six of the nine districts that should have been included in the big-district sample are located in the high-desegregation/low-loss quadrant, including all four of the districts larger than San Francisco. The remainder—Cincinnati, Newark, and Seattle—are located in the low-desegregation/high-loss quadrant. In short, *the two additions Coleman made to his subset of big districts for his second analysis contributed to the positive association between white loss and degree of desegregation; the nine he left out would have severely reduced the association.*

Figure 3 describes the same thirty urban school districts but relates the 1968 proportion black of total enrollment to declines in white enrollment from 1968 to 1973. Note the strong association that now emerges: those districts that had relatively high proportions of black students in 1968 tended to experience the largest decline in proportions white of total enrollment over the next five years $(r = -0.57)$. As Coleman has stated, though, such a strong predictor must be controlled to allow a fair test of the effect of desegregation.

Table 6 provides the relevant coefficients for the various subsets of large urban school districts. As figure 3 suggested, the Pearson correlation coefficients in table 6 show that the key variable associated with declines in white enrollment from 1968 to 1973 is the 1968 proportion black of total enrollment. In all five sets of districts, the first-order (column A), multiple (column D), and partial correlation coefficients (column E) are virtually identical. Neither degree of school desegregation nor school-system size is strongly related to the percentage decline in white enrollment over this five-year span. Controlling for proportion black and system size using desegregation as the independent variable (column F) does decrease the negative relationship between desegregation and decline in white enrollment, but the

FIGURE 3

Scatter Diagram of Proportion of Black Students in 1968 and White-Enrollment Losses, 1968-1973

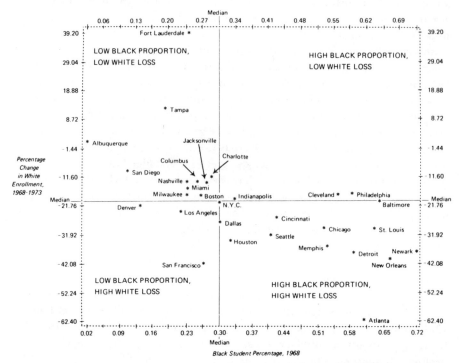

Black Student Percentage, 1968

coefficients (columns B and F) remain trivial. Moreover, small but interesting changes in the five partial coefficients for desegregation (column F) among the various subsets of districts further suggest that Coleman's choice of cases tainted his results. Indeed, the final two coefficients (column F, rows 4 and 5) show modest *negative* relationships between desegregation and decline in white enrollment, although they do not approach statistical significance.

The plot thickens as we push our analysis beyond Coleman's, which was largely confined to white Americans even though the policy issue even more crucially involves black Americans. Using the same format as table 6, table 7 repeats the analysis for the percentage *gains* in *black* student enrollment.

We should clarify one potentially confusing difference between tables 6 and 7. In table 6, following Coleman, we were using *declines* in white enrollment;

TABLE 6

Prediction of Decline in White Enrollment (1968-1973) for Various
Subsets of Large School Districts

| | First-order correlations of decline in white enrollment with: | | | Partial correlations of decline in white enrollment with: | | |
	A. Prop. black, 1968	B. Desegre- gation, 1968–1973	C. Natural log system size, 1972	D. Three- variable multiple correlation	E. Prop. black (size and desegregation held constant)	F. Desegre- gation (size and prop. black held constant)
1. Original 19 districts	.610	−.062	.003	.612	.610	.059
2. Original districts plus Denver and San Francisco	.522	−.026	−.048	.535	.531	.087
3. 27 districts whose cities rank in 50 largest	.577	−.174	−.081	.583	.556	.023
4. 21 districts of (2) plus Miami, Jackson- ville, Nashville, and Fort Lauderdale	.516	−.256	.034	.525	.470	−.108
5. Full 30 districts	.574	−.298	.020	.584	.523	−.123

Data Sources: For the original nineteen "largest" school districts plus those of Denver, San Francisco, Albuquerque, Newark, Charlotte, Cincinnati, and Seattle, the data for these analyses are taken from James S. Coleman, Sara D. Kelly, and John A. Moore, *'Trends in School Segregation, 1968–73*. The Urban Institute (Washington, D.C.: Aug. 1975), Appendix 3. For the four cities omitted from Coleman's analyses and Appendix 3 (Miami, Fort Lauderdale, Jacksonville, and Nashville), enrollment data are from the same HEW source utilized by Coleman; and the desegregation estimates are taken from Farley's index for elementary desegregation, 1967–1972, which for other districts closely approximates Coleman's index for all grade levels, 1968–1973.

now in table 7 we are looking at *gains* in black enrollment. These two dependent variables are negatively correlated for all thirty cities ($r = -0.34$). In other words, white and black enrollments across these large urban districts were positively associated, tending to rise or fall together during this five-year period.

The fact that both white and black enrollments decline in districts with high proportions of black students suggests that this variable acts as a surrogate for other factors. Thus, large cities with a high proportion of Blacks often have highly unfavorable tax bases, old housing stocks, declining employment, and other financial problems.

TABLE 7

Prediction of Black Enrollment Gains (1968–1973) for Various Subsets of Large School Districts

	First-order correlations with:				Partial correlations with:	
	A. Prop. black, 1968	B. Desegre-gation, 1968–1973	C. Natural log system size, 1972	D. Three-variable multiple correlation	E. Prop. black (size and desegregation held constant)	F. Desegre-gation (size and prop. black held constant)
1. Original 19 districts	−.583	.247	.000	.605	−.565	.198
2. Original districts plus Denver and San Francisco	−.490	.193	.056	.515	−.467	.145
3. 27 districts whose cities rank in 50 largest	−.486	.256	.162	.527	−.428	.145
4. 21 Districts of (2) plus Miami, Jackson-ville, Nashville, and Fort Lauderdale	−.491	.237	.060	.517	−.451	.132
5. Full 30 districts	−.505	.283	.126	.550	−.455	.175

Data Sources: Same as for Table 6.

Of greater interest is the contrasting operation of the desegregation variable in the two tables. In table 6, we have noted virtually no effect of desegregation upon white losses, although there was some slight variation according to which subset of big-city systems we used. Yet in table 7, across all five subsets of districts, desegregation has a modest but consistent *positive* association with black-enrollment gains (column B). Part of this relationship is indirectly due to the fact that cities with low proportions of Blacks have had more desegregation; thus, the coefficients are substantially reduced when we control for proportion black and system size (column F).

These analyses of white and black student enrollments lead to a conclusion that is in stark contrast to Coleman's. When viewed in a five-year perspective, *desegregation had no discernible effect on the general trend of decline in white enrollment in the nation's truly largest urban school districts*. It is particularly important for policy makers to observe that districts which are metropolitan in scope (Miami, Fort Lauderdale, Jacksonville, Tampa, Nashville, and Charlotte) seem especially resistant to the phenomenon (figure 2). Given that these districts are in the South, this resistance is especially noteworthy. Our analyses suggest further that desegregation *may* help enlarge black enrollments, perhaps by providing hope to black communities that public education for their children will improve. Our larger point is simply that a rounded scientific and policy perspective on interracial processes requires careful attention to black as well as white Americans.

A Proposed Resolution

Since all four of these "white flight" studies employ essentially the same HEW data base, there should be an underlying resolution of the discrepant findings. We believe that there is such a resolution, and that it consists of the following six generalizations that one or more of the four studies support and none contradicts.

There has been an enormous, long-term trend of Whites leaving the central cities for the suburbs and Blacks coming into the largest central cities. This trend began in many areas after World War I, gained momentum throughout the nation after World War II, and represents a "triumph of national housing policy."[63] Consistently during this period, federal programs such as urban renewal, public housing, Model Cities, discriminatory mortgage programs of the Veterans Administration and the Federal Housing Administration, and even federal highway construction have furthered the separation of the races between city and suburb. This separation antedated school desegregation by decades. This trend toward residential segregation has been so massive that school desegregation could have at most a relatively small impact. Inflation, energy shortages, the decline in black out-migration from the South, and the movement of Blacks to the suburbs could slow the trend in the future.

The studies indicate that desegregation has little or no effect on "white flight" in small and medium-sized cities. The few cases in which desegregation was accompanied by substantial decline in white enrollment often involved special factors unrelated to desegregation.

The studies also indicate that desegregation has little or no effect on "white flight" in metropolitan school districts. Figure 2 shows that the six southern metropolitan school districts in our sample of the thirty largest districts—Miami, Jacksonville, Tampa, Nashville, Charlotte, and Fort Lauderdale—experienced a high degree of desegregation and, correspondingly, a low decline in white enrollment.

[63] Orfield, pp. 18–20.

Court-ordered desegregation has had no greater effect on "white flight" than equivalent non–court-ordered desegregation. Rossell's data on this point are summarized in table 4.

The decline of both white and black enrollment in large urban school systems is related to the proportion of the system's enrollment which is black. This generalization must be qualified in two ways. First, this is not true for all cities, But in general, as revealed in tables 6 and 7, the relationship holds for both races. Second, the fact that both white and black enrollments varied in the same way with proportion black suggests that, in addition to racial factors, this variable is a surrogate for a range of variables—such as receding tax bases, old housing, and high unemployment rates—which characterize districts with relatively high percentages of Blacks.

Extensive school desegregation in the largest non-metropolitan school districts, particularly in the South, may hasten "white flight" in the first year of the process, but at least part of this effect may disappear in later years. Coleman showed only a one-year effect, part of which probably reflected neighborhood transition. Rossell also showed this effect in the first year for rapidly desegregating urban districts in the North. But she showed, too, that by the second and third years these same districts have an average rate of decline in white enrollment below both their own pre-desegregation rate and the rates of other districts (tables 4 and 5). It seems, then, that, with the onset of school desegregation, some white families may well hasten their already formed plans to move to the suburbs, especially if there is pro-segregationist political leadership as in Memphis and Boston. But a longer period of observation suggests that this first-year loss is often a short-term phenomenon and may be followed by a loss in later years which is lower than normal.

The Interviews Continue

The media continued to devote attention to Coleman's views throughout August and September. Walter Goodman published an interview in the *New York Times Magazine* entitled "Integration, Yes: Busing, No." Coleman repeated his now-familiar arguments and discussed his entitlement idea that central-city children be allowed to attend any school in their metropolitan area. Intermeshed with comments on his research were renewed attacks upon busing: "What's wrong with compulsory busing is that it's a restriction of rights. We should be expanding people's rights, not restricting them."[64]

[64] Goodman, p. 48.

In this interview, Coleman introduced two new pieces of data, both questionable, to support his argument. He stated flatly that "surveys indicate that a majority of blacks as well as whites oppose busing."[65] This assertion conflicts with the results of numerous national surveys. A November 1974 Gallup survey, for example, established that 75 percent of "non-white" respondents in a national sample favored "busing school children to achieve better racial balance in schools."[66] Coleman also chose this interview as the forum in which to present for the first time a large-district analysis which, he argued, indicated that school desegregation causes "white flight":

> Eleven cities out of the first 19 experienced little or no desegregation at all between 1968 and 1973. Based on the white loss that occurred in these 11 cities in 1968–69, they would have been expected to lose 15 percent of white students between 1969 and 1973; their actual loss was 18 percent, only slightly greater than expected. Eight cities experienced some desegregation; some of those experienced large desegregation, others not so large. Those eight cities, based on their losses in 1968–69, before desegregation occurred, would have been expected to lose only 7 percent of white students between 1969 and 1973; they actually lost 26 percent, nearly four times what would have been expected.[67]

This misleading statement actually refers to the *third* analysis, which had not yet been made public. This analysis, as we have seen, was to appear in modified form in the fourth version of Coleman's ever-changing study.[68] The casual Sunday *Times* reader might have concluded that even mild desegregation causes a fourfold increase in "white flight," instead of the more modest increase projected by Coleman's own earlier one-year models positing extreme conditions. Moreover, the *Times* reader had no way of knowing that "the first nineteen" cities were arbitrarily selected; that just three southern cities—Atlanta, Memphis, and New Orleans—provided virtually all of the "effect"; or that Tampa, the district with the most desegregation, was the only district of the nineteen to post a *gain* in white student enrollment from 1969 to 1973.

Many leading newspapers now began to run stories critical of Coleman's research and questioning the validity of his often-quoted opinions. John Mathews, a *Washington Star* staff writer, provided a detailed description of Coleman's study

65 Goodman, p. 48.
66 *Gallup Opinion Index Report 113* (Princeton, N.J.: The American Institute of Public Opinion, Nov. 1974).
67 Goodman, p. 11.
68 Coleman et al., Paper IV, pp. 69–70.

under the banner "IS COURT-ORDERED DESEGREGATION SELF-DE-FEATING?"[69] Unlike early stories, Mathews's article cited at length Reynolds Farley's research and took pains to describe the many cities in which large-scale school desegregation had occurred without massive "white flight." William Grant, education writer for the *Detroit Free Press*, contrasted Coleman's cautious style in academic settings with his free-wheeling manner in media interviews.[70] Grant quoted Coleman as saying: "Crime in the cities is clearly correlated with the proportion [of] blacks. It's not something people like to talk about, but . . . whether [whites] leave because of the fear of crime or whether because of the fear of blacks . . . I think it still adds up to the same thing." Coleman's argument, then, seems to be that the range of urban problems that might lead Whites to leave are themselves created by black citizens. This blaming-the-victim argument can, of course, be seriously challenged. In an extensive article that considered both Coleman's position and that of his critics, Steve Twomey, education writer for the *Philadelphia Inquirer*, stressed Coleman's novel metropolitan entitlement strategy and quoted his description of his critics as "a lot of . . . people who would rather pursue a common path and attempt to ignore the fact that this [desegregation] may be having unintended and undesired consequences."[71]

Coleman continued to make unfortunate *ad hominem* attacks on his critics in his second intervention in the Boston school-desegregation case. On August 27, 1975, he provided the anti-busing Boston Home and School Association with a second affidavit, much of which was a reply to criticisms of his work.[72] Coleman repeated the argument he had made in his *New York Times Magazine* interview, which implied that school desegregation multiplies "white flight" by a factor of four. This, he contended, ". . . should leave little doubt in any but the most fixed mind that substantial desegregation in a large city produces substantial increases in the rate of loss of whites from the city's schools."[73] Coleman predicted that "full-scale desegregation in Boston, occurring this fall, will have substantial effects in bringing about an additional loss of whites," and closed his affidavit with a blast at the present authors:

[69] "Is Court-Ordered Desegregation Self-Defeating?" *Washington Star*, 4 Sept. 1975, Sec. A, p. 1, cols. 1–6, and p. 10, cols. 3–8.

[70] "Sociologist's Busing Switch Based on Questionable Data," *Detroit Free Press*, 19 Aug. 1975, Sec. A, p. 3, cols. 6–8, and p. 16, cols. 1–8.

[71] "Busing Advocate Changes Course," *Philadelphia Inquirer*, 31 Aug. 1975, Sec. 1, p. 1, cols. 1–4, and p. 2, cols. 1–4.

[72] Coleman, Affidavit II.

[73] Coleman, Affidavit II, p. 5.

I cannot conclude without mentioning what seems to me an unfortunate phenomenon in social science. On certain questions, there appears to be a kind of conspiracy of silence, and then a rush to the attack when anyone dares to break the silence. I have the impression that if Professors Green and Pettigrew saw the fires in the sky during the riots of 1967, they would have attributed them to an extraordinary display of the Northern Lights. I believe that it does no one any good in the long run for us to blind ourselves to reality, because it is reality, not our fond hopes about it, which measures the effectiveness of government actions.[74]

Affidavits, unlike depositions, are not subject to cross-examination. But Coleman's second affidavit was answered two weeks later in an affidavit submitted by Norman Chachkin, the one lawyer who had participated in the review panel at The Urban Institute.[75] In addition to raising again some of the panel's methodological concerns, Chachkin made two points. First, Coleman had indicated in the panel discussion that his views on the proper role of the courts in school desegregation were personal and not based on the results of his study. Second, Coleman had also stated both in the discussion and in writing that his study was not intended for use in judicial proceedings. Chachkin quoted from the final printed version of Coleman's paper:

> It is useful also to point out that data such as these which show the indirect and unintended consequences of school desegregation actions may be relevant for certain desegregation actions, but not for others. They are relevant for an executive or legislative body which is attempting in its action to achieve a desirable social consequence. They are not relevant for a court decision which is acting to insure equal protection under the 14th Amendment.[76]

Coleman's public pronouncements continued unabated into the fall. He wrote another article reiterating his views in the October 1975 issue of *Phi Delta Kappan*. He now conceded that his findings could well be interpreted as affording "a strong argument in favor of eliminating segregation at the metropolitan level. . . ."[77] But he flatly rejected this possibility.

On September 22, 1975, Coleman rendered his third affidavit for the Boston Home and School Association. This time he replied to Christine Rossell's con-

---

74 Coleman, Affidavit II, pp. 5–6.
75 Affidavit of Norman J. Chachkin, Morgan v. Kerrigan, 9 Sept. 1975.
76 Coleman, Paper IV, p. 5.
77 "Racial Segregation in the Schools: New Research with New Policy Implications," *Phi Delta Kappan*, 57 (1975), 75–78.

flicting research, which the plaintiffs had submitted to the court.[78] In his July television appearance in Boston, his three affidavits, and his repeated interviews with Boston reporters, Coleman had given particular attention to that tense city even though the federal school-desegregation order had been handed down long before. Yet, except for admitting that his television appearance "may be mischievous," Coleman never publicly discussed the possibility that his warnings that Boston would experience a massive white exodus might act as a self-fulfilling prophecy.

Later in the fall, Coleman shifted his attention to Louisville, Kentucky, the nation's other desegregation trouble spot. On October 28, testifying along with Louisville and Kentucky officials before the Senate Judiciary Committee in Washington, he briefly reviewed his Analysis II and maintained that "policies of school desegregation which go beyond the elimination of *de jure* segregation . . . are counterproductive in our large cities. . . ."[79] He did not specify which, if any, federal court decisions had ever gone "beyond the elimination of *de jure* segregation." (We know of none.) Interestingly enough, Coleman opposed the proposed anti-busing amendments to the Constitution as improper. "This, I recognize, is not a very satisfactory position," he concluded, "because it leaves me with only the hope that the courts will themselves see the incorrectness of the precedent that has evolved; but it is the only position I find myself able to take."[80]

On December 5, Coleman delivered the major address at a national conference on busing alternatives held in Louisville. He repeated his anti-busing arguments and his "white flight" conclusions. In yet another telephone interview, he had told Berl Schwartz of the *Louisville Times* (October 8, 1975) that the conference could serve to "give legitimacy to anti-busing sentiments."[81]

Yet three days after the conference, at a special session of the United States Commission on Civil Rights in Washington, D.C., Coleman suddenly withdrew his firm conclusion about "white flight": "What is not clear is whether desegregation

[78] Reply Affidavit of James S. Coleman, Morgan v. Kerrigan, 22 Sept. 1975. Hereafter referred to as Affidavit III. Coleman noted some of the differences between Rossell's study and his own that we have discussed previously; he particularly stressed her different operational definition of "desegregation." He also overestimated the loss of white students from Boston's public schools during desegregation, because apparently he was unaware that the Boston School Committee had included Spanish-speaking pupils in the "white" total for 1973–1974 but excluded them in 1974–1975. This shifting designation of Latino children over recent years has also occurred in Florida and California and has probably caused Coleman's estimate of "white flight" in these areas to be inflated.

[79] James S. Coleman, "Testimony of James S. Coleman before the Senate Judiciary Committee," Washington, D.C., 28 Oct. 1975.

[80] Coleman, "Testimony," p. 4.

[81] Berl Schwartz, "Conference Being Set Up on Alternatives to Busing," *Louisville Times*, 8 Oct. 1975, Sec. B, p. 1, cols. 1–3.

itself induces an increased movement of whites from the desegregated district,"[82] Coleman told the Commission—thousands of headlines and eight months after he had initiated his campaign.

Coleman's Opposition to Court-Ordered School Desegregation

We have seen how limited Coleman's research results are, and how tenuous is their connection to his publicly expressed political views against court-ordered school desegregation. A review of his dozens of statements in articles, in affidavits, on television, and to interviewers suggests that his opposition to such judicial decisions as that in the *Swann* case derives, at root, less from his research than from two related and publicly expressed beliefs:

1. Change in racial relations should flow not from the federal courts, but from the will of the community. It is critical that Whites accept such change, for Whites ultimately have the power to defeat it.

2. Only a small part of segregation is *de jure,* that is, a result of state action. Most segregation, especially school segregation, is *de facto,* the result of individual actions, and thus beyond the appropriate reach of the law. Under the Fourteenth Amendment, federal courts are obliged to end all *de jure* segregation in public education; but they are wrong when they attempt to undo *de facto* school segregation as well, for in so doing they abridge individual rights.

Let us consider each of these beliefs in more detail.

The Will of the Community

Coleman's argument is remarkably similar to the position of the nineteenth-century Social Darwinists. "Stateways cannot change folkways" was their dogma, and this reasoning is embedded in the 1896 Supreme Court decision in *Plessy v. Ferguson*[83] which affirmed the legitimacy of "separate-but-equal" public facilities.

But the past generation has experienced change in racial relations that William Graham Sumner and his followers could not have foreseen. In 1954, the segment of white America most hostile to the reduction of discrimination against black people resided in the rural South. Yet in desegregating public facilities, the polls,

---

82 Coleman, "School Desegregation and Loss of Whites from Large Central-City School Districts," paper presented to the United States Commission on Civil Rights, 8 Dec. 1975, Washington, D.C., p. 7. Hereafter referred to as Paper VI.
83 163 U.S. 537 (1896).

and even schools, the rural South has made at least as much progress as any other part of the nation. To be sure, serious racial problems remain in the rural South, but the progress there is genuine and profound.

Most of this progress obviously did not flow from "the will of the community" but was imposed largely by government intervention—not the least of which was from the federal judiciary. How could this forward leap in the individual rights of the most oppressed portion of black America have taken place against the will of powerful white communities? Coleman himself, in his brilliant *Resources for Social Change: Race in the United States*, supplies part of the answer.[84] Blacks, even in the rural South, had personal and collective resources which could be converted into power and social change. Access to litigation was and is one of these resources, although Coleman rightly notes its limitations if unaccompanied by other assets.[85]

Another part of the answer to how such sweeping change has been possible in the rural South lies in the power of a *fait accompli*. Indeed, opinion surveys record that the most startling shifts in racial attitudes and behavior among white Americans occurred *after* racial desegregation had been achieved, often under court order.[86]

This is not to argue that mobilized white opposition cannot thwart progress in racial relations. Educational desegregation, like any other program, can be made to fail if national, state, or local leaders, such as those in Boston's school system, dedicate their efforts to making it fail. "White flight" at the onset of desegregation may even be induced, we suspect, by the dire predictions of such leaders. A principal objection to Coleman's position, then, is that, by implication, it takes the success of racist opposition to desegregation as reason for the United States to forsake its still unattained goal of racial justice.

De Facto *Segregation and Individual Rights*

Coleman's second underlying belief is remarkable for two reasons. It assumes that most racial segregation, especially in schools, is *de facto* and therefore should not fall under the "state action" provisions of the Fourteenth Amendment. It

---

84 *Resources for Social Change: Race in the United States* (New York: Wiley, 1971).

85 Coleman, *Resources*, pp. 54–60.

86 Gallup polls for May 1963, May 1966, July 1969, March 1970, and October 1973. The American Institute of Public Opinion, Princeton, N.J. Additional evidence that demonstrates the growth of pro-desegregation attitudes among white Southerners after desegregation is provided by Herbert H. Hyman and Paul B. Sheatsley, "Attitudes toward Desegregation," *Scientific American*, 211 (1964), 16–23.

further assumes that this segregation is *de facto* because of "individual actions"— Whites and Blacks freely making residential choices, unfettered by such structural limitations as government-sanctioned discrimination in housing and employment. We believe that both of these assumptions are wrong.

In the few available historical studies of the origins of school segregation within northern cities, virtually all segregation has been found to be *de jure* in origin. Racial discrimination and segregation do not just happen in America; they are planned and provided for, sometimes years in advance, by government agencies— school boards, city councils, state legislatures, and often federal bureaus as well.[87] The briefs of plaintiffs in Boston, Detroit, San Francisco, and other cities literally bulge with detailed evidence for these contentions. Such compelling evidence helps explain why conservative, strict-constructionist, federal district-court judges have repeatedly found system-wide *de jure* school segregation throughout the North. In so doing, they have not, as Coleman implies, abused judicial power; their decisions have been based on an overwhelming mass of evidence,[88] with which Coleman has apparently not acquainted himself.

Coleman emphasizes that the growing trend of school segregation between central city and suburb is caused mainly by individual actions and therefore should not be addressed by the courts with metropolitan remedies. Coming from a sociologist, this argument is perplexing, for its seems to deny institutional structure and to assume that society is composed simply of the sum of its freely acting individual members. It disregards a history of residential discrimination and of state action to bring about a pattern of black cities with white suburbs. The social-science research literature documents beyond dispute the federal government's involvement, since the passage of the first national housing act in 1935,[89] in creating this pattern. Inter-district segregation did not "just happen" any more than did intra-district segregation.

When Coleman argues that metropolitan remedies and extensive busing for desegregation are wrong because they limit individual rights, he is speaking largely of white rights and, in effect, of a white right to discriminate. Recall his entitle-

---

[87] For evidence on the widespread patterns of blatant *de jure* segregation and discrimination in the northern states even before the Civil War, see Leon F. Litwack, *North of Slavery* (Chicago: Univ. of Chicago Press, 1961). For historical evidence on education, see David B. Tyack, *The One Best System: A History of American Education* (Cambridge, Mass.: Harvard Univ. Press, 1974), pp. 109–25, 217–29, 279–85.

[88] Abrams.

[89] See Thomas F. Pettigrew, ed., *Racial Discrimination in the United States* (New York: Harper & Row, 1975).

ment plan, whereby each black child in the central city would have the right to attend any school in the metropolitan area up to a fixed percentage in each school. Notice how this proposed remedy, which constitutes his principal suggestion in 1975 for extending black rights, places the full burden of desegregation on the black child.

In short, Coleman would limit the federal courts in urban cases exclusively to intra-district remedies that would involve little or no busing or mixing of social classes. This is another point where his recommendations and his research findings diverge, for his data on the separation of the races between cities and suburbs show clearly that observing these limitations would effectively mean no racial desegregation of the public schools of large urban districts. Unless he is opposed to racial desegregation as a goal—and he has insisted in many interviews that this is not the case—we cannot reconcile his political position with his own data on urban school-desegregation trends.

In the last analysis, our major policy disagreement with Coleman involves the issue of metropolitan desegregation. His data and our own on the relationship between "white flight" and desegregation in six metropolitan districts indicate that metropolitan approaches are essential if desegregation is to be attained. Such remedies for segregation do not necessitate one huge school district. They can result in more districts than now exist, for they are meant only to disallow urban boundaries which function as racial "Berlin walls." In many areas, metropolitan approaches could *minimize* transportation as well as deter "white flight," and they could avoid placing the major burden of desegregation on working-class children, as in Boston. Inter-district arrangements would allow most schools to draw students from a wider geographical area and thus achieve a stable proportion of Blacks and Whites. In sum, metropolitan approaches to school desegregation could eliminate the constraints of present political boundaries.

We are not blind to demographic changes by race, although we believe that "black containment" is a more accurate descriptive term than "white flight." We do not believe that Coleman has convincingly proven that school desegregation *causes* "white flight," as he himself candidly admitted in his Civil Rights Commission paper. But we are aware—indeed, as race-relations specialists, we have for fifteen years been aware—that large central cities have long been becoming ever blacker and suburban rings ever whiter. We agree with Coleman completely that this is one of the most basic and threatening realities of modern race relations in America. We further agree that public policies brought this reality about—not court-ordered school desegregation in the 1970's but federal housing policies from the 1930's on. And under present housing policies these trends will continue with or without school desegregation.

Given this situation, what do we do about urban school desegregation? We agree that the present situation of court-ordered school desegregation confined within large central-city districts is not ideal. Coleman suggests that we should abandon such court orders and try interracial marriage and voluntary methods that have already failed. We believe that rather than abandoning the racial integration of public education, we should fashion our remedies to fit the problem. Since urban desegregation must overcome metropolitan-wide obstacles, it must be planned on a metropolitan-wide basis. This is why for over a decade we have sought support for metropolitan approaches to school desegregation.

Social Science and Public Policy

This article has not been easy to write. The information necessary to evaluate Coleman's much-publicized research has been consistently difficult to obtain. Throughout the furor created by Coleman's statements, there has been confusion about where his limited research ends and his sweeping opposition to court-ordered desegregation begins. When critics questioned his views, they repeatedly suffered *ad hominem* abuse. Some critics have hurled such abuse at Coleman. We regret all such *ad hominem* remarks deeply. They make good copy for the mass media, perhaps, but they cheapen the debate, lower the public's respect for social science, and divert public attention from real issues. Indeed, the whole episode goes beyond racial issues or attacks on personalities, to raise painful ethical questions about the relationship between social science and public policy.[90]

From April until August of 1975, the social-science community did not receive the analysis upon which Coleman's widely publicized statements were reportedly based. The details of the first analysis were never released; the second draft of the paper presented the details of an entirely new analysis with a radically different research design. All told, over an eight-month period, Coleman presented five editions of his paper (plus a thirty-nine–page erratum edition) containing three contrasting analyses of his data. Although Coleman's research was constantly changing, his expressed views remained substantially the same. Telephone calls to The Urban Institute in June requesting methodological detail were summarily

---

[90] See, for example, Thomas F. Pettigrew, "Sociological Consulting in Race Relations," *American Sociologist*, 6 (supplementary issue) (1971), 44–47.

rejected on the grounds that the analysis was "still in progress," yet there had already been two months of national publicity about policy recommendations said to flow from this still-in-progress research. Coleman's only statement about this serious problem appeared late in August in his second affidavit against the plaintiffs in the Boston desegregation case:

> First, many of the complaints in the Pettigrew-Green paper, the Weinberg paper, and the *New York Times* article are complaints about the absence of methodological detail in a paper presented orally to a lay audience. For example, in that presentation, I had no chance to state which 19 cities in the analysis as the largest central city school districts [*sic*]. Boston is one of these cities. . . . It is unfortunate that the full report was not available earlier to those commentators, and I am to blame for that.[91]

What made the four-month delay even more "unfortunate" was the consistent confusion between Coleman's personal opinions and his research findings. Most of the hundreds of articles and editorials about the episode presented Coleman's views as if they were the results of a new and massive study of urban desegregation. For example, the cover caption to his article in the October 1975 *Phi Delta Kappan* read: "HAS FORCED BUSING FAILED? JAMES COLEMAN OFFERS NEW INSIGHTS FROM RECENT RESEARCH." "New insights from [his] recent research" could not have concerned the success or failure of busing, of course, for the research did not even include a measure of busing.

Social scientists, like other citizens, have a right to express their political views on any subject without the support of research results. Problems arise, it seems to us, when a social scientist misrepresents or allows misrepresentation of personal opinions as results of extensive scientific investigation. If the social scientist in question is highly respected and popularly known, and if he or she chooses to engage in a mass-media campaign to influence public policy, these problems are exacerbated.[92]

Coleman's statements and personal attacks upon his critics suggest that he is certain his views are correct. His data, he told the Boston federal court, "should leave little doubt in any but the most fixed mind that substantial desegregation

---

[91] Coleman, Affidavit II, p. 1.

[92] Coleman has expressed surprise that two social scientists who have often expressed their views could criticize him for expressing his views. This misses our point completely. It is the persistent confusion of political opinions with new research findings in an intense media campaign which concerns us—not the exercise of Coleman's right to express his views.

in a large city produces substantial increases in the rate of loss of whites from the city's schools. . . ."[93] Those who dare disagree with him must suffer from "motivated blindness"; must be part of "a kind of conspiracy of silence"; must mistake race-riot fires for "an extraordinary display of the Northern Lights"; must be "people who would rather pursue a common path and attempt to ignore the fact that this [desegregation] may be having unintended and undesired consequences." Such summary dismissal of criticism is likely to cause a scientist to ignore the accumulation of contrasting evidence on the same issue that other competent and honest scientists have uncovered.

We firmly believe that social science can and should influence public-policy issues on which it can responsibly bring research and theory to bear. Perhaps specialized groups of social scientists, checked in part by peer review, could best perform this task. Individual social scientists could also carry out this function responsibly by basing their views on published and widely available material and by presenting them in situations, such as courtrooms and legislative committee hearings, where they are subject to formal cross-examination or at least to informed questioning. Mass-media campaigns are a hazardous way to introduce social science into public-policy debates. The Coleman episode of 1975 is the most extensive example of such a campaign in sociology, but it is by no means the first nor, we fear, the last.

Communicating material from the social sciences via the media is complicated by limitations in both institutions. Few social scientists other than economists have experience in dealing with the media. Until recently, sociologists, psychologists, and political scientists have seldom been taken seriously in matters of public importance. To be candid, academicians are often flattered by sudden attention from the media and offer bold views which contrast markedly with the cautious presentations they make to their colleagues. And professional associations offer little guidance.

Within the news media, social science has yet to be elevated to the status of a regular, specialized "beat." One television network and a few newspapers and magazines now have economics reporters, but the term "science writers" still refers largely to specialists in the physical sciences. All too often, non-specialists fit their stories into a "human-interest" format that emphasizes *ad hominem* charges and countercharges among the participants in a controversy, while ignoring the central issues.

93 Coleman, Affidavit II, p. 5–6.

The Russell Sage Foundation, Philip Meyer of the Knight Newspapers,[94] and a few other individuals and organizations have directed attention in recent years to this dangerous incongruity between the news media and the social-science profession. Unless structural changes are made in both institutions and each learns to take the other more seriously, the nation will continue to witness examples of extremely inadequate reporting of social-science findings relevant to public policy. In time, the public might understandably conclude that social scientists have nothing to contribute to policy debates except their own highly politicized opinions.

[94] Philip Meyer, *Precision Journalism: A Reporter's Introduction to Social Science Methods* (Bloomington, Ind.: Indiana Univ. Press, 1973). The Russell Sage Foundation sponsors a joint program in social science and journalism and periodically publishes papers from its studies.

B.

RESPONSE TO PROFESSORS PETTIGREW AND GREEN:

Pettigrew and Green, in a paper that appeared in the last issue of this journal [Thomas F. Pettigrew and Robert L. Green, "School Desegregation in Large Cities: A Critique of the Coleman 'White Flight' Thesis," *HER,* February 1976, pp. 1–53], carried out a detailed critique of my recent statements and writing on school desegregation and disputed the results of my research, which showed an accelerated loss of Whites when school desegregation occurred in large central cities. Their paper is only the latest in an enormous barrage of material designed to counter statements I have made and to undermine the results of my recent research. This barrage ranges from press conferences (two last June, others since) and symposia with the press in attendance, to papers in academic and semiacademic journals. One might ask why all the frantic activity, and I will ask that later. But first I would like to reply to points raised in the Pettigrew-Green paper.

The most important question is the substantive question: does desegregation in large central cities accelerate the loss of Whites from those cities, or not? My colleagues and I find that it does, while some others, including Reynolds Farley, Christine Rossell, and in their own analysis, Pettigrew and Green, do not. There are two basic reasons for the difference, along with some special reasons in the case of Rossell. One is that the three studies which find no effect confound metropolitan-area or county-wide desegregation with central-city desegregation. The other is that we examined losses in the year of desegregation itself, while Farley and Pettigrew-Green consider losses over a five-year period (although about half of the desegregation took place in the latter part of that period).

The confounding of central-city and metropolitan desegregation arises because Pettigrew-

From James S. Coleman, "Response to Professors Pettigrew and Green." In Correspondence, *Harvard Educational Review,* May 1976, *46*(2), 217-224. Copyright © 1976 by President and Fellows of Harvard College.

Green and Farley include in their analysis of large cities a number of cities not classified as central-city school districts by the U.S. Office of Education. This can be seen in Pettigrew-Green's figure 2, which relates loss of Whites to desegregation. In the upper left quadrant (high desegregation, low white loss) fall Fort Lauderdale, Tampa, Miami, Charlotte-Mecklenburg, Nashville, Jacksonville, and Albuquerque. *All* of these school districts are county-wide districts, covering all or nearly all the metropolitan area. Only three are classified by the U.S. Office of Education as central-city districts (and most are in the "sun belt" that is currently experiencing a population boom). In addition, most have a small proportion of Blacks. It is not surprising that these metropolitan areas do not experience the same loss of Whites when desegregation occurs as do central-city districts with large black populations in the large older cities.[1] Thus, the analyses include a mixture of low desegregation-induced losses in metropolitan-wide districts in growing urban areas with high desegregation-induced losses in central-city districts. This is compounded by the fact that there has been more desegregation in these metropolitan-wide low-proportion-black districts than in larger cities with already declining populations.

By separating these factors out, we showed in our analysis (equation 3 referred to by Pettigrew-Green) that one would expect negligible losses of Whites where the proportion black in the district is low and where there are no predominantly white suburbs. I do not fault Farley for not taking the latter into account, for when his analysis was carried out, it was not apparent that the availability of predominantly white suburban school districts in the metropolitan area was such an important factor in the acceleration of white loss when desegregation occurs. Pettigrew and Green, however, have no excuse, for their analysis was carried out in full cognizance of our findings on this point. By adding these metropolitan-wide districts, they have only restated results that we obtained; but they give the appearance of refuting those results.

Second, both Farley and Pettigrew-Green use the five-year losses, from 1967 to 1972 in Farley's case and from 1968 to 1973 in Pettigrew-Green's case. What happened is this: about half the desegregation occurred in the latter half of this period (whichever period is taken), so the use of five-year losses combines about equal quantities of *pre*-desegregation losses and *post*-desegregation losses. Thus for the desegregating cities, the pre- and post-desegregation losses are completely confounded by this procedure.

One might still say, however, that the post-desegregation losses, though diluted by this procedure, should nevertheless lead to enlarged five-year losses, even though the five years

1 In their analysis Pettigrew and Green added eight cities to my twenty-two largest central-city districts. Five were county-wide or metropolitan-wide districts which desegregated; three (Cincinnati, Seattle, and Newark) were cities that did not. All five of the desegregating districts had been *gaining* white student population before desegregation; all three of the non-desegregating districts had been losing. It is interesting to note, though Pettigrew and Green fail to do so, that even in these metropolitan districts that had been gaining Whites, four of the five experienced a loss of white students in the years they desegregated.

included on the average only about two and a half years of desegregation. The losses *are* enlarged by desegregation, but the reason this does not show up as larger losses than non-desegregating districts in Farley's and Pettigrew-Green's five-year method is that, on the average, desegregating districts had *lower* pre-desegregation losses than did non-desegregating district. Non-desegregating districts were, on the whole, larger, older, more in the North, with a higher proportion black, and with more white suburbs than desegregating districts. They had recent histories of greater population decline. For example, projecting the pre-desegregation losses of 1968–69 forward for the four additional years to 1973 would predict for the ten desegregating cities of the twenty-two large cities I studied a loss of 10 percent of the Whites by 1973. Projecting forward the 1968–69 losses for the twelve non-desegregating cities would predict a loss of 17 percent of the Whites. Again, Farley had no reason to suspect this, and cannot be faulted for not taking it into account; but again, Pettigrew and Green have no excuse for obscuring this fact; they were fully aware of it when they carried out their analysis.

It is, then, principally for these two reasons that the analyses of Farley and Pettigrew-Green give results different from ours. Rossell's analysis was of a different sort altogether. For her measure of desegregation, she uses the proportion of children reassigned by the district. This, however, does not measure the actual change in segregation. For example, she classifies Baltimore as having engaged in "medium desegregation" from 1970 to 1971 on the basis of "pupil reassignment." But Baltimore showed exactly the *same* degree of segregation in 1971 as in 1970: a value of .70 on the index of segregation in both years. Secondly, for her dependent variable, she did not measure the loss of Whites but the change in the proportion white in the system. As Pettigrew and Green note, this may be affected by changes in numbers of Blacks or other population groups, not only by changes in numbers of Whites. To exemplify how white loss is obscured in Rossell's analysis, she concluded in the case of Boston that the general trend in loss of Whites was not much affected in 1974 by desegregation.[2] But the figures tell a very different story: the average loss of Whites for the six years before 1974 was 3.7 percent per year; in 1974, when partial desegregation occurred, it was 16.2 percent.[3] When a method can obscure such a change as this, then the method obviously has serious shortcomings.

[2] Christine H. Rossell, "School Desegregation and White Flight," *Political Science Quarterly*, *90*, Winter 1975–76, 675–95. See footnote 24.

[3] Pettigrew and Green incorrectly state in footnote 78 that Spanish-speaking pupils in Boston were classified as "white" in 1973 and separated out in 1974. This is not so; in my data from HEW and the Boston School Committee, the Spanish-surnamed pupils are for all years considered separately. They constitute 5.4 percent of the total in 1972, 6.5 percent in 1973, 8.0 percent in 1974, and 8.4 percent in 1975. Thus the white loss is as I have stated it: 16.2 percent in 1974 (with a projected 7.9 percent loss in the spring of 1975, which grew to 18.9 percent by December 31, 1975, after Phase II of Boston's desegregation plan was implemented). I pointed this out to Green in December, yet their error persists.

There is a further issue about the particular cities used in the analysis. Apart from the implications by Pettigrew and Green that our selection of cities was a motivated one (a matter to which I will return), there is the substantive question of how strongly the results were influenced by the particular set of cities used. It is clear that for the simpler analyses, such as our equation 1 referred to by Pettigrew-Green, their own analysis, and those of Farley and Rossell, the particular cities would make a difference. However, in our analysis that took into account the availability of predominantly white suburban districts (equation 3), it is equally clear that the particular set of cities does not have a strong effect.[4] Even inclusion of Pettigrew-Green's non-central-city districts covering all or nearly all the metropolitan area would hardly have affected that result, for the result is very similar for two distinct sets of central cities: the largest twenty-one, and the next forty-six in size. These results, reproduced as table 1, indicate that the effects we found are not greatly distorted, as Pettigrew and Green argue, by Atlanta and Memphis, for Atlanta and Memphis are among the largest twenty-one, and not the next forty-six. The table shows the expected percentage of Whites lost in the year of desegregation (partial desegregation consisting of a reduction of .2 in the index of segregation) based on the desegregation experience of 1968–73. The losses vary in each column according to the proportion black in the district; and they vary in each row according to the availability of predominantly white suburban districts. The latter is measured by the "between-district segregation," which if high represents a high disparity between the racial composition of the city schools and those in the surrounding districts.

TABLE 1

Between-district Segregation	Largest 21* Proportion Black			Next 46 Proportion Black		
	.25	.50	.75	.25	.50	.75
.0	2%	10%	17%	3%	6%	9%
.2	9	16	24	8	11	15
.4	15	23	30	14	17	20

*Of the twenty-two cities referred to earlier, Washington is excluded because it is 97 percent black.

The figures for the two groups of cities are very similar, except for larger losses in the larger cities. The entry in the top line and left-hand column for each group shows the expected losses in metropolitan-area districts of the sort that Pettigrew and Green added to the sample: the expected losses are 2 percent and 3 percent—very small, as those metropolitan districts actually showed. But it is in the central-city districts with large proportions

---

4 Similarly, in our analysis of covariance in which each city was a covariate, the particular set of cities has only a small effect.

black and predominantly white suburban districts (the bottom row and third column) where the losses are very great when desegregation occurs—in both sets of cities.

There is one modification of our results that I would now make, but this is a modification that shows somewhat worse consequences of large central-city desegregation than we had found until now. It is important to discover whether it is true, as our data tentatively showed, that the desegregation-induced losses occur only in the year of desegregation, or continue beyond. For if they continue, the long-term consequences of school desegregation are much more dismal for maintaining cities with a racially mixed population than if the losses are confined to the first year. To obtain more evidence on this, I obtained enrollment data by race for 1974 and 1975 from the eight cities among the largest twenty-one that had carried out desegregation of .1 or more in a single year between 1968 and 1973, and for Boston, which carried out such desegregation in 1974. In general, the accelerated losses continue, not as high as in the year of desegregation, but higher than before desegregation. In one city, Memphis, which experienced the greatest desegregation loss (35 percent of the Whites) in 1973, the 1975 figures showed no loss over 1974, apparently because the returns from private schools balanced the other losses. But in most cities, the results were otherwise. This can be seen from the average losses of white students in the two years before desegregation, the year of desegregation, and the four years after, for these nine cities (see table 2). (The data are not as good as one would wish, because data for two years before and four years after desegregation are not available in all cases. Also, some districts annexed suburbs when desegregation occurred, thus understating the losses in the year of desegregation.)

TABLE 2

	Before Desegregation:		Year of Deseg- regation	After Desegregation:			
	2 Years	1 Year		1 Year	2 Years	3 Years	4 Years
Average % loss	4.1%	4.8%	12.4%	7.0%	6.7%	10.1%	8.1%
Number of cities	7	9	9	9	8	5	5

Note: If Memphis and Atlanta are excluded, as Pettigrew and Green would prefer (because their desegregation losses are large), the numbers are all smaller, but the same tendency exists: pre-desegregation, 3.7%, 3.1%; year of desegregation, 8.6%; post-desegregation, 5.2%, 5.6%, 6.1%, 5.2%.

This effect can also be seen by looking at individual cities. In Dallas, the rate of white loss rose from about 2 percent to 9 percent when partial desegregation involving compulsory busing occurred in 1971, and it has stayed there since; in San Francisco, the average rate of loss for the two years before partial desegregation was 6.9 percent, while the average rate after was 11.7 percent per year; in Houston, the rate before partial desegregation was 5.1 percent, and for the six years after has averaged 7.6 percent per year; in Atlanta, the rate in the year before partial desegregation was 7.5 percent, while the rate in the six years has averaged 19.1 percent per year; in Indianapolis, the average rate for the four years before partial desegregation was 4.8 percent and the average rate in the three years after was 7.4 percent; in Denver, the average for three years before partial desegregation was 1.1 percent per year, and for six years after was 6.4 percent. The conclusion that one must draw from these statistics for individual cities is, I believe, that current desegregation policies are having serious long-term demographic effects.

For example, if we consider a city that is 60 percent white and project forward for ten years the average of the two pre-desegregation losses from table 2 (4.1 and 4.8), then assuming the black student population remains constant, the white student population would be 49 percent of the total in ten years. If, however, we assume desegregation occurs and take the desegregation loss, the four post-desegregation losses, the white student population would be only 38 percent of the total. And this is not for an extraordinary city, but only for the average of these nine, which includes few of the oldest and largest American cities most susceptible to loss of Whites. As table 1 shows, the expected loss even in the first year is considerably higher than the average shown in table 2 when the city already has a high proportion black and predominantly white suburban districts outside it. Thus, school desegregation can be predicted to erode the population mix most strongly in those cities that are already least able to maintain a racially mixed population—cities like Detroit, Cleveland, Baltimore, Philadelphia, Chicago, St. Louis. It is in several of these cities, incidentally, that current desegregation suits and HEW administrative actions are being most strongly pursued. The prediction, considering these post-desegregation data, would be for a much greater long-term effect for such cities than shown in our table of projections which Pettigrew-Green include as their table 3. That is, the ten-year effect of strong desegregation for those cities would be expected to be considerably more than the 10 percent difference in proportion black that we showed in that table, because the effect apparently does not stop after the first year in most cities, as we assumed there.

I should add a sentence or two about the charade that Pettigrew and Green go through in examining changes in the black student population in large cities. That it is an empty gesture in the direction of "equity" is evident when one sees that they examine the wrong question. What is important for the integration of our large metropolitan areas is the maintenance of Whites in the central city and the movement of Blacks into the suburbs. Thus, what is important to examine is what's happening to the white student population in the central city and what's happening to the black student population *outside* the city, in the suburbs. In their rush to equity, Pettigrew and Green forget that the problem that has been plaguing Blacks for years, and one of the sources of the increasing segregation in our major cities, has been their exclusion from the suburbs and their enclosure in the city itself.

Pettigrew and Green go beyond an attempt to show that current desegregation plans do not produce white flight; they make a broad attack on various of my actions. They imply that our selection of cities was motivated by the expected results. It was, of course, not so. Pettigrew has known at least since August 4 that the criterion for selection was the largest twenty school districts classified by the U.S. Office of Education as central-city districts; and it was his complaint on that date that this sample contained too little Northern desegregation experience to allow generalization beyond the South that led me to add Denver and San Francisco—two of the next three districts in size, both of which were Northern and had undergone some desegregation. They complain that the data were not available; but the only written request for data from any investigator, made on July 15, was fulfilled on July 21.

Beyond this is the broad issue of my public statements, and the reaction they have produced, including the public statements of those who have declared themselves my opponents. By no means have I sought out the media, much less engaged in mass-media campaign. On the contrary, I remained largely unavailable to reporters, even unreachable by telephone throughout the summer. It was my self-declared opponents, including Pettigrew and Green, who engaged in an extensive campaign, of which the recent paper is a part. They have been aided in this by some nondeclared opponents in the media.

I have, however, written extensively on these matters, I have given testimony before Congress, and I have given affidavits in a court case; Pettigrew and Green have done likewise. I have done so because I believe that the integration actions currently imposed by the courts—most prominently and most recently, compulsory racial balance in large cities—go far beyond eradication of de jure segregation, and thus must be judged not on constitutional grounds but in terms of their consequences. And my research results convince me that these consequences in large central-city school districts are disastrous for the long-term integration of our society, by exacerbating the black-city white-suburb racial separation.

Pettigrew and Green apparently feel otherwise. They are free to express their opinions, and they certainly have done so in a variety of ways. I do not question their right to do so, indeed their obligation to speak out on policy they believe has important consequences. But they have not confined themselves to that. Instead, they have attempted from the outset to throw doubt on our research results and destroy the legitimacy of my opposition to current large-city desegregation actions. I believe the force of this reaction stems from their recognition that when opposition to desegregating actions gains legitimacy, there is no longer a simple division between 'the good guys" favoring any and all desegregating actions and "the bad guys" opposing all desegregation, and then the policies must be judged instead on their merits.

There is, I think, a common belief among those deeply committed to the current policies of compulsory racial balance that social-science research should be wholly in the service of those policies. Several actions follow from this belief. One is to attempt to suppress, counteract, or throw doubt on any research that leads to questioning of these policies.[5] Another is to use favorable research results (even when the research is poorly done) in a very fast and loose way, with no thought of ever being challenged. And the advocates seldom have been challenged, even when the excesses have been great. Eleanor Wolf, for example, shows this strikingly for the Detroit school desegregation case.[6]

I would like now to put professional matters aside, and refocus attention on the substantive issues at hand. Now, when the black population in central cities is stabilizing due to reduced rural-urban migration and reduced birth rates, and when many older cities have major inner-city rebuilding plans, is a time which brings an opportunity to create of our large cities stably integrated urban centers. For some cities, this is a last opportunity, because stabilization can occur only if there is a sufficiently racially-mixed population base in the cities. Affirmative integration policies in schools (for that is what the current court remedies have become, despite the protest that it is only de jure segregation that is being eliminated) should be directed to strengthening and stabilizing that racial mix—not toward destroying it, as many existing desegregation plans are doing.[7]

Because social-science research in this area has been largely in the service of the advocates of compulsory racial balance and their policies, the advocates have enjoyed a comfortable monopoly of legitimacy. Opponents could be labeled segregationists or racists, and guilt by association was a convenient and often-used tool. And now when the remedy can be legitimately questioned on the basis of its consequences, the advocates protest. What is serious and shocking to me is not that the questioning of compulsory racial balance in schools has now become legitimate, but that it has *only* now become legitimate—that social-science research has only recently broken the monopoly of legitimacy so that the policy can be examined on its merits.

If there is to be a lasting consequence of the turmoil that has surrounded my research and writing on this issue over recent months, I trust that it will be a mechanism for breaking such monopolies, such limitation on inquiry and expression, so that destructive policies can no longer be exempt from questioning.

JAMES S. COLEMAN
University of Chicago

[5] Pettigrew has shown such a disposition earlier; the role in which he has cast himself in this case is not a new one for him. In 1972, he engaged in a similar attack on David Armor, who had carried out research that threw into question the beneficial achievements and attitudinal consequences of desegregation that I and others had found earlier. See David Armor, "The Evidence on Busing," *The Public Interest*, Summer 1972; and Thomas Pettigrew et al., "Busing: A Review of 'The Evidence,'" and David Armor, "The Double Double Standard: A Reply," *The Public Interest*, Winter 1973.

[6] Eleanor Wolf, "Social Science and the Courts: The Detroit School Case," *The Public Interest*, Winter 1976.

[7] I have described such a policy elsewhere; see "Racial Segregation in the Schools," *Phi Delta Kappan*, October 1975.

C.

A REPLY TO PROFESSOR COLEMAN:

Professor Coleman's response to our recent article about his attacks upon court-ordered school desegregation serves to sharpen further our conflicting views about both research and racial justice ["School Desegregation in Large Cities: A Critique of the Coleman 'White Flight' Thesis," *HER*, 46 (Feb. 1976), 1-53]. Indeed, his retort illustrates again many of our central points, not only in what it states and the way it states it but even more by what it omits.

Coleman addresses only two of our many concerns about his research: his selected subset of the "largest" urban school districts, and the inability of other investigators to detect a *causal* relationship between "white flight" and school desegregation. He claims that he selected the nineteen largest central-city school systems as listed by the United States Office of Education. And he added Denver and San Francisco to his later analyses to meet our complaint on August 4 that his "sample contained too little Northern desegregation experience to allow generalization beyond the South. . . ."

But this explanation is insufficient. Unfortunately, Coleman does not here or elsewhere provide a citation as to where and when the U.S. Office of Education published such a list of "central city districts." Neither does he tell us how the office happened to concoct such a strange list nor why he employed it. Any listing of "largest" districts that includes one metropolitan district in Florida (Tampa—despite what Coleman now says about such districts in the "sun belt") but excludes three other districts all of which are larger (Miami, Jacksonvil!e, and Fort Lauderdale) is odd to say the least. Moreover, none of the officials at the Office of Education and the National Institute of Education contacted about this matter is aware of any such list as Coleman describes. To be sure, the office has had a number of listings over recent years of twenty "large cities," but those provided us all include Phoenix and San Antonio (not in Coleman's sample) and exclude Tampa and Atlanta (included in Coleman's sample, the latter of crucial importance to his argument).[1] Moreover, Denver and San Francisco (two more crucial cases) were added by Coleman in July and included in the second version of his paper issued in late July; hence, any discussions we had with him on August 4 could not possibly have influenced the inclusion of these two additional cities. Nor does this explanation account for the arbitrary line drawn

[1] For example, Betty J. Foster, *Statistics of Public Elementary and Secondary Day Schools, Fall 1971* (Washington, D.C.: G.P.O., 1972), pp. 10, 24; Betty J. Foster, *Statistics of Public Elementary and Secondary Day Schools, Fall 1972* (Washington, D.C.: G.P.O., 1973), pp. 20–21; and W. Vance Grant, *Digest of Educational Statistics, 1974* (Washington, D.C.: G.P.O., 1975), p. 36. We are not suggesting, as Coleman asserts, that his selection of large urban school districts was "a motivated one"; had it been, Tampa (a very negative case for his argument) would surely have been excluded. Our points are simply that: (1) there have been many listings of large central-city districts issued in recent years by the U.S. Office of Education; (2) whatever listing he employed is not so definitive as to be readily locatable today without a citation; and (3) the prior rationale for his utilization of such atypical listing is not obvious and should have been initially explained.

after San Francisco that excluded negative cases for his contentions (e.g., Newark, Seattle, and Cincinnati).

Other investigators (such as Professor Reynolds Farley[2] of the University of Michigan and ourselves) have failed to uncover "white flight" caused by school desegregation, in Coleman's opinion because we employed the wrong set of cities and the wrong method. A robust effect worthy of having sweeping national policies based upon it should be readily detected by a range of competent methods applied by various investigators on essentially the same data. But Coleman apparently believes that only his special sample of cities and his method can detect what he is confident is the complete truth of the matter. Actually, the reader may recall that our analysis failed to support his thesis even when we did use his particular subset of "largest" urban districts.

So the analyses over time utilized by Farley and ourselves become the crux of the matter. This method compares the number of white students in a school district at a time prior to much big-city desegregation (1967 or 1968) with the number in the district five years later. Coleman condemns this method on the grounds that post-desegregation losses are obscured, in two related ways, by the use of data from the late 1960s: any pre-desegregation white student increases, or lower-than-average pre-desegregation white losses relative to segregated districts. Save for metropolitan districts and Memphis (through annexation), however, none of the urban districts had pre-desegregation increases in white pupil enrollment. Yet his contention about the possible effects of below-average losses in 1968 and 1969 prior to most desegregation is a good point worth testing. So we redid our analyses for just 1970–1973, omitting the 1968–1969 years in question. The relevant findings are shown in table 1.

Following Coleman's equation 1, table 1 provides, for four subsets of cities, the partial correlations between school desegregation and the decline of white enrollments while holding constant the 1970 figures for the school districts' proportion of black students and total enrollments. Keep in mind that table 1 employs Coleman's data, his index of desegregation, his samples of cities, and his recommended three critical years of 1970 to 1973. Yet none of these relationships even approaches statistical significance—much less policy significance. Just as revealing is the change in signs between those subsets of cities that include Atlanta and Memphis and those that do not. Once these two Deep South cities are removed from the analysis, not even weak support is provided for Coleman's argument. These results answer Coleman's objection to the over-time method of analysis, and then emphasize again the crucial importance of just two atypical cities for his sweeping arguments.

[2] "Racial Integration in the Public Schools, 1967 to 1972: Assessing the Effects of Governmental Policies," *Sociological Focus*, 8 (1975), 3–26; and "Is Coleman Right?" *Social Policy*, 6 (Jan.–Feb. 1976), 14–23.

TABLE 1

School Desegregation and the Loss of White Students, 1970–1973

	N	Partial Correlation Holding Constant 1970 Black Student Proportion and Natural Log of 1970 District Student Size	P
Original Coleman sample of 19 cities including Atlanta and Memphis	19	+.300	.13
Original 19 cities including Atlanta and Memphis plus Denver and San Francisco	21	+.288	.12
Original 19 cities minus Atlanta and Memphis	17	−.276	.16
Original 19 cities plus Denver and San Francisco and minus Atlanta and Memphis	19	−.174	.26

Why, then, does the over time method used by Farley and ourselves not show the same magnitude of effects as Coleman's analysis? We advanced two possibilities in our paper, neither of which Coleman mentions in his response. The over time method substantially avoids two artifacts capitalized upon by Coleman's method of looking for white enrollment changes in the same year as the desegregation. Analyzing the problem over time lessens the "hastening up" effect caused by parents who, planning to move in any event, simply left the central city one or more years earlier than they would have without desegregation. It also avoids the "neighborhood transition" effect where schools in a residential area that is racially changing boast temporarily a greater degree of racial mixture. Here "white flight" actually causes the temporary school desegregation, but Coleman's analysis interprets it in the reverse causal sequence.

Similarly, Coleman rejects Rossell's conflicting research findings on the grounds that he likes his index of school desegregation better than the policy-oriented one she used. Actually, Rossell's measure of the student proportion which was reassigned to school for desegregation correlates highly across a wide range of urban districts (−.68) with Farley's dissimilarity measure of segregation, which in turn is essentially the same as Coleman's own measure (+.88).[3] There will be cases, of course, where the Rossell and Coleman mea-

[3] Christine H. Rossell and Robert L. Crain, "Evaluating School Desegregation Plans Statistically," unpublished paper, Center for Metropolitan Planning and Research, Johns Hopkins Univ.,

sures diverge; the most appropriate measure to use depends on the research focus. Coleman cites Baltimore, which had a busing program in one area of the city, whose desegregation effects were obscured at the district level by growing segregation in other areas. But he might also have cited San Diego, where his index revealed considerable school desegregation (largely from residential change), though the district had only one small busing effort.[4] One might have thought that his policy interests in busing and court orders would have led Coleman to favor an index such as Rossell's. But, in any event, both indices have value; and Rossell's disconfirmation of Coleman's "white flight" results in all but a few cities remains unanswered.

Coleman now readily, if belatedly, concedes that metropolitan districts are less likely to suffer significant white student losses when they desegregate. This fact, he assures us, is consistent with his earlier analysis. Metropolitan districts lack the two key characteristics which lead to large losses of white pupils "when desegregation occurs"—high proportions of black students in the system and predominantly white suburbs. But actually his own analyses reveal that these two factors relate to the loss of whites *whether or not there is desegregation*. Are these not additional arguments for metropolitan approaches to public school desegregation?

Much as he abandoned without further mention his initial analysis of April 1975 (labeled Analysis I in our paper), Coleman appears to be abandoning his arguments based on his three-variable equation 1 in preference for his five-variable equation 3 (Analysis II in our table 2).[5] Equation 3 uncovers interesting interactions between school desegregation and the black pupil proportion as well as between desegregation and the intra-district school segregation across central cities and their suburbs. Coleman now stresses the desegregation interaction with white suburbs, though its standard error (.494) approaches the magnitude of its coefficient (.561). Nonetheless, we welcome this shift, for we pointed out in our paper the potential importance of these findings "to the extent that any policy implications can be safely drawn from this work." Though equation 3 is also misspecified and devoid of demographic context, it does alert us to two potentially critical mediators of any possible loss of white students traceable to school desegregation. And both of these mediators—the black pupil proportion and predominantly white suburbs—are significantly modified by metropolitan approaches to school desegregation.

Baltimore, Maryland, Nov. 1973, p. 39; and Barbara Zolotch, "An Investigation of Alternative Measures of School Desegregation," *Institute for Research on Poverty Discussion Papers,* Univ. of Wisconsin, Madison, 1974.

[4] Rossell, private communication.

[5] For example, equation 3 is the basis of table 1 in his response. But, as we noted in our paper, the projections of this table are made questionable by the inflating assumption of an enormous .2 one-year drop in his desegregation index. This condition happened in only 6 percent of his 342 city/year observations.

The value of equation 3 relates, too, to a more generic point. It is not realistic to anticipate large first-order effects, positive or negative, from national programs that actually consist of literally hundreds or even thousands of different sub-programs at the local level. Does Headstart "work"? Does desegregation "work"? Such sweeping questions for such variegated programs are virtually meaningless and involve what has been called "the total effect fallacy." Likewise, Coleman finds great variability among his cities for his presumed "white flight" effect, though he has not emphasized that fact. Thus, more precise and answerable evaluation questions for national programs are: Where does the program "work"? Where does it not "work"? And what are the differences between these types of programs? Only Coleman's equation 3 and its two interactions, imperfect as they are, get at this needed specification of effects.

In addition, Coleman now presents in his table 2 new, if crude, data to argue his case. These data may be useful for political polemic, but they are of no scientific interest for two reasons. First, no control data for comparable segregated districts over these same years are provided. Second, as Coleman admits, "the data are not as good as one would wish," for the subset of cities changes across the critical later years.[6] Moreover, Coleman can hardly be demanding a realignment of national policy on the basis of five cases.

Unfortunately, Coleman does not address an array of other problems that have been raised about his research. To appreciate how much he has chosen to ignore, the reader should read our article in the last issue of this journal. Briefly stated here, Coleman has not responded to such matters as:

(A) His research on essentially a demographic problem has been conducted in a demographic vacuum, and he has omitted variables that other investigators have shown to predict the loss of white students better than school desegregation[7] (indeed, his new tables 1 and 2 repeat these difficulties).

(B) His future projections are inflated by unrealistic assumptions (this practice, too, is repeated in his table 1).

(C) An ecological fallacy is involved in his assertions of individual motivation ("white flight") from gross district-wide data.

Our basic point, however, is that the racial desegregation of schools has not been proven to *cause* so-called "white flight" in any rigorous sense. Recall that Coleman has conceded this point in a paper delivered to the U.S. Commission on Civil Rights last December, but

6 Inexplicably, Coleman states that "some districts annexed suburbs when desegregation occurred, thus understating the losses in the year of desegregation" without also mentioning that the largest annexation occurred in Memphis *before* desegregation, thus understating the losses prior to desegregation. Also note in table 2 that the removal of the two critical cities of Memphis and Atlanta alone reduces the reported post-desegregation white student losses by about a third.

7 For example, Gregg Jackson, "Reanalysis of Coleman's 'Recent Trends in School Integration,'" *Educational Researcher*, 4 (Nov. 1975), 21–25.

not mentioned in his response: *"What is not yet clear is whether desegregation itself induces an increased movement of Whites from the desegregated district"*[8] (italics added).

Turning to policy issues, we disagree with Coleman's assertion that "the most important question is the substantive question: does desegregation in large central cities accelerate the loss of Whites from those cities, or not?" First, our paper demonstrated that, even if his research could be accepted at face value, Coleman's findings argue strongly for metropolitan approaches to public school desegregation. Especially is this true now that he is emphasizing the interactions of equation 3. Second, it was demonstrated that there is at best "only a tenuous connection between Coleman's research findings and his political opposition to school busing for racial desegregation." Thus, "the whole episode raises serious questions about the relationship between social science and the mass media" as it involves public policy. Consider each of these points now in the light of Coleman's present response, for the "most important question" concerns the policy implications that have been drawn by Coleman and others from his research.

(1) *Metropolitan Desegregation vs. No Desegregation.* Rather than responding to our article's policy contentions, Coleman reacts sharply to his perception of self-styled " 'good guys' " who "in the rush to equity" favor "any and all desegregating actions. . . ." For the record, we have not and do not favor "any and all desegregating actions"; we have testified as expert witnesses in desegregation cases for southern school districts as well as for black plaintiffs; and we have opposed the rigid application of "racial balance" percentages.[9] Nor have we forgotten "the problem" of housing discrimination "that has been plaguing blacks for years"; indeed, we discussed it at length in our article and pointed out how Coleman had omitted it from his formulations. But more distressing is Coleman's failure to explain in his response why he so stoutly rejects current metropolitan efforts to achieve school desegregation even when his own research results clearly (as he concedes elsewhere)[10] point to that form of remedy. We can only repeat the policy statement of our article which Coleman virtually ignored:

[8] James S. Coleman, "School Desegregation and Loss of Whites from Large Central-City School Districts," paper presented to the United States Commission on Civil Rights, 8 Dec. 1975, Washington, D.C., p. 7.

[9] Throughout his reply, Coleman prefers the term "compulsory racial balance" to "school desegregation." The former is, of course, a politically loaded phrase that does an injustice both to our position and to that of the federal courts. No federal court to our knowledge is requiring a large city to meet narrow "racial balance" limits. The city often cited in this regard, Charlotte, North Carolina, operated last year with school percentages ranging roughly from 16 percent up to at least 40 percent. Rational discussion of social issues requires the use of less polemical and more accurate conceptualization.

[10] Coleman admitted that his findings could well be interpreted as affording "a strong argument in favor of eliminating segregation at the metropolitan level . . ." but he rejected the possibility. James S. Coleman, "Racial Segregation in the Schools: New Research with New Policy Implications," *Phi Delta Kappan,* 57 (1975), 75–78.

We are not blind to demographic changes by race, although we believe that "black containment" is a more accurate descriptive term than "white flight." . . . [A]s race-relations specialists, we have for fifteen years been aware that large central cities have long been becoming ever blacker and suburban rings ever whiter. We agree with Coleman completely that this is one of the most basic and threatening realities of modern race relations in America. We further agree that public policies brought this reality about—not court-ordered school desegregation in the 1970's but federal housing policies from the 1930's on. And under present housing policies these trends will continue with or without school desegregation. Given this situation, what do we do about urban school desegregation? We agree that the present situation of court-ordered school desegregation confined within large central-city districts is not ideal. Coleman suggests that we should abandon such court orders and try interracial marriage and voluntary methods that have already failed. We believe that rather than abandoning the racial integration of public education, we should fashion our remedies to fit the problem. Since urban desegregation must overcome metropolitan-wide obstacles, it must be planned on a metropolitan-wide basis. This is why for over a decade we have sought support for metropolitan approaches to school desegregation. (pp. 49–50)

(2) *Research Results and Political Beliefs.* Our article maintained that Coleman's opposition to such "destructive policies" as court-ordered school desegregation flowed less from his research than from two firmly held political beliefs: that change in race relations should come not from courts but from "the will of the community"; and that the courts are wrong when they reach beyond the small amount of de jure segregation that exists and attempt to eliminate de facto segregation. In his response, Coleman appears to accept this analysis. Rather than modifying these beliefs, he restates the second one even more trenchantly:

I believe that the integration actions currently imposed by the courts—most prominently and most recently compulsory racial balance in large cities—go far beyond eradication of de jure segregation, and thus must be judged not on constitutional grounds but in terms of their consequences. And my research results convince me that these consequences in large central-city school districts are disastrous for the long-term integration of our society, by exacerbating the black-city white-suburb racial separation.

Notice first that Coleman provides no citations to those cases where courts have gone beyond the requirements of the Fourteenth Amendment, though our article asked specifically for this information. We know of no such cases, nor do the constitutional law experts we have questioned on the point.[11] Remedies have been fit carefully to the demon-

---

[11] For the Boston case, which Coleman seems to regard as an example of his belief, see Roger I. Abrams, "Not One Judge's Opinion: *Morgan v. Hennigan* and the Boston Schools," *Harvard Educational Review*, 45 (1975), 5–16. More recently, the appellate court, in supporting the rulings of

strated constitutional violations. If Coleman is to construct his arguments upon this basic belief, he must come forward with the evidence of which legal scholars are as yet unaware.

Notice, too, that Coleman's revealing statement indicates his readiness to dispose of the relevant "constitutional grounds" in favor of judging the "consequences" as he views them. Courts, of course, do attempt to foresee the consequences of their rulings; but they must, and the society should, judge the consequences within the framework of the Constitution. We believe that this is precisely what the federal courts have in fact been doing. We agree with Coleman that social scientists can aid this process by providing competent and responsible testimony concerning the consequences of various options open to the courts; but we are not as willing as he to remove constitutional considerations from the school desegregation process. Finally, Coleman's statement reiterates the mistaken notion that his research investigated the consequences of court orders against de facto school segregation. Our article took pains to demonstrate that his research actually studied school desegregation resulting from any source and not just court action. Indeed, Rossell's data on court-ordered desegregation showed no differences on enrollments from other desegregation of comparable magnitude (table 4, p. 30).

(3) *Social Science, the Mass Media, and Public Policy.* Coleman also pays scant attention in his reply to our discussion of the problems involved with the mass media of communication serving as a principal mediator of social science influence upon public policy. He does tell us that one written request for his data from a federal agency was honored three-and-a-half months after he made his initial "white flight" speech. But he does not deny the fact that earlier requests for information about his research by individual social scientists were rejected by the Urban Institute.

Coleman also objects to our characterization of his activities last year as a "mass media campaign" on the grounds that he had "remained largely unavailable to reporters, even unreachable by telephone throughout the summer." Whatever you wish to call it, many dozens of media interviews were granted and together with television appearances and popular writings constitute unprecedented media coverage of a sociologist and his policy opinions. Even without a telephone last summer, for example, he granted interviews to, among others, *Newsweek, The New York Times, The New York Times Magazine, The Washington Star, The Detroit Free Press,* and *The Philadelphia Inquirer* as well as hour-long question-and-answer commercial televsion broadcast with over twenty-five reporters on Boston's WNAC-TV in July.[12] But our critical point was not Coleman's First Amendment right to engage in intensive media exposure, but rather the persistent media con-

---

Judge Arthur Garrity of Boston's federal district court, specifically held that Garrity's remedies had confined themselves to the demonstrated constitutional violations.

[12] Merrill Sheils and Diane Camper, "Second Thoughts," *Newsweek,* 23 June 1975, p. 56; Robert Reinhold, "Coleman Concedes Views Exceeded New Racial Data," *New York Times,* 11 July 1975, p. 1, cols. 3–4, and p. 7, cols. 1–2; Walter Goodman, "Integration, Yes; Busing, No," *New York Times Magazine,* 24 Aug. 1975, pp. 10–11, 42, 46, 48; John Mathews, "Is Court-Ordered Desegrega-

fusion, which he failed to correct, between his research and his political views. There is also the risk of the self-fulfilling prophecy entailed in such massive national coverage. Coleman cites 1975 data from Boston, for instance, without mention of his own possible role as a major figure in that embattled city's controversies.[13]

Another point that Coleman illustrates but does not respond to concerns the unfortunate use of harsh and often *ad hominem* remarks. Our analyses are a "charade"; and our article was immediately described to the media as "scurrilous."[14] Any questioning of his work is an attempt to maintain a "monopoly of legitimacy," "to suppress, counteract, or throw doubt on any research that leads to questioning of these [desegregation] policies." Here he ignores our published work that contains "negative" findings for school desegregation as well as our critiques of research with "positive" findings. He infers that our ideas are governed only by our politics, while his are those of an objective social scientist. If such behavior becomes the norm for policy debates within social science, will civil and fruitful discourse be possible?

Coleman's efforts may well have served, as he intended, to legitimate "opposition to desegregating activities" in Boston, Louisville, and elsewhere. But his extraordinary activities toward this single-minded end, we fear, have also hurt the legitimacy of social-science influence upon public policy in general.[15]

THOMAS F. PETTIGREW
Harvard University
ROBERT L. GREEN
Michigan State University

---

tion Self-Defeating?" *Washington Star*, 4 Sept. 1975, Sec. A, p. 1, cols. 1–6, and p. 10, cols. 3–8; William Grant, "Sociologist's Busing Switch Based on Questionable Data," *Detroit Free Press*, 19 Aug. 1975, Sec. A, p. 3, cols. 6–8, and p. 16, cols. 1–8; Steve Twomey, "Busing Advocate Changes Course," *Philadelphia Inquirer*, 31 Aug. 1975, Sec. 1, p. 1, cols. 1–4, and p. 2, cols. 1–4.

13 Coleman alleges only one factual error in our article regarding footnote 78 and the inflation of Boston's 1974 reported loss of white students due to an incorrect categorization of the Spanish-surnamed. If Coleman would check again the Boston data from the U.S. Department of Health, Education and Welfare, however, he would note that the footnote is correct and that the reported loss in 1974 was not 16.2 percent as he states but 14.4 percent (and how much of this is actually truancy and the unreliable record keeping of a resistant and inefficient school system, we may never know). This is a small correction for Boston. But Farley (personal communication) points out that the growing ethnic consciousness among Latinos in the United States together with changing school practices in designating "minorities" can inflate sharply and erroneously the estimates of "white loss" in such cities as Houston, Dallas, Denver, San Diego, and San Francisco—all of which Coleman relies on.

14 "Coleman Raps Critics of 'White Flight' Theory," *Boston Herald American*, 16 March 1976, p. 12, cols. 5–6.

15 Our fears are already being substantiated: see, for example, Noel Epstein, "The Scholar as Confuser: Or, Why the Busing Issue Is not about White Flight," *Washington Post*, 15 Feb. 1976.

20

ANOTHER HOUR, ANOTHER DAY: QUANTITY OF SCHOOLING, A POTENT PATH FOR POLICY

By

DAVID E. WILEY

If the purpose of evaluation research is to assist decision makers to formulate effective educational policies, investigators must ask "How much of an effect does schooling have?" According to David E. Wiley, a major shortcoming of studies on the effect of schooling is that the amount of schooling a child receives has not been included as a major variable in any statistical evaluation. Professor Wiley analyzes the relationship between the amount of schooling and actual educational achievement. To facilitate this analysis, he constructs a statistical model and uses actual data from the Detroit Metropolitan Area Sixth Grade Sample drawn from the Equality of Educational Opportunity Survey.

From David E. Wiley, "Another Hour, Another Day: Quantity of Schooling, a Potent Path for Policy." Pp. 225-265 in *Schooling and Achievement in American Society.* New York: Academic Press, 1976.

Assessment of School Effects
and Quantity of Schooling

In the last few years, we have been inundated with literature on a new mythology of schooling: From the report on *Equality of Educational Opportunity* (Coleman, Campbell, Hobson, McPartland, Mood, Weinfeld, and York, 1966) and the most recent reanalyses of its data (Mosteller and Moynihan, 1972) to Jencks' book, *Inequality* (Jencks, Smith, Acland, Bane, Cohen, Gintis, Heyns, and Michelson, 1972), we have been flooded with reports of the lack of effect of schooling. These reports have discouraged

The American College Testing Program, through its research institute, provided the basic financial but also much intellectual support for the research. Additional financial support was provided by the National Science Foundation (Grant No. GS-35642). The author further thanks the Max-Planck-Institut für Bildungsforschung, Berlin, for supplying facilities while the report was written.

The research reported herein was also supported, in part, by funds from the National Institute of Education, U.S. Department of Health, Education, and Welfare. The opinions expressed in this publication do not necessarily reflect the position, policy, or endorsement of the National Institute of Education (Contract No. NE-C-00-3-0102).

educational practitioners and have comforted and supported those who would reduce the resources allocated to education. However, the grounds for many of the investigators' conclusions are weak and those for the more popular policy interpretations even weaker. One has to consider the results of these analyses, but what is really needed is a more appropriate attitude toward assessing the effects of schooling. Rather than asking if there are any effects of schooling, we should be asking how much of an effect schooling has. If we regard the issue in this way, then we will be more successful in assessing these effects, and we will have a much clearer guide for educational policy.

To say that schooling has no effect is unwarranted. It is true that some middle-class children would learn to read even if they did not attend school and that school is not effective in teaching reading to some lower-class children. This does not mean, however, that children do not acquire appreciably better reading skills by attending school. It seems clear that some children, who learn to read, would not if they did not attend school and that some children, who would have learned to read, read much more capably because of their schooling.[1] The level of discussion, however, still has not risen above the question: Does schooling have any effect?

It is the degree of effect of schooling that is important for educational policy. If it were found, after a large concentration of resources in reading instruction, that only small gains in levels of competency were attained, then we might be dissatisfied with the return on our investment in this area. In this case, we would, perhaps, want to understand why there was such a small effect so that we could modify the conditions of our investment (i.e., change the curriculum), or we might wish to reduce our investment in this area, either to improve the yield of the system in another area, where we could use the same resources more valuably or to invest our resources in noneducational endeavours. In order to facilitate such educational decision making, we must be able to assess the extent of effect of a given amount of schooling. Under ordinary circumstances, the larger the effect of a given amount of schooling, the more we will value it. Our methods and our orientation must be directed toward assessing these impacts quantitatively, or our conclusions will be only tangentially useful for educational policy.

One distinct notion, which is also directly important in assessing the

---

[1] This example does not imply that achievement, especially in its most narrow sense, is all or the most important part of what schooling has to offer. Schooling occupies a major portion of the child's life in post-industrial societies and, as such, should have a major impact on the entire socialization process, including education in its broadest sense. Also, because of the major role it plays in childhood, attention must be given to its short-term effects and qualities as well as its long-term influences. For a more elegant exposition of these points, see Jackson (1973). This chapter is restricted to an assessment of the impact of schooling, using examples in the "achievement" category only, because of restrictions in the type and quality of data available.

impact of schooling, is the view of schooling itself, rather than its effect, as a quantitative rather than a qualitative phenomenon. We must not only begin to ask how much of an effect schooling has, we must also ask the more sophisticated question: What is the effect of a particular amount of schooling? A major mechanism for increments in resources allocated to a given instructional area is increasing the amount of instruction in that area.[2] If we wish to assess the impact of resources on outcomes useful for policy in a way, we must establish the relationship between the amount of schooling and achievement rather than attempting to answer the crude question of whether or not schooling has any effect. Husén (1972) has reviewed research findings with respect to the question: Does more schooling produce more achievement? Although he finds somewhat ambiguous results from prior studies, he concludes that an increase in the amount of schooling will not produce a proportionate increase in achievement. To us, his review does not seem to support his rather refined conclusion of nonproportionality, since the studies he reviews were neither originally designed nor reanalyzed to shed light on this issue. Our objective here is to detail our ideas about the ways in which school does affect achievement and to argue that this view dictates a drastic change in the ways in which data about schooling are collected and analyzed.

It is clear that if a child does not go to school at all, he will not directly benefit from schooling. If a child goes to school every day for a full school year, he will achieve his maximum benefit from that schooling, other circumstances being equal. If he attends school less than the full year but more than not at all, the benefits he derives from schooling should be intermediate. That is, the quantity of schooling should be a major determinant of school outcomes.

In addition, the effects of various components of schooling will probably vary with the child's exposure to them. If we assume that a teacher with a Master's degree is more effective in terms of achievement than one with a Bachelor's degree,[3] then, if a child does not go to school at all, that difference will not affect the child. If the child goes to school for the full year, that difference will have its maximum impact. If the child goes to school more than not at all and less than a full year, then that particular variable will have an intermediate impact.[4] The effects of various compo-

---

[2] A vital question, which is not addressed in this section, is concerned with the *measurement* of such a content area-specific quantity of instruction.

[3] The Master's versus Bachelor's degree dichotomy represents any of a number of alternative variables (e.g., library books, guidance counselors, field trips). Here the point applies to all of those aspects of school "quality" which investigators have used to "assess" the impact of schooling.

[4] Literally, of course, this difference cannot apply to a single child. The language is a shorthand used to describe the difference between two otherwise equivalent children.

nents of schooling should vary with the degree of exposure to them. If schooling has an influence on a child, it does so on a day-by-day basis, when he is present and subject to that influence, and cannot influence him when he is not there.

It seems, therefore, that Average Daily Attendance (ADA), the number of hours per day for which the school meets, and the number of days in the school year would be important characteristics of schools to assess. The average number of hours of schooling that a child in a given school receives may be calculated by multiplying the Average Daily Attendance by the number of hours in the school day by the number of days in the school year.[5] If schooling is quantified in this way, there are (see Table 8.10) variations of the order of 50% in the total number of hours of schooling per year; that is, typical pupils in some schools receive 50% more schooling than pupils in other schools. This indicates an enormous variation in exposure to schooling.

At a finer level of analysis, if one carries the concept of exposure to schooling even further, a deeper investigation of the amount of instruction in the school, that is, the amount of time that a pupil actually spends in a supervised educational experience, should result in a more valid measure of that concept. Carroll (1963) has, in fact, formulated a model of school learning in which the amount of time spent in learning plays the primary role. Extensions of that model would have been formulated by Wiley and Harnischfeger (1974) and an integrative conceptual framework has been developed more recently (Harnischfeger and Wiley, 1975). Work by Bloom (1971c) and his students have explored the implications of the time concept for modifying traditional methods of instruction.

If it is reasonable to believe that variations in exposure to schooling are as great as 50% and this factor is not taken into account, we might expect

[5] The maximum number of hours of schooling that a child in a given school may receive can be calculated by forming the product of the number of hours in the school day for the school in question and the number of days for which school met during the year. Each child in that school has a specific number of days of absence during the school year. The product, for a particular child, of the number of days for which he was present and the number of hours per day for which his school met, equals the total number of hours of schooling that the child received in the school year. The average of these figures, for all the children in the school, will yield the average number of hours of schooling in that school. The ratio of the hours of schooling received by a particular child to the maximum number of hours in that school defines his attendance rate since the hours per day in a particular school is constant. The average of these attendance rates is equal to the Average Daily Attendance (ADA) in that school. As a consequence, the average number of hours of schooling received in a school may be calculated by forming the product of the ADA and the maximum number of hours of schooling for that school. This is, of course, equal to the triple product of ADA, length of school day in hours, and length of school year in days for a particular school.

the effects of variables, such as teacher or school characteristics, to be obscured by the enormous variation in exposure. If we look at earlier studies from this perspective it is quite obvious that attendance was generally considered to be a student composition or background variable and, as such, was placed in the wrong category. One of the few exceptions to this generalization is a study by Douglas and Ross (1965). They investigated the effects of absence on primary school performance and found that effects depended on the child's social class level. Generally, absence had a larger detrimental effect on performance in lower-class children.

The first major influential study of the effect of schooling was the *Equality of Educational Opportunity* (Coleman *et al.*, 1966) survey. The report based on this study set the major precedents for school effects analyses and also became the primary exemplar for subsequent criticism. It is interesting that although it has occasioned the greatest amount of controversy, the analysis of the relations between school characteristics and achievement occupies but a small proportion of the report.[6] The first component of the analysis was a study of the school-to-school variations in achievement. Pupil background factors had an important role in explaining this variation. However, it was also found that achievement varied more within schools than between schools.

Student-body characteristics were also used to explain school-to-school variation in achievement.[7] This category illustrates the principles used to allocate the attendance variable, which can be considered a measure of quantity of schooling. Another explanatory category was school facilities and curriculum.[8] When the percentages of variance explained by school characteristics and by school characteristics plus student-body characteristics (over and above pupil background) were examined, it was found that school characteristics alone accounted for a relatively small proportion of the variance but that a considerably larger proportion was explained by the combination of school *and* student-body characteristics. From the perspective of this chapter, these results hint that the intensity of schooling rather than the particular kind of schooling has a larger effect on student achievement. This conclusion contradicts some of the more general earlier interpretations of these data, which tend to identify the detected effects of school characteristics with the true effects of schooling. Furthermore,

---

[6] This section of the report runs for only 40 pages, including an appendix, out of 547 pages of text and tables.

[7] For the sixth grade, these measures were attendance, student mobility (number of transfers), proportion of pupils whose families own encyclopedias, and teachers' perception of student body quality.

[8] In this category for sixth grade were the following variables: per pupil expenditure on staff, volumes per student in library, and school location (city, suburb, town, country).

teacher variables were used to explain pupil achievement.[9] This category of variables did contribute to achievement, but only to a minor degree as compared to pupil background.

It is apparent that the focus of the *Equality of Educational Opportunity* report on the distribution of educational resources led to a dichotomy in categorization of school variables. The quantity measure with which we are concerned here, attendance (ADA), was categorized as a characteristic of the student-body composition, whereas the resource measures formed separate categories since these could be physically allocated to schools. It seems relatively clear that the original intent of the study—description of the distribution of resources among racial groups—was not conducive to a theoretically based analysis oriented toward the conceptualization of how school influences children's achievement. As a consequence, there was no effort to analyze or interpret the data with the objective of determining the impact of the quantity of schooling on pupil achievement. This original orientation also has conditioned the work of many subsequent investigators who have attempted to correct and modify the original analysis. In addition, the models and procedures used in the *Equality of Educational Opportunity* study and by most subsequent investigators also precluded an appropriate assessment of school effects, even when the "quantity" issue is ignored.

The method of analysis of the *Equality of Educational Opportunity* report was variance decomposition. In each of the several types of decomposition, the total variance of an outcome variable is partitioned into component parts, each allocated to a "source" of variation and representing the "importance" of that "source" in determining the outcome. In the particular type used in the report, the several classes of variables were ordered, and the percentage of variance accounted for by each succeeding group was ascertained. As explained earlier, the classes of variables used, in order, were pupil background, student-body, school facilities and curriculum, and teacher. Such a variance decomposition is dependent on the order of the variables. Because of the ordering, only for the last category can the increment in variance accounted for be attributed solely to that category. In this case, only the increment due to teacher variables may be interpreted as unique.

A means of avoiding the dependence of the decomposition on the order of the categories has been suggested, most recently, by Mood (1971). This method attempts to distinguish the unique and common contributions of variables, although it does not solve the basic problem of variance

---

[9] These variables consisted of: the average educational level of the teachers' families, the average years of experience in teaching, the localism of the teachers in the school, the average level of education of teachers themselves, the average score on vocabulary tests self-administered by the teachers, the teachers' preference for teaching middle-class white students, and the proportion of teachers in the school who were white.

decomposition. We will show that the difficulty lies in arriving at an unambiguous interpretation of the components. Since variables in different categories are correlated, the sum of the unique variance accounted for by each category does not equal the total variance. For example, if we consider pupil background and Average Daily Attendance (ADA) as two distinct categories (or variables) that are positively correlated, then the sum of the unique variance accounted for by pupil background and that accounted for by ADA will be less than the total variance of the variable being accounted for. Depending on the interrelations among the categories, the amount of variance accounted for by each category uniquely may sum to more or less than the total variance accounted for by the variables of all the categories combined.[10] As a consequence, the percentage of variance accounted

[10] The variance decomposition, as it is usually done, is as follows: Assume that two variables, x_1 and x_2, account, partially, for a third, y. Suppose $y = \alpha + \beta_1 x_1 + \beta_2 x_2 + \epsilon$. Then the proportion of variance accounted for by x_1, ignoring x_2, is $\rho^2_{y \cdot x_1}$. The proportion accounted for by x_2, ignoring x_1, is $\rho^2_{y \cdot x_2}$. The proportion accounted for by x_1 and x_2, together, is the squared multiple correlation, $\rho^2_{y \cdot x_1 x_2}$. The unique proportion accounted for by x_1 is the difference between the proportion jointly accounted for by x_1 and x_2 and that accounted for by x_2 without x_1: $\rho^2_{y \cdot x_1 x_2} - \rho^2_{y \cdot x_2}$. Similarly for x_2, the proportion is: $\rho^2_{y \cdot x_1 x_2} - \rho^2_{y \cdot x_2}$. The proportion commonly accounted for is the difference between the proportion which is jointly accounted and that which is uniquely accounted:

$$\rho^2_{y \cdot x_1 x_2} - (\rho^2_{y \cdot x_1 x_2} - \rho^2_{y \cdot x_2}) - (\rho^2_{y \cdot x_1 x_2} - \rho^2_{y \cdot x_1}) = \rho^2_{y \cdot x_2} + \rho^2_{y \cdot x_1} - \rho^2_{y \cdot x_1 x_2}.$$

To illustrate, suppose the two variables, x_1 and x_2, are correlated ρ. Also suppose that $y = x_1 + x_2$ (i.e., $\beta_1 = \beta_2 = 1$ and $\epsilon \equiv 0$) and that $\sigma^2_{x_1} = \sigma^2_{x_2} = 1$. Then the correlations between x_1 and x_2, on the one hand, and y, on the other, are both $(1 + \rho)/\sqrt{(2 + 2\rho)}$. The proportion of variance accounted for by each x, ignoring the other, is $[(1 + \rho)/\sqrt{(2 + 2\rho)}]^2 = (1 + \rho)^2/(2 + 2\rho)$. The proportion accounted for by both (multiple correlation), jointly, is one (since $\epsilon \equiv 0$), so the unique proportion for each is:

$$1 - \frac{(1 + \rho)^2}{2 + 2\rho} = \frac{2 + 2\rho - 1 - 2\rho - \rho^2}{2 + 2\rho} = \frac{1 - \rho^2}{2(1 + \rho)}$$

$$= \frac{(1 - \rho)(1 + \rho)}{2(1 + \rho)} = \frac{1 - \rho}{2}$$

Therefore, the common proportion is:

$$1 - \frac{1 - \rho}{2} - \frac{1 - \rho}{2} = \frac{2 - 1 + \rho - 1 + \rho}{2} = \frac{2\rho}{2} = \rho.$$

In this case, the total decomposition is:

unique due to x_1:	$(1 - \rho)/2$
unique due to x_2:	$(1 - \rho)/2$
common between x_1 and x_2:	ρ
Total:	1.00

for—either uniquely by a class of variables (pupil background or ADA) or jointly with overlapping parts of other categories of variables (pupil background and ADA)—is not an adequate index to use in assessing the impact of a variable or category.

The unique proportion of variance accounted for is also typically used as a basis for significance testing. The use of the proportion for this purpose, rather than as an index of "importance," is valid. The significance test, in this case, assesses hypotheses about the contribution of a particular category of variables to the outcome, when the others are held constant. If a particular category is highly related to another, then the unique proportion of variance accounted for may be relatively small and, as a consequence, the power of the test of significance based on it may be very low. In addition, the confidence intervals for the regression coefficients of the variables in this category will be very broad. This implies that the data do not determine the effects of these variables very precisely.

In summary, a variance decomposition, whether ordered as in Coleman et al. (1966) or symmetric as that proposed by Mood (1971), does not offer a reasonable method for assessing the importance of the contribution of variables or categories to outcomes. Some of these criticisms have been made previously by Bowles and Levin (1968b).

Some investigators who reanalyzed the Coleman et al. data (Armor, 1972; Cohen, Pettigrew, and Riley, 1972) have used standardized regression coefficients, instead of variance contributions, as indices of the influence of variables. Standardized coefficients suffer from serious defects as well. As

When $\rho = .50$ the decomposition is:

unique x_1:	$(1 - .5)/2 =$	.25
unique x_2:	$(1 - .5)/2 =$	.25
common:		.50
Total:		1.00

This set of numbers seems reasonable since it implies that 25% of the variance in the outcome is unique to each independent variable while 50% is shared variation in common. If we examine the decomposition when $\rho = -.50$ we get a different impression:

unique x_1:	$(1 - (-.5))/2 =$	.75
unique x_2:	$(1 - (-.5))/2 =$	.75
common:		-.50
Total:		1.00

The finding that $-.50\%$ of the variance in the outcome is shared in common by both independent variables is obviously nonsense.

Variance decomposition is typically only meaningful when the sources of variation are orthogonal to (uncorrelated with) one another (see Tukey, 1954).

the variance of an independent variable decreases, the standardized regression coefficient also decreases, even though the unstandardized regression coefficient (structural relation) remains unchanged. To be more concrete, if a unit increase in an independent variable, such as Number of Possessions in the Home, produces a 1.23 point increase in an outcome variable, such as Verbal Achievement, the unstandardized regression coefficient is equal to 1.23. In one of the data analyses reported below, this value was actually found. In the same analysis, the corresponding standardized regression coefficient for the possessions variable was .21, its standard deviation being 1.57. If we were to change the circumstances in such a way that the structural relation (unstandardized coefficient) was unchanged (i.e., the effect of increasing the number of possessions by one was still 1.23 verbal score points) but the standard deviation of the independent variable (possessions) was half as large (about .79), then the standardized regression coefficient would also be half as large (about .10). The effect of any change in the independent variable would be the same, while the standardized coefficient would be different. As a consequence, the *standardized* regression coefficient is a reasonable measure of variable importance for policy purposes only when the standard deviations of independent variables are proportionately related to the amount of societal effort necessary to change the value of the policy variable in question.

Another problem with previous data analyses has been the use of large numbers of correlated explanatory variables. For example, M. Smith (1972: 334–335, Table J) reports a reanalysis of the Coleman et al. data containing 30 explanatory variables for verbal achievement. The problem is especially acute in the analysis of school data. When variables defined at the level of the individual pupil are aggregated to the level of the school, their correlations tend to increase. As a result, with large numbers of such variables, effective analyses are hindered by excessive collinearity (high relations among independent variables). When the number of such collinear variables becomes very large, the effects of individual variables become very difficult to detect. This is due to the decrease in precision, which we referred to earlier, when we discussed the effects of correlations among the categories of independent variables. The problem is also aggravated by limitations in the effective sample size. Whenever variables are defined at the school level, as are many of those derived from the *Equality of Educational Opportunity* survey, the appropriate unit of analysis is the school and the number of independent observations (and consequently the degrees of freedom available) is limited by the number of schools.

The effects of individual variables also become difficult to interpret when there are many. For most kinds of conceptual or theoretical structures, the operational variables used in the analysis overlap the conceptual explanatory variables in such a way that also makes interpretation of individual regression coefficients difficult. For example, the child's report of the presence of an encyclopedia in his home probably reflects several more basic variables as well, such as parental use of the encyclopedia, encouragement of the child to use it, number of other reference works in the home. Given that these variables may be interpreted in and of themselves or may be considered to be functions of or partial definitions of the social status of the child's home, interpretation becomes difficult. In addition, since other variables used in the data analysis, such as child's report of mother's education, may reflect some of the same underlying variables, the interpretation of the results becomes doubly difficult.

A small number of conceptually well defined variables is needed to account for outcomes. To be useful for policy purposes, these variables should be meaningfully defined at the school level, and unstandardized regression analyses should be performed using them. When the number of such variables is small, interpretation is usually less ambiguous, and ordinary scientific processes of model revision are easier. Unreasonable results can be easily detected by inspecting coefficients against the background of prior expectations. Unexpected results should lead to revisions of the model and conceptual redefinition of variables, when this is necessary.

Because of the confusion surrounding school attendance in previous analyses, some further exposition of its role in the model for pupil achievement is necessary. Jencks (1972a) included Average Daily Attendance (ADA) in his category of regional and community characteristics and did not include it in his category of exposure to school.[11] Coleman *et al.*, as mentioned earlier, included it in their category of student-body characteristics. Both investigations did not place ADA in any category representing exposure to schooling and even ignored it as an important moderator of the effects of school characteristics. Attendance is clearly influenced by the child's background and by his home and the community in which he resides, but it is not a background variable; it is a mediating variable for outcomes. An appropriate causal model would have three parts. The first would be an explanatory submodel for pupil attendance. This model would contain explanatory variables, reflecting the pupil's home background and characteristics of the community, and, perhaps, allow for the possibility of an effect of the school itself.[12] A second component model would define exposure to schooling in terms of ADA and other characteristics of the amount of instruction. A third submodel would explain pupil achievement in terms of home background, community characteristics, and exposure to

[11] Variables included in this category were automatic promotion, hold back slow learners, transfer slow learners, percentage of students on split sessions, days in school year, and length of school day. By Jencks' method of analysis, he found no effects of variables in this category.

[12] Such an effect of school on attendance would imply the use of what economists call a simultaneous equation system. A preliminary exploration of the use of such a model in this context is reported in Footnote 22.

schooling. These three models together would constitute an explanatory system for achievement. The analysis that follows is an attempt to partially explicate such a system using data from the *Equality of Educational Opportunity* survey.

In summary, it seems that one of the reasons that investigators have not found very many or very large effects of schooling is that they have not taken into account the amount of schooling the child receives and have not tried to measure it in a systematic and integrated fashion.

A Conceptual and Analytic Model for the Analysis of the Effects of Quantity of Schooling

As was discussed in the previous section, the analysis of the impact of schooling in general and of school characteristics in particular has been obscured by both methodological and conceptual faults. The methodological shortcomings in these analyses are threefold: inadequate indices used to characterize the importance of independent variables; the problem of excessive numbers of variables and collinearity; and the lack of appropriate units of analysis in data structures that are defined at several hierarchical levels (e.g., schools, classrooms/teachers, pupils) together with the implications of these units for model construction and data analysis. We have already suggested a means of correcting the first two faults; the first part of this section will be devoted to a discussion of the third.

The major features of the solution of the problem of appropriate units of analysis can be discussed within the context of a hierarchical data structure containing only two levels. In what follows, the concrete counterparts of these levels will always be schools and pupils.

The typical data set used for the analysis of school effects contains variables defined at the level of the individual pupil, such as the various home background variables measured in the *Equality of Educational Opportunity* survey and the achievement criteria tested in that survey. This data set also includes variables defined solely at the level of the school, such as length of the school day and the highest degree held by the principal. The latter category of variables takes on the same value for every individual pupil in a particular school. In addition to these variables, which are naturally defined at the level of the school, there are other variables that may assume the same value for all individuals in a school by aggregating (usually averaging) individually defined characteristics for all individuals in a particular school.

One of the problems plaguing the literature in recent years has been the separation of the effects of these aggregated variables into parts reflecting their individual-level effects, on the one hand, and their effects via school climate and organization, on the other. This problem has been labeled "context effect." Some of the common practices in handling this problem have been criticized by Hauser (1970a). Hauser (1971) has also treated more general problems in the hierarchical analysis of school effects. The model presented here is related to Hauser's but is more detailed and refined.

One way of describing an appropriate method of analysis is in terms of the general notions of confounding and control. If we wish to assess the impact of one explanatory variable on an outcome and it is correlated with another variable, then, if we ignore the second, we will attribute to the first not only its effect but also a spurious effect that is due to both the correlation between it and the second and the effect of the second. If we utilize an appropriate method of analysis which takes into account the second variable (i.e., its effects) and its relation to the first, we may obtain an adjusted assessment of the effect of the first variable which is not confounded by the second.

In examining the basic problem of the assessment of school effects on achievement, for example, we may think of it as the problem of disentangling the effects of variables defined solely at the level of the school, such as length of the school day and highest degree held by the principal, from those defined at the level of the individual pupil, such as home background characteristics. (In the most general case, we may denote the value of the vector for the ith school by z_i and the value of the vector for the jth pupil in the ith school by x_{ij}.) From this perspective, the problems of disentanglement may be seen as: (1) adjusting the *effects* of individual characteristics (denoted by β) on the outcome (denoted by y_{ij}) for those of the schools (denoted by γ) that the individuals attend and (2) adjusting the effects of school characteristics for those of the individuals. We may summarize the model implicit in this description by:

$$(1) \qquad y_{ij} = \gamma_0 + \gamma'z_i + \theta_i + \beta'x_{ij} + \epsilon_{ij},$$

where γ_0 is an additive constant and θ_i and ϵ_{ij} are errors or discrepancies defined at the school and individual levels, respectively. One means of obtaining the adjusted effect of one variable (e.g., home background) on another (e.g., achievement) is by adjusting each for the other variable and then relating the two adjusted variables.[13] Also, if we know the true effect of one variable or have a good estimate of it, we may calculate the adjusted

---

[13] This may be illustrated in the context of a simple linear model as follows: Assume,

$$y = \alpha + \beta_1 x_1 + \beta_2 x_2 + \epsilon,$$

then the regression coefficient of y on x_1, without x_2, is equal to

$$\beta_1 + \beta_2 \frac{\sigma_{x_1 x_2}}{\sigma_{x_1}^2}$$

since x_1 and x_2 are correlated.

effect of the other variable by relating a new variable, consisting of the criterion values minus the effect values of the first variable[14], to the other variable without adjustment. A common error, however, is to subtract the *unadjusted* effect value of the first variable from the criterion and then to estimate the effect of the second variable by relating it to the modified criterion. This procedure will not produce an appropriate adjustment, since subtracting the unadjusted effect value of the first variable does not remove all of its influence.

In the context of hierarchically defined school data, the key to finding appropriately adjusted estimates of the effects of individual-level variables

Thus, the adjusted y is equal to

$$y^* = y - \left(\beta_1 + \beta_2 \frac{\sigma_{x_1 x_2}}{\sigma_{x_1}^2} \right) x_1$$

$$= \alpha + \beta_1 x_1 + \beta_2 x_2 + \epsilon - \left(\beta_1 + \beta_2 \frac{\sigma_{x_1 x_2}}{\sigma_{x_1}^2} \right) x_1$$

$$= \alpha + \beta_2 \left(x_2 - \frac{\sigma_{x_1 x_2}}{\sigma_{x_1}^2} x_1 \right) + \epsilon.$$

The regression coefficient of x_2 on x_1 (ignoring y) is equal to

$$\frac{\sigma_{x_1 x_2}}{\sigma_{x_1}^2}.$$

The adjusted x_2 is equal to

$$x_2^* = x_2 - \frac{\sigma_{x_1 x_2}}{\sigma_{x_1}^2} x_1.$$

Consequently, the adjusted y may be written:

$$y^* = \alpha + \beta_2 x_2^* + \epsilon.$$

This implies that a linear regression relating the adjusted y (for x_1) to the adjusted x_2 (for x_1) will yield the correct (adjusted) coefficient for the effect of x_2 on y.

[14] Strictly speaking, we may only discuss the *effect* of a change in a variable and not the effect of a variable or one of its values. In the context of a *linear* model, the effect of a change of one unit in the value of the variable is always the same and is equal to the regression coefficient for that variable. As a consequence, in such a linear model we may talk about the effect of a change of one unit in the variable or, in shorthand, the effect of a variable. In general, when the model is nonlinear the effect of a change in a variable may depend on the value of the variable or even on the values of other variables (when there are interactions). In the text, when we discuss the "effect" of a variable, the reader should think in terms of a linear model. In this context, when we are discussing the general effect of a change in a variable, the effect is the regression coefficient of the variable. When we are discussing the adjustment of another variable, the effect *value* of a variable is the product of the regression coefficient and the value of the variable.

is to make sure that as many school based sources of variation as possible enter the adjustment. The simplest way to accomplish this is to adjust for all of them. We assume that if the model is completely specified at the school level (that is, all of the outcome-relevant school variables are measured) then $\text{cov}(\theta_i, \mathbf{x}_{i.}) = \mathbf{O}$, where $\bar{\mathbf{x}}_{i.}$ is the mean of $\mathbf{x}_{ij}$ for the ith school. The basic stance implied by this model is that individual-level variables have direct impact on outcomes only at the level of the individual; their effects at the school level are mediated through other variables, whether measured or not, defined at the level of the school. The covariance condition given above would only be expected to hold if *all* the mediating variables, which convey the indirect effects of aggregate individual variables at the school level, are specified in the model. If all such variables are not specified and measured, then $\text{cov}(\theta_i^*, \bar{\mathbf{x}}_{i.}) \neq \mathbf{O}$, where θ_i^* is the residual from the *measured* school variables. If this is the case, as it likely will be, direct fitting of the model will produce a biased estimate of β This source of bias may, however, be eliminated through analysis based on the variation within schools. This may be done by subtracting the relevant school means (school effect values) for the criterion variable and for each of the pupil-level explanatory variables from each of the individual values for these variables. An analysis using these adjusted (deviated) values will be effectively "controlled" or adjusted for all sources of variation among schools. This method of determining adjusted effects is an example of the application of the procedure, mentioned earlier, of adjusting both explanatory and criterion variable values. The covariance matrix of the adjusted (deviated) values is called the pooled within school covariance matrix. If this covariance matrix is computed for all individually defined variables and used as the basis for the regression of the outcome on the $\mathbf{x}_{ij}$ vectors, the resulting estimate of β, $\hat{\beta}$ will not be biased by specification errors at the school level.

Once the adjusted effects of the individual-level variables are determined, the average effect value for each school, aggregated over all the individual pupils, may be subtracted from the criterion mean for each school. Analyses, using the school as the unit with variables defined at the school level as explanatory and the modified criterion means as values to be explained, will produce estimates of the effects of the school variables adjusted for the effects of individually defined variables. That is, a school level analysis of

$$(2) \qquad \bar{y}_{i.} - \hat{\beta}'\bar{x}_{i.} = \gamma_0 + \gamma'\mathbf{z}_i + \phi_i,$$

where $\bar{y}_{i.}$ is the achievement mean for the ith school, will produce unbiased estimates of γ_0 and γ in the absence of specification error. If, however, as was our original concern, there is specification bias in the school-level model, this solution will not be adequate. The method of analysis may be refined in the following fashion. If we suppose that there is some specification bias at the level of school defined variables (perhaps some important variables are missing), then $cov(\theta_i, \bar{x}_{i.}) \neq O$ and $cov(\phi_i, \bar{x}_{i.}) \neq 0$. We may remove some of the bias (in the estimates $\hat{\gamma}_0$ and $\hat{\gamma}$) by including the sum of the average effect values $(\hat{\beta}'\bar{x}_{i.})$ of the individually defined variables as another variable in the school-level analysis—instead of just subtracting the sum from the school criterion mean. That is, we can fit the following model:

$$(3) \qquad \bar{y}_{i.} = \gamma_0 + \gamma'z_i + \lambda(\hat{\beta}'\bar{x}_{i.}) + \phi_i.$$

This (specifically the parameter λ) allows partial removal of some of the additional bias due to the omission of relevant school-level variables to the extent that the sum of these average effect values is correlated with the omitted variables.

In a situation where the number of schools is limited, this approach allows for the generation of a summary individual variable by using the great quantity of information available on variation and covariation among individuals within schools. At the same time, it saves the limited information on variation among schools for the assessment of school-level effects.

In summary, we have proposed a statistical model and method of data analysis for a data structure defined hierarchically (both at the level of the individual pupil and at the level of the school). In this approach, appropriate adjustments of the effects of variables defined at both levels of the hierarchy (e.g., length of school day at the school level and home background at the individual pupil level) can be readily and sensitively accomplished, without loss of important information at either level. The resulting economies are also helpful in solving the problem of excessive numbers of variables and their consequent collinearity, since all of the individual-level variables may be summarized into a single composite variable at the school level.

Effect of Quantity of Schooling: An Empirical Example

In the first section of this chapter we criticized the simplistic question: Does schooling have an effect? In its place, we substituted the question: How much of an effect does schooling have? Instead of attempting to establish the existence of schooling effects, we will analyze the relations between the quantity of schooling and quantitative measures of educational achievement. On the basis of the model outlined in the second section, we will give a concrete example of an analysis of the relationship between the amount of schooling and educational achievement. The data were obtained from the Detroit Metropolitan Area sixth-grade sample of the *Equality of Educational Opportunity* survey and had already been "laundered" to facilitate analyses.

Our model involves three categories of variables:

1. outcome variables,
2. variables defined at the school level,
3. explanatory variables defined at the level of the individual.

For the *outcome* category, we selected from the Coleman *et al.* survey the three variables that were most closely related to academic achievement: verbal ability, reading comprehension, and mathematics achievement. The *school* variables were chosen in order to derive an overall index of the quantity of schooling: Average Daily Attendance, number of hours in the school day, and number of days in the school year. As *individual*-level home background variables, we selected those most likely to be accurate indicators of the pupils' social background and home environment: the variables directly observable by the individual child. Indicators requiring inferences on the part of the child, such as parental education and occupation, are likely to be reported much less accurately than indicators which are observable to the child in his day-to-day environment. In their analysis of children's reports of father's occupation and parental education, Kerckhoff, Mason, and Poss (1973) find large reporting errors which are systematically related to actual parental status. This type of error has especially drastic consequences for regression analysis. The individual-level home background variables selected were the following: race, number of children in the child's family, and number of possessions in the child's home.

The selected variables were based on items and indices from the Coleman *et al.* (1966) survey. A detailed description of the variables follows.

1. *Outcome variables.* The verbal ability test was based on two sub-tests, a sentence completion and a synonym test, both of which were drawn from the Educational Testing Service's School and College Ability Test series. The test of reading comprehension was taken from the ETS Sequential Tests of Educational Progress (STEP) and required the pupils to answer questions identifying, interpreting, extracting and drawing inferences from passages of prose and poetry. The mathematics test was also selected from the STEP series. It consists of a series of verbally stated applied mathematics problems. All tests were scored with the number of correct responses.

2. *School variables.* Average Daily Attendance, defined as the average proportion of pupils attending a particular school during the school year in question, was obtained from the responses to the principal questionnaire.[15]

---

[15] The question is Number 42 on the principal questionnaire (Coleman *et al.*, 1966:662).

42. About what is the average daily percentage of attendance in your school?
    (A) Over 98%
    (B) 97–98%
    (C) 95–96%
    (D) 93–94%

Number of hours in the school day was obtained from the principal questionnaire[16] and number of days in the school year from the superintendent questionnaire.[17] The total number of effective hours of schooling for an average child in a particular school was defined as a product of these three variables yielding a number in the metric of hours per year. It should be noted that the effective-hours-per-year variable is an exact composition of these three variables.

3. *Individual explanatory variables.* The individual variables were obtained from the pupil questionnaire. The item on the pupil's race asked the pupil to choose one of five alternatives which he considered to best describe him.[18] The item on children asked for the number of children in the

---

    (E) 91–92%
    (F) 86–90%
    (G) 85% or lower
    These responses were coded: .99, .97, .95, .93, .91, .88, and .83, respectively. Missing data were coded .90.

[16] The question is Number 76 on the principal questionnaire (Coleman *et al.*, 1966:667).
    76. Approximately how long is the academic school day for pupils?
        (A) 4 hours or less
        (B) $4_{1/2}$ hours
        (C) 5 hours
        (D) $5_{1/2}$ hours
        (E) 6 hours
        (F) $6_{1/2}$ hours
        (G) 7 hours
        (H) $7_{1/2}$ hours
        (I) 8 hours or more
        These responses were coded: 4.0, 4.5, 5.0, 5.5, 6.0, 6.5, 7.0, 7.5, and 8.0, respectively. Missing data were coded as 5.5.

[17] The question is Number 34(A) on the superintendent questionnaire (Coleman *et al.*, 1966:700).
    34. Length of school term *1964–65*
        (A) The school year for *pupils:* How many *days* was school in session during the 1964–65 school year?
        (B) The school year for *classroom teachers:* How many *days*, including those when pupils were present, were teachers required to work?
        These responses.were coded in exactly the same way as they were given.

[18] The question is Number 4 on the pupil questionnaire (Coleman *et al.*, 1966:628).
    4. Which one of the following best describes you?
        (A) Negro
        (B) White
        (C) American Indian
        (D) Oriental
        (E) Other
        These responses were coded: White—1, Negro—0. Individuals who responded in any other way or who did not respond at all were eliminated from the analyses of these data.

family.[19] The variable, possessions in the child's home, was measured by summing the number of yes-responses to nine items. The child was asked if his family has a television set, telephone, record player (including hi-fi or stereo), refrigerator, dictionary, encyclopedia, automobile, or vacuum cleaner, or if his family gets a newspaper every day.[20]

Figure 8.1, which graphically illustrates the conceptual model linking these variables, shows the nine basic variables in the three categories. If we pick a particular outcome variable and focus on the implications of the model for a school-level analysis, then we need to consider three variables, and they correspond to the categories in the diagram. These variables are an achievement outcome, the summary measure of quantity of schooling, and the aggregate pupil background composite. In a complete analysis of these data, we would attempt to explain the quantity of schooling that a child receives by means of our background measure and then explain achievement by both background and quantity of schooling. This complete model is reflected in the diagram by the arrows linking the categories. However, the determination of quantity of schooling by pupil background does not require explication to validly analyze the subsequent determination of achievement by background and schooling. We will concentrate on the analysis of achievement.In Section II, we described a model and two data analysis processes consistent with that model. The first process was a

[19] The question is Number 8 on the pupil questionnaire (Coleman *et al.*, 1966:628).

8. How many children (under 18) are in your family? Count yourself.
   (A) 1—only me
   (B) 2
   (C) 3
   (D) 4
   (E) 5
   (F) 6
   (G) 7
   (H) 8
   (I) 9
   (J) 10 or more

These responses were coded using the numbers given in the alternatives.

[20] The questions are Numbers 19 through 27 on the pupil questionnaire (Coleman *et al.*, 1966:629–630).

19. Does your family have a television set?
    (A) Yes
    (B) No
20. Does your family have a telephone?
    (A) Yes
    (B) No
21. Does your family have a record player, hi-fi, or stereo?
    (A) Yes
    (B) No
22. Does your family have a refrigerator?
    (A) Yes
    (B) No

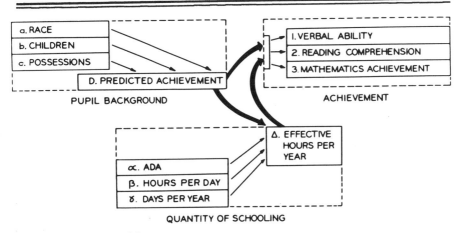

Figure 8.1 Basic model.

method of analysis that produced adjusted estimates of the effects of the individually defined variables. These estimates were to be computed from within-school regression analyses of the outcomes on the explanatory variables. This was actually accomplished by an analysis of variance and covariance. In addition to the adjustment of school-level effects, other parts of the variance and covariance analyses were used to characterize the extensiveness of the adjustments. The summary data set needed to perform the appropriate regression analysis is the pooled within-school covariance matrix. This within-school matrix is summarized in the form of the intercorrelation matrix of the individually defined variables together with their standard deviations in Table 8.1. The variance breakdown among and within schools for these six variables is given in the analyses of variance reported in Table 8.2.

---

23. Does your family have a dictionary?
   (A) Yes
   (B) No
24. Does your family have an encyclopedia?
   (A) Yes
   (B) No
25. Does your family have an automobile?
   (A) Yes
   (B) No
26. Does your family have a vacuum cleaner?
   (A) Yes
   (B) No
27. Does your family get a newspaper every day?
   (A) Yes
   (B) No
   The variable was coded as the total number of yes responses to the nine items. All other responses, including missing, did not contribute to the score.

TABLE 8.1

Within-School Standard Deviations and Correlations of Individual-Level Variables

	a	b	c	1	2	3	Standard Deviation
a. Race	1.000						0.302
b. Children	-0.061	1.000					2.195
c. Possessions	-0.008	-0.119	1.000				1.574
1. Verbal	0.135	-0.113	0.216	1.000			9.310
2. Reading	0.118	-0.082	0.165	0.765	1.000		6.751
3. Mathematics	0.173	-0.089	0.119	0.636	0.620	1.000	4.490

It is clear from that table that pupils are not randomly distributed among schools with respect to any of the background or achievement variables. Table 8.5 (Column 1), which reports the intraclass correlations (proportions of variance accounted for by schools) for each of these variables, shows that the largest degree of nonrandom allocation occurs for race (64% of the variance is among schools). The achievement variables and the possessions variable had between $11\frac{1}{2}$% and $15\frac{1}{2}$% of their variation among schools. The differences among schools were relatively small for the children variable

TABLE 8.2

Analyses of Variance for Individual-Level Variables

Source of Variation	Degree of Freedom	Mean Square	F-ratio
Among Schools	39		
a. Race		10.466	114.477
b. Children		22.813	4.736
c. Possessions		24.953	10.069
1. Verbal		883.355	10.192
2. Reading		423.976	9.304
3. Mathematics		256.406	12.719
Within Schools	2518		
a. Race		0.091	
b. Children		4.817	
c. Possessions		2.478	
1. Verbal		86.668	
2. Reading		45.571	
3. Mathematics		20.160	

TABLE 8.3

Results of the Within-School Regression Analyses for the Outcome Variables Using the Explanatory Variables

	Outcome Variable					
	1. Verbal		2. Reading		3. Mathematics	
Explanatory Variable	Coefficient	Standard Error	Coefficient	Standard Error	Coefficient	Standard Error
a. Race	4.053	0.593	2.591	0.436	2.526	0.289
b. Children	0.342	0.082	0.171	0.061	-0.134	0.040
c. Possessions	1.225	0.114	0.684	0.084	0.322	0.056
Squared Multiple Correlation (R^2)	0.072		0.045		0.049	
Standard Error of Estimate	8.976		6.602		4.382	

($5\frac{1}{2}\%$). These results are consistent with earlier analyses which found that by far the largest proportion of the variance was within rather than among schools.

One question to be asked, however, is: How much of the variation in the achievement scores among schools can be accounted for by the background variables, that is, how much of a difference in the among-school variation of achievement will adjustment for background make? In order to answer this question, we must examine the results of regressions of the achievement variables on the background variables within schools. The results of these regression analyses are presented in Table 8.3.

The percentages of variance explained—within school—are relatively small, ranging from $4\frac{1}{2}\%$ for reading to 7% for verbal ability. The results, however, in terms of the regression coefficients, are quite consistent from variable to variable and are rather precisely estimated. The difference between the races is 4 points on the verbal score and $2\frac{1}{2}$ on both reading comprehension and mathematics achievement. Each additional child in the family lowers the verbal score by about a third of a point and the reading and mathematics scores by .17 and .13 points, respectively. Each additional possession raises the verbal score by $1\frac{1}{4}$ points and the reading and mathematics scores by .7 and .3 points. The standard errors of these coefficients are uniformly small, relative to the sizes of the coefficients, indicating that none of the estimates are consistent with an hypothesis of no effect.

The results of the analyses of covariance, based on these regression analyses, are reported in Table 8.4. These results indicate that even after adjustment for the background variables, there is still nonrandom variation in the school achievement means for each of the outcome variables. When we turn to Table 8.5 again, however, we find that although there is nonrandom variation among schools after adjustment, it is much less than before adjustment. Table 8.5 (Column 2) displays the intraclass correlations (proportions of variance accounted for by schools) of the achievement variables after adjustment. These correlations are much smaller than the unadjusted ones. Column 3 displays the percentage change due to the adjustment. The largest adjustment occurs in the mathematics school means (82%), followed by verbal ability (75%) and reading (59%). Since all of the adjustments reduce the variance among schools by more than 50%, the adjustment obviously should have an important effect on the analysis of the school variation. Table 8.6 presents the correlations and standard deviations of the adjusted achievement variables within schools. The correlations and standard deviations are marginally smaller than before adjustment. These minimal adjustment effects were expected from the low values of the squared multiple correlations (Table 8.3). Note that there is no necessary relationship between the extent of adjustment for the within school versus among school variation. In this particular case, the adjustment was based on a within school analysis, and variation among schools had no influence. However, it made little difference within schools while having a quite large effect on the differences among schools.

TABLE 8.4

Analyses of Covariance for Outcome Variables, Adjusted for Explanatory Variables

Source of Variation	Degree of Freedom	Mean Square	F-ratio
Among Schools	39		
a. Verbal		246.183	3.056
b. Reading		182.880	4.195
c. Mathematics		51.857	2.701
Within Schools	2515		
1. Verbal		80.560	
2. Reading		43.591	
3. Mathematics		19.198	

The next stage in the analysis is to produce a school-level variable based on the adjusted effect values of the background variables. Since, in the analysis of covariance, the adjusted effects for the schools are equal to their unadjusted means minus the aggregated effect values, the aggregated effect values may be computed for each outcome variable by subtracting the adjusted from the unadjusted school means. Since the analysis of covariance subsumed the basic analysis, this method, which is an especially simple means of calculating the aggregate effects of the background variables, was used. Because of this method of calculation, the overall mean has been removed from each of the aggregated background variables. These variables, which are each in the metric of the corresponding achievement variable, will henceforce be labeled "predicted" (e.g., predicted verbal ability). The school means for verbal ability and predicted verbal ability (with the overall mean added back) are displayed in stem and leaf diagrams in Table 8.7.[21] The summary data for the predicted and

[21] The stem and leaf diagram (Tukey, 1970) is a method of displaying the data. It gives information about their distributional form as well as their actual values. In Table 8.7, the integer parts of the values are displayed between the parallel vertical lines, and the first decimal digits are displayed outside of those lines.

TABLE 8.5

Intraclass Correlations (Proportions of Variance Accounted for by Schools) of Individual-Level Variables and Outcome Variables, Adjusted for the Explanatory Variables, Together with Percent Change after Adjustment

	(1)	(2)	(3)
Variables	Unadjusted Intraclass Correlation	Adjusted Intraclass Correlation	Percent Change
Explanatory			
a. Race	0.640		
b. Children	0.055		
c. Possessions	0.124		
Outcome			
1. Verbal	0.126	0.031	75.2
2. Reading	0.116	0.048	58.9
3. Mathematics	0.155	0.028	82.0

unadjusted school achievement means are presented in Table 8.8, which shows their intercorrelations, means, and standard deviations together with those of other variables to be described later. Several things should be noted about this table. The intercorrelations of the school achievement means are much higher than the within school values. The predicted values, based on the background variables, are intercorrelated uniformly highly (from .98 to 1.00). Each of the predicted values has the same pattern of intercorrelation with the school achievement means, and these relatively high intercorrelations are consistent from variable to variable with the extent of the adjustment indicated by the percentage changes in the intraclass correlations (Table 8.5).

The summary characteristics of the quantity of schooling variables, discussed earlier, are also reported in Table 8.8. The distributions of three indices, days per year, hours per day, and Average Daily Attendance (ADA), are displayed in histograms in Table 8.9. The product of the three

TABLE 8.6

Correlations and Standard Deviations of Outcome Variables, Adjusted for Explanatory Variables

		1	2	3	Standard Deviation
1.	Verbal	1.000			8.976
2.	Reading	0.753	1.000		6.602
3.	Mathematics	0.619	0.604	1.000	4.382

components, which we have called "effective number of hours of schooling," is displayed in a stem and leaf diagram in Table 8.10.

A parallel diagram shows the natural logarithms of those values. After inspecting the interrelations between these variables and the other variables in the model, it became clear that uniformly more linear relations were obtained after logarithmic transformations than before these transformations. This can be seen in rows 7 and 8 of the intercorrelation matrix of Table 8.8. The logarithm of "effective hours per year" is uniformly more highly correlated with all of the other variables than is the untransformed variable. The analyses, subsequently reported in this chapter, all use the natural logarithms of the quantity variables.

A regression analysis was performed employing two explanatory variables for each of the three outcomes. The variables were the logarithm of the effective number of hours of schooling per year and the corresponding predicted value variable based on the three pupil background indices. The results of these analyses are given in Table 8.11. The Ln(effective hours per year) explanatory variable is related to each outcome. Typically, the ratio of the coefficient to its standard error is about three. The predicted outcome in each case has a coefficient (estimate of λ) significantly greater than one. This implies that, in fact, some of the specification error in the school-level model has been eliminated. The most encouraging finding, however, is the detectible impact of schooling on achievement.

The coefficients for Ln(effective hours per year) are 9.58, 9.57, and 4.08

TABLE 8.7

Stem and Leaf Diagrams for Aggregate Unadjusted and Predicted Achievement

Average		Stem		Average Predicted
Achievement				Achievement
	3	21		
	661	22		
	63	23		
	63	24		
Mean = 28.446	8871	25	67899	Mean = 28.445
Median = 28.62	41	26	12344556779	Median = 27.80
Standard Deviation	4110	27	3446	Standard Deviation
= 3.858	99851	28	018	= 2.196
Range = 14.60	5	29	148	Range = 6.49
	9884	30	23779	
	885210	31	01123679	
	0	32	1	
	8	33		
	81	34		
	93	35		

for verbal, reading, and mathematics, respectively. This implies that it would take an increase of 11% in the amount of schooling to augment the verbal and reading scores by one point, while it would require an increase of 28% to obtain the same result in mathematics. The discrepancy for mathematics achievement is not too surprising. Its standard deviation is only a little greater than two at the school level, while that of verbal ability is almost four. This discrepancy most likely reflects arbitrary differences in the measurement of these variables. What is surprising, however, is that the effect of schooling on reading comprehension is as large as that for verbal ability. The standard deviation for reading is only half a point higher than that for mathematics. If that value reflects the metric of the variable in

TABLE 8.8

Means, Standard Deviations, and Correlations of Aggregated Outcome Variables, Predicted Variables, and School-Level Explanatory Variables (N = 40 Schools)

	1'.	2'.	3'.	D1'.	D2'.	D3'.	Δ.	Λ'.	α'.	β'.	Y'.	Mean	Standard Deviation
1'. Verbal	1.000											28.446	3.859
2'. Reading	.919	1.000										19.228	2.585
3'. Mathematics	.896	.850	1.000									12.081	2.112
D1'. Predicted Verbal	.877	.782	.923	1.000								-.001	2.196
D2'. Predicted Reading	.865	.773	.922	.999	1.000							.000	1.342
D3'. Predicted Mathematics	.813	.732	.914	.978	.984	1.000						-.017	1.199
Δ. Effective Hours/Year	.387	.455	.345	.224	.218	.212	1.000					962.621	78.980
Λ'. Ln(Effective Hours/Year)	.403	.473	.360	.233	.227	.224	–	1.000				6.866	0.085
α'. Ln(Days/Year)	-.001	.001	.057	.101	.098	.151	–	.190	1.000			5.218	0.020
β'. Ln(ADA)	.219	.268	.170	.142	.125	.074	–	.299	.160	1.000		-0.085	0.030
Y'. Ln(Hours/Day)	.341	.395	.299	.166	.167	.170	–	.889	-.111	-.103	1.000	1.733	0.081

TABLE 8.9

Histograms for the Components of Quantity of Schooling

Days/Year

170	X
171	
172	
173	
174	
175	
176	
177	
178	
179	
180	XXXXXX
181	
182	XX
183	XX
184	XXXX
185	X
186	XXXXXXXXXXXXXXXX
187	XXXXXX
188	X
189	
190	X
191	
192	X

Average Daily Attendance

83	X
84	
85	
86	
87	
88	XXXXX
89	
90	XX
91	XXXXXXXXXXX
92	
93	XXXXXXXXXXXXXX
94	
95	XXXXXX
96	
97	XX

Hours/Day

40	X
45	
50	X
55	XXXXXXXXXXXXXXXXXXXXXXXX
60	XXXXXXXXXXXX
65	XXX

TABLE 8.10

Stem and Leaf Diagrams of Original and Ln-Transformed Values of Effective Numbers of Hours of Schooling per Year

Original Values[a]		Ln Original Values	
7	1	6.5	
7		6.5	6
8	2	6.6	
8	67	6.6	
9	02222333334444	6.7	1
9	5556667799	6.7	57
10	0012444	6.8	02222344444
10	668	6.8	5555666678899
11	1	6.9	112244
11	5	6.9	5779
		7.0	1
		7.0	5

[a]These values were divided by 10.

the same way that we assumed for the verbal and mathematics measurements, then this implies a much larger impact of schooling on reading than on verbal and mathematics achievement. A deeper assessment of the degree of impact of schooling on these variables will, however, be presented later; it involves comparisons to typical yearly increases in achievement.

The pattern of predictability of the outcome variables at the school level does not follow the pattern established in the within school regressions. The rank order of the variables, in terms of variance accounted for at the school level, is mathematics (86%), verbal (81%), and reading (69%). The mathematics and verbal variables have changed places in the rank ordering, and now those two variables are close and clearly higher than reading comprehension. In the within school analyses, verbal ability was discrepantly high.

An essential question concerning the analysis and the model on which it is based was raised earlier: Does schooling and the child's success within

TABLE 8.11

Results of Regression Analyses for Outcome Variables Using Ln(Effective Hours per Year) and Predicted Outcomes

	Outcome Variables					
	1. Verbal		2. Reading		3. Mathematics	
Explanatory Variable	Coefficient	Standard Error	Coefficient	Standard Error	Coefficient	Standard Error
Constant	-37.34	----	-46.50	----	-15.93	----
Δ Ln(Effective Hours/Year)	9.58	3.35	9.57	2.87	4.08	1.57
D. Predicted Outcome	1.46	0.13	1.35	0.18	1.55	0.11
Squared Multiple Correlation (R^2)	0.811		0.691		0.861	
Standard Error of Estimate	1.72		1.48		0.81	

the system influence attendance? This question must be answered with reference to a more complex model in which achievement influences attendance and vice versa. This "simultaneity" precludes the use of ordinary regression analysis as a method of estimating and testing the model. We have, however, attempted to explore the consequences of such an effect in order to discern possible biases that its exclusion from our model might have introduced. Fitting a model, which allows reciprocal influences, only slightly modifies the estimate of the effect of quantity of schooling. In the example that we analyzed extensively (verbal ability), the coefficient for Ln(effective number of hours per year) decreases from 9.58 to 8.85 after correction for the simultaneous determination of ADA and achievement.[22] This implies that the possibility that attendance may be

[22] In order to fit a simultaneous model for ADA and verbal ability, we must partially disaggregate the quantity-of-schooling variable into two parts: ADA and maximum number of hours of schooling per year. The school level variables used in this analysis are defined as follows:

1. z = predicted verbal ability
2. x_1 = ln(ADA)
3. x_2 = ln(maximum hours/year)
   = ln(hours/day) + ln(days/year)
4. x = $x_1 + x_2$ = ln(effective hours/year)
5. y = verbal ability

The model stated mathematically is:

(1) $$x_1 = \beta z + \lambda y + \theta$$
(2) $$x = x_1 + x_2$$
(3) $$y = \alpha x + \gamma z + \phi$$
$$= \alpha x_1 + \alpha x_2 + \gamma z + \phi,$$

which is simultaneous in y and x_1.

A path diagram illustrating the model is given in figure 8.2.

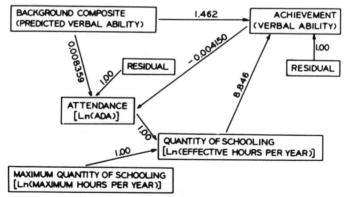

Figure 8.2 Path diagram for the simultaneous determination of ADA and verbal ability.

determined by achievement and vice versa does not affect the model substantially.

Another question left unanswered thus far concerns the simple product form of the aggregation of the three components of the quantity-of-schooling variable. The original effective-hours-per-year variable is the triple product of ADA, hours per day, and days per year. This implies that the logarithm of effective hours per year is the sum of the logarithms of ADA, hours per day, and days per year. Since the test of the simple product form involves comparing the adequacy of a model that uses the simple aggregate variable only with the adequacy of a model that uses each of the components of the aggregate as individual variables, the logarithmic transformation allows the specification of the latter model in a linear additive form rather than as a triple product. This greatly simplifies the estimation of the parameters in the disaggregated model and, thus, facilitates the comparison. Specifically, if those components are simply aggregable, then the regression coefficients for each of the three components should be equal to one another and to the coefficient for the aggregate variable.[23] We may test this hypothesis by performing a regression analysis using each of the three components as separate variables and comparing the result with the result of an analysis performed with the aggregate variable alone. The first analysis allows the coefficients for the three components to be different from one another, while the second analysis forces each of them to be equal to the coefficient for the aggregated variable. If the disaggregated analysis accounts for a larger proportion of the variance than the aggregated analysis, then only weighted versions of the variables can be consistently aggregated.

Table 8.12 summarizes the analyses of variance for testing this hypothesis. The sum of squares for the hypothesis of equality, for each outcome, is equal to the difference between the squared multiple correlations in the two analyses. The residual sum of squares is equal to one minus the squared multiple correlation from the disaggregated analysis, and it has as its

---

The estimates of the parameters obtained—any method of estimation will produce the same values since the model is just identified—are:

$$\hat{\beta} = .008359$$
$$\hat{\gamma} = 1.462$$
$$\hat{\alpha} = 8.846$$
$$\hat{\lambda} = -.004150.$$

[23] This is true because the aggregated model is:

$$y = \alpha + \beta \, ln(\text{effective hours per year}) + \gamma z + \epsilon$$
$$= \alpha + \beta \, ln[(\text{ADA})(\text{hours/day})(\text{days/year})] + \gamma z + \epsilon$$
$$= \alpha + \beta \, [ln(\text{ADA}) + ln(\text{hours/day}) + ln(\text{days/year})] + \gamma z + \epsilon$$
$$= \alpha + \beta \, ln(\text{ADA}) + \beta \, ln(\text{hours/day}) + \beta \, ln(\text{days/year}) + \gamma z + \epsilon$$

This is just the disaggregated model for the logarithms of the components with coefficients all equal to β, which is the coefficient for effective hours per year in the aggregated model.

TABLE 8.12

Analyses of Variance for Testing the Hypothesis of Equality of Regression Coefficients for the Logarithms of the Components of Effective Hours per Year of Schooling

Source of Variation	Sum of Squares	Degree of Freedom	Mean Square	F-ratio	Probability
1. Verbal					
Hypothesis	.019	2	.00950	1.955	.10 < p < .25
Residual	.170	35	.00486		
Total	.189	37			
2. Reading					
Hypothesis	.028	2	.01400	1.743	.10 < p < .25
Residual	.281	35	.00803		
Total	.309	37			
3. Mathematics					
Hypothesis	.017	2	.00850	2.436	p ≈ .10
Residual	.122	35	.00349		
Total	.139	37			

degrees of freedom the number of observations (schools) minus the number of parameters fitted in that model (40 minus 1—for the constant term—minus 4—for the regression coefficients—equals 35). The degrees of freedom for the hypothesis equal the difference between the number of parameters fitted in the disaggregated model and the number fitted in the aggregated model (5 − 3 = 2).

The probability levels for the tests of the aggregability nypothesis for each of the outcome variables did not reach significance. These results are not cause for doubting our original hypothesis of the simple aggregability of our quantity variable. This simple aggregability implies that a change in the total effective number of hours of schooling will have the same effect regardless of whether the change is in ADA, hours per day, or days per year. If this were not true, then a 10% increase in the quantity of schooling would have had different consequences for achievement depending on the mode of change. In the extreme, these components certainly ought to have detectibly different effects: Increasing the length of the school day by 10%, if pupils have already a long school day, would probably not have as large an impact as increasing the length of a long school year by an equivalent amount. The simple aggregability only holds when the values of the variables are near those in our sample.

A key question in interpreting the results of the final analyses is: Do these estimated effects of the quantity of schooling tell us anything of practical importance for educational policy? In order to answer this, we must determine whether or not feasible manipulations of the quantity of schooling result in valuable increases in the amount of achievement. First, we must define these manipulations and determine the value of their consequences. It seems that changes in the number of days in the school year, in the number of hours in the school day, and in the Average Daily Attendance are reasonable and practical policy moves. In fact, at the moment, such changes are being made in many school districts to save money. However, this is being done without prior knowledge of the consequences.

In the state of Michigan, the minimum length of the school year required by law is 180 days. All of the schools in the sample (Table 8.9), except one, are at or above the minimum level, and two of the schools met for 190 days or more. A possible increase in the length of the school year for some Detroit schools, whose cost could be evaluated, would be from 180 to 190 days. If the number of hours per day and the ADA in those schools remained the same, this manipulation would result in a 5.5% increase in the quantity of schooling (190/180 = 1.0555).

The consequences of manipulations of the total amount of schooling are shown in Table 8.13. The aforementioned policy action and its consequences are displayed in the first row of the table. Column 1 gives the assumed initial value of the policy variable. Column 2 the goal value, and Column 3 the percentage change. Columns 4, 7, and 10 list the changes in the score points in verbal ability, reading comprehension, and mathematics

TABLE 8.13

The Predicted Effects of Various Policy Manipulations in Quantity of Schooling

Policy Variable	Δ. Quantity of Schooling			1. Verbal Ability			2. Reading Comprehension			3. Mathematics Achievement		
	(1) Assumed Initial Value	(2) Assumed Goal Value	(3) Percent Change	(1) Score Point Change	(2) Month-Equivalent Change	(3) Year-Percent Change	(1) Score Point Change	(2) Month-Equivalent Change	(3) Year-Percent Change	(1) Score Point Change	(2) Month-Equivalent Change	(3) Year-Percent Change
Y. Days/Year	180	190	5.55	.52	1.00	8.33	.52	1.97	16.42	.22	1.00	8.33
β. Hours/Day	5.0 5.5	5.5 6.0	10.00 9.09	.91 .83	1.76 1.60	14.67 13.33	.91 .83	3.44 3.13	28.67 26.08	.39 .35	1.78 1.60	14.83 13.33
α. ADA	.88	.95	7.95	.73	1.41	11.75	.73	2.76	23.00	.31	1.42	11.83
Δ. Hours/Year	871[a]	1083[aa]	24.34	2.09	4.03	33.58	2.08	7.86	65.50	.89	4.07	33.92

[a] (180)(5.5)(.88) = 871

[aa] (190)(6.0)(.95) = 1083

achievement, respectively, that are expected on the basis of this assumed increase in quantity of schooling. This increase in the length of the school year is predicted to result in increases of .52, .52, and .22 score points for verbal ability, reading comprehension, and mathematics achievement.[24] Columns 5, 8, and 11 convert these score-point increases into grade-equivalent months.[25] These score-point increases correspond then to 1.00, 1.97, and 1.00 months. Columns 6, 9, and 12 express these grade-equivalent

[24] For example, the increase in verbal ability (.52), given in Column 4, was derived as follows: The predicted value based on the school-level regression of the number of verbal score points (y) for particular values of the quantity variable (x) and the predicted verbal outcome (z) is: $y = \hat{\alpha} + \hat{\beta}lnx + \hat{\gamma}z$. ($\hat{\alpha}$, $\hat{\beta}$, and $\hat{\gamma}$ are, respectively, the estimates of the constant term and the regression coefficients for the quantity variable and the predicted outcome.) The difference between the predicted values for 190 and 180 days of schooling is:

$$\hat{y}_{190} - \hat{y}_{180} = \hat{\alpha} + \hat{\beta}ln[(ADA)(hours/day)(190)] + \hat{\gamma}z$$
$$- \hat{\alpha} - \hat{\beta}ln[(ADA)(hours/day)(180)] - \hat{\gamma}z$$
$$= \hat{\beta}ln(190) - \hat{\beta}ln(180) = \hat{\beta}ln(190/180)$$
$$= \hat{\beta}ln(1.0555) = (9.58)(.054) = .52 \text{ points.}$$

Because of the logarithmic transformation, the components for ADA and hours per day are additive and subtract out along with the other parts of the equation which remain constant when the difference is calculated.

[25] The grade-equivalence conversions were established as follows: In the *Equality of Educational Opportunity* report (Tables 3.121.1, 3.121.2, and 3.121.3: 274–75), the standard deviation and grade-equivalent gaps between various subpopulations are given for verbal, reading, and mathematics test scores. Their ratios yield estimates of the standard deviation–grade equivalence conversion for each achievement variable. The midmeans—defined as the average of the middle 50% of the observations—for each variable were used as estimates of the conversions (see Tukey, 1970). This was done because it is less sensitive than the mean to extreme values, caused here by the report's rounding process. The following estimates were obtained for the grade-equivalent of one standard deviation.

Verbal Ability:	1.60 years
Reading Comprehension:	2.25 years
Mathematics Achievement:	1.86 years

These values were then used to calculate the score point equivalents in grade units. The standard deviations, used for conversions, were those of the Detroit sample.

The verbal ability standard deviation, for example, is 9.96 score points. Consequently, 9.96 points is estimated to be equivalent to 1.60 years or 19.2 months [= (1.60)(12)]. If we divide this by 9.96, we obtain an equivalence of one score point to 1.93 months (= 19.2/9.96). This value is close to Jencks' (1972a:112) equivalent of approximately two months to one score point. The results of applying this strategy to all three variables are as follows.

Verbal Ability:	1.93 months
Reading Comprehension:	3.78 months
Mathematics Achievement:	4.57 months

increases as percentages of a year (12 months). This conversion results in increases of 8.33, 16.42, and 8.33%.

We obtain somewhat larger effects if we change hours per day or ADA. An additional half hour in the school day (10% increase of a 5-hour day and 9% increase of a 5½-hour day) increases verbal ability and mathematics achievement by about 14% and reading comprehension by about 27%. Augmenting ADA from 88 to 95% improves these achievements about 12, 12, and 23%, respectively. If we simultaneously change days, hours (from 5 to 5½), and ADA, the consequent 24% increase in total effective hours of schooling results in 34, 34, and 66% gains in achievement.

Since we assume that a given percentage increase in schooling—Column 3—ought, on the average, to correspond to about the same percentage increase in achievement—Columns 6, 9, and 12—we are quite pleased with the predicted results of our policy actions: In every case, the gain in achievement exceeds the increase in schooling. Based on our estimates, Figure 8.3 displays in graphical form the expected percentage increase in each of the outcome variables for various percentages of increase in the quantity of schooling.

For verbal ability and mathematics achievement the ratios of the two percentage increases range from about 1.4 to 1.5, while for reading they range from 2.7 to 3.0. These results imply useful and important consequences of practicable manipulations of the amount of schooling for all outcomes. The benefits for reading comprehension even substantially exceed those for verbal ability and mathematics achievement.

We should also consider the precision of the computation of the expected consequences of policy manipulations. The coefficients from our analyses are not the real effects but only estimates of them. Therefore, the precision of the estimates must be considered in assessing the likely consequences of policy actions.

For example, the coefficient for quantity of schooling in the explanation of reading comprehension was 9.57, and its standard error was 2.87 (Table 8.11). If we establish a confidence interval for the coefficient—using the rough guide that 95% confidence may be placed in an interval bounded by the coefficient plus or minus twice its standard error—we obtain an interval indicating that the minimum effect of quantity of schooling on reading comprehension is 3.83 while the maximum is 15.31. These values can be used to predict the maximum and minimum changes in score points of a particular policy action in the same way that we calculated earlier the best single estimate of the change using the regression coefficient itself. If we do this for the policy action of increasing the total number of hours of schooling from 871 to 1083 (24% increase), we obtain a minimum score point increase in reading comprehension of .83 and a maximum of 3.34. This corresponds to a minimum increase of 3.15 grade-equivalent months and a maximum of 12.61 months, which are 26.3 and 100.5% of a grade-equivalent year, respectively. The minimum and maximum ratios of gain in achievement to increase in schooling are 1.08 and 4.13. These results are not only consistent with the inference of large effects of schooling, they imply them.

The purpose of presenting this example in such great detail was twofold. First, we wished to carry through, in a clearly understandable fashion, the application of what we think is the appropriate methodology for exploring the effects of schooling. Second, we wished to apply this methodology along a substantive path which will bring us to useful policy results in the assessment of school effects. We do not believe that our results have taken us to the end of that path, but we feel that these analyses lead in a new direction.

Our results should raise questions that are related to prior expectations about the effects of schooling: Is it reasonable to expect that a 24% increase in the quantity of schooling should result in a 65% gain in reading comprehension? Is this too large? If yes, why? Has the analysis been ineffective in controlling for pupil background? Is the quantity of schooling so stable over time that our analysis reflects the impact of more than one year? Is the Detroit sample atypical? These are the kinds of questions that need exploration if we are to produce a scientifically justifiable assessment of the effects of schooling.

Conclusions

A new mythology of schooling is snowing us. Based on a confusion between poor detective work and no clues, it tries to convince us of what is manifestly not true: Schooling has no effect. Instead of asking the inadequate question: Does schooling have an effect? We ask: What is the effect of a particular amount of schooling? The answer to the first question

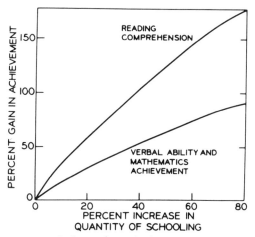

Figure 8.3 Percentage gain in grade-equivalent achievement for various percentages of increase in quantity of schooling.

must be "yes," regardless of the results of simplistic data analyses and their even more simplistic interpretations.

Our question would be a futile one if all pupils received the same amount of schooling. In fact, there are tremendous variations in the amounts of schooling pupils receive.

We view both schooling and its outcomes as quantitative phenomena. Consequently, our basic concerns are the measurement of: quantity of schooling, quantity of outcome, and the relationship between the two.

If our conceptualization of the effects of schooling is reasonable, why has this perspective never been taken before in the assessment of school effects? We have taken considerable space in an attempt to show that the most influential study of the effects of schooling, the Coleman *et al.* (1966) survey, from its original report to the most recent reanalyses of its data, has focused so intensely on issues of the allocation, to schools, of resources—such as, teacher training, textbooks, physics laboratories, and remedial instruction—that more general and basic sources of school effects, such as quantity of schooling, were neglected. All of these have mired in the swamps of inappropriate methodologies as well as the mudholes of conceptual misdirection.

As a path to dry land, we proposed unstandardized regression analysis, at the level of the school, with small numbers of conceptually well defined variables. These include, most importantly, a measure of the quantity of schooling.

To guide application, we have discussed in detail the logic of data analyses intended to assess the effects of schooling. The distinctive structure of these multi-level data requires special treatment and involves variables in at least three categories: outcome, school, and pupil. Outcome and pupil variables are defined for each individual, while school variables have the same values for all individuals in a particular school. Complete data sets may involve variables defined at many additional levels, such as state, school district, or teacher–classroom.

The problems inherent in data of this kind, especially those involving adjustment of variables in one category for those in another, have led to the formulation of a general statistical model. The elaboration of this model and a set of data analysis procedures consistent with it concretize our proposal for school-level unstandardized regression analysis. It also specifies a conceptually well-defined composite variable summarizing pupil-family-background variables.

Finally, we have detailed an empirical example of the application of the conceptual structure, statistical model, and analysis procedures to data from the Coleman *et al.* (1966) survey. Our intent was twofold: to illustrate our basic points in the most concrete fashion possible, and to provide a set of scientifically justifiable findings on the impact of schooling on achievement. We intended achievement to be only exemplary of the many effects of schooling. Some of the most important ones are very difficult to quantify. Our example was restricted because other data were not available.

We have concluded that

- our statistical model is useful for the generation of scientifically and policy useful analyses of schooling data;
- the quantity of schooling is an *important* determinant of achievement.

In addition, we have estimated the expected change in achievement for particular modifications in the quantity of schooling. We have also determined the effect of quantity of schooling in order to allow practicable policy actions with useful, predictable, and evaluatable implications.

Acknowledgments

The author wishes to thank Henry Levin for access to the data and for a critical comment, William Mason for his thoughtful and extensive criticisms, Richard Wolfe for insightful discussions concerning the statistical model, and especially Annegret Harnischfeger who participated in the statement of the thesis and the results so extensively that the main body of the paper grew from nine pages to its current length. Ward Keesling is a coinvestigator on this project and was of critical importance in the formulation of the structure of the analysis. Warm thanks to Angelika Neubauer for her assistance in typing the many drafts of this manuscript.

REFERENCES

Armor, D.J. School and Family Effects on Black and White Achievement: A Reexamination of the USOE Data. In F. Mosteller & D.P. Moynihan (Eds.), On equality of educational opportunity. New York: Vintage Books, 1972. Pp. 168-229.

Bloom, B.S. Learning for Mastery. In B.S. Bloom, J.T. Hastings, and G. Madaus (Eds.), Handbook on formative and summative evaluation of student learning. New York: McGraw-Hill, 1971. (c)

Bowles, S., & Levin, H.M. More on Multicollinearity and the Effectiveness of Schools. Journal of Human Resources, 1968, 3, 393-400. (a)

Carroll, J.B. A Model of School Learning. Teachers College Record, 1963, 64, 723-733.

Cohen, D.K., Pettigrew, T.F., & Riley, R.T. Race and the Outcomes of Schooling. In F. Mosteller and D.P. Moynihan (Eds.), On equality of educational opportunity. New York: Vintage Books, 1972. Pp. 343-368.

Coleman, J.S., Campbell, E.Q., Hobson, C.J., McPartland, J., Mood, A.M., Weinfeld, F.D., & York, R.L. Equality of educational opportunity. 2 Vols. Office of Education, U.S. Department of Health, Education, and Welfare. Washington, D.C.: U.S. Government Printing Office, 1966.

Douglas, J.W.B., & Ross, J.M. The Effects of Absence on Primary School Performance. British Journal of Educational Psychology, 1965, 35, 28-40.

Harnischfeger, A., & Wiley, D.E. Teaching-Learning Processes in Elementary School: A Synoptic View. Studies of Educative Processes, 1975, No. 9, University of Chicago. [Also in D.A. Erickson (Ed.), Reading in educational research: Educational organization and administration. American Educational Research Association, in preparation.]

Hauser, R.M. Context and Consex: A Cautionary Tale. American Journal of Sociology, 1970, 75, 645-664. (a)

Hauser, R.M. Socioeconomic background and educational performance. Washington, D.C.: American Sociological Association, Rose Monograph Series, 1971.

Husén, T. Does More Time in School Make a Difference? Saturday Review, 1972 (April 29), 32-35.

Jackson, P.W. After Apple-Picking. Harvard Educational Review, 1973, 43, 51-60.

Jencks, C.S. The Coleman Report and the Conventional Wisdom. In F. Mosteller and D.P. Moynihan (Eds.) On equality of educational opportunity. New York: Vintage Books, 1972. Pp. 69-115. (a)

Jencks, C.S., Smith, M., Acland, H., Bane, M.J., Cohen, D., Gintis, H., Heyns, B., & Michelson, S. Inequality: A reassessment of the effect of family and schooling in America. New York: Basic Books, 1972.

Kerckhoff, A.C., Mason, W.M., & Poss, S.S. On the Accuracy of Children's Reports of Family Social Status. Sociology of Education, 1973, 46, 219-247.

Mood, A.M. Partitioning Variance in Multiple Regression Analyses as a Tool for Developing Learning Models. American Educational Research Journal, 1971, 8, 191-202.

Mosteller, F., & Moynihan, D.P. (Eds.) On equality of educational opportunity. New York: Vintage Books, 1972.

Smith, M.S. Equality of Educational Opportunity: The Basic Findings Reconsidered. In F. Mosteller and D.P. Moynihan (Eds.), On equality of educational opportunity. New York: Vintage Books, 1972. Pp. 230-342.

Wiley, D.E., & Harnischfeger, A. Explosion of a Myth: Quantity of Schooling and Exposure to Instruction, Major Educational Vehicles. Studies of Educative Processes, 1974, No. 8, University of Chicago. [Also: Educational Researcher, 1974, 3, 7-12.]

21

USE OF NORMATIVE PEER DATA AS A STANDARD FOR EVALUATING CLASSROOM TREATMENT EFFECTS

By

HILL M. WALKER and HYMAN HOPS

Valid and reliable data about the evaluation of changes in human behavior attributed to specific treatments is both a concern and a challenge for researchers. Hill M. Walker and Hyman Hops design a model in which normative behavioral observation data can be utilized as a standard for evaluating the treatment effect for "behaviorally handicapped" children in the classroom. They are concerned with the generalizations from previous studies. They suggest that this can be useful in evaluating the effects of treatment on behavior in educational settings.

From Hill M. Walker and Hyman Hops, "Use of Normative Peer Data as a Standard for Evaluating Classroom Treatment Effects." *Journal of Applied Behavior Analysis,* 1976, *9*(2), 159-168. Copyright 1976 by the Society for the Experimental Analysis of Behavior, Inc.

This study illustrated the use of normative behavioral observation data as a standard for evaluating the practicality of treatment effects produced in other settings. Three groups of eight subjects each, displaying relatively low proportions of appropriate classroom behavior when compared with regular classroom peers, were selected for treatment within an experimental classroom setting. The three groups were exposed to intervention procedures designed to reinforce either direct academic performance and/or facilitative nonacademic classroom responses. The treatment was effective in changing levels of appropriate behavior (1) above baseline levels in the experimental classroom, and (2) to within normal peer-defined limits when reintegrated into the regular classroom. Further, the data reflect successful maintenance of these effects for a seven- to 12-week follow-up period. Several applications of a normative model for evaluating treatment, generalization, and maintenance effects were presented and discussed.

DESCRIPTORS: classroom behavior, maintenance, generalization, evaluation of treatment, methodology, mainstreaming of handicapped, reintegration, tokens, normative data, peers

As a rule, multiple criteria are used in evaluating procedures for changing human behavior. For example, Baer, Wolf, and Risley (1968) described effectiveness and generality criteria for assessing behavior change. The effectiveness criterion relates to the magnitude of behavior change attributable to specific treatment procedures, while the generality criterion refers to the persistence of treatment effects over time or to their generalization to untreated settings and behaviors.

These criteria can interact with each other in complex ways when used to evaluate effects of treatment. For example, some treatments may produce large-magnitude effects in the treatment setting, but no or limited generalization of those effects over time or to untreated settings. Other treatments may produce relatively small-magnitude effects during treatment, which then prove durable across time and settings. In the former example, the treatment effects may be sufficiently large to be of practical significance but for unknown reasons do not generalize. In the latter case, the obtained effects may generalize but may not be of practical significance due to their small magnitude. Without an established standard or a specified criterion level for judging when a treatment has achieved its goals, it becomes difficult to reach conclusive decisions regarding the effectiveness of specific treatment procedures.

A third criterion for evaluating treatment effects consists of normative observational data recorded on a target subject's peers. Normative peer data can be used as a standard against which the effects of treatment programs can be compared. These data also can be used to define normal limits as represented by the behavior of peers and can provide a measure of uncontrolled situational variables that may affect the target

[1]This research was performed pursuant to contract No. OEG-0-72-0702, Bureau of the Handicapped, Office of Education, U.S. Department of Health, Education, and Welfare through the Center at Oregon for Research in the Behavioral Education of the Handicapped. The authors wish to thank Nancy Todd for her extensive efforts in retabulation of the raw data. Thanks are also due Charles R. Greenwood for his critical reading of the manuscript. Reprints may be obtained from Hill M. Walker, CORBEH, 1590 Willamette St., Eugene, Oregon 97401.

subject's behavior during baseline, treatment or follow-up periods.

Patterson and his colleagues (Patterson, Cobb, and Ray, 1972; Patterson, Shaw, and Ebner, Note 2) were the first to employ a system of sampling the behavior of randomly selected peers in the classroom of a targeted subject to provide an additional criterion for evaluating intervention procedures. The procedure has been used in subsequent studies by Patterson (1974); Walker and Hops (1973); Walker, Hops, and Johnson (1975); Walker, Mattson, and Buckley (1971). This method makes it possible to evaluate treatments, not only in terms of their relative effectiveness and durability, but also in terms of whether they are instrumental in changing the target subject's behavioral level to within normal limits; if so, one can then judge whether the subject's behavior remains in the normal range over the long term by continuing to monitor simultaneously his/her behavior and that of peers.

The present study illustrates the use of normative behavioral observation data, based on targeted subjects' peers in the regular classroom, to evaluate treatment effects in other settings. Three different token reinforcement treatments, administered in an experimental classroom, were used for this purpose. The target subjects' levels of appropriate behavior were compared to their peers' before assignment to the experimental classroom and when they were reintegrated into the regular classroom.

METHOD

Subjects

Three groups of eight subjects each, exhibiting relatively low rates of appropriate classroom behavior, were selected from primary grades in regular classroom settings for this study. Target subjects were referred by classroom teachers in school district 4J in Eugene, Oregon. Children were identified by classroom teachers and accepted for short-term treatment in an experimental classroom setting if they dis-

played relatively low rates of behaviors that would appear to facilitate academic achievement in the regular classroom setting. These included listening to instructions, following directions, attending to task, completing assignments within specified time allowances, and so forth. Subjects in the three groups averaged 60% or less of observed time spent in appropriate classroom behavior as defined by the observation code used (see observations section). Subjects spent seven to 10 weeks in an experimental classroom setting and were then returned to the regular classrooms from which they were referred.

Of the 24 subjects, seven were female and 17 male. Group I consisted of four second graders and four third graders; Group II of one first grader, four second graders, and three third graders; and Group III of one first grader, five second graders, and two third graders.

Using the same observational code as for target subjects, normative observational data were recorded on each target subject's regular classroom peers during each phase of the study. All peers in the target subject's regular classroom were observed in each study phase; no peers were excluded from the observational procedure. Class sizes varied from 20 to 30 pupils across the 24 classrooms in which peers and target subjects were observed. The average teacher-pupil ratio in the Eugene school district was 1:24. Each target subject was at the same grade level as his respective peers.

Treatment Phases

The present study consisted of four phases: (1) baseline₁ (regular classroom), (2) baseline₂ (experimental classroom), (3) intervention (experimental classroom), and (4) follow-up (regular classroom). During baseline₁, the classroom behavior of experimental subjects and their respective peers was recorded in the regular classroom setting over a two- to three-week period.

Following baseline₁, experimental subjects were enrolled in an experimental classroom setting and assigned to a second two- to three-week baseline condition in that setting. The purpose of baseline$_2$ was to obtain baseline measures of child behavior under experimental classroom stimulus conditions in order to evaluate more clearly the effects associated with the subsequent introduction of formal treatment procedures in that setting.

The three different intervention procedures used in the experimental classroom are described in detail elsewhere (Walker and Hops, *in press*). Briefly, they consisted of token systems designed to reinforce direct academic performance and/or facilitative nonacademic classroom responses (see Cobb, 1972; Cobb and Hops, 1973; Hops and Cobb, 1973). Group I subjects were awarded points (exchangeable for backup reinforcers), paired with behavior-specific praise, for engaging in such behaviors as attending to task, listening to instructions, following directions, and volunteering. Points and praise were dispensed to Group II subjects for making correct academic responses, *e.g.,* papers finished correctly, problems completed correctly, and accurate reading responses. The two contingencies were combined for Group III subjects.

The follow-up period extended over two to three months beginning immediately after subjects were reintegrated into their regular classrooms. No attempts were made to program post-treatment maintenance of appropriate behavior for any of the experimental subjects.

Group I subjects were assigned to the experimental classroom from October to December and were followed up from January to March; Group II subjects were in the classroom from January to March and were followed up until the end of the school year; Group III subjects were in the classroom from March to June and were followed up during the first three months of the next school year.

Observation and Recording Procedures

The observation system was a modified 19-category time-sampling code originally developed by Cobb (Note 1). Definitions of the code categories are contained in Appendix A. Using this code, observers recorded the behavior of experimental subjects and their respective peers in successive 6-sec intervals.

Experimental subjects and their respective peers were observed weekly during baseline$_1$ and follow-up periods recorded in the regular classroom setting. Subjects were observed daily during baseline$_2$ and intervention phases while assigned to the experimental classroom. Table 1 contains the average number and range of minutes subjects and peers in each experimental group were observed per week during each study phase. The means reported for each experimental group are the average number of minutes observed for each experimental subject and his/her respective peers in that group.

During baseline$_1$ and follow-up periods, the behavior of experimental subjects and peers was recorded in alternate 6-sec intervals. The experimental subject was observed during the first 6-sec interval, a peer during the next interval, the experimental subject again during the third interval, and another peer in the fourth 6-sec interval. A new peer was observed every alternate interval until all peers had been observed once; then, the cycle began again and continued until the observation session was terminated.

While experimental subjects were assigned to the experimental classroom during baseline$_2$ and intervention phases, observers continued to record the behavior of peers weekly. The same rotating procedure was used as in baseline$_1$ and follow-up periods, except that experimental subjects were obviously excluded. Observers were free to code any of the 19 code categories during each 6-sec interval but only one instance of each category could be recorded in each 6-sec interval.

During regular classroom observations, the behavior of experimental subjects and peers was recorded across a variety of academic periods, including reading, math, social studies, science, and spelling, and during individual seatwork and teacher-led group activities. In the experimental classroom setting, observations were made during reading and mathematics periods only, where most of the academic work was individual seatwork.

Table 1

Mean weekly number of minutes observed for target subjects and their respective peers for experimental Groups I, II, and III.

	Subjects		Peers	
	$\bar{x}$ Number of Minutes Observed per Subject per Week	Range	$\bar{x}$ Number of Minutes Observed per Set of Peers per Week	Range
GROUP I				
Baseline$_1$	17.57	12.70-22.30	17.57	12.70-22.30
Baseline$_2$	33.40	10.50-56.30	16.50	*
Intervention	53.60	30.00-85.50	26.22	20.30-35.10
Follow-up	19.11	16.40-23.90	19.11	16.40-23.90
GROUP II				
Baseline$_1$	18.50	9.00-30.00	18.50	9.00-30.00
Baseline$_2$	51.20	37.50-73.00	19.50	15.50-22.00
Intervention	73.08	34.90-100.50	18.45	13.00-22.30
Follow-up	23.82	16.30-28.50	23.82	16.30-28.50
GROUP III				
Baseline$_1$	14.46	8.80-22.00	14.46	8.80-22.00
Baseline$_2$	86.65	80.30-93.00	23.60	20.10-27.10
Intervention	103.26	78.40-127.30	25.37	13.30-29.10
Follow-up	20.18	14.80-25.00	20.18	14.80-25.00

*Observation data were recorded for peers of Group I subjects during the second week of baseline$_2$ only.

RELIABILITY

Seven observers were used throughout this study. All were graduate or undergraduate students in either education or psychology, and each was trained for about six 1-hr sessions until he/she could achieve a criterion of five consecutive, 3-min observation sessions with reliability coefficients of 0.90 or better with the observer trainer/calibrater.

During the study, observers were rotated between the experimental classroom and the regular classroom settings from which the subjects had been referred. Observers were monitored via weekly recalibration spot checks with the observer/trainer to maintain their reliability (Reid, 1970; Taplin and Reid, 1973). All observer data recorded in weekly spot checks were included in the study. The recalibration checks were part of the regular observation periods.

Observer agreement was calculated using the per cent agreement method; observers had to agree on all behaviors coded in an interval for that interval to be counted as an agreement. An observer had to agree with the observer trainer

by code category, subject, and sequence for interobserver agreement to be coded in any 6-sec interval. Agreement was calculated by dividing the number of agreements by the total number of agreements and disagreements. Table 2 contains the average agreements per phase by experimental group for target subjects and peers throughout the study. The number of agreement checks per phase is given along with the range in agreement for both target subjects and peers

During initial training sessions, observer agreement averaged 90% across all observers and ranged from 30 to 100%. During weekly recalibration checks, agreement averaged 95% and ranged from 84 to 100%.

Dependent Measure

The dependent measure was the proportion of appropriate classroom behavior exhibited by experimental subjects and peers across phases. The following code categories were judged, on an · *a priori* basis, to be appropriate to the classroom setting: Approval (AP), Compliance (CO), Appropriate Talking with Teacher (TT+), Appropriate Interaction with Peer

Table 2

Number and range of agreement checks for target subjects and peers across study phases.

	Subjects			Peers		
	Number	Mean	Range	Number	Mean	Range
GROUP I						
Baseline$_1$	2	97.5	97- 98	2	97.5	97- 98
Baseline$_2$	14	95.2	88-100	10	96.4	88-100
Intervention	33	92.5	84-100	13	96.1	89-100
Follow-up	10	96.4	89- 98	10	95.4	89- 97
TOTAL	59	95.9	84-100	35	96.6	88-100
GROUP II						
Baseline$_1$	12	93.9	89-100	12	93.9	89-100
Baseline$_2$	10	95.8	91-100	6	95.7	91- 97
Intervention	28	96.0	86-100	11	96.4	88-100
Follow-up	9	94.1	91-100	9	94.1	91-100
TOTAL	59	95.0	86-100	38	95.0	88-100
GROUP III						
Baseline$_1$	6	96.9	92- 98	6	96.9	92- 98
Baseline$_2$	8	97.4	93-100	4	95.7	90- 97
Intervention	25	96.1	94-100	10	94.1	89-100
Follow-up	14	95.0	91-100	14	95.0	94-100
TOTAL	53	96.4	91-100	34	95.4	89-100

(IP+), Volunteer (VO), Initiation to Teacher (IT), and Attend (AT). The proportion of appropriate behavior was computed by dividing the total number of appropriate behavior categories recorded by the total number of behaviors recorded for each data point.

RESULTS

Figures 1, 2, and 3 contain plots of the weekly means for the proportion of appropriate behavior for target subjects and their respective peers for experimental Groups I, II, and III, across the four phases of the study. The phase means are presented in Table 3.

The peer data, although represented by peers in 24 different classrooms, indicate extremely stable trend lines (see Figures 1, 2, and 3). Each group's data were collected over a 21- to 24-week period, yet 62 of 64 data points fall between 60% and 80% appropriate behavior.

Examining the data within phases, it can be seen that during baseline$_1$ in the regular classroom, the levels of appropriate behavior for the target subjects, in all three groups, were well below that of their peers. A subsequent increase following their assignment to a second baseline condition in the experimental classroom eliminated this difference, although a decelerating trend was noted for experimental Group II.

With the application of the intervention procedures, all three experimental groups showed a further increase; the proportions of appropriate behavior for Groups II and III exceeding that of their respective peers, who remained in the regular classroom, for the entire phase. The follow-up data are marked by an immediate decrease in levels of appropriate behavior after the experimental groups were reintegrated into the regular classroom; the greatest decline is seen for Group III, which returned after a two-month summer holiday. Further, Groups I and II continued to show declining trends, while Group III's trend was increasing. The mean levels of appropriate behavior for the follow-up phase indicate differences between the target subjects and their peers. The trend lines show, however, that these differences are not consistent

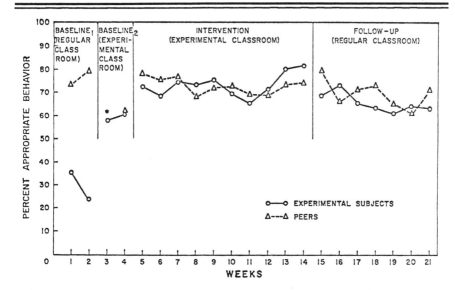

Fig. 1. Behavioral observation data for Group I subjects during successive treatment phases.

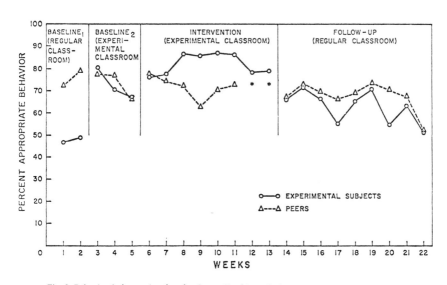

Fig. 2. Behavioral observation data for Group II subjects during successive treatment phases.

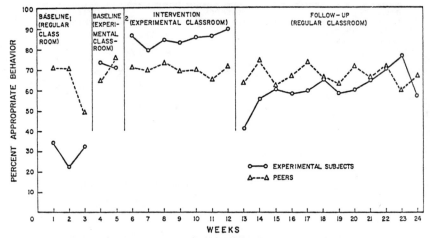

Fig. 3. Behavioral observation data for Group III subjects during successive treatment phases.

across the entire phase and that some overlap occurs in each group.

DISCUSSION

Comparison between the behavior of target subjects and their respective peers during the two experimental classroom phases are confounded in two respects. First, stimulus conditions and treatment conditions were radically different in the two settings. Second, the target subjects' behavior was recorded during reading and math periods in the experimental classroom, while the behavior of their peers in the regular classroom was recorded across instructional periods that included reading, math, social studies, science, and spelling. Thus, it is impossible to draw meaningful comparisons between target subjects and their respective peers during these two conditions. However, subjects and peers were observed under identical conditions both before and after assignment to the experimental classroom, thus making it possible to compare their performance during baseline₁ and follow-up phases.

These data indicate that the behavior of target subjects was changed at follow-up to within normal limits as defined by the behavior of their

Table 3

Mean proportions of appropriate behavior for target subjects and their respective peers during baseline, intervention, and follow-up phases.

	Baseline (Reg. Class)	Baseline (Exp. Class)	Intervention (Exp. Class)	Follow-up (Reg. Class)
GROUP I				
Target Subjects	32.73%	58.65%	73.42%	65.74%
Peers	75.87%	59.30%	72.90%	69.63%
GROUP II				
Target Subjects	49.64%	72.67%	82.14%	62.94%
Peers	73.25%	73.67%	71.47%	67.71%
GROUP III				
Target Subjects	27.74%	72.40%	84.86%	60.68%
Peers	68.08%	70.20%	69.94%	67.23%

peers. Further, these changes maintained within the peer-defined limits over the entire follow-up period. This was clearly not the case during the baseline₁ period recorded in the regular classroom before treatment.

A closer examination of the trends in follow-up suggests that whatever accounted for the gradual decelerating trend in Groups I and II target subjects may have produced similar trends in their peers' performance. In contrast, the divergent trend lines for subjects and peers in Group III could suggest that the influence on subjects' behavior may have been independent of classroom variables that could have affected the peers similarly.

The use of peer normative data as a standard for evaluating treatment effects has implications for treatments administered within the regular classroom as well as those administered in special settings followed by reintegration into the regular classroom. For example, the general failure to achieve generalization/maintenance of treatment effects across time and settings has been a persistent problem in the field of applied behavior analysis. This methodology has the potential for generating knowledge on parameters associated with both the achievement and nonachievement of generalization/maintenance effects. It also provides an additional source of information for judging the adequacy of posttreatment behavioral performance.

Normative peer data provides an operant measure of appropriate child behavior in any given classroom setting at any given point in time. It also provides a measure of variability and trends in this operant level over time as a function of changes in classroom stimulus conditions. These two parameters could affect placement/reintegration decisions either in the absence of or following formal treatment. For example, it may be that an individual subject's behavior would maintain better in a classroom where there is a high level of appropriate behavior with little variability over time. If this were the case, regular classrooms could be assessed along these dimensions as part of the decision governing selection of an optimum reintegration setting for a subject receiving treatment in a special setting.

Peer data also provide a measure of stimulus conditions during follow-up periods that can make interpretation of generalization/maintenance effects more meaningful. For example, if a subject were reintegrated into the regular classroom setting following treatment and his/her behavior approached baseline levels, the treatment would probably be judged ineffective. However, if peer data recorded under the same stimulus conditions in the regular classroom showed a substantial correlated decrease in level, one could argue that the lack of a posttreatment effect for the target subject may be attributable to uncontrolled variables operating in the posttreatment setting.

O'Leary and Drabman (1971) criticized research designs in which follow-up performance is measured by the use of occasional postchecks or probes. The limited sampling of a target subject's behavior does not provide a measure of intervening variables or events occurring between the termination of treatment and recording of follow-up measures. The simultaneous recording of target subject and peer data on a relatively continuous basis would provide considerable information for evaluating target subject performance during follow-up and in relating it to conditions occurring in the posttreatment period.

In the process of recording long-term follow-up measures on target subjects across school years, the technique offers a method for evaluating different classroom settings in which the subject is placed and relating this information to judgements about the relative durability of effects produced by a host of different treatments. Presumably, the probability of appropriate behavior being positively reinforced and maintained by either teachers and/or peers would vary considerably across classrooms.

In methodological terms, it is not intended that normative peer data would supplant any features of traditional intra- and intersubject research designs used for demonstrating causal relationships, *e.g.*, reversal, multiple baseline, and experimental/control group comparisons. Instead, peer data are seen as a potentially valuable informational supplement to each of these designs and would be used in conjunction with them. For example, the traditional features of such designs can be used to establish functional relationships between independent and dependent variables. Normative peer data can then provide a basis for evaluating the practical significance and durability of obtained treatment effects. Thus, given the addition of peer data, one is able to document causal relationships and also to evaluate the meaningfulness of changes represented by those relationships.

Some applications of the present methodology have been implemented in previous studies cited earlier. The information produced appears to be useful and relevant to the task of evaluating treatment, generalization, and maintenance effects. If the technique's potential utility is realized, many additional applications will probably be developed in the future, particularly in the area of mainstreaming the behaviorally handicapped in educational settings.

REFERENCE NOTES

1. Cobb, J. A. *Manual for coding academic survival skill behaviors and teacher/peer responses.* Eugene, Oregon: CORBEH, University of Oregon, 1590 Willamette St. 97401, 1971.
2. Patterson, G. R., Shaw, D. A., and Ebner, M. J. Teachers, peers, and parents as agents of change in the classroom. In F. A. M. Benson (Ed.), *Modifying deviant social behaviors in various classroom settings.* Eugene: University of Oregon, 1969, No. 1.

REFERENCES

Baer, D., Wolf, M., and Risley, T. Some current dimensions of applied behavior analysis. *Journal of Applied Behavior Analysis,* 1968, **1**, 91-97.

Cobb, J. A. Relationship of discrete classroom behaviors to fourth grade academic achievement. *Journal of Educational Psychology,* 1972, **63**, 74-80.

Cobb, J. A. and Hops, H. Effects of academic survival skill training on low achieving first graders. *The Journal of Educational Research,* 1973, **67**, 108-113.

Hops, H. and Cobb, J. A. Survival behaviors in the educational setting: Their implications for research and intervention. In L. A. Hamerlynck, L. C. Handy, and E. J. Mash (Eds.), *Behavior change: methodology, concepts and practice.* Champaign, Ill.: Research Press Co., 1973. Pp 193-208.

O'Leary, K. D. and Drabman, R. Token reinforcement programs in the classroom: A review. *Psychological Bulletin,* 1971, **75**, 379-398.

Patterson, G. R. Interventions for boys with conduct problems: multiple settings, treatments and criteria. *Journal of Consulting and Clinical Psychology,* 1974, **42**, 471-481.

Patterson, G. R., Cobb, J. A., and Ray, R.S. Direct intervention in the classroom: a set of procedures for the aggressive child. In F. W. Clark, D. R. Evans, and L. A. Hamerlynck (Eds.), *Implementing behavioral programs for schools and clinics.* Proceedings of the Third Banff International Conference on Behavior Modification. Research Press Co., 1972.

Reid, J. B. Reliability assessment of observation data: a possible methodology problem. *Child Development,* 1970, **41**, 1143-1150.

Taplin, P. S. and Reid, J. B. Effects of instructional setting and experimenter influence on observer reliability. *Child Development,* 1973, **44**, 547-554.

Walker, H. M. and Hops, H. The use of group and individual reinforcement contingencies in the modification of social withdrawal. In L. A. Hamerlynck, L. C. Handy, and E. J. Mash (Eds.), *Behavior change: methodology, concepts and practice.* Proceedings of the Fourth Banff International Conference on Behavior Modification. Research Press Co., 1973. Pp. 269-307.

Walker, H. M. and Hops, H. Increasing academic achievement by reinforcing direct academic performance and/or facilitative non-academic responses. *Journal of Educational Psychology (in press).*

Walker, H. M., Hops, H., and Johnson, S. M. Generalization and maintenance of classroom treatment effects. *Behavior Therapy,* 1975, **6**, 188-200.

Walker, H. M., Mattson, R. H., and Buckley, N. K. The functional analysis of behavior within an experimental class setting. In W. C. Becker (Ed.), *An empirical basis for change in education.* Chicago: Science Research Associates, 1971. Pp. 236-263.

APPENDIX A

Definitions of Codes

In the following list, code definitions are applicable to both behavior of the subject and to responses from teachers and peers unless noted otherwise.

Approval (AP): a person gives clear verbal, gestural, or physical approval to the students.

Complies (CO): the person does what another person has requested, *e.g.*, teacher asks class to take out notebooks and pupil does.

Appropriate Talking with Teacher (TT+): the pupil talks with the teacher about academic material whether in private as in independent work situations or answers questions in other situations.

Appropriate Interaction with Peer (IP+): the pupil is interacting wth peer about academic material and is not violating classroom rules.

Volunteering (VO): by verbal or nonverbal means the student exhibits behaviors associated with volunteering information of an academic nature.

Initiation to or by Teacher (IT): pupil or teacher *initiates* or *attempts* to initiate interaction with each other, but not in conjunction with volunteering.

Attending (AT): to be a subject response, the subject is looking at the teacher when the teacher is talking, looking at any materials in the classroom that have to do with the lesson, working on assignments, and engaging in other behaviors appropriate to the academic situation. To be a teacher or peer consequence, the behavior need not be in regard to academics, *i.e.*, teacher or peer looks at the child or engages in other behaviors that indicate they are paying attention to the child.

Physical Negative (PN): use of this category is restricted to times when a person attacks or attempts to attack another person with the possibility of inflicting pain.

Destructiveness (DS): a person destroys or attempts to destroy some object.

Disapproval (DI): a person gives clear verbal, gestural, or physical disapproval of another person's behavior or characteristics.

Noisy (NY): the person talks loudly, yells, bangs books, scrapes chairs, or makes any sounds that are likely to be actually or potentially disruptive to others.

Noncompliance (NC): the person does not do what is requested.

Play (PL): a person is playing alone or with another person.

Inappropriate Talk with Teacher (TT−): used whenever content of conversation with teacher is negative or nonacademically oriented or when classroom rules do not allow interaction with teacher.

Inappropriate Interaction with Peer (IP−): peer or pupil interacts with or attempts to interact with another about nonacademic matters or when classroom rules are being violated.

Inappropriate Locale (IL): student is in classroom area that is inappropriate for academic activity that is occurring.

Self-Stimulation (SS): the person attempts to stimulate himself in such ways as swinging his feet, rubbing his nose, ears, forehead, tapping his fingers, scratching, *etc.*, to such an extent that attention to other ongoing activities is precluded.

Look Around (LO): the subject is looking around the classroom environment or staring at something or someone that is not relevant to the current academic activity.

Not Attending (NA): the subject is in the appropriate area and is looking at other things in the immediate environment than those aspects that have to do with the current academic activity.

22

THE DEVELOPMENT OF INSTITUTIONS OF HIGHER EDUCATION: THEORY AND ASSESSMENT OF IMPACT OF FOUR POSSIBLE AREAS OF FEDERAL INTERVENTION

By

GEORGE B. WEATHERSBY, GREGORY A. JACKSON, FREDERIC JACOBS, EDWARD P. ST. JOHN, and TYLER TINGLEY

The Developing Institutions Program, Title III of the Higher Education Act of 1965, is the largest federal program providing direct aid to postsecondary institutions. In a well documented pioneer study, the authors consider three possible areas of impact: (1) structural development of colleges and universities, (2) levels of various collegiate activities, and (3) relative efficiency with which colleges provide instruction, research possibilities, and public service. In addition, they examine the determinants of student demand, focusing especially on those institutional actions which affect choice of college.

Although the legislative history of the program suggests that the program is, in part, designed to facilitate structural development, there currently are no measures of structural development which have been collected and reported by the Title III program. Using some of the available data, the authors find that institutions funded under the Title III basic program have activity levels not meaningfully different from colleges that were not funded or that never applied for funding. They found, in addition, that colleges which provided similar services showed wide variations in their resource use. Finally, this study suggests that student-aid policies have a greater impact on student attendance decisions than on any other single characteristic.

From George B. Weathersby et al., "The Development of Institutions of Higher Education: Theory and Assessment of Impact of Four Possible Areas of Federal Intervention." Report prepared for the United States Office of Education, January 1977.

EXECUTIVE SUMMARY

We believe there are four areas of college and university characteristics
which are relevant to the broad policy concerns of the Title III, "Developing
Institutions," program. These four areas are: (1) the structural development
of colleges and universities; (2) the levels of various collegiate activities
such as the number of students, faculty, library volumes, or terminal degree
recipients on the faculty; (3) the relative efficiency with which colleges and
universities provide instruction and, where appropriate, public service and
research; and (4) the determinants of student demand with a special focus on
those institutional actions which affect individuals' college going choices.
It is very important to be clear about these four areas when stating
objectives, organizing a funding program, selecting evaluation criteria, collecting program data and reaching conclusions about program effectiveness.
In the past decade the rhetoric of Title III has been almost entirely about
structural development (area 1); the eligibility criteria have all been
activity indicators (area 2); there has been little focus on relative efficiency (area 3); and one of the major effects attributed to the Title III
program, the increased enrollment of low income and ethnic minority students,
is probably more appropriately attributed to the massive increases in
federal student assistance (area 4).

Furthermore, our research and that of others suggest that these
four areas may be largely independent. That is, that colleges can mature
structurally without becoming larger or more expensive. Similarly, colleges
can undertake more activities without structural change or increased
efficiency. In practice, generous grant programs may reduce the rate of

structural development and/or remove the incentives for efficiency while simultaneously increasing the levels of institutional activities. If the assumption is that higher institutional activity levels attract students and serve a previously neglected clientele, there is no supporting statistical evidence for this assumption. If the expectation is that Title III funding enables colleges to expand their activity levels faster than they would otherwise, there is also no supporting evidence for this expectation (among Basic Program funded schools).

There are currently no measures of structural development collected and reported by the Title III program and, therefore, we are not able to reach any conclusions about this area. (1) In the absence of these data, we cannot test statistically the relationships among the four areas. What we do conclude from our own research and our analysis of previous research is:

- . These four areas should be recognized explicitly in any program design and evaluation of Title III;

- . Title III Basic Program funded institutions have activity levels not meaningfully different from colleges which were not funded or never applied;

- . Colleges providing apparently similar services have wide variations in resources used suggesting that significant improvements in efficiency are possible if encouraged; and

- . Public programs aimed at increasing the attractiveness of colleges through increased college activities and/or through increased financial aid should be considered as alternatives and analyzed jointly. Our statistical results indicate that student aid policies have a greater impact on student attendance decisions than do college characteristics, especially activity indicators.

II.   INTRODUCTION

Title III of the Higher Education Act of 1965 authorized federal
financial support of "developing institutions" of higher education.[1]
Financial assistance provided under Title III, Strengthening Developing
Institutions, was similar in form to the general institutional support provided through the two Morrill Acts. However, it departed significantly from
the student assistance and the categorical contracts which had characterized
most previous federal assistance for higher education.

Over the past decade the Developing Institutions program has become
the major federal medium to support institutions directly, assisting one
quarter of the higher education institutions in the United States. More
recently, the Education Amendments of 1972 (as amended in 1976) have extended
a philosophy of general institutional support beyond developing institutions
to encompass all institutions meeting desired criteria. While these new
institutional support provisions have not been funded, they manifest institutional support as a policy of accomplishing national objectives in higher
education.

The present study grew out of two general concerns: How does one
conceptualize developmental sequences for institutions of higher education?
If such sequences exist, how does outside financial assistance alter the rate
at which institutions progress through these sequences? More generally,
how effective is federal institutional assistance in accomplishing national
objectives for higher education such as student access and choice, program
and institutional diversity, and institutional growth and survival? We
cannot fully answer these broad questions, but we do suggest a framework

within which answers can be sought.

The essence of our framework is that there are four areas in which objectives for funding programs should be specified, and to which evaluative criteria should be applied. These four areas are: (1) the structural development of colleges and universities; (2) the levels of activities within colleges (students, faculty, courses, degrees, etc.); (3) the relative efficiency of resource use; and (4) student choice, including the impacts of college characteristics. The next four chapters address these four areas in sequence.

It is important to point out that this study does not evaluate program management by the Developing Institutions Division of the U.S. Office of Education nor the specific guidelines they are now employing. Instead, this study focuses on the effects on colleges and universities of receiving Title III funds. We have studied existing data bases, historical documents on Title III, and literature on institutional development and institutional resource use. We have used these to explore the impact of federal funds on the structural development of institutions, on institutional activities, on the efficiency of resource use, and on student decisions about higher education.

Context of Evaluation

The context in which we now review the consequences of Title III differs drastically from the mid-1960's context in which the Congress enacted it. At the time there were a burgeoning economy and low unemployment. Student unrest and the Vietnamese War were not yet major diverse issues. Enactment of civil rights legislation was a major national issue: the New Frontier, the Great Society, and the War on Poverty were major banners of activist government intervention. In 1965 there were explicit federal concerns for black colleges, although the legislative language called them institutions "out of the mainstream." There was an idea that unaccredited colleges, if given a small amount of federal assistance, might become accredited and thereby expand the number of accredited educational opportunities. Moreover, during this period of increasing enrollments, student access and choice could be facilitated by strengthening existing institutions (only institutions at least five years old are eligible for Title III) to complement the increasing number of new institutions, particularly in the public sector.

By the late nineteen-sixties and early nineteen-seventies the concept of federal support to developing institutions had expanded to encompass six to seven hundred public and private, two- and four-year institutions annually. The U.S. Office of Education gradually codified the vague eligibility criteria contained in the legislation and institutions meeting these criteria began to view the program as an entitlement.

A countervailing force to the entitlement concept was that of a developmental sequence. If funds were awarded to enable colleges to move along a sequence of development, would not some colleges ultimately develop and no longer need federal funding? This argument yielded the Advanced Institutional Development Program, intended for institutions which had received one or more years of Title III funding and advanced to a point where three to five years of additional funding would enable them to enter the "mainstream" of American higher education. This program essentially doubled the funding of Title III, from 55 to 110 million dollars a year. "Advanced" institutions were only to be eligible to receive advanced funds, and presumably any Title III funds, for a total of five years. However, this "up and out" phenomenon has not occured, and probably will not occur under the revised Title III guidelines.

As a result, after a decade the Title III program constitutes a natural experiment of providing financial assistance to colleges and universities to alter their developmental pattern or increase the delivery of services to their clientele. The program was not consciously designed thus; there was no carefully randomized control group, and "treatment" has been very idiosyncratic. However, there is adequate variation among the non-applicant, applicant, and funded populations to provide some insight into the impact of a general funding program. In this context we established our approach and methodology for this study.

In addition to this introduction, which outlines the plan and major caveats of the study, this report summarizes the results of our investigations into the impact of Title III on funded institutions. Succeeding chapters of the report discuss sequences of development, the impact of Title III funds on institutional activities, methods of assessing efficient resource use, and the possibly confounding student-aid effects on student choice. Each of these topics is treated in more detail in the various appendices; the last receives extensive treatment in a separate technical report.

Study Approach and Methodology

From the beginning, this study was limited by USOE to the use of existing data. We first identified all the existing national data bases which might shed some light on the institutional or student characteristics in higher education. Appendix F and the corresponding technical report give a complete description of the data bases we obtained and of the final integrated data base which we developed. All of the national surveys have been organized by topics, such as finance, enrollment, racial and ethnic composition of the student body, and earned degrees. These surveys have been administered in different years with varying longitudinal consistency.

We reorganized existing data bases so that all data pertaining to a single institution would be assembled as compactly as possible in one place. The sheer volume of data on each institution (over 40,000 characters) made it impracticable to create one record for each institution, but we came rather close to this ideal.

At the same time, we reviewed existing theories of institutional development which might be relevant to colleges and universities. Drawing upon previous studies of the Developing Institutions programs, and more fruitfully upon the general literature in organizational development, we developed a three-stratum framework for describing sequences of structural development in areas relevant to postsecondary education. The literature review and the detailed description of these theories of structural development constitute Appendix B. We identified from previous studies, the general literature, and the programs' own eligibility criteria a series of institutional characteristics which would be appropriate to the study of institutional development.

A small subset of these characteristics actually existed in the national data bases, and we analyzed these. At the descriptive level, we wanted to know whether Title III applicants differed substantially from non-applicants, and whether schools which received Title III funding differed substantially from applicants not funded. We developed an ad hoc measure of meaningful difference to determine whether distributions on each characteristic overlapped or differed for these groups. (Because we were dealing with the entire universe of higher-education institutions, traditional statistical sampling measures are not appropriate. Appendix C describes our analytic procedure in detail.)

Our descriptive analysis provides some evidence whether providing direct financial assistance to institutions produces observable changes in their characteristics. It is not, however, sufficient to answer more complicated questions related to resource use. We were interested in the relationship between Title III funding and funds from other sources. Does the receipt of Title III funds result in an increase or decrease in support from other sources? How efficiently are institutions using the resources they now receive? Are there rearrangements in these resources use patterns which could result in greater efficiency, with or without changes in a college's developmental sequence?

Since most of the funds of Title III recipients are primarily engaged in instruction and community service rather than research, we were also interested in student choice. How are student choices about whether to go to college and which college to attend related to institutional characteristics? In terms of student access and choice, what have been the relative impacts of federal student assistance and federal institutional assistance? We could not address these questions directly, but we did examine the effects of financial aid offers high school graduates postsecondary decisions in 1973.

Cautions to the Reader

One major constraint of this study is that at Government behest it was limited to existing data. While large amounts of data on institutions and on students have been collected, few measures relevant to institutional development have been collected and reported nationally. Furthermore, the data previously collected display many inconsistencies over time and among institutions in terms of definition, collection procedure, reporting accuracy, and many other characteristics. As described in the appendices, it was necessary to edit the data files received from various federal agencies to eliminate obviously erroneous data. While this process has been carefully documented, there is still room for error both in those data elements which were retained and in those data elements which were eliminated. Thus our statistical results are far from definitive.

Since the data were collected at the institutional level, we could not analyze intra-institutional differences in patterns of development or efficiency of resource use.

Our statistical procedures are at best correlational and provide no evidence of causality. This point is particularly important for the analysis of substitutive effects. We have tried to restrict our conclusions to statements of association rather than inferences of causality, although we know that for public policy purposes causality is the major concern. At the same time, we have presented a theoretical construct of patterns of institutional development to inform judgments of causality from our data on association.

The reader should keep these shortcomings and uncertainties in mind as he or she proceeds. However, our conclusions have policy implications which we summarize in the concluding section. The limitations are important, but it is equally important that the reader not lose sight of the overall perspective.

III. SEQUENCES OF STRUCTURAL DEVELOPMENT

Most higher education institutions enroll students, hire faculty, acquire library volumes, construct and maintain facilities, employ staff, enter into contracts, and undertake myriad other activities. Without external financial support, there are limits to an institution's ability to undertake these activities given only a paying student clientele. As a matter of public interest, state and national governments support directly the public institutions which enroll over three-quarters of the college and university students in the United States. To a much lesser extent, there is direct public support for the private or independent institutions which enroll the remainder. Most public policy toward higher education is aimed at expanding institutional activities, including community service, research and development, special services for educationally-disadvantaged individuals, health-science professional training, and a variety of specially-targeted programs. Similarly, publicly provided student assitance expands individuals' financial capacity to attend collegiate and other postsecondary education, and therefore should increase the proportion of adults who take advantage of their postsecondary educational opportunities. Again, this strategy will, if anything, increase institutional activities. With the American penchant for growth, public support has primarily been available to expand activity levels, not to contract them.

What distinguishes Title III from other Federal programs is the premises of institutional development on which the Developing Institutions program is based: structural development is possible, direct federal support can influence the rate of structural development, and more evolved forms of structural development are preferable in terms of public policy. Thus the program should develop capacities within institutions as well as expand activities. However, it has been difficult to implement this concept, and the indicators used to determine eligibility and disburse Title III funds measure activity rather than structural development.

We began our investigation into institutional development by considering observable sequences of structural change. Do colleges and universities progress through a series of structurally different stages of development, or do they simply undertake more or less of a variety of activities? If there are distinguishable patterns of structural development, are some more stable, capable of dealing flexibly and resourcefully with the financial exigencies of an uncertain future? Or is an institution's ability to make choices about its future virtually unaffected by its pattern of development? If general sequences of structural development exist in colleges and universities, can interventions by outside agents, such as the federal government or philanthropic foundations, affect either the rate or the sequence of development? Does an institution's structural development affect the delivery of services or the efficient use of resources to accomplish its objectives?

These are key questions for public policy toward institutional support. They are also difficult questions to answer. This report initiates answers to some of them. We present here some important dimensions of structural development and suggest measures which might indicate the extent to which institutions are involved in these processes.[2] In summary, we believe that:

(1) there are distinguishable structural patterns of development, especially in the areas of technology and decision making;

(2) these patterns of structural development do affect the efficiencies of resource use and the capacities of institutions to deal with the financial and other crises which beset them;

(3) some forms of outside assistance may help institutions change their patterns of development;

(4) activity expansion may induce structural development, but not necessarily of institutional capacities to cope with crises other than growth; and

(5) general subsidies may enable institutions to postpone institutional transformations necessary for adaptation to new, long-term demographic and economic conditions.

In this section we consider three views of structural development for colleges and universities: shifts in the technologies of instruction and management available to higher education institutions; the sequential development of institutional decision structures; and patterns of qualitative development in institutional instruction and decision process. Finally, we assess existing measures of institutional change in light of this three-level framework.

Developmental Patterns of Technological Change

The instruction, research, and public-service functions of colleges and universities are constrained by prevailing technologies. Lecture instruction, for example, reflected the dearth of reading material: only hand-copied books were available, so the lecturer or reader would stand in front of the class and read from the book. The printing press and the photocopy machine now enable each student to have his or her own copy. The size of the audience was initially limited by the range of the human voice; today, telecommunication provides virtually limitless audiences. Neither of these potentials is often realized. The computer has made possible a scale of numerical calculations for statistics and mathematics unheard of two decades ago. The same can be said for a number of computer-based managerial advances in college and university administration. The important point here is that the rate of technological advance does not depend on the organizational development of colleges and universities. On the other hand, the structural development of colleges and universities does depend substantively on the rate of technological development. For example, in television based institutions, the patterns of institutional development have been and probably will continue to be different from those of a face-to-face instructional college.[3]

The discussion of this view is based on W. W. Rostow's (1960) stages of economic growth. Rostow's model is based on changes in the dominant technology being employed in the economy of developing nations. This model can be used to consider the implications of current shifts in technology on the higher education industry as a whole.

Rostow's concept also provided the intellectual basis for the stages of college and university development proposed by Hodgkinson and Schenkel (1974) in a previous study of the Title III program. There is an understandable appeal in dividing institutions into stages called preconditions for take-off, take-off, drive to maturity, and high mass consumption. Although Hodgkinson's model used this terminology, it did not take into account shifts in use of technology and the resulting distributions of income, labor, and capital. It is difficult to apply these economic concepts to educational institutions because most have essentially the same technology, or at least the same technological possibilities. It is very difficult to distinguish the technology of instruction used at a "well-developed" institution from that used at a "developing" institution.

In the "academic procession" there are a few leading institutions which establish the dominant pattern and technology of instruction followed by most other institutions.[4] It is unlikely that the application of different technologies in existing institutions either reflects or causes different patterns of institutional development. For example, if an established campus adopts new technologies, like computers and television, it is not likely that the dominant mode of pedagogy will change. Therefore, it is unlikely that changes in technical possibilities or in the application of technology to education will have a substantial impact on the structural organization of educational institutions.

Structural Patterns of Decision Making

A second way of understanding patterns of institutional development is to focus on the making and implementing of decisions rather than the output-producing processes such as instruction, research, or public service. The research of Larry E. Greiner (1972) and others suggests a developmental sequence in the decision making patterns of institutions of higher education.

Colleges and universities tend to emerge through a series of phases: a creative phase with a small number of individuals organized to accomplish a particular task; a direction phase in which the beginnings of functional specialization occur in academic as well as administrative arenas; a delegation phase which has extensive differentiation of academic and administrative functions and specialties; a coordination phase in which new administrative planning and analysis structures emerge and policy formulation becomes distinct from policy implementation, at least formally; and a collaboration phase in which individuals play multiple roles and at the same time integrate the concerns for policy formulation and policy implementation. These phases are points along a continuum and not distinct categories; they represent common clusterings of characteristics rather than precisely differentiable forms of organizations. Transitions between phases often occur, at least in theory, as part of the resolution of problems generic to each phase. In addition to the substantive problems which face an organization, there are also problems inherent in the organization structure by which substantive decisions are implemented. These inherent "managerial crises" provide both a threat to organizational survival and an opportunity for organizational growth.

According to this perspective, creative organizations are typically very informal; policy formation and decision making occur over a cup of coffee or around the water cooler. Implementation is similarly ad hoc. Frequently a charismatic leader is the major stimulus for the formation of a new organization. Moreover, individuals who forsake more traditional alternatives to commit their energies and efforts to a new venture need substantial degrees of personal autonomy.

The creative phase, with its informal administrative structure and style of decision-making, typically confronts a crisis of leadership. It is essential for someone to speak for the organization when financial crises severely threaten the continuation of the status quo, when student unrest brings increased political pressure from government or trustees, or when anything places severe strain on the decision-making process of a creative organization. The decisions of who is in charge, who can commit the future course of theorganization, and who defines the vision and the mission of the organization resolve the crisis of leadership. If internal dissension is high and the crisis is severe, creative organizations might split into several smaller units instead of resolving the crisis of leadership at the entire organizational level. Alternatively, they could choose to have key leaders differentiate their roles along a variety of areas within academic and administrative affairs, and between administrative affairs and policy oversight, so it is clear who speaks about what for the organization. This is the beginning of a directive structure.

Directive structures, in turn, confront the crisis of autonomy. This occurs when individuals find the visions which originally attracted them to the organization are no longer widely shared among the administrative officers, their own sphere of action is being circumscribed, and their ability to be a free agent and yet participate in every decision has been greatly reduced. At this point many key people may leave seeking a more receptive environment elsewhere, or start their own organization. To adjust, the college or university may increasingly differentiate the functions to give each actor his or her own turf. This highly delegated structure, resembling the multiple departments in even our smallest liberal arts colleges, is a structural response to the crisis of autonomy.

The crisis of control tends to occur in a delegated structure. Increases in the number of actors with powers of initiation, the distance between the operating and the policy levels, the formality of interaction, and non-faculty and non-policy staffs in the middle management of an institution raise the probability that trustees and chief executives will view the organization as being out of control. In this context, control relates to the degree of congruity between the goals and purposes of the

institution and the activities followed by the members of the institution.
As the complexity of an organization increases, so does the likelihood that
the whole is far less than the sum of the parts. With increasing form-
alization, the major response to the crisis of control is to create another
level of bureaucracy with the purpose of planning and coordination within an
institution.

The red-tape crisis results from successful implementation of the
coordination phase. As the proportion of total resources devoted to
administrative overhead increases in an organization, it becomes increasingly
clear to most observers that a more efficient way has to be found both to
coordinate the activities of an institution and to reduce the administrative
overhead costs. This is the basis of a collaborative organization which,
in many senses, may resemble the creative organization.

This spiral evolution, coming full circle but slightly displaced in
terms of structural development and capacity, may be followed by many
organizational subunits as well as by entire organizations. There is no
"best" level of development. Neither is there any assurance that a particular
crisis once resolved will not recur or that the resolutions found are
entirely appropriate. The theory leaves unspecified the appropriate match
between style and type of leadership and the structural phase of an
organization. There appears to be a direct relationship here, but the
available research is far too limited to say what it is.

While there is neither evidence nor reason to suggest that more
evolved stages of development are better, the differences of perspective
associated with each stage may be helpful in understanding organizational
crises. For example, a college president might view faculty workload as an
issue reflecting a general, underlying concern for accountability,

perceive it as a crisis of control, and therefore advocate a planning or coordinating structural response. On the other hand, faculty might well interpret the institution to be in a crisis of autonomy and react by demanding a more delegated structure. An unresponsive administration might find itself in a collective bargaining situation which solidifies a delegated structure. The substance of an issue might appear to be the same from two perspectives but the organization's structural context (or prevailing crisis) may be perceived to be very different from different perspectives.

Sequential Development of Interpersonal Systems

A third way to understand patterns of institutional development is to focus on the interpersonal relationships that are at the heart of educational enterprise--relationships among students, faculty and administrators. Qualitative changes in the interpersonal dynamics and decision-making process operating on a campus are related to, although not necessarily dependent on, the development of new learning technologies and more differentiated administrative structures. The literature on organizations calls bureaucracy an advanced form of organizing interpersonal relationships, and depicts it as a system of defined relationships, roles, and procedures. Most campuses are successful in developing to a bureaucratic stage, but few move beyond it. Recent history suggests, however, that students and others on many campuses have become dissatisfied with this mode of organizing, and indeed several organization theorists suggest that there is a more advanced form of organizing than bureaucracy.

Especially during the past decade, campuses have experimented with qualitatively different patterns of organizing. They have modified existing structures and programs by placing more emphasis on individual students' learning goals than on predefined educational requirements and on developing collaborative, rather than authoritative, methods of decision-making. This has yielded experiments with post-bureaucratic forms of organizing, known variously as "snared authority," "beyond bureaucracy," or "openly chosen structures." William R. Torbert's (1974/75) concept of openly chosen structures can be applied to higher education. Openly chosen structures require higher-education institutions to hold an atypical set of values. Ironically, in many ways, openly chosen structures in higher education would not differ drastically from those dictated by now-forgotten mid-nineteenth century concepts of liberal education: organizing the curriculum to enhance the moral development of students; providing educational experiences that help students adjust to numerous future career options; and creating an environment that encourages higher quality, ongoing exchanges and relationships among students and faculty.

The qualitative factors distinguishing an organization with openly chosen structure from one operating in predefined-productivity or bureaucratic stage can be considered measures of viability for institutions and programs, in that institutions that explicitly examine their relations with external communities and organizations are more advanced. Although it is not necessary according to Torbert's description, in our opinion institutions that involve faculty and students as well as administrators in policy formulation and implementation decisions are also more advanced. Increased student and faculty participation can concomitantly increase commitment to the institution. When an institution's students and faculty feel committed to a new program because of their involvement in it, the program may have a greater impact than one with a limited investment on the part of the individuals it is supposed to benefit.

Openly chosen structure also emphasizes interpersonal relations and the development of the individual. In higher education researchers have long paid attention to the students' maturation and intellectual growth, and therefore many institutions consider these factors when developing programs. Educational programs' ability to meet the educational needs of individuals at different stages of development have been a more recent concern. And there appears to be a parallel concern about faculty and administrators' development. Consideration of what institutional plans and their implementation imply for the development of individuals in the institutions--whether through educational programs for students or staff development for faculty and administrators--may be an increasingly important measure of institutional and program viability in the future.

For the modern campus, openly chosen structure can take the form of individually centered rather than institutionally centered curricula; developing procedures that encourage the involvement of students as well as faculty and administration in decisions that directly affect them; and considering campus decisions in light of community as well as campus interests. Enhancement of how people learn is, after all, a major objective of most collegiate education. Although central to the purposes of the institutions, these interpersonal dynamics are very removed from federal decisions and are the least likely to be influenced by federal interventions.

Possible Measures of Structural Development

In the following discussion of measures, we suggest a series of indicators appropriate to the three types of institutional development. We offer these tentative measures more to widen vision and make specific some of the developmental concepts than to propose a formal extension to what is already too large a data collection effort at the national level. If these measures could only capture the intuition and common sense of experienced observers, they would be very helpful in understanding the complex patterns of institutional development.

The first set of measures in Table I relates to the development of the technology used by institutions. Technological development in its broadest sense refers to the relative sophistication of the means used in institutional activities. It includes both traditional and nontraditional teaching, service, research, and management activities. The first dimension relates to observable characteristics of institutional activities, including such quanitative measure as enrollment, number of faculty, faculty with doctorates, faculty salaries, and library volumes. The technological characteristics have been further broken down into two categories, hardware and software. Software comprises development in instructional programs-- basic skills, individualized instruction, work experience, and assessment of prior experience. Hardware, in contrast, refers to the use of equipment (e.g., television, film, and computers) in the instructional delivery process. Closely related but nevertheless distinct is the relative efficiency with which institutions and institutional programs use resources.

The phase of development of an institution's decision structure and the appropriateness of the management system to that phase can be described by a second set of measures. Phase can best be assessed either from institutional case histories or by identifying the types of managerial crises that predominate: leadership, autonomy, control, or red tape. Considering the types of crises facing an institution can have useful implications for institutional management as well; a predominance of one type of crisis suggests an institution's decision structures and information system may no longer be the most appropriate.

The development of interpersonal processes in the institution and its programs--that is, the openness of the system and its impact on individuals in the institution--can be identified by a third set of measures. Subjective judgments by students and surveys by social science professionals measuring individual change can be used to evaluate program impact, while case histories, analysis of decisions, and examination of the governance process (participation in policy making and implementation) can be used to evaluate openness. Qualitative changes are the most difficult of the three types of development to measure usefully for evaluation, but they are important nevertheless.

Relevance for Policy

For every policy action directed at a perceived deficiency in a college or university's activities, there is, almost as if it were a social law of motion, some kind of reaction among the structural characteristics of that institution. This reaction may contribute to the purposes of initial action, but we suspect the structural consequences of most activity-oriented policies are both unplanned and unperceived. Thus, increasing the income of the institution for a short period of time, which is an activity-directed intervention, might not alter the institution's pattern of development or even its level of service. Similarly, one must not assume that increasing the level of service--for example, meeting all enrollment demands--positively affects the structural development of the institution.

These different perspectives on development suggest some ways in which outside agents could intervene constructively in the developmental sequence of a college or a university. The most effective strategies would differ, depending upon the sort of development one wants to affect. Purely financial changes are unlikely to lead systematically to evolution along any of the developmental dimensions discussed in this section. It is very likely, however, that changes in financial conditions will produce or reflect changes in institutional activities, on which we focus in the next section.

IV. ACTIVITY INDICATORS FOR COLLEGES AND UNIVERSITIES

From the legislative origins of Title III to the present, the Developing Institutions Program has been greatly concerned with institutional activities, whether or not they reflect development. In this section, we examine the activity indicators which the Office of Education has used recently to determine institutional eligibility for Title III funding. These indicators are given in Table 2.

Using Title III application data, we compared the activity characteristics of institutions which received funding to institutions that did not. Using Higher Education General Information Survey (HEGIS) data for virtually all institutions of higher education, we compared institutions which did not apply for Title III funding to applicant institutions, both receipient and non-recipient.

In essence, we were trying to determine whether the program distinguished categories of institutions according to the activity indicators used for eligibility. Using the same data plus additional information on private giving, we also examined interrelationships among sources of income to see whether the receipt of Title III funds affected the magnitude of funds received from other sources.

It is important to understand that from the beginning of the activity analysis we were not attempting to discover those institutional characteristics which do distinguish Title III funded from all other institutions. Essentially, the quanitative analysis of institutional data could be used for at least two purposes: to determine those correlational

factors which "best" describe or predict the funding decisions of the Title III
program staff or to determine whether the Title III program eligibility
criteria meaningfully distinguish non-applicant from applicant and recipient
from non-recipient institutions. Consistent with our overall study design
in which we were not evaluating program management, we have not developed a
statistical model of program funding decisions among eligible institutions.[5]
What we have focused on is whether the eligibility criteria, which are all
activity measures, actually sort institutions out into substantively different
groups, whether the recipient institutions have activity measures similar
to non-recipient institutions, and whether over the five years of data we
examined the activity measures of the recipient institutions changed at a
rate appreciably different from the rate of change of activity measures of
the non-recipient institutions.

Findings of Descriptive Analyses

When the level (two-year or four-year) and control (public or
private) of institutions were taken into account, the three activity indicators used as eligibility criteria by the Title III program and also
available from HEGIS, consistently showed the non-applicant group to be
larger in total FTE enrollment and educational and general expenditures.
However, there were no meaningful differences in the ratio of educational
and general expenditures to FTE enrollment for the four institutional groups
examined (Figures 1, 2, 3). Although these institutions appear different
when means are compared, tnese differences are neither substantial or
meaningful in light of the within-group variation. Further detail is available in Appendix C.

Figure 1

Generated Total FTE Enrollment

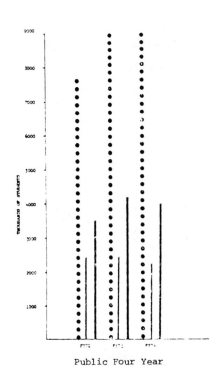

Public Four Year

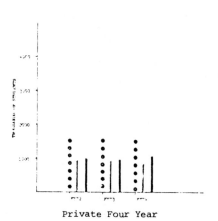

Private Four Year

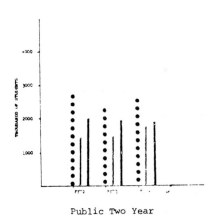

Public Two Year

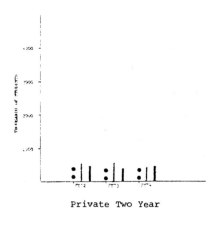

Private Two Year

Source: HEGIS Data Base

Figure 2

Total Education and General Purpose

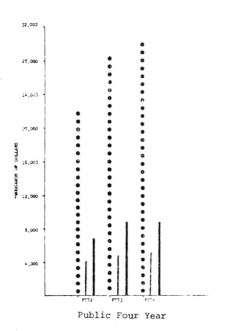

Public Four Year

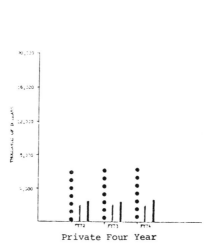

Private Four Year

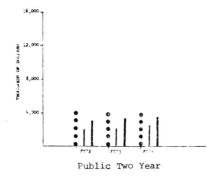

Public Two Year

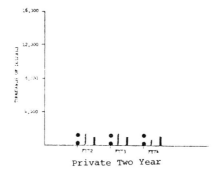

Private Two Year

Source: HEGIS Data Base

Non Funded (Basic Applicant)
Basic Funded
● ● ● ● ● ● ● Non Applicant

Figure 3

Education and General Purpose Expenditures/
FTE Student

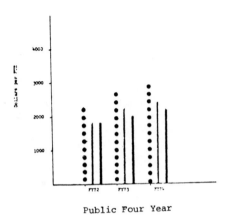

Public Four Year

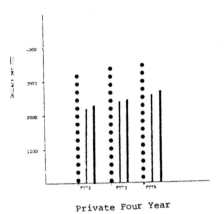

Private Four Year

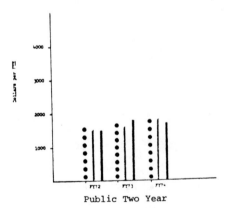

Public Two Year

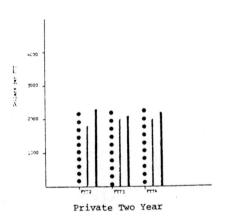

Private Two Year

Source: HEGIS Data Base

The recipients of Advanced Institutional Development Program (AIDP) funding, on the other hand, clearly differed from other institutions. AIDP institutions enrolled more students, spent more, possessed larger library collections, employed a higher proportion of faculty with doctoral degrees, and so forth than institutions funded in the Basic program or non-funded applicant institutions (Table 3 a-h). Subsequent analysis comparing funded and non-funded AIDP applicants substantiated this general finding. AIDP-funded institutions were again consistently larger on most characteristics. These latter findings are slightly misleading, however, because institutions could apply for both the Basic and Advanced programs for the years covered by our data. Often, applicant institutions denied funding under the Advanced programs were funded under the Basic Program (see Appendix C).

We have observed the three categories of institutions--non-applicants, non-funded applicants, and funded applicants--over a period of three to five years based on existing data. During this time, the Title III recipient institutions indicate increasing activity levels: increasing enrollment, increasing total budget, increasing library holdings, increasing proportion of faculty with doctoral degrees, and so forth. However, during the same time period, non-funded applicant institutions and non-applicant institutions showed a very similar pattern of increased activity levels. (Again, see Appendix C for a full data presentation.) In summary, there is no evidence to suggest that Title III recipient institutions have increased their levels of activity at a rate any different than other institutions of higher education.

Institutions of higher education have many sources of funds including: federal, state, and local governments, students, endowment, gifts, and revenues from auxiliary enterprises. We examined the interaction among these income sources by calculating the simple correlation co-efficients among all the sources of income for all Title III institutions reporting data, classified by Carnegie category and control. Table 4 sumarizes our results. With relatively few exceptions, we observed positive correlations between other sources of income and Title III funding. With the exception of alumni gifts to private liberal-arts colleges, which were negatively and substantially correlated with Title III funding, all the other sources appear to vary positively with the Title III funding. This suggests either that institutions which successfully obtain Title III funds also obtain funds from other sources or that institutions' ability to secure funds from other sources is enhanced by the receipt of Title III funds. In fact, most correlation coefficients were positive. That is, institutions which secure income from one source also secure it from most others. In any event, there appears to be very little substitution of Title III funds for funds from other sources; apparently the federal govern-ment is indeed increasing the resources available to an institution rather than simply changing distribution of sources.

We recognize that activity indicators provide little information on the actual patterns of institutional development. However, they have been used to assess program eligibility and, for that reason, their distribution merited investigation. We found that:

(1) While institutions which do not apply to the Title III program tend to be larger than applicant institutions in both FTE enrollment and educational and general purpose expenditures, they are not meaningfully different in the ratio of expenditure to enrollment.

(2) Basic-funded institutions' activity indicators increased over the past five years, but at about the same rate as non-recipients.

(3) AIDP recipients are meaningfully different from institutions funded in the Basic Program and from non-funded institutions. AIDP recipients tend to be larger on almost every indicator than those schools which were denied funding.

(4) There is little evidence of substitution among income sources in response to Title III; there is some evidence that Title III funding does increase the total amount of resources available to the institution.

V. EFFICIENCY OF INSTITUTIONAL RESOURCE USE

In addition to concern about structural development, which we could not measure and about increased effectiveness of the institutions, which we could measure crudely using activity-level indicators, a third area of concern is the relative efficiency with which colleges and universities use resources. Effectiveness, to us, is a measure of the degree to which objectives are accomplished, while efficiency provides a measure of the magnitude of resources used to accomplish those objectives.[6] In our general framework, an outside agent such as the federal government can seek to increase the delivery of services by higher education institutions by increasing (1) the rate or congruity of institutional development, (2) the level of activity within the existing state of development, (3) the efficiency with which current institutional technology is applied, or (4) the choice patterns of individuals seeking educational services.

In this section, we discuss some of the available evidence on the relative efficiency of resource use by colleges and universities, particularly as it relates to instruction. For the one or two hundred major research universities, graduate instruction and research greatly confound any attempt to use undergraduate instruction as a primary outcome of the institution. For most other institutions, however, providing direct student instruction is a major activity and therefore outcome of those institutions. The research of the last ten years is described in Appendix D and suggests that it is appropriate to use student instruction as an outcome measure to distinguish institutions which use resources in a relatively efficient manner from all other institutions providing similar services or producing comparable

outcomes. Assessing comparability of outcomes is a long and complicated
process still in its preliminary stages of development, but some work has
been using Carnegie categories and public or private control as points of
departure (see Carlson, 1975, described below).

Institutions providing comparable outcomes typically vary in patterns
of resource use. For any given level of total resource input, we will
observe institutions providing a wide variety of outcome levels of a given
quality, such as the number of students enrolled in various programs.
There will be some institutions which provide more of a given outcome than
others. We label the set of institutions which provides the most outcome
of comparable quality for any given level of input as the efficient set
(Figure 4). The efficient set of institutions provides two useful benchmarks
simultaneously: the most output observed for a given amount of total input,
and the minimum amount of input found necessary to yield a given level of
output. Many if not most institutions are below the efficient set; that
is, they use more resources than they need to produce the same levels of
output. This is not to say that higher education institutions are careless
or wasteful, but rather that there have been few incentives to maximize their
efficiency. There have been clear incentives, for example, to increase
faculty salaries, decrease faculty work load, decrease average class size,
and increase student services, some of which also contribute to increased
quality of outcomes. But all of these incentives contribute to increased
costs.

Most of the previous studies of institutional resource use--unit-
cost studies, ratio analyses, and the usual comparative statistics collected
and reported by USOE, educational associations, and special studies--have
focused on the average use of resources by groups of institutions. By

Figure 4
Efficient Set of Institutions

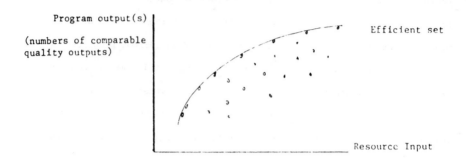

The Efficient Set comprises those institutions for which no
more output can be produced with the same resources and no
fewer resources can be used to produce the same quantity of
output.

definition, about half of the institutions are more efficient and approximately half are less efficient than the average institution. From a public-policy perspective, increasing the relative efficiency of existing institutions would increase the level of services they are able to provide at current or even reduced levels of resource input. From the institution's perspective, there are obvious incentives for increasing the amount of input for a given level of output because these resource increases are shared in personally by faculty, administrators, and students.

In some analyses, linear programming is used to identify the efficient set, then multiple regression analysis is used to estimate a continuous function through the efficient set which describes how resources can be translated into outcomes--for example, student enrollment outcome (see Appendix G). This approach has been used many times before to analyze industrial production analyses, and on one or two previous occasions to study the outcomes of educational institutions.[7]

While it is difficult to reach general conclusions about all institutions based on the existing literature and on the preliminary analysis we have performed, the previous work of Daryl Carlson (1975) and others substantiates the general finding: a significant proportion of institutions lie below the efficient set and could, therefore, increase their output with existing resources by reorganizing their use of those resources.

For example, Carlson examined 1972-73 HECIS data by the linear programming techniques of estimating the efficient surface (or frontier) and calculated the results shown in Tables 5, 6, 7 and 8 for 106 private, highly selective liberal arts colleges and for 95 public comprehensive colleges. As shown in Tables 6 and 8, the average institutions spends about 80% more per student than the efficient institutions. Alternatively,

if an average institution spent its resources like an efficient institution
it would have about 40% of its cost per student to save or devote to other
purposes. The amount of funds absorbed by technical inefficiency, as
measured by Carlson, is far greater than even the largest Title III awards
to institutions. Furthermore, Carlson shows that his results are relatively
insensitive to the proportion of part-time students, the size of the
institution, the number of graduate students, or the level of research
(Tables 5, 6, 7 and 8).

To the extent institutional effectiveness as measured by activity
indicators is a significant goal for public policy, it seems to us
efficiency should also be sought. This research gives us some indication
that this policy alternatives would be valuable. There is also some evidence
that traditional assumptions about the economy of scale and the relative
desirability of capital versus operating support for institutions are not
completely valid (see Appendix G). At this time, these findings yield
questions without definitive answers, in part because of inadequacies in
the available data and in part because the requisite analyses go beyond the
intended scope of this project. However, these questions can be answered
and, perhaps for policy purposes, should be answered instead of continuing
to act on the assumptions they challenge.

VI.   STUDENT CHOICES AND EFFECTS OF STUDENT AID PROGRAMS

Title III accounts for only about 5 percent of federal spending under the Higher Education Act (as amended). Most of the remainder goes to direct student aid under the Basic and Supplemental Educational Opportunity Grants, College Work-Study, and Student Loan Programs. Each of these presumably has influenced the likelihood prospective students would enroll, and the ensuing changes in enrollment might well have counter-acted or enhanced the impact of Title III on institutions' ability to grow.

With a view toward disentangling these effects, we attempted in a sub-study to estimate how student aid programs might have changed enrollment.[8] We estimate federal student-aid programs brought aid to four to nine percent of college applicants who would not otherwise have received aid. This suggests these programs have had relatively little impact on enrollment nationally, increasing the overall attendance rate among applicants by a total of 0.3 to 2.0 percentage points from fall 1969 to fall 1972. (The rapid growth in Basic Educational Opportunity Grants is not reflected in currently available longitudinal data.) Since the enrollment rate actually declined over these years, countervailing forces evidently existed. Institution-specific aid might have helped Title III institutions draw additional applicants, since student aid's competitive effects are larger than its attendance-inducing ones, but it is likely other schools would have done the same and canceled any advantage.

The study provided some useful, interesting descriptions of the forces that move high-school graduates into colleges. First, students' backgrounds, academic performance, and aspirations predominate in students' decisions whether to apply, how many and what sorts of schools to apply to, and whether or where to attend. This places limits on programs which fail to modify these forces; for example, programs which focus on high-scoring students will eventually yield no new enrollees unless they also increase the stock of such students by improving other students' performance.

Second, fewer than half the applicants apply to more than one school, and those who do so apply to remarkably homogeneous ones. This suggests preselection is a critical stage in the college-going process, and that institutional changes or policies invisible to a student at preselection time will have little impact on where he or she attends.

Third, colleges' admission decisions have very little substantive impact on where students go to college. Under 20 percent of three-application students' first-choice applications elicited rejections. Overall, only about 8 percent of first-choice applications were rejected; only 3.3 percent of students were rejected by all of their choices. The conventional wisdom on this point is that multi-applicants' first choices are seldom fulfilled dreams, an assertion not borne out here. Either the myth has never been true or it has become self-fulfilling at the preselection stage.

Fourth, college characteristics other than financial aid have little effect on students' decisions whether to attend, and only highest offering and financial aid appear to influence selection among several offers of admission. This reflects the preselection phenomenon we mentioned above.

Finally, the effects of financial aid on students' decisions span socioeconomic, regional, and academic-ability boundaries: financial-aid offers increase the likelihood students will attend at all by about

8.5 percentage points and increase the likelihood they will choose a particular school rather than another offering no aid by about 11.5 percentage points. There are undoubtedly extremes for which these amount/ eligibility trade-offs are not valid, but these are the effects observed in practice.

Although they provide little of interest to Title III per se, the results of our demand study place fairly strict limits on the enrollment changes to be expected from universal financial-aid programs. In 1972 about 21 percent of all college admission offers were accompanied by aid offers; we estimate that had every admission carried an aid offer enrollment among applicants would only have risen by 6.3 percentage points. Presumably some students would have applied who did not, but it unlikely enough would have done so to change the thrust of these conclusions. Financial aid is on its face an effective way to give money to needy students so that they may attend college if they wish; there is little evidence here or elsewhere that it is an effective or efficient way to induce large numbers of them to do so.

What is of direct interest to those seeking to evaluate the impacts of Title III using the numbers and characteristics of students is that we have no statistical evidence that institutional characteristics beyond the highest degree offered (which sorts out two-year, four-year and graduate institutions) and whether or not aid was offered have any impact on student choice. With over 90% of college applicants admitted to their first choice institutions and over 95% of college applicants admitted to one of their choices, there is also no evidence of frustrated choices or pent-up demand constrained by inadequate institutional resources. The vast majority of college applicants are apparently admitted wherever they apply and go

where they choose. What is not so clear is that individuals' preselections
of where to apply are made with full and current knowledge of institutional
characteristics, or what the actual effects on preselections depend on
the perhaps erroneous information that guides them.

VII.   CONCLUSIONS AND RECOMMENDATIONS

In this report we have argued there are four different areas of concern relevant to the history and the practice of the Developing Institutions program. These four areas of concern are: (1) the structural, developmental sequence or sequences which colleges and universities experience; (2) the levels of activities undertaken by institutions; (3) the relative efficiency of resource use by institutions in offering various activities and services; and (4) the institutional and environmental factors which affect student choice both whether to attend some form of postsecondary education and which particular institution to attend. All four of these areas represent important and significant concerns of national policy; all reflect arguments advanced during the legislative debate leading to Title III of the Higher Education Act. To some extent, these areas of concern suggest different bases for program planning and evaluation. One obvious conclusion, therefore, is that planning, program implementation, and evaluation should be done consistently according to the area or areas chosen as the basis for the program. It is inconsistent, for example, to use a set of activity measures for program eligibility and a series of development measures for program evaluation.

The legislative history, program history, and evolution of eligibility criteria all reinforce the conclusion that the current Title III program is focused primarily on increasing the activities of funded institutions. With some exceptions, our basic conclusion is that the quanitative measures of institutional activity available to us show no significant differences between funded and other similar institutions. The notable exceptions are twofold: the Advanced program has funded institutions

which have previously achieved high activity levels, and the Basic program
has selected a set of institutions with proportionately greater enrollments
of low-income and ethnic-minority students.

This latter observation suggests there is some intention to serve
such students, perhaps based on the assumption that institutional characteristics will affect such students' choices whether to attend college. There
is no empirical support for this latter assumption.

In our conversations with individuals concerned with this program, a
constant theme has been the developmental sequence through which institutions
are assumed to emerge. The quantitative data currently available provide no
meaningful measures of institutional development. Consequently, we cannot assess
the impact of Title III funds on institutional development. However, we have
suggested a series of measures which might provide some insight into sequences
of institutional development, and we recommend later in this section a pilot
testing of these measures to determine the feasibility of a new data-collection
and analysis process.

Based on our review of the literature and our own analysis, we see no
reason to assume the levels of activity undertaken by an institution necessarily
relate to its location on some pattern or sequence of development. In other
words, we see no reason to believe that "developed" institutions spend more
money per student, have more library volumes, have a higher proportion of
faculty with doctoral degress, have a higher proportion of low income or ethnic
minority students, admit a higher proportion of clever students, have a larger
development office, undertake more curricula reform, or indeed differ on any
other traditional activity measures.[9] More important, the converse may equally
be true: active institutions need not be developed. Increasing budgets,
student enrollments, numbers of faculty, number and variety of courses offered,
or any other activity need not cause a change in the pattern of institutional

development.

Although the evidence on institutional efficiency is relatively limited, we believe it is possible to identify institutions which use their resources in a relatively efficient manner to produce observable and measurable outcomes. We believe it is possible to describe these relatively efficient institutions by conventional economic production functions which represent the efficient production possibilities even though most academic institutions share a value system of relatively inefficiency -- that is, administrators and faculty generally seek higher faculty salaries, lower faculty work loads, smaller classes, and lower student/faculty ratios. From the student or government point of view, these pressures against relatively efficient resource use should raise serious questions about the likely impact of the financial support they provide these institutions as clients.

Following through with a careful analysis of the relatively efficient institutions along the lines we have suggested would provide some indication of the minimum level of support needed for a particular level of activity.[10] The provision of additional resources to expand the levels of activity in institutions is essential only for those institutions that are relatively efficient. One obvious public strategy would be to provide information about the variety of resource-use characteristics of institutions along the efficient surface and to predicate financial support to institutions on the capabilities of the relatively efficient institutions, thereby creating some incentive for other institutions to use their own resources more efficiently.

While colleges and universities have many complex and sometimes conflicting purposes, one common objective is to serve students who seek to continue their eduction at the collegiate level. In the last decade maximizing student access and freedom of choice have become important objectives to institutions and to state and federal funders. Although research on the determinants of student choice is relatively recent and still quite limited, the available evidence suggests that institutional characteristics play a relatively small role in individuals' choices (or preselection) whether or where to secure higher eduction. On the other hand, pricing and financial-aid decisions of institutions and governments appear to have some impact on student choice. The available evidence indicates that student financial aid is likely to be much more efficient means to use public money to alter student attendance patterns than institutional support.

While we have attempted to describe what is discernible from existing quantitative data bearing on the four areas of important concern to the Title III program, it has become increasingly clear to us that the most significant data either have not been collected or, if collected, have not been made available coherently. In particular, the area of the patterns of institutional develop-ment, the available data do not speak at all to the types of measures we have suggested. We believe the measures we have suggested should be pilot tested and refined for a limited number of institutions. If they prove to effectively identify the various patterns of institutional development experienced by these pilot institutions, a more substantial effort could be mounted to determine the patterns of institutional development experienced by institutions in general. Observing institutions over time and comparing those institutions which receive Title III funds with those which do not would yield some indication of the developmental impact of Title III funding. Given the decline in demand for traditional undergraduate education anticipated in the early nineteen-eighties, we think it important to begin to understand these patterns of institutional development. With such understanding, institutions could prepare themselves structurally to deal with what in all likelihood will be a declining market.

TABLE 1   MEASURES OF STRUCTURAL DEVELOPMENT IN POSTSECONDARY EDUCATION

DEVELOPMENTAL CONCEPTS	DIMENSIONS	MEASURES
1. Technological (Institutional characteristics, and viability)	a) Technological Characteristics 1) Software 2) Hardware	- Institutional Characteristics, Capital Investment - Types of programs and services, proportion of spending on software - Types of technologies, proportions of instruction budget spent on technological aids
	b) Program Efficiency	- Labor productivity, cost-effectiveness (efficient surface)
2. Decision Structure Development (Developmental phase of institutions based on internal history and observable characteristics)	a) Organizational Phase	- Match organizational pattern and developmental phase - Management responses to institutional crises (decision analysis)
	b) Management Efficiency	- Complexity measures, differentiation of staff, % overhead
3. Qualitative Change (Assessment of openness of the decision process and the impact of the program on students)	a) Systems Openness	- Match of organizational stage with diagnosis of organizational climate (case history) - Determination of degree of participation and decision centricity
	b) Program Impact	- Individual change, individual commitment to institution and program, comparison of student and institutional goals

Table 2

Title III
Eligibility Criteria

Percentiles for FY '74 Grantees (AIDP and BIDP)
Using Data from '74 Applications

2—Year Public

	5%	25%	50%	75%	95%
FTE Enrollment	395	766	1,217	2,304	4,122
Full-Time Enrollment	275	672	890	1,609	3,045
% of Faculty with Masters	40	70	79	83	91
Average Faculty Salary	7,800	8,822	10,113	11,041	14,800
% of Students from Low-Income Families[1]	14	33	47	63	86
Total E & G Expenditures	681,212	1,118,202	1,542,652	2,488,819	6,790,000
E & G Expenditures/FTE	621	1,066	1,341	1,680	2,300
Volumes in Library	10,750	20,913	27,505	34,179	47,000

2—Year Private

	5%	25%	50%	75%	95%
FTE Enrollment	147	205	419	592	1,204
Full-Time Enrollment	123	178	384	546	1,196
% of Faculty with Masters	60	67	74	81	86
Average Faculty Salary	6,225	7,100	7,886	8,424	9,432
% of Students from Low-Income Families[1]	17	23	38	80	94
Total E & G Expenditures	315,562	379,777	672,865	990,788	1,407,697
E & G Expenditures/FTE	555	973	1,462	2,144	4,001
Volumes in Library	5,510	18,893	21,179	29,239	40,418

4—Year Public

	5%	25%	50%	75%	95%
FTE Enrollment	672	1,702	2,372	3,224	5,290
% of Faculty with PhD	20	28	32	38	95
Average Salary/Professor	11,460	14,040	15,467	16,315	17,888
Average Salary/Instructor	8,000	8,696	8,905	9,485	10,840
% of Students from Low-Income Families[1]	15	42	63	79	52
Total E & G Expenditures	988,633	2,916,696	3,917,770	5,395,140	10,280,000
E & G Expenditures/FTE	1,101	1,617	1,863	2,402	3,183
Volumes in Library	45,000	75,233	95,000	120,430	242,191

4—Year Private

	5%	25%	50%	75%	95%
FTE Enrollment	346	532	704	1,027	1,865
% of Faculty with PhD	12	24	31	40	49
Average Salary/Professor	9,750	12,000	12,854	13,802	15,840
Average Salary/Instructor	6,883	7,650	8,330	8,871	9,470
% of Students from Low-Income Families[1]	10	24	44	77	94
Total E & G Expenditures	801,890	1,108,871	1,590,827	2,140,888	3,987,714
E & G Expenditures/FTE	1,040	1,820	2,186	2,590	3,746
Volumes in Library	27,500	48,000	57,530	69,000	96,768

[1]For purposes of this subpart a low-income family is one whose adjusted family income is less than $7,500. (20 U.S.C. 1052)

Source: Federal Register, Vol. 40, No. 107—Tuesday, June 3, 1975, p. 23859.

Total FTE Enrollment
Table 3a
Two Year

	FY70	FY71	FY72	FY73	FY74	FY75
PUBLIC						
Advanced Funded						
Mean					4,486	2,864
S.D.					1,736	1,963
N=					5	16
Basic Funded						
Mean	1,334	1,520	1,545	1,584	1,752	1,770
S.D.	1,277	1,330	1,386	1,619	2,096	2,219
N=	195	185	188	192	154	120
Not Funded						
Mean	2,285	2,249	1,886	2,163	1,858	1,070
S.D.	2,604	2,539	1,779	2,532	2,096	2,219
N=	61	91	114	77	113	120
PRIVATE						
Advanced Funded						
Mean					1,716	1,422
S.D.					2,063	1,967
N=					2	3
Basic Funded						
Mean	506	536	568	635	555	689
S.D.	538	677	791	758	738	823
N=	46	42	44	47	35	31
Not Funded						
Mean	502	473	603	344	470	445
S.D.	415	492	566	277	351	248
N=	28	283	28	15	26	29

Four Year

	FY70	FY71	FY72	FY73	FY74	FY75
PUBLIC						
Advanced Funded						
Mean					2,804	3,633
S.D.					1,820	1,947
N=					5	13
Basic Funded						
Mean	2,028	2,191	2,313	2,356	2,179	2,165
S.D.	1,106	1,359	1,196	1,208	1,355	1,486
N=	75	73	66	68	67	65
Not Funded						
Mean	2,329	2,792	2,793	3,077	2,712	2,367
S.D.	1,805	2,024	2,109	2,535	2,304	1,409
N=	27	42	40	14	15	9
PRIVATE						
Advanced Funded						
Mean					1,547	1,368
S.D.					621	708
N=					12	26
Basic Funded						
Mean	920	234	939	907	778	772
S.D.	742	804	699	652	566	629
N=	153	145	141	160	158	133
Not Funded						
Mean	967	959	854	822	881	873
S.D.	991	859	545	753	793	712
N=	101	89	91	59	52	63

Percentage of Faculty with Doctorates of FTE Faculty
Table 3b

	FY70	FY71	FY72	FY73	FY74	FY75
Two Year						
PUBLIC						
Advanced Funded						
Mean					4	6
S.D.					2	4
N=					4	15
Basic Funded						
Mean	3	3	4	6	6	6
S.D.	4	4	4	10	7	8
N=	196	178	183	187	146	112
Not Funded						
Mean	4	4	5	6	7	9
S.D.	5	4	6	11	11	14
N=	61	93	115	75	101	123
PRIVATE						
Advanced Funded						
Mean					5	17
S.D.					3	19
N=					2	3
Basic Funded						
Mean	4	6	6	7	7	10
S.D.	5	6	7	11	7	8
N=	47	40	44	48	34	28
Not Funded						
Mean	7	7	6	6	8	8
S.D.	7	7	5	5	8	6
N=	27	28	28	13	24	25
Four Year						
PUBLIC						
Advanced Funded						
Mean					30	39
S.D.					4	9
N=					4	12
Basic Funded						
Mean	23	24	29	33	45	36
S.D.	11	12	10	9	87	10
N=	73	64	69	71	63	58
Not Funded						
Mean	28	31	32	33	40	42
S.D.	15	14	15	14	10	11
N=	27	40	42	14	15	9
PRIVATE						
Advanced Funded						
Mean					41	37
S.D.					10	10
N=					11	25
Basic Funded						
Mean	23	25	27	29	35	34
S.D.	10	12	12	13	60	11
N=	147	145	143	157	149	123
Not Funded						
Mean	27	26	27	24	28	28
S.D.	14	13	13	16	15	18
N=	102	90	91	55	50	56

Average Salary of Full Professors
Table 3c
Two Year

	FY70	FY71	FY72	FY73	FY74	FY75
PUBLIC						
Advanced Funded						
Mean					18,073	20,614
S.D.					0	0
N=					1	1
Basic Funded						
Mean	11,909	13,236	12,632	14,608	14,895	14,803
S.D.	1,852	2,553	3,731	3,038	3,113	4,329
N=	34	41	38	47	40	34
Not Funded						
Mean	12,279	14,950	15,615	15,433	15,904	16,423
S.D.	1,592	3,009	2,592	2,756	2,702	2,622
N=	23	38	33	25	36	42
PRIVATE						
Advanced Funded						
Mean					0	0
S.D.					0	0
N=					0	0
Basic Funded						
Mean	9,326	10,107	8,415	12,333	11,290	12,531
S.D.	2,197	1,926	4,166	2,750	2,304	2,855
N=	9	5	8	15	11	13
Not Funded						
Mean	10,018	11,707	12,485	9,717	18,736	10,891
S.D.	1,959	2,997	3,499	2,241	22,531	2,843
N=	9	14	13	9	12	10

Four Year

	FY70	FY71	FY72	FY73	FY74	FY75
PUBLIC						
Advanced Funded						
Mean					16,891	17,018
S.D.					1,057	5,200
N=					5	13
Basic Funded						
Mean	12,557	14,130	14,917	15,572	16,193	16,758
S.D.	1,888	1,754	1,839	1,846	1,966	1,956
N=	65	63	65	70	64	60
Not Funded						
Mean	13,310	14,992	15,497	14,740	15,659	16,341
S.D.	1,724	2,191	3,082	1,330	1,899	1,382
N=	24	42	39	13	14	8
PRIVATE						
Advanced Funded						
Mean					16,059	15,635
S.D.					1,479	2,003
N=					11	25
Basic Funded						
Mean	10,979	12,491	12,973	13,311	13,585	13,957
S.D.	1,773	1,970	1,876	1,854	1,772	1,829
N=	146	141	129	156	150	125
Not Funded						
Mean	11,744	12,600	12,836	13,997	13,324	14,248
S.D.	2,409	2,179	2,810	2,532	2,834	2,814
N=	92	80	77	43	46	50

Average Salary of Instructors
Table 3d
Two Year

	FY70	FY71	FY72	FY73	FY74	FY75
PUBLIC						
Advanced Funded						
Mean					11,899	12,570
S.D.					1,898	2,343
N=					3	5
Basic Funded						
Mean	8,811	9,284	9,415	10,057	10,813	11,146
S.D.	1,555	1,307	1,558	1,924	1,891	1,875
N=	82	42	40	93	78	65
Not Funded						
Mean	9,427	10,123	10,181	10,801	10,913	11,359
S.D.	1,598	2,045	1,789	2,191	2,438	2,495
N=	35	41	33	49	66	77
PRIVATE						
Advanced Funded						
Mean					0	8,800
S.D.					0	0
N=					0	1
Basic Funded						
Mean	7,113	7,193	6,112	7,970	8,538	8,888
S.D.	961	873	2,829	1,098	1,211	1,550
N=	15	7	8	22	18	19
Not Funded						
Mean	6,689	7,818	8,410	7,824	8,248	8,638
S.D.	987	1,054	928	1,183	1,078	1,337
N=	14	14	13	10	16	15

Four Year

	FY70	FY71	FY72	FY73	FY74	FY75
PUBLIC						
Advanced Funded						
Mean					9,755	10,290
S.D.					534	303
N=					5	12
Basic Funded						
Mean	8,047	8,666	9,013	10,439	9,652	10,148
S.D.	1,208	974	1,006	9,373	986	1,066
N=	69	62	65	70	63	58
Not Funded						
Mean	8,131	8,827	9,150	8,965	9,828	10,542
S.D.	1,960	798	1,461	729	995	1,302
N=	25	42	39	13	14	8
PRIVATE						
Advanced Funded						
Mean					9,346	9,438
S.D.					660	612
N=					11	25
Basic Funded						
Mean	7,403	7,954	8,296	8,475	8,784	9,108
S.D.	787	902	1,026	885	1,023	1,083
N=	145	140	130	153	145	119
Not Funded						
Mean	7,567	8,034	8,202	8,278	8,598	9,081
S.D.	877	1,048	1,054	1,335	1,391	1,315
N=	91	78	76	47	45	50

Percentage of Total Students with Family Income
Less Than $7500 of Total Enrollment

Table 3e

Two Year

	FY70	FY71	FY72	FY73	FY74	FY75
PUBLIC						
Advanced Funded						
Mean					38	40
S.D.					20	21
N=					11	16
Basic Funded						
Mean		39	41	41	44	44
S.D.		25	22	22	25	25
N=		194	184	193	120	120
Not Funded						
Mean		28	30	36	36	36
S.D.		22	21	22	22	21
N=		100	114	79	141	136
PRIVATE						
Advanced Funded						
Mean					99	83
S.D.					0	16
N=					1	3
Basic Funded						
Mean		43	44	44	38	38
S.D.		29	25	25	24	24
N=		43	44	48	31	31
Not Funded						
Mean		46	32	40	41	39
S.D.		106	24	35	28	28
N=		28	28	15	31	29

Four Year

	FY70	FY71	FY72	FY73	FY74	FY75
PUBLIC						
Advanced Funded						
Mean					52	55
S.D.					32	26
N=					5	13
Basic Funded						
Mean		45	53	53	70	48
S.D.		32	28	27	190	27
N=		74	66	71	67	65
Not Funded						
Mean		25	37	45	34	33
S.D.		22	27	27	16	20
N=		42	41	14	15	9
PRIVATE						
Advanced Funded						
Mean					47	53
S.D.					32	28
N=					12	25
Basic Funded						
Mean		37	44	38	39	36
S.D.		29	31	29	51	28
N=		149	142	160	158	133
Not Funded						
Mean		20	25	25	26	22
S.D.		20	21	22	25	21
N=		91	91	55	52	63

Total Expenditures for Education and General Purposes
(in thousands of dollars)
Table 3f
Two Year

	FY70	FY71	FY72	FY73	FY74	FY75
PUBLIC						
Advanced Funded						
Mean					7,271	4,462
S.D.					4,141	3,650
N=					5	16
Basic Funded						
Mean	860	1,656	1,903	2,189	2,305	2,570
S.D.	763	1,297	2,848	2,169	2,007	3,531
N=	203	194	186	158	154	120
Not Funded						
Mean	1,101	2,033	2,301	2,006	2,287	2,541
S.D.	1,149	2,453	2,161	1,901	2,285	2,463
N=	77	100	116	114	113	136
PRIVATE						
Advanced Funded						
Mean					3,967	3,198
S.D.					4,556	3,801
N=					2	3
Basic Funded						
Mean	279	656	769	956	764	772
S.D.	244	765	1,035	1,160	541	675
N=	47	43	44	37	35	31
Not Funded						
Mean	266	600	764	514	566	662
S.D.	221	530	623	329	340	357
N=	30	29	28	26	26	29

Four Year

	FY70	FY71	FY72	FY73	FY74	FY75
PUBLIC						
Advanced Funded						
Mean					7,117	8,239
S.D.					1,119	4,123
N=					5	13
Basic Funded						
Mean	1,560	3,644	3,852	4,400	4,602	4,533
S.D.	1,039	2,348	2,161	2,795	2,977	2,787
N=	80	77	69	93	67	65
Not Funded						
Mean	1,763	4,259	4,053	3,839	4,243	4,266
S.D.	1,473	3,580	3,004	1,923	2,751	2,962
N=	30	44	42	14	15	9
PRIVATE						
Advanced Funded						
Mean					4,779	4,009
S.D.					3,162	2,584
N=					12	26
Basic Funded						
Mean	723	1,615	1,794	1,914	1,761	1,668
S.D.	557	1,181	1,199	1,443	949	904
N=	157	151	143	164	158	133
Not Funded						
Mean	874	1,748	1,402	1,582	1,842	1,945
S.D.	1,212	1,870	1,190	1,479	1,627	1,554
N=	106	94	91	58	52	63

Education and General Purposes Expenditures/FTE Student
(in thousands of dollars)
Table 3g
Two Year

	FY70	FY71	FY72	FY73	FY74	FY75
PUBLIC						
Advanced Funded						
Mean					1.6	1.6
S.D.					.5	.9
N=					5	14
Basic Funded						
Mean	.8	1.2	1.3	1.4	1.7	1.6
S.D.	.6	.4	1.2	.5	1.3	1.0
N=	195	185	183	191	153	119
Not Funded						
Mean	.7	1.2	1.3	1.5	1.4	1.4
S.D.	.3	.6	.6	.9	.8	.6
N=	59	90	113	77	153	134
PRIVATE						
Advanced Funded						
Mean					2.6	2.1
S.D.					.4	.0
N=					2	2
Basic Funded						
Mean	.6	1.4	1.5	1.6	1.9	1.5
S.D.	.3	.63	.7	.8	1.1	.8
N=·	46	42	44	47	35	29
Not Funded						
Mean	.6	1.6	1.6	2.1	1.5	1.6
S.D.	.2	.9	.8	1.7	.9	.5
N=	29	29	28	15	26	29

Four Year

	FY70	FY71	FY72	FY73	FY74	FY75
PUBLIC						
Advanced Funded						
Mean					2.1	2.5
S.D.					.5	1.1
N=					4	12
Basic Funded						
Mean	.8	1.7	1.7	2.0	2.1	2.1
S.D.	.3	.8	.7	.6	.8	.7
N=	74	72	66	68	63	60
Not Funded						
Mean	.9	1.6	1.6	1.5	1.7	1.8
S.D.	.4	.7	.6	.4	.4	.4
N=	27	42	40	14	15	9
PRIVATE						
Advanced Funded						
Mean					3.0	2.7
S.D.					1.0	.9
N=					12	24
Basic Funded						
Mean	.8	1.8	2.1	2.2	2.4	2.2
S.D.	.3	.6	1.4	.6	.6	.6
N=	153	145	141	160	153	126
Not Funded						
Mean	1.0	1.9	2.0	2.6	2.1	2.2
S.D.	1.0	.6	.8	4.2	.8	.9
N=	101	89	91	54	50	59

Number of Library Volumes
(in thousands of volumes)
Table 3h
Two Year

	FY70	FY71	FY72	FY73	FY74	FY75
PUBLIC						
Advanced Funded						
Mean					40	42
S.D.					11	15
N=					5	12
Basic Funded						
Mean	22	24	26	26	29	29
S.D.	10	11	13	14	19	17
N=	196	193	181	190	151	119
Not Funded						
Mean	26	27	24	26	27	31
S.D.	20	22	19	25	19	22
N=	61	98	112	76	107	127
PRIVATE						
Advanced Funded						
Mean					23	23
S.D.					0	0
N=					1	2
Basic Funded						
Mean	20	22	23	22	24	24
S.D.	7	9	9	9	11	12
N=	47	42	43	45	34	28
Not Funded						
Mean	21	22	23	19	19	24
S.D.	13	10	9	8	6	10
N=	28	28	43	15	24	27

Four Year

	FY70	FY71	FY72	FY73	FY74	FY75
PUBLIC						
Advanced Funded						
Mean					170	179
S.D.					68	92
N=					5	11
Basic Funded						
Mean	78	87	99	103	111	113
S.D.	50	57	57	57	59	54
N=	76	76	65	70	61	59
Not Funded						
Mean	88	96	109	118	126	128
S.D.	64	69	92	68	65	53
N=	27	42	40	14	15	9
PRIVATE						
Advanced Funded						
Mean					154	124
S.D.					107	94
N=					12	25
Basic Funded						
Mean	56	62	66	70	65	66
S.D.	32	37	41	44	29	22
N=	151	148	139	161	154	126
Not Funded						
Mean	69	63	65	60	71	75
S.D.	68	37	42	49	59	59
N=	102	91	87	59	50	57

Table 4

Correlation Matrix

Title III Award with Income Sources

PUBLIC INSTITUTIONS

	Comprehensive Colleges and Universities (Carnegie Codes: 21 & 22)			Two Year Colleges (Carnegie Code: 41)		
	1972	1973	1974	1972	1973	1974
Income: E & GP	.41811	.64011	.57975	.16536	.05740	.17338
Income: Federal – T3	.36370	.44340	.45531	.13092	.03432	.16905
Income: State Government	.38378	.50625	.45941	.02860	-.02006	.10808
Income: Local Government	*	*	*	.29222	.15682	.21631
Income: Student Aid	.45668	.46392	.40155	.29688	.04596	.37945
Income: Endowment	*	-.48078	-.49072	*	*	*
Direct Corporate Support	*	.45819	.36303	*	-.19794	*
Alumni Support	*	.40243	.42470	*	-.25445	*
Foundation Support	*	.28891	.28461	*	.34152	*
NonAlumni Support	*	-.01416	.16469	*	-.02414	*

PRIVATE INSTITUTIONS

	Liberal Arts Colleges II (Carnegie Code: 32)			Two Year Colleges (Carnegie Code: 41)		
	1972	1973	1974	1972	1973	1974
Income: E & GP	.48185	.48488	.52676	.01223	.18798	.31693
Income: Federal – T3	.11827	.02018	.30469	-.02000	-.02552	.31158
Income: State Government	*	.40508	.56883	*	*	*
Income: Local Government	*	*	*	*	*	*
Income: Student Aid	.55049	.55439	.58232	.31833	.17238	.31412
Income: Endowment	.13381	.05697	.06129	.46860	-.00039	-.14819
Direct Corporate Support	.33291	.19100	.28051	*	.54543	*
Alumni Support	-.21480	-.19556	-.29588	*	-.23687	*
Foundation Support	.26803	.25797	.46030	*	.43608	*
NonAlumni Support	.10713	.53563	.33419	*	.40608	*

* Number of available cases for this variable less than 15.

Table 5 Student-Faculty Ratios for Private Highly
Selective Liberal Arts Colleges

	Total Enrollment/Faculty
Average	13.8
Frontier: typical institution	18.7
high level of research	17.5
large number of fields	16.5

Table 6 Cost-Per-Student Ratios for Private Highly
Selective Liberal Arts Colleges

	Cost/Total Enrollment
Average	$1,371
Frontier: typical institution	768
low level of part-time undergraduates	796
high level of part-time undergraduates	719
small institution	780

Table 7 Student-Faculty Ratios for Public Comprehensive
Colleges and Universities

	Total Enrollment/Faculty
Average	23.5
Frontier: typical institution	32.1
no teaching assistants	29.8
large number of fields	31.6
low level of part-time undergraduates	29.2
high level of part-time undergraduates	33.6

Table 8 Cost-Per-Student Ratios for Public Comprehensive
Colleges and Universities

	Cost/Total Enrollment
Average	$863
Frontier: typical institution	514
high level of graduate students	525
no research	499
high level of research	533
small institution	515

Source: Carlson (1975) p. 50

NOTES

1. Appendix A provides a detailed review of the legislative history of Title III of the Higher Education Act of 1965, as amended.

2. These theories are described in much greater detail in Appendix B.

3. Sunrise Semester, the University of Mid-America and the British Open University are examples of media-based institutions.

4. David Riesman is credited with developing the concept of the "academic procession" (Riesman, 1956).

5. The recently published General Accounting Office (U.S. Comptroller General, 1975) report on Title III uses discriminant analyses to identify factors which "explain" Title III staff decisions whether to fund and how much to fund an applicant institution.

6. Here we are referring to "resource use efficiency" or "production efficiency" or "technical efficiency". See Wallhaus (1975).

7. A full discussion of the history and technical approaches of these various forms of analysis is given in Appendix D.

8. Appendix E provides the technical description of our statistical estimation of these effects.

9. The variability in resource use of private highly selective liberal arts colleges given in Tables 5 and 6 support this observation.

10. There is no implication that all efficient institutions are homogeneous in any respect. While these institutions have only recently been identified, they have not been studies to any degree to determine their actual characters.

References

Detailed bibliographies on the topics covered in this report are included in the Appendices. The following references were specificallv referred to in this report.

Carlson, D.A., "Examining Efficient Joint Production Processes," Measuring and Increasing Academic Productivity, R.A. Wallhaus (ed.), New Directions in Institutional Research, vol.2, no.5, S.F. Jersey-Bass, 1975.

Greiner, L.E., "Evolution and Revolution as Organizations Grow," Harvard Business Review, 1975, 50, 37-46.

Hodgkinson, H.L. and Schenkel, W. A Study of Title III of the Higher Educations Act: The Developing Institution Program, Berkeley: C.R.D.H.E., 1974.

Riesman, D. "The Academic Procession," in Constraint And Variety in American Education, University of Nebraska Press, 1956; Garden City, N.Y.: Anchor Books, 1958.

Rostow, W.W., The Stages of Economic Growth: A Non-Communist Manifesto, Cambridge, England: Cambridge University Press, 1960.

Torbert, W.R., "Pre-Bureaucratic and Post-Bureaucratic Stages of Organizational Development," Interpersonal Dynamics, 1974/5, 5, 1-25.

U.S. Comptroller General, Report to the Congress: Assessing the Federal Program for Strengthening Developing Institutions of Higher Education, Washington, D.C.: General Accounting Office Pubn. MWD-76-1, 1975.

Wallhaus, R.A. "The Many Dimensions of Productivity," Measuring and Increasing Academic Productivity, R.A. Wallhaus (ed.) New Directions in Institutional Research, vol. 2, no. 5, S.F. Jossey-Bass, 1975.

PART 5

STUDIES IN CRIME AND JUSTICE

23

THE EXPLOSION IN POLICE DIVERSION PROGRAMS: EVALUATING THE STRUCTURAL DIMENSIONS OF A SOCIAL FAD

By

**MALCOLM W. KLEIN, KATHIE S. TEILMANN, JOSEPH A. STYLES,
SUZANNE BUGAS LINCOLN, and SUSAN LABIN-ROSENSWEIG**

The authors of this study do not claim to answer the question of whether diversion programs are successful. Instead, they analyze the structure of the juvenile justice system and its relationship to the diversion program. Their investigation indicates that lack of information along with the conflicting goals of different participating agencies make the operation of diversion programs cumbersome. In this study, the relationships between the participating agencies are clarified, and the complexity of the system is fully captured. In order to develop meaningful evaluation studies of these diversion programs, the authors suggest that the multiple objectives and values of the various groups involved be identified. Evaluators will then be able to utilize more specific measures to decide which of the set goals have been met.

From Malcolm W. Klein et al., "The Explosion in Police Diversion Programs: Evaluating the Structural Dimensions of a Social Fad." Pp. 101-119 in M.W. Klein (ed.), *The Juvenile Justice System.* Beverly Hills, Calif.: Sage Publications, 1976.

Evaluation technology has slowly but steadily grown both in sophistication and in acceptance by those involved in public policy (Struening and Guttentag, 1975; Guttentag and Struening, 1975). Concurrently, simplistic reliance on idealized experimental designs has yielded to more comprehensive if less controlled approaches to the "so what" questions about social programs. We pay more attention to the objectives and values or "utilities" (Edwards et al., 1975) of various audiences or publics related to such programs. This paper deals with a type of social program to which such thinking is just beginning to be applied. By pinpointing selected structural dimensions of the program as it has developed in the past few years, we can highlight an assortment of evaluative criteria to which attention must be paid. We believe these are prototypical of dimensions and criteria in many components of the juvenile justice system.

AUTHORS' NOTE: *Materials for this chapter were gathered in part with support from Grant No. MH26147-01 from the National Institute of Mental Health and from Grant No. 74-NI-99-0045 from the National Institute of Law Enforcement and Criminal Justice, Law Enforcement Assistance Administration, U.S. Department of Justice. Points of view or opinions stated in this document are those of the authors and do not necessarily represent the official position or policies of HEW or the Department of Justice.*

The type of program to which we refer is generally called *diversion*. In the present instance we shall concentrate specifically on police diversion programs for juvenile offenders.

The importance of specifying measurable dimensions for evaluating police diversion programs has been underscored by conclusions from a recent, exhaustive review of published and unpublished reports on these programs:

> The central results of the . . . project surround the analysis of the twenty-two police diversion evaluation studies located. These were subject to severe limitations in the Internal Validity area in that they tended not to formulate problems clearly or to frame and test hypotheses carefully. Often the target population of the study was not exactly described and there was little hope of determining whether or not the programs "worked" because objective tests of this question were absent.
>
> In the Methodology area, far too often study populations were inadequate, analytic methods were inexplicit and of questionable utility, appropriate data were lacking, statistical tools utilized were limited, "treatment" influences were only some among many possible explanations for results, supportive evidence from extra-study sources was non-existent, and logical leaps were involved in moving from data analysis to discussions of conclusions.
>
> Studies reviewed tended to be consistently superficial or to major on one or two (often semi-extraneous) aspects of diversion at the expense of several others. Typical differences in analytic rigor involved careful analysis of cavalierly collected data, or vice-versa, and great attention to the possible program implications of findings resting on almost no data collection at all.
>
> The studies inclined toward inconsistency. Changes in analytic approaches repeatedly crept into studies mid-stream. Worse, often one could not tell whether there was any internal consistency or not, save unflawed lack of clarity.
>
> The External Validity question goes to whether or not studies of the same or like phenomena achieved similar results. It is difficult to determine whether structured diversion programs increase the level of diversion—one of their main purposes. Whether or not diversion leads to less penetration of the criminal justice system and less recidivism remains unknown. It can be concluded that sometimes diversion programs "work;" by no means all of them do. What distinguished the successful approaches is not known. There may be no structural components that can guarantee effectiveness. [Neithercutt and Moseley, 1974]

We use the term diversion henceforth to refer only to the process of turning suspects or offenders away from the formal system. *Referral* will mean the process by which the police initiate the connection of the juvenile to a non-justice-system agency, public or private (Klein, 1973). Thus one can have diversion with or without referral, and one can have referral with or without successful contact and treatment at the referral agency. The distinction between diversion and referral is critical to much of the following discussion. With this distinction in mind, we now move to six issues which raise major evaluative questions, each such question providing objectives and values associated with the many audiences of diversion programs.

1. THE DIVERSION EXPLOSION

Easily the most striking single dimension of diversion programming is its enormous recent growth. Significantly stimulated by the President's Commission (1967), nurtured by the "national strategy" for delinquency prevention promulgated in the early 1970s (Gemignani, 1972; Polk and Kobrin, 1972), and given enormous funding by regional and state arms of the Law Enforcement Assistance Administration in the mid-1970s, diversion has national backing and scope and is almost epidemic in proportions.

Some measure of recent changes can be made by reference to descriptions of the diversion and referral situation in Los Angeles County in 1970 and 1971. Research was carried out in those two years to determine the level of referral activity of all the police departments in the county. These included the two behemoths, the Los Angeles Police Department and the Los Angeles County Sheriff's Department, and 45 smaller independent departments serving cities ranging in population size from 1,000 to 400,000 persons. On the basis of interviews with 77 juvenile officers and over 40 police chiefs and on the basis of data available from the departments, Klein (1975) concluded:

> Juvenile officers do not seek out, nor are they urged to seek out, suitable referral agencies. By the same token, few private agencies offer themselves as willing absorbers of delinquency. Thus the modal number of private agencies known to our smaller-city juvenile officer respondents . . . was two! In six cities, the officers in 1970 could not name a single private agency to whom youngsters might be referred.
>
> Nor is this "accidental" or temporary ignorance of resources. Exactly half of the 1971 respondents reported *belonging to no* community organizations in the communities they served. Half did not live in the community served. Yet the median number of police associations for these same officers was two and a half. The situation was even worse in the LAPD and LASD. In these two agencies, officers in one quarter of the stations could not name *any* community resources.

Lack of information is not the only problem; the nature of the occasional referral process was often less than wholehearted. About half of the 45 independent cities reported making referrals *directly,* that is, by contacting the referral agencies personally. In the LAPD and LASD, only 2 of 31 officers reported using such direct referrals. The others merely told the arrested youth or his parents that they should go to selected agencies. Twenty percent of the officers in the smaller departments and 45% of those in the LAPD and LASD said they *never* made referrals. The modal response in the other departments was that they made "two or three a month." Clearly, then, police referrals of juveniles to community agencies was at best a minor practice and an ill-defined policy area.

Corroboration for this conclusion comes from a survey of 119 private agencies which were selected for a survey on the basis of their reported appropriateness for police referrals in Los Angeles County. A summary statement from that survey concludes (Klein, 1975):

> The first conclusion we can offer is that the diversion process is, at best, minimal. Of 119 private agencies queried for the year 1969, three reported receiving referrals from LAPD, two from LASD, and eight from one or more of the other . . . departments. In all, these connections led to 428 referrals. By way of contrast, there were 6,142 referrals to 84 of the 119 agencies from probation, court, and correctional components of the system. Available private agencies are used for rehabilitation, but not for diversion. . . . These data come from personal interviews and question-naires. Almost none of the police agencies keep a *record* of referrals to community agencies. The recording necessitated by the FBI and the state's Bureau of Criminal Statistics likewise makes no explicit reference to such referrals. That is, the "System" expresses no interest in and therefore receives no information about the workings of its input and diversion module.

There is no reason to think that this situation described for the Los Angeles area would not have applied equally well to any metropolitan area in the early 1970s. That the referral level did not *have* to be so low was amply demonstrated by a pilot project carried out in one police station in 1970 and reported recently by Lincoln (1975). This station had made almost no referrals in the prior year. Yet under the leadership of a police lieutenant who sought out available agencies and proselytized his juvenile officers,[1] a total of 35 juvenile offenders were referred to local agencies during the first 40 days of the pilot project. Thirty-two of these made the agency connection and initiated counseling. The experience with this pilot project became the opening wedge for officials in Los Angeles County to expand referrals in the Sheriff's Department. From a 1968-69 figure of 119, the Department increased its "referrals to social agencies" to 896 in 1971-72, 1,349 in 1972-73, and 1,646 in 1973-74. The 1974-75 figure has been projected to 2,098 by the head of the juvenile diversion unit.

This particular department's obvious enactment of a diversion policy and dramatic increase in referrals is impressive, yet it is typical of what has been taking place generally. A survey of police departments in Los Angeles County in 1973, conducted by a County agency, described active diversion/referral programs in 14 departments, and minor or informal programs in 20 others. Our own detailed survey only a year later, in 1974, identified diversion/referral programs in 37 departments. It was the plan of the Regional Criminal Justice Planning Board, the local dispenser of LEAA funds, to have 60 cities involved in its diversion system by the end of 1975. The board designated over four million dollars to support these programs within the county during that year.

A recent review of diversion programs throughout the state of California provides equally impressive numbers (Bohnstedt, 1975). Seventy-four projects funded by the state planning agency and active in 1974 were identified, to the exclusion of those funded from other sources. Of these 74, 9 were located in Los Angeles County and involved, at most, 15 police departments. Using what we know in detail about the Los Angeles County figures and the percentages of projects funded specifically by the state planning agency, we can extrapolate from these figures to estimate that there were probably between 150 and 200 projects throughout the state. And even more have been funded in 1975. The overall rate of expansion is shown by the data taken from this same state survey: of the 74 projects, 12 were in their third year, 27 were in their second year, and 35 were in their first year. The explosion in diversion projects is continuing.

Finally, it should be noted that the federal government itself, through the Law Enforcement Assistance Administration, is launching its own direct participation. Using funds authorized under the Juvenile Justice and Delinquency Prevention Act of 1974, LEAA has announced the decision to underwrite an eight-and-a-half million dollar program for the development of model juvenile diversion programs across the nation. Fortunately, it is planned to commit a portion of these funds to evaluating these model programs. This diversion program follows directly on the heels of another eight-and-a-half million dollar program to fund model programs for the deinstitutionalization of status offenders, a clear form of juvenile diversion. In reality, then, we are speaking of a seventeen million dollar direct federal investment in juvenile diversion projects.

2. ALTERNATIVE RATIONALES FOR DIVERSION

As clear as it has become that there is a diversion "explosion," it has become equally clear that the rationales for diversion are multiple, are conflicting, and are both manifest and latent. The explosion seems to be serving several ends, with the obvious implication that any comprehensive evaluation of diversion programs must concern itself with the degree to which each of these several ends is attained.

A concise and hard-hitting summary of diversion activities in California (Public Systems Inc., 1974, chap. 4) has noted four major rationales underlying the current explosion. The first of these is that increased diversion overrides "the system's inherent biases" in releasing and detaining suspects by stressing and legitimating explicit criteria which, ipso facto, are more equitable and universalistic. This fits nicely with the growing "professionalism" of police work as the latter is defined in terms of the application of less personal discretion (Wilson, 1968).

The second rationale is that increased diversion will decrease the volume of cases inserted into the juvenile justice system. Since the vast majority of these cases do not consist of serious adult-like offenses, there is indeed considerable opportunity to find alternative means for handling them outside the system. These alternatives range from intensive community treatment programs, to outright release, to what Edwin Schur has designated as "radical non-intervention" (1973). So long as diversion *does* mean movement away from the system of cases otherwise destined for system insertion, and does not mean nonsystem treatment of cases formerly released without treatment (Vorenberg and Vorenberg, 1973), then this rationale seems well served by police diversion programs. The fact is, however, that programs actually launched by police departments are often characterized by the second meaning more than by the first, that is, providing treatment in lieu of outright release.

The third rationale is simply that, ceteris paribus, diversion processing is less expensive than system processing, certainly to the system itself and probably to the overall community as well, even if alternative treatment programs are provided. The volume by Public Systems Inc. (1974) provides savings estimates ranging from thousands of dollars on the local level, to billions of dollars on the national level.

The fourth rationale is the one with the greatest theoretical import, the avoidance of stigmatization as delinquent, "bad," or criminal. In this sense, diversion is the practitioner's operationalization of labeling theory. Although the esoterics of labeling theory are not known to most system officials, the basic implications of self-image changes and differential societal reaction are frequently encountered. So long as these implications are not explicitly juxtaposed against the implications of a deterrence philosophy, many police are sympathetic to actions that will avoid stigmatizing juvenile offenders. This seems particularly true of juvenile officers and higher officials with command responsibilities. It seems least true of experienced or older patrol officers.

In addition to these four rationales, two others are frequently encountered both in the field and in the relevant social science literature. Often voiced by the police, in particular, is the concern that relatively naive young offenders will become contaminated through contact with more sophisticated and recalcitrant offenders during periods of detention or incarceration. To the extent that diversion prevents the exposure of the one to the other, it is seen as an effective preventive measure.

Finally, there is the widely held desire to find procedures, outside the juvenile justice system, to provide help for young offenders whose very status *as* offenders seems to signal the need for help. Diversion *from* the system with referral *to* a helping agency satisfies the various personal and institutionalized propensities to respond to the need to provide service as well as to prevent recurrence of the problem behavior. To most people, help offered within the context of the justice system is suspected of having little effective impact; help offered in an alternative context—one already accepted and established, such as the mental health and/or welfare system—is "known" to be effective. As the Vorenbergs have noted, a diversion program " . . . offers the promise of the best of all worlds: cost savings, rehabilitation, and more humane treatment" (1973: 151).

If the foregoing material does indeed represent more than a summary of the views of various writers and policy makers, if it does indeed represent the acting rationales of the practitioners who carry out juvenile diversion programs, then it should be possible to document this in interviews with such practitioners. Recent interviews with juvenile officers in 35 police departments with diversion programs have been completed by the writers of this chapter. The results do *not* yield the same picture.

The interviews reveal that police motives for diversion are often not what is commonly implied by the term "diversion." The criteria which the police state they use in deciding to refer a juvenile are examples of this subtle change in the meaning of diversion. Asked specifically about criteria for referral, 18 of 35 officers mentioned "offense seriousness" as a factor, but probing indicated that it is *low* seriousness which convinces the officer to refer the juvenile. Similarly, greater willingness to be referred, not resistance, leads to referral; shorter prior arrest records (two priors or less) lead to referral; younger offenders are preferred for referral over older ones; if the officer's estimation is that the youngster is not likely to be rearrested, that youngster is preferred for referral over the one judged more likely to be arrested. Thus the composite picture of the more referable offender seems to be of the young, minor offender with little or no record, who is unlikely to be rearrested in any case. This picture fits the profile of the youngster who heretofore would have been released outright, for whom referral represents *increased* intervention rather than diversion *from* system intervention.

Thus, it can be suggested from these interviews that, while there is clearly a desire in some police departments to divert juveniles from the system, the more common feeling is that referral should be used as an alternative to simple release. In short, the meaning of diversion has been shifted from "diversion from" to "referral to." Ironically, one of the ramifications of this is that, in contrast to such earlier cited rationales for diversion as reducing costs, caseload, and the purview of the justice system, diversion may in fact be extending the costs, caseload, and system purview even further.

For anecdotal illustration, we cite the case of one rather large department which has attempted to explicate diversion and referral criteria by specifically listing cases for which diversion may *not* be employed. Cases may not be diverted and referred in this department if they involve:

(1) felony offenses resulting in death or serious injury;

(2) known gang members;

(3) more than two prior arrests;

(4) offenders already on probation or parole;

(5) crimes against police officers, school personnel (teachers, administrators, or any other regular employee), or employees of the recreation department;

(6) offenses that disrupt school or recreation department activities or destroy property of school and recreation departments;

(7) use or possession of a deadly weapon;

(8) offenders judged physically dangerous to the public because of a mental or physical deficiency, disorder, or abnormality;

(9) escapees from probation institutions;

(10) selected vehicle code violations, primarily hit and run, auto theft, and driving under the influence of or in possession of drugs, liquor, or weapons;

(11) a prior arrest with a referral to a treatment agency.

Obviously, this is a department that believes very strongly in a deterrent philosophy and is testing the notion of diversion and referral much as a bather tests his bath water—toes only. This department's overall release rate has varied over the years between 10% and 20%, as opposed to the oft-cited national average of about 50%. Obviously, referrals from this 10% to 20% pool, given the restrictions listed, must yield a miniscule referral rate. This represents the bottom line in juvenile referral programs.

The top line may be represented by another department, located right next to this one, in which almost *every* juvenile slated for release is referred to a local agency; or perhaps by another adjoining department which has established its *own* referral agency. In any event, there has developed a paradox not unlike that in other human service areas. There is a need to provide more effective service for those presenting the most serious problem, a concommitant need to show program impact which is unlikely among the most serious problem cases, and finally a concommitant need to prevent others from becoming serious cases but without knowing who these will be. To date, the dominant trend has been to resolve the paradox by "ignoring" the serious cases while diverting and referring those less in need but more likely to yield pleasing results, since the less serious cases seldom recidivate.[2] Rationales have yielded to practicality and administrative/political considerations.

3. ALTERNATIVE ENCAPSULATION

There are several other issues less critical to the diversion movement than its explosive nature and its rationales, which nevertheless are directly pertinent to the evaluation of the movement and its constituent programs. Among these is what was somewhat facetiously labeled "alternative encapsulation" at a recent working conference called by the U.S. Justice Department's Law Enforcement Assistance Administration.

There is a danger that the attempt to remove young offenders from the juvenile justice system may do so merely by inserting them into another system which might be characterized as the mental health, welfare, or social service system. So long as it is felt that diverted offenders, or "deinstitutionalized" offenders, need service or treatment when we turn them away from the justice system, then ipso facto we are inserting them into an *alternative* system which may be equally pervasive or *encapsulating*. For all we know, it may be equally stigmatizing although admittedly less costly.

One agency administrator recently estimated that 75% of her police referral cases in a diversion project were of the type which normally would be released and would not receive agency counseling. This same spokesman indicated that, if other things were equal, the police referral would receive priority in enrollment into the agency program over regular (nondiversion) clients. Similarly, the developer of a multi-million dollar diversion program stated to us that his clients, however minor their problems might be, would have to take precedence in assignment of treatment resources over "regular" agency clients. "Are you concerned about these 'bumped' clients?" we asked. "Well," came the answer, "I guess that's the way the cookie crumbles." Here, then, we see more than alternative encapsulation: we also see a questionably appropriate set of clients supplanting a traditional set of clients. There is a conflict between two legitimate concerns: the well-being of diversion clients and that of traditional clients.

A major police department makes the relationship between referral and minor offenders explicit in a departmental directive: "Referral agencies should be used *whenever possible with the beginning offender.* 'Counseling and releasing' of offenders should be considered *only in very minor cases* and only when the subject is not likely to repeat deviate behavior" (emphasis added). Ordinarily, first offenders are released by the police unless the offense is so serious as to require petitioning into the juvenile court. Yet in an established diversion program in one large police department under our purview, over two-thirds of the *referred* offenders were first offenders. A special project subsequently initiated by this department which stressed diversion of more serious cases could only reduce this rate to 50% first offenders. To create the diversion population, it was necessary, it seems, to draw heavily from the pool of offenders normally released. Now these offenders are referred to community agencies; they are inserted into a new social service system. Are we merely trading new service for old?

A hint comes from data recently collected on three cohorts of offenders referred to agencies by the department last mentioned. These cohorts of 41, 52, and 27 referred offenders received means of seven, eight and a half, and almost twelve hours of counseling. In a comparable cohort of 82 youths for whom petitions were filed, 20 were subsequently released at intake without treatment, 30 were assigned to "informal probation" with minimal treatment, and all but 6 of the remainder were sent home on probation. Such figures do *not* make it clear that referral is less encapsulating than petitioning. In fact, it becomes clear that referral is equally or even more encapsulating.

4. EXPANSION OF THE SERVICE SYSTEM

If thousands of new clients are being diverted from one system and referred to a second, we might expect the second system to undergo some modification and, most specifically, to expand in sheer size. Clearly such modifications and expansion are now taking place.

Of twelve programs funded by "Probation Subsidy" funds in Los Angeles County in 1973, ten were juvenile diversion programs. Among these, the funds were used to expand police staffing in six instances and referral agencies in four instances. The largest known diversion agency in Los Angeles County was, by its own account, saved from closing its doors by an influx of funds from police diversion activities which purchased agency services. Another had to open a second office as its budget suddenly increased by a third and its counseling load doubled.

In an as yet unpublished report, Dennison and associates (1975) have described one setting in which a small agency with a $50,000 budget quickly expanded into a central mental health facility with a budget of $600,000. They describe another setting in which an agency opened three branches and became a training center for a prominent school of psychology. The authors note, "If there is some chagrin manifested by agencies that feel they have not received their portion of referrals, a number of others have been rescued from extinction."

No head count of new "diversion" agencies or personnel has been undertaken, yet within Los Angeles County alone the authors have seen a number of new agencies and dozens of new staff members. Things have moved far enough for there to have been, in 1975, a *third annual conference* of a new organization called the California Association of Diversion and Youth Service Counselors.[3]

Site visits undertaken by the authors to numerous cities throughout the United States confirm that a similar expansion among service agencies is taking place and accelerating in many localities. We are amused, on occasion, to find the associated jargon to be less than uniform (diversion becomes "divergence," "diversionary," or "deferrment"), but we find this linguistic confusion to be overshadowed by the conceptual and definitional confusions in the rapidly increasing professional literature on diversion. We may only be describing some typical growing pains of a new social welfare movement, but there is a legitimate concern over whether such a service expansion is a healthy and useful development or not.

If the services provided do in fact reap benefits for the referred delinquent clients, reduce the load on the justice system, and accomplish these ends without harm to other client groups, then the concern disappears. But many agencies, programs, and funders have failed to evidence genuine concern with demonstrating and *testing* such benefits. If on the other hand, the services provided amount primarily to a new form of overreach, a larger net within which to encapsulate the diversion client, then the concern must be taken seriously and a moratorium declared until the impact of such alternative encapsulation can be assessed.

If, finally, the service expansion takes on a semblance of permanence, of a new, full-blown system, then its very existence may pose a danger. New systems and new bureaucracies often become self-perpetuating phenomena; they may become resistant to change; they may become attuned to their own needs often at the expense of (or even in ignorance of) client needs. Much of the current activity in diversion, deinstitutionalization, and decriminalization can be interpreted as recognitions of this pattern and attempts to counteract it. But we may be counteracting by creating counterparts, by putting our wolves in sheep's clothing.

5. POLICE CONTROL

There are two control dimensions of immediate concern. The first describes the degree to which diversion programs maintain control over their clients, determining their activities, their options, and the likelihood that additional antisocial behaviors will reinsert them into the justice system. The second control dimension describes the degree to which diversion programs are under the control of, or accountable to, the juvenile justice system—in our case, to the police.

The first issue, program control over clients, has several facets; but we will allude briefly to only two, overreach (i.e., who is controlled) and extensiveness (i.e., how much one is controlled). Interviews with referring officers in 35 police departments, as well as preliminary analyses of data on samples of arrested juveniles in these and other departments, have convinced us that "over-reach" is the predominant pattern. To a very considerable extent, diversion practices are being applied to juveniles who formerly have been released by the police without further action. Thus control is being extended to a larger and less seriously involved sector of the juvenile population. Other writers have recently reported similar findings with unbroken consistency (Vorenberg and Vorenberg, 1973; Kutchins and Kutchins, 1973; Blomberg, 1975; Mattingly and Katkin, 1975).

Extensiveness of control over client lives is illustrated by the range of restrictiveness of treatment programs for referred offenders. At the high control extreme are residential treatment centers in which offenders eat, sleep, often work, may receive educational instruction and other "betterment" lessons (from grooming to encounter therapies), and so on. Control mechanisms may include curfew and grounds restrictions, daily schedules, and behavior modification procedures with specific rewards for approved behaviors and negative sanctions for disapproved behaviors.

More typically, referral agencies vary their control over clients living at home by contracting for expectations, by requiring certain numbers of treatment hours or visits at the agency, by maintaining contact with adults significant to the client (parents, school personnel, peers), and by retaining varying levels of contact with police and court officers concerned with the case. Thus control over clients can be achieved by mutual "contract," by suggestion and expectation, and by threat of reinvolvement with the police, probation, or court.

The other dimension, system control over programs, has emerged with some clarity from the plethora of diversion programs recently instituted. In many—perhaps most—instances, the level of control is determined by the philosophy of the referring agency. For example, one recent paper describes a court volunteer program in which the volunteers may have become merely another arm of the law (Berger, 1975). A report from Cook County describes how juvenile officers, antagonistic to a diversion program, used a legal loophole to subvert the program and actually brought about a 53% increase in incarceration (NCCD, 1975). Thus, to evaluate the impact of control, we need to recognize the means by which the police exercise varying levels of control over program. We list six of these for illustration:

a. *In-house counselors.* Some police departments hire or arrange for the transfer of counselors to work in the department and treat referred offenders. Some of the counselors are probation officers, others are agency counselors on loan, others are private counselors on the police payroll, and occasionally they are, themselves, police officers. In each instance, they are housed in the department, a part of the police milieu, and they are often formally and informally accountable to police officials. The clients, of course, may interpret their counselor's role and their relationship to it as a function of this departmental context.

b. *Police-based agency.* Occasionally, one finds a referral setting established by or in very close collaboration with the police and staffed by a mixture of police and counseling personnel. It may be located on departmental premises or in another, often public, building (school, probation office, welfare office). It may be called a Youth Services Bureau, even though these bureaus were originally designed to be independent of the justice system. The singular feature of this type of program is the sheer visibility of police involvement in the diversion/referral process. To the client, it must be clear that diversion has not meant his "escape" from the justice system. For the nonpolice staff, it must be equally clear that they are intrinsically involved in police business.

c. *Selected referral resources.* Perhaps the most common and understandable means by which control is exerted by the police is through the selection (and occasional modification) of referral agencies. We have found rather consistently a police preference for professionally (psychologically) staffed agencies, agencies without the "flavor" of minority militancy, agencies that do not condone or excuse minor transgressions, such as the use of marijuana, but counsel specifically against each of these, and agencies willing to keep the police informed about client progress or continuation of a delinquent pattern. This latter can be either informal or formal via feedback reports on client progress or renewed misbehavior. This is not to say that the police commonly reject agencies that refuse to provide feedback to them, but such agencies do seem less preferable to those who will join in a more collaborative (and thus controlling) operation.

As a tangential note to this pattern, we can report the increasingly common pattern of police referrals to firemen who serve offenders in some variation of a Big Brother role. For the police, firemen are good bets as referral resources. They are often "cleared" through police files prior to acceptance in the fire department, they have official authority, and they are seen as brothers-in-arms by the police. The young boy looking up at the fireman with adulation and respect is an image peculiarly suited to the police-endorsed, Norman Rockwell mythology of a "straight" America.

d. *Purchase of service.* An increasingly common procedure is for the police to purchase the service of community agencies for treatment of referred offenders. The fee usually is paid contingent upon a minimum number of clients, or a minimum number of treatment hours or visits per client. Obviously, agencies that do not provide what the police want may be cut off from further payments; control may be achieved financially. The epitome of this is an arrangement whereby an agency receives a minimum fee for accepting a client and provides a specified level of treatment, for instance $50 for six client visits. Then, if the client stays "clean"—that is, does not recidivate—for a given period of time such as six months, the agency receives an additional stipend several times as large as the original. Thus it is worth the agency's while to provide effective intervention specifically pinpointed if possible to the reduction of delinquent behaviors. From the police viewpoint, what is being purchased is maximum and time-extended attention to the production of legal conformity. In one such program observed by the authors, this arrangement did indeed yield significantly greater levels of treatment in accordance with the desire of the police agency involved.

e. *Program organization.* On a number of occasions, diversion programs have been initiated by police departments out of frustration with the ineffectiveness of existing procedures. This initiation—an unusual stance for a public agency which is more typically *re*active than *pro*active—includes seeking out, coordinating, and motivating community agencies, seeking public funds and writing grant proposals, seeking facilities and political support, and convincing normally hesitant factions within the police department itself. Once such an effort is expended, there is little inclination to loose the reins and turn control over to others. The stamp of the initiator remains visible, and the program is likely to thrive or die in proportion to the continued concern and involvement of the police. As a result, the character of the program is highly responsive to the philosophy and concerns of the police department.

f. *The directorate.* Many diversion programs, especially those involving more than one municipal jurisdiction, are governed, directed, advised, and supported by boards of directors and advisory boards. Often, one finds police representation on these boards to be disproportionately heavy. Experience also suggests that their voice on such boards is a strong one; one "nay" vote from the police can effectively block a diversion program. McAleenan (1975) has recently described a project with two boards, one of which is comprised solely of community agency personnel while the other is half police and half school personnel. Dennison and associates (1975) portray two projects with advisory boards. In one, 4 of 18 members are police officials; in the other, 5 of 12 including the chairman represent the police.

Other forms of control are obviously possible; our purpose in presenting these, each of which we have observed, has been to highlight the variety of control procedures possible and to make it clear that this control dimension is indeed a prominent one. Diversion programs are far from independent of the juvenile justice system, even though diversion is supposed to mean diversion *from* that system. It seems clear, as well, that programs high on the police control dimension are more likely to be higher on the client control dimension.

However, it is important to emphasize that we have observed a number of police-diversion programs in which the police connection with referral agencies is truly minimal. Diversion here is not so much a project as a habit.

6. COMMITMENT TO DIVERSION

In the preceding sections we have characterized diversion as a fad serving multiple and conflicting goals. Now we turn to the final concern of this chapter, police commitment to diversion. If commitment is genuinely low, then perhaps the question of appropriate evaluation dimensions is moot. But if commitment is more than low—high commitment is perhaps not a realistic expectation—then the evidence for commitment is worth pursuing. Despite the reservations and cautions expressed throughout this chapter concerning the way in which police diversion programs are being carried out, we are satisfied that police commitment to the diversion philosophy is, in general, too entrenched currently to be considered "low." Of course, this still does not characterize it as "high."

Our own interviews in 47 police departments suggested to us as being involved in diversion yielded 35 which characterized themselves as so involved. In 33 of these 35, we inspected 100 randomly selected case files, finding referrals to community agencies in 26 of 33; 7 stations who think of themselves as having referral programs yield *no* referrals in 100 cases.

Still, that leaves 26 who are referring juveniles for treatment of some kind. The range of referral rates is from 1 in 100 to 28 in 100, with most of the stations having fewer than 10. Taking the 33 departments that characterized themselves as having diversion programs, we find a mean referral rate of 8%: 8 in 100 arrestees are referred. Commitment to referral is certainly not high, but the low of a decade ago has been raised considerably.

As important as level of commitment, if we are to understand the relevant issues, are the variables associated with police commitment to diversion. Two sets of variables have been suggested by current research. In their comparison of two multi-city diversion programs, Dennison and associates (1975) have related commitment implicitly to (a) levels of political involvement and (b) degree of success sensed by police personnel. Political involvement emerges as paramount in this analysis, especially as exhibited in interorganizational relationships and in threats to organizational "turfs." The authors note, "The lesson is that funding agencies should be thoroughly familiar with the regions to be served before attempting to impose organizational guidelines, and that the regions should be small and well-defined" (1975: 16).

The second set of variables relates directly to the control issue explicated earlier. Specifically, the present authors found from interview data in 34 departments that commitment to diversion was related to whether the counseling was all done within the police department or was placed in community-based agencies. An interesting and rather clear pattern of differences emerges.

First, as might be expected, inhouse programs are positively associated with the structural additions of new divisions or details and new staff. Not so obviously, inhouse programs are positively associated with initiation of the program from inside the department. Conversely, departments using outside referrals were more likely to have remained structurally unchanged and their programs were more likely to have been initiated from the outside, usually by a state or regional planning agency.

Second, inside initiation and inside development of the program are associated with structural changes and with having a period of civic funding, or no funding at all, at some point in the program's history.

The composite picture so far then is one set of programs that were self-initiated and developed, were operating without funds or with civic funding for a period of time, have added staff, and have an inhouse counseling arrangement. Another set of programs, initiated and developed with the help of outside agencies (usually the state planning agency) have always operated on outside government funding, have yielded no structural changes in the department, and refer offenders to outside counseling agencies.

Perhaps more interesting, these historical and structural variables were found to be closely associated with certain attitudinal variables. These represent a dimension of optimism versus pessimism about the program and its effects, including prospects for changing the crime rate, confidence in counselors, and possible effects on public relations. Clearly, optimism was associated with the inhouse programs and pessimism with the outside referral programs. It should be noted that 17 of the 34 programs were strictly outside referral ones.

Thus, although there are a number of departments having self-initiated, self-developed, self-funded programs that have resulted in structural changes in the department—in short, a group of "committed" practitioners of diversion and referral—there are many others that cannot be so described. This latter group, making up a substantial proportion of the recent diversion "explosion," has been induced from the outside to begin programs about which they are not especially optimistic. From our informal contacts and from data inferences, it is clear that the inducement is government money. The question immediately arises: what happens when federal money is withdrawn, as it inevitably will be? Does referral become a thing of the past? Probably not for the self-initiated programs which are clearly operated by juvenile officers committed to diversion. However, it is just as clear, at this point, that the government-initiated programs will probably die unless something happens which changes the attitudes of those officers.

In line with this last remark, it is appropriate to note that, in general, the government-funded projects started more recently than the self-initiated ones. It is possible that there has not been time for the officers in these programs to see positive results and therefore become convinced of the merits of diversion. The opposite possibility is, of course, equally probable. It might be advisable for the state planners to turn their attention to this problem. Succinctly put, funders must face the fact that rationales and commitment behind funding and planning at an administrative level do not necessarily filter down to the operating level of the juvenile officer.

CONCLUSION: EVALUATION DIMENSIONS

The reader may have noted by now that this chapter has paid almost no attention to whether or not diversion "works," especially in the sense of reducing recidivism rates. This omission does not reflect a view that the recidivism criterion is of little consequence; quite to the contrary, we consider it of paramount importance. However, we have been concerned here with a different matter, trying to elucidate a number of additional evaluative criteria which emerge from a structural analysis of diversion programs. These other criteria are often given great emphasis by policy makers. Further, they deal more directly with the connections between the police, as one component of the juvenile justice system, and the system, community, and political contexts within which police programs must operate.

To attend to all criteria may ask too much of any single evaluation group or project. To ignore most criteria has been the history of most groups and projects. But with a reasonable amount of planning, and given the large number and varying forms and settings of diversion programs, a comprehensive evaluation methodology is conceivable. The existence of scores of state and local criminal justice planning agencies should make such comprehensive evaluation possible, or even mandatory. To date, it has not.

NOTES

1. A printed sign on the wall admonished, "Think Referral."

2. McAleenan (1975) has recently noted the case of the diverted juvenile offender aged four and a half years, as well as several others aged five, seven, and nine.

3. Recruitment was facilitated by an announcement from the U.S. Department of Health, Education, and Welfare (OYD, 1975).

REFERENCES

BERGER, R. J. (1975) "An evaluation of a juvenile court volunteer program." Ann Arbor: Institute for Social Research, University of Michigan, mimeo.

BLOMBERG, T. G. (1975) "Diversion: a strategy of family control in the juvenile court process." Tallahassee: School of Criminology, Florida State University, mimeo.

BOHNSTEDT, M. (1975) The Evaluation of Juvenile Diversion Programs. Sacramento: California Youth Authority.

DENNISON, L., L. HUMPHREYS, and D. WILSON (1975) "A comparison: organization and impact in two juvenile diversion projects." Claremont: Claremont Graduate Schools, mimeo.

EDWARDS, W., M. GUTTENTAG, and K. SNAPPER (1975) "A decision-theoretic approach to evaluation research," in E. L. Struening and M. Guttentag (eds.) Handbook of Evaluation Research, Vol. I. Beverly Hills: Sage Publications.

GEMIGNANI, R. J. (1972) "Youth service systems." Delinquency Prevention Reporter. Washington, D.C.: Government Printing Office.

GUTTENTAG, M. and E. L. STRUENING (1975) Handbook of Evaluation Research, vol. 2. Beverly Hills: Sage Publications.

KLEIN, M. (1973) "Issues in police diversion of juvenile offenders: a guide for discussion," pp. 375-422 in G. Adams, R. M. Carter, J. D. Gerletti, D. G. Pursuit, and P. G. Rogers (eds.) Juvenile Justice Management. Springfield, Ill.: Charles C Thomas.

——— (1975) "On the front end of the juvenile justice system," in R. M. Carter and M. W. Klein, Back on the Street: The Diversion of Juvenile Offenders. Englewood Cliffs, N.J.: Prentice-Hall.

KUTCHINS, H. and S. KUTCHINS (1973) "Pretrial diversionary programs: new expansion of law enforcement activity camouflaged as rehabilitation." Presented at the Pacific Sociological Association Meetings, Hawaii, mimeo.

LINCOLN, S. B. (1975) "Juvenile referral and recidivism," in R. M. Carter and M. W. Klein (eds.) Back on the Street: The Diversion of Juvenile Offenders. Englewood Cliffs, N.J.: Prentice-Hall.

MATTINGLY, J. and D. KATKIN (1975) "The Youth Service Bureau: a re-invented wheel?" Presented at the Society for the Study of Social Problems Meeting, San Francisco, mimeo.

McALEENAN, M. M. (1975) "The politics of evaluation in a juvenile diversion project." Los Angeles, Occidental College, mimeo.

NCCD (1975) note in Criminal Justice Newsletter 6 (April 14), p. 2, Hackensack, N.J., mimeo.

NEITHERCUTT, M. G. and W. H. MOSELEY (1974) Arrest Decisions as Preludes to ?: An Evaluation of Policy Related Research, Vol. II. Davis, Calif.: National Council on Crime and Delinquency.

Office of Youth Development (1975) note in Youth Reporter, 75-26030. Washington, D.C.: Government Printing Office.

POLK, K. and S. KOBRIN (1972) Delinquency Prevention Through Youth Development. (SRS) 72-26013, Washington, D.C.: Government Printing Office.

President's Commission on Law Enforcement and Administration of Justice (1967) The Challenge of Crime in a Free Society and Task Force Report: Juvenile Delinquency. Washington, D.C.: Government Printing Office.

Public Systems Inc. (1974) California Correctional System Intake Study. Sunnyvale, Calif.

SCHUR, E. M. (1973) Radical Non-Intervention: Rethinking the Delinquency Problem. Englewood Cliffs, N.J.: Prentice-Hall.

STRUENING, E. L. and M. GUTTENTAG (1975) Handbook of Evaluation Research, vol. 1. Beverly Hills: Sage Publications.

VORENBERG, E. W. and J. VORENBERG (1973) "Early diversion from the criminal justice system: practice in search of a theory," pp. 151-183 in L. E. Ohlin (ed.) Prisoners in America. Englewood Cliffs, N.J.: Prentice-Hall.

WILSON, J. (1968) "The police and the delinquent in two cities," pp. 9-30 in S. Wheeler (ed.) Controlling Delinquents. New York: John Wiley.

24

THE NEUTRALIZATION OF SEVERE PENALTIES: SOME TRAFFIC LAW STUDIES

By

H. LAURENCE ROSS

H. Laurence Ross states that "sharp measures in formal penalties tend to be subverted by contrary adjustment in the behavior of those who apply the law." To support his hypothesis, the author uses indirect data collected from relevant cases to illustrate that whenever sentences are particularly harsh, there is an inverse adjustment process in which the behavior of those who apply the law softens almost in direct contrast to the harshness of the sentence. The study shows in how sophisticated a manner time series analyses can be used.

From H. Laurence Ross, "The Neutralization of Severe Penalties: Some Traffic Law Studies." *Law & Society Review*, 1976, *10*(3), 403-413. Copyright 1976 by the Law and Society Association.

Between the formal law of statute books and appellate courts and the informal law of routine dispositions intervene a variety of actors, exemplified by policemen and insurance adjusters, some of whom have not traditionally been regarded as "legal" actors. However, one of the most important contributions of sociology to the understanding of law has been the demonstration that the attitudes and values of these actors and the pressures embodied in their roles produce a comprehensible divergence between the prescriptions of the formal law and the regularities exhibited in the informal law (Skolnick, 1966; Ross, 1970). This paper discusses some instances of discrepancy between the formal and informal law when formal penalties are suddenly and greatly increased. Its principal hypothesis is that sharp increases in formal penalties tend to be subverted by contrary adjustments in the behavior of those who apply the law. The data to be presented come from four of my studies on the effectiveness of changing traffic laws. As these studies were not designed to test the present hypothesis, their evidence is indirect, and the presentation is exploratory rather than demonstrative.

The hypothesis is consistent with empirical generalizations by observers of legal institutions as well as with the high-level generalizations of functionalist theory in sociology. An example of the former is James Q. Wilson's (1975: 187) observation on the tendency to legislate mandatory penalties to deter currently fashionable crimes: "No one should assume that any judicial outcome can be made truly 'mandatory'—discretion removed from one place in the criminal justice system tends to reappear elsewhere in it." Functionalist theory's "homeostatic principle" is exemplified by such assertions as "So far as it impinges on institutionalized patterns of action and relationship, therefore, change is never just 'alteration of pattern' but alteration *by the overcoming of resistance*" (Parsons, 1951:491, italics in original).

There are a variety of points of discretion in the application of legal sanctions, and the examples to be considered suggest that homeostatic resistance to change may be found at a number of these points. Police may stabilize or reduce the number of arrests for the violation subjected to increased penalties; prosecutors may reduce the number or severity of the charges through plea bargaining; judges and juries may fail to convict the accused or may find reason to mitigate the penalties; and those convicted may find means to avoid the sanctions prescribed. As suggested by Wilson, the attempt to control discretion at one such point may merely result in the shifting of its exercise to another point, much as—to use a slithery analogy—the serpent held by one coil of his body may wriggle more energetically elsewhere.

The Connecticut Speed Crackdown of 1955. The most extensive data come from my study, with Donald T. Campbell, of the increase in the penalty for speeding introduced into Connecticut by Governor Abraham Ribicoff in 1955 (Campbell and Ross, 1968). The change in penalty was achieved by the Governor by means of the threat not to reappoint judges who failed to punish drivers found guilty of speeding with a 30-day license suspension on the first offence.

According to the contemporary press, the new penalty in Connecticut was considered to be unusually stringent by all concerned. Our analysis of the accident data failed to produce evidence that the change promoted highway safety. However, some other effects were apparent from the same analysis. The number of arrests for speeding fell drastically, from 4377 in the first six months of 1955 to 2735 in the comparable period of 1956. The official explanation for this phenomenon was that drivers were speeding less often but we were tempted to believe that part of the diminution was the result of police failing to make arrests in marginal cases. Our speculation was supported by an otherwise unexplained simultaneous rise in vaguely defined offenses such as "careless driving" which did not carry the mandatory license suspension that accompanied speeding.

We also found that the proportion of drivers accused of speeding who were found not guilty seemed to rise spectacularly in Connecticut at about the time of the crackdown. This is a diagrammed in Figure 1. Unfortunately, this figure is not unambiguous in its message, for increases in not-guilty findings also occurred in 1954 and 1955. However, the 1955-1956 increase is

Figure 1. Percentage of speeding violators judged not guilty in Connecticut.

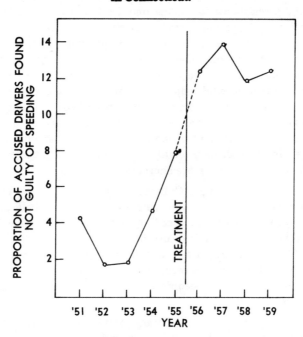

the largest, and accelerates the prior trend, in keeping with the interpretation that judges were reacting to the increase in penalty in that year. If, as we suspect, the population of accused drivers following the crackdown lacked marginal cases through police discretion, the 1955-1956 increase in not-guilty findings becomes more meaningful. Whether because of a harder fight by the defendants or a disposition to leniency on the part of the judges, the increased penalty upon conviction may have made that conviction less likely.

Because the crackdown limited the discretion of judges in sentencing, once the accused was found guilty, we may assume that license suspension was the near-universal penalty in practice. The data in Figure 2, however, indicate that an unintended result of the crackdown was to increase the number of violators of license suspension orders. The guilty were apparently taking their own steps to avoid the prescribed penalties.

Jail for drunk drivers in Chicago. In another administrative action, a mandatory seven-day jail sentence for driving while intoxicated was prescribed by the Supervising Judge of Chicago's Traffic Court at Christmas of 1970. The claimed success of this

**Figure 2. Arrested while driving with a suspended license,
as percent of suspensions, Connecticut**

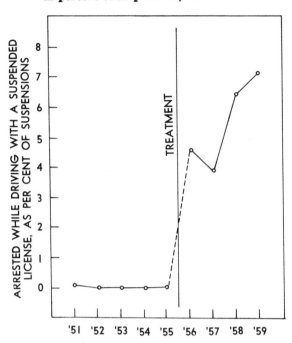

threat in reducing fatalities produced a continuation of the policy
into the first six months of 1971. Again, analysis failed to produce scientifically acceptable evidence of effectiveness of the legal change in achieving its goal of fewer fatalities, but changes
could be detected in the operation of the system (Robertson, Rich
and Ross, 1973). Although the threat was made in universal
terms, the jail sentence was in fact seldom applied. Chicago police arrested more than 1100 drivers each month for drinking and
driving during the period in question, but the total number of
7-day jail sentences for all traffic offenses for the first six months
of 1971 was only 557. This did represent an increase over the
357 such sentences given in the comparable months of the preceding year, but the obvious inference is that despite enormous publicity the judges were not applying the sanction at the threatened
level. One course of action producing this effect was signaled
by a small increase in findings of not guilty, but we believe that
the principal explanation lies in judges failing to sentence the
guilty drivers as prescribed by administrative fiat.

The Denver Court study. Departure from prescribed sanctions on the part of judges was also noted in an experimental

study of various treatments for drinking-and-driving offenders in Denver (Ross and Blumenthal, 1974). An agreement was reached between the Presiding Judge of the County Court and researchers at the University of Denver (at the request of the former) whereby penalties would be alternated during arbitrary time periods between a fine, probation, and a clinical or educational program, in order to determine the comparative effectiveness of each. Although the trial judges were parties to the agreement and faithfully promised adherence, they compromised the study by substituting the defendants' preferred treatment, a fine, for the other scheduled treatments in a large proportion of cases. The data are presented in Table 1, which shows that the proportion of broken judicial promises was negligible when a fine was prescribed, but it was nearly a third in the case of probation and more than half in the clinical-educational case, the latter being most disliked by the defendants. Judges' defections were much more numerous where a lawyer was present than for unrepresented defendants, but even among the latter the judges frequently avoided what were regarded as harsh penalties.

TABLE 1. Sanctions administered to drivers found guilty of DUI in Denver Court experiment.

		Scheduled Sanctions		
		Fine (N=166)	Probation (N=157)	Therapy (N=164)
Sanctions received	Fine	95%	32%	41%
	Probation	5	68	12
	Class or Clinic	1	0	47
	TOTAL	100%	100%	100%

The Finnish drinking-and-driving legislation of 1950. A statute greatly increasing the maximum severity of prison sentences for drinking and driving was passed by the Finnish Parliament in 1950. The maximum penalty had previously been two years in prison. Henceforth it became four years, with the possibility of six years if the offence produced serious bodily injury and seven years if it caused death. The potential punishment for drinking and driving was thus raised 250 percent at one stroke.

My analysis of the Finnish legislation (Ross, 1975: 303-308) again found no evidence for effectiveness of severe penalties in lowering crash or fatality rates. Previously unpublished data did, however, reveal the interesting fact that the *increase* in the maximum penalty was accompanied by a *decrease* in the number of long sentences meted out be Finnish courts in cases of drinking and driving. This phenomenon is documented in Figure 3. Also,

Figure 3. Prison sentences of 6 months or more per 10,000 registered vehicles, 1931-1968. Finland (1938-1944 omitted)

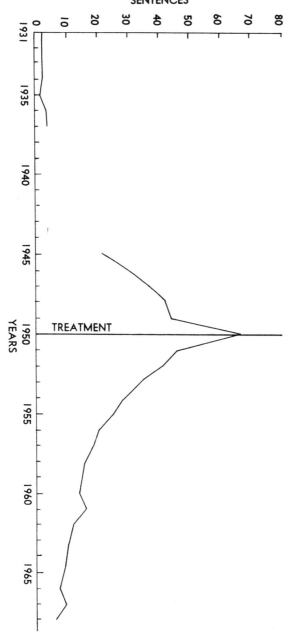

following 1950, prosecutions for drinking and driving followed a declining trend. The legislature's apparent intent to increase penalization of drinking-and-driving offences was not only moderated but was in some manner actually reversed in the operation of the system of police, prosecutors, and courts.

Other studies. Some studies of increased arrests for drinking and driving have shown outcomes similar to those noted above

Figure 4. Court dispositions of driving-while-intoxicated charges in Hennepin County, Minnesota.

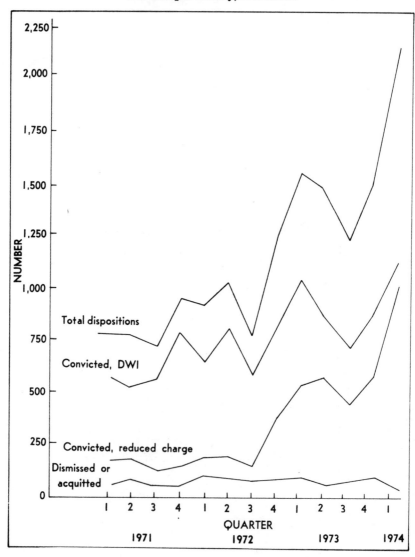

in cases of increased penalties. The U.S. Department of Transportation's Alcohol Safety Action Programs aimed to increase arrests. Figure 4, from the ASAP evaluation report (U.S. Department of Transportation, 1975) shows the experience of the Hennepin County, Minnesota, ASAP. The program was in fact able to effect a manifold increase in the arrest rate without affecting dismissals or acquittals, but plea-bargaining apparently reduced the consequences of these arrests for a very large proportion of arrested drivers. Likewise, a study in progress by Marc Galanter and associates at the State University of New York at Buffalo, shows "skyrocketing" arrests by State Police for drinking and driving, yet only a very slow rise in convictions for the offence charged and a steep rise in convictions for lesser offences.

Beyond traffic law violations, with their peculiarities in representing the criminal law, it has been noted by various observers that harsh formal penalties are seldom applied in action. One example is the fact that the relatively frequent death sentences meted out in Great Britain in the late 18th and early 19th centuries were seldom executed. Tobias (1968:200) states: "Most people thought the death penalty tended to promote crime, believing that it did not deter the criminal, who regarded it as a risk of the calling and accepted it as a soldier accepted the risk of death in battle, but that it did deter the prosecutor, magistrate, jury and judge, who were tempted to strain the law to avoid the risk of what was felt to be an unjust penalty." He notes that the Statistical Branch of the Home Office, in an 1841 memorandum, pointed out that the ratio of convictions to charges fell in the years after a death sentence was carried out for a crime, and that this ratio grew when Britain abolished capital punishment. A similar belief has been cited by conservative, punishment-oriented, legislators in support of moves to reduce penalties for the use of marijuana. (Galliher, McCartney and Baum, 1974.)

Discussion. The evidence from four diverse studies of increased penalties for traffic offences suggests that where the discretion of actors is relatively broad there occurs a mitigation or even an annulment of the increase. Compatible findings can be cited from observations of related issues in traffic and in general criminal law. Speculation may be offered concerning the mechanisms that produce this effect.

First, penalties exceeding established and accepted levels of severity may conflict with norms of fairness. This is especially likely when the penalty is increased beyond the level that fits current notions of the relative seriousness of the offence in an effort to realize greater general deterrence, as in most of the cases described. Moreover, legal actors can readily rationalize discretionary departures from a given standard by the doctrine of equity, which legitimizes individualized and deviant treatments for "exceptional" cases, which may in fact become routine (Ross and Blumenthal, 1975).

Second, legal actors respond to pressures from others on whom they depend for routine functioning. In this way the expectations of individual parties, even if they are criminal defendants, can become effective demands, spreading throughout the system. As Wilson notes (1975:179):

> . . . . the more severe the penalty, the more unlikely that it will be imposed. To ensure a conviction, avoid an expensive trial, reduce the chances of reversal on appeal, and give expression to their own views of benevolence, prosecutors and judges will try to get a guilty plea, and all they can offer in return is a lesser sentence. The more severe the sentence, the greater the bargaining power of the accused, and the greater the likelihood that he will be charged with a lesser offence. Extremely long mandatory minimum sentences do not always strengthen the hand of society; they often strengthen the hand of the criminal instead.

In conclusion, although the data presented in this paper are largely indirect, they support a theoretical and practical view of the legal system as embodying a homeostatic principle or law of inertia when confronting the introduction of severe penalties. The system minimizes the change through the exercise of discretion by various legal actors, apparently to satisfy the actors' values and to minimize pressures upon them from other participants in the system. Comparable consequences might be predicted for a sudden and severe lowering of penalties from an accepted standard, for example with the decriminalization of some kinds of immoral behavior. In support of this prediction can be cited pilot observations by my students and associates concerning the 1972 decriminalization of homosexual behavior in Colorado, which show that local police activity directed against homosexuals (e.g., for soliciting) remained high despite the decriminalization at the state level.

All but one of the four instances of severe penalties for traffic law violations cited here were put into effect in an effort to deter dangerous behavior, and deterrence is probably a goal for many other instances of sharply increased severity of punishment. In all cases studied, the actual punishment of offenders increased much less than might have been expected, and in the Finnish case actual punishment even decreased. Although such action may possibly increase the general perception of punishment for the offence and thus achieve a deterrent effect (Geerken and Gove, 1975), it is also possible that experience will subvert the credibility of the threat. In none of the studies cited could any deterrent effect of increased penalties be proved, so they cannot enlighten the question at hand. However, in my study of the British Road Safety Act of 1967, which found a strong deterrent effect for an increase in the apparent certainty of punishment, the gap between the threat and actuality appeared to produce learning which undermined the deterrent effect of the legislation over time (Ross, 1973). The studies described here do suggest that if levels of actual punishment are to rise as intended, it may be necessary for the law-giver simultaneously to limit the discretion of legal actors and reduce their ability to resist the initiated change. Bearing in mind the complexity of the legal system and the manifold points of discretion, this is no simple order. If it is to inflict the mandated punishment, the legal serpent may have to be grasped on every coil.

REFERENCES

CAMPBELL, Donald T. and H. Laurence ROSS (1968) "The Connecticut Crackdown on Speeding: Time-series Data in Quasi-Experimental Analysis," 3 *Law & Society Review* 33.

GALLIHER, John F., James L. McCARTNEY, and Barbara E. BAUM (1974) "Nebraska's Marijuana Law: A Case of Unexpected Legislative Innovation," 8 *Law & Society Review* 441.

GEERKEN, Michael R. and Walter R. GOVE (1975) "Deterrence: Some Theoretical Considerations," 9 *Law & Society Review* 497.

PARSONS, Talcott (1951) *The Social System*. Glencoe, Ill.: The Free Press.

ROBERTSON, Leon S., Robert F. RICH, and H. Laurence ROSS (1973) "Jail Sentences for Driving while Intoxicated in Chicago: A Judicial Action that Failed," 8 *Law & Society Review* 55.

ROSS, H. Laurence (1970) *Settled Out of Court: The Social Process of Insurance Claims Adjustment*. Chicago: Aldine Publishing Company.

——————— (1973) "Law, Science and Accidents: The British Road Safety Act of 1967," 2 *Journal of Legal Studies* 1.

——————— (1975) "The Scandinavian Myth: The Effectiveness of Drinking-and-Driving Legislation in Sweden and Norway," 4 *Journal of Legal Studies* 285.

——————— and Murray BLUMENTHAL (1974) "Sanctions for the Drinking Driver: An Experimental Study," 3 *Journal of Legal Studies* 53.

——————— and ——————— (1975) "Some Problems in Experimentation in a Legal Setting," 10 *American Sociologist* 150.

SKOLNICK, Jerome (1966) *Justice without Trial*. New York: John Wiley & Sons.

TOBIAS, J. J. (1968) *Crime and Industrial Society in the 19th Century.* New York: Schocken Books.

U. S. DEPARTMENT OF TRANSPORTATION (1975) *Alcohol Safety Action Projects: Evaluation of Operations, 1974.* Washington: Government Printing Office.

WILSON, James Q. (1975) *Thinking about Crime.* New York: Basic Books.

25

SENTENCING COUNCILS: A STUDY OF
SENTENCE DISPARITY AND ITS REDUCTION

By

SHARI SEIDMAN DIAMOND and HANS ZEISEL

It is commonly recognized that there is a disparity in sentencing between judges even when cases are comparable. Sentencing councils have been established in federal district courts in an attempt to alleviate this disparity. In their study, Shari Seidman Diamond and Hans Zeisel develop a method which measures sentence disparity. They describe the various methods for examining this disparity, such as random assignment, selection of comparable groups of cases, and analysis of identical cases. Their study concludes with recommendations which can help to reduce disparity in sentencing.

From Shari Seidman Diamond and Hans Zeisel, "Sentencing Councils: A Study of Sentence Disparity and Its Reduction." *The University of Chicago Law Review,* 1975, *43*(1), 109-149. © 1976 by the University of Chicago Law Review.

The fundamental premise in the idea of impartial judges and rules of law is that certain kinds of decision-making, for example, by judges, can by institutional arrangements and role discipline be made to show less variance and less correlation to personal factors than other kinds of decision-making . . . . Beyond this there is the question of whether different arrangements will produce different degrees of impersonality in decision-making.[1]

HARRY KALVEN, JR.

The severity of a criminal sentence depends to some extent on the identity of the sentencing judge. Comparable cases will not always receive comparable sentences. Although all would acknowledge that such sentence disparity among judges exists, there is disagreement both about the magnitude of the disparity and how it might be reduced.

One institutional arrangement used in some federal courts to alleviate sentence disparity is the sentencing council. The council enables the sentencing judge, before imposing sentence, to meet with his colleagues in order to learn what sentences they would impose if they were the sentencing judge. This article first reviews the problems sentence disparity has created and recounts earlier

---

f Assistant Professor of Criminal Justice and Psychology, University of Illinois, Chicago.

†† Professor of Law and Sociology Emeritus, The University of Chicago.

* This study is part of a larger research program on the problems of reducing sentence disparity. The research is supported by a grant from the Law Enforcement Assistance Administration to the Center for Studies in Criminal Justice at The University of Chicago Law School. We are grateful to Edwin A. Robson, Chief Judge of the United States District Court for the Northern District of Illinois, and to Judge Hubert L. Will, chairman of the sentencing council in that court; to Jacob Mishler, Chief Judge of the United States District Court for the Eastern District of New York; and to all the judges of both courts for their generous cooperation. The central retention of the sentencing court records by the Probation Department of the Chicago court greatly facilitated our work. Not the least of our thanks go to Judith Peyton and the Computation Center of the University of Illinois in Chicago for their dependable assistance. We also would like to thank our colleague Franklin B. Zimring, the Director of the Center for Studies in Criminal Justice, for his counsel and gentle impatience.

[1] Kalven, *Toward a Science of Impartial Judicial Behavior, Symposium: Empirical Approaches to Judicial Behavior*, 42 U. CIN. L. REV. 594 (1973).

efforts to study the phenomenon. It then develops a measure of disparity that might prove useful in future research and uses it to assess the magnitude of sentence disparity in two federal district courts: the Northern District of Illinois (Chicago) and the Eastern District of New York (Brooklyn). Finally it describes the operation of the sentencing councils in these two courts and tries to assess their ability to reduce disparity.

I. THE PROBLEM

Under any system of law, unless there is but one mandatory penalty, the sentence of an offender will depend partly on the identity of the sentencing judge. Under American law, the trial judge's views and values can play a particularly important role. The law provides practically no guidelines regarding the weights to be given to the many aggravating and mitigating circumstances of the crime, the offender, and the victim. Unlike his colleagues outside the Anglo-American tradition, the American judge need not and generally does not give reasons for his sentencing decision. Since the legal sentencing frames are normally broad, especially for the more serious crimes, similar offenders who commit similar offenses under similar circumstances may receive substantially different sentences. Moreover, because American law does not allow an independent appeal of the sentence,[2] the trial judge's sentence is generally final, subject to adjustment only by parole or executive pardon.[3]

Sentence disparity is a matter of concern to the offender, the judge, and the criminal justice system as a whole. The person most directly affected is the offender. As James V. Bennett, a former director of the Federal Bureau of Prisons, observed:

> The prisoner who must serve his excessively long sentence with other prisoners who receive relatively mild sentences under the same circumstances cannot be expected to accept his situation with equanimity. The more fortunate prisoners do not attribute their luck to a sense of fairness on the part of the law but to its whimsies. The existence of such disparities is among the

---

[2] The propriety of the sentence may be indirectly called into question on appeal in certain circumstances. *See generally* M. FRANKEL, CRIMINAL SENTENCES: LAW WITHOUT ORDER (1973).

[3] *But see* ME. REV. STAT. ANN., tit. 15, §§ 2141-44 (1965), which requires state judges to give reasons for their sentences. And ten states permit some sentencing appeal. *See, e.g.*, ALASKA STAT. §§ 12.55.120, 22.10.020 (1970); ARIZ. REV. STAT. ANN. §§ 13-1717 (1956); COLO. REV. STAT. ANN. § 40-1-509 (1971). *See also* S.B. 1, 94th Cong., 1st Sess. (would allow separate appeal of a sentence).

major causes of prison riots, and it is one of the reasons why prisons so often fail to bring about an improvement in the social attitudes of their charges.[4]

Judges, too, are disturbed by these variations. At the urging of the federal judiciary, the Congress, in 1958, passed a law providing for sentencing institutes where federal judges could exchange information on sentencing alternatives and practices with the aim of reducing undesirable sentence disparity.[5] More recently, Judge Marvin E. Frankel discussed the problem in his landmark book, *Criminal Sentences: Law Without Order:*[6]

> [I]n the great majority of federal criminal cases . . . a defendant who comes up for sentencing has no way of knowing or reliably predicting whether he will walk out of the courtroom on probation, or be locked up for a term of years that may consume the rest of his life, or something in between.

The costs of disparity to the system are high. As Mr. Justice Jackson said when he was Attorney General of the United States:

> It is obviously repugnant to one's sense of justice that the judgment meted out to an offender should depend in large part on a purely fortuitous circumstance; namely the personality of the particular judge before whom the case happens to come for disposition.[7]

For all concerned, sentence disparity offends a shared concept of fairness.

II. APPROACHES TO THE STUDY OF DISPARITY

In order to measure sentence disparity caused by differences among judges, all other factors that may affect the sentence must be controlled. This goal has been approached in three ways.

A. Random Assignment

If a court assigns cases at random to its judges, they will receive comparable groups of cases.[8] Differences in sentences must then be

---

[4] J. BENNETT, OF PRISONS AND JUSTICE, S. Doc. No. 70, 88th Cong., 2d Sess. 319 (1964).

[5] H.R. REP. No. 1916, 85th Cong., 2d Sess. (1958).

[6] M. FRANKEL, *supra* note 2, at 6. *See also* JUSTICE IN SENTENCING: PAPERS AND PROCEEDINGS OF THE SENTENCING INSTITUTE FOR THE FIRST AND SECOND UNITED STATES JUDICIAL CIRCUITS (L. Orland & H. Tyler, Jr. eds. 1974); K. DAVIS, DISCRETIONARY JUSTICE 133-41 (1969) (considers the problem in a wider context).

[7] 1940 ATT'Y GEN. ANN. REP. 5-6.

[8] Within the limits of the sampling error.

due to differences among the judges; such random assignment creates a natural controlled experiment. The earliest studies of sentence disparity relied on this design, but were not alert to its operational limitations.

The first of these was Everson's study in 1919, which compared the sentencing patterns of forty-two magistrates in New York City.[9] He found that after conviction for public intoxication the frequency of suspended sentences varied from less than 1 percent to 83 percent among the magistrates; moreover, the frequency of suspended sentences tended to reflect the magistrate's ethnic background. In 1933 Gaudet et al. published their first finding from a study of 7,442 sentences imposed by six county judges of a New Jersey court that claimed to distribute its cases randomly.[10] The most lenient judge ordered incarceration in 34 percent of his cases, the most severe judge for 58 percent of the offenders he sentenced. The sentencing patterns showed no change over time for three of the judges, while two became more severe and one more lenient. In 1938 Gaudet published disparity figures by type of crime.[11]

These studies have limitations. Random assignment will produce initially comparable groups only if correctly applied across a large number of cases. In practice, considerations of court management or simple carelessness may interfere with the operation of the random assignment rule.[12] Moreover, even if assignment is random, cases are usually assigned before they reach the sentencing stage. Although sensible for the court, by the time the randomly assigned cases reach the sentencing stage, their mix is likely to differ from judge to judge. Differential rates of guilty pleas and convictions after trial, factors that are themselves partly functions of personality differences among the judges, will then affect the mix of cases and, in turn, the sentences.

B. Selecting Comparable Groups of Cases

Without prior random assignment, comparability might be

---

[9] Everson, *The Human Element in Justice*, J. CRIM. L. & CRIMINOLOGY 90 (1919).

[10] GAUDET, HARRIS & JOHN, *Individual Differences in the Sentencing Tendencies of Judges*, 23 J. CRIM. L. & CRIMINOLOGY 811 (1933).

[11] Gaudet, *Individual Differences in the Sentencing of Judges*, 32 ARCH. OF PSYCHOLOGY 1 (1938).

[12] In the federal courts, a judge will occasionally be bypassed if he is already burdened with cases requiring an unusual amount of trial time. The random assignment rule is also distorted when a new judge comes to the court and receives his first cases by transfer from his colleagues; if he came from the U.S. Attorney's Office, he will not be assigned criminal cases prepared during his time at the Office.

sought in the following manner: first, the cases of each judge are divided into subgroups according to characteristic factors likely to affect the sentence, such as the crime, the defendant, and the victim; second, comparisons are drawn among judges for cases within each subgroup. As the subgroups become more specific, they will approach comparability. The analyst can never be certain, however, that the groups are perfectly comparable because he cannot rule out the possibility that some unknown variable affecting the sentences is more heavily represented in the cases of one judge than in those of another.[13]

One of the more elaborate examples of this approach to the study of sentence disparity is Green's investigation of the Philadelphia criminal court during the late 1950s.[14] Based on the 1,437 convictions obtained during a seventeen-month period in 1956-57, he analyzed the sentencing patterns of the eighteen judges in cases where the severity of the crime, the offender's criminal record, and other important factors were held constant. Green's data arrangement was appropriate, but his conclusions were not. In contrast to earlier disparity studies, he claimed to have found only minimal sentence disparity. But Green misread his data, which clearly show sentence disparity, especially in the middle ranges of severity.[15]

The ready availability of precise statistics for all United States federal court cases has generated several studies of sentence disparity within the federal system. One of the first comparisons of this kind was presented to the Pilot Institute of Sentencing, held in Boulder, Colorado, in the summer of 1959. One participant reported:[16]

> The most shocking exhibit . . . was a chart showing the disparity of sentences in income tax cases over a period of 12 years. In one district all of the defendants who were convicted or pleaded guilty were sent to prison. The percentage of those sent to prison in other districts varied widely, from under 5 percent to over 90 percent.

The magnitude of the differences in the sentencing patterns of var-

---

[13] *Cf.* D. CAMPBELL & J. STANLEY, EXPERIMENTAL AND QUASI-EXPERIMENTAL DESIGNS FOR RESEARCH (1966); F. CHAPIN, EXPERIMENTAL DESIGNS IN SOCIOLOGICAL RESEARCH (1955); H. ZEISEL, SAY IT WITH FIGURES (5th ed. 1968).

[14] E. GREEN, JUDICIAL ATTITUDES IN SENTENCING (1961) (Cambridge Studies in Criminology). *See also* R. HOOD, SENTENCING IN MAGISTRATES' COURTS, A STUDY IN VARIATIONS OF POLICY 123 (1962); Zeisel, *Methodological Problems in Studies of Sentencing*, 3 LAW & SOC'Y 621-33 (1969).

[15] *Id.* at 134-38.

[16] Thomsen, *Sentencing in Income Tax Cases*, 26 FED. PROBATION, March 1962, at 10.

ious districts is so great that it is reasonable to infer that the judges' differing sentencing philosophies are a primary cause of the disparity; this inference assumes that the mix of cases in the different districts does not vary enough to account for the observed sentence disparities. In order to test this assumption, it would be necessary to break down the mix of cases into comparable subgroups as described above. Rau has made a trial step in this direction by analyzing sentences for ten major crime categories controlling for the offender's prior record.[17] He found significant disparities among the circuits. Additional disparities might have emerged had he looked at districts within each circuit.

A study now in progress by Tiffany, Avichai, and Peters, sponsored by the American Bar Foundation, promises to carry this type of analysis several steps further. They have collected detailed data on all offenders convicted in the federal system during a two year period, the crimes of which they had been convicted, and their type of plea. The authors will be able to analyze the sentencing patterns in the various districts by comparing those cases that share particular combinations of characteristics likely to affect the sentence.[18] It would be useful to push the analysis still further and compile comparative data on individual judges in order to see the interplay among judges, districts, and circuits.[19]

While these refinements promise more specific disparity measures, the approach has natural limits. There are only a certain number of convictions in the system, and every refinement step makes each subgroup smaller and each comparison less reliable.[20] The sample of cases, moreover, cannot be safely expanded by including cases from more years, because sentencing patterns may change over time as judges retire and are replaced.

C. Identical Cases

A third approach to the study of sentence disparity requires different judges to "sentence" an identical group of cases, thereby ensuring absolute comparability. Because criminal sentences in

---

[17] Rau, Sentencing in the Federal District Courts (1972) (mimeographed paper prepared for the National Institute of Law Enforcement and Criminal Justice (LEAA)).

[18] They have published a partial analysis of their data but have not yet made comparisons by districts. *See* Tiffany, Avichai & Peters, *A Statistical Analysis of Sentencing in Federal Courts: Defendants Convicted After Trial, 1967-1968*, 4 J. LEGAL STUDIES 369 (1975).

[19] One might extend the comparison to the state courts in the federal districts to learn whether sentencing standards in the two systems affect each other.

[20] Beyond a certain level of refinement, some subgroups will lose all their cases and thus lose their comparative value.

American courts are always imposed by a single trial judge, this approach must to some extent rely on simulated sentencing decisions, whereby each judge states the sentence he would give if he were the sentencing judge.[21]

The first such attempt was made in 1961 by federal judges at the Sentencing Institutes held by the Fifth Circuit in New Orleans[22] and by the Sixth, Seventh and Eighth Circuits in Highland Park, Illinois.[23] The sentences handed down in the sample cases by the conference judges varied widely. In one case of income tax evasion, for example, the recommended sentences ranged from a six-month suspended prison sentence to a five-year prison sentence with a $20,000 fine.[24] In an embezzlement case the sentences ranged between probation and five years custody.[25]

The Federal Judicial Center recently conducted a systematic study of disparity using simulated sentencing.[26] Second Circuit judges read presentence reports and made sentence recommendations in thirty cases. Substantial disparities were found; in sixteen of the twenty cases submitted to all of the judges, there was disagreement in regard to the propriety of incarceration.

In England, Rupert Cross, throughout his career concerned with the problems of sentencing, has made informal experiments with sentencing. One of them was designed to show that judges too are human. The case involved manslaughter through grossly negligent driving. Some of the judges received the case ornamented by a legally irrelevant variable: the negligent driver was accompanied by a married woman, not his wife. Throughout, the man with the woman received a more severe sentence.[27]

---

[21] In many countries, especially on the European continent, sentences for major crimes are determined by a tribunal of several judges. Such a system would permit disparity to be measured without simulation. But this seemingly perfect "naturally controlled experiment" suffers from a potential difficulty: the unavoidable bargaining process may move some judges to make their initial recommendation artificially high or low for negotiating purposes.

[22] *Sentencing Institute and Joint Council for the Fifth Circuit, New Orleans, 1961*, 30 F.R.D. 185 (1962) [hereinafter cited as *New Orleans Conference*].

[23] *Seminar and Institute on Disparity of Sentences for Sixth, Seventh, and Eighth Judicial Circuits, Highland Park, Illinois, 1961*, 30 F.R.D. 401 (1962) [hereinafter cited as *Highland Park Conference*].

[24] *New Orleans Conference* at 226.

[25] *Highland Park Conference* at 500.

[26] A. Partridge & W. Eldridge, The Second Circuit Sentencing Study, Federal Judicial Center (August 1974).

[27] From a personal communication to Hans Zeisel. Cross thus anticipated a favorite experimental pastime of present-day psychologists. *Cf.* Landy & Aronson, *The Influence of the Character of the Criminal and Victim on the Decisions of Simulated Jurors*, 5 J. EXPERIMENTAL & SOCIAL PSYCHOLOGY 141-52 (1969); Sigall & Ostrove, *Beautiful But Dangerous:*

Roger Hood, who earlier had studied sentence disparity in the English magistrate courts by the "comparable cases" method, studied sentence disparity by submitting identical cases of serious driving offenses to a panel of judges. To make the simulation more realistic, he included excerpts from the trial record, highlighted the testimony, and gave a careful description of the offender.[28]

Despite such precautions, simulated sentencing recommendations may differ from real sentencing decisions. To impose a long prison term is a difficult task even after years on the bench; a simulated sentence sends no one to jail. Moreover, simulated sentencing is based on a written record which, however carefully prepared, cannot substitute for information gained from a sentencing judge's presence in court. It is reasonable to suppose that a less complete picture of the case leaves more to the judge's imagination and increases the likelihood of disagreements over the sentence.[29] In addition, the judge may suspect that the experiment is designed to measure his "severity" and, if only unconsciously, may seek to dispel an unwanted reputation by deviating from his normal sentencing practice.

The many cautionary notes we have added to the description of these earlier studies must not lead to a general distrust of them. As studies of the same problem using various research approaches proliferate, the valid ones, whatever their individual imperfections, tend to support each other by mutual corroboration.[30]

The "identical case" approach offers the best opportunity for measuring disparity, and the sentencing council provides the optimal arrangement of this approach. While elements of simulation remain, the participating judges know that their recommendations can and often do have a real impact on the sentence actually imposed. Under present law no more realistic arrangement can be devised that will allow several judges to sentence one offender.

III. The Sentencing Council

The first sentencing council was started in the Eastern District of Michigan in 1960,[31] followed by the Eastern District of New York

Effects of Offender Attractiveness and Nature of the Crime on Juridic Judgment, 31 J. PERSONALITY AND SOCIAL PSYCHOLOGY 410-14 (1975).

[28] R. HOOD, SENTENCING THE MOTORING OFFENDER (1972).

[29] This is probably a special case of a more general proposition, applicable to all experiments which use abbreviated materials, such as abstracted trial scripts in jury experiments.

[30] *See generally* H. ZEISEL, *supra* note 10, at 200-39 (ch. 13, Triangulation of Proof).

[31] *See* Doyle, *A Sentencing Council in Operation*, 25 FED. PROBATION, Sept. 1961, at 27;

in 1962,[32] the Northern District of Illinois in 1963,[33] and, more recently, the District of Oregon. All four councils are still in operation. Data from the New York[34] and Chicago[35] courts form the basis of this study.

The New York and Chicago courts generally hold weekly meetings of the sentencing council. Several days before the meeting, each participating judge receives a copy of the presentence report prepared by the court's probation office for each offender. The report contains a short description of the offense and the background of the offender. The judges then record their sentence recommendations. The cases and recommendations are discussed at the next council meeting. After hearing the discussion and the sentences recommended by his colleagues, the sentencing judge makes his final decision. The council is purely advisory; the sentencing judge retains complete discretion in making the final decision.

The Chicago and New York councils differ in important respects. In New York, every case is considered by panels of three

---

Hosner, *Group Procedure in Sentencing: A Decade of Practice*, 34 FED. PROBATION, Dec. 1970, at 18; Kaufman, *Sentencing: The Judge's Problem*, 24 FED. PROBATION, March 1960, at 3; Levin, *Toward a More Enlightened Sentencing Procedure*, 43 NEB. L. REV. 499 (1966); Smith, *The Sentencing Council and the Problem of Disproportionate Sentences*, 27 FED. PROBATION, June 1963, at 5; *cf.* Sigurdson, The Federal Sentencing Council: An Attempt at Disparity Reduction, 1964 (summary of unpublished master's thesis, U. of Michigan School of Social Work).

[32] Zavatt, *Sentencing Procedure in the U.S. District Court for the Eastern District of New York*, 41 F.R.D. 469 (1966).

[33] B. Meeker, Values of a Sentencing Council, Oct. 1964 (paper presented at the Institute and Joint Council on Sentencing, Lompoc, Calif.) (The University of Chicago Law Library).

[34] The New York sample is composed of 624 of the cases considered by the council panels during the calendar year 1973. The judges keep the records in their personal files. Nine judges provided access to them, leaving three judges whose cases were not included in the sample; one had died, another had retired, the third was a visiting judge.

Administrative Office statistics indicate that the number of offenders sentenced during 1973 was around 1,089 (Courtesy of James McCafferty, Chief of the Operations Branch of the Administrative Office of U.S. Courts). Until 1974 sentences imposed during the summer, some 20 percent of all cases, did not come before the council. Zavatt, *supra* note 32. The 624 cases, representing twelve judges, constitute therefore approximately 57 percent of all cases. Three-fourths of the cases came before the regular three-member panels; one-fourth of the cases came before two judges. In 14 cases no record could be found of a judge's recommended sentence.

[35] The Chicago sample of 1,619 cases consisted of all the cases sentenced during the eighteen month period between January 1, 1972, and June 30, 1973. Of these, 518 were brought before the sentencing council; 566 belonged to judges who did not participate in the council; and 535 cases were not brought before the council by the judges who otherwise participated in its deliberations. The sample does not include 17 cases for which indictment was filed before 1971; it also omits 24 cases for which the identity of the sentencing judge could not be determined.

judges: the sentencing judge and two of his colleagues assigned more or less in rotation. In Chicago council participation is voluntary, and each case comes before the full council of participating judges.[36]

This study measures the degree of existing disparity in both courts, discusses the ability of each council to reduce disparity, and evaluates the effects of the organizational structures of the two councils. First, however, it will be necessary to define sentence disparity more precisely.

IV. THE MEASUREMENT OF DISPARITY

Sentence disparity can be measured at various levels. The first level of disparity is disagreement among judges over the type of sentence—custody (prison) or noncustody (probation or fine). At a second level, differences in the duration of recommended sentence can be measured within each type. Finally, disparity may be measured on a scale that considers the duration as well as the type of sentence. Table 1 gives an overview of the sentences at the disposal of a federal judge:[37]

Table 1

SIX MAJOR SENTENCING FRAMES FOR FEDERAL CRIMES

	Sentencing Frames		Examples of Crimes in that Frame
	Minimum	Maximum	
1	Probation	$1,000 fine and/or 1 year	a) Mail theft of property up to $100 (18 U.S.C. § 1708) (b) Embezzlement by employee of bank—up to $100 (18 U.S.C. § 656)
2	Probation	a) 3 years	a) Destruction of letter boxes or mail (18 U.S.C. § 1705)
		b) $1,000 fine and 3 years	b) Impersonating a federal officer (18 U.S.C. § 912)
3	Probation	a) $2,000 fine and 5 years	a) Mail theft of property over $100 (18 U.S.C. § 1708)
		b) $5,000 fine and 5 years	b) Sale or receipt of stolen vehicles (18 U.S.C. § 2313)
		c) $10,000 fine and 5 years	c) Selective Service violation (50 U.S.C. § 462(a))

[36] Originally, the sentencing council in Chicago consisted of two panels of six members each. Eventually, one panel stopped meeting, and the members who wished to remain on the council joined the other panel. At the time of this study, nine members of the court were participating in council activities, though not all of them all of the time.

[37] A few rare offenses carry different upper limits, e.g., 18 U.S.C. § 701 (1970) (illegal use of a government insignia); 18 U.S.C. § 3 (1970) (violation of a government park regulation); 18 U.S.C. § 114 (1970) ($1,000 and/or seven years for maiming).

4	Probation	a)	$5,000 fine and/or 10 years	a) Theft from interstate shipment over $100 (18 U.S.C. § 659)
		b)	$10,000 fine and 10 years	b) Interstate transport of stolen goods (18 U.S.C. § 2314)
5	Probation	a)	$5,000 fine and 20 years	a) Bank robbery with force (18 U.S.C. § 2113(a))
		b)	$10,000 fine and 20 years	b) Extortion (18 U.S.C. § 894)
6	10 years	a)	Life imprisonment	a) Murder or kidnapping during commission of bank robbery (18 U.S.C. § 2113(e))
		b)	$100,000 fine and life imprisonment	b) Narcotics violation indicating a continuing criminal enterprise (21 U.S.C. § 848(a))

A. Levels of Disparity

1. *Type of Sentence.* A federal judge can almost always choose between ordering imprisonment or probation. He also can mix the two by imposing a short prison term of six months or less, followed by a longer period of probation.[38] In most cases he can also impose a fine, and sentences for more than one count may be imposed concurrently or consecutively.

The most crucial part of the sentencing process is the decision whether the offender is to be imprisoned. Stability of job and family life are at stake, even if the sentence is only a short one. This first level of disparity, between custody and noncustody, is reflected in Table 2.

Table 2

AGREEMENT AND DISAGREEMENT ON THE ISSUE OF CUSTODY
(AMONG THREE JUDGES)

	Chicago* %	New York %
Agree to impose *no* custody	27.8	11.4
Agree to impose custody	40.8	58.9
Total agreement	68.6	70.3
Disagree on whether to impose custody	31.4	29.7
	100%	100%
	(439)	(460)

*simulated for three-judge panels

---

[38] *See* 18 U.S.C. § 3651 (1970).

The two courts show almost identical figures on this first level of disparity.[39] In 30 percent and 31 percent of their respective cases, the judges of the New York and Chicago councils disagree whether the offender should be incarcerated. The distribution of the cases in which they agree, however, reveals that the sentencing pattern is more severe in the New York court. The proportion of agreed-upon noncustody cases is 11 percent in New York; it is 28 percent in Chicago. The custody cases show the reverse pattern.

2. *Duration of Sentence*. The second level of potential disparity is disagreement over the length of the sentence, as shown in Table 3.

Table 3

AGREEMENT AND DISAGREEMENT ON DURATION OF SENTENCE

	Custody Sentences		Noncustody Sentences	
	Chicago*	New York	Chicago*	New York
Agree on Duration	12%	10%	98%	82%
Disagree on Duration	88%	90%	2%	18%
	100%	100%	100%	100%
Percent of all Council Cases in which there was agreement on type of sentence (See Table 2)	(40.8%)	(58.9%)	(27.8%)	(11.4%)

*Simulated for three-judge panels

If all judges agree on custody, there will be disagreement over its length in nine out of ten cases, both in New York and in Chicago. If all favor probation, there will be disagreement over its length in New York 18 percent of the time, in Chicago only 2 percent of the time.

3. *Disparity as to Type and Duration of Sentence*. Measuring disparity for both type and duration of sentence requires a yardstick that converts both dimensions to a common measure. The Administrative Office of the United States Courts has developed a scale for that purpose which we have slightly modified to provide finer detail at the upper end of the scale and to reduce the importance of differences in length of probation (Table 4).

---

[39] Because the incidence of agreement is artificially affected by the number of participating judges, the Chicago disparity figures were computed by simulating the three-judge panels of the New York court. This was done by randomly selecting two judges from the group of consulting judges that participated in the particular case, and treating them as the two advisors to the sentencing judge.

Table 4

POINT SCALE OF SENTENCE SEVERITY

	Developed by the Administrative Office of the U.S. Courts		As Modified
Fine	1		1
Probation (months)			
1-12	1		1
13-36	2		2
Over 36	4		3*
Split-Sentence			
(Jail + Probation)	4		4
Prison (months)			
1-6	3		3
7-12	5		5
13-24	8		7
25-36	10		9
37-48	12		11**
49-60	14		13
61-120	25	61-72 months	15
over 120	50	73-84 months	17

(Add two points for every year.)

*underlined figures are our modifications

**following the example of the Federal Judicial Center study (note 23 *supra*), custody sentences under the Youth Corrections Act count as four year terms.

Even as modified, the scale fails to reveal minor differences among sentences. For example, both two and three years of probation have a point value of 2; a fine and one year of probation both have a value of 1. Moreover, the scale provides no information on whether special conditions, such as participation in a drug-abuse program, are attached to the sentence. On the whole, therefore, the scale will understate slightly the differences among sentences.

We propose to define and measure disparity as follows:

> Sentence disparity is the expected percent difference between two sentences if two judges, randomly selected from the court, were to sentence the same case independently. Their two sentences are expressed as a percentage of their common mean.

Using the modified scale, we can derive the disparity figures from the sentencing council data. The measure can, of course, be applied to the disparity among more than two judges, by averaging the disparities between all possible combinations of two judges. The following example is for the case of three judges, and thereby describes the computation method for the New York council (Table 5).

Table 5

EXAMPLE FOR COMPUTING
SENTENCE DISPARITY AMONG THREE JUDGES

	Example		
	Judge	Sentence	Points
(1) Translate the sentences recommended by each judge into their respective point values:	A	3 yrs.	9 pts.
	B	5 yrs.	11 pts.
	C	7 yrs.	13 pts.
(2) Compute mean sentence		(33 ÷ 3 =)	11pts.
	Judge Combinations		
(3) Compute point differences between each pair of judges:	A & B		2 pts.
	A & C		4 pts.
	B & C		2 pts.
(4) Compute mean difference		(8 ÷ 3 =)	2.67 pts.
(5) Express mean difference as percentage of mean sentence		(2.67 ÷ 11 =)	24 percent

The sentence disparity in the example given in Table 5 is 24 percent. Averaging the disparity measures in a great number of cases from a court in which all judges participate in council panels yields a disparity measure for the court.

It would be possible to express disparity in terms of the absolute point difference between two judges, by omitting operation (5). The percent measure adopted here, on the other hand, considers the sentence difference between one and three years to be more important than the difference between ten and twelve years,[40] even though the absolute disparity is two years in either case. The percent measure also corresponds to an important practical difference between these two cases: for the parole board, which ultimately determines how much time the offender will actually serve, the difference between one and three years is undoubtedly more critical than that between ten and twelve years.

The disparity measures for the two courts, as derived from the council data, are presented in Table 6 (page 123). Two judges will thus differ, on the average, by between one-third and one-half of the mean sentence.

---

[40] The scale of the Administrative Office already makes this adjustment to a limited extent; in the lower prison sentence ranges one point represents four months, in the higher ranges, six months.

Table 6

AVERAGE SENTENCE DISPARITIES OF THE TWO COURTS

Chicago*	36.7 percent (Std. Dev. 33.0%)
New York	45.5 percent (Std. Dev. 22.9%)

*for the one-third of the cases brought before the council

B.   Differences in Severity Among Judges

One cannot necessarily infer from the existence of sentence disparity that some judges are generally more severe than others. Even if sentence disparity were present, it might be true that all judges sentenced, on the average, with equal severity. Each judge might simply fluctuate around the same average. This situation does not exist, however, in either of the two courts studied; in both, some judges are clearly more severe than others.

The differences in severity among judges can be shown by measuring the deviation of each judge's sentencing recommendation from the mean of all sentences proposed in any one case, taking into account whether the deviation was toward the severe (+) or the lenient (−) side. Since each judge takes part in numerous council deliberations in all possible combinations with his colleagues, a reliable average deviation for each judge, in all cases in which he participates, may be computed:

Table 7

SEVERITY OF JUDGES*

	Chicago			New York	
Judge	Percent Deviation	Number of Cases	Judge	Percent Deviation	Number of Cases
A	−11	(329)	A	− 5	(172)
B	+10	(311)	B	−12	(201)
C	+ 7	(293)	C	−11	(104)
D	+ 4	(312)	D	+ 7	(164)
E	− 1	(385)	E	−11	(110)
F	−10	(331)	F	+21	(128)
G	+ 5	(161)	G	+24	(59)
H	+ 3	(48)	H	−10	(28)
			I	−21	(61)
			J	+58	(27)
			K	+20	(77)
			L	− 2	(5)

*percent average deviation from the mean recommendation of all judges

If a judge always stood at his "average severity" position (which, of course, he does not), Chicago Judge *B* would always be 10 percent more severe than the average, and Judge *F* would always be 10 percent less severe than the average. Their sentences would vary between 110 percent for Judge *B* (100 + 10) and 90 percent for

Judge F (100−10), a difference of about 20 percent. But none of the judges on either court sentence with consistent severity, as, for example, the New York voting pattern illustrates. Hence, in any given case the difference between any two judges will, as a rule, be larger or smaller than their average severity figures would indicate (Table 8).

Table 8

VOTING POSITION OF NEW YORK JUDGES*

	Judge						
	A	B	C	D	E	F	K
	%	%	%	%	%	%	%
least severe	22	26	22	14	28	10	17
shares least severe position with at least one other judge	24	21	24	15	19	8	8
all judges agree or the sentencing judge is in the middle	24	28	33	26	33	24	21
shares most severe position with at least one other judge	13	14	7	17	12	18	8
most severe	17	11	14	28	8	40	46
	100	100	100	100	100	100	100

*with 75 or more cases

Therefore, it is not simply the fluctuation of sentences that causes disparity; some judges are in fact more severe than others.[41] Such differences in sentencing philosophies appear to be a major cause of the sentence disparity that sentencing councils are designed to reduce.

V. COUNCIL EFFORTS TO REDUCE DISPARITY

The primary purpose of the sentencing council is to reduce sentence disparity by confronting the sentencing judge with the views of his colleagues. If disparity is revealed, it is assumed that the sentencing judge will change his sentence to reduce the disparity. To test this assumption, it is necessary to consider, first, how often and under what circumstances the sentencing judge alters his

---

[41] Actually, the situation is somewhat more complex. Judges will vary in their relative severity level according to the particular type of case. These patterns will be examined in a separate article along with the case characteristics that appear to promote disparity and disparity reduction.

original sentence decision and, second, the extent to which such changes reduce disparity.

As Table 9 shows, sentencing judges in both courts change their sentences in only about one-third of the cases they bring before their councils. Roughly half of these changes involve shifts in sentence type; the other half alter sentence length.

Table 9

CHANGES BY THE SENTENCING JUDGE
BETWEEN RECOMMENDATION AND DISPOSITION

	Chicago %	New York %
Increases Sentence	13	7
in type	(4)	(3)
in duration	(9)	(4)
Reduces Sentence	20	35
in type	(11)	(20)
in duration	(9)	(15)
Total Changes	33	42
No Change	67	58
	100%	100%
	(N = 434)*	(N = 460)*

*Cases with at least 3 judges in which the sentencing judge recorded an initial recommendation

Table 9 also shows that in both courts sentence reductions outnumber sentence increases. New York shows a higher frequency of change (42 percent) than Chicago (33 percent). One might have expected the participating judges in Chicago to be more amenable to change, since participation in this council is voluntary. On the other hand, Chicago judges might change less than the New York judges because initial disparity was lower in Chicago. Another interesting difference is that the imbalance between increases and reductions is more pronounced in New York (7 to 35) than in Chicago (13 to 20). It will be shown, however, that the major part of this greater imbalance in New York is unrelated to the council.[42]

Under what circumstances, then, will the judge change his original position? It is reasonable to assume that the extent of his disagreement with his fellow judges will be a critical factor in determining whether the sentencing judge changes his sentence. Table 10

---

[42] See text at note 44 infra.

supports this assumption. The six columns for each court represent the six possible positions in which the sentencing judge may find himself in relation to his colleagues.[43]

In the Chicago court (Table 10), if all the counseling judges favor a more severe sentence (col. 1), the sentencing judge will increase his sentence in 46 percent of the cases. If some judges recommend a higher sentence, but at least one shares the sentencing judge's recommendation (col. 2), the judge will increase his sentence in only 17 percent of the cases. On the other hand, if all judges vote for a more lenient sentence (col. 6), the sentencing judge will reduce the severity of his sentence in 74 percent of the cases; he will reduce the sentence 36 percent of the time even if only some of his colleagues vote for a more lenient sentence as long as none votes for a higher one. Finally, the sentencing judge may move in either direction if the counseling judges split and recommend sentences both higher and lower than his original recommendation. The pattern of the New York court is similar, even though that court has a more dramatic imbalance between sentence reductions and sentence increases.

Table 10 shows the frequency and direction of changes by the sentencing judge after the case has been before the council. Two types of changes cannot plausibly be attributed to the council. The first type (marked with an asterisk) are changes where the sentencing judge moves in the opposite direction from that recommended by the counseling judges. If none of the counseling judges favor a more lenient sentence (cols. 1, 2, 3) but the sentencing judge reduces the sentence anyway, or if none recommend a more severe sentence (cols. 3, 5, 6) but the sentencing judge nevertheless increases the sentence, the council cannot have caused the change.

Second, there are cases in which the sentencing judge, although changing in the direction recommended by his colleagues, moves beyond the position held by the most extreme counseling judge. In one case, for instance, the sentencing judge proposed a three-year prison term, his colleagues recommended two years and one year respectively, and the judge ultimately imposed a six-month sentence. Table 11 treats both of these kinds of changes as if the sentenc-

---

[43] By subdividing the sample into groups based on the initial location of the sentencing judge, the possibility of regression—that is, of the greater likelihood of extreme values to move toward the mean upon a second measurement—arises. The role of regression in this study is difficult to determine, however, since the very purpose of the council is to pull extreme values back toward the mean. The second measure is thus not only independent of the first, but the council is most likely to reduce disparity precisely where the regression phenomenon is most likely to occur.

Table 10

COUNCIL VOTE AND SUBSEQUENT CHANGES

Action of Sentencing Judge / Position of Counseling Judges	(1) All judges are more severe (++) %	(2) Some judges are more severe, at least one shares the trial judge's view (+) %	(3) All judges agree with sentencing judge (=) %	(4) Judges disagree in both directions (+−) %	(5) Some judges are less severe, but at least one shares the trial judge's view (−) %	(6) All judges are less severe (−−) %	Total %
Chicago							
becomes more severe	46	17	9*	10	2*	2*	13
does not change	50	77	88	67	62	24	67
becomes less severe	*4*	6*	3*	23	36	74	20
	100 (25)	100 (149)	100 (33)	100 (129)	100 (60)	100 (38)	100
Share of all Cases	(6%)	(34%)	(8%)	(29%)	(14%)	(9%)	100% (N=434)
New York	%	%	%	%	%	%	%
becomes more severe	28	7	-	8	-	-	7
does not change	57	68	77	62	54	28	58
becomes less severe	15*	25*	23*	30	46	72	35
	100	100	100	100	100	100	100
Share of all Cases	(16%)	(20%)	(13%)	(20%)	(14%)	(17%)	(100%) (N=460)

*unexplained changes

Table 11

MAXIMUM FREQUENCY OF COUNCIL-INDUCED CHANGES

Action of Sentencing Judge	(1) All judges are more severe (++) %	(2) Some judges are more severe, at least one shares the trial judge's view (+) %	(3) All judges agree with sentencing judge (=) %	(4) Judges disagree in both directions (+ −) %	(5) Some judges are less severe, but at least one shares the trial judge's view (−) %	(6) All judges are less severe (− −) %	Total %
Chicago							
becomes more severe	42	17	-	10	-	-	11
does not change	58	83	100	70	72	29	73
becomes less severe	-	-	-	20	28	71	16
	100	100	100	100	100	100	100
New York							
becomes more severe	28	5	-	8	-	-	7
does not change	72	95	100	69	66	36	73
becomes less severe	-	-	-	23	34	64	20
	100	100	100	100	100	100	100

ing judge made no change in his sentence and thereby represents as changes only those shifts that could have been induced by the council.[44] The figures it presents, moreover, represent the estimates of the maximum frequency of council-related changes.

In both cities, the maximum frequency of council-related change is 27 percent. In 73 percent of the cases, the council did not cause the judge to change. Sentence reductions in Chicago (16 percent) and increases (11 percent) are fairly balanced; in New York, reductions occur three times as often as increases.

We have thus far assumed that nearly all decreases in columns 4, 5 and 6 are due to the council's influence. But since unexplained reductions occurred in columns 1, 2 and 3, it is likely that at least some of the reductions in columns 4, 5 and 6 are also noncouncil-related. We estimate the frequency of these unrelated changes by computing the mean percent of unexplained reductions from columns 1, 2 and 3 and applying the resulting figures (5 percent in Chicago and 21 percent in New York) to the remaining columns. The procedure is reversed to obtain the unrelated increases, which only occur in Chicago:

Table 12

"Unexplained" Sentence Changes

	Chicago	New York
Reductions*	5%	21%
Increases**	4%	0

*mean of reductions in columns 1, 2, and 3 of Table 10
**mean of increases in columns 3, 5, and 6 of Table 10

Removing these additional unrelated changes yields an estimate of the minimum frequency of council-induced changes, represented in Table 13.

Somewhere between the maximum figures in Table 11 and the minimum figures in Table 13 lies the true frequency of council-induced changes. In Chicago the sentencing judge changes as a result of the council in between 25 and 27 percent of the cases. In New York the range is between 20 and 27 percent.

---

[44] Conceivably, there could be an indirect relation to the council; the sentencing judge may at times place an artificially severe sentencing proposal before the council intending to make a later reduction in order to deter protracted disagreement. There is some indirect statistical evidence to that effect: "noncouncil-related" reductions are slightly more apt to occur if the counseling judges are on the severe side.

Table 13

MINIMUM FREQUENCY OF COUNCIL-INDUCED CHANGES

Position of Counseling Judges →	Chicago				New York			
	(4) Judges disagree in both directions (+ −)	(5) Some judges are less severe, but at least one shares the trial judge's view (−)	(6) All judges are less severe (− −)	Total	(4) Judges disagree in both directions (+ −)	(5) Some judges are less severe, but at least one shares the trial judge's view (−)	(6) All judges are less severe (− −)	Total
Action of Sentencing Judge ↓	%	%	%	%	%	%	%	%
becomes more severe	6	-	-	9*	8	-	-	7
does not change	76	69	31	75	83	75	49	80
becomes less severe	18	31	69	16	9	25	51	13
	100	100	100	100	100	100	100	100

*The Chicago "more severe" figures are altered because of the unexplained increases in columns 3, 5, and 6 (Table 10).

Given this estimate of the frequency of change: by how much does the sentencing council reduce sentence disparity?

VI. MEASURING DISPARITY REDUCTION

Sentence disparity has been operationally defined as the expected percent difference between two sentences if two judges, selected at random from the court, were to sentence the same case independently. To measure the extent to which sentencing councils reduce disparity under this definition would require data about how the council changes the views of the counseling judges as well as that of the sentencing judge. In the absence of reliable data on this point[45] we propose to measure disparity reduction indirectly.

Considering the following model of a sentencing council procedure:

> Every sentencing case is brought before the council, which consists of all judges of the court. After the sentencing judge has effectively shared all of the relevant information on the case with his brethren, each judge independently recommends the sentence he considers appropriate. Under these conditions of complete and equal information and responsibility, the court accords equal weight to each recommendation. *The judges have agreed that the mean of the recommended sentences will become the sentence of the court.*

Such a system would not necessarily remove disparity between individual judges. But in the important sense of whether two offenders under identical circumstances would receive the same sentence, this procedure would remove disparity. To the offender it does not matter whether his sentence came about because every judge thought it to be the best sentence or whether they simply agreed on the procedure of averaging their sentences. This procedure would effectively remove disparity between any two judges, since each judge, irrespective of his own position, would have to impose the same sentence—the mean of all recommended sentences.

While the adoption of such a council rule would not be without

---

[45] In Chicago, the counseling judges are asked to write down their final recommendations at the end of the meeting. Those judges change their recommended sentences about half as frequently as the sentencing judge does. We were privately informed, however, that the second notations by the counseling judges are not always accurate gauges of their true opinions. Perhaps they hope to minimize intra-court disharmony by reducing the apparent disparity.

merit, it is introduced here only to make clear that as the sentencing judge moves toward the mean sentence of all the judges, he reduces the disparity. We propose to measure disparity reduction indirectly, since the two distances—the disparity between any two judges and the deviation of the sentencing judge from the mean—are related. Using the deviation measure, then, will make it possible to measure disparity reduction without knowing the extent to which counseling judges' opinions are changed by the council.[46] Thus, on the average, if the sentencing judge removes a fraction of his distance from the mean, we shall conclude that he thereby removes that fraction of the disparity between any two judges.

Table 14 shows the schematic relationship between the two measures.

Table 14

SCHEMATIC RELATIONSHIP BETWEEN "BASIC DISPARITY"
AND "VISIBLE DEVIATION"

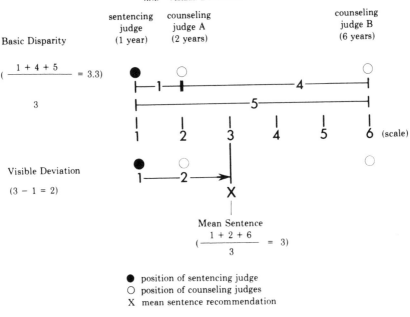

● position of sentencing judge
○ position of counseling judges
X mean sentence recommendation

---

[46] The mean deviation multipled by $\left[\dfrac{n^2}{2(n-1)}\right]^{\frac{1}{2}}$ of a sample from any distribution is greater than the standard deviation of that sample. 1 M. KENDALL & A. STUART, THE ADVANCED THEORY OF STATISTICS 45 (2d ed. 1963). Furthermore, for any distribution, the average standard deviation is greater than the average mean difference divided by the square root of two. Therefore, the ratio of the average mean deviation to the average mean difference for any distribution is greater than $\dfrac{n-1}{n}$. If the sentences are normally distributed the ratio is $\left(\dfrac{n-1}{2n}\right)$. 1 M. KENDALL & A. STUART. *supra* at 240 n.1.

The New York court, unlike its counterpart in Chicago, does not sit en banc but rather in three-judge panels. The mean sentences of these panels will deviate somewhat from the mean sentence the entire court would have imposed. That difference is a disparity invisible to the sentencing judge because he can only know the panel's mean. Even if he accedes to that mean, the New York judge will not have removed all disparity relative to the court's mean. Statistical theory allows us to compute the size of that invisible difference (2b in Table 15),[47] and, by adding it to the visible one, it is possible to estimate the deviation of the New York sentencing judge from the mean sentence of the entire court. Table 15 compares the deviations from the mean in the two courts.

The basic disparity is higher in New York (45.5 percent) than in Chicago (36.7 percent). The lower figure for the Chicago council probably stems from its voluntary character; the judges who choose to participate in the council are relatively likeminded. The visible deviation of the sentencing judge from the mean of the council is the same in both courts (23.3 and 23.5 percent), but once the "invisible" deviation is added to the visible deviation from the mean in the New York council, the latter shows a greater total deviation.

The judges in the two courts studied, unlike those in the hypothetical sentencing council, seldom impose a sentence that is the mean of all council judges' recommendations. At times they remove only part of their deviation from the mean, and at times they even increase the deviation by moving away from the mean. The following diagrams illustrate the four types of moves open to the sentencing judge:

---

[47] There are 56 possible ways of selecting 3 judges from a court of 8 judges. The mean deviation for each of the 56 three-judge panels could be calculated theoretically, but in reality the only calculation that can be made is for the combination that actually occurs in a particular case. The average of the 56 mean deviations is different from the mean deviation of all 8 of the judges in the council. How is the mean deviation of a three-judge subgroup related to the mean deviation of all 8 judges? Averaged over sentences that are normally distributed, the average of the 56 mean deviations is smaller than the mean deviation of all 8 judges and accordingly an upward adjustment of 15 percent must be made in the mean deviation for the three-judge panels. For a panel of n judges and subgroups of size k, the upward adjustment is:

$$\left[\left(\frac{n-1}{n} \right)^{1/2} \Big/ \left(\frac{k-1}{k} \right)^{1/2} -1 \right] \times \ 100\%$$

Table 15

RELATIONSHIP BETWEEN BASIC DISPARITY AND DEVIATION OF THE SENTENCING
JUDGE FROM THE MEAN IN THE TWO COURTS

	Chicago	New York
Basic Disparity (1)		
Average difference between the sentence imposed in the same case by any two judges randomly selected from the court	36.7%	45.5%
Visible Part of the Deviation (2a)		
Distance of sentencing judge from the mean of all participating council judges	23.5%	23.3%
Invisible Part of the Deviation (2b)		
If the council does not consist of the entire court but only of smaller sub-groups, the difference between the means of those subgroups and the (potential) mean of the entire court in each case is invisible. For 3-judge panels that difference is on the average 15% of the visible deviation	-*	3.5%
Total Deviation (2a + 2b)		
Total distance of sentencing judge from the mean of all judges of the court	23.5%	26.8%

*In the Chicago council all participating judges sit *en banc*.

(a) The judge moves toward the mean and stops either at or before it, thereby reducing deviation from the mean.

(b) The judge moves beyond the mean but stops at a point closer to the mean than was his original recommendation, thereby achieving a net reduction of deviation.

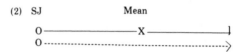

(c) The judge moves beyond the mean and stops at a point at least as far from the mean as was his original recommendation. He thus increases deviation or leaves it unchanged.

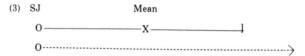

(d) When the sentencing judge occupies the middle position, he is often so close to the mean that in changing his sentence he moves away from it, thereby increasing disparity.

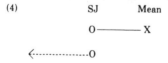

Table 16 shows the frequency of the four types of moves by the sentencing judges on each court.

The majority of these moves reduce sentence disparity, yielding a net reduction of deviation (Table 17). The sentence changes shown in Table 17 are those developed in Table 11 and hence represent the maximum estimate of changes attributable to the council.

For the 73 percent of the cases in which the sentencing judge does not change his original recommendation, the average deviation in each court is 20 percent. In the 27 percent of the cases in which the judge does change, his original deviation averages 33 percent in Chicago and 36 percent in New York, from which the changes remove 9 percentage points (of 33 and 36 percent, respectively), or about one-quarter of the deviation (27 and 25 percent, respectively).

Table 16

FREQUENCY OF THE FOUR TYPES OF MOVES BY
THE SENTENCING JUDGE IN THE COUNCIL

	Chicago %	New York %
Reduces deviation by moving		
(1) toward the mean	24	24
(2) beyond the mean, still reducing deviation	33	32
	57	56
Increases deviation by moving		
(3) so far beyond the mean, that deviation is increased or unchanged	31	16
(4) away from the mean	12	27
	43	44
	100%	100%

Table 17

REDUCTION OF THE SENTENCING JUDGE'S VISIBLE DEVIATION *
(IN PERCENT OF THE MEAN SENTENCE)

Chicago**	Share of Cases %	(1) Average Size of Deviation	(2) Reduction in Council	(2) as Percent of (1)
Sentencing Judge				
Does not change	(73)	20	0	0%
Changes	(27)	33	9	27%
Total	(100%)	23.5	2.5	10.6%
New York				
Sentencing Judge				
Does not change	(73)	20	0	0%
Changes	(27)	36	9	25%
Total	(100%)	23.3	2.5	10.7%

*From the mean
**Only for the one-third of the cases coming before the Chicago council

The initial average visible deviation in each city was about 23 percent. In each city, these figures were reduced as a result of the sentencing council by 2.5 points, or a little over 10 percent. The drops from 27 and 25 percent to roughly 10 percent in the last column reflect the fact that the council fails to move the judge in 73 percent of the cases.

We now apply the share of the deviations removed by the council to the basic disparity[48] and thereby arrive at the final evaluation of the council's effectiveness in reducing disparity (Table 18).

Table 18

EFFECT OF THE COUNCIL ON SENTENCE DISPARITY
(AVERAGE DIFFERENCE BETWEEN THE SENTENCES
IMPOSED IN THE SAME CASE BY ANY TWO JUDGES,
RANDOMLY SELECTED FROM THE COURT)

	Chicago	New York
Disparity prior to council deliberation	36.7	45.5
Percent removed by council	−10.6	−9.6*
Disparity remaining after council	32.8	41.1

*adjusted by reducing the 10.7 share (Table 17) by 10 percent for "invisible deviation" in New York (Table 15)

In each court the council removed about 10 percent of the existing disparity, thus reducing disparity in New York from 45 to 41 percent, in Chicago from 37 to 33 percent.

VII. COMPARING THE TWO COURTS

The amount of disparity reduction is strikingly similar in the two courts. But this similarity should not mask the different processes that produced the result. In order to assess the relative impact of the two sentencing councils, their structure and operation must be compared in terms of case composition, council size, and whether participation was voluntary.

A. Differences in Case Composition

The urban character and the population of the New York and Chicago districts are roughly comparable but the composition of the cases that come before the two courts differ in a number of ways, as Table 19 shows.

---

[48] The ratio of these deviations to the disparity in those courts, .59 in New York and .64 in Chicago, corresponds well with the theoretical value. *Cf.* note 47 *supra.*

Table 19

DISTRIBUTION OF OFFENSES

	Chicago	New York
	%	%
Narcotics	7.8	29.2
Marijuana and Other Drugs	4.3	9.0
Bank Robbery	3.0	8.3
Theft and Interstate Transport of Stolen Goods	28.1	12.9
Other Property Crimes	19.5	11.2
All Other Crimes	37.3	29.4
	100.0%	100.0%

Over 38 percent of all New York cases were drug-related, compared to 12 percent in Chicago. Chicago also had fewer bank robberies than New York, perhaps because Illinois does not permit branch banking and hence reduces the opportunities for committing that crime. The Chicago court, on the other hand, had a higher frequency of theft, fraud, and interstate transport of stolen property, probably because Chicago is centrally located and has numerous road and railway transport systems passing through it.

The crime mix for which the New York offenders were convicted was somewhat more serious. Taking the maximum sentence the law allows for a given offense as a measure of seriousness, the average of these maximum years was 11.2 years for New York and 10.0 years for Chicago.[49] This difference in seriousness of the crimes may account for some of the differences observed between the two courts.

B. Council Size

The New York council meets in three-judge panels on a rotation basis, whereas the Chicago council meets en banc. Because the Chicago council is much larger than the New York panel, two countervailing factors may influence the sentencing judge. First, the sentencing judge may be more likely to heed the council's advice if he is opposed by a larger number of his colleagues. In New York, a

---

[49] The recommendations and sentences of the sentencing judges reflect this difference. The average recommendation was 8.5 in New York and 5.1 in Chicago; the average sentence in New York was 7.4 and in Chicago it was 4.9. The size of the difference suggests that factors other than the severity of the case may contribute to the different severity levels in the two courts. New York also has a higher share of convictions after jury trial (16%) than Chicago (10%). Bench trial convictions are more frequent in Chicago (5%) than in New York (2%).

maximum of two judges can oppose the sentencing judge; in Chicago, many more may oppose him (Table 20).

Table 20

LIKELIHOOD OF SHIFT DEPENDING
ON THE VOTING POSITION OF THE SENTENCING JUDGE

Position of Sentencing Judge	Chicago	New York
All judges more severe	42%	28%
Some judges more severe, none less severe	13%	7%
Judges on both sides	24%	17%
Some judges less severe, none more severe	31%	25%
All judges less severe	69%	51%

In each voting position, the Chicago judge is more likely to change than his New York counterpart. On the other hand, as the size of the council becomes larger, the sentencing judge will find himself less frequently in an extreme position, as shown in Table 21:

Table 21

DISAGREEMENT CONSTELLATION VIS-À-VIS THE SENTENCING JUDGE

	Chicago	New York
	%	%
all more severe	5	16
some more severe	34	20
all agree	8	13
disagree in both directions	30	20
some less severe	14	14
all less severe	9	17
	100%	100%

The Chicago judge is less frequently in an extreme position, but when he finds himself there he may feel more pressure to alter his original recommendation. It may well be that the countervailing effects produced by the larger council size of the Chicago court simply cancel each other.

C. Voluntary Participation

Participation in the Chicago council is voluntary, and some judges do not take part. Even those who do participate do not bring all their cases before the council. Table 22 gives an overview of this limited participation, and Table 23 breaks down the total number of cases sentenced by the six judges who do not participate in the council and by the eight who do.

Table 22

PERCENT OF CASES BROUGHT BEFORE THE CHICAGO COUNCIL
BY EACH OF THE 14 JUDGES OF THE COURT

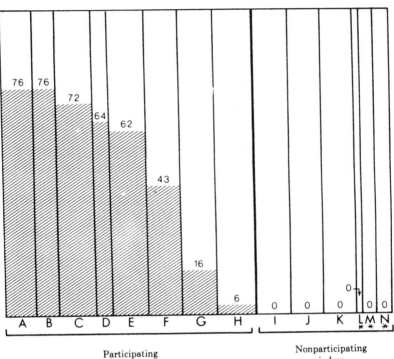

Participating
judges

Nonparticipating
judges

The width of the bar indicates the judge's share of cases in the sample.

*senior judges with reduced caseloads

There are thus three groups of cases that reach the sentencing stage, each accounting for about one-third of the total.

Table 23

SHARE OF THE CHICAGO CASES BROUGHT BEFORE THE COUNCIL

	Percent
Cases not brought before council	68
cases of participating judges	(33)
cases of nonparticipating judges	(35)
Cases brought before council	32
	100%

number of cases (1619)

The voluntary and limited participation in the Chicago council raises certain questions. First, what distinguishes the nonparticipating from the participating judges? Second, what distinguishes the cases withheld by the participating judges from those brought before the council? Finally, how much further would disparity in Chicago be reduced if council participation were obligatory? Table 24 helps answer the first question: one characteristic that distinguishes nonparticipating judges from the participating judges is their age.

Table 24

AGE AND YEARS ON THE BENCH
OF PARTICIPATING AND NONPARTICIPATING JUDGES

Participating Judges			Nonparticipating Judges	
Age	Years on Bench		Age	Years on Bench
46	*		66	5
49	*		66	8
51	1		68	9
54	*		69**	31
55	1		71	10
58	10		75**	20
60	10		76**	19
63	6			
			Average 70	15 yrs.
Average 54	3 yrs.			

*Less than 1 year
**Senior judges

There is a clear division: all judges under 65 participate; judges over that age do not. Years on the bench is related to age, but this factor does not clearly divide the two groups of judges. Although all five of the new members of the court participate, they are joined by three of the more experienced judges, two of whom have been on the bench for ten years. The council thus allows the newer judges to become familiar with the court's sentencing practices.[50]

There are two criteria that distinguish the cases the participating judges withhold from the council from those they bring before it: the seriousness of the offense and whether the conviction was handed down by a jury. Judges are most likely to bring before the council the more serious criminal cases and those cases in which conviction was obtained by jury trial (Table 25).

Table 25

PROPORTION OF CASES BROUGHT TO THE COUNCIL
BY SEVERITY OF THE CRIME* AND TYPE OF CONVICTION
(PERCENTAGE ARE BASED ON THE NUMBER OF CASES IN EACH CELL)

	No Custody	Custody
Guilty Plea	35% (573)	60% (318)
Bench Trial	42% (19)	61% (37)
Jury Trial	83% (18)	73% (84)

*as measured by the sentence actually imposed for noncouncil cases and by the sentencing judge's initial sentence recommendation in council cases.

Sixty percent of all guilty plea cases likely to result in prison sentences were brought to the council; only 35 percent of the non-custody guilty plea cases were brought to the council.[51] Possibly the judge considers the duration of a prison sentence to be a more important issue than the length of probation and therefore is more interested in his colleagues' advice.[52] Another reason may be that there is greater variation in the length of custody sentences. These percentages hardly change if the conviction was obtained after a bench trial. But if there was a jury trial, the proportion of cases brought to the council was high, regardless of whether the case was likely to end in a custody sentence.

Finally, the voluntary character of the Chicago council weakens its power to reduce overall sentence disparity in the court, because

---

[50] Two of the three more experienced participating judges bring few of their cases before the council, thus reinforcing the notion that the council serves an educative function.

[51] The classification custody-noncustody is based upon the initial recommendation of the sentencing judge.

[52] We have not determined for this article the types of cases—distinguished by crime, defendant, and mode of conviction—in which the sentencing judge is more (or less) likely to accept the advice of the council.

only one-third of all cases come before the council. To estimate the council's effect on the entire court, it is necessary to estimate the disparity in the two-thirds of all cases not brought before the council.

The participating judges fail to bring one-half of their cases before the council; this represents one-third of the total cases. There is evidence that these cases tend to be low-sentence, noncustody cases,[53] which have a somewhat lower average disparity.[54] On the other hand, the one-third of all cases heard by nonparticipating judges will tend to involve above-average disparity: four of the six nonparticipating judges are found at the extremes of the severity spectrum; one near the lower extreme, two near the upper extreme, and one judge so severe that he exceeded the upper extreme.[55]

If we assume that these two deviations offset each other, we may conclude that the two-thirds of all cases that do not come before the council have the same average disparity as the one-third that come before it. A 10.7 percent reduction in disparity was found for the one-third of the Chicago cases brought before the council. Assuming that the remaining two-thirds have the same average disparity, this 10.7 percent decrease in disparity must be reduced by two-thirds to reflect the council's effect on all cases sentenced in the Chicago court. Therefore, the council reduces the sentence disparity of all cases in the Chicago court by not quite 4 percent.

VIII. THE NONCOUNCIL-RELATED CHANGES

At an earlier stage of our analysis we decided temporarily to disregard changes by the sentencing judge that could not be meaningfully related to the council's deliberations. We tentatively assumed these changes were induced by events that occurred after the council finished its deliberation. By definition, all of these changes were away from the mean, and hence would have increased

[53] See Table 25 supra.

[54] The New York court shows the same pattern:

Chicago	
Mean Severity	Percent Disparity
.01 - 3.49	29.8
3.5 - 6.99	46.7
7.0 or higher	36.4

[55] This ranking was derived from the net percentage of cases in which a judge imposed custody if the Probation Department recommended probation, minus the cases where the judge gave probation where the Probation Department recommended custody. This was the only severity measure for which we had data on all judges, including those who did not participate in the council.

disparity. They, too, constitute a major difference between the two courts: in Chicago, their number was negligible, between 6 and 8 percent of all cases, depending on the mode of computation; in New York, their number was between 15 and 22 percent.[56] The judges in New York explained that these changes, all sentence reductions, were made on the basis of the information conveyed in the sentencing hearing. There the prosecutor, as a rule, stands silent and only the defense speaks. Although all of these moves were in the direction away from the counseling judges' recommendations, we decided not to consider them as increasing disparity, under the optimistic assumption that the counseling judges would have changed with the sentencing judge had they become aware of the new information. But, since only New York shows this high frequency of unexplained reductions, the puzzle remains. We hope to resolve it eventually by tracing these changes and having them explained as they occur.

IX. DISCUSSION AND CONCLUSIONS

We have analyzed many facets of the sentencing councils, and we shall now summarize our findings and discuss their limitations. We shall also propose possible alternatives a court might adopt to help reduce sentence disparity.

Here, first, is the summary of our findings—the amount of sentence disparity that exists among the judges of the two courts, the amount removed by the sentencing council, and the amount of disparity that remains (Table 26).[57]

In each court the council is able to reduce about 10 percent of the sentence disparity in the cases that come before it. In Chicago, since only one-third of the cases are brought before the council, the reduction in all cases is under 4 percent.

To evaluate this statistic, one must see its limitations. First, the roughness of the measuring scale fails to detect such minor but potentially important nuances as special treatments or conditions accompanying a sentence.[58]

---

[56] *See* text at note 44.

[57] *See* Table 18 *supra*.

[58] In our one observation of a council meeting in Chicago, we could see several instances of this role of the council. In one case, discussion turned on whether the offender should be sentenced under the provisions of the Youth Corrections Act which allows the conviction record to be expunged. In another case, the judges discussed the feasibility of a work-release form of incarceration which would allow the offender to keep his job. A third discussion hinged on the probation officer's recommendation that the offender be required to move his residence in order to avoid the temptation of further gang activities.

Table 26

EFFECT OF COUNCIL ON DISPARITY
(LIKELY DIFFERENCE IN THE SENTENCES
OF TWO JUDGES SELECTED RANDOMLY FROM THE COURT)*

		Cases before the Council	Chicago — All Cases	New York — All Cases
(a)	Disparity Prior to Council Deliberation*	36.7	36.7	45.5
(b)	Percent of Disparity Removed by the Council*	10.6	3.6**	9.6
(b x a)	Percentage points removed by Council	3.9	1.3**	4.4
(a-b x a)	Disparity after Council Reduction*	32.8	35.4	41.1

*From Table 18
**Because of voluntary participation, only 1/3 of all cases

More importantly, the study observes reduction only within the narrow time interval between discussion in the council and the imposition of sentence. It thus does not indicate anything about the possible long-range effect of the council. It may be that the very existence of the council tends to reduce disparity and that the disparity observed among initial recommendations would be greater were it not for the experience gained by the judges in previous meetings.

In order to determine whether the council has this long-range effect, it would be necessary to measure its disparity at different points in time and to compare these data with parallel measurements in a court with no council. We retrieved rudimentary data on such a comparison from the study of the Second Circuit by the Federal Judicial Center.[59] That study asked each district judge in the Second Circuit for his sentence recommendations on an array of twenty selected cases. By comparing the judges of the Eastern District (who participate in a sentencing council) with those of the Southern District (who do not), we were able to compute the sentence disparities for the two districts (Table 27).

The disparity in the Eastern District is not smaller, and is even somewhat larger, than in the Southern District. Table 27 provides an important by-product. The disparity figure computed for the

---

[59] See note 26 supra (our computation).

Table 27

SENTENCE DISPARITY IN A COURT WITH A
SENTENCING COUNCIL AND IN A COURT WITHOUT ONE

	Eastern District of New York (Before Discussion by Council)	Southern District of New York
From the Federal Judicial Center Study of Simulated Cases	47.8%	42.0%
From the Sentencing Council Data	45.5%	

Eastern District from the Federal Judicial Center study is nearly identical to the disparity measure derived from the sentencing council, suggesting that simulation results may parallel sentencing council results.

The data are only suggestive, since the comparison refers to only one point in time and we do not know the disparity with which each court began. But to sustain the notion of a long-range effect of the council in reducing disparity, we would have to assume that the original sentence disparity in the Eastern District was even larger than the observed 47.8 percent. This is a difficult notion to sustain since the two districts are adjacent and similar and their judges come from the same reservoir.

There are inherent difficulties in measuring reduction in disparity over time. The sentencing practices of individual judges may change, and the composition of the court will change as judges retire and are replaced. To assess the full impact of the council on this learning process, it would be necessary to trace the sentencing patterns of individual judges over time.

Again, a substitute measure was developed by grouping the judges according to their years on the bench and then comparing their average percent distance from the mean, as in Table 28.

TABLE 28

AVERAGE PERCENT DISTANCES FROM THE MEAN FOR
JUDGES* GROUPED BY YEARS ON THE BENCH

	1 year to 2 years	Over 2 years to 5 years	Over 5 years
Chicago	26%		26%
New York	29%	26%	27%

*for all cases in which judge gave a recommended sentence

Although this table does not indicate the disparity of the more experienced judges when they first joined the bench, the near uniformity of disparity levels suggests that further research may not disclose that disparity significantly declines over time in a court with a sentencing council.

Finally, the present study was primarily actuarial, comparing the sentences recommended before the council convened with the sentences eventually imposed. We have observed no council meeting in New York and only one in Chicago. Council meetings may be useful simply as a relief from the isolation in which the judge finds himself. One participant in the sentencing council of the United States District Court for the Southern District of Michigan described the process with sensitivity:

> It is here, in the give and take of fraternal discussion, that points are emphasized or subordinated according to the judgment of the individual judges, with the result that there is a close approach to a common meeting ground. The weights assigned to the various factors thought to be controlling as to disposition of the case are sometimes modified by the sentencing judge in the light of the experience of his brother judges with their own previous sentences.[60]

These qualifications notwithstanding, a simple balance remains: against an effort of some two to three hours per week for each judge, the sentencing council cures not more than 10 percent of the disparity in the cases that come before it. In New York, disparity is reduced from 45 to 41 percent. In Chicago, the original disparity of some 37 percent is reduced by 4 percent in the cases that come before the council, and thus only 1 percent across all cases.

There might be ways of improving the effectiveness of the council. One would be to require the sentencing judge to adopt the median[61] of the recommended sentences. While such a rule would effectively reduce disparity, it might reduce the autonomy of the judges to an unacceptable degree.[62] The ultimate goal of all arrangements

---

[60] Quoted in Smith, *supra* note 31, at 9.

[61] The median is the point at which half of the recommended sentences are more severe, and half are less severe. Unlike the mean, it cannot be influenced by judges who try to increase their weight by submitting a recommendation more extreme than the sentence they would actually impose.

[62] Sherwood Zimmerman, a student of Professor Leslie Wilkins at the State University of New York at Albany, simulated group sentencing decisions under three different procedures: (1) the group has purely advisory capacity; (2) consensus should be reached after deliberation; (3) the mean sentence of a secret ballot becomes the sentence of the court. He

to reduce disparity must not be to average the various sentence recommendations but to bring the initial recommendations closer together.

A promising way to achieve that goal might be to expand upon the information role performed by the council in acquainting the sentencing judge with the sentences his colleagues would impose. Courts could set up internal reporting systems of all sentences imposed by their judges or the judges of their circuit. Already used in many courts, computers could provide the judges with the distribution of sentences, together with their means and medians for any combination of crime and offender. Eventually, such data could form the foundation for meaningful sentencing guidelines, especially if they included information about the parole board decisions and hence the relationship between sentence and actual time served.[63] One might consider developing such an information system either as a supplement to the council or as a substitute for it. This approach should be particularly helpful in nonmetropolitan districts, where judges, because of the geographic isolation, are unable to attend council meetings.

At this time, the most determined efforts to reduce disparity through clear but flexible guidelines are made at the last stage of the regular sentencing process by the United States Parole Board.[64] The sentencing council, even if its reduction effect is small, represents one of the very few institutional attempts to resolve the disparity problem. The participating judges, although aware of its modest impact, like the council and find the time they devote to it well spent.

found procedure (1), modeled after the sentencing council, least likely to reduce disparity within and between groups and procedure (3) most likely to reduce it; procedure (2) leads to intermediate results.

[63] The multiplicity of sentencing choices available to the courts, and the varying attitudes between sentencing judges results in a wide disparity in the lengths of sentence imposed on persons convicted of similar offences and often who possess similar backgrounds. To a very real degree, the Board of Parole tends, in practice, to equalize this disparity whenever it is not bound to the one-third maximum line required in regular sentences.

UNITED STATES BOARD OF PAROLE, BIENNIAL REPORT 1968-1970, at 13 (1970).

[64] Through bold integration of research and policy making, Professor Wilkins, *supra* note 62, under another grant from the Law Enforcement Assistance Administration, has joined the U.S. Parole Board in a broad reform move. The examiners and the board are now operating under clear guidelines, which take into consideration the gravity of the commited crime and the record of the offender. The prisoner's behavior in the institution allows the examiner to deviate slightly from the guidelines. If he cares to exceed the limits, he needs approval of the board. Unless, therefore, the sentencing judge prescribed a minimum sentence, the parole board imposes in fact a de novo sentence. This is an interesting reflection on the sentencing system and might well hasten its reform. Some of the underlying thinking is reported in W. AMOS & C. NEWMAN, PAROLE (1975).

We cannot disagree. In the absence of legislative reform efforts,[65] the sentencing council is a progressive innovation that deserves support, if only as the first step in the resolution of a troublesome problem. An average sentence disparity between any two judges of around 40 percent is too much.

---

[65] Some state courts have attempted to reduce sentence disparity through sentence review by a panel of three trial judges, which may not include the sentencing judge, *after* sentence has been pronounced.

26

WORK RELEASE AND RECIDIVISM:
AN EMPIRICAL EVALUATION OF A SOCIAL POLICY

By

GORDON P. WALDO and THEODORE G. CHIRICOS

The return of convicts into the mainstream is a process which some describe as "unlocking the second gate." In this study, Gordon P. Waldo and Theodore G. Chiricos pose a challenge to policymakers who have supported the growth of the work release program without having evaluated its rehabilitative consequences. The authors conducted an evaluation analysis to determine whether or not members of work release programs and a control group differed in recidivism. Their findings indicated that work release programs have no rehabilitative success. However, the authors feel that since so little is known about the effect of other rehabilitative programs the work release program should be allowed to continue until our knowledge base in this area is richer.

From Gordon P. Waldo and Theodore G. Chiricos, "Work Release and Recidivism: An Empirical Evaluation of a Social Policy." *Evaluation Quarterly*, 1977, *1*(1), 87-108.

This study is an empirical assessment of the work release program in the Florida Division of Corrections. An experimental design was used in which, randomly, 188 persons were assigned to a work release group and 93 to a control group. Follow-up interviews were conducted in the community, and recidivism data were obtained from Division of Corrections files and from FBI rap sheets. Eighteen different indices of recidivism were examined, using both discrete and continuous measures. The work release and control groups showed no appreciable differences on any of the recidivism measures and length of time in work release also failed to be consistently related to recidivism. Controls were introduced for 16 demographic, prior record, and job-related variables, which did not alter the original findings. Policy implications of the results are discussed.

$\mathcal{W}$hile suggesting that policy-makers and administrators in the field of corrections have been "overactive on the basis of too little knowledge," Leslie Wilkins (1969: 9) has further observed that:

> It is a surprising and perhaps even shocking fact that our present day society is engaged in many activities which have no more support in terms of reliable evidence than the incantations of medicine men and the potions of witches.

Such an observation might be reasonably applied to the practice of work release or work furlough, which has become an established fact of community-based correctional policy in most states. How *well* established is suggested by a recent accounting that reported a total of 42 states with operative work release programs administered at either state or county levels (Swanson, 1973). This acceptance of work release into the mainstream of applied criminology has been accomplished, for the most part, since 1965, when the Federal Prisoners Rehabilitation Act authorized work release from federal institutions. (A major program in North Carolina that began in 1957 is an exception). Between 1965 and 1972, the legislatures of at least 39 states authorized or expanded work release programs and several states have made sizable commitments to the practice.

Given the rapid acceptance of work release, one might assume that legislators and administrators have been impressed with the demonstrated effectiveness of the programs. However, one's faith in such an assumption is readily shaken by a review of the available empirical "evidence" relative to work release, which lends credence to Glaser's (1965: 11) more general observation that: "In the judicial and correctional areas, so many decisions radically affecting the lives of others are made by vague, subjective impressions, untested rules of thumb, and nonrational prejudices."

As the review of pertinent work release literature by Waldo and Chiricos (1974: 15-49) clearly demonstrates, the implementation of work release has *not* been founded on empirical evidence of its "rehabilitative" consequences. Indeed, almost none of the research needed to demonstrate the effectiveness of work release has been undertaken, and certainly none of any substance was available during the period 1965-1968, when the flurry of legislative enthusiasm for work release reached a peak. If one may judge from what has been written about work release, especially by its proponents, it would appear that the establishment of work release has been based upon its appeal to the good economic sense of legislators and the sound "common sense" of correctional professionals and laymen who seem to argue that something as "obviously" good as work release *must* work.

The fiscal "effectiveness" of work release has been persuasively demonstrated.[1] However, the saving of taxpayers' money—though a laudable objective for any public agency—could prove a false saving in a field such as corrections, if those for whom agency costs have been reduced are more likely to return to crime and, eventually, to the courts and prison system. In short, as noted by Glaser (1973: 12) the effectiveness of any "people-changing" process like corrections, must be reflected in its ability to change people as well as in its ability to save money.

Several theoretical perspectives within criminology provide a sound rationale for expecting that work release would have positive rehabilitative consequences for participants. For example, strain or opportunity theory, control theory, cultural deviance, learning and differential association theories, and labeling theory—each for different reasons— would lead one to hypothesize that participation in work release should reduce the potential for future law violations.[2] Most of the proponents of work release, however, have ignored both theoretical premise and empirical evidence in asserting that work release (1) develops a sense of responsibility and self-discipline (Richmond, 1968; Johnson, 1967); (2) enhances the opportunities for employment upon release from prison (Grupp, 1965; Richmond, 1968); (3) mitigates the debilitating and demoralizing effects of prolonged and exclusive contact with incarcerated criminals (Grupp, 1965; Johnson, 1967; Shah, 1971); and (4) bridges the substantial gap between life in an authoritarian total institution and life in a presumably free society (Alexander, 1966; Moeller, 1968; Johnson, 1970).

Having reviewed the available research evidence relative to work release, Saleem Shah (1971: 14) was forced to conclude that:

> To gain further information on the impact of work release programs . . . controlled experiments would appear to be necessary. Such experiments would *randomly assign inmates eligible for release to control and experimental groups* [emphasis added].

The research reported herein has employed such a methodology, and provides the kind of evaluative criteria that should be a prerequisite to any policy decisions to expand or implement a program such as work release.

RESEARCH METHODS

A classical experimental design using random assignment was employed in this study. The Florida Division of Corrections permitted the researchers to assign inmates randomly to the work release and nonrelease groups from the pool of inmates meeting the minimal eligibility requirements for work release. Between July 1, 1969 and December 31, 1969, every third person meeting the minimal requirements was placed in a control group, and the other two-thirds were placed on work release—providing 188 work releasees and 93 nonreleasees for the study. Those not selected for work release continued to participate in the correctional programs in which they were then involved. Length of participation in work release ranged from two to six months, with the maximum being determined by state law.

In order to ascertain that the selection process had yielded comparable groups, the work release and control groups were compared on a number of specific dimensions, and it was determined that no statistically significant differences existed between the two groups in terms of age, racial composition, educational attainment, IQ, reading level, weekly income prior to arrest, anticipated income upon release, number of prior arrests, number of prior felony convictions, number of prior misdemeanor convictions, total amount of time spent in correctional institutions, age at first arrest, age at first commitment, number of juvenile commitments, sentence length, time in state prior to last arrest, and time in county prior to last arrest. In short, we may be reasonably certain that the selection procedure rendered truly comparable experimental and control groups.

The dependent variable in this study was recidivism. The concept of recidivism has been operationalized in previous criminological research in many ways, ranging from counting any new arrest to considering a person as a recidivist only if he were reincarcerated for the same type of offense for which he was originally imprisoned. Rather than attempting to determine what the "best" measure of recidivism might be, the present study has defined the concept very broadly and has utilized 18 different indicators of "recidivism" (see Appendix). It is recognized, of course, that these different indices are highly intercorrelated. However, since the concern of the present analysis is with whether or not work releasees and control group members differ in terms of recidivism, regardless of how it is operationally defined, it seemed advantageous to examine the question in as many different ways as possible. In several instances, the concept of "recidivism" is being stretched considerably; however, the term is used as a convenient label for all of the measures involved.

FINDINGS

Table 1 shows the proportion of subjects from Florida's experimental and control groups who have recidivated or, for those measures that are continuous, the proportion from each group that is above the

TABLE 1
Recidivism Within Experimental and Control Groups

Symbols*	Recidivism Measure and Cutting Point	Data Source*	Experimentals		Controls		x^2	P
			%	(of N)	%	(of N)		
A1	Arrests: ever (no/yes)	SR	70.4	(98)	66.7	(48)	.07	.79
A3	Arrests: number (≤1/>1)	FBI	48.9	(188)	53.8	(93)	.40	.53
A4	Arrests: rate per month (≤.037/>.037)	FBI	48.9	(188)	52.7	(93)	.22	.64
C1	Bookings: number (0/>0)	SR	66.7	(64)	65.2	(30)	.0004	.99
C2	Charges: number (≤2/>2)	FBI	46.8	(188)	48.4	(93)	.01	.90
C3	Charges: rate per month (≤.048/>.048)	FBI	51.1	(188)	49.5	(93)	.02	.90
C4	Convictions: number (0/>0)	SR	58.3	(56)	54.3	(25)	.07	.79
R1	Reincarceration: ever (no/yes)	SR	47.3	(43)	55.8	(24)	.54	.46
R2	Reincarceration: ever (no/yes)	DC	19.7	(188)	21.5	(93)	.04	.84
R7	Reincarceration: number (0/>0)	FBI	35.6	(188)	31.2	(93)	.37	.54
R8	Reincarceration: number of felonies (0/>0)	FBI	26.1	(188)	20.4	(93)	.79	.37
S1	Severity: total (0/≤20.036/>20.036)	FBI	37.8	(188)	30.1	(93)	1.64	.44
S2	Severity: average (0/≤5.80/>5.80)	FBI	35.1	(188)	35.5	(93)	.27	.87
S3	Severity: most severe crime (0/≤6.16/>6.16)	FBI	37.8	(188)	37.6	(93)	.07	.97
S4	Reincarceration: sentence received (≤21/>21 mos.)	DC	54.1	(37)	60.0	(20)	.02	.88

*See Appendix for explanation of symbols and sources.

median level of recidivism for all subjects. Considering first the arrest data for both groups, it may be observed that no significant differences were found between work release participants and nonrelease controls in the percentage of subjects who were ever arrested (A1), or were arrested more than once (A3), or were above the median rate of arrest (A4). For both measures of arrest compiled from FBI data (A3, A4), the control group was slightly more recidivistic than were the experimentals but, again, such differences are minimal.

Considering the recidivism data that measures self-reported *bookings* (C1) and *charges* (C2, C3) filed against a subject by the police, it may again be observed that no significant differences were obtained in the comparison of experimental and control groups. In fact, the percentage of work releasees who were booked (C1 = 66.7%), were charged with two or more crimes (C2 = 46.8%) or were above the median rate of charges (C3 = 51.1%) is less than two percentage points different from the corresponding percentages for the control group (65.2%; 48.4%; 49.5%). A minimal difference is observed for self-reported *convictions* (C4), inasmuch as 58.3% of the experimentals and 54.3% of the controls report at least one or more convictions. Thus, as with arrests, participation on work release appears to have no bearing upon the likelihood of being booked, having charges filed, or being convicted.

A similar conclusion must be reached with regard to the findings for reincarcerations that were derived from self-reports (R1), Division of Corrections' files (R2), and FBI records (R7, R8). Though the absolute number of those reporting one or more reincarcerations varies from one measure to another, the discrepancy between work release participants and nonrelease controls remains small for self-reports (R1 = 8.5%), prison files (R2 = 1.8%) and "rap sheet" data (R7 = 4.4%) alike. When the proportion of both groups with one or more *felony reincarcerations* (R8) is examined, the experimentals (26.1%) are slightly more likely to recidivate than are the controls (20.4%), but such a difference is not statistically significant. The data for R7 and R8, which are derived from FBI sources and receive input from all 50 states, provide an interesting comparison with the data for R2, which are derived from the prison records of Florida. It is the latter measure (return to a given prison system) that is most often used to assess postrelease recidivism rates in correctional research; and the data from Table 1 show that, while the more broadly based FBI measures do, indeed, reflect understandably higher levels of reincarceration, the comparison of experimentals and controls is not substantially changed by the more inclusive measures. However, while the Division of Corrections data (R2) might suggest slightly higher rates of reincarceration for the nonrelease control group, the FBI measures (R7, R8) show slightly higher rates of reincarceration for the work release experimental group. Having a variety of measures that seem to vary no more than might be expected by chance strengthens the apparent conclusiveness of the finding of no difference between experimentals and controls in rates of reincarceration.

Finally, Table 1 shows the percentage of experimentals and controls who, on the basis of crimes charged (S1, S2, S3) or sentence received upon reincarceration (S4) are in the *highest* category regarding the seriousness of the crime. A new index developed by Rossi et al. (1974) was used to assign seriousness scores to the offenses charged to all Florida subjects and recorded on the FBI "rap sheets." Distributions of the total severity of all charges (S1), the average severity of all offenses (S2), and the single most serious of all charges (S3) were trichotomized for the cross-tabulations summarized in Table 1. Similarly, the severity of sentence received was presumed to be an indirect and somewhat imprecise index of the seriousness of offense, and it is employed in that context for the present . analysis. While work release participants (37.8%) are more likely than controls (30.1%) to be represented in the highest category of total severity, and controls (60.0%) are more likely than participants (54.1%) to be above the median in severity of reincarceration sentence, these differences are not statistically significant. Furthermore, when the average seriousness of all offenses (S2) is examined, as well as the most serious offense charged (S3), less than one percentage point difference is observed in the proportion of experimentals and controls falling within the "most serious" category.

In short, Table 1 shows that no more than chance differences can be observed in the proportions of experimental and control groups that have been arrested, booked, charged, convicted, readmitted to prison within Florida or anywhere in the United States, or charged and sentenced for serious offenses. At this initial point in our analysis, it would appear that participation in work release has no bearing on the rates of recidivism for all subjects in the present inquiry.

A second kind of analysis employed only those measures of recidivism that are continuous (A2, A3, and so on) rather than discrete or dichotomous (A1, R1, . . .) variables. For the continuous measures, it is possible to compute mean levels of recidivism for experimental and control groups and to test for the significance of differences between those means (t-test). In many respects, such analysis is more descriptive of the *extent* of recidivism as opposed to the *occurrence* of recidivism, which was the principal focus of the previous section. Table 2 reports the mean level of recidivism for work release participants and non-release controls, utilizing 15 measures of recidivism. Also reported are the respective t-values and levels of statistical significance (p).

Considering first the average number of self-reported arrests (A2) and the number and rate of FBI recorded arrests (A3, A4), it is strikingly clear from Table 2 that no difference can be found between the two groups in the extent of postrelease arrests. The consistency with which the self-reported and the FBI reported data show the experimentals and controls almost identical lends strong support to the reliability of the conclusion that work release participation is unrelated to levels of postrelease arrests.

A very similar conclusion must be reached with regard to self-reported bookings (C1), the number (C2) and rate (C3) of charges recorded by the FBI, and the number of self-reported convictions (C4). If there is any trend among the statistically insignificant findings for these measures of recidivism, it may be that the experimental group is barely higher than the control group on each of the measures. But the discrepancies are so slight that, despite their consistency, we must conclude that no real difference has been observed in the levels of bookings, charges, and convictions experienced by experimentals and controls.

No significant difference between experimental and control groups is again reflected in the "extent of reincarceration" measures reported for both groups in Table 2. While the extent of reincarceration for both groups is almost identical when measured by returns to the Florida Division of Corrections (R6) and the total of all reincarcerations recorded by the FBI (R7), slightly larger differences may be noted for the two remaining reincarceration indices. It appears that the work release participants remained free prior to reincarceration (R5) for a slightly longer period (18.25 months) than did the controls (15.80 months); but the average level of felony reincarcerations was greater for the experimental group (0.32) than it was for the control group (0.23). Thus, what little difference exists—and it is not statistically significant—is somewhat conflicting, and it must be concluded that no real difference exists in the extent of reincarceration for the two groups.

For two measures of the severity of postrelease recidivism: average severity of crimes charged (S2) and severity of most serious crime

TABLE 2
Mean Recidivist Data and T-Tests for Experimental and Control Groups

Symbols*	Recidivism Measure	Data Source*	Experimentals X̄	(N)	Controls X̄	(N)	t-value	P
A2	Arrests: number	SR	1.37	(94)	1.35	(46)	.08	.93
A3	Arrests: number	FBI	2.22	(188)	2.25	(93)	.08	.93
A4	Arrests: rate	FBI	.06	(188)	.06	(93)	.57	.57
C1	Bookings: number	SR	1.22	(96)	1.20	(46)	.09	.93
C2	Charges: number	FBI	3.45	(188)	3.23	(93)	.43	.67
C3	Charges: rate	FBI	.10	(188)	.08	(93)	.89	.38
C4	Charges: number	SR	.90	(96)	.83	(46)	.36	.72
R3	Reincarceration: months prior to	DC	18.25	(36)	15.80	(20)	.99	.33
R6	Reincarceration: number	DC	.24	(188)	.28	(93)	-.49	.63
R7	Reincarceration: number	FBI	.53	(188)	.55	(93)	-.18	.85
R8	Reincarceration: felonies	FBI	.32	(188)	.23	(93)	1.30	.19
S1	Severity: total	FBI	27.76	(134)	24.46	(64)	.36	.72
S2	Severity: average	FBI	5.73	(134)	5.73	(64)	-.03	.98
S3	Severity: most serious	FBI	6.28	(134)	6.28	(65)	.00	.99
S4	Severity: sentence received	DC	61.24	(37)	30.50	(20)	1.23	.22

*See Appendix for explanation of symbols and sources.

charged (S3), almost identical levels of severity (S2 = 5.73; S3 = 6.28) were reported for both experimental and control groups. The total severity of all crimes charged (S1) was only slightly higher for work release participants (27.76) than for nonrelease controls (26.46); however, a substantial difference can be observed in the length of sentence received (S4) upon reincarceration with the Florida Division of Corrections. While the average recidivism sentence received by experimentals was 61.24 months, the corresponding sentence for controls was only 30.5 months, or slightly less than half as severe. Because the number of cases involved is rather small, such a difference is not statistically significant, but it clearly represents one of the largest differences between experimental and control groups that have been generated by these recidivism data.

The final portion of this analysis is concerned with the impact of extent of participation in work release. To this point, simple participation versus nonparticipation on work release has been shown to have almost no bearing upon either the occurrence or the extent and seriousness of postrelease recidivism. These measures of recidivism now will be reexamined in relation to the time spent (in days) in the work release program. If simple comparisons between the experimental and control groups could reveal little advantage for participation in work release, then perhaps some advantage can be observed for those who spent longer periods of time in the program. For present purposes, time spent on work release has been employed both as a dichotomous variable (median = 82 days) for use in cross-tabulations (Table 3) and t-tests (Table 4) and as a continuous variable for use in product-moment correlations (Table 5).

Table 3 shows the proportion of subjects who recidivated or were above the median on recidivism measures for two groups of experimentals: those who participated on work release for 82 days or less, and those who participated for more than 82 days. Chi-square values and p-levels are also reported. The most general observation to be made about Table 3 is that no statistically significant differences were found in the proportions of recidivism by extent of participation. Considering arrests, the largest percentage difference was obtained in the comparison of self-reported arrests (A1) for those with "low" participation on work release (76.2%) and those whose participation is "high" (61.9%). Although such a difference is not statistically significant, it is consistent with other differences obtained for self-reported measures of recidivism. That is, for both self-reported bookings (C1) and self-

TABLE 3
Recidivism for Short- and Long-Term Work Releasees

Symbols*	Recidivism Measure and Cutting Points	Data Source*	Up to 82 Days on Work Release		More than 82 Days on Work Release		X^2	P
			%	(of N)	%	(of N)		
A1	Arrests: ever (no/yes)	SR	76.2	(42)	61.9	(42)	1.39	.24
A3	Arrests: number (≤1/>1)	FBI	48.1	(77)	48.7	(80)	.005	.94
A4	Arrests: rate per month (≤.037/>.037)	FBI	46.8	(77)	50.0	(80)	.06	.80
C1	Bookings: number (0/>0)	SR	73.8	(42)	59.5	(42)	1.33	.25
C2	Charges: number (≤2/>2)	FBI	41.6	(77)	52.5	(80)	1.47	.23
C3	Charges: rate per month (≤.048/>.048)	FBI	45.5	(77)	55.0	(80)	1.07	.30
C4	Convictions: number (0/>0)	SR	69.0	(42)	50.0	(42)	2.42	.12
R1	Reincarceration: ever (no/yes)	SR	46.2	(39)	46.2	(39)	.05	.82
R2	Reincarceration: ever (no/yes)	DC	23.4	(77)	18.8	(80)	.27	.61
R7	Reincarceration: number (0/>0)	FBI	36.4	(77)	28.7	(80)	.72	.39
R8	Reincarceration: felonies (0/>0)	FBI	28.6	(77)	21.2	(80)	.77	.38
S1	Severity: total (0/≤20.036/>20.036)	FBI	32.5	(77)	41.2	(80)	1.85	.40
S2	Severity: average (0/≤5.80/>5.80)	FBI	32.5	(77)	32.5	(80)	1.81	.40
S3	Severity: most severe crime (0/≤6.16/>6.16)	FBI	35.1	(77)	38.7	(80)	1.47	.48
S4	Severity: sentence received (≤21/>21 mos.)	DC	44.4	(18)	60.0	(15)	.29	.59

*See Appendix for explanation of symbols and sources.

reported convictions (C4), the comparison of "low participation" and "high participation" experimentals shows a consistently higher percentage of recidivators (C1: 73.8% versus 59.5%; C4: 69.0% versus 50.0%) among those who spent less time on work release. For self-reported reincarcerations (R1), the proportion of recidivists (46.2%) was identical for both groups. Considering additional reincarceration measures that are based upon Florida Division of Corrections' data (R2) and FBI sources (R7, R8), the small differences again favor those experimentals who spent the longer period on work release. Finally, with regard to three of the severity measures (S1, S3, S4), longer participation in work release is associated with more severe charges and sentences after release. However, the same percentage of both groups (32.4%) was found to be in the highest category of average seriousness (S2) for postrelease offenses. In general, however, the differences observed in Table 3 are small, nonsignificant, and warrant the conclusion that length of participation on work release is *not* consistently related to the occurrence of recidivism.

It is possible that length of participation, if not related to the *occurrence* of recidivism, may be related to the *extent* of recidivism, when the relevant recidivism measures are treated as continuous variables. The remaining analysis, both of mean recidivism (Table 4) and correlations of recidivism with length of work release participation (Table 5), utilize the continuous nature of many of the recidivism indices. Table 4 shows the mean arrest, charge, conviction, reincarceration, and severity levels for subjects with shorter and longer participation in work release. Again, it appears that no significant difference can be observed between the $\overline{X}$s for those who spent up to 82 days on work release and those who spent more than 82 days. For 12 of the 15 continuous recidivism indices, the observed discrepancy, though slight, favors those who spent more time on work release. That is, with the exception of self-reported arrests (A1), number of charges (C2), and total severity (S1), the mean levels of recidivism are higher for those who spent less time on work release. However, most of the differences are so slight as to make any valid inferences impossible. The data from Table 4, again, suggest the conclusion that length of participation in work release makes little or no difference for recidivism.

Table 5 contains the product-moment correlations between length of work release participation—treated as a continuous variable—and the various continuous recidivism measures. From these data, there is some slight indication that length of participation in work release is

TABLE 4
Mean Recidivist Data and T-Tests for Short- and Long-Term Work Releases

Symbols*	Recidivism Measure	Data Source*	Up to 82 Days on Work Release		More than 82 Days on Work Release		t-value	P
			$\bar{X}$	(N)	$\bar{X}$	(N)		
A2	Arrests: number	SR	1.45	(40)	1.67	(42)	.92	.36
A3	Arrests: number	FBI	2.27	(77)	2.16	(80)	.26	.80
A4	Arrests: rate	FBI	.07	(77)	.05	(80)	1.32	.19
C1	Bookings: number	SR	1.36	(42)	1.05	(42)	1.06	.29
C2	Charges: number	FBI	3.23	(77)	3.75	(80)	-.76	.45
C3	Charges: rate	FBI	.11	(77)	.09	(80)	.79	.43
C4	Convictions: number	SR	1.02	(42)	.76	(42)	1.14	.26
R3	Reincarceration: months prior to	DC	20.29	(17)	15.93	(15)	1.27	.21
R6	Reincarceration: number	DC	.30	(77)	.24	(80)	.66	.51
R7	Reincarceration: number	FBI	.61	(77)	.43	(80)	1.26	.21
R8	Reincarceration: felonies	FBI	.36	(77)	.28	(80)	.88	.38
S1	Severity: total	FBI	28.27	(51)	28.55	(60)	-.06	.95
S2	Severity: average	FBI	5.72	(51)	5.66	(60)	.39	.69
S3	Severity: most serious	FBI	6.36	(51)	6.15	(60)	1.01	.31
S4	Severity: sentence received	DC	53.17	(18)	26.87	(15)	1.12	.27

*See Appendix for explanation of symbols and sources.

associated with recidivism. For self-reported bookings (C1) and self-reported convictions (C4), the product-moment correlations with time on work release (-.19; -.18) are statistically significant and negative, as expected, though of moderately small magnitude. For the several FBI measures of recidivism, including arrest, charge, reincarceration, and severity data, the strongest correlation is r = -.08 (number of felony reincarcerations) and none is statistically significant. The strongest correlation from among all the recidivism measures (r = -.26 for months prior to reincarceration) provides additional evidence that is contrary to the rehabilitative expectations for work release since a positive correlation was expected. That is, the more time spent on work release, the less time it seems to have taken for experimentals to incur a reincarceration (R3). Though such a finding is only marginally significant (p < .08) it further qualifies any conclusions of support for work release that are suggested by the data in Table 5. In sum, twelve correlations were not significant, two were significant in the expected direction, and one was nearly significant in the direction opposite to that which would be hypothesized by the proponents of work release.

Disregarding the generally negative results thus far, it is possible that beneficial consequences of participation in work release may occur for some types of inmates and not for others. To examine this possibility, the relationship between participation in work release and recidivism was examined for particular kinds of offenders. Basic demographic, prior record, and job-related control variables were introduced, and the same forms of comparisons were made within the categories of these variables as previously examined in Tables 1-5. Controls were included for race, IQ, education, marital status, age at release, number of prior arrests, number of felony convictions, original offense, sentence length, time served in prison, amount of money at release, number of jobs since release, rate of job change since release, status of jobs held since release, mean income since release, and status difference between pre- and postprison jobs.

When the relationships are examined within the control categories with regard to participation in the work release program, there are no statistically significant differences found between work releasees and the control group in the likelihood of recidivism (contingency tables) or the extent of recidivism ($\overline{X}$s and t-tests) for any of the control categories. In short, there is no evidence that participation on work release makes any difference in recidivism, regardless of the operational definition of recidivism or the control variables utilized.

Length of participation in work release was also examined within the control categories using product-moment correlations. The modest correlations noted in the zero-order relationship in Table 5 were also found in the control categories; however, many of these correlations failed to reach statistical significance. Out of a total of 480 correlations within the control categories, 42 are statistically significant. Of these 42 relationships, 29 are in the expected direction and 13 are in the opposite direction. It should be noted that we would expect 24 of the 480 correlations to be significant at the .05 level simply by chance; therefore, the number of correlations that are significant represents minimal gain over what would be predicted by probability theory. Several of these relationships are considerably stronger than the zero-order correlations: however, few meaningful or logically consistent patterns emerge that would greatly alter the findings derived from Table 5.

TABLE 5
Product-Moment Correlations Between Time in Work Release and Recidivism

Sym-bols*	Recidivism Measure	Data Source*	r	r^2	(N)	P
A2	Arrests: number	SR	-.17	.0289	(82)	.06
A3	Arrests: number	FBI	-.02	.0004	(157)	.40
A4	Arrests: rate per month	FBI	-.07	.0049	(157)	.20
C1	Bookings: number	SR	-.19	.0361	(84)	.05
C2	Charges: number	FBI	.03	.0009	(157)	.34
C3	Charges: rate	FBI	-.05	.0025	(157)	.25
C4	Convictions: number	SR	-.18	.0324	(84)	.05
R3	Reincarceration: months prior to	FBI	-.26	.0676	(32)	.08
R6	Reincarceration: number	DC	-.06	.0036	(157)	.21
R7	Reincarceration: number	FBI	-.07	.0049	(157)	.18
R8	Reincarceration: felonies	FBI	-.08	.0064	(157)	.15
S1	Severity: total	FBI	.02	.0004	(111)	.42
S2	Severity: average	FBI	.01	.0001	(111)	.48
S3	Severity: most serious	FBI	-.07	.0049	(111)	.22
S4	Severity: sentence received	DC	-.16	.0256	(33)	.18

*See Appendix for explanation of symbols and sources.

CONCLUSIONS

At this point, it is reasonable to ask two questions. First, how is it possible that a program such as work release could be allowed to grow and become established policy without any empirical justification of its presumed rehabilitative consequences? And further, now that we have reasons to doubt that work release accomplishes the rehabilitative tasks expected by many, how will this knowledge affect policies toward .he program?

It would appear that work release has become established policy in the absence of empirical justification because (1) it saved money; (2) it appealed to the intuitive "common sense" of legislators and correctional policy-makers; and (3) such empirical justification has simply not been encouraged, facilitated, or considered relevant by most correctional administrators. In this regard, the director of the correction agency involved in the present research is to be commended for his early recognition of the need to conduct a sound evaluation of work release. As noted by Twain et al. (1970: 2-3) such recognition in the field of corrections is rare: "All too often important decisions of social policy and programmatic change are based on speculation, hearsay or personal experience."

The absence of systematic evaluation of correctional policies can be attributed to a variety of factors, among which are budgetary limitations that prevent correctional agencies from evaluating adequately their own programs; a distrust or fear of research that derives from a lack of understanding and exposure to the objectives and methods of empirical research; and the moral and practical difficulties of doing truly experimental research with human subjects.

With regard to the first point, we may observe somewhat optimistically that in recent years many states have greatly increased the research capabilities of their state correctional agencies. While this increase in staff and budget for research has the potential for giving meaningful input to policy decisions, such input is in no way insured, because much of the work that research staff members are asked to perform serves the needs of accounting and record-keeping requirements or justification—though not evaluation—of existing programs. Both of these needs, but particularly the latter, are most acutely felt during those periods when the legislature is in session and demanding some justification of programs that require continued or additional funding. The result is that research staff frequently serve the purpose of putting out administrative brushfires, rather than conducting sound evaluative research.

In terms of the fear and distrust of research, one can only hope that with the passage of time, and the infusion of more graduate-trained criminologists into administrative and policy-making positions, this fear of the unknown will dissipate. Perhaps as administrators come to learn that research can help them put out brushfires, they will also make the observation that sound research input to their policy decisions will prevent many of the fires they spend so much time putting out.

With regard to the human considerations of experimental research, there is little we can add to the substantial literature dealing with the ethics of such research (e.g., Kelman, 1968; Sjoberg, 1967; Rivlin and Timpane, 1975). We might observe that with regard to correctional programs, the problem of withholding certain "control" subjects from an experimental program with presumed benefits—such as work release—may not be doing any irreparable harm, inasmuch as we have yet to find anything in corrections that really accomplishes the purpose of "rehabilitation." Indeed, it is frequently the case that those who are withheld from the correctional innovation actually "benefit" more than those selected. In the case of an established program such as work release, which was widely presumed to have positive consequences and which was actively sought by many inmates, there are the additional problems of resentment and disappointment on the part of those eligibles who are refused participation in work release and kept in the "control group." Rather extraordinary pressure was put on correctional administrators from inmates, superintendents who nominated them for the program, and even from local congressmen who wanted to know why the inmate in question did not receive work release when he was so obviously qualified. Such pressure is likely to make administrators reluctant to conduct truly experimental research projects in the near future. We suspect that this pressure has been a major impediment to such research in many other states that have failed to evaluate correctional programs.

Finally, we expect that policies will be little changed with regard to work release, despite our findings that it does not have the rehabilitative consequences anticipated. We suspect that commitment to the program is so great that policy-makers will point to shortcomings in the research (for example: it involved a sample drawn several years ago, and the present program is different) to denigrate its immediate import. Further, we suspect that the justifications given for work release and for expanding the program will simply have less to say about its rehabilitative consequences and, in these days of fiscal restraint, more to say about its economic utility. In addition, supporters of work release can, with some justification, argue that the present research shows that the program does no harm, and on that account should be continued. The present researchers would not argue for the elimination of work release programs since they might be justified on humanitarian or economic grounds. This research indicates, however, that policy-makers should not attempt to "sell" work release on its rehabilitative merits and should be prepared to discard it when better programs can be demonstrated. Unfortunately, since so few correctional programs have been adequately evaluated, we are unable to compare the relative merits of different policies in terms of the rehabilitative consequences.

In the long run, we suspect that economic utility is what legislators (and consequently correctional administrators) are most concerned with—even in those fields where "people changing" is the presumed mission of the organization.

NOTES

1. See, in particular, McMillan (1965); Ashman (1966); Cooper (1967); and Moeller (1968).

2. On strain or opportunity theory, see Merton (1938); Cohen (1955); Cloward and Ohlin (1961). Hirschi (1969); Reckless and Dinitz (1967); and Matza (1969, 1964) have addressed the notion of control theory. On learning and differential association theories, see Miller (1958); Sutherland (1947); Burgess and Akers (1966). Finally, on labeling, see Lemert (1951); Becker (1963); Lofland (1969); and Schur (1971).

REFERENCES

ALEXANDER, M. E. (1966) "Current concepts in corrections." Federal Probation 30 (September): 3-8.

ASHMAN, A. (1966) "Work release in North Carolina." Popular Government 32 (June): 1-5.

BECKER, H. S. (1963) Outsiders: Studies in the Sociology of Deviance. Glencoe, Ill.: Free Press.

BURGESS, R. L. and R. L. AKERS (1966) "A differential association-reinforcement theory of criminal behavior." Social Problems 14 (Fall): 128-147.

CLOWARD, R. A. and L. E. OHLIN (1961) Delinquency and Opportunity. Glencoe, Ill.: Free Press.

COHEN, A. K. (1955) Delinquent Boys: The Culture of the Gang. Glencoe, Ill.: Free Press.

COOPER, W. D. (1967) "An economic analysis of the work-release program in North Carolina." M.A. thesis, North Carolina State University at Raleigh.

GLASER, D. (1973) Routinizing Evaluation: Getting Feedback on Effectiveness of Crime and Delinquency Programs. Rockville, Ill.: National Institute of Mental Health.

——— (1965) "Correctional research: an elusive paradise." J. of Research in Crime & Delinquency (January): 1-11.

GRUPP, S. E. (1965) "Work release and the misdemeanant." Federal Probation 29 (June): 6-12.

HIRSCHI, T. (1969) Causes of Delinquency. Berkeley: Univ. of California Press.

JOHNSON, E. H. (1970) "Work release: conflicting goals within a promising innovation." Canadian J. of Corrections 12: 67-77.

——— (1967) "Work release—a study of correctional reform." Crime & Delinquency 13: 521-530.

KELMAN, H. C. (1968) A Time to Speak: On Human Values and Social Research. San Francisco: Jossey-Bass.

LEMERT, E. M. (1951) Social Pathology. New York: McGraw-Hill.

LOFLAND, J. (1969) Deviance and Identity. Englewood Cliffs, N.J.: Prentice-Hall.

MATZA, D. (1969) Becoming Deviant. Englewood Cliffs, N.J.: Prentice-Hall.

——— (1964) Delinquency and Drift. New York: John Wiley.

McMILLAN, D. R. (1965) "Work furlough for the jailed prisoner." Federal Probation 29 (March): 33-34.

MERTON, R. (1938) "Social structure and anomie." Amer. Soc. Rev. 3 (October): 672-682.

MILLER, W. B. (1958) "Lower class culture as a generating milieu of gang delinquency." J. of Social Issues 14: 5-19.

MOELLER, H. G. (1968) "Corrections and the community: new dimensions." Federal Probation 32: 25-29.

RECKLESS, W. C. and S. DINITZ (1967) "Pioneering with self-concept as a vulnerability factor in delinquency." J. of Crim. Law & Criminology 58: 515-523.

RICHMOND, M. S. (1968) "The practicalities of community based corrections." Amer. J. of Corrections 30: 12-18.

——— (1966) "On conquering prison walls." Federal Probation 30 (June): 17-22.

RIVLIN, A. M. and M. P. TIMPANE (1975) Ethical and Legal Issues of Social Experimentation. Washington, D.C.: Brookings.

ROSSI, P. H., E. WAITE, C. BOSE, and R. A. BERK (1974) "The seriousness of crimes: normative structure and individual differences." Amer. Soc. Rev. 39 (April): 224-237.

SCHUR, E. M. (1971) Labelling Deviant Behavior: Its Sociological Implications. New York: Harper & Row.

SHAH, S. A. (1971) "Graduated release." National Institute of Mental Health, Center for Studies of Crime and Delinquency, Bethesda, Md.

SJOBERG, G. (1967) Ethics, Politics, and Social Research. Cambridge, Mass.: Schenkman.

SUTHERLAND, E. H. (1947) Principles of Criminology (4th ed.). Philadelphia: J. B. Lippincott.

SWANSON, R. M. (1973) Work Release: Toward an Understanding of the Law, Policy and Operation of Community-Based State Corrections. Carbondale: Southern Illinois University, Center for the Study of Crime, Delinquency and Correction.

TWAIN, D., E. HARLOW, and D. MERWIN (1970) Research and Human Services: A Guide to Collaboration for Program Development. New York: Jewish Board of Guardians, Research and Development Center.

WALDO, G. P. and T. G. CHIRICOS (1974) Work as a Rehabilitation Tool: An Evaluation of Two State Programs. Washington, D.C.: U.S. Department of Justice, Law Enforcement Assistance Administration, Final Report.

WILKINS, L. T. (1969) Evaluation of Penal Measures. New York: Random House.

APPENDIX
Indices of Recidivism

The 18 indices of recidivism were derived from three separate sources—Self-Report (SR) from follow-up interviews with released inmates, Florida Division of Corrections files (DC), and FBI Rap Sheets (FBI)—and may be clustered into four distinct dimensions: (A) arrest data; (C) charge, booking, or conviction data; (R) reincarceration data; and (S) severity of offense data. The follow-up period between point of release and the various measures of recidivism ranged from a low of 24 months on the follow-up interviews to a high of 46 months on the FBI rap sheet data. A brief description of each recidivism measure used in this study follows:

A1: Arrests—ever. SR question: "Have you been arrested since you have been out of prison?"

A2: Arrests—number. SR question: "How many times have you been arrested since you have been out of prison?"

A3: Arrests—number. FBI recorded arrests since the date of release from prison.

A4: Arrests—rate. FBI recorded arrests per month since release from prison.

C1: Bookings—number. SR question: "Were you booked?"—asked of those who may have been taken into custody (and technically arrested) but released without having charges filed against them.

C2: Charges—number. FBI recorded charges since release.

C3: Charges—rate. FBI recorded charges per month since release.

C4: Convictions—number. SR question: "Were you found guilty of the crime for which you were arrested?"—(sum of "yes" response for each arrest).

R1: Reincarceration—ever. SR question: "What was the outcome of the arrests?"—(scored "yes" if one of the responses to that item was "sent to prison").

R2: Reincarceration—ever. DC record of reentry to one of its institutions. (This index, frequently used in recidivism studies, has the advantage of being available for all subjects, but has the disadvantage of representing only those felony incarcerations taking place within Florida.)

R3: Reincarceration—months until. DC record of number of months between release and reincarceration. (There is no overlap between length of participation in work release and the length of time the person was out of prison prior to reincarceration.)

R6: Reincarceration—number. DC record of number of times subject was returned to state prison.

R7: Reincarceration—number. FBI-recorded incarcerations (felony or misdemeanor) in excess of 30 days.

R8: Reincarceration—number of felonies. FBI-recorded reincarcerations for a period in excess of one year (directly comparable to R6 except includes out-of-state cases).

S1: Severity—total. FBI-recorded offenses, summed total of all severity scores (Rossi et al., 1974).

S2: Severity—average. FBI-recorded offenses, S1 divided by the number of charges (indication of the average level of seriousness of the crimes alleged for a particular subject).

S3: Severity—most severe crime. FBI-recorded offense with the highest seriousness score.

S4: Severity—sentence received. DC-recorded number of months for the first reincarceration.

PART 6

STUDIES IN HUMAN SERVICES: HEALTH AND LABOR

27

MONITORING AND ANALYSIS OF
MENTAL HEALTH PROGRAM OUTCOME DATA

By

JAMES A. CIARLO

This study discusses the various means by which mental health program managers can integrate statistical data into planning and decision making. James A. Ciarlo designs a process by which patient information and program outcome data can be utilized. He hopes that such a system will assist program managers in monitoring and analyzing programs in mental health.

From James A. Ciarlo, "Monitoring and Analysis of Mental Health Program Outcome Data." *Evaluation* (4:1, 1977) © Minneapolis Medical Research Foundation.

The routine use of statistical data about clients and treatment process information in mental health program planning and decision-making is still a relatively rare phenomenon. Such use would require a high quality data system, one or more full-time staff operating it, and program managers who are reasonably comfortable and adept with respect to the nature and use of statistical information. For the small number of mental health programs which have come this far along in program evaluation, this progressive state of affairs represents a considerable achievement.

Even more rare, perhaps not yet achieved anywhere in the country, is the routine use of client and program *outcome* data in the regular decision-making and program monitoring process. In this case, the same data system, evaluation staff, and data-experienced managers are necessary, but with the additional requirements of (1) regular collection of outcomes or client-state data, and (2) some capability to relate treatment career or events to better or worse outcome scores. These additional requirements represent not a small extension of the initial set, but rather a quantum leap ahead because of the large number of outcome measurement considerations that must now be addressed and handled. For example, obtaining client-state scores following treatment requires some type of follow-up of clients no longer in regular periodic treatment; otherwise, the needed score will either not be obtained at all, or the treatment system (clinicians) will be contributing such scores on the basis of out-of-date impressions.

The outcome measure itself is not problem free; it should be equally applicable to all types of clients and possess demonstrated validity and reliability. There should be no question as to whether a score for one client indicates the same client state as a similar score for another client. This allows individual scores to be aggregated meaningfully into *program* outcome scores. "Individualized" or unique outcome scales constructed anew for each client appear to us to be fraught with problems in this respect. There are also additional problems in obtaining scores unbiased by method of client selection, administration of the outcome instrument, and attrition of members of the group chosen for follow-up which must be faced and reasonably resolved. For these reasons, competent outcome evaluation represents a sizeable increment of investment in program resources over and above those dedicated to needs assessment and process evaluation.

In 1971, a system for continuous monitoring of outcome data was designed for the large urban community mental health center operated by Denver General Hospital (later named the Northwest Denver Mental Health Center). Operationalizing and implementing the system took several years as we addressed the problems described above. It has been essentially operational since early 1974, although some major obstacles to achieving full effectiveness still remain to be resolved. In 1972, our Mental Health Systems Evaluation Project completed its first version of a client-oriented outcome questionnaire. It was designed to assess several major aspects of a client's mental health from a *community* perspective, covering not only his personal functioning and satisfaction with services, but also his relations with family and friends, engagement in socially productive activities, use of public resources for self-maintenance, and a variety of negative consequences of alcohol or drug abuse. It seemed essential to us to determine outcome in terms of the actual condition of the treated person at some later point in time, rather than using such arbitrarily influenceable "outcome" criteria as inpatient admission, state hospitalization, later readmission, length of treatment or "drop-out" rate, etc. We chose the client himself, rather than relatives or friends, as a primary source of information about his functioning, partly because of the importance of some subjective information which only he would have (e.g., experiencing distress or feelings of satisfaction with treatment). Another determinant was the fact that we service a catchment area heavily populated with isolated individuals and disrupted families. We also selected administration of the questionnaire by a nonprofessional in a face-to-face interview with a client in his own home. This procedure, we believed, would maximize the outcome assessment's relevance to actual in-community functioning and behavior, would help reduce "please-the-doctor" biases usually involved in asking clients about their current condition right where they receive treatment, and would also insure that we would lose no clients through such selection factors as not having a telephone, inability to read or write on a questionnaire form, or unwillingness to be frank and truthful in an impersonal mailed questionnaire.

Since 1973 this outcome questionnaire has been standardized on a random sample of the Denver population, has been administered to typical members of various client groups at intake, and has routinely been applied to quarterly samples (or cohorts) of similar clients about 90 days following their intake into one of our treatment services. The resulting data for each cohort on each dimension of functioning (we regularly use eight dimensions) are plotted on a single graph of the type depicted in Figure 1. This allows direct comparison of scores of treated clients at time of follow-up with typical client scores at intake, and also with nonclient community norms. Thus, a continuous "picture" is generated of how typical client groups are functioning at intake relative to the Denver community, how much better (or worse) they are functioning at follow-up, and how far they are at follow-up from the Denver community average in each functioning area. Depending upon the results, we may be pleased or displeased at our apparent success at moving clients from relatively poor functioning at intake to more "normal" functioning at follow-up. The larger the differences between admission and follow-up levels, and the closer the follow-up level to community norms, the more pleased we can be. Note, however, that in the absence of suitable untreated comparison groups, the

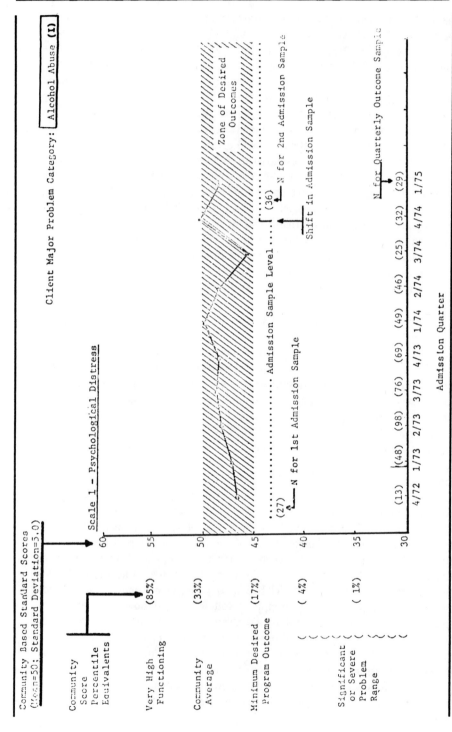

Figure 1: QUARTERLY OUTCOME SCORE FORMAT EXPLANATION

data establish only the fact that clients have changed, for possibly many reasons—only one of which might be the treatment received. Nevertheless, we believe that such graphic information is much of what is needed to overcome obstacles to utilization of outcome data in decision-making on a regular basis. For example, it was encouraging that the 13 alcoholics admitted to treatment in the fourth quarter of 1972 earned an average score of about 47 in the area of experiencing Psychological Distress at the time of follow-up. While this was not as favorable as the Denver community's average score of 50, it was nevertheless considerably better than the intake or Admission Sample average of 43. The improvement also placed the outcome score above the '45' level, which was chosen as our minimum desired program outcome level because it represents scores falling just one standard deviation below the community average. In a very real sense, the '45' level represents our minimum aspirations for clients relative to "normal" community functioning. Since it is a level below which only about one-sixth of the community itself falls, it implies that we are conservative in aspiring to restore our clients to this level. Trying to move severely impaired clients up to the community average is, for most mental health programs, quite ambitious and possibly unrealistic. Of course, we prefer to see scores in the upper part of the "zone of desired outcome," but normally we would not be too disturbed if they were nearer '45' or '50'. Again, we find the representation of admission, follow-up, and community norm data on the same graph to be extremely helpful in depicting how far our clients as a whole have progressed, and how much farther they still must move before a satisfactory outcome level is reached.

The next important feature of the graph in Figure 1 is the time dimension. Follow-up scores for successive cohorts of clients are plotted as a continuous series, so that major changes in client functioning at follow-up can be visually detected and interpreted. In the example of Figure 1, client outcomes on the Psychological Distress dimension improved steadily between the last quarter of 1972 and the first quarter of 1974; after that, a fairly sharp decline in outcome level was seen for the next two quarters, followed by a sudden return to the highest outcome level in the series in the fourth quarter of 1974. It is sometimes possible to correlate such outcome changes with simultaneous changes in the treatment program itself—staff reductions, changes in length of treatment use of different drugs, and similar factors. This process can be misleading, however, and such changes in outcome level cannot definitively be assigned to any such hypothetical cause *after the fact*. What becomes possible with this methodology, however, is detecting the effect of a *future* change in the program intended to affect the score level. If, for example, a new treatment regime were instituted for our alcohol abusers in the second quarter of 1975, and if later scores show a timely and sustained increase in outcome level, the new regime can be judged responsible for the improvement, barring the unlikely coincidental occurrence of some powerful extraneous factor at exactly the same time as the treatment change. This "interrupted time-series" design is already frequently used in other fields, such as economic forecasting and financial monitoring by corporations; it has not yet received extensive attention in the behavioral sciences or the field of health services delivery and evaluation, although the technology involving its use is developing rapidly (for example, see Glass et al., 1975).

A complete set of eight graphs for the most severely disturbed client group treated by our Center ("Disorganized Behavior and Thinking") is shown in Figure 2. Several features of this data set are noteworthy. First, the scores of both Admission samples on Psychological Distress are extremely low—below 40, or at about the third percentile of the Denver community distribution. Ninety days later, however, the follow-up groups score within the zone of desired outcomes (45-50). Second, this client group is quite isolated from both family and friends, and our treatment services (or other factors) do not seem to change this very much. Third, Client Satisfaction scores (standardized on a random Center client sample in 1973) run slightly below the average of all types of clients followed up. Finally, outcome scores are fairly stable over successive quarters, except that the most recent data are somewhat poorer on several scales. As this may possibly reflect the beginning of an unfavorable outcome trend, the next few data points will be watched carefully for signs of confirmation of the trend or reversion to previous levels.

Making program changes which will increase outcome levels, or which might at least hold program outcome levels constant while costs are decreased, is an important management objective. The success or failure of such alterations can be assessed with the succeeding data, thus providing reasonably definitive feedback to program managers within a fairly short time (perhaps 6 to 9 months) following the change. Stimulating managers and clinicians to try out such alterations or innovation thus becomes one of our evaluation project's major functions. We therefore also undertake a wide variety of quasi-experimental and nonexperimental analyses of the same outcome data in relation to treatment career variables such as type of medication used, length of treatment career, type of treatment modality employed, clinician training or degree level, and costs involved. For example, we have recently completed nonexperimental and quasi-experimental analyses of the effects of three major treatment variables upon outcomes for several types of outpatients. In general, the results suggested that there was little association of number of treatment sessions received with functioning at follow-up, even when demographic and clinical differences at admission were statistically controlled. The same result occurred in comparing outcomes for four different outpatient teams which differed to some extent on the average number of treatment sessions they provided to similar clients. At the same time, for one client group ("Disorganized Behavior and Thinking"), use of major tranquilizers and anti-Parkinsonism drugs was substantially associated with better functioning at follow-up.

In another analysis, individual therapy seemed to have little, if any, advantage over group psychotherapy when drug therapy and total number of sessions received were statistically controlled; yet the costs differed appreciably, as would be expected. Accordingly, we constructed a simple computer model of outpatient treatment and used it to find the cost savings which might be realized if clients were assigned more frequently to groups than they currently are. Results of these

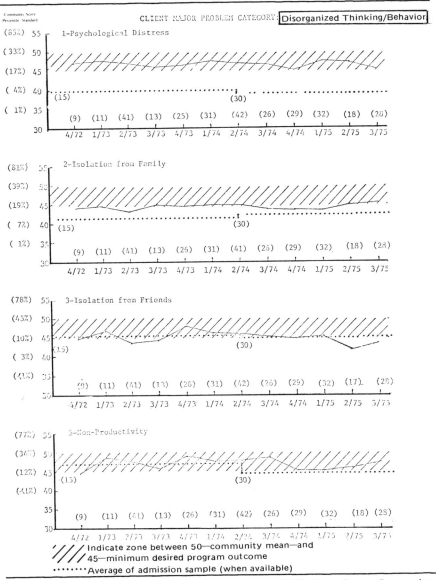

Figure 2: QUARTERLY PROGRAM OUTCOME SCALE SCORES (From Denver Community Mental Health Questionnaire Follow-Ups)

analyses have been fed back to managers, not as definite proof of the particular influence of any one of these factors upon outcome, but rather as a stimulus to program revision or innovation which could subsequently be evaluated through changes in the outcome level over time. While it is too early to determine the full effects of this type of evaluation stimulus to our management upon our programs'

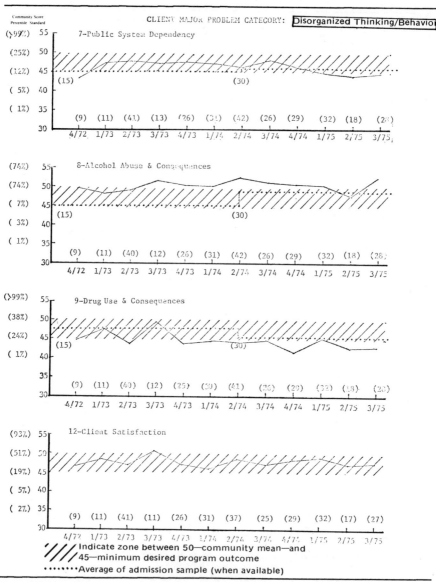

Figure 2 (continued)

effectiveness, we can make a few general observations regarding our current prospects and the obstacles which still lie ahead of us.

First, the mere idea of continuously monitoring selected program data is quite new to mental health clinicians and clinically trained managers. Most have had no training about or exposure to research or evaluation reports of this type, which often seem "cold-blooded" and hopelessly abstruse to the clinicians. Over the past two to three years, however, our top managers, program coordinators, and service element leaders have experienced continuous feedback of statistical data and process evaluation data from our section, and have gradually increased their awareness, use, and now even reliance on such data for program direction. A good deal of leadership in this regard has been asserted by a small number of senior staff who are both clinically innovative and interested in tracking the impact of their ideas by means of evaluation data. These persons have successfully communicated the idea that monitoring program data reflects a progressive and effective managerial style. Their use of it has also helped the Center staff to feel that the data are the *Center's* data, not just the evaluator's proprietary product.

Assuming that our program managers have come to feel comfortable with the continued presence of data in the managerial arena, a final obstacle nevertheless remains. In order to capitalize on the informational opportunities inherent in an outcome information monitoring system program, managers and staff must adopt, at least periodically, a more tentative and less doctrinaire style of thinking about their professional activities than is customary. Wildavsky (1972) put it well:

> The ideal organization would be self-evaluating. It would continuously monitor its own activities so as to determine whether it was meeting its goals or even whether these goals should continue to prevail. When evaluation suggested that a change in goals or programs to achieve them was desirable, these proposals would be taken seriously by top decision makers. They would institute the necessary changes; they would have *no vested interest* in continuation of current activities. Instead they would steadily *pursue new alternatives* to better serve the latest desired outcomes. [Italics mine.]

But most managers and staff are ordinary mortals who find it difficult to suspend their own theoretical and personal biases regarding proper treatment of clients in order to be willing to make a significant program change, even if only on a temporary basis. This is not surprising. One can find a parallel phenomenon in the business world; management literature and casebooks are replete with evidence that major business enterprises often find it difficult to shift to new products or processes, even when their profits have shown a steady declining trend. In the business arena, however, acceptance of profitability as a corporate goal is so strongly established that a continued decline in this indicator normally *does* result in significant changes (eventually in management, if not in operations). In the mental health area, in contrast, no set of program outcome indicators has yet become so compelling to program managers and governing or regulatory boards. Hence, the pressures for program change generated by the outcome data are much weaker than in the business example, and the operation of previously held opinions and ideologies is correspondingly much more prevalent. There are, of course, many factors involved in timely and effective organizational change which are neglected in the above analyses to make the point regarding the significance of data; the reader may refer to Davis (1971) for a brief but encompassing perspective on this topic.

The new federal legislation requiring a commitment by every community mental health center to evaluation of its programs and their impacts may eventually have a momentous effect upon the use of outcome data in routine managerial decision-making, as clinical and administrative staff become increasingly exposed to program data and the congruences or disparities with ultimate values and goals which they highlight. As in other areas of human endeavor, change will follow the introduction of new tools, and the pace of change in programs will probably escalate. This does not disturb us too much from our perspective; there is much in our clinical service programs that seems soundly based, and this will prevent whimsical or cataclysmic unheavals in programs on the basis of tentative outcome data. Instead, we look forward to gradually increasing program simplicity, efficiency, and staff satisfaction as the shape of programs is increasingly influenced by their effects as well as by their roots in humanistic and community concerns.

REFERENCES

DAVIS, H.R. (1971). Planning for creative change in mental health services: A manual on research utilization. DHEW Publication No. (ADM) 74-14. Washington, D.C.: U.S. Government Printing Office.

GLASS, G.V, WILSON, V.L., and GOTTMAN, J.M. (1975). Design and analysis of time-series experiments. Boulder, Colo.: Colorado Associated University Press.

WILDAVSKY, A. (1972). "The self-evaluating organization." Public Administration Review, 32(September/October).

28

RELATIONS BETWEEN NUTRITION AND COGNITION
IN RURAL GUATEMALA

By

HOWARD E. FREEMAN, ROBERT E. KLEIN,
JEROME KAGAN, and CHARLES YARBROUGH

The authors conducted an interesting study on the relationship between nutrition and cognitive development in rural Guatemala. They measured nutritional status of three- and four-year-old children by height and head circumference as related to cognitive performance in four rural Guatemalan villages. The relationships persist when social factors are taken into account.

Families in two of the villages participated in a voluntary, high-protein, high-calorie supplementation program. In the other two villages, the families received a vitamin and mineral supplement with about one-third of the calories. Although the longitudinal study is still ongoing, there is some evidence that the children who receive the high-calorie supplement (or whose mothers received it during pregnancy and lactation) are most likely to score high in cognitive performance. The results support other animal and human studies that report an association between nutrition and cognitive development. The findings suggest the work of nutrition intervention programs in rural areas of lesser developed countries.

From Howard E. Freeman et al., "Relations Between Nutrition and Cognition in Rural Guatemala." *The American Journal of Public Health,* 1977, *67*(3), 233-239.

Abstract: The nutritional status of three and four year old children, as measured by height and head circumference, is related to cognitive performance in four rural Guatemalan villages. The relationships persist when social factors are taken into account.

Families in two of the villages participate in a voluntary, high protein-calorie supplementation program. In the other two villages, the families receive a vitamin and mineral supplement with about one-third of the calories. Although the longitudinal study still is ongoing, there is some evidence that the children who receive the higher calorie supplement (or whose mothers received it during pregnancy and lactation) are most likely to score high in cognitive performance. The results support other animal and human studies that report an association between nutrition and cognitive development. The findings, while not diminishing social environmental explanations of differences in cognitive function, suggest the worth of nutrition intervention programs in rural areas of lesser-developed countries. (Am. J. Public Health 67:233–239, 1977)

During the 1960s, a number of investigators studying children in various regions of the world reported an association between severe protein-calorie malnutrition and intellectual functioning.[1-5] Laboratory studies with animals in the 1960s and early 1970s also provided important findings of the profound effects of malnutrition on neurological development[6,7] and on learning patterns and other individual behaviors.[8,9] The demonstration of a linkage between severe protein-calorie malnourishment and cognitive performance of children, bolstered by the animal studies, received widespread attention since an estimated three per cent of the world's children experience one or more episodes of severe malnutrition before five years of age.[10]

In relation to the incidence of mild and moderate protein-calorie malnutrition, however, severe nutritional deficiencies are relatively unique events. It is estimated that fully one-half of the children in lesser developed nations are suffering from mild-to-moderate protein-calorie malnutrition,[11] as well as varying but critical numbers of children in low-income families in industrialized countries.[12] The finding that severe nutritional deficiencies of children appear to limit their mental development, when extrapolated to moderately and mildly malnourished children, has resulted in one

of the important scientific and policy debates of the past decade. In part, the controversy centers around accepting a causal relationship on the basis of epidemiological data between measures of nutritional status and psychological test scores.[2,13] In part, it is the result of the efforts of well-intentioned policy makers and humanitarians who marshal all possible evidence to justify large-scale nutrition interventions.

The presumed causal link between malnutrition and intellectual development is challenged by the findings of numerous investigations of the influence of the social environment on the child's cognitive functioning. Evans and associates, for example, found that malnourished South African children and their healthier siblings *both* attain similar scores on cognitive tests.[5] The widely-known Coleman report as well as less ambitious but more rigorous investigations provide support for an association between aspects of the child's social environment and cognitive development.[14] Economically advantaged children obtain larger values on the anthropometric indicators commonly used to measure nutritional status. Thus, many have suggested the covariation between economic and nutritional indices accounts for the relation between mild malnutrition and poor cognitive functioning.[15]

The intentioned and unintentioned efforts of scientists and policy makers to downgrade the influence of either nutrition or the social milieu is understandable in terms of both the disciplinary orientations of investigators—biological and medical on the one hand, and social and psychological on the other—and the passions that come into play among policy makers competing for limited funds, particularly those provided by industrialized countries to less developed ones.

Address reprint requests to Howard E. Freeman, Department of Sociology, University of California at Los Angeles, Los Angeles, CA 90024. Authors Klein and Yarbrough are with the Institute of Nutrition of Central America and Panama (INCAP); author Kagan is with Harvard University. This paper, submitted to the Journal December 29, 1975, was revised and accepted for publication October 28, 1976.

By the mid-1960s, there was a widely acknowledged need to develop and implement investigations that took into account *both* nutritional and social determinants of cognitive development. The need to study both nutritional and social factors involves complex issues of conceptualization, design, and analysis. The number of variables that must be quantified and introduced into any reasonable design requires respectable sample sizes, extensive data collection and collation, and complex data analysis. Further, the immature state of the nutritional and behavioral sciences does not allow complete solutions to the major problems of method, including the operationalization and measurement of the several sets of key variables (see Klein, et al., for an expanded discussion of this point[15]).

The data reported here came from a long-term longitudinal investigation of nutrition and mental development being undertaken in Guatemala by the Institute of Nutrition of Central America and Panama (INCAP) and begun in 1968 (see McKay, et al. and Mora, et al. for discussions of related ongoing projects[16, 17]). The INCAP investigation, although still in its data collection phase, has resulted in a large number of papers on various substantive and methodological aspects of the project (see Klein, et al., for a recent review[18]). In a 1972 paper,[15] early data were reported that bear directly on the contributions of nutritional and social factors to cognitive functioning. The results of this analysis suggested that both domains of measures are related to cognitive development, and that the relative importance of nutritional and social factors depended on the particular cognitive dimension selected as the criterion variable; further, that the sex of the children must be taken into account. There were major sex differences in the amount of variance accounted for by the different social and nutritional measures included as independent variables. Given the limited robustness of the findings, the sample size at that time, and the inevitable methodological weaknesses of a complex field study, we were forced to conclude that, while the results hint at the importance of nutritional as well as social factors, the findings were insufficient to advocate wide-scale social action programs that are predicated on nutritional status being related to cognitive functioning.

In this paper, we summarize a considerably larger body of data from the INCAP study on the contributions of nutritional and social factors to cognitive development. It is still a progress report since much of the longitudinal analysis awaits some two additional years of data collection. But the information at hand allows for a more definitive examination of the competing viewpoints.

The INCAP Study

The study population consists of children from four small, Spanish-speaking Guatemalan villages. The families in them are poor with average incomes less than $300 per year, most cannot read or write, live without indoor sanitary facilities, and drink water contaminated with enteric bacteria. Corn and beans are the major diet and animal protein is less than 12 per cent of total protein intake.[19] Height and weight of both adults and children are strikingly low in comparison with standards for children in developed countries.

Study Design

The study can most properly be described as a quasi-experiment. In two of the villages, pregnant and lactating mothers and children are offered a protein-calorie supplement (11 gms. of protein per 180 ml. of supplement). In two other villages, a supplement that contains no protein is provided. The second supplement, a "Kool-aid" type drink, contains one-third of the calories of the protein-calorie supplement (59 total calories compared with 163 per 180 ml.).* Both preparations contain the vitamins, minerals, and fluorides possibly limited in the home diets. Attendance at the twice-daily supplementation program is voluntary, there are no restrictions on how much can be ingested, and a wide range of intake is observed in each village.

The supplementation of two of the four villages with a high-calorie diet, however, provides a study group that includes sufficient children and lactating mothers with an adequate calorie intake, even in families with minimal economic resources. The intervention is necessary because the proportion of poor families in rural Guatemalan villages with malnourished children is so large that it is not possible to examine thoroughly the relations between social-environmental variables, measures of nutritional status, and cognitive functioning. As reported elsewhere, the physical growth of young children in the set of villages receiving the high-calorie supplement is significantly higher than in the set receiving the low-calorie one.[20] In addition, preventive and curative medical care is provided in all villages by a physician-supervised resident nurse. Appropriate referrals are made to regional hospitals in cases of serious illness. Severe malnutrition is treated upon discovery in all four villages.

The Study Group

The longitudinal study group at the time of this report consisted of 1,083 children, 671 born alive since the field work started in 1969, and 412 alive and under three years of age when data collection commenced. The study group reported on here consists of those children from the 1,083 in the longitudinal panel who are old enough so that data are available at either age three (N = 573), age four (N = 536), or both ages. This point requires some amplification. When data are presented by age, the age designation refers to the information collected at a particular time-point; in other words, information reported for age three and then for age four includes many of the same children in the two analyses, but the data differ by time-point collected. The study group sizes are as follows:

3-year-old males	300
3-year-old females	273
4-year-old males	278
4-year-old females	258

---

*The protein-calorie supplement will be referred to as the "high calorie" supplement or diet in this paper.

Exact study group sizes for each analysis presented vary somewhat because of missing data. In general, the tables contain about 95 per cent of the subjects reported above.

Variables

The project has collected an unusually large corpus of data on health status and medical treatment, food consumption, nutritional supplementation, physical growth, and social environmental factors. Because of the pressure to implement the field study, early data collection included many measures later discarded as either irrelevant or unreliable. In this paper, selected measures from three domains of variables are employed.

1. Dependent Variables

The cognitive measures come from a specially designed "preschool" battery. As in the previous report,[15] we use three variables selected from this battery.

Language Facility. The score is based on the child's ability to name and recognize pictures of common objects and to note and state the relations among orally presented verbal concepts.

Short-term Memory for Numbers. The child's score is based on his recall of increasingly long strings of numbers read to him at the rate of one per second.

Perceptual Analysis. The child's score is based on his ability to locate hidden figures embedded in a complex picture or to detect which of several similar variations of an illustrated object was identical with a standard.

Test-retest reliabilities differ somewhat by age but are in the generally accepted range of .7 to .8 when the scores are obtained one month apart. Consistent with current thinking about cognitive performance, particularly the utility of Western-oriented tests to underdeveloped populations,[21] the general strategy has been to develop a set of measures that "sample" a domain of separate cognitive processes. For heuristic purposes, however, it also seemed useful to develop a single score reflecting the overall cognitive performance for each child. Since the earlier paper was published, a number of efforts based on theoretical considerations and factor analytic studies have been undertaken to develop a composite measure. The one that seems to satisfy both theoretical and psychometric requirements consists of 12 tests that represent the child's ability to memorize, recognize, perceive, infer, and verbalize. This measure, labeled *cognitive composite*, is included as a fourth dependent variable in the analysis. The test-retest reliability when the cognitive composite battery was administered the second time after one month was .88 for three-year old children.

2. Social Environmental Measures

These measures were developed from first administering a large number of items, inspecting intercorrelations between items, and identifying scales that correlate with psychological test scores. Reliability of the measures in many cases was found to be too low to continue their use. Al-

though the villages are relatively "flat" in stratification, nevertheless there is evidence of structural and life-style variation. It was decided to continue using three measures and to obtain family data repeatedly on them. The measures are the following:

Quality of house: Rating based on the type of construction, interior design and condition of dwelling. (Test-retest reliability = .80.)

Mother's dress: Rating based on whether or not the mother possessed particular items of commercially manufactured clothing. (Test-retest reliability = .65.)

Task instruction: Rating based on family members' reports of teaching the child to perform household tasks and to travel to a nearby town. (Test-retest reliability = .50.)

The first measure, quality of house, is conceived as a social-economic stratification measure. The second, mother's dress, reflects modernity as well as income. The third, task instruction, is viewed as an indicator of the parents' efforts to provide adult modeling and purposeful learning opportunities. Reliability of the two stratification measures is reasonably high, particularly the quality of house measure. The task instruction measure's reliability is border-line. Reliability of measures is increased by pooling the scores, usually three in number, that are obtained in repeated annual interviews. In part of the analysis, these three variables are combined. The composite measure is referred to as the *social factor index*. The test-retest reliability of the social factor index is .85.

3. Nutritional Data

The child's head circumference and total height are used as indices of nutritional status. Both variables presumably reflect the child's history of protein-calorie intake, although genetic background and illness experience also influence head size and height. Height is generally the best indicator of extended nutritional deficiency; head circumference is most sensitive to malnourishment before the age of two years.[20] Extensive field trials conducted as part of the INCAP program argue for the utility of anthropometric measures as indicators of nutritional status.[20] In villages in which children receive an annual intake of more than 20 liters of the high calorie food supplement, children's physical growth velocities are similar to those recorded for children in the U.S. In villages receiving the low-calorie supplement, these velocities are significantly lower. In part of the analysis, these two measures (height and head circumference) are combined. The composite is referred to as the *nutrition index*.

4. Supplementation Data

Children and their mothers receive and drink the supplements under supervision and the amount is recorded for each visit. In this study, two separate measures are used. The first is the total caloric intake of mothers during their pregnancy and the period of their lactation. The second is the total calories consumed by the mothers and by the child directly.

In the two villages receiving the high calorie supplement, the mothers of the children tested at three years of age, during pregnancy and lactation, ingested approximately twice as many calories as mothers in the villages receiving the vitamin-mineral supplement (67,000 calories compared with 32,000). The mothers of the four year old children averaged 53,000 and 24,000 calories respectively. The children themselves at three years of age had consumed an average of 97,000 calories in the two high calorie supplement villages compared with 15,000 calories in the two low calorie supplement villages; at four years of age the comparable figures were 121,000 and 31,000 calories respectively.

Results

A multiple-regression analysis was employed. For each of the four cognitive measures, separate analyses were undertaken by age and sex with the data pooled for the four villages. A large number of repeated analyses were performed for three reasons. First, in order to estimate the independent and joint effects of variables reflecting the different domains of measures, the variables were "forced" into the analyses in different orders, e.g., the social factor measures first and then the nutritional measures. Second, analyses were undertaken with the individual measures and with the composite indices. The indices greatly reduce the number of variables, advantageous in conserving degrees of freedom and in simplifying the interpretation and presentation of findings. The measures in the composite indices are not highly correlated, however, and thus the amount of variance explained may be reduced. Third, analyses were undertaken with and without taking into account the interaction effects between variables. There were no interaction effects deemed useful to include in the data presented since the variance explained by them was small and outweighed by the loss of degrees of freedom. A further refinement was to adjust the correlations for the estimated reliability of these measures. Again, this procedure does not modify the results.

Nutrition and Cognitive Performance

In Table 1, the zero-order correlations of the two measures of nutritional status, the composite nutrition index, and the test-scores are presented. The R^2 values between these two variables and the psychological scores also are included.

In most cases, the correlations are statistically significant at the .05 or lower level. There are considerable variations in the magnitude of the correlations, by both psycholog-

ical score and by age-sex group. Values are consistently lower for boys at age three than for the other groups, possibly related to age-sex maturation differences.

The variations in the correlations of height and head circumference to the test scores is difficult to explain. Both are conventional measures that reflect nutritional status. Perhaps age-sex maturation patterns account for the differences. In any event, consistent with epidemiological studies of nutritional status and intellectual development, and the findings reported in our previous paper, there is a reasonably clear association between nutritional status and cognitive measures.

Social Factors and Cognitive Performance

Social-environmental factors, as well as nutritional status, are related to cognitive scores. In Table 2, the zero-order correlations are reported for the three individual measures—quality of house, mother's dress, and task instruction—and for the social factor index. In addition, the R^2 values are presented when the three individual measures are regressed on the test scores.

The social variables are significantly related to the psychological scores at the $p < .05$ level or lower in a number of instances. Only a few of the correlations between quality of house measure and the test scores are statistically significant. This social measure was a much better predictor of cognitive scores in the data reported on earlier.[15] The general direction of the correlations, however, is consistent enough to argue for a link between social-environmental differences and psychological performance. The relationship is most clear for the language measure.

Independent and Joint Contributions of Nutrition and Social Factors

As reported in studies primarily focused on *either* nutrition *or* social-environmental factors as explanatory variables, the INCAP data suggest that both domains of variables are related to psychological test performance. The issue is whether any general statement can be made about the unique contributions of nutritional status and social factors to mental development. Put another way, do the nutrition measures predict cognitive functioning after all the variance attributed to the social variables has been acknowledged, and vice-versa?

TABLE 1—Correlations between Nutritional Status and Cognitive Scores

Nutritional Measures	Cognitive Measures															
	Language				Memory				Perception				Cognitive Composite			
	3 yrs		4 yrs		3 yrs		4 yrs		3 yrs		4 yrs		3 yrs		4 yrs	
	M	F	M	F	M	F	M	F	M	F	M	F	M	F	M	F
Nutritional Index	.20**	.34**	.29**	.30**	.05	.31**	.06	.14*	.14*	.25**	.09	.14*	.17**	.39**	.26**	.30**
Height	.24**	.26**	.29**	.27**	.11	.28**	.14*	.18*	.13*	.19*	.11	.14*	.20**	.30**	.28**	.29**
Head Circumference	.10	.31**	.19**	.25**	−.01	.26**	−.04	.09	.11	.24**	.05	.11	.09	.36**	.15*	.09
Multiple R^2	.06**	.12**	.09**	.10**	.02*	.10**	.02*	.03**	.02*	.07**	.01	.02*	.04**	.16**	.08**	.08**

*P < .05
**P < .01

TABLE 2—Correlations between Social Measures and Cognitive Scores

	Cognitive Measures															
Social Measures	Language				Memory				Perception				Cognitive Composite			
	3 yrs		4 yrs		3 yrs		4 yrs		3 yrs		4 yrs		3 yrs		4 yrs	
	M	F	M	F	M	F	M	F	M	F	M	F	M	F	M	F
Social Factor Index	.22**	.12*	.21**	.25**	.15*	.08	.10	.10	.16**	.04	.08	.08	.23**	.10	.18**	.23**
House Quality	.08	.11	.06	.23**	.04	−.01	.05	.15*	.02	.02	−.06	.05	.05	.04	.04	.19**
Mother's Dress	.18**	.07	.22**	.19**	.15*	.06	.11	.10	.12*	.00	.16*	.07	.18**	.06	.22**	.19**
Task Instruction	.20**	.05	.19**	.12**	.12*	.05	.10	−.06	.18**	.01	.10	.03	.22**	.03	.16*	.10
Multiple R^2	.06**	.01*	.07**	.07	.03	.00	.02	.04*	.04*	.00	.04*	.00	.07*	.00	.06*	.06*

*P < .05
**P < .01

Multiple regressions were undertaken in which the social variables were forced in first, followed by the nutritional terms and the interactions between these measures. Likewise, in other regressions, the measures and the height × head circumference interaction were forced in first, followed by the social variables. The analysis was undertaken by the composite indices as well as by the separate variables.

In Table 3, we show the proportion of variance explained when the composite nutrition and social factor indices are regressed on the psychological measures. The total amount of variance explained tends to be somewhat lower when the composite indices are used instead of the separate variables. The results are substantially the same, however, and the use of the indices economizes on degrees of freedom.

In one-half of the regressions, the amount of variance explained by the nutrition index is statistically significant even when the social factor effects are first taken into account. When the procedure is reversed, the social factor index sometimes continues to explain a significant amount of variance, but primarily in the case of the language measure. The amount of variance explained by the social factor index is generally less than the nutritional measures.

These findings are consistent with the results reported in the earlier report. Further, there are differences by both age-sex group and cognitive domain. The earlier analysis was undertaken with the first 342 cases in the study, data were available for the memory and perception tests on slightly more than 200 children. Here, the size of the study group—over 500 children—and scores at two age-points provide strong evidence for the contribution of nutrition measures to cognitive performance, especially to language.

Impact of Supplementation

The data previously discussed make a substantial case for the view that inadequate nutrition is associated with lower cognitive performance. Statements of a causal nature, however, are risky from epidemiological data. Fortunately, the nutrition intervention is far enough along to use its results as supporting evidence of the identified relationships. In Table 4, the findings on supplementation and cognitive performance are shown. The variable labeled supplementation is the sum of calories consumed during pregnancy and the lactation of the tested child by the mother, added to calories consumed by the child up until each testing point. The analysis was also undertaken using only calories con-

TABLE 3—Proportion of Variance Explained by Nutrition and Social Factor Measures

	Cognitive Measures															
Factors	Language				Memory				Perception				Cognitive Composite			
	3 yrs		4 yrs		3 yrs		4 yrs		3 yrs		4 yrs		3 yrs		4 yrs	
	M	F	M	F	M	F	M	F	M	F	M	F	M	F	M	F
Nutrition Index Alone	.04**	.12**	.08**	.09**	.00	.09**	.00	.02*	.02*	.06**	.01	.02*	.03**	.15**	.07**	.09**
Social Factor Index Alone	.05**	.02*	.05**	.06**	.02*	.01	.01	.01	.03**	.00	.01	.01	.05**	.01	.03**	.05**
Nutrition and Social Indices Combined	.07**	.12**	.11**	.12**	.02*	.10**	.01	.03*	.04**	.06**	.01	.02	.06**	.15**	.08**	.11**
Nutrition Index with Social Factor Index First Removed	.02*	.11**	.06**	.06**	.00	.03*	.00	.02	.01	.00	.00	.00	.02	.05**	.05**	.06**
Social Factor Index with Nutrition Index First Removed	.03**	.00	.03**	.04**	.02	.00	.01	.01	.02*	.00	.00	.00	.03**	.00	.01	.02*

*P < .05
**P < .01

TABLE 4—Amount of Variance Explained by Supplementation, Social Factors, and Nutrition

Factors	Cognitive Measures															
	Language				Memory				Perception				Cognitive Composite			
	3 yrs		4 yrs		3 yrs		4 yrs		3 yrs		4 yrs		3 yrs		4 yrs	
	M	F	M	F	M	F	M	F	M	F	M	F	M	F	M	F
Supplementation only	.02*	.01	.02*	.02*	.00	.03*	.00	.00	.01	.00	.00	.00	.00	.01	.01	.01
Supplementation with Social Factor Index Removed	.03**	.01	.03*	.03*	.00	.03*	.00	.00	.01	.00	.00	.01	.01	.01	.01	.01

*P < .05
**P < .01

sumed by the mother during pregnancy and lactation. Results are the same and this variable is not shown. As discussed elsewhere,[18] the INCAP results suggest that adequate nutrition of pregnant and lactating mothers, rather than the direct supplementation of children after weaning, may be the more important determinant of differences in young children's cognitive performance. Supplementation of young children, however, may be beneficial in terms of current and future health status and physical growth.

The data have their weaknesses. Ideally, it would be desirable to have measures of home diet-intake as well. Although home nutrition surveys are regularly undertaken, they are not precise enough for family members for use here. They do provide evidence that the interventions are "true supplementations" and do not substitute for food normally eaten by the children. Also, since over one-half of the children were born before the study started, many mothers in the study group were not exposed to the intervention while pregnant and lactating, and some one-quarter of the children were similarly unexposed to supplementation during early life.

Nevertheless, the results are encouraging from an intervention standpoint. Out of the 16 estimates of variance explained that are presented in the first line of Table 4, four are significant at the .05 level and five others are greater than zero. In all cases, the values are accounted for by direct relationships between nutritional status and test scores. The social factor index, however, is negatively related to the supplementation measure, although not always significantly. The direction of the relationships between the social factor index and the supplementation measure suggests that the "needier" children are benefiting most from the supplementation program. Removing the variance explained by the social factor index first, in some cases, raises the amount of variance explained by supplementation. With the social factor index removed first, 11 out of 16 times there are direct relationships between the amount of supplement ingested and cognitive test scores. These direct relationships account for all of the values greater than zero that are shown in the second line of Table 4.

In this analysis, the composite social and nutritional indices were employed to preserve degrees of freedom. Results are similar when the individual nutrition and social measures are employed. Although the amount of variance explained by the supplement is small, the findings lend support for the causal character of the relationship between nutrition and cognitive development.

Limitations of the Study

A number of criticisms can be addressed at this analysis. We are aware of the validity problems surrounding the variables selected. Even though there were strenuous efforts to develop reliable variables, some unreliability remains in both the social and psychological measures. As noted, however, adjusting the correlation coefficients by the estimated reliability of these measures does not substantially change the findings. We recognize that many of the measures are metrically inelegant and we have not met all of the statistical assumptions required for some of the analyses performed. Additional indices of either nutrition and growth of social characteristics could have been included and may have modified the findings. Moreover, the two nutrition variables are not sensitive indices of the severity, duration, or age at onset of nutritional insult. The nutritional heterogeneity of the groups may account for some of the irregularities of the findings. Finally, the association may not be sustained as children approach adulthood. Rather, nutritional condition may simply postpone cognitive development temporarily.

Nevertheless, the analysis suggests that supplementation of pregnant and lactating mothers and young children is related to the latters' pre-school cognitive performance, and it is reasonable to suggest that the relationship is causal. The amount of variance explained by the nutrition measures is not always substantial, but consistent with the magnitudes of findings of most social-epidemiological investigations. Indeed, it is a fair assertion that given more reliable measures, and ones with better metric properties, the variance explained might be larger. Further, although we present only the results for three psychological variables and a composite score, the findings are generally consistent when other cognitive test measures are used as the dependent variables.

Finally, it is puzzling that the effect of nutrition is greater for a nondynamic cognitive variable like size of vocabulary than it is for memory, which requires focused attention and cognitive strategies. Indeed, supplementation or the nutritional index, with social class removed, made a minimal contribution to memory or perceptual analysis. A child's vocabulary knowledge is the cognitive variable that consistently shows the highest correlation with social class of family—across cultures and time. It is also the best single correlate of the total IQ on intelligence tests which sample a variety of cognitive talents. Hence, the fact that vocabulary correlates best with nutrition indicates that vocabulary is either an extremely sensitive index of the quality of cognitive functioning or that social-cultural differences not captured by our social factor index, but nevertheless linked to cognitive performance, accounts for the high vocabulary score for the physically larger children.

Implications

The findings presented strongly suggest that calorie intake affects cognitive development as well as physical growth and general health status. There are a number of plausible explanations for the results. Either a lack of adequate total calories or a deficiency of protein may impede the development of the neurological system. Another hypothesis is that the poorly nourished child, pre- and post-partum, has insufficient energy to take advantage of opportunities for social contacts and learning. Finally, it may be that adults and older children treat the larger child as a more mature individual, which leads to increased social learning opportunities. Clearly, the state of knowledge, as Evans and associates have noted,[5] in neither the nutritional nor the social sciences is sufficient to suggest a single, primary explanation.

It bears emphasis that the findings do not diminish social environmental explanations of difference in cognitive functioning. The generally persistent correlations between the social factor variables and cognitive functioning support the reasonableness of various views on the consequences of deficient family milieux. Moreover, the fairly systematic findings on the amounts of variance explained by nutritional and social measures from one cognitive dimension to the next suggest that the social and nutritional inputs into a child's life have different magnitudes of importance in determining performance on various cognitive dimensions.

At the same time, it is important to note that at least in rural Guatemala nutrition intervention programs are relatively easy to implement in comparison to most other social action efforts. In terms of the human and economic resources required for broad-scale, sustained social milieu interventions, and the political and cultural barriers to their rapid implementation, there is sound reason to stress nutrition intervention efforts in the formulation of social and community development policies for rural Guatemala and perhaps for other lesser-developed countries as well.

REFERENCES

1. Cabak, V., and Najdanvic, R. Effect of undernutrition in early life on physical and mental development. Archives of Disease in Childhood 40:532–534, 1965.
2. Cravioto, J., DeLicardie, E. R., and Birch, H. G. Nutrition, growth and neurointegrative development: An experimental and ecologic study. Pediatrics 38:319–372, 1966.
3. Monckeberg, F. Effects of Early Marasmic Malnutrition on Subsequent Physical and Psychological Development. In Malnutrition, Learning and Behavior, edited by Scrimshaw, N. S., and Gordon, J. E., pp. 269–278. M.I.T. Press, Cambridge, 1968.
4. Stoch, M. B., and Smythe, P. M. Undernutrition During Infancy and Subsequent Brain Growth in Intellectual Development. In Malnutrition, Learning and Behavior, edited by Scrimshaw, N. S., and Gordon, J. E. M.I.T. Press, Boston, pp. 278–289, 1968.
5. Evans, D. E., Moodie, A. D., and Hansen, J. D. L. Kwashiorkor and intellectual development. S. A. Medical Journal 45:1413–1426, 1971.
6. Chase, H. P., Lindsley, W. F. B., and O'Brian, D. Undernutrition and cerebellar development. Nature 221:554–555, 1969.
7. Dobbing, J. Effects of Experimental Undernutrition on the Development of the Nervous System. In Malnutrition, Learning and Behavior, edited by Scrimshaw, N. S., and Gordon, J. E. M.I.T. Press, Boston, pp. 181–203, 1968.
8. Barnes, R. H., Moore, A. U., and Pond, W. G. Behavioral abnormalities in young adult pigs caused by malnutrition in early life. J. Nutrition 100:149–155, 1970.
9. Dobbing, J., and Smart, J. L. Clinics in Development Medicine. Heinemann Radical Publications, London, 1972.
10. Béhar, M. Prevalence of Malnutrition among Preschool Children in Developing Countries. In Malnutrition, Learning and Behavior, edited by Scrimshaw, N. S., and Gordon, J. E. M.I.T. Press, Boston, p. 30, 1968.
11. Jelliffe, D. B. The Assessment of Nutritional Status of the Community. World Health Organization, Geneva, 1966.
12. U.S. Department of Health, Education, and Welfare, National Center for Health Statistics. Height and Weight of Children: Socioeconomic Status. Vital and Health Statistics, Series 11, No. 119, DHEW Publication No. (HSM) 73–1601, 1972.
13. Birch, H. G. Malnutrition, learning and intelligence. Am. J. Public Health 62:773–784, 1972.
14. Hertzig, M. E., Birch, H. G., Thomas, A., and Mendez, O. A. Class and Ethnic Differences in the Responsiveness of Preschool Children to Cognitive Demands. Monographs of SRCD 33:(Serial No. 117), 1968.
15. Klein, R. E., Freeman, H. E., Kagan, J., Yarbrough, C., and Habicht, J-P. Is big smart? The relation of growth to cognition. J. Health and Social Behavior 13:219–225, 1972.
16. McKay, H. E., McKay, A. C., and Sinisterra, L. Behavioral Effects of Nutritional Recuperation and Programmed Stimulation of Moderately Malnourished Preschool Age Children. Paper presented at the Meeting of the American Association for the Advancement of Science Symposium, 1969.
17. Mora, J. O., Amezquita, A., Castro, L., and associates. Nutrition and social factors related to intellectual performance. World Review of Nutrition and Dietetics 19:205–236, 1974.
18. Klein, R. E., Lester, B. M., Yarbrough, C., and Habicht, J-P. On Malnutrition and Mental Development: Some Preliminary Findings. In Nutrition, edited by Chavez, A., Bourges, H., and Basta, S., Vol. 2, pp. 315–321. S. Karger Basel, Switzerland, 1975.
19. Mejia-Pivaral, V. Características Economicas y Socio-culturales de Cuatro Aldeas Ladinas de Guatemala. Guatemala Indigena. Vol. VII, No. 3. Instituto Indigenista Nacional, Guatemala, 1972.
20. Yarbrough, C., Habicht, J-P., Martorell, R., and Klein, R. E. Physical Anthropology and Mild to Moderate Malnutrition: A Definition of the Problem. Wenner-Gren Foundation/Fels Research Institute, NY, 1974.
21. Berry, J. W., and Dasen, P. R. Culture and Cognition: Readings in Cross-Cultural Psychology. Methuen and Co. Ltd., London, 1974.

ACKNOWLEDGMENTS

The data for this study are drawn from the Guatemalan growth and development project by Contract N01-HD-5-0640 of the National Institute of Child Health and Human Development, N.I.H. This investigation is part of a program of collaborative research and Uniform Measures of Social Competence by H. E. Freeman, J. Kagan, R. E. Klein, and A. K. Romney and is supported by the National Science Foundation (Grant GS-33047) and the Grant Foundation.

29

CORONARY ARTERY SURGERY:
THE USE OF DECISION ANALYSIS

By

STEPHEN G. PAUKER

In treating patients with coronary heart disease, most physicians are confronted with having to make decisions without the support of reliable and comprehensive data. In light of this, Stephen G. Pauker proposes combining medical knowledge and patient's preference in order to determine treatment. As a consequence of this mutual process, the physician is aided in making a responsible medical decision and the patient is better informed about his condition and its possible outcomes.

From Stephen G. Pauker, "Coronary Artery Surgery: The Use of Decision Analysis." *Annals of Internal Medicine*, 1976, *85*(1), 8-18.

The choice between coronary by-pass surgery and medical therapy in patients with angiographically documented coronary artery disease was examined. This decision analysis included consideration of patient preferences, severity of disease, prognosis with medical therapy, surgical mortality rate, graft patency rate, the probability that surgery will provide both short-term and long-term pain relief, and the probability that surgery will alter long-term survival. Coronary surgery was found to be the preferred therapy in many patients with disabling angina; it was rarely found to be the preferred therapy in asymptomatic patients, even those with proximal obstruction of the left anterior descending coronary artery. The therapeutic decision was strongly affected by differences in patient attitudes and differences in the past results of the prospective surgeon. This paper presents both a data base and a methodology that allow the physician to apply decision analysis to individual patients with coronary artery disease.

THE PHYSICIAN IS A DECISION-MAKER: given a patient with coronary artery disease, he must decide between coronary by-pass surgery and conservative medical therapy. This complex decision involves balancing the risk of operative complications against the potential long-term benefits of decreased disability and increased life expectancy.

In contrast, some clinical decisions are straightforward and require little analysis. For example, given a patient with probable acute appendicitis, the physician usually can elect laparotomy with impunity because the risks are low and the potential benefits are high (1). Except in extraordinary circumstances, the decision does not depend strongly upon the surgeon's skill or the patient's desires.

Unfortunately, such is not the case with coronary artery surgery, where pain relief (at least in the short run) is highly likely, but where operative risks are significant and where long-term benefits on life expectancy and pain relief remain unproved. Thus in an individual patient, the selection of optimal therapy is not straightforward; consequently, both the skill of the prospective surgeon and the preferences of the individual patient may strongly influence the choice of therapy.

Such complex clinical problems can, however, be ap-

► From the Department of Medicine (Cardiology) and the Clinical Decision Making Group, New England Medical Center Hospital and Tufts University School of Medicine; Boston, Massachusetts; and the Clinical Decision Making Group, Laboratory for Computer Science, Massachusetts Institute of Technology; Cambridge, Massachusetts.

proached through *decision analysis* (1-9). Briefly, this technique includes consideration of all possible outcomes of therapy, both the probability of each outcome and the utility, or the relative worth, of each outcome. These probabilities and utilities are then combined to determine which therapeutic option can be expected to be of greater value to the patient.

This paper illustrates how decision analysis can be used as an aid in the management of individual patients with chronic ischemic heart disease. The first step in using this technique was to formulate a model of prognosis. This formulation encompassed much of the published data about prognosis, both with medical management alone and with coronary by-pass surgery. This prognostic model was then used to determine the optimal therapy for a spectrum of patients with differing severities of coronary artery disease and with differing attitudes about the utility of each possible outcome.

This analysis required many *explicit* assumptions about prognosis and patient preferences. Any rational decision-making process must, however, involve similar assumptions, although perhaps implicitly. Although some controlled studies of prognosis after by-pass surgery are now in progress, the physician cannot wait until those data are available: patients present with coronary disease *now* and by-pass surgery is available now. Thus the physician must consider that mode of therapy for these patients. Although any analysis of the surgical therapy of coronary disease would be more convincing if detailed data were available, this study deals with the spectrum of available prognostic data and suggests which therapeutic choices are best in the light of the current uncertain data. If a physician disagrees with the values chosen in this study, he can still use this technique by substituting the values that he prefers.

The Problem Stated

Consider a patient with known coronary artery disease. Three main variables determine the value of by-pass surgery: [1] the prognosis with medical therapy, which is largely dependent upon the severity of the patient's coronary disease and upon his ventricular function, [2] the potential short-term and long-term surgical results, including the operative risks, and [3] the patient's preferences (how he views the relative importance of pain relief and life expectancy). The first two factors affect the likelihoods of the various outcomes, while the last influences the relative desirability of the outcomes.

In this analysis, patients were divided into four categories of disease severity. In addition, based on past operative results, the prospective surgical teams were divided into three groups, giving a total of 12 clinical cohorts. Patient preferences were also grouped into four types; thus, a total of 48 situations were considered. These situations are not meant to encompass all patients with coronary artery disease, but rather they constitute a set of prototypical analyses. Furthermore, using the techniques outlined later in this paper, the physician can apply decision analysis to individual patients with coronary artery disease (*see* Appendix).

SEVERITY OF DISEASE

Coronary anatomy was classified as "good" if there was a coronary arterial obstruction that occluded more than 75% of the lumen of the vessel, if the lesion was surgically accessible and if distal run-off was good. It was termed "fair" if there were distal lesions and if run-off was marginal. A separate category ("LAD") described a lesion in the left anterior descending coronary artery, proximal to the first septal perforating branch, with good distal run-off and with disease elsewhere in the coronary tree. Ventricular function was labelled "good" if the ejection fraction was above 40% and "fair" if it was between 25% and 40%.

This study considered patients with [1] "good" anatomy and "good" ventricular function, [2] "fair" anatomy and "good" ventricular function, [3] "good" anatomy and "fair" ventricular function, and [4] "LAD" anatomy and "good" ventricular function. For the purposes of exposition, it was assumed that patients in the first three categories had disabling angina, refractory to medical therapy, whereas patients in the fourth category ("LAD") were asymptomatic*.

MEDICAL THERAPY

The severity of the patient's disease dictates the natural history (the course without surgery, but with optimal medical therapy). Data about prognosis with medical therapy were derived from published reports (10-20). The frequencies of spontaneous regression and reappearance of disabling angina were derived from the opinions of experienced cardiologists, because such information was not available in the literature.

SURGICAL THERAPY

Although the probabilities of the various outcomes after surgery depend upon the extent of the patient's disease, they are also a function of the previous results *of the prospective surgical team*. Consideration of both the short-term and the long-term post-operative course, derived from published data (11, 12, 16, 21-30), allowed classification of previous results into three types: [1] "excellent," [2] "good," and [3] "average" results.

PATIENT PREFERENCES

The *utility*, or relative worth, of each outcome is deter-

---

* An unusually high mortality rate is associated with proximal obstruction of the left anterior descending coronary artery. Therefore, relatively asymptomatic patients with this lesion may be candidates for by-pass surgery.

mined by the preferences of the patient. This analysis was limited to two dimensions of preference: [1] length of life and [2] quality of life. The quality of life was determined by the presence or absence of disabling angina and by the pain and suffering necessitated by coronary by-pass surgery.

In dealing with issues such as death and chronic disability, many people prefer a *guaranteed* moderately good outcome to a gamble on either a very good or a very poor result. These patients are termed *risk-averse* (2, 7, 31, 32). For such a risk-averse patient, the utility of having "pain for 2½ years" *for certain* is *greater* than the utility of an even chance at "5 years with pain" and "5 years free of pain." Thus for risk-averse patient "a bird in hand is worth two in the bush."

If one tabulates an individual's utility for a variety of outcomes, one generates a *utility function*, which, in the case of ischemic heart disease, might be a function of length of life and freedom from pain. A graph of the utility function of a risk-averse individual (vide infra) is convex when viewed from above, that is, as explained previously, the utility of any guaranteed outcome is *greater* than the utility of an even chance at a better or a worse outcome (which corresponds to the average of the utilities for two such points on the curve). Previous studies (7) have shown that risk-averse utility functions can be approximated by an exponential of the form: Utility $= k_0 (1 - e^{-k_1 \text{time}})$. Constant k_0 is arbitrary and is used for purposes of scaling. Constant k_1 is positive and increasing it corresponds to increasing the degree of risk-aversion. People concerned with life expectancy have been shown to be more risk-averse than those concerned with disability alone (for example, $k_1 = 3$ versus $k_1 = 1$, respectively).

This study divided patient preferences into four groups: two extreme types of preference and two intermediate types. The patient preferences considered were [1] Type "Pain," patients who were primarily concerned with time free of *pain* and chronic disability, [2] Type "Life," patients who were primarily concerned with length of life, [3] Type "Either," patients in whom *either* time free of pain or increased life expectancy was important and who would accept increased time free of pain at the cost of decreased life expectancy and vice versa, and [4] Type "Both," patients in whom *both* these factors were of such importance that pain relief was not acceptable unless life expectancy was also increased and vice versa.

Methods

The first step in this analysis was to construct a *decision tree* that contained all the relevent outcomes of the problem. For simplicity, "quality of life" was considered in only two states: "Pain" (chronic disabling angina) and "NoPain."

THE DECISION TREE

A tree for chronic ischemic heart disease is shown in Figure 1. The square node denotes the decision at hand (to do coronary by-pass surgery or to use medical therapy alone); the circular nodes denote chance happenings, that is, occurrences not under the direct control of the physician. If surgery is elected, perioperative death may occur or the patient may survive surgery. After operation the patient may be improved (NoPain) or may remain disabled (Pain). All surviving pa-

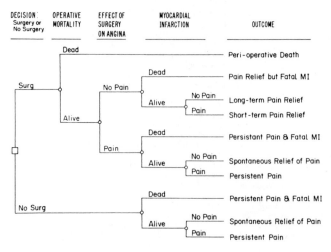

Figure 1. Decision Tree for chronic coronary artery disease. The decision between surgical and medical therapy is denoted by a square node. The circular nodes denote chance occurrences. Fatal MI refers to the occurrence of a fatal myocardial infarction during the time horizon under consideration.

DECISION: Surgery or No Surgery
OPERATIVE MORTALITY
EFFECT OF SURGERY ON ANGINA
MYOCARDIAL INFARCTION
OUTCOME

Surg — Dead — Peri-operative Death

Alive — No Pain — Dead — Pain Relief but Fatal MI

Alive — No Pain — Long-term Pain Relief

Pain — Short-term Pain Relief

Pain — Dead — Persistant Pain & Fatal MI

Alive — No Pain — Spontaneous Relief of Pain

Pain — Persistent Pain

No Surg — Dead — Persistent Pain & Fatal MI

Alive — No Pain — Spontaneous Relief of Pain

Pain — Persistent Pain

tients are subject to subsequent myocardial infarction, which may result in death or which may alter their pain status. Survivors may be pain free or may be disabled.

If one considers a time horizon of 2 years and the possibility of a single myocardial infarction (MI) occurring at the end of Year 1, then the first outcome implies immediate death, whereas outcomes "Pain Relief but Fatal MI" and "Persistent Pain and Fatal MI" imply 1-year survival. The other outcomes denote survival for at least 2 years and varying periods of time free of pain.

Figure 1 is, however, a schematic representation of only a portion of the tree analyzed in this study. It depicts only one myocardial infarction. The tree actually used in this study contained five possible myocardial infarctions, one for each year considered, and thus contained many more branches*.

PROBABILITIES OF OUTCOMES

Table 1 summarizes the data upon which this prognostic model was based. It gives the probabilities of the outcomes for each chance event. Each column corresponds to one combination of coronary anatomy, ventricular function, and past surgical results.

To simplify this analysis, the following assumptions were made: [1] no more than one myocardial infarction occurs each year; [2] late failures (Surg → NoPain → Pain) occur at the graft closure rate (although the late reappearance of pain relates to both graft closure and disease progression, it was assumed that the graft closure *rate* approximates the *rate* of reappearance of pain); [3] the spontaneous disappearance of pain occurs with the same frequency in surgically treated (Surg → Pain → NoPain) and medically treated (No Surg → No Pain) patients; [4] successful surgery increases survival only if the graft remains patent†; [5] early or late surgical failures decrease survival, because they have adverse effects on the coronary circulation (33); [6] the rates of the spontaneous disappearance and reappearance of pain are constant from year to year; and [7] reoperation after graft closure is not considered.

* Detailed analysis has shown that the larger tree can be *approximated* by the simple 10-branch tree with little error. Thus the tree shown in Figure 1 can be used in tailoring the decision to individual patients (*see* Appendix).
† This assumption is examined in detail in the sensitivity analysis presented in Table 3C, below.

VALUES OF THE OUTCOMES

Figure 2 summarizes the utility function for each type of patient considered. For each patient the scale is arbitrary: the conclusions of this analysis do not depend on the scale chosen. The time horizon is limited to 5 years. These utility functions are based on the exponential equation described above. For Type "Pain" patients, the position on the utility curve is determined by the number of years free of pain, while for Type "Life" patients it is determined by survival. For Type "Pain" patients (whose main concern is freedom from pain) the function is only slightly curved ($k_1 = 1$), whereas for the more risk-averse Type "Life" patients (whose main concern is survival) the function is sharply curved ($k_1 = 3$). Thus, as shown in Figure 2, an outcome with survival for 3 years, 2 of which were free of pain, would have a utility of 52 for Type "Pain" patients but a utility of 88 for Type "Life" patients. For Types "Either" and "Both" patients, the particular line on each graph is determined by the survival while the position on that line is determined by the number of years of freedom from pain. Because Type "Either" patients were concerned with *either* pain relief or increased life expectancy, their utilities were obtained by simply averaging the utilities of Types "Pain" and "Life" for the same outcome. Thus, for the outcome with 3-year survival, 2 of which were free of pain, the utility for Type "Either" patients would be $(52 + 88)/2$ or 70. In contrast, Type "Both" patients valued *both* factors and would assign a low utility to an outcome with either short survival or little time free of pain. Because it is a property of the geometric average of two numbers that if either number is small the average is small‡, the utilities for Type "Both" patients were obtained by a geometric average of the utilities of Types "Pain" and "Life." Thus for the outcome with 3-year survival, 2 of which are free of pain, the utility for Type "Both" patients would be $(52 \times 88)^{1/2}$ or 68.

In the immediate postoperative period, patients experience *increased* pain and disability. Thus patients concerned with pain must assign slightly less utility to the outcomes associated with surgery, compared with similar outcomes reached by medical therapy. This analysis considered the *cost of surgery* by subtracting 1 year from the "time free of pain" for each surgical outcome. Thus an outcome whereby patients underwent

‡ For example, the geometric average of 1 and 100 is $(1 \times 100)^{1/2}$ or 10, in contrast to the simple average which is $(1 + 100)/2$ or 50.5.

Table 1. Probabilities of Chance Events*

Coronary Anatomy Ventricular Function Past Surgical Results	Disabling Angina									Asymptomatic		
	Good Good Exc	Good Good Good	Good Good Avg	Fair Good Exc	Fair Good Good	Fair Good Avg	Good Fair Exc	Good Fair Good	Good Fair Avg	LAD Good Exc	LAD Good Good	LAD Good Avg
Outcome												
Surgery												
Operative mortality	0.01	0.03	0.06	0.02	0.06	0.12	0.04	0.12	0.24	0.02	0.04	0.08
Operative success with pain cure	0.90	0.85	0.80	0.80	0.70	0.60	0.88	0.80	0.70	0.95	0.90	0.85
Graft closure year	0.05	0.10	0.15	0.10	0.20	0.30	0.07	0.15	0.25	0.05	0.05	0.15
Annual mortality with patent graft	0.04	0.04	0.04	0.07	0.07	0.07	0.12	0.12	0.12	0.05	0.05	0.05
Annual mortality with closed graft	0.07	0.07	0.07	0.12	0.12	0.12	0.18	0.18	0.18	0.12	0.12	0.12
Spontaneous pain cure year	0.03	0.03	0.03	0.02	0.02	0.02	0.03	0.03	0.03	0.03	0.03	0.03
Spontaneous pain recurrence year	0.04	0.04	0.04	0.04	0.04	0.04	0.04	0.04	0.04	0.04	0.04	0.04
Natural history												
Annual mortality	0.05	0.05	0.05	0.10	0.10	0.10	0.15	0.15	0.15	0.10	0.10	0.10
Spontaneous pain cure year	0.03	0.03	0.03	0.02	0.02	0.02	0.03	0.03	0.03	0.03	0.03	0.03
Spontaneous pain occurrence year	0.04	0.04	0.04	0.04	0.04	0.04	0.04	0.04	0.04	0.04	0.04	0.04

* LAD = proximal obstruction of the left anterior descending coronary artery. Exc = excellent, Avg = average.

surgery and survived 4 years, all of which were pain-free, was assigned the utility of a 4-year survival, 3 years of which were pain free.

The Assessment of Utilities: Rather than use the prototypical utility functions shown in Figure 2, one can debrief *individuals* of their own preferences (2, 7, 31). Consider three possible outcomes: [1] "immediate death," [2] "5 years of life with severe pain," and [3] "2½ years of life without pain." The patient is first asked to choose the best and the worst of these alternatives, *for him.* Assume that he chooses "immediate death" as the worst and "2½ years of life without pain," as the best. Arbitrarily assign a utility of zero to "immediate death" (U$_{worst outcome}$), and a utility of 100 to "2½ years without pain" (U$_{best outcome}$). What remains is to assign a value to the outcome of "5 years of life with severe pain" (U$_{unassigned outcome}$), which is consistent with the values assigned to the other outcomes.

In using this techique, the physician explains that there exists an imaginary game such that if the patient wins the game he will be *guaranteed* "2½ years without pain" (the best outcome), whereas if he loses the game he will be *guaranteed* "immediate death" (the worst outcome). Now suppose the game were an "even money bet," that is, a probability of 0.5 of either winning or losing. The patient is asked whether he would prefer to take his chances with the game or take a *guaranteed* outcome of "5 years of pain" (the unassigned outcome). If he prefers the game, he is then asked what he would do if the probability of winning the game were only 0.25. If he then prefers "5 years of pain," he is asked what he would do if the probability of winning the game were 0.4. By such successive approximations, it is possible to find a *point of indifference,* where the patient cannot choose between the game and the unassigned outcome.

Given this indifference point one can now assign a *consistent* utility to the unassigned outcome. If the odds of winning the game were P, at this point of indifference, then U$_{unassigned outcome}$ is [P(U$_{best outcome}$) + (1-P) U$_{worst outcome}$]. Because U$_{worst outcome}$ was chosen to be zero, and U$_{best outcome}$ to be 100, one has that U$_{unassigned outcome}$ = 100P. For example, if the patient's indifference point were 0.3, then the utility of "5 years of pain" would be 30. By repeatedly applying this technique, one can assign a consistent utility to each outcome.

ANALYSIS

The relative worths of surgical and medical therapy were determined for all combinations of the 12 situations in Table 1 and the four utility structures in Figure 2. The time horizon for the analysis was 5 years. The tree included 190 end states, 127 surgical, and 63 medical*. The "expected value of surgical

* Each survivor was considered to be subject annually to myocardial infarction.

therapy" (EV$_{surg}$) and the "expected value of medical therapy" (EV$_{No surg}$) were calculated by multiplying the probability of each end position by the utility of that end position and summing over all end positions possible for that therapy (*see* Appendix).

Decision theory states that one should select the therapy that has the larger expected value (1-5, 7)‡. The difference between the expected values of surgical and medical therapy is a measure of the degree to which surgery is preferable. Thus

‡ Actually the larger expected utility.

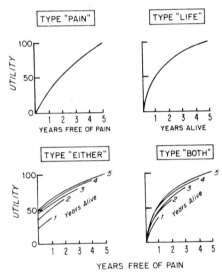

YEARS FREE OF PAIN

Figure 2. Utility curves for the four patient types considered. Types "Pain" and "Life" consider only a single factor. The Type "Life" curve is steeper (more risk-averse) than the Type "Pain" curve. Types "Either" and "Both" consider both freedom from pain and survival. For each of these latter types, the choice of line is determined by the survival and the position on the line is determined by the number of years free of pain.

Table 2. Benefits of Surgery and Expected Values*

	Disabling Angina									Asymptomatic		
Anat	Good	Good	Good	Fair	Fair	Fair	Good	Good	Good	LAD	LAD	LAD
Funct	Good	Good	Good	Good	Good	Good	Fair	Fair	Fair	Good	Good	Good
Surg	Exc	Good	Avg	Exc	Good	Avg	Exc	Good	Avg	Exc	Good	Avg
Patient type†												
Pain												
	58.2‡	47.4	37.9	43.8	28.5	17.1	44.2	30.0	16.7	−15.7	−26.5	−36.6
	64.0§	53.3	43.7	47.2	31.9	20.5	48.5	34.3	21.0	80.8	80.8	80.8
Life												
	−0.4‡	−2.5	−5.6	−0.3	−4.6	−10.5	−1.9	−9.4	−20.5	1.9	−0.4	−4.6
	95.4§	95.4	95.4	91.1	91.1	91.1	87.0	87.0	87.0	93.0	91.1	91.1
Either												
	28.9‡	22.5	16.1	21.8	12.0	3.3	21.1	10.3	−1.9	−6.9	−13.4	−20.6
	79.5§	73.1	66.7	69.0	59.2	50.5	66.8	55.9	45.7	85.9	85.9	85.9
Both												
	63.9‡	53.5	43.9	50.2	34.5	22.0	50.6	35.7	21.0	−12.3	−22.8	−33.2
	71.4§	61.0	51.4	54.6	38.9	26.4	56.2	41.3	26.6	85.2	85.2	85.2

* The time horizon is 5 years and the cost of surgery is equivalent to 1 year of disabling angina. Anat = coronary anatomy, Funct = ventricular function, Surg = past surgical results; LAD = proximal obstruction of the left anterior descending coronary artery, Exc = excellent, Avg = average.
† Patient Type = type of patient preferences (utilities); Type "Pain" is concerned with freedom from pain; Type "Life" is concerned with life expectancy; Types "Either" and "Both" are concerned with both. For details, see text.
‡ The first number is the benefit of surgery (EV$_{Surg}$—EV$_{NoSurg}$), where EV$_{Surg}$ is the expected value of surgery and where EV$_{NoSurg}$ is the expected value of medical therapy; a positive benefit implies that surgery is preferable, whereas a negative benefit implies that medical therapy is preferable.
§ The second number is the expected value of the better choice.

this difference (EV$_{Surg}$—EV$_{NoSurg}$) is the net *benefit* (1) of surgery. Since the utility curves (Figure 2) are not linear, more information is conveyed by considering both the "benefit of surgery" and the expected value of the optimum therapy for each situation*.

Because the data used in this analysis have not been firmly established by controlled studies, the model was then examined to determine the effect on the decision of changes in some of the probabilities in Table 1. Parameters examined in this *sensitivity analysis* (1, 2) included [1] the operative success rate, [2] the graft closure rate, [3] the mortality rate with a patent graft, and [4] the spontaneous pain cure rate. Finally, the model was examined for the effect on the decision of changes in the cost of surgery, the time horizon considered, and the amount of detail represented in the decision tree.

Results

Table 2 presents the benefit of surgery and the expected value of the better decision for each of the 48 analyses. The twelve columns correspond to the different medical cohorts, whereas the four rows correspond to different patient preferences. The upper number for each analysis is the "benefit" of surgery, while the lower number is the expected value of optimal therapy in that situation. If the benefit of surgery is positive, surgery is the preferred therapy; whereas if it is negative, medical therapy is preferable.

The preferred therapy for Type "Pain" patients (who cared most about pain relief) was surgery, except when they were asymptomatic. The better choice for Type "Life" patients (who cared most about life expectancy) was medical therapy, except when they had "LAD" disease with "good" ventricular function and the past results of the

* Consider two situations in which the "benefit of surgery" is 1 additional year of pain-free survival. In the first situation assume that medical therapy offers an expected survival of 20 years, whereas surgical therapy offers an expected survival of 21 years; in the second situation assume that medical therapy offers an expected survival of 6 months and surgical therapy offers an expected survival of 18 months. Although the "benefit of surgery" is the same in both situations, the two situations are clearly different; a surgical procedure might be more readily chosen in the latter situation than in the former.

prospective surgical team were "excellent." Although the better therapy for Type "Either" and "Both" patients was, in general, surgery if they were symptomatic, the better therapy for Type "Either" patients was medical therapy when ventricular function was only "fair" and the past results of the surgical team were only "average."

In every situation Type "Pain" patients had the lowest expected values and Type "Life" patients had the highest. With the exception of the Type "Life" patients, the asymptomatic patients with "LAD" disease had higher expected values than did the symptomatic patients. The "good" anatomy, "fair" function cohort, and the "fair" anatomy, "good" function cohort had similar expected values.

SENSITIVITY ANALYSES

Figure 3 shows the concept of the *threshold* (1) probability, that is, the probability where the expected values of the two treatments were equal. The expected values of medical and surgical therapy were plotted against the variable being analyzed. At the point where the expected values are equal the threshold, there is indifference between the therapies. To the left of the threshold surgery is preferable, while to the right of the threshold medical therapy is preferred.

Table 3 shows the results of four sensitivity analyses. For each variable analyzed, the table contains the threshold probability at which EV$_{Surg}$ equals EV$_{NoSurg}$. The term "Any" implies surgery was preferable for any value of the variable, whereas the term "None" implies medical therapy was preferable for all values. For comparison, the corresponding probabilities contained in Table 1 are displayed in the row labelled "Base." Those clinical settings where the threshold probability was within 0.25 (an arbitrary value chosen for clarity of exposition) of the "Base" probability (and hence where revised data might be expected to influence the decision) are italicized in Table 3.

Operative Success Rate: Part A of Table 3 shows the threshold operative success rates, *above* which surgery was the preferred therapy. For Types "Pain" and "Both" patients these threshold success rates were quite low ($P =$ 0.03 to 0.09), if the patient was symptomatic. These thresholds reflected the low likelihood of a spontaneous cure of disabling angina and the importance of pain relief to these patients. For Type "Life" symptomatic patients medical therapy was preferable, except when there was "fair" anatomy, "good" ventricular function, "excellent" past surgical results, and almost a guaranteed ($P = 0.89$) operative success. For symptomatic Type "Either" patients, thresholds were intermediate.

For asymptomatic patients, medical therapy was uniformly preferable, except for the Type "Life" patient (concerned mainly with life expectancy), and even those thresholds were high.

Graft Closure Rate: Part B of Table 3 shows the threshold graft closure rates *below* which surgery would be preferable. With the exception of Type "Life" patients, surprisingly high thresholds were found for symptomatic patients. These thresholds again reflected the low likelihood of spontaneous pain cure and the high benefit of even short-term pain cure to severely disabled patients.

Mortality Rate with Patent Graft: Part C of Table 3 shows the threshold annual mortalities *below* which surgery was preferable. Interestingly, for all symptomatic patients except for Type "Life," the threshold mortalities shown here were above the natural history mortalities. Not surprisingly, patients concerned with relief of pain would be expected to accept an increased mortality to obtain pain cure. For Type "Life" patients annual mortality might be lowered to acceptable levels with "excellent" surgery if the patients were symptomatic, but might be acceptable with either "excellent" or "good" surgery if the patients had a highly lethal ("LAD") lesion. In many settings, the base and threshold probabilities were within 0.25 of each other, and consequently, the corresponding decisions were sensitive to changes in the mortality rate with a patent graft.

Spontaneous Pain Cure: Part D of Table 3 presents the threshold natural history pain cure rates *below* which surgery was preferable. These thresholds were quite high and reflected the high initial operative success rate of coronary by-pass surgery.

Implications of the Sensitivity Analyses: These threshold probabilities show that the choice of therapy in the four patient types and 12 situations examined would be little affected by small changes in prognosis. Certainly large changes would alter many decisions, but given the available data base, changes of that magnitude seem unlikely. The decisions showed the most sensitivity to the annual mortality with a patent graft. Even for that parameter, however, the choice of therapy was very sensitive only for the Type "Life" patients, who were concerned primarily with survival. Thus one might expect that the decisions represented in Table 2 are quite stable.

CHANGES IN THE MODEL

The model was modified by changing [1] the cost of

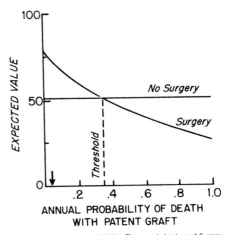

Figure 3. The threshold probability. The expected values of Surgery and NoSurgery are plotted against the variable analyzed, in this case the annual mortality rate with a patent graft. As this mortality rate increased, the expected value of surgery fell; the expected value of NoSurgery did not depend on this parameter. The threshold probability is the point where the two expected values were equal. For annual mortalities below the threshold surgery is preferred; for annual mortalities above the threshold, medical therapy is preferred. The small arrow on the probability axis indicates the "Base" value of this mortality found in Table 1. This plot refers to Type "Either" patients with "good" anatomy and "good" ventricular function and to surgeons with "good" past results.

surgery, [2] the time horizon, and [3] the number of myocardial infarctions considered. These modifications had little effect on the preferred therapies. Although the decision was sensitive to the mortality rate of surgical therapy, it was relatively *insensitive* to the other costs of surgery (the increased pain and suffering associated with operation), that is, it was not changed within a reasonable *range* of these surgical costs. The left-hand portion of Figure 4 illustrates this point. The expected value of surgery was plotted for various costs of surgery; the expected value of medical therapy was not affected by variations in the cost of surgery. Although the expected value of surgery declined with increasing surgical cost, the fall was gradual and surgery remained preferable.

The right-hand portion of Figure 4 shows a similar analysis for changes in the time horizon. With longer time horizons, the excepted value of medical therapy increased gradually because survival was longer. The expected value of surgery increased sharply at first (because the operative mortality was unchanged and because a longer time horizon allowed the costs of surgery to be partially offset) but then declined gradually as the expected number of graft closures increased.

Finally, the analysis was repeated with a 5-year time horizon, but with a very coarse model that assumed only a single myocardial infarction occurring after 2½ years. This coarse model corresponded exactly to the 10-branch

Table 3. Probabilities Where EV$_{Surg}$ Equals EV$_{NoSurg}$

Anat Funct Surg	Good Good Exc	Good Good Good	Good Good Avg	Fair Good Exc	Fair Good Good	Fair Good Avg	Good Fair Exc	Good Fair Good	Good Fair Avg	LAD Good Exc	LAD Good Good	LAD Good Avg
				Disabling Angina							Asymptomatic	
Patient type												
A. Probability of operative success with pain cure												
Base	0.90	0.85	0.80	0.80	0.70	0.60	0.88	0.80	0.70	0.95	0.90	0.85
Pain	0.04	0.04	0.05	0.03	0.04	0.06	0.04	0.06	0.09	None	None	None
Life	None	None	None	*0.89*	None	None	None	None	None	0.61	*0.97*	None
Either	0.07	0.12	0.19	0.08	0.18	*0.41*	0.14	0.33	*0.82*	None	None	None
Both	0.04	0.04	0.05	0.03	0.04	0.05	0.04	0.06	0.09	None	None	None
B. Annual graft closure rate												
Base	0.05	0.10	0.15	0.10	0.20	0.30	0.07	0.15	0.25	0.05	0.10	0.15
Pain	0.91	0.90	0.88	0.93	0.92	0.89	0.91	0.88	0.83	None	None	None
Life	None	None	None	None	None	None	None	None	None	0.82	None	None
Either	0.86	0.79	0.68	0.88	0.70	*0.46*	0.79	0.53	*0.18*	None	None	None
Both	0.94	0.93	0.92	0.96	0.94	0.92	0.94	0.92	0.88	None	None	None
C. Annual mortality with patent graft												
Base	0.04	0.04	0.04	0.07	0.07	0.07	0.12	0.12	0.12	0.05	0.05	0.05
Pain	0.81	0.79	0.77	0.87	0.84	0.78	0.84	0.81	0.73	None	None	None
Life	*0.03*	*0.00*	None	*0.07*	None	None	*0.09*	None	None	*0.08*	*0.04*	None
Either	0.39	0.35	0.30	0.41	0.32	*0.17*	0.43	*0.31*	*0.08*	None	None	None
Both	0.83	0.82	0.80	0.89	0.86	0.82	0.86	0.83	0.77	None	None	None
D. Annual spontaneous pain cure rate												
Base	0.03	0.03	0.03	0.02	0.02	0.02	0.03	0.03	0.03	0.03	0.03	0.03
Pain	0.84	0.61	0.45	0.69	0.39	*0.22*	0.80	0.44	*0.23*	None	None	None
Life	None	None	None	None	None	None	None	None	None	Any	None	None
Either	0.82	0.54	0.35	0.68	0.30	*0.09*	0.71	*0.26*	None	None	None	None
Both	0.83	0.60	0.44	0.70	0.40	*0.23*	0.78	0.43	*0.23*	None	None	None

*EV$_{Surg}$ = expected value of surgery, EV$_{NoSurg}$ = expected value of medical therapy; Anat = coronary anatomy, Funct = ventricular function, Surg = past surgical results; LAD = proximal obstruction of the left anterior descending coronary artery, Exc = excellent, Avg = average.
† Patient Type = type of patient preferences (utilities); Type "Pain" is concerned with freedom from pain; Type "Life" is concerned with life expectancy; Types "Either" and "Both" are concerned with both. For details, *see* text.
‡ None implies that surgery would never be the preferred therapy; Any implies that surgery is always the preferred therapy; Base probabilities are taken from the appropriate row in Table 1; *Italicized* probabilities are within 0.25 of base, thus the decision is quite sensitive to changes in those parameters.

tree in Figure 1, rather than the 190-branch tree used in deriving Table 2. Again the results did not differ substantially from those in Table 2, implying that the physician might calculate the 10-branch tree for an *individual* difficult patient (*see* Appendix).

Discussion

Considerable disagreement exists about the indications for coronary by-pass surgery (11, 12, 18, 21, 34, 35). This study considered the choice between medical and surgical therapy in patients with chronic coronary artery disease. It applied decision analysis to four groups of patient preferences, four categories of disease severity, and three classes of past surgical results. Coronary by-pass surgery was, in general, found preferable in severely disabled patients, but medical therapy seemed preferable in asymptomatic patients. The decision between medical and surgical therapy was sensitive to patient attitudes and to the quality of surgery available. This sensitivity depended on the strong relation, assumed in this model, between operative mortality and long-term graft patency rates. Variation in disease severity and patient preferences influenced the decision more strongly than did variation in operative statistics.

THE VALIDITY OF THE MODEL

Consider the validity of the model upon which this

analysis is based. Certainly the tree represented by Figure 1 is over-simplified: the time horizon can be longer than 5 years; more than one "event" can occur each year; coronary anatomy and myocardial function fall into more classes than those considered here; other factors, such as serum lipids (36), smoking, and blood pressure, are involved in determining prognosis; disability is not a discrete, two-valued function (Pain and NoPain); the cost of surgery is not really equivalent to the loss of 1 year of pain-free survival; monetary costs should not be neglected. Nevertheless, this prognostic model is a reasonable approximation of the major factors that physicians *now* consider. In addition, sensitivity analyses have shown that many of these added complexities do not affect the decision.

This analysis required a number of assumptions about prognosis and patient preferences. However, the physician's implicit decision-making must include some consideration of these same factors and thus must include a similar number of *implicit* assumptions. Decision analysis attempts, however, to make *explicit* those factors involved in the decision.

THE ADEQUACY OF THE DATA BASE

Any analysis of therapeutic decisions must consider the validity of the data upon which it is based. Certainly the studies summarized in Table 1 were not all well-controlled and dealt with highly selected patient populations. Nevertheless, today's clinician must make decisions concerning today's patients; he cannot defer such decisions until better data become available. Therefore, one might reasonably ask how improved prognostic data, when available, might affect the choice of therapy. That question can be answered, in part, with the type of *sensitivity analysis* (1, 2) used in this study. This analysis delineates the *range* of prognoses over which the decision is stable and the range of prognoses over which the decision should be changed.

Table 3 summarizes the sensitivity analyses for four of the most controversial prognostic parameters. For example, Part C deals with the affect of successful surgery upon mortality: for the asymptomatic patient with a proximal lesion in his left anterior coronary artery, medical therapy would continue to be preferable even if the mortality after successful surgery approached zero. The only exceptions were the Type "Life" patients with prospective surgical teams having had "excellent" or "good" past results. The sensitivity analyses also show which parameters are unlikely to affect the decision. For example, in most severely disabled patients, the graft closure rate (Table 3, Part B) will have little influence upon the decision because it is unlikely to be so high as to exceed these thresholds.

Thus, as more complete data upon prognosis become available, the results in Table 3 can help to determine whether the optimal therapy in an individual patient should be altered. However, until such data are collected, the analyses in Tables 1, 2 and 4, in conjunction with the technique shown in the Appendix, should help the clinician choose the best therapy for his present patients with

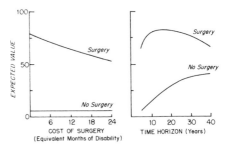

Figure 4. The effects of the cost of surgery and the time horizon In the **left-hand diagram,** the expected values of Surgery and No-Surgery are plotted for various costs of surgery, measured in equivalent months of disability. With increasing cost of surgery there was a slight decrease in the expected value of surgery. This plot refers to Type "Pain" patients with "good" anatomy and "good" ventricular function and to surgeons with "excellent" past results. In the **right-hand diagram,** the expected values of Surgery and NoSurgery are plotted against the time horizon used in the analysis. This plot refers to Type "Pain" patients with "good" anatomy and "good" ventricular function and to surgeons with "excellent" past results.

coronary artery disease.

Decision analysis cannot itself improve the data upon which therapeutic choices are based. It does, however, allow such choices to be made in a clear and logical fashion, and it exposes in an explicit manner the numerous assumptions underlying the decision making process. These data and assumptions can then be discussed and improved.

Table 4. Probabilities of Outcomes*

Coronary Anatomy Ventricular Function Past Surgical Results			Disabling Angina									Asymptomatic		
			Good Good Exc	Good Good Good	Good Good Avg	Fair Good Exc	Fair Good Good	Fair Good Avg	Good Fair Exc	Good Fair Good	Good Fair Avg	LAD Good Exc	LAD Good Good	LAD Good Avg
	Years Alive	Years Free of Pain												
Outcome														
Surgery														
Perioperative death	0	0	0.01	0.03	0.06	0.02	0.06	0.12	0.04	0.12	0.24	0.02	0.04	0.08
Pain relief but Fatal MI	2.5	2.5	0.17	0.17	0.16	0.26	0.24	0.20	0.42	0.36	0.29	0.23	0.24	0.23
Long-term pain relief	5.0	5.0	0.57	0.41	0.29	0.33	0.16	0.07	0.31	0.18	0.08	0.57	0.41	0.29
Short-term pain relief	5.0	2.5	0.15	0.24	0.30	0.19	0.26	0.25	0.11	0.16	0.17	0.13	0.22	0.27
Persistent pain and fatal MI	2.5	0	0.03	0.05	0.06	0.09	0.13	0.17	0.07	0.11	0.14	0.02	0.04	0.07
Spontaneous relief of pain	5.0	2.5	0.01	0.01	0.02	0.01	0.01	0.02	0.01	0.01	0.01	0.01	0.01	0.01
Persistent pain	5.0	0	0.06	0.09	0.11	0.10	0.14	0.17	0.04	0.06	0.07	0.02	0.04	0.07
Medical therapy														
Persistent pain and fatal MI	2.5	0†	0.23	0.23	0.23	0.41	0.41	0.41	0.56	0.56	0.56	0.41	0.41	0.41
Spontaneous relief of pain	5.0	2.5†	0.10	0.10	0.10	0.05	0.05	0.05	0.06	0.06	0.06	0.49	0.49	0.49
Persistent pain	5.0	0†	0.67	0.67	0.67	0.54	0.54	0.54	0.38	0.38	0.38	0.10	0.10	0.10

* Time horizon is 5 years. LAD = proximal obstruction of the left anterior descending coronary artery, Exc = excellent, Avg = average, fatal MI refers to the occurrence of a fatal myocardial infarction during the 5-year time horizon.
† Number applies to patients with disabling angina. For asymptomatic patients, number should be increased 2.5 years.

THE VALUE OF THE OUTCOMES

Obtaining general utility curves for any individual is a complex task (37), but in this analysis the physician might consider only the 10 outcomes shown in Figure 1. The utilities corresponding to these outcomes can be collected directly from the patient by the technique described in this paper. This has been done in a limited number of cases and patients accept the procedure well. Such debriefing can usually be accomplished within 30 minutes. In addition, explicit questioning of the type described here increases the patient's understanding of his disease and of the therapeutic options involved.

Once such utility curves have been obtained, the physician can use them to gain further insights into the benefits of surgery. Table 2 shows that for Type "Pain" patients with "good" anatomy and "good" ventricular function and surgeons with "good" past results, the benefit of surgery is 47.4 and the expected value of the optimum therapy is 53.3. Because the benefit of surgery is positive the optimum therapy is surgery. Thus the expected value of medical therapy would be (53.3 − 47.4) or 5.9. Referring to the Type "Pain" graph in Figure 2, the physician can see that a utility of 53.3 is equivalent to 2 years free of pain, while a utility of 5.9 is equivalent to 3 months free of pain. Thus, for these patients, the benefit of surgery is equivalent to a gain of 21 months of freedom from pain.

ASYMPTOMATIC DISEASE

For the asymptomatic patient with nonisolated LAD disease, even if "excellent" surgery was available, surgery seemed preferable only in patients of Type "Life," and then only marginally (benefit of surgery was 1.9 units). One might argue that surgery might be preferable in patients at even higher risk, that is, those with left main coronary artery disease. Some recent data (14, 38-40) suggest, however, that the natural history mortality for left main coronary disease is similar to that assumed in Table 1 for "LAD" disease, although other recent data (41-44) suggest that the mortality is considerably higher.

A further argument might be made that timely surgery in asymptomatic patients might prevent or delay the occurrence of disabling angina. Some data concerning unstable angina (45, 46) support that view, but data even suggestive of that conclusion in asymptomatic patients are lacking.

INDIVIDUAL PATIENTS

The decision between surgical and medical therapy in many patients with chronic ischemic heart disease is difficult. It depends upon the severity of the patient's disease, the patient's desires, and the ability of the operating surgeon. Because it is appropriate to fully inform the patient, the physician often presents the patient with information about prognosis with both medical and surgical therapies. The patient often has difficulty absorbing this complex data and making a truly *informed* decision: he often asks the physician for a recommendation. Although the physician may be familiar with the data (shown in Table 1), he may have difficulty combining these data with the patient's attitudes and preferences and giving the patient appropriate advice. Decision analysis combines both medical expertise and patient preferences into an explicit method of clinical decision making. The use of the decision tree, shown in Figure 1, and an examination of patient preferences, as explained here, facilitate the education of the patient about his options and their consequences.

ACKNOWLEDGMENTS: Grant support: in part by the Health Resources Administration, U.S. Public Health Service, under grant 1 R01 MB 00107-01 from the Bureau of Health Manpower and under grant HS 0091101 from the National Center for Health Services Research.

Received 2 January 1976; revision accepted 14 April 1976.

►Requests for reprints should be addressed to Stephen G. Pauker, M.D.; New England Medical Center Hospital, 171 Harrison Avenue; Boston, MA 02111.

Appendix

CALCULATION OF EXPECTED VALUES AND BENEFIT OF SURGERY FOR INDIVIDUAL PATIENTS

Three illustrative cases are presented to show the application of this model to the choice of therapy in individual patients. For the convenience of the physician who wishes to apply this technique to his own patients, Table 4 provides the probabilities of the 10 outcomes shown in Figure 1, with a 5-year time horizon. This table was derived from the data presented in Table 1. Note that for a one-time event like death, $P_{5yr} = [1-(1-P_{1yr})^5]$. Thus if the annual mortality is 0.05, the 5-year mortality is $(1-0.95^5)$ or 0.23.

Case 1: A 45-year-old truck driver had severe disabling angina of 6 months' duration. He had been treated with nitrates and propranolol, but he continued to have four to five severe attacks of angina daily. He found it difficult to continue working. Cardiac catheterization showed a 90% occlusion of the right coronary artery in its proximal third, a similar lesion in the middle third of his left anterior descending coronary artery, and a 50% occlusion in his circumflex system. Distal run-off was good. Ejection fraction was 37%. Previous results of the surgical team were "good."

Analysis: Assume the coarse model of Figure 1 with a 5-year time horizon. From the results of the catheterization, coronary anatomy can be considered "good" and

Appendix Table 1. Sample Calculation of Expected Value*

Outcome†	Probability	× Utility	= Expected Value
Perioperative death	0.12	0	0.0
Pain relief but fatal MI	0.36	60	21.6
Long-term pain relief	0.18	100	18.0
Short-term pain relief	0.16	80	12.8
Persistent pain and fatal MI	0.11	30	3.3
Spontaneous relief of pain	0.01	80	0.8
Persistent pain	0.06	60	3.6
Total for surgery	*1.00*		*60.1*
Persistent pain and fatal MI	0.56	40	22.4
Spontaneous relief of pain	0.06	90	5.4
Persistent pain	0.38	70	26.6
Total for medical therapy	*1.00*		*54.4*

* Probabilities are taken from Table 4. Utilities were obtained by debriefing patient.
† Fatal MI refers to the occurrence of a fatal myocardial infarction during the 5-year time horizon.

ventricular function can be considered "fair." Thus, the probabilities of the outcomes can be taken from Table 4. These probabilities, along with the utilities of these outcomes obtained from debriefing the patient, are shown in Appendix Table 1. The expected value of each course of action was calculated by multiplying the probability of each outcome by its utility and summing. Thus, the expected value of surgery is 60.1, the expected value of medical therapy is 54.4, and the benefit of surgery is 5.7. Surgery would, therefore, be the preferable therapy, although only marginally so.

Case 2: A 35-year-old man was catheterized after his first myocardial infarction. He was asymptomatic, but he had a strong family history of premature coronary artery disease. He did not smoke and was not overweight. Serum lipid profile was normal. Coronary angiograms showed a 95% occlusion in his proximal left anterior descending coronary artery and a 75% occlusion of his right coronary artery in its middle third. Ejection fraction was 65% and past surgical results were "excellent."

Analysis: Make the same assumptions as in the previous case. Assume the patient was debriefed and his utilities were "Peri-operative Death" = 0, "Pain Relief but Fatal MI" = 40, "Long-term Pain Relief" = 90, "Short-term Pain Relief" = 70, "Persistent Pain and Fatal MI after Surgery" = 30, "Spontaneous Relief of Pain after Surgery" = 70, "Persistent Pain after Surgery" = 60, "Persistent Pain and Fatal MI" = 50, "Spontaneous Relief of Pain" = 100, and "Persistent Pain" = 80. Using the data in Appendix Table 1, for this patient with "good" ventricular function and "LAD" anatomy, one can show that the expected value of surgery is 72.1 and the expected value of medical therapy is 77.5. Medical therapy would, therefore, be preferable.

Case 3: A 65-year-old retired executive had 10 years of long-standing angina. He had altered his life style but had tolerated his medical therapy fairly well. He was catheterized and shown to have 80% occlusions in his proximal third of his right and circumflex coronary arteries. Distal run-off was good. His ejection fraction was 55% and past results of the prospective surgical team were "good."

Analysis: Assume the patient was debriefed and his utilities were "Peri-operative Death" = 0, "Pain Relief but Fatal MI" = 70, "Long-term Pain Relief" = 100, "Short-term Pain Relief" = 80, "Persistent Pain and Fatal MI after Surgery" = 50, "Spontaneous Relief of Pain after Surgery" = 80, "Persistent Pain after Surgery" = 70, "Persistent Pain and Fatal MI" = 60, "Spontaneous Relief of Pain" = 90, and "Persistent Pain" = 80. The probabilities of the outcomes for this patient with "good" anatomy and "good" function are available in Table 4. One can calculate that the expected value of surgery is 81.7 and that of medical therapy is 76.4. Surgical therapy appears preferable for this patient.

References

1. PAUKER SG, KASSIRER JP: Therapeutic decision making: a cost-benefit analysis. *N Engl J Med* 293:229-234, 1975
2. RAIFFA H: *Decision Analysis.* Reading, Massachusetts, Addison-Wesley, 1968
3. SCHWARTZ WB, GORRY GA, KASSIRER JP, et al: Decision analysis and clinical judgment. *Am J Med* 55:459-472, 1973
4. GORRY GA, KASSIRER JP, ESSIG A, et al: Decision analysis as the basis for computer-aided management of acute renal failure. *Am J Med* 55:473-484, 1973
5. GIAUQUE WC: *Prevention and Treatment of Streptococcal Sore Throat and Rheumatic Fever—A Decision Theoretic Approach* (Doctoral thesis). Cambridge, Massachusetts, Harvard School of Business Administration, 1972
6. LUSTED LB: *Introduction to Medical Decision Making.* Springfield, Illinois, Charles C Thomas, 1968
7. GINSBERG AS: *Decision Analysis in Clinical Patient Management with an Application to the Pleural-Effusion Syndrome.* Rand Corporation, R-751-RC/NLM, 1971
8. FEINSTEIN AR: *Clinical Judgment.* Baltimore, Williams and Wilkins, 1967
9. MCNEIL BJ, ADELSTEIN SJ: The value of case finding in hypertensive renovascular disease. *N Engl J Med* 293:221-226, 1975
10. KANNEL WB, BANAS JS, SCHIFFMAN J: The natural history of coronary disease: implication for prophylactic surgical revascularization of the myocardium, in *Paul D. White Symposium: Major Advances in Cardiovascular Therapy.* Baltimore, Williams and Wilkins, 190-205, 1973
11. RUSSEK HI: Prognosis in severe angina pectoris: medical versus surgical therapy. *Am Heart J* 83:762-768, 1972
12. ARONOW WS, STEMMER EA: Two-year follow-up of angina pectoris: medical or surgical therapy. *Ann Intern Med* 82:208-212, 1975
13. REEVES TJ, OBERMAN A, JONES WB, et al: Natural history of angina pectoris. *Am J Cardiol* 33:423-430, 1974
14. WEBSTER JS, MOBERG C, RINCON C: Natural history of severe proximal coronary artery disease as documented by coronary cineangiography. *Am J Cardiol* 33:195-200, 1974
15. BURGGRAF GW, PARKER JO: Prognosis in coronary artery disease. *Circulation* 51:146-156, 1975
16. GENSINI GG, ESENTE P, KELLY A: Natural history of coronary disease in patients with and without coronary bypass surgery. *Circulation* (Suppl 2) 49-50:98-102,1974
17. BRYMER JF, BUTER TH, WALTON JA, et al: A natural history study of the prognostic role of coronary angiography. *Am Heart J* 88:139-143, 1974
18. DUNKMAN WB, PERLOFF JK, KASTOR JA, et al: Medical perspective in coronary artery surgery—a caveat. *Ann Intern Med* 81:817-837, 1974
19. HUMPHRIES JO, KULLER L, ROSS RS, et al: Natural history of ischemic heart disease in relation to arteriographic findings. *Circulation* 49:489-497, 1974
20. BEN-ZVI J, HILDNER FJ, JAVIER RP, et al: Progression of coronary artery disease. *Am J Cardiol* 34:295-301, 1974
21. MATHUR VS, GUINN GA, ANASTASSIADES LC, et al: Surgical treatment for stable angina pectoris. *N Engl J Med* 292:709-713, 1975
22. GOTT VL: Outlook for patients after coronary artery revascularization. *Am J Cardiol* 33:431-437, 1974
23. NAJMI M, USHIYAMA K, BLANCO G, et al: Results of aortocoronary artery saphenous vein bypass surgery for ischemic heart disease. *Am J Cardiol* 33:42-48, 1974
24. CANNON DS, MILLER DC, SHUMWAY NE, et al: The long-term follow-up of patients undergoing saphenous vein bypass surgery. *Circulation* 49:77-85, 1974
25. MCNEER JF, CONLEY MJ, STARMER CF, et al: Complete and incomplete revascularization at aortocoronary bypass surgery: experience with 392 consecutive patients. *Am Heart J* 88:176-182, 1974
26. BENCHIMOL A, FLEMING H, DESSER KB, et al: Postoperative recurrence of angina pectoris after aortocoronary venous bypass graft. *Am Heart J* 88:11-12, 1974
27. LEA RE, TECTOR ALJ, FLEMMA RJ, et al: Prognostic significance of a reduced left ventricular ejection fraction in coronary artery surgery. *Circulation* (suppl\2) 46:49, 1972
28. ASSAD-MORELL JL, FRYE RL, CONNOLLY DC, et al: Relation of intraoperative or early postoperative transmural myocardial infarction to patency of aortocoronary bypass grafts and to diseased ungrafted coronary arteries. *Am J Cardiol* 35:767-773, 1975
29. MUNDTH ED, AUSTEN WG: Surgical measures for coronary heart disease. *N Engl J Med* 293:13-19, 75-80, 124-130, 1975
30. SHELDON WC, RINCON G, EFFLER DB, et al: Vein graft surgery for coronary artery disease. *Circulation* (suppl 3) 184-189, 1973
31. KEENEY RL: *Multidimensional utility functions: theory, assessment and application.* Technical Report 43. Cambridge, Massachusetts, Operations Research Center, Massachusetts Institute of Technology, 1969
32. BARNOON S, WOLFE H: *Measuring the Effectiveness of Medical Decisions.* Springfield, Illinois, Charles C Thomas, 1972

33. PASTERNAK R, COHN K, SELZER A, et al: Enhanced rate of progression of coronary artery disease following aortocoronary saphenous vein bypass surgery. *Am J Med* 58:166-170, 1975

34. MCNEER JF, STARMER CF, BARTEL AG, et al: The nature of treatment selection in coronary disease. *Circulation* 49:606-614, 1974

35. HULTGREN HN, TAKARO T, FOWLER N, et al: Evaluation of surgery in angina pectoris. *Am J Med* 56:1-3, 1974

36. ALLARD C, GOULET C, GRONDIN C, et al: Patency of aorto-coronary vein grafts and serum triglycerides. *Am J Cardiol* 33:679-680, 1974

37. INGELFINGER FJ: Decision in medicine. *N Engl J Med* 293:254-255, 1975

38. LAVINE P, KIMBRIS D, SEGAL BL, et al: Left main coronary disease. *Am J Cardiol* 30:791-796, 1972

39. ZEFT HJ, MANLEY JC, HUSTON JH, et al: Left main coronary stenosis: results of coronary bypass surgery. *Circulation* 49:68-76, 1974

40. KOUCHOUKOS NT, OBERMAN A, RUSSELL RO, et al: Surgical versus medical treatment of occlusive disease confined to the left anterior descending coronary artery. *Am J Cardiol* 35:836-842, 1975

41. COHEN MV, GORLIN R: Main left coronary artery disease. *Circulation* 52:275-285, 1975

42. TALANO JV, SCANLON PJ, MEADOWS WR, et al: Influence of surgery on survival in 145 patients with left main coronary artery disease. *Circulation* (suppl 1) 52:105-111, 1975

43. SUNG RJ, MALLON SM, RICHTER SE, et al: Left main coronary artery obstruction. *Circulation* (suppl 1) 52:112-118, 1975

44. LIM JS, PROUDFIT WL, SONES FM: Left main coronary arterial obstruction: long-term follow-up of 141 non-surgical cases. *Am J Cardiol* 36:131-135, 1975

45. BERTOLASI CA, TRONGE JE, CARRENO CA, et al: Unstable angina-prospective and randomized study of its evolution, with and without surgery. *Am J Cardiol* 33:201-208, 1974

46. BERNDT TB, MILLER DC, SILVERMAN JF, et al: Coronary bypass surgery for unstable angina pectoris. *Am J Med* 58:171-176, 1975

30

THE IMPACT OF EMPLOYMENT AND TRAINING PROGRAMS

A Policy Statement by the
NATIONAL COUNCIL ON EMPLOYMENT POLICY

Traditionally, manpower programs in the United States have lacked cohesiveness. There have been noticeable shortcomings in the following: defining what the program intended to do, assessing the needs and goals of the target group, and relating these goals to the general scheme of program planning and evaluation. The most severe shortcoming lies in the area of evaluation where the work of program evaluators generally does not relate to the need of the policymakers and program operators for reliable and comprehensive information. The need for a systematic study of the development, implementation, and evaluation of manpower programs is not only an academic challenge but also a necessity that could positively influence the quality of information for the policymakers and program operators of manpower programs.

This policy statement by the National Council on Employment Policy gives the reader an overall picture of the present status of employment policy.

From a Policy Statement by the National Council on Employment Policy, "The Impact of Employment and Training Programs." November 1976.

ASSESSING EFFECTIVENESS

Federal outlays for training, placement, and work support efforts totalled more than $9 billion in fiscal 1976. Fifteen years earlier, less than a quarter of a billion dollars went for such activities. Is this substantial and expanded commitment warranted? Have employment and training programs worked?

There are no easy answers. Prior to the Comprehensive Employment and Training Act of 1973 (CETA), there were numerous federally-directed categorical programs with distinct service appraches, target groups and delivery mechanisms. Decentralization and decategorization under CETA may have increased diversity as state and local sponsors were encouraged to develop programs and priorities best suited to their individual needs. Aggregate assessment is, therefore, problematic. Job creation cannot be judged by the same standards as placement; services for the most disadvantaged are not directly comparable to those for more advantaged workers displaced by the recession; programs operated by community groups may have different inputs and effects from those run by state and local bureaucracies; efforts in high unemployment areas face greater obstacles than those in tight labor markets. To complicate matters further, there are a number of unresolved conceptual issues in measuring program impacts, as well as practical constraints on the precision of evaluations. Judgments rest ultimately on normative standards of success or failure. In the mid-1960s, when optimism prevailed about the potentials of government action, manpower programs were declared a success. The same evidence was used to document their shortcomings when gainsaying later became fashionable. The facts had not changed, but rather the standards of judgment.

Recognizing these complications, what can be said about the effectiveness of employment and training programs after more than fifteen years of experience and the millions of dollars spent on research and evaluation? Based on a comprehensive review of the literature and its own participation in the evaluation effort, the National Council on Employment Policy offers the following judgments:[1]

1. The overwhelming body of evidence indicates that institutional training, subsidized private sector on-the-job training, and public service employment substantially improve the economic well-being of participants.

2. Benefits measured in dollars and cents usually exceed costs, suggesting that the investment of scarce societal resources is profitable. There

are a number of uncertainties, however, and benefit-cost analysis cannot serve as the primary measuring rod of effectiveness.

3. Employment and training programs have had favorable impacts on reducing poverty, improving the trade-off between unemployment and inflation, providing a "piece of the action" for the disadvantaged and improving the status of minorities. However, resource constraints and policy decisions have limited the desirable spillovers and much more could be achieved.

4. Employment and training policies must rest on informed judgments rather than unequivocal findings. Evaluations can be improved, but even the best studies will leave many questions unanswered. Thus, decisionmaking standards are critically important. If it must be proven beyond a reasonable doubt that efforts work, there is no such proof. Yet the weight of the evidence substantiates the positive impacts of employment and training programs, and there is more proof of effectiveness than for any other major social welfare activity.

EARNINGS IMPACTS

The primary goal of employment and training programs is to raise the earnings of participants by increasing labor force participation, reducing unemployment and augmenting wages. Employment status data have been collected at entry and exit for participants under most programs, and these have been supplemented by scores of follow-up studies. While the dependability and sophistication of the findings vary widely, they support some generalizations.

Measured Pre-/Post-Gains

The evidence is consistent and convincing that participants are better off after receiving services than before. Institutional training under the Manpower Development and Training Act (MDTA-Institutional) has been studied extensively. According to one follow-up analysis of 1960 through 1963 participants, there was more than a $1500 jump in earnings from the year before to the year after training.[2] A detailed study of MDTA in four cities in 1969 and 1970 found an increase of $1100.[3] A nationwide survey of 1969 participants estimated a $1900 improvement.[4] More comprehensive analyses, based on social security records, have calculated gains ranging from $1300 to $1600.[5] These figures are representative of the distribution found in most other studies. According to program statistics, the first jobs after training paid 38 cents more per hour than the last jobs before entry for fiscal 1969-1972 participants.[6] By most estimates, hourly wage gains accounted for between a fifth and a fourth of earnings increases, with greater regularity of employment accounting for the rest.[7]

The average gains of on-the-job trainees are apparently somewhat higher, in part because of the greater likelihood of being employed at the end of training and also because enrollees, usually selected by employers, tend to be less disadvantaged than institutional trainees. A national sample of 1966 MDTA-OJT participants gained an estimated $1200 in annual income.[8] Studies based on social security earnings records of 1964, 1967 and 1968 on-the-job trainees indicated annual earnings gains of $1600, $1900 and $1900, respectively.[9] Under the Job Opportunities in the Business Sector (JOBS) program, the earnings of participants rose between $1000 and $2400 according to different studies.[10]

Offering varying mixes of counseling, placement and training, the Work Incentive (WIN) program for welfare recipients, Opportunities Industrialization Centers (OIC) for the more motivated among the disadvantaged, and the Concentrated Employment Program (CEP) targetted for residents of poverty areas, have been less extensively studied than institutional and on-the-job training under MDTA. The data suggest that they have had a lesser, but still substantial, impact on average earnings. For instance, a 1971 four city survey found that annual earnings of OIC enrollees rose $400 and of WIN enrollees $800.[11] A study of CEP in Philadelphia estimated $500 improvements for males and $200 for females in 1969.[12] Countercyclical public employment programs have had a very significant earnings impact reflecting the fact that jobless workers were moved into relatively well-paying temporary positions from which a large proportion transitioned directly into permanent jobs.[13]

Estimated Relative Gains

While the gains of participants are clearcut, these cannot be ascribed directly to services received. Any group selected on the basis of its employment problems is likely to show improvement since many of the problems are only temporary. The maturation of individuals and economy-wide increases in wage rates push up the earnings of most persons over time. It is necessary to compare them with changes for similarly disadvantaged individuals not participating in the programs being assessed. There are substantial difficulties in selecting a control group. Undetected, differences between participants and controls may significantly affect their comparative future success. Nevertheless, there is a consistency in the findings of many different studies with different comparison group selection methods. This consistency bolsters the credibility of their generally favorable findings (Table).

Among the analyses of institutional training, the only negative findings are those of an unpublished Department of Labor study which compared a large sample of 1968 participants with a control group matched on the basis of age, race, sex and previous earnings using social security records. Although the results became generally known, the study was never officially released because of methodological problems which clearly biased the findings negatively.[14] A reanalysis of the same data indicated that institutional trainees experienced statistically significant gains relative to control groups. [15] There is no disagreement about the effectiveness of on-the-job training. It has been found to raise relative earnings for all participant groups in all major studies.

There are fewer evaluations of other employment and training efforts which yield reliable estimates of the gains relative to controls. The best studies of the out-of-school Neighborhood Youth Corps (NYC) suggest that it had a slight but positive impact on future earnings. OIC, WIN and CEP raised relative earnings modestly. There are widely varying estimates of the Job Corps' initial impact; the duration of benefits is uncertain and control group selection is a real problem because Corps members are so severely disadvantaged. [16]

The most comprehensive assessment of available evaluation studies has concluded that skill training has increased earnings for participants between $400 and $800 per year relative to comparable nonparticipants; subsidized employment under public employment programs and JOBS has resulted in a long-term gain averaging between $300 and $700 per year; pre-employment assistance efforts such as OIC, CEP, WIN and the Job Corps have produced net gains between $200 and $400 per year; and work experience under NYC and Operation Mainstream has had a more modest earnings impact, adding less than $200. [17] The most recent studies not included in this assessment tend to fall within these ranges. [18] It is important to note, however, that there are no good estimates of program effectiveness during the severe recession which began in 1974. The economic slump unquestionably affected placement rates of participants, although the employment opportunities for comparable nonparticipants were also lowered.

The overwhelming body of evidence, then, supports the conclusion

Table. Estimated annual income gains of trainees compared to controls.

Institutional training	Males Both Races	Whites	Nonwhites	Females Both Races	Whites	Nonwhites
Hardin & Borus 1		$ 557	$1151		$ 895	$1095
Farber (1964) 2		- 48	129		132	211
Sewell 3			429			
Prescott & Cooley 4		719	587		527	624
Farber (1968) 2		- 676	- 732		- 368	- 364
Ashenfelter 5						
Assumption I		97	221		398	440
Assumption II		276	366		571	547
Goodfellow 6						
Assumption I	$ 778			$ 417		
Assumption II	369			797		
Kiefer 7		- 200	+ 256		+1316	+1456
On-the-job training						
Farber (1964) 2		350	551		291	620
Sewell 3			384		756	756
Prescott & Cooley 4		842	755			
Farber 2		88	44		104	300
Goodfellow 6						
Assumption I	897			660		
Assumption II	617			338		
Kiefer 7		108	432		728	1640

1 Einar Hardin and Michael E. Borus, Economic Benefits and Costs of Retraining (Lexington: D. C. Heath & Co., 1971) p. 162.

2 David J. Farber, "Highlights: Some Findings From a Follow-Up Study of Pre-and Post-Training Earnings Histories of 215,000 Trainees Participating in Two 1964 and Four 1968 Training Programs," unpublished U. S. Department of Labor study, 1971.

3 David O. Sewell, Training the Poor: A Benefit-Cost Analysis of Manpower Programs in the U. S. Antipoverty Program (Kingston, Ontario: Industrial Relations Centre, Queen's University, 1971) p. 85.

4 Edward C. Prescott and Thomas F. Cooley, "Evaluating the Impact of MDTA Programs on Earnings Under Varying Labor Market Conditions," report prepared for the Employment and Training Administration, U. S. Department of Labor, 1971, p. 11.

5 Orley Ashenfelter, "Estimating the Effect of Training Programs on Earnings With Longitudinal Data," paper presented to the Conference on Evaluating Manpower Training Programs, May 6-7, 1976, Princeton University. mimeo.

6 Gordon Goodfellow, "Estimates of Benefits From Training," paper presented to the Conference on Evaluating Manpower Training Programs, May 6-7, 1976, Princeton University. mimeo.

7 Nicholas M. Kiefer, "The Economic Benefits of Four Manpower Training Programs," paper presented to the Conference on Evaluating Manpower Training Programs, May 6-7, 1976, Princeton University. mimeo.

that employment and training efforts have had a positive impact on participant earnings. The gains have varied widely among programs and client groups and between completers and dropouts. The duration of benefits and their responsiveness to the mid-1970s recession are uncertain. As a general rule, however, and under normal economic circumstances, there is no doubt that such government assistance has resulted in improved employability and employment.

THE RETURN ON SOCIETY'S INVESTMENT

Investments in new plants or equipment are not undertaken unless the current value of expected returns exceeds their costs. Training and other manpower services result, or are intended to result, in increased participant earnings. The current value of these returns from the investment in human resources may be compared with costs, just as in the case of business decisions. If benefits exceed costs, the outlay is then presumably justified as a prudent and profitable investment.

This benefit-cost approach, providing a seemingly rigorous and exact standard for assessing government activities, was in vogue during the 1960s.

However, human experience proved difficult to measure by a monetary standard alone. The arbitrary assumptions necessary in estimating benefits and costs were critically important to the outcomes and left a wide range of uncertainty. Yet if benefit-cost analysis cannot provide all the answers, it remains a useful tool in weighing comparable approaches and in considering whether earnings gains are of a reasonable magnitude.

Benefit-Cost Estimates

Despite great diversity in the underlying assumptions, benefit-cost studies of institutional training present a definite consensus that future benefits exceed costs by a substantial margin. A synthesis of nine studies of the MDTA-Institutional program which standardized the findings by assuming a ten-year benefit duration and a 10 percent discount rate found that seven of the benefit/cost ratios were between 1.8 and 3.1, with one of 9.3, another of 12.2, and an average of 3.9 (Chart). A 20 percent return (or 1.2 benefit/cost ratio) would probably be considered a quite lucrative payoff by most businessmen; hence, institutional training is apparently a sound public investment.

On-the-job training is equally profitable for society. Again under standardized assumptions, the estimated benefit/cost ratios for seven studies of MDTA-OJT and JOBS ranged from 1.7 to 9.6 with an average of 4.0. The benefits of pre-employment assistance under CEP apparently exceeded the costs. Out-of-school NYC had a benefit/cost ratio exceeding 1.0 in three of four studies, and only slightly below it in the other. Only in the case of the Job Corps, where the provision of room and board as well as comprehensive services raises the cost per enrollee above that of other training programs, is there doubt about a positive payoff. In five of the nine Job Corps studies, the benefit/cost ratios were less than 1.0, although the one study with the most meticulous methodology indicated a modestly favorable return. It is worth noting that the performance of the Job Corps has improved substantially since the last of these studies while costs have declined in real terms, so that the present rate of return would be higher. [19]

The Implications

These benefit/cost ratios would change under different assumptions. If it were assumed that the gains measured in the period immediately after termination would last less than ten years, the ratios would all be lower. Longitudinal studies provide some evidence of diminishing increments between the earnings of male participants and controls, though the relative benefits for female participants do now seem to erode.[20] These, however, are very

Chart. Benefit-cost ratios from available studies standardized assuming a ten-year duration of benefits and a ten percent discount rate.

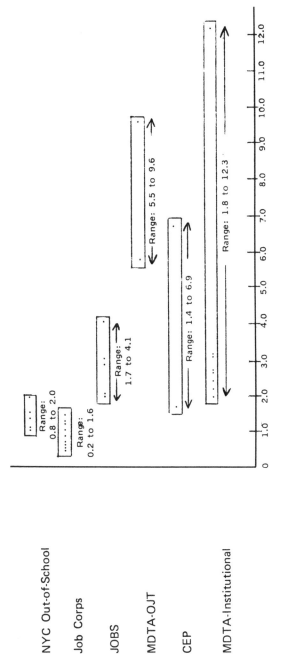

Source: Joe N. Nay, John W. Scanlon and Joseph S. Wholey, Benefits and Costs of Manpower Training Programs: A Synthesis of Previous Studies With Reservations and Recommendations (Washington: The Urban Institute, 1971), p. 7.

tentative conclusions. Rates of return may be underestimated to the extent that benefits other than immediate earnings gains are rarely considered while conservative assumptions are usually adopted in calculating the impact of participation. Given the substantial margin by which benefits exceed costs under most studies, technical adjustments would probably not negate, and might further support, the general conclusion that employment and training efforts pay off in dollars and cents.

Employment and training efforts might be considered worthwhile even if benefit/cost ratios were less than 1.0. Society or the individual involved might prefer a dollar of extra earnings to a dollar of transfer income which would also have a benefit/cost ratio of 1.0. Some consider it worth a substantial price to try to help those trapped by their social and economic handicaps even if only a few are able to benefit.

SECONDARY EFFECTS

In addition to direct impacts on participant earnings, employment and training efforts have other positive spillovers. They are, intrinsically, an instrument of government economic policy, affecting the functioning of the labor market. To the extent they focus on the disadvantaged and minorities, they are also instruments of antipoverty and equal opportunity policy.

Labor Market Impacts

Manpower programs have been responsive to changing macro-economic conditions, emphasizing training for the socioeconomically disadvantaged in the tight labor markets of the 1960s, then shifting to job creation for the victims of the recession in the 1970s. The expansion of employment and training programs has increased their importance as an adjunct to monetary and fiscal policies. The fact remains, however, that the United States is far from having an "active manpower policy" of the Swedish variety in which training, employment, placement and relocation programs have a major impact on the functioning of the labor market. Despite the implementation of emergency job creation programs, the 2.8 million first-time enrollments in 1975 represented only an eighth of persons experiencing unemployment during the year. In the tight labor market of 1969, first-time enrollments were 1.0 million compared to the 11.7 million persons experiencing joblessness.

If employment and training programs are not of a magnitude to significantly alter macroeconomic conditions, there is no doubt that they have desirable impacts. Manpower programs have reduced unemployment among those segments of the labor force which are least effectively reached by monetary and fiscal measures. In fiscal 1971, when expenditures for manpower programs were a third of their present level, the Department of Labor estimated that the programs reduced the measured rate of unemployment by .3 percentage points by providing work support or alternatives to unemployment. [21] (Participants in work experience programs are usually counted as employed while trainees are considered outside the labor force). The effect is at least twice as great today. It has also been estimated that expenditures on manpower training have double the job creation impact of other nondefense spending. [22] The overwhelming majority of enrollees and a comparatively large share of administrators and functionaries have been drawn from the ranks of the less skilled and of minorities.

These employment effects are supplemental to the long-term impacts of services on participants. In theory, placement services can reduce the length of job search and can improve the job/man match leading to increased employment stability. Training can upgrade unskilled workers into labor shortage occupations. Employment programs directed to the unskilled reduce the great disparities in unemployment rates and create jobs directly rather than as the result of a trickle-down of increased outlays. Institutional changes to eliminate discrimination and artificial credentials barriers improve the functioning of the labor market.

These theoretical impacts have been limited in practice. Participants have too frequently been placed into dead-end jobs. Training has usually been of short duration and hence in less skilled occupations. Public employment programs have developed into a two-tiered system of very menial jobs for the disadvantaged and higher paying jobs filling local public service needs for unemployed workers with experience. The community action approach to institutional reform, which was an integral part of the manpower effort in the mid-1960s, has been abandoned; now, employment and training resources may make change easier to manage but there is less federal pressure.

There is little doubt, however, that programs have had a favorable effect. They have clearly increased the employment stability of participants who are primarily the disadvantaged unable to find jobs even at low rates of aggregate unemployment. Studies have suggested that public service employment programs are a much faster and much more cost-effective way to create jobs than the traditional monetary or fiscal measures. [23] Finally, some institutional changes have been achieved, such as revisions of civil service hiring requirements, the creation of new entry level jobs and a reduction in racial discrimination. These are desirable developments and will improve the functioning of labor markets even if they do not markedly alter the relationship between inflation and unemployment. A massive commitment would be needed to improve the overall economic picture. Whether employment and training programs on such a massive scale are warranted is a legitimate subject of debate, but given the level of commitment, past and present efforts cannot be condemned because of their limited macroeconomic impact.

Fighting Poverty

Manpower programs were an essential weapon in the War on Poverty. The idea was to attack the causes rather than the symptoms of low income by making the disadvantaged more productive and attractive to employers, thereby increasing their capacity for self-support. Expectations and rhetoric were sometimes inflated in the 1960s. Subsequent experience has demonstrated that limited services are not likely to drastically alter future prospects, and even the most comprehensive aid will lead to a quantum leap in employability for only a small minority of disadvantaged participants. Under MDTA-Institutional, the average annual earnings after training ranged from $2300 to $3600 according to different estimates. For OJT, post-enrollment earnings were apparently somewhat higher, $3100 to $4100. [24] They were less for participants in NYC, Operation Mainstream and the Job Corps. In other words, many enrollees remained in poverty or near poverty despite improvements.

The poverty line is arbitrary, and the crucial question is not the number of persons or families raised from a dollar below to a dollar above the threshhold, but rather whether low-income persons received attention and benefitted significantly. Employment and training programs have traditionally emphasized the "disadvantaged," defined officially as persons who are poor and handicapped by either age, race, sex or limited educaiton. The disadvantaged represented seven of ten CETA participants in fiscal 1976. While this proportion was lower than in earlier years because of the need to help the victims of the recession, and while the number of disadvantaged may have been exaggerated, there is no doubt that most services have gone to low-income persons.

Those who casually dismiss gains of several hundred dollars should consider what this means to a participant who previously earned wages below the poverty level. Whether or not added earnings push income above the poverty threshhold, they certainly reduce hardship. While disadvantaged participants tend to drop out of programs more frequently than persons with less serious difficulties, their improvements relative to comparable persons not receiving assistance are often greater. Serving the disadvantaged also makes sense in terms of reducing future transfer payments and alleviating imbalances in the labor market.

Equalizing Opportunity

Employment and training programs have been closely related to the civil rights movement. Minorities are overrepresented among the disadvantaged, representing a sixth of the unemployed in 1975, but they have benefitted from a proportionately even greater share of manpower enrollments. From 1965 through 1972, blacks accounted for 46 percent of enrollees and other minorities for five percent. The black share declined in the 1970s while that of other minorities rose slightly. Still, more than two-fifths of all participants under CETA were minorities in fiscal 1976. As a general rule, nonwhite participants tend to do worse than whites in terms of placement and subsequent wage rates, but this reflects their greater disadvantages at enrollment and the discriminatory barriers they face in the labor market. The gains of nonwhites, especially of nonwhite women, tend to equal or exceed those of white participants, particularly when compared to similar individuals not receiving services. Minority women benefit substantially from institutional training, while minority males realize their greatest gains under job development programs.

Since minorities gain as much or more than other participants, and since all enrollees gain on the average relative to nonparticipants, the overrepresentation of minorities in employment and training programs clearly helps to improve their relative labor market status over the long-run. There is also a substantial short-run impact. For instance, fiscal 1976 minority enrollments equalled a fourth of the number of nonwhites experiencing unemployment at some point during the year. In the nonsummer months of fiscal 1974, the unemployment rate of nonwhites under age 22 would have been a fourth higher if participants had instead been unemployed. In the summer months of 1975, more than half of nonwhite teenagers would have been jobless rather than a third.[25] Jobs within the manpower establishment have also provided upward mobility routes for many minority group members.

Though there is no measure of the impact, employment and training programs have helped to change attitudes in American society toward the poor and minorities. Research and programatic experience demonstrated the widespread need for remedial aid and the existence of formidable barriers to employment for the disadvantaged. The principle was firmly established that competitive forces in the labor market were not, alone, an assurance of equality of opportunity. It became clear, for instance, that hiring standards were frequently unrealistic. The sticks and carrots of manpower programs were used to change employer practices. The large bureaucracy established to serve persons at the end of the hiring queue became an institutional force working for those who had earlier been ignored. Employment and training resources were central to the community action effort to organize the poor and give them a voice in local governments. As a result, elected officials in most jurisdictions can no longer ignore with impunity the needs of the disadvantaged.

THE UNCERTAINTIES

It is deceptively easy to assess the impact of employment and training programs. Their primary goal is to improve the labor market status of participants, so that comparison of the earnings changes for enrollees with those of a perfectly matched sample should suggest the effect of participation. Unfortunately, it is not this simple.

Comparison Group Selection

The scientific approach would be to deny services to one group of acceptable applicants and to compare their subsequent experience to that of participants. There is an understandable reluctance to use human beings as social guinea pigs; therefore, various alternatives have been employed to select proxy control groups based on demographic variables such as age, race, sex, education and socioeconomic status. Yet those who ask for and receive public help may be different, in terms of motivation or prospects, from those who do not. Most studies have attempted statistical adjustments, but there is no proof, and there is indeed reason to doubt, that such procedures compensate fully for differences unrelated to measured variables. This is especially true for the younger cohorts, because their limited experience in the labor market provides little basis for predicting future success. Another control group selection approach is to use "no-shows," i.e. persons who applied for and were accepted into programs but who chose not to participate. Again, the factors which led to nonparticipation may have had a significant though undetermined impact on later outcomes. The same holds true when dropouts are compared to completers.

Another problem in control group selection is determining the base period for comparison. The labor force status of participants tends to deteriorate immediately before entry, in part because of a conscious effort to qualify for or bide time until enrollment, but mostly because those with current problems are the ones selected for aid. If participants are matched with controls on the basis of the status of both in the entry week, the control group is much more disadvantaged than if the matching is done on the basis of the previous year's experience.[26]

Net Effects and Their Duration

The differential success of enrollees compared to controls may not be an accurate measure of program impact. If employment and training programs simply become a rationing mechanism through which participants get jobs which would otherwise have gone to persons with similar characteristics, then participants will necessarily do better than controls. Even where programs provide upward mobility routes there is some loss for those who would otherwise have gotten the better positions. On the other hand, where services improve the relative position of the disadvantaged, they leave fewer competitors for low level positions, so that those who do not participate may also be better off. The relative importance of displacement effects in the former case and vacuum effects in the latter is unknown.

There are other considerations. In subsidy programs for hiring and training the disadvantaged, employers who normally hire the less skilled will be the first to apply for aid in "training" enrollees for the same slots; some subsidies may thus be paid for "business as usual." Under public employment programs, state and local governments may cut back their own payrolls in response to expanded, federally subsidized employment. The extent of such offsets can only be guessed. Some critics have claimed, for instance, that 90 percent of the jobs created under federally-funded public employment programs are offset by cutbacks in state and local payrolls. In truth, however, these assertions are totally dependent on the underlying assumptions and much smaller offsets would result from different but also plausible assumptions. It is nearly impossible to tell what would have happened in the absence of governmental intervention.

The duration of impacts is another uncertainty. Do incremental gains deteriorate or remain constant over time? We have learned little about the long-run pattern of benefits despite an increased number of longitudinal evaluations. One reason is that there is difficulty in multiyear follow-up. The proportion of any sample which can be located declines appreciably over time, and if there are systematic differences between those who are lost and those who are located, this can bias outcomes. Social security data facilitate more complete tracking despite limitations of income coverage. But longer-range assesssment puts a greater burden on control group selection procedures. For instance, if the comparison group for a youth cohort contains more current or potential college enrollees than the participant sample, the earnings differences will not be noticeable immediately but will increase over time. Social security records alone are not adequate for control group selection, especially where youthful participants are matched with a sample chosen on the basis of past earnings. [27]

Estimating Benefits and Costs

The uncertainties are most visible in benefit-cost analysis when assumptions must be detailed in estimating benefits and costs. Over half of outlays for MDTA went for enrollee stipends. Are such transfer payments a training cost or does a dollar of cash aid produce a dollar of benefits whatever its impact on employability? The same question applies to child and health care and other supportive services offered under manpower programs. Should costs be calculated only for completers or should aggregate benefits be expected to amortize total outlays? In assessing the rate of return on a college education, the usual approach has been to compare the average cost of four years of college with the average earnings gain of college graduates. If the costs to noncompleters were added in, as is done in evaluating remedial training programs, the estimated rate of return on a college education would be substantially lower. What is the value to the participant of greater self-esteem or reduced chances of crime or illegitimacy? What is the payoff to society if there is less violence on the streets during the summer months? What is the productive output of persons hired under subsidized employment programs?

Even if all these questions could be answered and benefits straightforwardly compared to costs, there would remain many uncertainties. A benefit/cost ratio greater than 1.0 does not necessarily mean that expansion is warrante The critical issue is the likely payoff of an additional expenditure, i.e. the marginal rather than average rate of return. Sometimes additional outlays can improve payoffs, sometimes they are subject to diminishing returns.

In assessing the profitability of an investment, it is important to recognize the high start-up costs which are frequently experienced. The payoff in the first few years may be less than that subsequently. Most available studies of manpower programs are based on the experiences of persons enrolled in the 1960s. These programs were then relatively new and the manpower system has been dramatically changed since. To the extent that there is a steeply sloped learning curve, past assessments may understate current effectiveness. Evaluations of long-standing programs such as the Job Corps suggest that there has, indeed, been a great deal of improvement over time.

The decentralization and decategorization of manpower programs under CETA, combined with the worst recession since the Great Depression, has complicated the picture considerably. Advocates of CETA anticipated improved performance after a shakedown period. The implementation of emergency public employment programs undermined an orderly transition to local control. It will be several years, then, before new employment and training arrangements can be reasonably assessed. With the diversity of local efforts and the limitations of reported data, it will be difficult to determine whether CETA is more effective than the federal, categorical programs it replaced, much less to determine whether the overall investment has paid off in benefit-cost terms.

Living With Uncertainty

There is no need to apologize for our ignorance. It is a fact of life that practical and theoretical problems seriously limit what we have learned and can learn about the effectiveness of employment and training programs. Despite our best efforts, the rigorous, unequivocal answers desired by policy-makers are not available and are an unlikely prospect.

If the success of employment and training programs has not been and cannot be proven beyond a reasonable doubt, the weight of evidence is unquestionably positive. We know enough to say quite definitely that these efforts improve the earnings experience of the average participant. We are equally certain of the direction if not the degree of the impact in fighting poverty, improving the trade-off between unemployment and inflation, reforming labor market institutions and helping to achieve equal employment opportunity.

The National Council on Employment Policy believes that there is need for increased resource commitments and a much more active manpower policy which supplements monetary and fiscal policies. The Council also believes that the effectiveness of employment and training programs can be, and is being, substantially improved. But these conclusions rest on additional arguments and assumptions. The message of this statement is more basic: As far as we can measure the impact of employment and training programs with our limited tools, they seem to have worked. We should approach the challenges ahead with faith in our capacity for positive action, rather than carrying on a sterile debate about our ability or inability to measure with complete precision the success of our efforts.

FOOTNOTES

1. This statement is based on the work of the Council and its members over the last decade. Specifically, Dr. Gerald Somers reviewed the evaluations of employment and training programs for the Council. A more detailed analysis by Dr. Bernard Anderson, in conjunction with associates at the Wharton School, was a source of much information, while Dr. Garth Mangum's recently published study, Employability, Employment and Income, provided perspective. The interpretative synthesis is based largely on the assessment of manpower programs in The Promise of Greatness by Drs. Sar Levitan and Robert Taggart.

2. Einar Hardin and Michael E. Borus, Economic Benefits and Costs of Retraining (Lexington: D.C. Heath and Company, 1971) p. 47.

3. Garth L. Mangum and R. Thayne Robson, The Metropolitan Impact of Manpower Programs, A Four City Study (Salt Lake City: Olympus Publishing Company, 1973) pp. 235-259.

4. Decision Making Information, "MDTA Outcomes Study," report prepared for the Employment and Training Administration, U. S. Department of Labor, 1972, Chapter VII, pp. 7-10.

5. David J. Farber, "Changes in the Duration of the Post-Training Period and in Relative Earning Credits of Trainees: The 1965-1969 Experience of MDTA-Institutional and OJT Trainees, Class of 1964," unpublished U. S. Department of Labor report, 1971.

   Edward C. Prescott and Thomas F. Cooley, "Evaluating the Impact of MDTA Training Program on Earnings Under Varying Labor Market Conditions," report prepared for the Employment and Training Administration, U. S. Department of Labor, 1972, p. 4.

6. Bernard E. Anderson, Herbert R. Northrup, Charles R. Perry and Richard L. Brown, The Impact of Government Manpower Programs (Philadelphia: University of Pennsylvania, The Wharton School, 1973) p. 113.

7. Ibid. p. 55.

8. Allan H. Muir et al., "Cost-Effectiveness Analysis of On-the-Job and Institutional Training Courses," Planning Research Corporation report prepared for the Employment and Training Administration, U. S. Department of Labor, 1967, p. 14.

9. David J. Farber, "Changes in the Duration of the Post-Training Period and in Relative Earning Credits of Trainees, op. cit.; Edwin C. Prescott and Thomas F. Cooley, op. cit., p. 4; and David J. Farber, "Highlights - First Annual Follow-Up: 1968 JOBS Contract and Noncontract Program," unpublished U. S. Department of Labor study, 1971.

10. U. S. Congress, Senate Subcommittee on Labor and Public Welfare, Subcommittee on Employment, Manpower and Poverty, The JOBS Program: Background Information, 91st Congress, 2nd Session, April 1970, p. 169; and Greenleigh Associates "The Job Opportunities in the Business Sector Program: An Evaluation of Impact in Ten Standard Metropolitan Statistical Areas," report prepared for the Employment and Training Administration, U. S. Department of Labor, 1970, p. 91.

11. Garth Mangum and R. Thayne Robson, op. cit., pp. 235-259.

12. Richard D. Leone et. al., Employability Development Teams and Federal Manpower Programs: The Philadelphia CEP's Experience (Philadelphia: Temple University Press, 1972) p. 126.

13. Sar A. Levitan and Robert Taggart, eds., Emergency Employment Act: The PEP Generation (Salt Lake City: Olympus Publishing Company, 1974) pp. 11-58.

14. Herman P. Miller, "Critique of David Farber's Method of Evaluating the Gains in Earnings of MDTA Trainees," National Council on Employment Policy, mimeo. September 1972.

15. Orley Ashenfelter, "Estimating the Effect of Training Programs on Earnings With Longitudinal Data," paper presented to the Conference on Evaluating Manpower Training Programs, May 6-7, 1976, Princeton University. mimeo.

16. Bernard E. Anderson, et. al., op. cit., pp. 64-79.

17. Ibid. p. 76.

18. Orley Ashenfelter, op. cit.; Gordon Goodfellow, "Estimates of Benefits from Training"; Nicholas M. Kiefer, "The Economic Benefits of Four Manpower Training Programs"; papers presented to the Conference on Evaluating Manpower Training Programs, May 6-7, 1976, Princeton University. mimeo.

    Pacific Consultants, The Impact of WIN-II, draft report to the Employment and Training Administration, mimeo. August 1976.

19. Sar A. Levitan and Benjamin H. Johnston, The Job Corps: A Social Experiment That Works (Baltimore: Johns Hopkins University Press, 1975).

20. Orley Ashenfelter, op. cit.

21. Sylvia S. Small, "Work Training Programs and the Unemployment Rate," Monthly Labor Review, September 1972, pp. 7-13.

22. Bureau of Labor Statistics, Expenditures and Manpower Requirements for Selected Federal Programs Bulletin 1851 (Washington: Government Printing Office, 1975) p. 5.

23. Congressional Budget Office, Temporary Measures To Stimulate Employment: An Evaluation of Some Alternatives (Washington: Government Printing Office, September 1975).

24. Bernard E. Anderson, et. al., op. cit., pp. 39-79.

25. Robert Taggart, "Employment and Training Programs for Youth," From School to Work: Improving the Transition (Washington: Government Printing Office, 1976), p. 132.

26. Orley Ashenfelter, op. cit.

27. Herman P. Miller, op. cit.

31

THE FISCAL SUBSTITUTION EFFECT OF ALTERNATIVE APPROACHES TO PUBLIC SERVICE EMPLOYMENT POLICY

By

GEORGE E. JOHNSON and JAMES D. TOMOLA

Since their inception, manpower programs' goals and substance have undergone multiple changes. The Manpower Development and Training Act, initiated in 1962, emphasized the need for retraining unemployed workers. Under the Comprehensive Employment and Training Act of 1973, local authorities became the primary sponsors of manpower programs. Federal funds were distributed to local manpower authorities who were responsible for generating employment. In a comprehensive study, George E. Johnson and James D. Tomola analyze the effect of the Public Service Employment Program on fiscal policy. By measuring the impact of the substitution effect, the authors wish to determine whether a public employment program is a countercyclical policy or a form of revenue sharing.

From George E. Johnson and James D. Tomola, "The Fiscal Substitution Effect of Alternative Approaches to Public Service Employment Policy." *Journal of Human Resources*, 1977, *12*(1), 3-26.

ABSTRACT

The size of the fiscal substitution effect is important in evaluating public service employment as either a counter-cyclical policy or as revenue-sharing. Empirically, the effect appears to be very small for one or two quarters, but rises to about 100 percent after five quarters. From an anti-poverty perspective, however, composition effects are most important. Although PSE program employees appear representative of the total labor force, the proportion of the disadvantaged among PSE participants is greater than the proportion of them in state and local government employment.

I. INTRODUCTION: THE FISCAL SUBSTITUTION EFFECT OF PSE

During the 1970s the emphasis of manpower policy has shifted from training programs to public service employment (PSE) programs. First, under the Emergency Employment Act of 1971, which was renamed the Public Employment Program (PEP), the federal government transferred slightly in excess of one billion dollars per year to state and local governments (S&Ls) during fiscal years 1972 and 1973 for purposes of employment creation, and the program continued on a reduced scale through 1975. In the Comprehensive Employment and Training Act of 1973 (CETA), responsibility for formulating and operating man-

Johnson is Professor of Economics in the Department of Economics and Institute of Public Policy Studies, University of Michigan. Tomola is a graduate student in economics at Harvard University.

* This paper was written while both authors were with the Office of Evaluation, ASPER, U.S. Department of Labor, and the views expressed do not represent any sort of official position of that agency. It was prepared for ASPER-USDOL under Contract No. J-9-M-6-0009. We are particularly indebted to James L. Blum and Robert S. Smith for useful comments and suggestions. [Manuscript received September 1974; accepted August 1976.]

power programs was shifted to the S&Ls, and under Titles II and VI of CETA a large increase in the funding of PSE programs was provided. During the first half of fiscal year 1976, for example, $1.8 billion was allocated to the various parts of CETA for PSE, as compared to $.8 billion for training programs under Title I, and some of the Title I funds were used for S&L employment creation rather than training. During the past two years, numerous proposals have been brought before Congress to expand PSE programs many fold, but thus far most of them have not been enacted.

One of the principal limitations of the PSE approach is that it is quite possible that the S&Ls will use their PSE subsidies to pay for incumbent employees or, more subtly, for workers who would have been hired even in the absence of the program. The literature on the impact of general revenue-sharing on S&L expenditures establishes a presumptive case that this "fiscal substitution effect" may be fairly large.[1] However, in both the PEP and CETA programs, various "maintenance-of-effort" restrictions were in effect, so it is not necessarily appropriate to treat the impact of PSE as a straightforward lump-sum transfer. Moreover, under both PEP and CETA, a great deal of publicity accompanied their introduction into communities, and it is conceivable that this created a constituency that expected "jobs" and thus tended to mitigate the fiscal substitution effect. On the other hand, not all regulations are enforced (or are enforceable), and S&L officials could placate interest groups by altering the distribution of jobs. Thus, although our knowledge of the effect of general revenue-sharing points to a potential problem with PSE, the size of the fiscal substitution effect is, at bottom, an empirical question.

There were two early studies of the impact of the PEP program on S&L employment. The first, which was prepared by the National Planning Association [12], was able to utilize data from a sample of high-impact demonstration areas in which the quantity of PSE slots was about five times the average for all localities on a per capita basis. The investigators then estimated a fiscal substitution effect of .46 after one year. The NPA data have been reworked in a recent paper by Michael Wiseman [14], and he has revised this estimate down to .39. A second study, which was prepared by the present authors [10], utilized aggregate time-series data on eight quarters of experience with PEP and obtained a point estimate of the fiscal substitution effect of .60 after one year. The model, however, was subject to a number of limitations, including a rather crude lag structure and the short time-span over which the PSE approach had been operating at that time.

It is somewhat interesting to ask why the size of the fiscal substitution effect might be of interest to policy-makers. The answer depends on whether PSE is viewed primarily as (1) a counter-recession policy, (2) an antipoverty pro-

---

1   See, for example, [5]. The inferential implications of the Gramlich-Galper model for public employment programs have been explored by Fechter [4]. For direct estimates of federal grants on S&L employment, see [1].

gram, or (3) a form of disguised revenue-sharing.[2] If one is interested in increasing aggregate employment as much and as rapidly as possible, a PSE program can be more effective (per unit of budget deficit) in the short run than any other form of fiscal policy if the fiscal substitution effect is small (see [8]). A given increase in expenditure on PSE will have the same effect on private sector demand as a tax cut of equivalent size, but it will also increase public sector employment. In the most extreme case of fiscal substitution, there is no net increase in public employment, S&L taxes are reduced by the amount of the subsidy, and the impact of the PSE program on total employment is the same as a policy of cutting federal taxes. Thus, although the size of the substitution effect influences the degree to which PSE is an effective instrument of counter-recession policy, at worst PSE is as effective as a tax cut in reducing unemployment in the short run.[3]

The importance of the size of the fiscal substitution effect concerning the efficacy of PSE as an antipoverty program is upon first reflection rather straightforward: to the extent that substitution approaches 100 percent, PSE is not a manpower program at all. This conclusion, however, must be tempered by the possibility that the PSE program is successful at altering the *composition* of S&L employment toward those groups that are relatively disadvantaged with respect to the labor market even if there is a large amount of substitution. For example, consider a situation in which a local government hires 100 police officers from the ranks of the long-term unemployed with CETA funds. After a few months the city council decides that the community does not need so many police and orders a halt to the filling of vacancies so that by attrition the number of police officers falls to the pre-CETA level. The local labor force now contains 100 individuals who are qualified to be police officers, but because of CETA they are forced to find work in the private sector.[4] Presumably they are better able to do this than are the CETA participants, so despite the fact that, by construction of the example, there is 100 percent substitution, the program has been successful

---

2 For a lucid exposition of the relevance of the first two of these distinctions, see Wiseman [13].

3 According to the new conventional wisdom in macroeconomics, in the longer run (after two or three years) it is unlikely that *any* fiscal policy will have much influence on the rate of unemployment. Indeed, an increase in PSE jobs of, say, 100,000 will simply reduce private sector employment by approximately that number after adjustment. Thus, from a longer-run point of view, a high fiscal substitution effect is probably desirable. See [8], Section 4-5.

4 New York City provides an example of a similar strategy for the use of CETA funds. During the summer of 1975 New York apparently used CETA funds to hire new employees performing the same jobs as permanent employees who had recently been laid off. However, in conjunction with bargaining for a wage freeze, the unions achieved the firing of many of these CETA employees and the subsequent rehiring of laid-off workers with the CETA funds. See *New York Times*, July 9, 1975, p. 1:7; August 5, 1975, p. 24:7; and August 6, 1975, pp. 44:4.

as a manpower policy. On the other hand, if the city uses CETA funds to pay for 100 incumbent police officers (or, as time goes on, for 100 police officers it would have hired without the CETA subsidy), there is 100 percent substitution *and* no manpower program. To go further with this example, suppose that the city uses the CETA funds to pay for 100 additional police officers with the same sort of labor market attributes (that is, fairly highly skilled) as the incumbent police officers and that without the subsidy the additional personnel would not have been hired. In this case, the rate of substitution is zero, but it is not clear that from a social point of view this would be as desirable as the first case—that in which the city effectively replaced 100 police officers who are advantaged with respect to the labor market with 100 individuals who are much less so.[5]

Thus, the size of the fiscal substitution effect does *not* have unambiguous implications concerning the efficacy of PSE as an antipoverty program *if* it can be established that the program shifts the composition of labor demand in the public sector toward those who would have inordinate difficulty obtaining employment in the private sector.

The third possible objective—the pure revenue-sharing motive for PSE—is, of course, best satisfied when there is 100 percent substitution *and* no alteration in the composition of S&L employment away from that which maximizes the cost effectiveness of the provision of public services. Local governments are worse off the smaller is the fiscal substitution effect. Such a program, however, is of relatively little interest from the point of view of aggregate employment policy and of no interest whatsoever from the point of view of national labor market policy.

In the remainder of this paper we will reexamine the question of the size and importance of the fiscal substitution effect of PSE programs. In Section II, a conceptual model of the determination of the level of S&L employment is set out and, in particular, the implications of three variants of PSE programs—wage subsidies, federalized programs, and lump-sum grants with maintenance-of-effort restrictions—are explored. In Section III the model is applied to aggregate time-series data in an effort to estimate the relevant parameters, including the fiscal substitution effect of current PSE programs, for an evaluation of the relative efficacy of the alternative approaches for increasing S&L employment. In Section IV we explore further the conceptual interdependence of the fiscal substitution effect and impact of PSE on the composition of S&L employment by "quality" of labor. Finally, in Section V we present a summary of our conclusions.

---

5 From a longer-run point of view, the distinction between the counter-recession and antipoverty objectives is not so clear. Again from the point of view of the new macroeconomics, a PSE program will have a positive effect on total employment in the economy after two or three years if it focuses on individuals who are "unemployable" in the private sector.

II. A CONCEPTUAL FRAMEWORK FOR ANALYZING THE IMPACT OF PSE ON GOVERNMENT EMPLOYMENT

It is useful to specify first how a community would decide how many workers should be hired by its local government in the absence of any federal programs designed to influence this variable. In this section we assume that there is only one quality of labor, but this assumption will be relaxed in Section IV. Following the approach of Ehrenberg [3, Ch. 2], we assume that perceived community welfare (the utility of the median voter) depends on the consumption of private goods and services (C) and the flow of services produced by the local government (X), say

$$(1) \qquad U = U(C,X), \qquad\qquad U_c > 0, \; U_x > 0$$

Government output depends on public employment (E) and nonlabor inputs (M) according to a production function

$$(2) \qquad X = \phi(E,M)$$

Given that the local government budget must be balanced, the community faces the budget constraint

$$(3) \qquad C + wE + vM = Y_n = Y - T + G$$

where Y is the total income of the community, T is the tax paid by the community to the federal government, G is lump-sum transfers by the federal government back to the local government, and w and v are the prices of labor and nonlabor inputs, respectively. Y_n is defined as net community income.

To determine the desired level of local government expenditure, substitute (2) for X in (1) and then maximize U with respect to E and M subject to the budget constraint. The first-order conditions imply that in general the optimal level of government employment in the community depends on net community income and the input prices. For present purposes it is useful to write out the demand for employment functions as

$$(4) \qquad E = F(Y_n,w)$$

Presumably, $\partial E/\partial Y_n > 0$ and $\partial E/\partial w < 0$, although, of course, it is possible from the theory that E is an inferior good or a Giffen good. Of particular interest for the policy question at hand are the income and wage elasticities of the demand for local government employment. These are defined as $\epsilon_Y = \partial \log E/\partial \log Y_n$ and $\epsilon_w = -\log E/\partial \log w$, respectively.

The first question concerning the impact of PSE programs is the effect on E of an untied lump-sum transfer from the federal to the local government, an increase in G. Its effect on E will depend in part on the extent to which federal taxes are increased to pay for the increase in G (versus financing G through a deficit or by cutting back other federal programs), and we will specify that $dT = \lambda dG$, $\lambda \geqslant 0.$[6] Differentiating (4) with respect to G, we see that

(5) $$\partial E/\partial G = (1 - \lambda)\partial E/\partial Y_n$$

and the number of government jobs created by a grant of size w is

(6) $$w(\partial E/\partial G) = (1 - \lambda)\epsilon_Y s$$

where $s = wE/Y_n$ is the share of community net income allocated to the local government wage bill.

The value of s has averaged .085 over the past 10 years in the United States, so it is unlikely that the size of the job-creation effect of a lump-sum transfer will be very large unless local government employment is subject to very high income elasticity of demand. Moreover, if federal taxes are raised by the increase in the lump-sum transfer, the average value of λ will be unity, and the program will have no effect on local employment. Some communities, presumably the less wealthy ones, will receive a larger grant than the amount they pay out in additional taxes, but this will be offset by the effect of a fall in Y_n in other communities.

The principal qualification of the conclusion that an untied lump-sum transfer program will have a relatively small impact on local government arises when one considers the possibility of transitory declines in Y_n due to economic recessions. If it is assumed that (1) local governments must balance their operating budgets each year, and (2) their tax rates cannot be altered in the short run, then a decline in $Y - T$ may force the local government to reduce E below the level it would choose if it could either increase taxes or run a temporary budget deficit.[7] (This is especially true if the other inputs in the production of local government expenditures are fixed in the short run—for example, interest on bonds.) In this case, an increase in G may result in a much larger increase in E than would be implied by (6).[8] On the other hand, the existence of such a program may alter the behavior of local governments in such a way that they no longer run surpluses in boom periods in order to smooth their employment levels over the business cycle; instead they would collect lower taxes over the course of time and would rely on federal subsidies to get them through periods of low tax

---

6   Increases in Y_n due to a Keynesian multiplier effect (when $\lambda < 0$) are obviously ignored in this formulation. In the subsequent empirical work, however, it is controlled for.

7   This is true only to the extent that S&L government revenues depend on $Y - T$. In 1970 approximately 35 percent of total S&L taxes came from the property tax, a source that may not vary directly with $Y - T$.

8   A policy along the lines of this approach is Title II of the proposed Public Works and Economic Development program, the so-called "counter-cyclical revenue sharing" provision. By this program, federal grants to S&Ls to "maintain customary services" would be triggered if the national unemployment rate exceeded 6 percent for three consecutive months.

revenues. The question of the degree to which local government administrators make such "rational" intertemporal allocations must be held open, *especially* in the light of recent casual evidence.[9]

In addition to untied lump-sum grants, federal programs to provide resources to local governments for purposes of expanding their employment levels can take three alternative forms. First, the federal government can provide a *wage subsidy* to each local government in a certain proportion to its total wage bill. Second, the federal government could actually hire workers and assign them to the local government—a federalized PSE program. Third, the federal government could provide lump-sum transfers to local governments coupled with legal and administrative "maintenance-of-effort" *restrictions* designed to yield a unit increase in local employment per federally funded PSE slot. Although both the PEP and CETA programs take the third form (with a sprinkling of a variant of the second), we will work out the analytics of each of them, for the empirical results in the following section will allow us to assess their relative job-creation potential.

If the federal government provides a subsidy of some fraction, say g, of the local government wage bill, the marginal cost of labor is reduced from w to $(1 - g)w$. E is then increased by a movement along the demand curve. To obtain an expression for the effect of g on E, differentiate (4) totally (that is, $dE = f_Y dY_n - wf_w dg$) and note that $dY_n = -dT = -\lambda gwdE - \lambda wEdg$. Solving for dE, we see that the effect on E of the rate at which the wage bill is subsidized is

(7) $$dE/dg = [\epsilon_w - (1-g)\lambda\epsilon_Y s]E/(1-g)(1 + \lambda g\epsilon_Y s)$$

To convert this into the ratio of the increase in wE to the increase in the total

---

9 If the two conditions for the efficacy of counter-cyclical revenue-sharing hold, then, other things equal, we would expect that S&L employment would be more cyclically sensitive than private sector employment, for private employers are not subject to a balanced budget constraint in all periods. As a crude test of this proposition, we regressed annual percentage changes in both private sector and S&L employment on the percentage change in real GNP and its lagged value from 1954 through 1974. The results were:

$$\Delta E_{priv} = -1.56 + .67\Delta Y + .32\Delta Y_{-1} \qquad R^2 = .71, \text{D.W.} = 1.53$$
$$\phantom{\Delta E_{priv} = -1.56} (.66) \quad (.10) \qquad (.11)$$

$$\Delta E_{S\&L} = 3.90 + .02\Delta Y + .22\Delta Y_{-1} \qquad R^2 = .25, \text{D.W.} = .95$$
$$\phantom{\Delta E_{S\&L} = 3.90} (.51) \quad (.08) \qquad (.09)$$

This suggests that although S&L employment is sensitive to changes in aggregate economic activity, it is only a fourth as sensitive as private sector employment. These results, however, should be interpreted with caution. The S&L sector is much more skill-intensive than the private sector (see Section IV), and the demand for highly skilled labor is relatively insensitive to variations in output. Work by one of the authors to resolve this question is currently in progress.

subsidy to the local government, we use the fact that $d(gwE)/dg = w[E + g(dE/dg)]$. Thus, the number of jobs created per w of the total subsidy is

$$(8) \qquad [dE/d(gwE)]\,w = [\epsilon_w - (1-g)\lambda\epsilon_Y s] / [1 - g(1 - \epsilon_w)]$$

For a relatively small program (say, under \$10 billion) g can effectively be ignored, and (8) reduces to $\epsilon_w - \lambda\epsilon_Y s$.

A second option, the possibility of which has been suggested by Killingsworth,[10] is to federalize the PSE program. Under this format the federal government would hire F employees to work in the particular local community, but the degree to which they would be subject to the control and supervision of the local government authorities is an open question. At one extreme they could be federally paid police officers fully integrated into the local government's police department; at the other extreme, they could be put to work fixing the roadbed of the railroad running through the community. In the first instance, they would be performing regular community services; in the second, they clearly would not be.

To formalize this option somewhat, assume that with the federalized PSE program the local government's production function may be rewritten as

$$(9) \qquad X = \phi(E + \theta F, M)$$

where θ is an efficiency parameter that reflects how useful the federally paid workers are to the local government. For the case of police officers, θ would be one; for the roadbed improvement gang, it would be (at least very close to) zero. The implications of this modification are most clearly seen by introducing the flow of efficiency units of labor from the point of view of the local government, $Z = E + \theta F$. Making the appropriate substitutions, the utility function for the community becomes $U = U[Y_n + w\theta F - wZE - vM, \phi(z,M)]$, and it is clear that the demand function for total employment takes on exactly the same form as (4), that is

$$(10) \qquad Z = f(Y_n + w\theta F, w)$$

An increase in F increases the flow of efficiency units of total employment through the income effect. The number of locally hired government employees is

$$(11) \qquad E = Z - \theta F,$$

$$= f(Y_n + w\theta f, w) - \theta F$$

and the impact of an increase in F on E is

---

10   See Killingsworth [11]. To be fair, Killingsworth does not propose that PSE be federalized. Instead, he argues that the question of the size of the fiscal substitution effect is unimportant because if there *were* substitution, the program could always be federalized.

(12) $$\partial E/\partial F = \epsilon ys(\theta - \lambda)(E + \theta F/E)(Y_n/Y_n + w\theta F) - \theta$$

Notice first that if the program simply hires employees to perform regular local government functions ($\theta = 1$), but increases taxes by the amount necessary to pay for them ($\lambda = 1$) the F PSE workers simply displace regular employees on a one-to-one basis. At the other extreme, however, if the F PSE workers perform tasks that have no relevance to normal local government operations ($\theta = 0$), E is only reduced by the income effect, for small values of F/E by $-\lambda\epsilon ys$, and the increment to total local employment is $1 - \lambda\epsilon ys$, which is undoubtedly positive.[11]

A third variant of PSE programs is to provide lump-sum transfers to the local government, coupled with restrictions on and exhortations about how the funds should be used. This description comes closest to depicting the PEP and CETA programs. The question in this case concerns how successful is the federal government in getting the local government to hire the same number of employees it would have hired in the absence of the program *plus* all the PSE participants. In other terms, the community wants to hire E_C local government workers, where $E_C = F(Y_n, w)$, but the federal authorities expect them to hire $E_f = f[Y_n - (1 - \lambda)wP, w] + P$ workers, where P is the number of PSE participants. Now $f[Y_n - (1 - \lambda)wP, w] \approx f(Y_n, w) - (1 - \lambda)wPf_Y$, so $E_f = E_C + [1 - (1 - \lambda)\epsilon ys]P$. Taking the actual employment level to be a weighted average of the community preference and the federal preference, we have

(13) $$E = \gamma E_C + (1 - \gamma)E_f$$

$$= f(Y_n, w) + (1 - \gamma)[1 - (1 - \lambda)\epsilon ys]P$$

where γ is the weight given to the community as opposed to the federal preference.

Differentiating with respect to P, we see that the impact of a marginal PSE slot on local government employment is

(14) $$\partial E/\partial P = \gamma(1 - \lambda)\epsilon ys + 1 - \gamma$$

If $\gamma = 1$ (that is, if the community is able to do what it wants with the grant), an additional PSE slot will have the same impact on E as any other form of general revenue-sharing—zero if $\lambda = 1$. On the other hand, if maintenance-of-effort

---

11   The analytics of this "federalized" case also apply to a small portion of the CETA program. For example, the allocation under the control of the governor of Massachusetts goes in part to the Local Initiative Program (MLIP), patterned after a Canadian program with the same name. Under MLIP, citizen groups are encouraged to submit proposals for projects to satisfy "unmet needs" in their communities in areas such as conservation, child care, public safety, and the like. Interestingly, the requests-for-proposals for the program states that projects must not "result in the substitution of MLIP funds for other funds for work which would otherwise be performed," which means that they want to keep θ as close to zero as possible in order to maximize the program's impact on total employment.

TABLE 1

EMPLOYMENT IMPACT OF ALTERNATIVE FORMS OF PSE PROGRAMS

Program Type	Jobs Created per w of Transfer
Unrestricted grant	$\epsilon_Y s(1 - \lambda)$
Wage subsidy	$\epsilon_w - \lambda \epsilon_Y s$
Federalized program	$1 - \theta + \epsilon_Y s(\theta - \lambda)$
Grant with restrictions	$1 - \gamma + \gamma \epsilon_Y s(1 - \lambda)$

restrictions are completely successful ($\gamma = 0$), E will increase by one for each PSE slot.

A summary of the predicted effects on local government employment of a transfer of W from the federal government for the three approaches to PSE programs appears in Table 1. These results assume that the program is relatively small (that is, g and F/E are both close to zero). To contrast the relative sizes of these effects, first notice that an unrestricted grant has a smaller effect than a wage subsidy as long as $\epsilon_w > \epsilon_Y s$, and, since $s = .085$, this is satisfied unless ϵ_w is very small relative to ϵ_Y. The wage subsidy format is more effective than the federalized program format so long as $\epsilon_w > 1 - \theta + \epsilon_Y s\theta$, and for $\theta = 0$ this is so only for $\epsilon_w > 1$. Wage subsidies are more effective than the subsidies with restrictions format if $\epsilon_w > 1 - \gamma[1 - (1 - \lambda)\epsilon_Y s]$; for $\lambda = 1$, this condition reduces to $\epsilon_w > 1 - \gamma$ and for $\lambda = 0$ to $\epsilon_w > 1 - \gamma(1 - \epsilon_Y s)$. Finally, a federalized PSE program will create more jobs per dollar of transfer than a restrictions program if $\theta < \gamma - [\epsilon_Y s/(1 - \epsilon_Y s)]\lambda (1 - \gamma)$, and this amounts essentially to the question of whether the federal authorities are better at getting local governments to hire more employees than they "want" (γ as close to zero as possible) or at selecting projects the local government would not have done with its own resources (θ close to zero).

III. ESTIMATES OF THE EMPLOYMENT-CREATION POTENTIAL OF ALTERNATIVE APPROACHES TO PSE

As we have pointed out, the PEP and CETA programs are basically examples of the grant-with-restrictions approach, and the principal question with respect to their performance concerns the value of γ, the extent to which each local government is able to treat PSE subsidies as completely unrestricted transfers. Bearing in mind that the size of the fiscal substitution effect is only a *part* of the story, we now proceed to attempt to estimate this as well as the other parameters of the model on aggregate time-series data.

To estimate a model along the lines of (13), we propose an estimating equation of the form

(15) $$N(t) = a_0 + a_1 Y_n(t) + a_2 W(t) + a_3 K(t) + a_4 P(t) + u(t)$$

where $N(t)$ is per capita non-PSE employment in the S&L sector, $Y_n(t)$ is real per capita income (including federal grants) potentially available to S&L governments, $W(t)$ is the average real wage of S&L employees, $K(t)$ is children ages 5–19 per capita, $P(t)$ is the number of PSE slots per capita, and $u(t)$ is a random disturbance term.[12] The variable $K(t)$ has been added to the employment equation to reflect changes in the demand for employment in the educational sector as the number of school-age children changes. The estimated coefficient on the PSE variable will be an estimate of $- [\gamma + (1 - \gamma) (1 - \lambda)\epsilon_Y s]$ or simply $-\gamma$ if it is assumed that federal taxes are increased by exactly the amount of the change in the expenditure on the PSE program (that is, $\lambda = 1$).

Because of the lack of data on the prices of nonlabor inputs in the S&L production process and of other shift variables in the demand function, time is included as an explanatory variable and seasonal dummy variables are also included. (See the Appendix for the complete specification of the model.) All four of the explanatory variables in (15) were initially entered in the form of Almon variables (restrictions: second degree polynomial with the coefficient on the variable lagged six quarters constrained to zero), but the initial results revealed that the current value of $w(t)$ was all the information necessary for that variable. The results for the period 1966-I–1975-IV are

(16) $$N(t) = -.037 + 7.19 \Sigma_0^5 \delta_i^1 Y_n(t - i) - 3.57 w(t)$$
$$(.011) \quad (1.74) \qquad\qquad (.52)$$

$$+ .184 \Sigma_0^5 \delta_i^2 K(t - i) - 1.02 \Sigma_0^5 \delta_i^3 P(t - i)$$
$$(.035) \qquad\qquad (.55)$$

$$+ .00034 t - .00010 S1 - .000008 S2 - .00123 S3$$
$$(.00004) \quad (.00010) \qquad (.00010) \qquad (.00027)$$

where $R^2 = .9982$, D.W. = 1.76, and the values in parentheses are the standard errors of the estimated coefficients. (The sum of the δ_is in each case is one.)

The implied values of the income and wage elasticities at the means of relevant variables are $\epsilon_Y = .62(.15)$ and $\epsilon_w = .56(.08)$. These estimates are quite close to the elasticities reported in other studies using different data and methodologies.[13] Notice that (16) implicitly assumes that grants have the same effect‑

---

12 See the Data Appendix for the definitions and source of each variable.

13 For example, in their time-series/cross-section study, Ashenfelter and Ehrenberg [1] obtain average estimates of $\epsilon_Y = .78$ and $\epsilon_w = .71$. Notice that (16) implicitly assumes that grants have the same effect on employment as community disposable income, and this may be tested explicitly by adding separate Almon variables for $Y_n(t) - G(t)$. The results yielded a higher point estimate of the sum of coefficients on grants than on disposable income, probably reflecting the fact that many federal grants are matching in nature. This difference, however, was not statistically significant, and we thus continue to use $Y_n(t)$ rather than its decomposition.

TABLE 2

ESTIMATED MARGINAL AND CUMULATIVE FISCAL SUBSTITUTION EFFECTS
AND S&L JOBS CREATED BY QUARTER AFTER INTRODUCTION OF PSE SLOT[a]

Quarter After Introduction of PSE Slot	Effect of PSE Variable		Effect of Grant	S&L Jobs Per 100 PSE Slots	
	Marginal $-a_4 \delta_i^3$	Cumulative $-a_4 \Sigma_0^i \delta_i^3$	$\epsilon_Y s \Sigma_0^i \delta_j^i$	$\lambda = 1$	$\lambda = 0$
1	-.015 (.174)	-.015 (.174)	.025 (.008)	102 (17)	104 (18)
2	.141 (.104)	.126 (.256)	.039 (.012)	87 (26)	91 (28)
3	.235 (.123)	.361 (.312)	.049 (.013)	64 (31)	69 (33)
4	.268 (.147)	.629 (.389)	.051 (.014)	37 (39)	42 (40)
5	.240 (.138)	.869 (.479)	.052 (.014)	13 (48)	18 (49)
6	.151 (.090)	1.020 (.545)	.053 (.013)	-2 (55)	3 (56)

a   Estimated standard errors of predicted effects in parentheses.

on employment as community disposable income, and this may be tested explicitly by adding separate Almon variables for $Y_n(t) - G(t)$ and $G(t)$. The results yielded a higher point estimate of the sum of coefficients on grants than on disposable income, probably reflecting the fact that many federal grants are matching in nature. This difference, however, was not statistically significant and we thus continue to use $Y_n(t)$ rather than its decomposition.

The sum of the lag coefficients on the PSE variable is -1.020, but its standard error is .545 which, although the estimated value of a_4 is significantly less than zero by conventional test standards, is such that the extent of fiscal substitution cannot be estimated very precisely. This is, of course, not very surprising, for PSE represents at most 2.8 percent of total S&L employment during the sample period. Qualifications aside, this point estimate suggests that in the long run the fiscal substitution effect of PSE is not significantly different from 100 percent. This implies that 100 PSE slots will cause a reduction of 2.0 S&L jobs in the long run if the program is financed by a tax increase ($\lambda = 1$) or an increase of 3.3 jobs if the program is financed by either deficit spending or an equivalent reduction in some set of other federal programs.

These estimates, however, refer to the long run, which in this case is six quarters, and it is interesting to examine the time path of the estimated impact of PSE programs on S&L employment. This is shown in Table 2 in which the lag structure for the relevant impact variables is sorted out. The first column shows the marginal fiscal substitution effect (the negative of the lag coefficient for each quarter) and the second column the cumulative effect. Interestingly, the fiscal substitution effect is negligible for the first one or two quarters after a PSE slot is filled, but then it gets very much larger until there is (a *point* estimate of) complete substitution after a year and a half. The third column shows the predicted number of jobs created in the S&L sector by an increase in lump-sum government grants equal to the wage rate, and it is clear that the mean response time of S&L employment to Y_n is shorter than to PSE slots. The last two columns show the predicted increase in S&L employment in response to 100 PSE slots, first under the assumption that federal taxes are raised to pay for the program and then on the assumption that the funds come from somewhere else. Because $\epsilon_Y S$ is only equal to .053, the effects of the two policies are quite similar.

It is worth stressing that PSE does appear to be a *potentially successful policy in influencing the level of S&L employment in the short run*—for two or three quarters after a slot is filled. This period corresponds to the budget cycle of local government decision-making. If *unanticipated* federal subsidies are received by a community in order to hire new employees, the city council will put people to work performing some functions that would not have been performed otherwise. When planning for the next budget takes place, however, the city administrators will attempt to use the PSE funds to finance regular government functions.[14] Still, the results are consistent with the view that PSE can be effective as a short-run counter-cyclical weapon. The major qualification to this arises from the possibility that if a particular program is institutionalized, local government administrators will come to anticipate revenues from it and modify their budgetary behavior accordingly. PEP and CETA were unexpected, so they had a short-run impact on S&L employment. On the other hand, a program such as Title II of the proposed Public Works and Economic Development bill is triggered as a result of fairly predictable events, and this might give S&Ls a lead-time in setting up a strategy for fiscal substitution.

It could be argued that PEP and CETA were different programs and that they might have different impacts. PEP, for example, was heralded as a short-term program (recall the use of the word "emergency" in its original title), and CETA may be viewed as more permanent. Given the large standard error of the

---

14　As an example, in February 1975 Los Angeles put 373 laborers to work cleaning city streets and alleys. City Councillor Louis Nowell said, "We clean up the alleys today and tomorrow they are dirty." (*Los Angeles Times*, February 8, 1975, p. 1). We have no information on what happened in this case, but we suspect that these particular PSE workers will not be doing this function too far into the next budget cycle.

estimated coefficient on the PSE variable, however, there seems only faint promise in attempting to distinguish between the effects of its components. Nevertheless, separate variables, *PEP* and *CETA*, both in Almon form, were entered into an equation that was otherwise identical with (16). As expected, the point estimates were smaller for *PEP* than for *CETA*. The results yielded an estimated sum of lag coefficients of -.22(.74) for *PEP* and -1.29(.58) for *CETA*. Neither of these coefficients is significantly different from minus one (complete substitution), however, and the null hypothesis that PEP and CETA slots had the same impact on S&L employment cannot be refuted ($F = 2.33 < F_{2,28}^{.05} = 3.34$).

To test the robustness of our results with respect to the PSE variables, we introduced an alternative specification—the stock adjustment model. This model has the disadvantage of implicitly assuming that S&L employment adjusts to all variables at exactly the same rate (which our Almon results suggested was not true). The point estimate of the long-run fiscal substitution effect was .82, and this is reached very quickly (for example, 65 percent substitution in the first quarter rather than the Almon estimate of, in effect, zero). We also extended the sample period back another 10 years and, again using the Almon technique, obtained estimated coefficients on *PEP* of -1.77(.59) and *CETA* of -1.12(.80). The residuals of this equation were highly autocorrelated, and further tests revealed that the model was subject to fairly serious structural change over the period. The obvious point is that despite plausibility of some aspects of the results in (16) (especially the time path, if not the level, of the fiscal substitution effect), they should be used cautiously.[15]

The results also permit us to make estimates of the probable impact of alternative approaches to PSE policy, and these are presented in Table 3. With respect to the wage subsidy approach, the effect of a transfer of sufficient size to hire 100 additional workers will, in the absence of a corresponding increase in federal taxes, cause an increase of 100 ϵ_w = 56 S&L workers. Since we found that *w* influenced *E* immediately, this effect does not vary over time. (Recall, however, that Ashenfelter and Ehrenberg [1] obtained an estimate of ϵ_w = .71, which would make a wage subsidy relatively more desirable than would our esti-

---

15 In [10] we estimated the fiscal substitution effect for PEP to be 68 percent. However, that result was subject to several qualifications: (1) only eight quarters of data on PEP were available; (2) the stock-adjustment model imposed a potentially inappropriate lag structure on the PEP variable; (3) the model was estimated only for employment in the noneducation sector; (4) the wage rate was not included as an independent variable; (5) results were presented only for the longer sample period, 1956-I–1973-II. When the current Almon lag model in (16) is estimated for 1956-I–1973-II, the sum of lagged coefficients on PEP is -1.14(.47), i.e., effectively complete displacement after six quarters; for 1966-I–1973-II, the estimate is -1.41(.55). Thus, although our original results suggested a large fiscal substitution effect, correcting for (2)–(5) by using the current model would have suggested complete substitution in the long run, but the results would still have been subject to (1), the availability of only eight quarters of data on PEP.

TABLE 3

PREDICTED IMPACT OF 100 PSE SLOTS ON S&L EMPLOYMENT
FOR ALTERNATIVE PSE POLICIES

Program Type	λ	Quarter					
		1	2	3	4	5	6
Unrestricted grant	0	2	4	5	5	5	5
Wage subsidy	0	56	56	56	56	56	56
	1	54	52	51	51	51	51
Federalized, $\theta = .3$	0	71	71	72	72	72	72
	1	69	68	67	67	67	67
Federalized, $\theta = .7$	0	31	32	33	33	33	33
	1	29	29	28	28	28	28
Restrictions	0	104	91	69	42	18	3
	1	102	87	64	37	13	-2

mate.) If federal taxes are increased to pay for the wage subsidy, the impact of the program will be the result for λ = 0 less the effect of an unrestricted grant— 54 in the first quarter and 51 in the third quarter and thereafter. (The corresponding long-run effect in this case from the Ashenfelter-Eherenberg estimate is 64 jobs.)

Estimates of the effect on S&L employment of a federalized program depend on the unknown parameter θ, the degree to which the federalized PSE programs are absorbed into regular local government functions. Without prejudging what its probable value might be in a real-world program, we assume two values, .3 and .7 (that is, federalized are worth 30 and 70 percent, respectively, of what a regular S&L worker is worth in terms of getting normal S&L functions done). Predictably, this leads to an employment increase of 70 or 30, plus or minus as λ is 0 or 1, in the two cases.

Finally, our point estimates for the job-creation impact of PSE programs are presented for the restrictions case. This obviously has a larger short-run job-creation impact and a smaller long-run impact.

IV. THE EFFECTS OF PSE ON THE COMPOSITION OF STATE AND LOCAL GOVERNMENT EMPLOYMENT

As we pointed out in Section I, if PSE is viewed as an antipoverty program, the most crucial question about PSE is whether or not it induces local governments to hire workers who are at the low end of the skill distribution. Although this question is largely irrelevant to the evaluation of PSE as a counter-recession policy, it is very important in assessing the longer-term macroeconomic (that is, inflationary) impact of PSE. Finally, the composition question is quite important if the objective of PSE is pure revenue-sharing; a finding that S&Ls use the money to hire the same *quality* as well as quantity of labor would be interpreted as favorable in this case. We thus turn to the question of how PSE influences the composition of S&L employment.

First, the composition question is to a large extent related to the fiscal substitution issue. Suppose a particular local government hires two types of labor, "skilled" and "unskilled" for lack of better terms, in a particular combination depending on their relative wages (as determined by the local labor market or, increasingly, as negotiated with trade unions) and the technology of the production process. A lump-sum grant that is not accompanied by an increase in taxes will cause an increase in the desired employment level along the lines of the model outlined in Section II, and in the present case the demands for the two types of labor will increase in the same proportion.[16]

A PSE program with restrictions on the type of workers that can be hired (such as wage ceilings, eligibility restricted to the unemployed, etc.) will *presumably* force the local governments to use their PSE funds to hire unskilled workers. This, however, causes the local government to be out of equilibrium, for it has "too many" unskilled workers. (To use the Los Angeles example, it has a number of persons to clean up the alleys, but no one to supervise them.) Thus, as time goes on, the local government will allow its unskilled work force to decline and will use the funds to increase its skilled work force (*and*, to the extent there is fiscal substitution similar to the point estimate in the preceding section, to reduce taxes and/or increase expenditure on nonlabor inputs). What this means is that fiscal substitution is likely to be skill-specific, and it implies further that even if it can be shown that PSE participants are drawn from the low end of the skill distribution, it does not *necessarily* mean that the program increased the relative demand for labor with low skills.

On the other hand, a necessary (but, because of the possibility of skill-specific fiscal substitution, not sufficient) condition for the conclusion that PSE is an effective antipoverty program is that PSE participants are taken from the low end of the skill distribution.[17] It thus appears interesting to attempt to make an assessment of the skill distribution of PSE participants.

The approach we will take is based on the notion that some identifiable group (with characteristics tending to be the opposite of white, male, prime age,

---

16 We are implicitly assuming a homothetic production function in the two types of labor.

17 A negative finding on this point would not, however, be necessary in order to conclude that PSE was satisfying the pure revenue-sharing objective because of the possibility of skill-specific fiscal substitution. It would not be sufficient either unless there were a high rate of fiscal substitution for all skills.

and highly educated) in the economy face inordinate difficulties in securing steady employment and thus experience high average unemployment rates. Part of the cause of this imbalance is the existence of various institutional rigidities in the wage structure, the implication of which is that, conditional on the perpetuation of conditions that create these rigidities, the social opportunity cost of placing disadvantaged members of the labor force in PSE positions will be less than their observed wage levels.[18]

Let the equilibrium unemployment rate of the ith individual be given by

$$(20) \qquad U_i = f(C_i, B_i)$$

where C_i is a set of observable characteristics, and B_i is a set of unobservable (or, at least, unobserved) characteristics. The C_i would include the standard variables such as age, education, and sex, and the B_i would include variables such as ability, motivation, and the like. Treating C_i and B_i as composite variables, the linear form of (20) is

$$(21) \qquad U_i = \mu_0 + \mu_1 C_i + \mu_2 B_i$$

where the variables are defined so that the μs are positive. To obtain the equilibrium unemployment rate for the jth subset of the population, for example, of PSE participants, one can simply replace C_i and B_i with their means for the group, or

$$(22) \qquad \bar{U}_j = \mu_0 + \mu_1 \bar{C}_j + \mu_2 \bar{B}_j$$

To compare the equilibrium unemployment rate of PSE participants with that of the jth group, we have

$$(23) \qquad \bar{U}_{PSE} - \bar{U}_j = \mu_1(\bar{C}_{PSE} - \bar{C}_j) + \mu_2(\bar{B}_{PSE} - \bar{B}_j)$$

The jth group can be the entire labor force, regular S&L employees, or whatever.

An important limitation of this approach is that μ_2, the vector of coefficients on the unobservable characteristics, cannot, by definition, be estimated, and we will get to this shortly. We are, however, able to estimate the other parameters. To do so, it is necessary to use a year in which the aggregate labor market was close to "equilibrium"—that is, the aggregate unemployment rate was neither too high nor too low. Fortunately, in 1970 the aggregate unemployment rate was 4.9 percent, probably just about exactly the value of the natural unemployment rate at that time (see [6]), and, of course, 1970 was also a Census year. To conform with available statistics on the characteristics of participants of various manpower programs, we obtained Census data on unemployment rates for 346 age-education-sex-race cells and then regressed the unemployment rate in the ith cell on two age dummies (YNG = age less than 22, MID

---

18 See [7], esp. pp. 744–45; see also [9]. Hall argues further that indeed the opportunity cost of the low unemployment groups is *above* their observed wage rate.

TABLE 4

DISTRIBUTION OF SELECTED SKILL CHARACTERISTICS FOR SELECTED MANPOWER PROGRAMS AND GROUPS IN LABOR FORCE

| Variable | Age | PSE | | Training | | | | Experienced Civilian Labor Force[d] | S&L Government[e] | |
| | | PEP[a] | CETA[b] | MDTA[c] | | | CETA[b] | | All | Excluding Teachers |
				1964	1968	1973				
YNG	<22	31	24	25	39	36	27	13	11	11
MID	22–44	57	63	44	50	57	62	51	50	46
—	>44	12	13	11	11	7	10	36	39	43
Education										
LOWED	<12	30	24	48	59	36	39	39	18	24
HISK	12	41	44	45	35	54	42	35	28	39
—	>12	29	32	7	6	10	19	26	54	37
Sex										
—	Male	72	71	60	55	67	54	63	50	55
FEM	Female	28	29	40	45	33	46	37	50	45
Race										
—	White	60	66	61	36	49	53	84	85	84
BLACK	Black	22	23	28	45	35	32	11	11	12
SPAN	Spanish	14	8	9	15	12	12	4	3	3
—	Other	4	3	2	4	3	3	1	3	3
—	EEUR	5.8	5.2	6.0	7.8	6.8	6.2	5.0	3.6	3.8

a Public Employment Program statistics obtained from Department of Labor for participants in fiscal year 1973.
b *Continuous Longitudinal Manpower Survey*, Report No. 1, prepared for Department of Labor by Westat, Inc., Contract No. 23-24-75-07, January 1976, Table 3–1. These data apply to enrollees in the third quarter of fiscal year 1975.
c *Manpower Report of the President*, Washington, 1974, Table F–5, p. 362.
d U.S. Bureau of the Census, *Industrial Characteristics*, PC(2)-7B, 1970, Table 3.
e U.S. Bureau of the Census, *Government Workers*, PC(2)-7D, 1970, Table 5.

= age between 22 and 44), two education dummies ($LOWED$ = education less than 12, $HISK$ = education equal to 12 years), two ethnic dummies ($BLACK$ and $SPAN$), and one sex dummy (FEM). The excluded group is thus white, male, more than high school education, older than age 44. The generalized least squares (weighted by the square root of the labor force in each cell) results were

$$(24) \quad UN_i = .49 + 6.75\,YNG + 1.27\,MID + 3.21\,LOWED + 1.06\,HISK$$
$$(.24)\ (.28) \qquad (.20) \qquad (.23) \qquad\quad (.23)$$
$$+ 2.21\,BLACK + 1.51\,SPAN + 1.15\,FEM$$
$$(.28) \qquad\quad (.43) \qquad\quad (.18)$$

where R^2 = .801 and the standard errors of the estimated coefficients are in parentheses below the coefficients.

Table 4 shows the distribution of these skill characteristics for various groups in selected government programs and the labor force as a whole. It is difficult to make comparisons solely on the basis of the table. For example, PSE participants are younger and more likely to be from minority groups, but they are also more educated and less likely to be women. The evidence, so to speak, is mixed. Thus, we calculated an estimated equilibrium unemployment rate (EEUR) for each of the groups on the basis of the coefficients in (24); these figures are presented on the bottom line of the table.

Before we discuss these comparisons, we must point out *two serious difficulties* associated with this procedure. First, the method of calculating EEUR is based on the assumption that each of the variables influences the unemployment rate additively. For example, being female raises the equilibrium rate of unemployment for a particular group by 1.15 percentage points regardless of age, education, or ethnicity. This is, of course, not true in general.[19] An interactive model, however, would require cross-tabulation of characteristics, and for most groups in Table 4 these are not available. Thus, for example, if PSE participants under age 22 were more (less) inclined to be black than were all PSE participants, the EEUR for PSE is, ceteris paribus, biased down (up), for young blacks have very high unemployment rates.[20]

---

19 For example, adding interaction terms between *FEM, BLACK,* and *SPAN* and each of the four age and education dummies suggested that generally being older and more educated lowered *UN* more for these groups than for white males. The test that the addition of these 12 variables added to the explanation of *UN* yielded F = 7.40, which is significantly different from zero at the 1 percent level.

20 In principle, the interactive problem can be attacked by analyzing the unemployment propensities of demographic groups with microeconomic data (e.g., the CPS) and then obtaining weighted EEURs for alternative programs with program data on the joint characteristics of participants. Work along these lines is in progress, and the initial results suggest that the EEUR is biased upward for PSE participants and downward for participants in CETA training programs. The extent of the bias, however, is fairly small.

Second, the validity of the method of calculating the EEURs is also subject to bias due to the fact that the average value of the unobservable characteristics may vary across groups.[21] With respect to the EEUR for PSE, it is possible that the true long-run employability potential of PSE participants is lower than the four observable characteristics would indicate. One indication of this possibility is the fact that they were unemployed at the time of entry. (More strictly for CETA-PSE, we know that 76 percent of participants were unemployed the *day* before entry.) On the other hand, local governments may screen potential PSE participants to eliminate those who appear unlikely to be useful employees (have high B_is), and this would lessen the possible positive covariance between B_i and PSE participation. Needless to say, questions concerning the average value of the unobservable characteristics for the various groups is unresolvable, but the bias possibility should be borne in mind as comparisons involving the EEURs are made.

Turning to the EEURs, the estimated values for the two PSE programs are 5.8 for PEP and 5.2 for CETA. These values are only slightly higher than the EEUR for the aggregate labor force. Notice, however, that the EEUR in the S&L sector is 3.6 (3.8 excluding teachers), so there is no question but that PSE participants were less employable in a long-run sense than was the average S&L employee. However, this points out a fundamental problem with the PSE approach *as an antipoverty program*. The S&L sector is very skill-intensive, and it is therefore difficult to expand low-skill jobs in that sector. Taken at face value (that is, ignoring the possibility of skill-specific fiscal substitution and the two possible sources of bias in the EEURs), the results suggest that while S&Ls lowered their hiring standards to accommodate the PSE program, their initial standards were so high that the effect of the program was *neutral* with respect to the composition of aggregate labor demand with regard to skill.[22]

---

21 To some extent this bias will be eliminated because of the covariance of the unobservable variables with education. For example, less able and less motivated people will generally obtain less schooling, biasing the coefficient μ_2 away from its "true" value which is good in this case.

22 Table 4 also shows the distribution of skill characteristics and the associated EEURs for three separate years of MDTA Institutional and for CETA Employability Development programs. PSE programs, of course, focus on groups with lower equilibrium unemployment rates. Notice that the values of the EEURs for 1964 and 1968 are in line with what is commonly believed about MDTA—that in the latter part of the 1960s the program shifted from an emphasis on reducing unemployment in the aggregate as much as possible (and thus choosing to train the most job-ready) to a focus on the most disadvantaged members of society. A subsidiary issue in the overall evaluation of CETA, including training programs under Title I, concerns whether the fall in the EEUR for MDTA for 1973 and to CETA in 1975 occurred because of the increase in the aggregate unemployment rate or because of the defederalization of training programs. That question, however, is clearly outside the scope of this paper.

V. SUMMARY OF MAJOR CONCLUSIONS

We have examined the questions of the size and nature of the fiscal substitution effect of public service employment programs (the possible tendency of state and local governments to use a major portion of their federal grants, which are supposed to be used for net employment creation, to finance government services that would otherwise have been financed from local revenues) from a number of perspectives. Our conclusions are as follows:

1. The importance of the size of the fiscal substitution effect in assessing the efficacy of PSE depends on the objectives of the program. If PSE is viewed as a counter-cyclical employment policy, the size of the substitution effect is a factor in comparing its impact with that of other forms of fiscal policy, but even with 100 percent substitution, PSE is as effective as a federal tax cut. If PSE is viewed as a tool of antipoverty policy, a large fiscal substitution effect is not important if it can be established that the program alters the composition of S&L employment toward individuals who are at the low end of the skill distribution. If such individuals are not employed, PSE is not an effective instrument of labor market policy, especially if the fiscal substitution effect is large. Finally, a third possible objective of PSE is pure revenue-sharing, which is best accomplished when the fiscal substitution effect is 100 percent.

2. There are several ways in which PSE programs can be set up, and four alternatives are examined from a theoretical point of view with respect to their employment-creation potential. They include: (a) untied lump-sum grants, (b) a wage subsidy on S&L employment, (c) a federalized program, and (d) grants with maintenance-of-effort restrictions. The current PSE component of CETA contains elements of (a), (c), and (d), but it is presumably dominated by (d). How successful a restrictions variant of a PSE program is depends on how well the federal authorities coerce local governments to hire more labor than they would choose to, and the degree to which they do can, in principle, be estimated.

3. The empirical results for an analysis of aggregate S&L employment between 1966-I and 1975-IV suggest that the fiscal substitution effect of PSE is very small for one or two quarters after introduction of a PSE slot, but then rises to about 100 percent after five quarters. Taken at face value, this finding is consistent with notions of the local government business cycle. It also suggests that PSE may be a very effective counter-recession tool in the short run, but not over longer periods of time. These results, however, are subject to a fairly wide error band, for PSE programs have been small factors in the overall determination of S&L employment, and they should, accordingly, be used with caution.

4. On the basis of the other parameters estimated in the model, estimates of the job-creation potential of alternative approaches to PSE are derived. The point estimates suggest that the traditional PSE format, as represented by PEP

and CETA (and, to an extent, by Title II of the proposed Public Works and Economic Development bill), is probably more effective than a wage subsidy in increasing S&L employment up to a year after triggering of the program, but thereafter the reverse is true.[23]

5. An analysis of the effect of PSE on the composition of employment demand by skill suggests that although PSE participants are much less employable in a long-run sense than the average S&L employee, they are not much different in this respect than the average member of the aggregate labor force. This conclusion, however, must be qualified by the possibility that fiscal substitution is skill-specific (that is, local governments hire their low-skilled participants through PSE but fail to maintain their low-skilled non-PSE work forces at their pre-PSE levels) and by the existence of the two sources of bias in our measures of employability.

DATA APPENDIX FOR SECTION II

Our basic quarterly model of S&L government employment determination is:

$$
\frac{E - PSE}{POP}(t) = a_0 + a_1 \Sigma_0^5 \delta_l^1 \frac{Y + SLBTAX - FTAX + G}{POP*P}(t-1)
$$
$$
+ a_2 \ w/P \ (t) + a_3 \ \Sigma_0^5 \ \delta_l^2 (K/POP)(t-1)
$$
$$
+ a_4 \ \Sigma_0^5 \ \delta_l^3 (PSE/POP)(t-1) + a_5 t + a_6 S1
$$
$$
+ a_7 S2 + a_8 S3 + u(t)
$$

where E = total S&L semployment; PSE = PEP + CETA participants; POP = population; Y = personal income; $SLBTAX$ = S&L indirect business taxes; $FTAX$ = federal taxes; G = federal grants to S&L governments; P = personal consumption deflator; w = average wage of S&L employees; K = children ages 5-19; t = time; and $S1, S2, S3$ = seasonal dummy variables.

The definition of community personal income, $Y + SLBTAX - FTAX/POP*P$, was suggested by Roger Bolton [2].

The wage rate is constructed by dividing total compensation of S&L employees by total S&L employment.

The data sources are as follows: Personal income, federal taxes, state and local indirect business taxes, grants to state and local governments, personal consumption deflator, and compensation of S&L government employees through 1974-IV are from U.S. Department of Commerce, *Survey of Current Business*, Vol. 56, Part II (January 1976), Tables 2.1, 3.2, 3.4, 3.2, 7.11, and 3.7, respec-

---

23 Judgment about the efficacy of a federalized program with respect to job creation requires knowledge of the value of a parameter that cannot be estimated until such a program is in place.

tively. Data for 1975-I-IV are from the *Survey of Current Business* (February 1976), National Income and Product Tables, pp. 7-14.

Total S&L employment is a quarterly average of monthly data in U.S. Department of Labor, Bureau of Labor Statistics, *Employment and Earnings, United States, 1909-72*, Bull. 1312-9, p. 604, and monthly publications of *Employment and Earnings*, Table B-2.

Population and children ages 5-19 are quarterly interpolations of annual values in *Economic Report of the President* (Washington: U.S. Government Printing Office, 1976), Table B-21, p. 195.

Employment levels for CETA and PEP are quarterly averages of monthly figures obtained through the Office of the Assistant Secretary for Policy Evaluation and Research, U.S. Department of Labor. The CETA figures include public service employment under Titles I, II, and VI.

REFERENCES

1. Orley Ashenfelter and Ronald G. Ehrenberg. "The Demand for Labor in the Public Sector." In *Labor in the Public Sector*, ed. Daniel S. Hamermesh. Princeton, N.J.: Princeton University Press, 1975. Pp. 55-78.
2. Roger E. Bolton. "Predictive Models for State and Local Government Purchases." In *The Brookings Model: Some Further Results*, ed. James S. Duesenberry and others. Chicago: Rand McNally and Co., 1969.
3. Ronald G. Ehrenberg. *The Demand for State and Local Government Employees*. Lexington, Mass.: D.C. Heath and Co., 1972.
4. Alan Fechter. *Public Employment Programs*. Washington: American Enterprise Institute for Public Policy Research, 1975.
5. Edward M. Gramlich and Harvey Galper. "State and Local Fiscal Behavior and Federal Grant Policy." *Brookings Papers on Economic Activity* (1: 1973): 15-58.
6. Robert E. Hall. "The Process of Inflation in the Labor Market." *Brookings Papers on Economic Activity* (2:1974): 343-93.
7. ———. "Turnover in the Labor Force." *Brookings Papers on Economic Activity* (2:1972).
8. George E. Johnson. "Evaluating the Macroeconomic Effects of Public Employment Programs." In *Evaluating the Labor Market Effects of Social Programs*, eds. Orley Ashenfelter and James Blum. Princeton, N.J.: Princeton University Press, forthcoming.
9. ———. "The Labor Market Displacement Effect in the Analysis of the Net Impact of Manpower Training Programs." Working Paper No. 84, University of Michigan, January 1976.
10. George E. Johnson and James D. Tomola. "An Impact Evaluation of the Public Employment Program." Technical Analysis Paper No. 17. Washing-

ton: Office of Evaluation, ASPER, U.S. Department of Labor.

11. Charles C. Killingsworth. "CETA and Manpower Program Evaluation." In *Proceedings of the 27th Annual Winter Meeting, Industrial Relations Research Association.* Madison, Wis.: The Association, 1975. Pp. 203–13.

12. National Planning Association. *An Evaluation of the Economic Impact Project of the Public Employment Program.* Prepared for the Manpower Administration, U.S. Department of Labor, under Contract No. 42-2-001-11. Final Report, May 1974.

13. Michael Wiseman. "On Giving a Job: The Implementation and Allocation of Public Service Employment." Working Paper No. 58, Institute of Industrial Relations, University of California, Berkeley, February 1975.

14. ――――. "Public Employment as Fiscal Policy." *Brookings Papers on Economic Activity* (forthcoming).

32

THE COMPREHENSIVE EMPLOYMENT AND TRAINING ACT

By

WILLIAM MIRENGOFF and LESTER RINDLER

The Comprehensive Employment and Training Act of 1973—CETA —resulted from the need for assimilation of diverse manpower programs. The purpose of this new legislation was based on the assumption that local authorities have better understanding of local needs and, therefore, can be more effective in designing programs to meet local needs. This article is a chapter from William Mirengoff and Lester Rindler's The Comprehensive Employment and Training Act. *In it they thoroughly assess the impact of CETA on manpower programs and enrich the reader's comprehension of the changes involved in shifting from categorized manpower programs to local control.*

From William Mirengoff and Lester Rindler, "Overview." Pp. 1-19 (Chapter 1) in *The Comprehensive Employment and Training Act—Impact on People, Places, Programs: An Interim Report.* Staff paper prepared for the Committee on Evaluation of Employment and Training Programs, Assembly of Behavioral and Social Sciences, National Research Council, National Academy of Sciences, 1976.

INTRODUCTION

The antecedents of manpower programs can be traced to the 1930s and earlier, but the current emphasis dates from the Area Redevelopment Act of 1961 and the Manpower Development and Training Act of 1962 (MDTA). Two distinct periods are identifiable: from 1963 to 1970, and from 1971 to the present. The earlier period focused on structural problems in the labor market--the intractable difficulties of the poor and disadvantaged who lacked the preparation, experience, and skills to get and hold a job. New programs providing remedial education, training, and work experience would, it was hoped, enhance their employability. These were authorized by the MDTA, the Economic Opportunity Act (EOA), and civil rights legislation. The economic setting was favorable; during most of the period, employment demand was expanding. It was possible to find jobs for some of the disadvantaged workers in the interstices of the job market.

The current period, beginning in the early 1970s, was marked by counter-cyclical programs in response to rising unemployment levels. The Emergency Employment Act of 1971 (EEA), which subsidized state and local public service jobs for a two-year period, was designed to put unemployed people--not necessarily the most disadvantaged--into employment quickly while providing badly needed public services in local communities.

By the end of the 1960s, there were more than 17 programs, each with its own legislative and organizational base, funding source, and regulations. Out of these so-called categorical programs flowed 10,000 or more specific manpower projects, often several in the same community competing for the same clientele and resources. These programs generally were conducted through public and nonpublic agencies but not through the local governments themselves.

Although there had been general dissatisfaction with this patchwork approach for some time, it was not until the end of 1973 that Congress and the Administration

SUMMARY OF THE COMPREHENSIVE
EMPLOYMENT AND TRAINING ACT

The Comprehensive Employment and Training Act of 1973 (PL 93-203, as amended) has seven titles:

Title I establishes a program of financial assistance to state and local governments (prime sponsors) for comprehensive manpower services. Prime sponsors are cities and counties of 100,000 or more, and consortia, defined as any combination of government units in which one member has a population of 100,000 or more. A state may be a prime sponsor for areas not covered by local governments.

The prime sponsor must submit a comprehensive plan acceptable to the Secretary of Labor. The plan must set forth the kinds of programs and services to be offered and give assurances that manpower services will be provided to unemployed, underemployed, and disadvantaged persons most in need of help.

The sponsor must also set up a planning council representing local interests to serve in an advisory capacity.

The mix and design of services is to be determined by the sponsor, who may continue to fund programs of demonstrated effectiveness or set up new ones.

Eighty percent of the funds authorized under this Title are apportioned in accordance with a formula based on previous levels of funding, unemployment, and low income. The 20 percent not under the formula are to be distributed as follows: 5 percent for special grants for vocational education, 4 percent for state manpower services, and 5 percent to encourage consortia. The remaining amount is available at the Secretary's discretion.

State governments must establish a state manpower services council to review the plans of prime sponsors and make recommendations for coordination and for the cooperation of state agencies.

Title II provides funds to hire unemployed and underemployed persons in public service jobs in areas of substantial unemployment. Title III provides for direct federal supervision of manpower programs for Indians, migrant and seasonal farm workers, and special groups, such as youth, offenders, older workers, persons of limited English-speaking ability, and other disadvantaged. This title also gives the Secretary the responsibility for research, evaluation, experimental and demonstration projects, labor market information, and job-bank programs. Title IV continues the Job Corps. Title V establishes a National Manpower Commission. Title VI, added in December 1974 under the Emergency Jobs and Unemployment Assistance Act, authorizes a one-year appropriation of $2.5 billion for a public service employment program for all areas, not just for areas of substantial unemployment. Title VII contains provisions applicable to all programs, such as prohibitions against discrimination and political activity.

agreed upon a manpower reform bill, and the Comprehensive Employment and Training Act (CETA) was passed.

The new law, which became effective in July 1974, transferred control of Department of Labor manpower programs to state and local officials. Cities and counties of 100,000 or more (and combinations thereof) may under Title I receive federal funds to develop and run the types of manpower programs that they find most useful for their needs.

Major shifts in methods of delivering government services occur infrequently, hence a study of the changes resulting from CETA affords an opportunity to examine the impact of such a major shift on human resources programs. The central issue is the impact of decentralization and decategorization--the essential features of CETA--on places, programs, and people, and on the administration of manpower programs.

The confluence of several forces made the enactment of CETA in December 1973 possible. First, Congress and federal manpower administrators were convinced of the need to overhaul the burgeoning profusion of manpower programs. Second, the Nixon Administration had embraced the New Federalism and embarked upon a drive for revenue-sharing legislation. CETA was viewed as the first of several special revenue-sharing programs. Third, state and local governments, generally bypassed in manpower programs, were interested in assuming a strategic role. Finally the Watergate crisis loosened rigidly held positions and made differences between the legislative and executive branches of governments easier to resolve.

Although opinions differ as to whether CETA is in fact a revenue-sharing program, it is generally agreed that its purpose is to shift control over the multibillion-dollar manpower program, within broad limits, from federal to local officials and to increase flexibility in the use of these resources by local prime sponsors.

The rationale for the key elements of the legislation--decentralization and decategorization--is both pragmatic and ideological. The pragmatists assume that local control is a superior way to plan and administer manpower programs. It was expected that programs would be designed to meet local needs, that ineffective ones would be weeded out, that comprehensive programs would replace fragmented ones, and that innovations would be introduced.

The ideological underpinning is the belief that a decentralized system is a better expression of popular will. It was assumed that under CETA there would be greater community involvement and that local decision makers would be more closely attuned to the electorate and to the clients served.

EXTENT OF DECATEGORIZATION
AND DECENTRALIZATION

Although the purpose of the new legislation is to provide training and employment opportunities through a decategorized and decentralized system, CETA in fact still operates to a large extent through categorical programs and with substantial federal involvement. Of the four titles in the original statute that authorize operating programs, three establish programs for special purposes or for particular groups. Title II sets up a public employment program for areas of substantial unemployment; Title III authorizes programs for Indians, migratory farm workers, and other groups with special problems; Title IV continues the Job Corps for disadvantaged youths. However, the Act permits prime sponsors to interchange funds among several Titles. 2/

Title I (Comprehensive Manpower Services), which is the main focus of this report, authorizes a decategorized manpower system. It replaces numerous programs, each with its own set of regulations and supportive bureaucracy, with a flexible system of manpower services. However, the extent of decategorization that actually occurs locally rests with the prime sponsors. They are free to retain or establish as few or as many special programs as they deem necessary.

In terms of funding, 34 percent of the original fiscal 1975 CETA appropriation went to titles that authorize categorical programs. However, the enactment of a special public service employment program (Title VI) in December 1974 3/ and appropriations for a summer youth program radically altered the picture. Now 58 percent of CETA funds are earmarked for special use. Thus, before CETA was well off the ground, it was turned back toward a prescribed system of specific programs for special problems.

Congressional intent to shift control of programs and funds from federal to state and local authorities was originally reflected only in Titles I and II. The addition of Title VI and a summer youth program as decentralized (although categorized) activities brought the proportion of CETA resources managed by local authorities to 89 percent in fiscal 1975. 4/

2/ The act permits use of Title II and Title VI (Public Service Employment) funds for Title I (Comprehensive Manpower Services) or Title IIIA (Special Target Groups) programs at the option of the prime sponsor, while Title I funds may be used for public service employment.
3/ Emergency Jobs and Unemployment Assistance Act of 1974.
4/ Some funds authorized by those titles are for the discretionary distribution by the Secretary of Labor (see Table 3, p. 33).

Although Congress clearly intended to decentralize most manpower programs, the nature and degree of this local autonomy is qualified. It was not expected that the Department of Labor would simply "put the money on the stump and run." On the contrary, the act explicitly provides for federal oversight responsibilities and has built specific intervention points, such as the approval of local plans, into the administrative process. In addition, there are detailed regulations and other requirements that set limits on the degree of local freedom.

The line between local control and federal oversight responsibilities is not finely drawn and this irresolution is reflected in the relationship between prime sponsors on the one hand, and local program operators and regional offices of the Manpower Administration on the other. Complete prime sponsor control would require that the independence of individual local project operators be subordinated to prime sponsor authority, and that regional office control be replaced by an oversight and technical assistance role. The survey findings suggest that the first condition has been met, the second only partially so.

There seemed to be a general uncertainty on the part of federal as well as local officials as to the appropriate role of regional offices. The survey found considerable variation, ranging from domination to neutrality, in the extent to which regional staff were involved in local programs. Differences are explained by the unequal capabilities of prime sponsors as well as varying perceptions of role by federal staff. The pressure of time, the urgency of meeting planning schedules, changes in national program directions, and new legislation brought with them bursts of federal activity.

Some prime sponsors believe the amount of regulation, the number of reports, and the federal presence in general to be excessive; a few felt that these might reverse the decentralization of manpower programs. What some viewed as undue interposition, others considered a reasonable exercise of oversight responsibilities. The gray area between these views may become reconciled and the relationship between the principals more comfortable as prime sponsors gain experience and regional offices adjust to a more modest role.

On balance, the early CETA program appears to be neither completely decategorized nor completely decentralized, yet significant strides have been taken, especially in decentralization. Institutions are being built that will set new forces into motion and generate additional changes.

CETA PLANNING: EXPECTATIONS AND FINDINGS

Inherent in the rationale for a decentralized system is the premise that local authorities are in the best position to understand needs for manpower services, and to plan and provide them.

In a situation of local control, planning was presumed to be more relevant to community needs, more closely related to decision making, and more integrated into local government activities. What has happened under Title I becomes clearer if a distinction is made between the preparation of a specific planning document and planning as a continuing process.

There is little evidence to indicate that the first formal CETA plans were markedly superior to their predecessors, in some cases they were strikingly similar. Given the constraints in terms of time, staff, and know-how with which the CETA planner had to cope, a different outcome is difficult to envision. In the few weeks (somtimes days) that the prime sponsors' staffs were given to prepare the grant applications, there was hardly time to do more than dig out, adapt, and staple together existing material. Moreover, most prime sponsors were unable to start with a clean slate; there were ongoing programs to consider. Under the unremitting pressure to meet deadlines, many CETA planners did little more than provide, pro forma, the items necessary to pass muster and trigger the allocation of funds. Second-year operations may provide a better basis for assessing manpower plans in a decentralized system.

When manpower planning is viewed as a process, CETA planning represents the latest stage in a development that started with the Cooperative Area Manpower Planning System (CAMPS) in the mid-1960s. Pre-CETA planning, even at its most advanced, was primarily an information exchange far removed from the locus of power and with very little effect on decision making. The planning system under CETA, however, is closely integrated into the local government structure and planners have access to the prime sponsors. In many cases CETA planners are also manpower administrators and decision makers.

Decentralization is welcomed not only by practical administrators who see it as a more effective way of conducting manpower business, but also by those who equate decentralization with a more democratic system. It was assumed that decision making would be brought closer to the people by publishing CETA plans, providing an opportunity to comment on them, establishing advisory councils, and placing program control in the hands of elected officials answerable to the community. Decentralization implies that the smaller the unit of government, the closer it can be to the people and thus the more representative of their interests.

On the whole, the publication of CETA plans in newspapers was a formality and the exposure of the plans for comments, largely cosmetic. Time pressure precluded the possibility of any meaningful participation from the public. Faced with a choice between full ventilation of plans and speedy implementation of the program, the prime sponsors opted for the latter, perhaps on the assumption that the additional time required for comments would not produce significantly greater public involvement.

Public advisory councils, which Congress hoped would become the instrument for community participation in all aspects of CETA, were established. Although the scope of their responsibilities is wider than their pre-CETA counterparts, the membership is much the same and their role remains advisory. The survey found that, in the main, they tend to be passive. The dominant influence on the councils is usually exercised by the CETA administrator and staff. Nevertheless, CETA councils are more viable than their predecessors; their role and composition are legitimized by legislation; they are concerned with a wide range of activities and are closer to the decision makers; in a few places they have exercised considerable independent influence.

ADMINISTERING LOCAL PROGRAMS

For decentralization of whatever degree to become operational, prime sponsors must establish the necessary administrative machinery to assume command of the manpower programs in their jurisdictions--this has largely been accomplished. Units have been set up in all areas to handle centrally such administrative functions as fiscal accounting, reporting, and contract supervision.

Many prime sponsors have gone further and consolidated or coordinated recruitment, referral, job development, and placement services. In a few cases, the prime sponsors have designed a comprehensive manpower program. Decentralization of federal programs seems to be accompanied by centralization at the local level.

How well prime sponsor control is being exercised and what the effect of decentralization is on program operations have yet to be established. It is clear that the new responsibilities are seriously straining the capa-

bilities of the local governments, half of whom had no
prior experience with what are now Title I programs. An
assessment of 402 prime sponsors made by the Department of Labor Manpower Administration in May 1975
found 114 to be marginal performers; 52 were characterized as "significant underperformers." (A later survey, made in September, showed that most of these had
brought their programs up to acceptable levels. The
number of marginal performers had dropped to 19, and
only 3 remained on the list of significant underperformers.)

Survey responses cited as major obstacles inexperi-
ence, the complexity of the programs, cumbersome and
changing procedures, and repeated program interruptions occasioned by funding changes and new legislation.
The enactment of Title VI and the all-out push for public service employment programs overwhelmed many
prime sponsors in their efforts to implement Title I.

In vesting control in state and local prime sponsors,
Congress stipulated that organizations operating manpower
programs before CETA would not necessarily continue to
manage them. There were to be no "presumptive deliverers" of manpower services. This position, it was assumed, would result in competition for program contracts
and selection by the prime sponsor of the best performers; however, there was some equivocating on this point.
Although prime sponsors are given authority to contract
with organizations best able to deliver services, the
statute urges maximum feasible use of existing agencies.
Some Manpower Administration regional offices have
delayed approval of prime sponsor plans on this issue.

The study results indicate that although, on the whole,
the same program operators were used, important
changes did occur. Most significant is the role of prime
sponsors. In addition to centralizing administrative
functions, many began to conduct their own programs.
This occurred mainly at the expense of local employment
service offices and community action agencies.

On the other hand, community-based organizations
such as the Urban League, Opportunities Industrialization Center, and Services, Employment, and Redevelopment benefited from more funds and an increase in the
number of local programs. Along with other program
operators, however, they lost some degree of freedom
they enjoyed as independent sponsors funded directly by
the federal government. CETA has added an administrative layer between program operators and the Department of Labor. Some community-based organizations
are uneasy about the trend towards consolidation, which
they see as a threat to their identity as agencies serving
special racial and ethnic groups.

According to the Department of Labor estimates,
1,970 organizations were directly funded by local prime
sponsors in fiscal 1975 to provide manpower services
under Title I--500 more service deliverers than were
operating prior to CETA. The net increase results from
720 new service deliverers and a decrease of 210 that
were not selected. This proliferation reflects the funding of programs for the first time, especially in counties,
and the decisions of many prime sponsors to deliver
some services to participants through their own staff
units.

The shift of control from federal to local levels was
expected to lead to greater involvement of elected officials in manpower matters. There has undoubtedly been
increased participation, but in most cases it has been
limited to key decisions such as hiring a CETA administrator and allocation of local manpower resources among
programs and client groups.

CETA decentralized political as well as program
responsibility. Placing the manpower program under
the aegis of state and local elected officials puts it in
the political arena and subjects it to the local political
process. Local elected officials tend to be more accessible than federal administrators and perhaps more susceptible to politically potent groups with interests to
protect or to advance. However, the political process
is subject to abuse at any level, and the survey did find
some instances of political patronage, but this was not
typical of Title I programs.

CETA PARTICIPANTS

It is too early to tell whether local control will
result in better job preparation for the labor market--
the most important question in assessing manpower programs. It is possible, however, to detect some changes
in the kinds of people being served under Title I. The
manpower program clients before CETA were nearly all
poor, with little job experience or training. Participants
in Title I are higher on the socioeconomic ladder; relatively fewer of the disadvantaged, youth, and high school
dropouts are being enrolled. These findings are consistent with the direction of forces impinging upon CETA,
such as: 1) broader eligibility requirements, 2) greater
participation of suburban communities, 3) increasing use
of programs by victims of the recession, and 4) the inclination of some program managers to enroll persons
most likely to succeed rather than those most in need of
manpower training. There are some countervailing
pressures, such as the influence of community-based

organizations, the personal commitment of some CETA staff to serve minorities and the disadvantaged, and the intervention of some regional offices.

EFFECTS OF DECATEGORIZATION

Decategorization and decentralization are comple- mentary. To decentralize without giving localities the freedom to put together a mix of programs tailored to local needs would be to provide the trappings but not the substance of local control. CETA furnishes this flexibility by decategorizing earlier specialized programs.

Besides enabling the prime sponsor to fashion programs relevant to local needs, decategorization was expected to: 1) eliminate the duplication characteristic of earlier programs; 2) encourage new programs that are comprehensive, organizationally integrated, and liberally laced with innovations; and 3) eliminate or modify inadequate programs.

Despite their newly acquired authority and flexibility, prime sponsors did not rush to reshape manpower programs. Their flexibility was circumscribed by internal and external constraints. Insufficient time, lack of staff and experience, institutional pressures, and political considerations all operated against change. Most important, prime sponsors inherited a full complement of programs that could not immediately be turned around. Most programs were therefore continued, although some were stripped of their intake, administrative, and job placement functions; they were often consolidated and centralized. Because certain groups of clients require specialized manpower services, some categorical programs may well be indicated. The objections to pre-CETA programs referred to overlapping activities and lack of integration rather than to special programs as such.

Notwithstanding the pressures facing sponsors, they have been able to adjust quickly to a changing labor market. This has been demonstrated by their ability to shift from on-the-job training to work experience projects as the recession developed and deepened.

EMERGING ISSUES

Changing Nature of Program and Clientele

A number of issues have begun to emerge in the early transition period. Perhaps most important is the shifting of manpower programs away from the chronic,

structural problems of the labor market toward an increasing emphasis on the immediate cyclical problem of
unemployment. This change was accompanied by a
broadening of eligibility for manpower services.

Social, economic, and political developments all
played a part in this new orientation. The social fer-
ment of the 1960s and the organizational support for
social action had diminished to a considerable extent.
Governmental enthusiasm for "Great Society" programs
dampened and public interest in coping with the problems
of the disadvantaged waned, particularly since instant
cures did not materialize.

Soon after the enactment of CETA, the economy
faltered badly. Employment opportunities for graduates
of manpower programs declined. It was difficult to persuade employers to accept on-the-job trainees while
they were laying off their regular work force. The ranks
of manpower program applicants swelled with newly unemployed workers who did not normally compete for
slots in those programs. The response of prime sponsors to these conditions was to concentrate on subsidized
work experience and public service employment
programs.

On the political level, the looser eligibility requirements of CETA and the delegation of decision making
to some 400 elected officials invited a broader participation in manpower programs. The addition of a large public service employment program (Title VI) changed the
emphasis of manpower programs from its earlier structural to a counter-cyclical orientation. The shift was
welcomed by local officials who recognized the political
attractiveness of a program that not only created jobs
but also could be used to provide fiscal relief for hard-
pressed communities.

The change in the nature of manpower programs and
participants suggests a retreat from the 10-year effort
to grapple with the employability problems of the disadvantaged. It raises the question of how to insulate the
hard-core unemployed from the competition of better
prepared program applicants.

A closely related issue is the advisability of addressing the problems of cyclical unemployment (Title VI)
through a program (CETA) designed principally to deal
with labor market maladjustments of a structural nature.
Incorporating a public service employment component
into CETA is consistent with the general objective of
designing a comprehensive manpower system, and increases the prime sponsor's options in dealing with local
manpower matters. Presumably, efficiency of program
administration would also be increased. On the other
hand, Title VI is basically a different kind of program

for a different group, authorized for a more limited time
period. The relative attractiveness of its job-creation
program puts other less glamorous programs at a disadvantage in terms of the time, interest, and attention
of the prime sponsors. Finally, housing both programs
together tends to obscure the differences between structural and cyclical manpower programs.

Tendencies to bifurcate the system of manpower
programs are already discernible. There are distinctions between the work-ready applicants enrolled in
public service employment programs and those less prepared who are placed in pre-employment training activities. Moreover, the two kinds of programs are frequently
administered through separate organizational units.

Issues in Public Service Employment

Although most of the field work for this study was
completed before the enactment of Title VI, there was
some opportunity to identify a number of issues associated with public service employment. The most serious
obstacle to the attainment of the Title VI objective of
creating additional jobs is likely to be the practice of
substitution; that is, there are increasing indications
that federal funds are being used for positions that might
otherwise have been financed through regular local
revenues--not to create new jobs. However, some local
jurisdictions are experiencing actual budget stringencies
and unavoidable layoffs.

There are also worrisome institutional problems.
Conflicts between the objectives of a national public service employment program and the interests of established
institutions in the public sector are not uncommon. Most
of these arise from the relationship between CETA enrollees and the regular civil service employees with respect
to civil service hiring qualifications, entry-level jobs,
promotional opportunities, and the order of layoffs.

Political patronage, if not the most serious problem
to emerge, is probably the most publicized one. Some
indications appeared early in the Title I program. However, opportunities for such practices are much greater
in the public service employment program and will be
covered in the next phase of the study.

National Policies and Local Decisions

Framers of the original CETA legislation faced the
problem of reconciling a commitment to local discretion
with the need to address national problems. In the ab-

sence of any new major development, it was assumed
that programs fashioned by 400 prime sponsors would be
congruent with national needs and priorities.

However, Congressional action since CETA suggests
an inclination to revert to a categorical approach in meeting new national developments. The enactment of the public service employment program as a new categorical
title is one indication of this tendency; handling the summer
youth program through a separate appropriation is another.

The problems associated with public service programs
(especially that of substitution) and the proclivity to spin
off new and visible programs have generated new initia-
tives in Congressional committees. The chairman of the
House subcommittee dealing with manpower has drafted
legislation to extend and enlarge the public service employment program, as well as to centralize control in
the regional offices of the Department of Labor. Funding
would be made to a wider spectrum of public bodies as
well as to private nonprofit organizations. In effect, a
large part of the manpower program would be recentral-
ized. The ranking minority member of the subcommittee
has introduced legislation that would establish a series of
national categorical programs. Taken together, they
could spell recentralization and recategorization. Although these are not yet fixed positions, they do suggest
the way the Congressional wind is blowing.

Other Issues

In addition to the general issues just discussed, a
number of specific problems are coming into focus.

The allocation of Title I resources is a potential
source of difficulty. Prime sponsors are guaranteed at
least 90 percent of their prior year's funding level. Despite this stabilizer, which tends to prevent abrupt
changes, at constant funding levels the amount available
for many large cities is likely to decrease over a period
of years. There are also technical problems in measuring unemployment and low income and in designing measures to allocate resources to those most in need.

Advisory councils are still struggling with identity
problems. Increasingly, the objectivity of council members whose agencies provide program services to the
prime sponsor is being questioned. In some instances
they have been excluded from council membership or
have not been permitted to vote on issues on which they
are an interested party.

The relationship between the employment service,
which had been the major pre-CETA manpower agency,
and the present prime sponsors is frequently unsettled,
especially in situations in which the role of the employ-